KU-998-851

Government Assistance
in Eighteenth-Century France

By SHELBY T. McCLOY

PROFESSOR OF HISTORY, THE UNIVERSITY OF KENTUCKY

DURHAM, N. C.

DUKE UNIVERSITY PRESS

1946

COPYRIGHT, 1946, BY THE DUKE UNIVERSITY PRESS

PRINTED IN THE UNITED STATES OF AMERICA BY THE
SEEMAN PRINTERY, INC., DURHAM, NORTH CAROLINA

TO
MINNIE LEE

PREFACE

THE PURPOSE of this volume is to give an account of government assistance to the needy in France in the eighteenth century. Nothing has hitherto been published in English on the subject save a 179-page survey by Miss Emily Balch (*Public Assistance of the Poor in France*, Baltimore, 1893), covering several centuries, and a few articles in learned journals. Even in French no work has appeared treating the entire field. Among the notable studies dealing with certain aspects is the four-volume encyclopaedic treatise by Martin-Doisy (*Dictionnaire d'économie charitable . . .* , edited by the Abbé Migne, Paris, 1855-64), surveying government, ecclesiastical, and private charities through the centuries, with observations by the author. Lacking footnotes or many references to authorities, this work is nevertheless unbiased and rests upon much study. A four-volume *Histoire de la charité* (Paris, 1902-12) by the Oratorian scholar, Léon Lallemand, while heavily documented and at places more detailed than the work by Martin-Doisy, is nevertheless sketchy, and is strongly Catholic. Lallemand has more to say concerning private and ecclesiastical charities than government relief. By far the best study is the volume by Camille Bloch, *L'assistance et l'état en France à la veille de la Révolution (généralités de Paris, Rouen, Alençon, Orléans, Chalons, Soissons, Amiens) (1764-1790)* (Paris, 1908, pp. lxiv, 504), presented as a doctoral treatise in law at the University of Paris. Based upon years of research in French archives as well as a thorough examination of the printed sources, the book is a splendid treatment within its limits of the period preceding the Revolution. Two brief but commendable studies by Ferdinand-Dreyfus, *Un philanthrope d'autrefois: La Rochefoucauld-Liancourt, 1747-1827* (Paris, 1903, pp. xvi, 547) and *L'assistance sous la Législative et la Convention (1791-1795)* (Paris, 1905, pp. 180) deal with the Revolutionary era. None of these works, however, has the scope of the present volume. They do little more than mention such subjects as flood and fire relief, epidemics and epizootics, pensions, aid to large families, relief to refugees, and educational aid. The present volume is not itself designed to cover all French charities, but is restricted primarily to the assistance rendered by the state and provincial governments, touching only incidentally municipal, church, and private charities.

Realizing the importance of the archival material, the author spent the summer of 1937 in the Archives Nationales and the manuscript room of the Bibliothèque Nationale, at Paris. In late July, 1939, he returned to France, on a year's leave of absence from teaching duties at Duke University, to spend thirteen months in further archival study, but unhappily was interrupted by the outbreak of war after only five weeks of work in the Archives Nationales. Advised by the American Embassy to leave France, the author proceeded to Bordeaux, where happily the Archives de la Gironde were still open, and during a week's work prior to sailing he found much valuable material. Thence he went to Washington and spent some months at work on printed sources in the Library of Congress. It was with the keenest regret that the author forewent his year in the French archives, and he feels confident that he would have plowed a deeper furrow with the additional archival material than it has been possible to do without it.

In his research and the preparation of the book the author has received aid from various quarters. To the officials of Duke University he is indebted for the leave of absence during the academic year 1939-40. To the Research Council of Duke University he is indebted for several grants-in-aid for the acquisition of printed and filmed material, for two grants providing secretarial assistance, and for a special grant-in-aid toward the expense of publication. To the Social Science Research Council he gratefully acknowledges two grants-in-aid toward work in French archives: one on its general fund, in 1937; the other, on its fund for Southern scholars, in 1939. To his wife, who accompanied him to France and Washington, he expresses his appreciation for patiently sharing vicissitudes, for copying manuscript and printed material, and for twice typing his entire manuscript.

To various others he is indebted for assistance in the critical revision of his manuscript: to Professor W. T. Laprade, Chairman of the History Department at Duke University, who besides his encouragement of the undertaking from the first has read the entire manuscript with detailed suggestions; to Professor Earl J. Hamilton, of the Department of Economics at Northwestern University, who read the entire work and offered detailed suggestions on certain chapters; to Professor Charles Woolsey Cole, of the Department of History at Columbia University, who read the entire manuscript, offering many suggestions, detailed and general; to Professor Joseph J. Spengler, of the Department of Economics of Duke University, for critical observations on two chapters; to Mr. David K. Jackson, of the Duke University Press, for many improvements in expression; and to Professor Loring B. Walton, of the Department of Romance Languages of Duke University, for assistance in the felicitous rendering of several passages of translation quoted in the text. The writer, however, assumes responsibility for the blemishes still to be found in his work.

He wishes to acknowledge the kindness of archive and library officials and their staffs. He has labored in the Duke University Library, the Library of Congress, the Library of the Surgeon-General of the United States, the Bibliothèque Nationale, and in the Archives Nationales, the Archives de l'Assistance Publique, and the Archives de la Gironde. He has availed himself of the Inter-Library Loan Service of American Libraries, receiving books or bound periodicals from the University of North Carolina, the Library of Congress, Columbia University, Harvard University, Yale University, Princeton University, the University of Chicago, the University of Michigan, the University of Louisiana, and the John Crerar Library of Chicago. From the Archives de la Seine-Inférieure he has received microfilmed copies of manuscript material. To the officials and staffs of these institutions he is grateful for courteous service.

Finally, the editors of certain presses and learned journals have granted permission to reprint (with some revision) articles published for the author years ago. Acknowledgments are due to the University of Chicago Press and the *Journal of Modern History* for the privilege of reprinting as Chapter VI an article from the March, 1941, issue, entitled "Flood Relief and Control in Eighteenth-Century France"; to the same press and the *Social Service Review* for permission to reprint as Chapter VII an article published in June, 1938, entitled "Government Assistance during the Plague

of 1720-22 in Southeastern France"; and to the University of Louisiana Press and the *Louisiana Historical Quarterly* for the use as a
part of Chapter XVI of an article originally published in July, 1938,
entitled "French Aid to the Acadians, 1755-1799."

SHELBY T. McCLOY

Lexington, Kentucky
November 13, 1945

CONTENTS

Government Assistance
in Eighteenth-Century France

CHAPTER I

THE "GREAT WINTER" OF 1709

An ever-present task of government officials in eighteenth-century France was to assure each Frenchman of a sufficiency of food. Incredible as it may seem, eighteenth-century France, the most cultured country in the world, then lived almost continually on the verge of famine. Indeed, almost every second or third year saw hunger in one or more parts of the country. In the province of Guyenne alone there were famines or near-famines for thirty-four years during the period 1700-89.[1]

But with or without a famine, French officials were ever concerned over the supply of food, which formed no mean part of the correspondence every year between the controller-general of finance and the intendants of the provinces. Since the sixteenth century, the French government had annually investigated the probable size of each forthcoming harvest.[2] In the sixteenth century this information was required of the *baillis* and other local officers, but in the eighteenth, of the thirty-odd intendants of provinces and their subdelegates.[3] Like the government forecasts of United States crops in our own times, this information was not always reliable; yet as a rule it approached accuracy sufficiently to be indispensable. Upon it as a basis the government, or to speak more precisely the controller-general of finance and the council of finance, made plans in advance for importation or exportation of grain, as the need might be, for

[1] In the years 1708-09, 1712, 1716, 1718-19, 1722, 1725, 1727, 1730, 1737, 1742-44, 1746-49, 1751, 1759, 1766-73, 1777-78, and 1787-89 (E. Bourgoüin, "Une disette en Guyenne à la fin de l'ancien règime (1777-78)," *Revue historique de Bordeaux*, XI, Bordeaux, 1918, 146-147). Guyenne, a superior winegrowing region, was probably exceptional; but even Brittany, one of the leading grain regions, experienced many famines during the century. The "most terrible" were perhaps those of 1709, 1725, 1759, 1768, 1772, 1775, 1785, 1790 (J. Letaconnoux, *Les subsistances et le commerce des grains en Bretagne au XVIIIe siècle: Essai de monographie économique*, Rennes, 1909, p. 138).

[2] A. P. Usher, *The History of the Grain Trade in France, 1400-1710* (Cambridge, 1913), p. 234.

[3] Michel Lhéritier, *Tourny, intendant de Bordeaux* (Paris, 1920), p. 43; F. Dumas, *La généralité de Tours au XVIIIe siècle: administration de l'intendant du Cluzel (1766-1783)* (*Mémoires de la Société archéologique de Touraine*, Vol. XXXIX) (Tours, 1894), pp. 236-258.

France was then under the mercantile system, with a strongly paternalistic government that endeavored to foresee and provide for the needs of its people through elaborate plans and regulations.

Detailed accounts of certain leading famines of the century disclose not only the work of the government in provisioning but also the care and vexations of government officials and their precise methods of procedure. Government relief in its relation to local relief, too, is revealed by them.

Perhaps France's most severe famine of the century, that of 1709 was ushered in by the "Great Winter" of 1708-09, one of the coldest in French annals, and occurred in the midst of the War of the Spanish Succession (1702-13), in which the French had lost battle after battle to the genius and arms of Marlborough and Prince Eugene, and in which their soil had been invaded. Acute economic distress had prevailed almost continuously since 1690.[4] Vauban's *Projet d'une dixme royale,* published in 1706 and written a few years earlier,[5] provides a description of the misery of the French masses. Almost the same conditions prevailed in 1709 during the famous period of cold and famine.

The *débâcle* began in late December, 1708, with a heavy snow that reached two feet in depth in some parts of France. Snow was still on the ground on January 6, when a frigid north wind hit all the country, indeed all of Western Europe, producing sub-zero temperatures, and lasted until January 17. At Paris temperatures of $-21.3°$ (centigrade) on January 14, and of $-20.6°$ on the twentieth, were reached;[6] at Bordeaux, temperatures of $-23.2°$ on Jan-

[4] For a discussion of this distress and its several causes, see Henri Sée, *L'évolution commerciale et industrielle de la France sous l'ancien régime* (Paris, 1925), pp. 148-152.

[5] First written in the period 1697-99; presented to the king in MS late in 1699; revised in 1704; and published in 1706 (despite the date 1707 printed on the first edition) (A. de Boislisle, ed., *Mémoires de Saint-Simon,* XIV, Paris, 1899, 327 n. 3, 330 n. 3, 335 n. 1; P. Lazard, *Vauban, 1633-1707,* Paris, 1934, p. 564; Daniel Halévy, *Vauban,* Paris, 1924, pp. 188-194).

[6] Auguste Bramard, *La dernière famine: l'hiver et la famine de 1709 en France, en Bourbonnais* (Moulins, 1932), p. 20. Bramard, who designates himself a member of the Meteorological Society of France, states (*ibid.,* p. 9) that the centigrade thermometer did not exist in 1709, but that a number of savants in different parts of Europe took readings with other types of thermometers, employing alcohol, mercury, or air, and published their report in learned journals. It has thereby been possible for later students to transfer these readings to the centigrade scale.

According to A. Wolf (*A History of Science, Technology, and Philosophy in*

uary 11 and −23.8° on January 20;[7] at Moulins, temperatures from −24° to −26° on January 10 and 11.[8]

Whether or not the thermometer reached its nadir for all time in France in 1709, perhaps no other year of modern times produced such disastrous effects in frigidity, and the winter is still known, in France and elsewhere in Continental Europe, as the "Great Winter" of 1709. At Bordeaux the rivers Dordonne and Garonne and at Lyons the rivers Saône and Rhône froze so hard that carriages could be driven across them. Along the coast of Provence the surface of the Mediterranean was frozen, and at Venice, where allegedly (of course without verification) the coldest winter in six hundred years prevailed, the Adriatic was so thick with ice that carriages could be drawn over its surface. In Belgium, Holland, and Germany the rivers, canals, and adjacent seawaters froze, and troops and artillery were transported over the frozen Rhine and Elbe. In Copenhagen harbor ice reached the thickness of twenty-seven inches, and pedestrians crossed the Sund to Sweden.[9]

At Versailles it was so cold that not only ink froze in its wells, but wine and oil froze in their casks, and even liqueurs froze and broke their bottles in heated rooms and in cabinets beside heated chimneys.[10] Wine at Bordeaux froze in the chalices during the celebration of mass, and priests heated it on the altars to keep it liquid. Bread got so hard from freezing that it had to be cut with a hatchet or saw.[11] According to Nicolas Delamare, author of a

the 16th & 17th Centuries, New York, 1935, pp. 90-91), the Fahrenheit thermometer was not invented until about 1714, the Réaumur in 1730, and the centigrade in 1742-43. Of earlier thermometers he gives an account (*ibid.*, pp. 82-90).

[7] M. Labuchelle, "Bordeaux il y a 200 ans, la misère à Bordeaux et au département de la Gironde," *Revue historique de Bordeaux*, II (Bordeaux, 1909), 31.

[8] Bramard, *op. cit.*, p. 22. Whether these readings were taken before dawn, when temperatures would have been lowest, or after sunrise, is not indicated. It has been pointed out by Michelet (*Histoire de France*, XIV, Paris, 1862, 307) that these temperatures were equaled in France in 1788 and 1829, and that they occur often in various parts of Germany and Poland.

[9] Labuchelle, *op. cit.*, II, 32; J. B. Monfalcon, *Histoire monumentale de la ville de Lyon*, III (Paris and Lyon, 1886), 192; Bramard, *op. cit.*, p. 24; A. de Boislisle, "Le grand hiver et la disette de 1709," *Revue des questions historiques*, N.S., XXIX (Paris, 1903), 465-466. In the British Isles the effects were somewhat less severe.

[10] Saint-Simon (*Mémoires*, new ed. . . . by A. de Boislisle, XVII, Paris, 1903, 195) wrote: "The violence . . . was such that the water of the queen of Hungary, the strongest elixirs, and the most spirituous liqueurs broke their bottles in the closets of heated chambers and surrounding chimney pipes, in several apartments of the château of Versailles, where I have seen many. . . ."

[11] Labuchelle, *op. cit.*, II, 34.

celebrated work on the police, the ground froze to a depth of two feet, making burials difficult and in some instances impossible.[12]

On January 23 a thaw set in, lasting until February 4. Rivers became flooded from the melted snow and ice, and bridges, mills, and dikes were destroyed as huge ice-cakes struck them. Roads became impassable with mud, and the fields were inundated with water. Much of the planted grain as yet not frozen was killed by flooding. One writer reports that sap began to rise in the trees.[13] This mild period terminated on February 4, when a second frigid spell set in. It continued until February 27, with temperatures of −9.8° on February 24 and −12.7° on the twenty-fifth. This second period, somewhat less cold than the first, was perhaps more responsible for the havoc.

By the alternate periods of freeze and thaw France had been devastated. Not only was the greater part of the forthcoming wheat crop ruined, but almost all of the vines, the fruit trees, the chestnut and walnut trees, even the olive trees of southern Provence and Languedoc were killed to their roots. At Bordeaux the greater portion of a magnificent grove of giant cypresses (like those still standing in the city's Jardin des Plantes) were killed. Many of the oaks throughout France succumbed to the low temperatures, as did also most of the cork trees in regions near Spain.[14] Never in the memory of living man had France experienced so cruel a winter.[15]

Most of the birds and domestic fowl, the wild and domestic animals, were killed.[16] Throughout France, human beings, too, died of cold and hunger, and the bodies of many were found on the roads and streets.[17] The *Journal de Verdun* of December, 1709, denied that any had died of hunger;[18] nevertheless, the evidence from other contemporary sources that many Frenchmen did die

[12] *Traité de la police*, 2d ed. enlarged, II (Paris, 1722) supplement, 1.

[13] Whether this would have been possible with the mercury reaching daily minimums of −3° and −4° is of course questionable (*ibid.*, II, 39).

[14] *Ibid.*, II, 34-35; Boislisle, *op. cit.*, XXIX, 463; Saint-Simon, *op. cit.*, XVII, 27, 196.

[15] *Ibid.*, XVII, 195; J. Tissier, *L'hiver de 1709 dans le diocèse de Narbonne* (reprinted from the *Bulletin de la Commission archéologique de Narbonne*) (Narbonne, 1895), pp. 3-4.

[16] Boislisle, *op. cit.*, XXIX, 466-467.

[17] *Ibid.*, XXIX, 459-461; Bramard, *op. cit.*, Foreword and p. 16; Pierre Rambaud, *L'assistance publique à Poitiers jusqu'à l'an V*, I (Paris, 1912), 361.

[18] Quoted by Boislisle, *op. cit.*, XXX (Paris, 1903), 524-525.

from hunger and cold at this time appears conclusive. Moreover, fatalities were existent not only among the poor—the poor whose bodies lay on the streets and the highways—but even among the upper nobility, who supposedly had adequate food and fuel for their needs.[19] Paris, Rouen, indeed many parts of France, experienced outbreaks of scurvy and dysentery, brought on by the narrowed diet; and the hospitals were filled to capacity.[20] An "infinite number of families" were ruined, and "cascades of evils of every sort" developed.[21]

No part of France apparently escaped the disastrous consequences of the terrible cold and lack of food. Southern France was even more severely hit than northern France, and the rural folk suffered more than the urbanites, since the officials at Paris and the intendants were more solicitous to give aid to the cities, lest riots occur, and since the cities had relief agencies of their own, not found in the rural districts.

It was traditional in France, and the practice continued throughout the eighteenth century, for the poorer people of the rural regions and villages to pour into the cities in times of famine and unemployment in search of work or food. Thousands of them ("beggars" they were frequently called) were to be found on the streets of the larger French cities in this crisis of 1709. Their presence was not only embarrassing but dangerous, since the cities had their own poor to care for. Industry and commerce suffered heavily in this crisis; for example, at Lyons, the leading industrial city after Paris, the silk factories were largely closed during June and July, and, according to estimates, half of their forty to fifty thousand workers were unemployed.[22] Most of them turned to begging, and many were so insolent that Lyonese merchants were afraid to go to the exchange lest they encounter them. An attempt

---

[19] *Ibid.*, XXIX, 467.

[20] *Ibid.*, XXIX, 467-468; A. M. de Boislisle and P. de Brotonne (eds.), *Correspondance des contrôleurs généraux des finances avec les intendants des provinces*, III (Paris, 1897), Nos. 361, 369, 415, 422, 543, 656, 719, 817, 874. In the small town of Montargis 800 died. To Montargis and other places the government sent "skilled physicians." Large quantities of "remedies" by Helvétius, and printed directions on their use, were sent in care of various intendants for distribution among the poor of their generalities. The epidemics ran from early 1709 through the spring of 1710.

[21] Saint-Simon, *op. cit.*, XVII, 204, 206.

[22] Boislisle and Brotonne, *op. cit.*, III, No. 344.

at raising a collection for the poor in the city yielded only the contemptible dole of 16 sous monthly a person.[23] Amid these circumstances Lyons did not care to see additional thousands of hungry rustics pour into the city and walk the streets in discontent. They could only be inflammable material for riots.

This dangerous situation prevailed in other French cities, and most of them from the outset (as was customary) passed ordinances demanding that the nonresident "beggars" return at once to their homes. It is not known how many left. Some formed large bands of a hundred or more and pillaged the countryside. When they could find nothing to plunder, they returned home to subsist on any herbs or roots that could be found.[24]

The commonly accepted theory in eighteenth-century France was that charity should be localized as much as possible.[25] Each parish, each city, each province, was expected as nearly as possible to care for its own relief needs. Only as a last resort, after local agencies had done all within their power, was it the practice of the royal government to lend assistance.

Acting on this long-established principle, almost every city and town in France rushed to the rescue of its needy in the early days of the crisis of 1709. Curés employed church offerings,[26] and city officials and other prominent persons solicited voluntary relief funds. Occasionally the officials of church and city united in sponsoring the same collection. In most instances the sums were small. Even in the large and wealthy cities of Paris, Lyons, and Bordeaux, the

[23] The rich were reluctant to give anything. So wrote Ravat, provost of merchants (mayor) of Lyons, to the controller-general on July 28. He recommended, among other things, that the silk-factory owners should be forced to give the poor employment, and suggested that since coin was rare, paper might be used (*ibid.*, III, No. 448).

[24] Bramard, *op. cit.*, pp. 50-51; Labuchelle, *op. cit.*, II, 41-42. In Touraine bands of 400 to 500 roamed and plundered the countryside in April, 1709 (Boislisle and Brotonne, *op. cit.*, III, No. 38).

[25] Camille Bloch, *L'assistance et l'état en France à la veille de la Révolution* . . . (Paris, 1908), p. 55; Marcel Fosseyeux, *Le budget de la charité à Paris au XVIIIe siècle* (Extrait de la *Revue des Etudes historiques* for juillet-octobre 1919) (Paris, 1919), pp. 7-8; Jacques Necker, *De l'administration des finances de la France*, III (Paris, 1785), pp. 160-161; M. F. Buchalet, *L'assistance publique à Toulouse au dix-huitième siècle* (Toulouse, 1904), p. 33.

[26] Boislisle (*op. cit.*, XXIX, 490) pays tribute to the clergy for their part in organizing relief in 1709, but (pp. 461-462) mentions criticism of them by lawyers that they selfishly stood apart in their charities.

nobles and bourgeoisie were parsimonious in their contributions, and the offerings were trivial in comparison with the needs.

The cities and provinces borrowed what money they could to help meet the situation. Bordeaux in December, 1708, borrowed of a group of bankers at Nantes 60,000 livres for a period of six months, in order to increase the funds available for the purchase of wheat for its population. Realizing that this supply was not enough, its *jurats* (aldermen) on January 9, 1709, ordered its *consul de la bourse* to import into the city an additional 40,000 pounds (livres) of wheat. To facilitate this importation, they exempted all ships engaged in the undertaking from the normal duty of 50 sous per ton.[27] The city of Rochefort borrowed 20,000 livres, with the intendant's approval and personal endorsement, for the purpose of feeding its poor. The *jurats* made themselves the custodians of the funds, and delivered to the bakers the wheat which they purchased with the understanding that the bread made from it was to be sold at a stipulated price. Their action, according to historians of that city, saved the large population of the poor in Rochefort.[28] The generality of Provence, in which Marseilles was situated, borrowed 300,000 livres to meet partial payments on the wheat imported during 1709 and 1710.[29] Burgundy, one of the hardest hit of the provinces,[30] also borrowed heavily in this crisis.[31]

With the money raised by voluntary offerings or municipal appropriations, the cities attempted to purchase through grain agents wheat, rye, barley, or buckwheat, when and how they could. They set up one or more *marmites* (large cauldrons), from which soup rich in rice, beans, and any other obtainable vegetables was served free to the poor. In a few instances municipal bakeries were established to provide bread at a cheap price for the needy. More commonly local authorities subsidized the losses to bakers and forced

[27] Labuchelle, *op. cit.*, II, 46-47. The city was forced to borrow more than a million livres for expenses in 1708-09 (*ibid.*, II, 273).

[28] J. T. Viaud and E. J. Fleury, *Histoire de la ville et du port de Rochefort*, I (Rochefort, 1845), 257.

[29] *Inventaire-sommaire des archives départementales antérieures à 1790 . . . Bouches-du-Rhône*, C 63 (f 173v).

[30] Saint-Simon, *op. cit.*, XVII, 201 with n. 1. Dangeau is cited as stating that "misery is greater in Burgundy than anywhere else."

[31] *Inv.-som . . . Côte d'Or*, C 2983 (f 186). Mention is made of the borrowing of 3,400,000 livres by the generality, but whether all was borrowed to meet this crisis is not clear.

the sale of bread to the poor at a sub-market rate. Finally, in some instances coin was distributed among the poor to enable them to purchase for themselves the necessities of life.[32] In Paris bread, soup, and even meat were served daily to large numbers of the needy from the home of De Pontchartrain, chancellor under Louis XIV.[33] In Marseilles great quantities of rice were given to the poor.[34] In Bordeaux four public ovens for baking bread, and some *marmites* for making free soup, were set up. Public fires also were provided.[35] Libourne, too, provided public fires, and even distributed wood.[36] At Auxerre more than thirteen hundred persons daily received soup.[37] The poor in the towns of Moulins and Montluçon were served food regularly from the beginning of March, partly through municipal aid and partly through aid from the intendant.[38]

Realizing that these local efforts were inadequate, the central government finally lent its assistance. Twice in early 1709 it made grants of 2,000 livres to the city of Paris to subsidize the losses to bakers necessitated by the compulsory sale of bread to the poor at sub-market rates.[39] On May 21 the council of state ordered that the curés furnish lists of indigents unable to buy salt at the *gabelle* stores, and directed the stores to furnish salt free (at government expense) until October 1.[40] Eventually, on October 22, a royal declaration set up a special tax designed to raise 600,000 livres for the poor in Paris alone. All property owners and leading renters were assessed a sum twice in amount what they had formerly paid for the cleaning and lighting of the streets.[41]

[32] Boislisle and Brotonne, *op. cit.*, III, No. 475.

[33] Saint-Simon, *op. cit.*, XVII, 207 n. 1.

[34] Labuchelle, *op. cit.*, II, 125-126.

[35] *Ibid.*, II, 38, 50-51.

[36] *Ibid.*, II, 38.

[37] Boislisle and Brotonne, *op. cit.*, III, No. 462. More than a third of them were fed by the clergy.

[38] Bramard, *op. cit.*, p. 50.

[39] Commandant Herlaut, *La disette de pain à Paris en 1709* (offprint from the *Mémoires de la Société de l'Histoire de Paris et de l'Ile-de-France*, XLV) (Paris, 1918), p. 20.

[40] *Ibid.*, pp. 42-43.

[41] *Ibid.*, p. 92 n. 4; Boislisle, *op. cit.*, XXIX, 497-498; Saint-Simon, *op. cit.*, XVII, 207. Saint-Simon refers to it in critical terms. "An indiscreet and tyrannical charity," he says, "contrived some taxes and an *impôt* for the poor." The effect was the virtual ruin of "an infinite number of men" already overburdened with taxes, the drying up of private contributions, and, as he suggests that "the employment of these taxes was perhaps badly managed," "the poor were much less alle-

In several cities (for example, Paris, Bordeaux, Rouen, Amiens, and Orléans) the establishment of charity workshops, to provide relief through labor, was contemplated.[42] This method had already been employed in various regions of France in the famines of the 1680's and 1690's, and was regarded with some favor. In Rouen charity workshops were in actual operation in July, with the men repairing the streets, and the women spinning cotton.[43] De Bouville, the intendant at Orléans, wrote in April to the controller-general that he planned to open at once three public workshops for the large number of poor in that city and that he would compel the nonresidents to leave, observing that they were able to work at the levees of the Loire.[44] Whether the workshops contemplated at Amiens and Bordeaux actually came into operation is not clear, but the intendants at both cities sought them inasmuch as the need was great.[45] At Paris two charity workshops were opened on August 20, but because of rioting in one of them both were closed the same day.[46]

The Parisian workshops were handled in a disgraceful manner. Since April, Desmaretz, the controller-general, had entertained the idea of establishing workshops in the capital for the needy, and Daguesseau *fils*, the procurer-general (prosecuting attorney) to the parlement of Paris, had supported him. On April 19 the parlement of Paris issued an order creating them. This *arrêt* was confirmed on June 8. Women and children as well as men were to be put to work, the former at spinning and various forms of light labor, the men at the heavier tasks. But the workshops were not immediately set up. Much legal tape was necessary, and it was not until August

viated." Further, he says, the king made these taxes permanent, after moderating them slightly, and appropriated to himself funds originally set up for the poor.

As a matter of fact, a poor tax had been collected at Paris since 1544 (Baron Dupin, *L'administration des secours publics, ou analyse historique de la législation des secours publics* . . . , Paris, 1821, p. 361; cf. Boislisle, *op. cit.*, XXIX, 497 with n.).

[42] Boislisle and Brotonne, *op. cit.*, III, Nos. 339, 369, 384, 410, 475. Boislisle (*op. cit.*, XXIX, 498-499) states that all these cities save Bordeaux actually set up the workshops.

[43] Boislisle and Brotonne, *op. cit.*, III, 181, No. 475.

[44] *Ibid.*, III, No. 369.

[45] *Ibid.*, III, Nos. 178, 339, 369, and 410. The intendant of Bordeaux even as early as September, 1708, requested for the purpose 40,000 livres. The government granted him the funds, which apparently were used in the election of Agen; and in May, 1709, he asked a similar sum for *ateliers de charité* at Bordeaux.

[46] *Ibid.*, III, No. 522; Herlaut, *op. cit.*, pp. 62-73. Boislisle (*op. cit.*, XXIX, 500-501), however, implies that they were continued a week longer.

6 that a royal declaration called for their establishment. Parlement duly registered this declaration on the twelfth, and provision was made to open the workshops on the twentieth. To finance them, 30,000 livres were raised by subscription, part coming from the city officials, part from the archbishop, and part from the first president of the parlement of Paris.

From the first the workshops met with opposition. Whereas the controller-general of finance and the parlement of Paris favored them, the two leading city officials, Bignon, provost of merchants (mayor), and D'Argenson, lieutenant general of police, were both opposed. Perhaps there was rivalry between Daguesseau *fils* and D'Argenson over the problem of relief work in the city. At any rate, the police force on hand to maintain order was inadequate when on August 20 the two workshops were opened, one on the Mont de Parnasse, with six hundred workers, the other on the *butte* Saint-Martin, with two thousand.[47]

The relief measures which have thus far been described were of relatively small value. The most useful form of relief during the famine evidently was importation of grain, which was almost entirely the work of government officials, i.e., the controller-general of finance and the intendants of provinces. These officials corresponded on the subject with French diplomatic and consular representatives in other countries, and sent out grain agents with passports to virtually all parts of Continental Europe, North Africa, and the Near East. In some instances bankers and grain wholesalers were

---

[47] Workers in both camps were divided into brigades of 200 each, with inspectors and timekeepers. All went well at the smaller workshop, but at the larger a horde of some 8,000 persons of both sexes and of all walks of life soon appeared, demanding work and food. These mingled with the 2,000 who had submitted their credentials and been accepted for work, and took their tools. So great became the disorder that the workshop officials fled. Thereupon the 8,000 plundered the house, in which around 4,000 loaves of bread were kept for the workers. The mob then set out on a plundering tour of bakers' shops until stopped by Villars and his guards. Some shots in the air failing to disperse the mob, the soldiers fired into it, killing a man and his wife. Thereupon the mob fled. The workshops were closed. The alternative of continuing them with military or greater police protection apparently was not even considered.

The riot was but one of several score that occurred in various French cities in 1709. Boislisle (*op. cit.*, XXX) devotes several pages to them. In some instances the rioters attacked the nobility, the intendants, and threatened the leading officials of Paris. No class of society was safe. The mobs of 1709 were almost as daring and insolent as those of 1789-94.

empowered to make purchases abroad through their own representatives.

Not until April did Desmaretz, the controller-general and a nephew of the great Colbert, become alarmed over the grain situation, though as early as September, 1708, he had been warned by letters from the intendants of certain of the important grain-growing regions that France would face a considerable shortage during the forthcoming winter and should make adequate importations. But Desmaretz, confident of his own opinions, was convinced that France enjoyed a surplus of wheat, and throughout the autumn months permitted exports to Lorraine, Germany, and Switzerland.[48] Not until early 1709 was he prevailed upon to halt exportation. By that time some of the provinces (for example, Normandy and Provence), fearful of famine, were taking steps to buy grain stocks abroad. The eldest of the famous Paris brothers, leading bankers of their day, was engaged by the cities of Rouen, Calais, and Dunkirk to purchase their quota of wheat toward supplying the army.[49]

The banker's agent wrote from Holland to the controller-general in mid-January (despite the fact that the United Provinces were at war with France) that he had purchased two hundred thousand sacks of grain, two thirds of it wheat and one third rye, and reported that he could make further purchases. He awaited the orders of the French government. But Desmaretz, still unconvinced that the country needed importations, apparently missed this remarkable chance to obtain a large stock of grain from abroad. According to Boislisle, author of the authoritative study of this famine, France failed to get even the two hundred thousand sacks that were purchased.[50] In February other grain agents were sent to Holland, but only one of them met with success.[51] In March the Dutch forbade any future shipment of grain from their country, and the French were obliged to look elsewhere.

Desmaretz deserves severe criticism for his stubbornness and hesitancy in late 1708 and early 1709. A more alert controller-

[48] Boislisle and Brotonne, *op. cit.*, III, No. 264. They were permitted to Switzerland even as late as January 5, 1709.

[49] Boislisle, *op. cit.*, XXIX, 472.

[50] *Ibid.*, XXX, 519.

[51] This man managed to purchase 6,600 quintals of wheat at Amsterdam with funds advanced by the French government (Boislisle and Brotonne, *op. cit.*, III, No. 275).

general of finance might have forestalled a famine. When in the spring of 1709 he came to realize the true situation, it was difficult for France to make importations through the fleets of Britain and Holland, then blockading both her Atlantic and Mediterranean shores.

Desmaretz later tried hard to make up for lost time. He sent French agents to Sweden and Poland in June and July in search of grain. He made overtures to the merchants and shippers of Danzig, where large quantities of grain were available. On June 8 he wrote to De Besenval, the French *envoyé extraordinaire* to Sweden, asking him to make known to all Danzig merchants and shippers the advantages that France would offer them for bringing grain to French ports: first, exemption from the port duty of 50 sous per ton, and all other duties; secondly, permission to get a return cargo in French ports, or ballast, as the shipmasters preferred; thirdly, permission to call at an enemy port, if desired, before returning to Danzig; and fourthly, monetary awards to the captains.[52] But few if any Danzig captains ventured the risk of capture.

Late in June the representative of King Stanislas of Poland, who acted also as a French grain agent, wrote to the controller-general that it was possible for the French to get wheat from Danzig, and even from Hamburg, if they would have it consigned by water to the Polish consul at Lisbon. The captain of the vessel carrying it could proceed leisurely and at the first opportunity call for unloading at a French port. Nothing, however, came from the suggestion, for Desmaretz was reluctant to take the risk of capture. Similarly, a French agent at Stockholm wrote that the Swedes had wheat to sell but dared not attempt to run the British and Dutch blockade.[53]

It appears possible that Desmaretz could have obtained ample quantities of grain from Northern Europe even at that late moment, had he been willing to make payment in advance and assume all monetary risks for the vessels in case of capture. Whether any of the vessels would have succeeded in slipping through the blockade is of course uncertain. Many did slip through the British-Dutch Mediterranean blockade, and considering the desperate condition of the French populace, the venture might well have been tried. Here

[52] Labuchelle, *op. cit.*, II, 268.
[53] Boislisle and Brotonne, *op. cit.*, III, No. 275.

again, however, there was a great difficulty: the coffers of the French government were virtually empty. It had been unable to pay an indebtedness of approximately 600,000 livres to peasants in Picardy for drayage in 1707 and 1708, and in fact did not pay it until 1712. It was forced in 1709 to declare suspension of payment on the principal and interest of government securities until peace should be made.[54] For some time the troops had not been paid, and though in 1709 an increase of two sous was made in the pay of soldiers to maintain their morale during the crisis, only a part was paid.[55] Even in previous years they had been paid with the greatest difficulty.[56] Thus Desmaretz faced overwhelming obstacles.

Of the grain agents in the north who met with success, the most fortunate was Fargès, who made importations into Hainaut (French Flanders) from the Palatinate, from Luxemburg, and allegedly from the Netherlands. He had furnished Hainaut with about four thousand sacks of grain and was the only agent able to get grain past the enemy lines into that province.[57]

In the Mediterranean area France had much more success. Large quantities of wheat and other grains were imported from Italy, the Aegean islands, Egypt and the Levant, and, above all, the Barbary States.[58] The *Journal de Verdun* of December, 1709, gloated over the remarkable success of the grain boats in slipping through the blockade. The ships docked and unloaded grain at Marseilles, Toulon, and other ports, whence it was distributed over France in convoys by land and by river traffic. No summary figures have been found, but, according to Boislisle, the importations caused a con-

---

[54] Saint-Simon, *op. cit.*, XVII, 205 n. 1.

[55] The troops in the generality of Amiens were paid in August or September (Boislisle, *op. cit.*, XXX, 535). At this time France had five armies in the field (Bramard, *op. cit.*, pp. 38-39).

[56] Arthur Hassal, *Louis XIV and the Zenith of the French Monarchy* (New York, 1899), p. 377. The troops were fed during this crisis, although they had a bitter time of it. Provinces with grain stocks were assigned quotas to supply to specific bodies of troops. Often these were not sent. Desmaretz stated in his *Compte rendu* that the government procured 557,900 sacks of grain for the army in 1709, and more than 730,000 in 1710, at a cost of more than 25,000,000 livres (Boislisle, *op. cit.*, XXX, 532-537, 540). Voltaire (*Siècle de Louis XIV* ["Oeuvres de Voltaire," ed. Beuchot, Paris, 1830, XX], II, 286) says that provisioning of the army in 1709 cost the government "forty-five millions."

[57] Boislisle and Brotonne, *op. cit.*, III, No. 476.

[58] Boislisle and Brotonne, *op. cit.*, III, No. 359; Boislisle, *op. cit.*, XXX, 524-525; Bramard, *op. cit.*, pp. 36-37; J. Tissier, *op. cit.*, pp. 9-10.

siderable drop in the price of grain, and went far, though belatedly, toward meeting the food crisis.[59]

Within France freedom of trade in grains was established by a royal order of December 8, 1708, and later extended throughout 1709. All tolls and duties on grains carried from province to province were suspended, and no grain was to be seized either for the *taille* or other taxes.[60] But while in theory shipments of grain were to be made freely from one province to another without duties, no purchases were to be made without the knowledge of the intendants of selling regions, who had the liberty to halt the export from their generalities when they deemed it necessary. This a number of them did.[61] Provincial estates, subdelegates, and the populace interposed on occasion to prohibit the removal of grain from their province.[62] Even authorization for a city to purchase grain was sometimes sought.[63] The alleged freedom of trade in grains in 1709 was therefore by no means what one would understand by the term today.

Not many regions of France grew large quantities of grain. Prior to the eighteenth century the only regions which grew much grain for export were Brittany, Aunis, and Languedoc.[64] It was traditional for Paris to draw her grain supplies chiefly from Champagne and Picardy; Bordeaux, from Brittany and Poitou; Marseilles, from Languedoc; and Lyons, from Burgundy. In all these instances the grain could be carried by water as well as by land. In 1709 these metropolitan areas attempted to fall back upon their customary granaries, but the results were unhappy. The grain-producing regions became panicky and attempted to reserve their stocks for themselves. Guyenne (whose capital was Bordeaux) made heavy importations from Brittany. On February 6, 1709, the intendant at Rennes wrote to the controller-general that his generality could not continue them, since it had to supply the army in Flanders and to keep grain in

---

[59] "These importations saved France" (*op. cit.*, XXX, 523). Herlaut (*op. cit.*, p. 99) holds the same opinion.

[60] Boislisle, *op. cit.*, XXX, 510-511; Letaconnoux, *op. cit.*, p. 179; Herlaut, *op. cit.*, pp. 26-27.

[61] Boislisle and Brotonne, *op. cit.*, III, Nos. 335, 344, 352, 406, 409.

[62] *Ibid.*, III, Nos. 294, 335, 346.   [63] *Ibid.*, III, No. 388.

[64] "France was not characteristically a grain-exporting country. Brittany, Languedoc, Aunis, Picardy, and Normandy sent grain to foreign countries, but only in the case of Brittany, Languedoc, and Aunis was the grain a staple export. Exportation was a relatively incidental problem in France . . ." (Usher, *op. cit.*, p. 238).

reserve for planting purposes.[65] Burgundy had little grain to spare in 1709, and the city of Lyons suffered severely in consequence. Regions about Lyons, it was claimed, were better cared for.[66] Languedoc made shipments of wheat in early 1709, but in March its intendant announced that thenceforth the province would make none, retaining its stores for itself. The controller-general, however, refused to permit this action, and further shipments were made to other provinces.[67] Evidently Paris fared better than any other large city. Frantic measures were taken at an early stage for its provisioning. The parlement of Paris issued orders virtually commandeering all surplus stocks of wheat in its domain in northern France for the city's use. Similar measures were taken by the government officials. Dozens of commissioners and grain agents were sent into the provinces, under orders from both the city and the central government, to purchase for the city any and all available grain stocks. Whatever else happened in France, it was imperative that Paris be fed! From Champagne, Brittany, Alsace, and Lorraine, shipments of grain poured in by water and land.[68]

In short, grain shipments from one part of France to another continued throughout the worst part of the famine, the summer of 1709. The movements indeed were slow, and frequently attended by popular uprisings, both in the regions of origin and in those traversed by the convoys. Since the police proved unequal to the situation, it became necessary for detachments of troops to accompany the grain-wagons and boats. Even then clashes occurred. At Saint-Flour, Rouen, Bayeux, Reims, Montauban, Lyons, Amiens, Soissons, Angers, Marseilles, and numerous other places, crowds attacked the troops engaged in this enterprise.[69] There were also instances of alleged sabotage.[70] On the Loire boatloads of grain were purposely damaged, and in Picardy the peasants tied their horses in the woods lest they be drafted for carrying grain.[71] It is amazing that the

[65] Boislisle and Brotonne, op. cit., III, No. 298.
[66] Monfalcon, op. cit., II, 192.
[67] Boislisle, op. cit., XXX, 510.
[68] Herlaut, op. cit., pp. 81-82; Boislisle, op. cit., XXX, 516; Usher, op. cit., pp. 328-329; P. de Crousaz-Crétet, "La question du pain à Paris en 1709," La revue hebdomadaire, XI (Paris, 1917), 478-479. Lorraine was not at that time a part of France.
[69] Boislisle, op. cit., XXIX, 506-508.
[70] Saint-Simon, op. cit., XVII, 197 with n. 6.
[71] Boislisle, op. cit., XXX, 509.

people faced the problem with so much hysteria. The intendants were more or less helpless to enforce the controller-general's orders that all regions with grain share it with those destitute. Even parishes which had food refused to share it with their unfortunate neighbors.

On March 27 the government ordered a census of all the grain in France, but was unable to obtain correct information. Many, perhaps most, of those with grain concealed it or misrepresented its amount. Repeated orders were given, without success, that all hoarders report their stocks, under penalty of a fine of 3,000 livres and confiscation if caught and found guilty. In order to encourage informing, one half of the fine was offered to anyone who reported a case.[72] That a few hoarders were apprehended and their stocks seized did not greatly improve the situation.[73]

As was customary throughout the eighteenth century in time of famine, many accused the bakers of hoarding and profiteering, with the result that plundering of bakers' shops by mobs was frequent during the crisis. Many, according to Saint-Simon, accused government financial officials of speculation in grain in an endeavor to enrich both the king and themselves.[74] Desmaretz's hesitancy and lack of initiative, however, were largely to blame for the bad situation. Had he been more alert or less stubborn, France might conceivably have escaped the famine altogether.

Desmaretz was variously praised and blamed for issuing his notorious order in the spring of 1709 forbidding farmers to replant their wheat, even with other cereals, after the charge was commonly made that most of the wheat in the ground had been killed. In this he was motivated by a desire to avoid the waste of any more grain than necessary. A few weeks later, when according to his critics it was too late to plant cereals, he countermanded his order, directing farmers to do any replanting that was necessary and to use for the

[72] False declarations concerning stocks of grain carried a fine of 1,000 livres (Boislisle and Brotonne, *op. cit.*, III, No. 498; Herlaut, *op. cit.*, pp. 25-26). Saint-Simon (*op. cit.*, III, 109), on the contrary, reports that informing was discouraged, and that a poor man who went to Desmaretz with some secret information was "rudely chastized."

[73] Labuchelle, *op. cit.*, II, 49, 125, 273; Viaud and Fleury, *op. cit.*, pp. 132-133; Boislisle, *op. cit.*, XXX, 497-498; Herlaut, *op. cit.*, p. 25 n. 1.

[74] *Op. cit.*, XVII, 197. More recent writers have dismissed as unfounded this accusation against the officials.

purpose grains other than wheat. His original order, however, had been unheeded by many farmers, and no doubt the intendants closed their eyes to the violations.

It turned out that not all of the wheat had been killed. The crop of 1709 was, indeed, a short one. Much further importation was necessary, and the shortage lasted until the crop of 1710 became available. Some aspects of the famine persisted into 1710, but the worst was over by the autumn of 1709.

The effects of the famine lasted for years. The shortage in grain could be quickly relieved, but two or three years were necessary for the vines, which in most sections of France had been killed to their roots, to reach maturity again. And much longer time was required for the apple trees of Normandy, the olive trees of Provence and Languedoc, the cypresses, chestnuts, and cork trees of Guyenne, and the walnuts of Touraine, to grow up again from sprouts.[75]

When throughout France hordes of peasants contemplated migration, the government came to their aid.[76] To all who wanted it, the government advanced seed in the summer and autumn of 1709 for planting the 1710 crop.[77] A royal declaration of June 11, 1709, called upon all farmers, proprietors, and tenants to cultivate every possible bit of their land; and it extended to any person whatsoever the privilege of working land as yet untilled a fortnight later, regardless of its ownership.[78] This made it possible, at least legally, for any person, no matter how poor, if he had tools and a willingness to work, to borrow seed from the government and cultivate unused land. To all those planting their lands, the royal declaration extended certain relaxations in the collection of taxes for a period.

To virtually every province the government, as was its custom, made heavy remissions in taxes, in recognition of the losses and the extraordinary expenditures that the provinces and cities had been obliged to make in meeting the distress brought on by the cold and the famine. To Languedoc alone, one of the richer provinces, the

[75] Labuchelle, *op. cit.*, II, 275; Dumas, *op. cit.*, p. 291.
[76] Alexandre Giraudet, *Recherches historiques et statistiques sur l'hygiène de la ville de Tours* (Tours, 1853), pp. 93-94.
[77] Boislisle, *op. cit.*, XXX, 491.
[78] The essential preamble may be found in the *Recueil général des anciennes lois françaises, depuis l'an 420 jusqu'à la Révolution de 1789* . . . , by MM. Jourdan . . . Decrusy . . . [and] Isambert, XX (Paris, n.d.), 541; Delamare (*op. cit.*, II, supplement, 10-13) reproduces the entire declaration.

capitation was reduced in 1709 from 1,800,000 to 1,00,000 livres, and was left at this lower figure until 1717.[79]   Furthermore, from 1709 to 1715 the government granted indemnities each year of 350,000 livres to be distributed among those who had lost olive trees, to aid them in replanting; from 1715 to 1717 it granted annually 290,000 livres.[80]   To Burgundy a remission of 100,000 livres was made on the *don gratuit*.[81]   To Bourbonnais were remitted 400,000 livres on the *taille* of 1710.   Almost every generality received a heavy remission in one or more taxes, with the result that the royal government generously wiped from its slate many millions.   According to Voltaire, Louix XIV remitted 9,000,000 livres of the *capitation* alone, "at a time when he did not have the wherewithal to pay his soldiers."[82]

Louis XIV played an obscure part in meeting the crisis.   Saint-Simon criticized certain of his actions.[83]   Voltaire, on the other hand, wrote that "the king sold some of his gold plate," obtaining for it "four hundred thousand francs [livres]."[84]   The suggestion that the king sell his own crown jewels, which would bring 2,000,000 livres, and use the money for the relief of the needy in Paris was made by Daguesseau *fils* to Desmaretz in a letter dated September, 1709. Daguesseau declared, possibly for prudence, that the proposal had been made to him by one of the leading jewelers of the capital, who assured him that the jewels would have a ready sale.   The controller-general was distinctly embarrassed by this proposal, and with a short explanation rejected it, apparently without bringing it to the attention of the king.   Daguesseau replied with a long letter, countering Desmaretz's objection; but Desmaretz had made up his mind,

---

[79] Boislisle and Brotonne, *op. cit.*, III, No. 471; Ernest Roschach, "Etudes historiques sur la province de Languedoc," *Histoire générale de Languedoc*, . . . by dom Cl. Devic and dom J. Vaissete, XIV (Toulouse, 1876), 2085.

[80] *Ibid.*, XIV, 2082.

[81] Boislisle and Brotonne, *op. cit.*, III, No. 487.

[82] *Op. cit.*, II, 286.

[83] He criticized his rebuffing of two parlements, and cowing the others, in regard to the offering of suggestions.   He repeated a widespread rumor that the famine was being used by government officials for speculation in grains, and that the king's treasury was to benefit.   He commented sardonically that the tax instituted in 1709 to aid the poor was permitted to continue after the famine, and was used by the king for other purposes (*op. cit.*, XVII, 197-203, 207).

[84] *Op. cit.*, II, 73.   "The greatest lords," he added, "sent their silver plate to the Mint.   For some months Parisians ate only black bread.   Several families, even at Versailles, lived on oaten bread.   In this, Madame de Maintenon set the example."

and he did not care to pass on such a suggestion to the "Sun King."[85]

If Louis XIV had succeeded in his attempt in the spring of 1709 to bring the War of the Spanish Succession to an end, this would have afforded a greater measure of relief than any other, since food importations on a large scale could shortly have been made from the northern countries.[86] To this end he sent Torcy to the Hague to make peace proposals to the Allies. France was willing to give up much, but the Allies demanded more than she could accept. Louis was willing to accede to French withdrawal from the war, but not to the employment of French arms against his grandson on the Spanish throne. That would have been inconsistent with honor. In early June the negotiations broke down, and Louis recalled his envoy. In a letter to the French people, published and circularized throughout the provinces on the advice of Torcy, he confided to them what had taken place, the destitution of the treasury, and the weakness of France, and asked for their loyalty in carrying on the war until there could be peace with honor.[87] The response was electrical, and its record will ever form one of the most gallant pages of French history.[88]

So much for the *Grand Hiver* and the famine of 1709. Relief in many respects was not handled as such a disaster would be in the twentieth century. In fact, it was managed with greater slowness and bungling and more consequent misery than were certain famines of the second half of the seventeenth century, notably those of 1662, 1679, 1684, 1693-94, and 1698.[89] The most important phase of the relief problem was handled by Desmaretz and his lieutenants, but Desmaretz did not cover himself with glory in handling this crisis.

[85] Boislisle and Brotonne, *op. cit.*, III, 552; Boislisle, *op. cit.*, XXX, 522.
[86] Voltaire (*op. cit.*, II, 72-73) wrote that Holland had ample stores.
[87] Hassal (*op. cit.*, p. 382) quotes part or all of the letter.
[88] Boislisle, *op. cit.*, XXX, 538-542.
[89] *Ibid.*, XXX, 519.

CHAPTER II

LATER EIGHTEENTH-CENTURY FAMINES

The Famine of 1747-48 in Guyenne

AMONG the numerous famines in France after 1709 was that of 1747-48 in Guyenne. This province, of which Bordeaux, the famed wine center, was the capital, did not grow a great amount of grain under any circumstances. In 1747, partly because of a severe hailstorm, its wheat crop was only two fifths of the normal production.[1] Even in late July and early August fear of a forthcoming famine spread rapidly throughout the countryside. Few shipments of grain were made, and some of them were pillaged along the way by the panicky population. Tourny, the intendant, in dismay wrote letter after letter in August to the officials in Paris and to the intendants of other provinces for additional grain supplies. On his own initiative he hastily made arrangements with a grain dealer in Bordeaux to import 40,000 bushels of wheat, 25,000 bushels of rye, and 15,000 bushels of beans, and afterwards asked the approval of the controller-general. He also seized large wheat shipments that were being sent by way of the Garonne to the army in Provence.

Machault, the controller-general of finance, himself a former intendant, disapproved of the hasty actions of Tourny, realizing that his frantic efforts would only result in heightening grain prices and hoarding in the adjacent provinces. Guyenne would thus find it much more difficult to purchase wheat than if Tourny went about the matter calmly. Moreover, the fear of a famine might be so injected into the neighboring provinces as to set up an artificial famine in them. Machault was well informed on the grain situation in all the provinces, had been in constant communication with their intendants and subdelegates, and was aware that France had a mediocre but ample harvest and could care for the situation in Guyenne. Accordingly, he abrogated Tourny's precipitate arrangements and sent to his assistance Bouret, a clever government agent with expe-

[1] M. Marion, "Une famine en Guyenne (1747-1748)," *Revue historique,* XLVI (Paris, 1891), 244.

rience in Provence,[2] to make such purchases of grain as would be necessary to tide Guyenne through the crisis.

Bouret was unpopular in Bordeaux from the moment of his arrival, for the people did not like Machault's action in depriving them of grain supplies which they had within their grasp. This unpopularity became intense when Bouret, after some weeks of waiting, proceeded to engage as underagent Ribes, a wholesale merchant of Toulouse. The choice of a stranger, rather than some Bordeaux merchant or merchants, for this important transaction was displeasing. Tourny, also possibly irked, insisted that the 100,000 bushels of rye and 200,000 bushels of wheat that Bouret set about to purchase would be only half enough to meet the needs of the province.[3]

Quickly tiring of being *persona non grata*, Bouret suggested a change to the intendant: he proposed that instead of his acting alone, a committee of the leading merchants of Bordeaux be formed to co-operate with him in provisioning the province. Accordingly, Tourny convoked a meeting at his home on September 13, bringing together with himself and Bouret the procurer-general, the *jurats* (aldermen), and twenty-five leading merchants of the city. Eight of the merchants at length agreed to act as commissioners along with Bouret in making the necessary grain purchases for the province. They agreed to import within four months from October 1, 1747, a total of 200,000 bushels of wheat and 100,000 bushels of rye; for their efforts they were to receive the modest commission of 15 sous per bushel of wheat and 12 sous per bushel of rye.[4]

The royal government placed at the disposal of the province a loan of 300,000 livres for the purchase of grain,[5] and later, in early 1748, made a gift of 100,000 livres, to be used for the distribution of food or alms among the poor.[6] Much of the gift was employed in the distribution of rice. Even after the worst of the famine, the government furnished 2,000 livres a month to procure food for the poor, both in the city of Bordeaux and throughout the province.[7]

[2] Some months earlier Bouret adroitly had ended an artificial famine in Provence by bringing in several boatloads of sacked material passing for wheat. Immediately hoarders and speculators dumped their stocks on the market, and the situation was righted. Only a portion of the sacks, however, had grain in them; the rest were dummies, filled with sand or other matter (Lhéritier, *op. cit.*, p. 211).

[3] Marion, *op. cit.*, pp. 248-250.   [4] *Ibid.*, p. 251.

[5] *Ibid.*, p. 250. For the first six months the loan was to run without interest.

[6] *Inv.-som . . . Gironde*, C 1388.   [7] *Ibid.*, C 1404.

The importations by the company of commissioners set up in mid-September went slowly. Difficulties beset them on every hand. The intendants of Poitou and Languedoc, two of the great grain-growing regions, would permit only small exportations, and the intendant of Brittany also wished to limit his sales to Guyenne.[8] Panic had already reached these regions. From Brittany it was difficult to ship even the grain that had been purchased. These circumstances made for slowness in supplying the needs of Guyenne. By December 31, 1747, although 230,000 of the 300,000 bushels desired had been purchased, a mere 46,000 had arrived at Bordeaux.[9] Even by mid-February, when the purchases were larger, only 58,376 bushels of wheat and 52,671 bushels of rye had been received.

Tourny, meanwhile, had grown frantic. He then sought to purchase grain in Spain, Portugal, Poland, Touraine, Orléanais, Montauban, Auch, Languedoc, and the Isle of Oleron. Only some trifling importations resulted, for the alarm increased abroad, and the situation within Guyenne became more desperate. The circumstances that Machault wished to avert were taking place in spite of his efforts.

In April, with importations still slow, Tourny addressed letter after letter to Machault depicting the distress of his generality. Each became more piteous than the former. On April 20 he wrote: "There are perhaps in my generality more than 10,000 persons who look less like living persons than walking skeletons, their food for some time being almost nothing except bran and herbs, and even bran is often lacking . . . ; my heart breaks with grief and despair, tears fall from my eyes as I write you, so deeply am I touched by these unfortunates; I wish that my blood could be transformed into grain; I would draw it to the last drop. . . ."[10] On April 27 he wrote another distressing letter; on the thirtieth he informed Machault that Bordeaux had food for only eight or ten more days; on May 4 he reported that four persons had died of hunger and that half the population faced death unless food arrived as speedily as possible. On May 5 he sent Machault by special courier yet another letter, more distressing than the others. In short, he asserted that his predictions had at last come to pass: "Death escorted by

[8] Marion, *op. cit.*, XLVI, 252-253.
[9] *Ibid.*, XLVI, 254.
[10] Quoted, *ibid.*, XLVI, 262.

Famine stalks through all the parishes of Médoc, Blayais, Bourgez, Cubzagues, Entre-Deux-Mers, and other sections of the Bourdelais: it carries off some inhabitants continually, and is ready to enter Bordeaux, where its ravages, preceded by all sorts of disorders, would be very much greater. . . ."[11] Machault, who could resist no longer, decided that he had been mistaken, and Tourny right, in estimating the needs of the province. Quickly he purchased from the Palatinate, with government funds, 60,000 bushels,[12] and urged upon other officials in Paris and in the provinces the need of dispatching at once aid to stricken Guyenne. Furthermore, on April 30 the government hastily signed the preliminary terms of the peace of Aix-la-Chapelle, bringing the War of the Austrian Succession to a close.[13]

Within a few days after the signing of the peace proposals, grain began to flow into Bordeaux from all sides. The importations of Bouret and of the company of commissioners made their tardy appearance. Heavy purchases, permitted to Tourny after his heart-rending letters, were quickly filled. Additional supplies were received from England by individuals, for the government had so altered its former position as to allow any and all persons in Guyenne to import grain. Besides, 60,000 bushels were purchased by the government from the Palatinate. It was the end of a melodrama: aid was rushed from all sides to the need of the desperate province. To cap the climax, the hoarders of grain and bread in Guyenne now placed their holdings on the market. Within a few days after the signing of the peace terms the bakeshops had, so to speak, no purchasers of bread, the markets no purchasers of wheat. Tourny in humiliation was obliged to admit to Machault that he had misjudged the situation, and that Guyenne had never been so seriously in need of grain as he had imagined. He was even compelled to beseech Machault to halt the shipments from the Palatinate, since his province was now submerged in surplus grain.[14]

Naturally Machault was provoked at Tourny because of these vexatious actions, and his anger doubtless lingered for years.[15] In

[11] Quoted, *loc. cit.*   [12] *Ibid.*, XLVI, 264.

[13] Marion (*op. cit.*, XLVI, 263, n. 1) believes that the distressing news from Bordeaux was probably responsible for "the vexatious precipitation with which this treaty was concluded."

[14] *Ibid.*, XLVI, 263-265.   [15] Lhéritier, *op. cit.*, pp. 227-229.

handling this famine the controller-general of finance played a more capable role than in 1709, while the intendant, or intendants, played a weaker part. By way of further contrast, only one province in 1748 experienced famine, and the shortage of grain was due to over-estimation rather than underestimation.

During the crisis the province had imported, through its company of commissioners, headed by Bouret, a total of 432,973 bushels of grain, about half wheat and half rye, at a cost of 4,672, 979 livres.[16] From the sale of this grain in Guyenne only 3,798,561 livres were obtained, leaving a deficit of 874,418 livres, most of it due to the drop in prices after the signing of peace. Naturally the province assumed responsibility for the deficit. Tourny apportioned one third of it to the city of Bordeaux and two thirds to the rest of the province. To raise the funds from the province, he assigned an increase in the *taille*, a tax that fell almost entirely upon the middle and lower classes.[17] Since the city of Bordeaux was not subject to payment of the *taille*, other means of raising the money were found. Payment in full, however, was apparently not made until 1756 or later,[18] and then it turned out to be another trying experience for Tourny.[19]

The Famine Period of 1767-75

The winter of 1766-67 was one of the coldest in the eighteenth century. According to a country curé of Brittany, the temperature was nearly as low as in 1709, but the cold weather lasted longer, with disastrous results.[20] It marked the beginning of a period of misery that lasted for a decade in France. Each year saw poor harvests in some part of the kingdom. In some provinces such as Limousin (1768-74), Touraine (1768-75), Guyenne (1766-73), and Brittany (1767-70, 1772-75), the famine ran, with fluctuations, throughout the greater portion of the period. In other provinces, such as Orléanais (1768-69) and Normandy (1769-70), it was of shorter duration, but severe while it lasted. In Orléanais children died in large

[16] An additional 9,928 bushels had been purchased, but were captured by the British or lost (Marion, *op. cit.*, XLVI, 270, n. 1, 274, with n. 1).

[17] Marion (*ibid.*, XLVI, 275) criticizes Tourny for choosing to increase this tax rather than the more representative taxes, the *dixième* and the *capitation*.

[18] [Pierre] Bernadau, *Histoire de Bordeaux* . . . (Bordeaux, 1837), p. 124.

[19] Marion, *op. cit.*, XLVI, 273-285.

[20] Paul Caraman, "Le journal d'un curé de campagne (1763-1792)," *Revue historique de Bordeaux*, VI (Bordeaux, 1913), 334.

numbers, either from the lack of food or from epidemics that were almost an invariable accompaniment of eighteenth-century famines.[21]

The times were reminiscent of the prolonged era of economic depression from 1690 to 1713, which had likewise had many years of bad crops. In 1767-75 the people, like those of the earlier period, suffered from the effects of war. Turgot in letters to the controller-general of finance attributed much of the indebtedness and penury of his generality (Limousin) to the war (1756-63).[22] But war had little or nothing to do with the crop failures of these last years. Floods, hailstorms, and other caprices of nature were mainly responsible.[23]

Of the 1769 wheat crop in Touraine, many elections (townships) harvested no more grain than had been planted; even in the most fortunate sections, only a seminormal crop was raised. "Misery was general," according to report. The municipal officers of certain towns wrote to the intendant, Du Cluzel, exposing the sad living conditions of the poor in their vicinities: "There are some walking spectres, devoured by need and hunger. One sees them go about the cities with emaciated children. Everything tends to destruction, to depopulation, to want."[24]

In May, 1770, some rural inhabitants resorted to the practice of mixing baked fern roots with grain in their bread.[25] In Limousin similar conditions prevailed. Turgot, writing in 1770, described the past year as "one of the worst in memory" in that province.[26] Not only was the grain crop a heavy failure, but the inhabitants were able to get very poor prices for their wine and livestock. To make matters worse, an epizootic among the cattle broke out in certain parishes. The distress thus was very great. The larger portion of the families in his generality, Turgot asserted, were compelled to sell "at a vile price" whatever commodities they had on hand, even to their personal and household effects, in order to get some money with which to purchase grain.[27]

Happily less hysteria prevailed than in 1709 and in 1747-48, and, as a result of wise management on the part of Terray and his in-

[21] Bloch, op. cit., p. 12.

[22] Oeuvres de Turgot, ed. Daire, I (Paris, 1844), 581, 618.

[23] Inv.-som . . . Seine-Inférieure, C 111 and 268; Dumas, op. cit., p. 342; Turgot, Oeuvres, I, 597, 608.

[24] Quoted by Dumas, op. cit., pp. 342-343.

[25] Ibid., p. 344.   [26] Op. cit., I, 601.   [27] Ibid., I, 599, 604.

tendants, sufficient quantities of grain were imported from the more fortunate French provinces and from abroad.[28] Large quantities of grain were obtained, through agents, from Holland, Germany, and Poland.[29] Turgot alone spent 200,000 livres for grain in 1770-71, getting most of it from Danzig and Stettin.[30] This money, in the form of diminutions, was advanced by the government.[31]

Considerable quantities of beans and rice were distributed among the poor by the intendants. In Touraine, Du Cluzel distributed 20,000 pounds (livres) of rice, but according to his biographer, F. Dumas, "100,000 were needed to aid the eighty-four thousand poor of the generality."[32] Du Cluzel also printed a simple memoir to instruct the populace how to prepare the rice. To Brittany the government sent 30 quintals of rice for distribution,[33] and to the generality of Rouen 400 quintals. In Limousin, Turgot spent a total of 47,200 livres for rice and beans for distribution in the two years 1770 and 1771.[34] Writing to the controller-general in late 1770, Turgot reported that he had been obliged to provide food gratuitously to approximately one fourth of the inhabitants of his province.[35]

The most interesting feature of government assistance in 1770, however, was the embarkation on a large scale of a plan to aid the unfortunates through provision of work. Considerable sums of money were provided to all, or virtually all, of the generalities for the establishment of charity workshops (ateliers de charité), in which the unemployed could be employed for a season at repairing roads, at draining swampy lands, or at other projects of a communal value in which unskilled labor could be used. The charity workshop was an old institution in France, having been adopted at intervals for two or three centuries. It had been resorted to occasionally in periods of famine in the eighteenth century, and its popularity had been slowly growing. In 1770 it was made an important institution by the Abbé Terray, and retained this importance throughout the re-

[28] According to Turgot (ibid., I, 609) "misery" was "about universal in the kingdom" during 1769-70, and his province was one of those that suffered most.

[29] Ibid., II, 75; Dumas, op. cit., pp. 347-348.

[30] Op. cit., II, 75, 84.   [31] Ibid., I, 595.   [32] Op. cit., p 344.

[33] Memorandum of the controller-general's office, 1770 (Arch. Nat., H 565).

[34] Op. cit., II, 84.

[35] He estimated that there were about 700,000 in the province (ibid., I, 593, 595).

mainder of the century. No total figure for the sums granted by the government to the provinces for charity workshops in 1770 is available, but the *Inventaires-sommaires des archives départementales antérieures à 1790* for the various provinces commonly makes mention of grants for the purpose and lists documents on the matter.[36] Illustrative of the size of the grants is that to Limousin of 80,000 livres; Brittany, 28,000 livres; and Touraine, 25,000 livres.[37]

Frequently in earlier periods the mistake had been made of restricting the workshops to the larger cities and thus attracting a swarm of the needy from the smaller towns and rural sections, a result always undesirable inasmuch as large gatherings of malcontents furnished tinder for riots and uprisings. Partly to avert this, partly to carry aid to the rural communities, the charity workshops of 1770 and the following years were distributed in several, sometimes many, places in each generality. The results were gratifying.

In some of the charity workshops of the period women and children worked with the men, but had lighter tasks. Turgot employed a small portion of the sum allowed his province to establish some charity workshops in spinning *(ateliers de filature)* at Limoges for the employment of women and children.[38]

In 1770 Turgot expended a total of 85,000 livres on charity workshops. Since his workshops were concentrated in the canton of Montagne, a large portion of which belonged to the Marshal De Soubise, the Marshal contributed the additional pittance of 6,000 livres.[39] In 1771 Turgot scattered the workshops over the whole generality, as had been done in Touraine, Brittany, and other provinces, spending on them a total of 218,404 livres (greatly exceeding his allowance of 80,000 livres).[40] Turgot did not hesitate to overspend. He exceeded his allowances in all matters of relief for the two years 1770-71 by considerable sums; yet, according to his own computation and hedging, he showed a deficit of only 90,000 livres on expenditures of 1,240,000 livres, all employed in famine relief work in Limousin.[41] In earlier periods of the eighteenth century this overspending might have brought an intendant a sharp repri-

---

[36] Turgot (*op. cit.*, I, 608-609) wrote that all the provinces got aid for this purpose.

[37] *Ibid.*, II, 72; memorandum of the controller-general's office, 1770 (Arch. Nat., H 565); and Dumas, *op. cit.*, p. 347 with n. 2.

[38] For this purpose he used 1,691 livres 15 sous (Turgot, *op. cit.*, 74).

[39] *Ibid.*, II, 82, 84.   [40] *Ibid.*, II, 84.   [41] *Ibid.*, II, 84-97.

mand or even dismissal, but by 1770 France had entered on a period of liberality, and Turgot's action was not only approved but admired, and in 1774 he was appointed controller-general of finance, succeeding Terray.[42]

While the period between the harvests of 1769 and 1770 was that of the greatest dearth and suffering in this decade (1766-75), misery of the populace continued, and government assistance was necessary. In most of the generalities charity workshops were continued through 1774 or 1775. Illustrative of the sums spent by the government for this purpose are those assigned to the generality of Tours. In 1771 this generality was allowed 30,000 livres; in 1772, 100,000 livres; in 1773, 90,000 livres; in 1774, 100,000 livres.[43] Importations of grain from abroad and from French provinces enjoying a surplus continued to be made, gratifications being paid to the importing agents.[44] Considerable amounts of rice were distributed to the needy, as in Touraine, where Du Cluzel employed curés at the task. Moreover, in Touraine, in Limousin, and in Guyenne,[45] charity funds were raised by levy or taxes, commonly on the rich.

In 1773-74 riots in Touraine and Guyenne were accompanied by pillaging of bakers' shops and grain markets. The worst riot in Touraine occurred at Tours, February 22, 1774, when the rabble pillaged two boats loaded with wheat on the Loire and the Cher and threatened to burn the city. It was necessary for the mounted police (maréchaussée) to charge the mob with the flat of their swords and to fire their muskets (but without shot) in order to disperse it. Four of the principal rioters were later hanged, on the king's orders; amnesty was extended the rest.[46] In Guyenne the rioting was chiefly in the late spring and early summer of 1773. Bordeaux had experienced a procession of bad harvests in grain since 1766, but that of 1772 was the worst, following a crop of only half the normal size.

[42] His handling of relief in Poitou had much to do with this appointment.

[43] Dumas, op. cit., pp. 345, 354.

[44] Turgot wrote in his "Compte-rendu au contrôleur-général" in 1771 that the customary commission and gratification to agents in these circumstances was 2 per cent. His expenditure in this respect for 1770-71 had been 15,474 livres (Oeuvres, II, 85).

[45] Dumas, op. cit., p. 355; Turgot, op. cit., I, 595 with n.; P. Caraman, "La disette des grains et les émeutes populaires en 1773 dans la généralité de Bordeaux," Revue historique de Bordeaux, III (1910), 317.

[46] Dumas, op. cit., pp. 355-356.

At the end of July, 1772, the outlook for the province appeared desperate. Some Bordelais and Parisian agents were then employed to provide it with grain, and reportedly they did their job well.[47] Nevertheless, much discontent prevailed, grounded in part on the popular dislike of one Bethman, a member of the Bordeaux firm of provisioners. Rumors spread that the provisioners were enriching themselves. Food was scarce, prices were high, begging was widespread, and misery general. At length in May riots broke out in a dozen or more places in the generality. On May 8 one occurred in Bordeaux, brought on according to some by the cupidity of the bakers, according to others by the poor quality of the bread. From Bordeaux riots spread throughout the province. Sometimes the same rioters went from village to village. Homes and shops were ransacked; their food was taken and their wine was drunk. Four boats were pillaged, two loaded with grain (for the province) and two apparently with wine (for the colonies).[48] Millers and others with stocks of grain were compelled to sell at reduced prices; when some refused, the rioters seized their stocks without payment. In some communities the middle- and upper-class citizens organized themselves into bodies of vigilantes, in anticipation of the National Guard of the Revolution, and maintained order.[49] The arrival of two regiments of troops did more than anything else to restore calm. Additional food supplies from Languedoc came about the same time and helped. Nevertheless, some of the convoys were plundered, and in July there was a slight recrudescence of plundering, the mobs taking food as well as other objects.[50]

Throughout this famine period of 1767-75 the government made remissions or diminutions in taxes to the various provinces that had suffered, as had long been its practice. Though covering only a small portion of the losses to these regions, they helped. The in-

[47] Caraman, op. cit., III, 298, 314.

[48] "They pillaged 'two boats loaded with grain, and two others loaded with approximately 500 barrils [sic] de minots for the colonies had the same fate'" (ibid., III, 303).

[49] Ibid., III, 306.

[50] Caraman (ibid., III, 319) finds in these riots the beginnings of the Revolution. While this view may well be taken, it should be mentioned that bread riots and plundering of bakers' shops were a common feature of seventeenth- and eighteenth-century famines. Cf. P. Clément, La police sous Louis XIV (Paris, 1866), pp. 252-255, 258-261, 283, 319; Boislisle and Brotonne, op. cit., III, Nos. 324, 344, 346, 361.

tendants always asked for more than they got. Thus Turgot asked for diminutions of at least 600,000 livres because of the miserable harvest of 1767, and received only 220,000 livres.[51] The 600,000 livres were but a fraction of the losses of the generality. Turgot estimated that the losses through importing food from outside the province had been approximately 3,600,000 to 4,000,000 livres.[52] For each of the next several years his estimate of losses through importations was approximately the same as was his request for aid, and the remission was proportional. Brittany was granted a remission of 100,000 livres in 1770, on condition that 28,000 of it be employed on a charity workshop for the poor.[53] Languedoc was allowed remissions of 400,000 livres for 1768, 100,000 for 1771, 203,400 for 1774, and 400,00 for 1776.[54] The generality of Bordeaux was extended 20,000 livres annually for 1772 and 1773; after the riots in May, 1773, the controller-general made an additional grant of 200,000 livres for that year.[55] The other generalities that suffered from famine or shortage of crops, because of accidents of nature, received similar treatment. The total remissions each year were large.

The Famine of 1788-89

The fifteen years in France prior to the Revolution were, according to the economist Charles Gomel, "a prosperous period."[56] Even so, from 1783 they were marked by a succession of economic disasters that culminated in the crisis of 1789. First was the frigid winter of 1783-84, with temperatures so low that for weeks almost all industry and commerce in many cities came to a standstill, making conditions hard for the laborers. This disaster was followed in early 1784 by perhaps the worst floods that France experienced in the eighteenth century, with staggering property losses and increased misery for the lower classes. The crops of 1784 and 1785 were not

[51] *Oeuvres*, I, 577, 579.　　　　[52] *Ibid.*, I, 593.
[53] Memorandum of the controller-general's office, 1770 (Arch. Nat., H 565). There were other charity workshops in Brittany in 1770. This particular one was to be devoted to road construction or reconstruction. In another at Morlaix, the workers were employed at cleaning the harbor *(le curage du port)* *(Inv.-som . . . Ille-et-Vilaine*, C 667).
[54] *Histoire générale du Languedoc*, XIII, 105, 108, 110, 115. Remissions were commonly made for the year following the calamity or loss experienced by a province.
[55] Caraman, *op. cit.*, III, 317.
[56] *Les causes financières de la Révolution française: Les derniers contrôleurs généraux* (Paris, 1893), p. 567.

good in certain provinces. In 1786 the trade treaty with England provided that the duties on English hardware and textiles entering France should be reduced in return for similar reductions on French wines and liqueurs entering England. The treaty, which was in part the result of agitation by the physiocrats, worked well for England but wretchedly for France. France was flooded with English goods, manufacturing establishments throughout her provinces had to close down or limit their production, and scores of thousands of industrial workers were thrown out of employment. Thirty thousand were unemployed in Lyons alone. This economic crisis, beginning in 1786, deepened steadily until it reached its nadir in the dire events of the summer and autumn of 1789.

France would probably have weathered the industrial and commercial crisis of the late 1780's peacefully had it not been accompanied by a still more frightful agricultural crisis, the result of a wretched harvest in 1788.[57] Large sections of France, both north and south, were devastated by a hailstorm and a flood on July 13, so violent in nature that, according to a report from Picardy, houses, mills, and trees were uprooted, the harvest of hemp and hay was ruined by the water, and all the lowlands were left flooded.[58] The damage to the grain crop of France, according to the Abbé Tessier,[59] amounted to 25,000,000 livres in value, and he estimated that other hailstorms did further damage to the extent of 7,000,000 livres. France thus was left with perhaps the smallest grain harvest since 1708.

[57] Georges Lefebvre (La grande peur de 1789, Paris, 1932, p. 13) calls it a "detestable" harvest: Abbé Tessier, in the article "Disette," in the Encyclopédie méthodique, Agriculture, Vol. IV, writes that even in the more fortunate provinces the harvest was "mauvaise." On the other hand, Gomel, citing Arthur Young, English traveler and student of scientific agriculture, designates the crop of 1788 as "mediocre" throughout France despite some hailstorms which hit certain regions (op. cit., pp. 551-552). Gomel and Young insist that the famine was largely a fictitious one, brought on by Necker's imprudent expressions of alarm and public announcements of his grain purchases abroad (ibid., pp. 564-565). There is thus a difference of opinion among authorities, and even among contemporaries of 1788, on the size of the French harvest of that year. The present writer finds it difficult to agree with Gomel and Young, because of the gigantic grain importations which France made in 1788-89, and because these importations led to no price drops after the abundant harvest of 1789 came in, as would certainly have happened had the famine of 1789 been in large part a psychological one.

[58] Petition from "Les administrateurs de la Somme" to De Lessart, May 21, 1791 (Arch. Nat., F15, 101).

[59] Loc. cit.

Since the harvest in 1787 had been excellent, and grain from a new harvest was not properly seasoned for grinding and use before mid-October,[60] it might be expected that even the scanty crop of 1788 would tide all except perhaps industrial workers over into 1789. According to Professor Lefebvre, however, the city of Troyes had 10,200 unemployed in October, 1788, of whom 6,000 were nonresidents who had poured into the city, presumably from the villages and countryside, in search of work and food. Paris, Cherbourg, and other cities experienced this drift of indigents that was the accompaniment of every famine. Some of the unemployed were put to work on the dike at Cherbourg and on certain canals in Picardy and central France.[61] Paris and other cities opened charity workshops.

The government subsidized the distribution among the poor of great quantities of rice, as well as smaller quantities of Irish potatoes and beans, either without charge or at a very low price, throughout the larger towns and cities.[62] On December 10, 1788, Necker, the director-general of finance, wrote to Berthier, the intendant of the generality of Paris, approving heartily of the distributions of Irish potatoes which Berthier was making, and urging him to double the amounts if necessary, should more critical moments arrive.[63] Doubtless the *marmites*, or soup kitchens, with which almost all cities were provided, furnished considerable quantities of soup to those who came and stood in line.

Everywhere private contributions were made to alleviate the situation. In some places they were large. In Orléans the sum of 211,869 livres was subscribed in November to care for local needs.[64]

[60] J. S. Bailly, *Mémoires*, II (Paris, 1822), 272, 383, 407. The harvest of grains in Picardy, one of the chief supply regions in northern France for the city of Paris, ran from late July to early September. Rye was cut in late July; wheat and oats were harvested somewhat later. Threshing and grinding came afterwards, and "lasted throughout the entire winter," being delayed by the necessity of making immediate planting of seed for the winter (Eugène Creveaux, *Le ravitaillement de Paris par le département de l'Aisne pendant la Révolution*, Paris, 1936, p. 232).

[61] *Op. cit.*, pp. 11, 17.

[62] Bibl. Nat., Fonds français, 6801, ff. 30, 35, 37-38, 40, 172-174, 176-179, 180-181, 186, 197-199; Arch. Nat., H 1420, note to Tarbé dated December, 1788. Paris alone was furnished 1,500 quintals of rice in December, 1788, at a cost of 37,500 livres.

[63] Gustave Bord, *Histoire de blé en France: le Pacte de Famine; histoire, legende* (Paris, 1887), pp. 46-47.

[64] "Liste des personnes qui ont voulu contribuer aux Approvisionnemens de la Ville . . ." (Arch. Nat., H 1420).

Paris made large offerings, even if they were slow in coming. The archbishop of Paris, De Juigné, went in debt 400,000 livres through his gifts to charities on this occasion.[65] In July, 1789, the proceeds of three performances of the Comédie Française were given to the cause.[66] In September the Duc de Charost made a *don patriotique* of 100,000 livres to the government treasury, which may be considered as a private contribution to meet this situation. The king and queen, in like manner, sent their silverware to the mint as a *don patriotique*.[67] But, taken as a whole, these private contributions were but a drop in the bucket. While some individuals gave generously, the greater number of those in a position to give held back, waiting for the municipalities, the provinces, and the royal government to meet the situation. Chaos would have prevailed had not the government assumed the responsibility.[68] The fatalities from famine might have been as great as they were in 1709; but thanks to the government's huge importations of grain, apparently no deaths were due to famine. This achievement in itself was no small feat for the government.

The winter of 1788-89, like that of 1709, was one of great severity. "From the middle of November there were some extremely cold spells which were felt over all France; the waters of the Seine, the Loire, the Saône, the Rhône, and the Garonne were for several weeks covered with ice; the harbors of several Channel ports froze; and even the port of Marseilles was covered with ice. During the night of December 30, the Réaumur thermometer registered 18½° below zero at Paris, and the temperature did not moderate until fifteen days later. In brief, the winter of 1789 was the most terrible experienced in France since 1709; work in the cities and in the country ceased; the use of boats for the transportation of grain and flour was suspended; and the working class, famished and shaking with cold, saw itself deprived of every means of existence."[69] At Bordeaux, where the thermometer went one degree lower than it had in the cold winter of 1766, the people invaded

---

[65] Gomel, *op. cit.*, p. 572.
[66] Bailly, *op. cit.*, II, 99. The proceeds of the third performance were first offered to the French Guards, who refused in favor of the needy.
[67] *Ibid.*, II, 389.
[68] Gomel (*op. cit.*, pp. 552-555), however, scoffs at the government's provisioning as being unnecessary, and even harmful.
[69] *Ibid.*, p. 572.

the grounds of the convent of the Chartreuse and cut down its great osiery in order to get firewood with which they could warm themselves.[70]   In Provence the cold killed the larger portion of the vines and olive trees.[71]

It was customary for the French government in times of famine in the eighteenth century to halt all exportation of grain[72] and to grant freedom of trade in this commodity throughout France. Therefore, when Necker became director-general of finance in August, 1788, he proceeded almost at once (September 7), on account of the short harvest, to forbid further exportation,[73] and to order liberty of internal commerce in grain.[74]   To prevent secret buying by speculators, Necker in November, 1788, revoked the privilege of selling grain anywhere except in open markets.   Moreover, to encourage the importation of grain from other countries by large grain dealers, he offered prizes to all who brought in grain from abroad.[75]

Agents representing the government, individual provinces, and cities, were engaged to make importations.   Steps in this direction were begun early, and according to *La grande encyclopédie*[76] the government expended 12,000,000 livres in 1788 alone in making provision for the emergency which it knew lay ahead.   Little of this grain, however, arrived in France before January, 1789.   One of the earliest shipments was a cargo of 7,746 sacks of wheat from Boston, consigned to Leleu Frères of Corbeil, who since 1774 had been grain agents of the French government.[77]

In 1789 the government further spent 70,000,000 livres on the importation of grain, securing a total of 4,436,970 quintals.[78]   Ac-

[70] Bernadau, *op. cit.*, p. 73.   [71] *Inv.-som . . . Bouches-du-Rhône*, C 1010.
[72] For the fluctuating history of the right to import and export in France, see Letaconnoux, *op. cit.*, pp. 175-200.
[73] Gustave Bord (*op. cit.*, p. 104) reports that France had made enormous exportations in 1787-88, and had almost completely disposed of her surplus from the big harvest of 1787.
[74] This action, twice reaffirmed by the National Assembly, was without salutary results (Letaconnoux, *op. cit.*, p. 184).
[75] Lefebvre, *op. cit.*, pp. 27-28; Gomel, *op. cit.*, pp. 554-555.   The old eighteenth-century practice of offering prizes in times of famine had been employed by various controllers-general and intendants.
[76] Art. "Famine."   [77] Bord, *op. cit.*, p. 74.
[78] *La grande encyclopédie*, art. "Famine"; Tessier, *op. cit.*   There were 2,643,-270 quintals of flour, 917,693 quintals of rye or rye and wheat mixed, 351,343 quintals of flour, 97,477 quintals of oats, 462,774 quintals of barley, buckwheat, maize, and other small grain (*menus grains*), 232,415 quintals of beans, peas, and other vegetables, 115,998 quintals of rice.

cording to the Abbé Tessier, "These items were late in arriving, since the most of them were not in our ports until in July, that is to say near the time of the harvest, which happily was abundant." While these precautions did not therefore have their total effect, they were "very useful," and without them, he adds, inroads would have been made on the new harvest before it was cut. Even as it was, according to Professor Lefebvre,[79] a considerable amount of unripe wheat was cut in June and July, 1789, by irresponsible bands which wandered from parish to parish.

The imported wheat in most instances was resold to the public at a price lower than cost. Generally this reduction was made by the government directly to the bakers, who were a numerous, powerful, and much hated group; and they, in turn, were required to sell to the poor, at prices set by the government, varying according to the quality of the bread. One purpose in selling the grain and flour below cost was to force the market price downward and prevent speculators from exploiting the public; a second purpose was to prevent riots. From January through October, 1789, there were dozens, scores, perhaps even hundreds, of bread riots.[80] Not since 1709 had there been anything like such a general breakdown of law enforcement. Convoys of mounted police and troops had long been used to protect grain trains in France, but convoys in 1789 were frequent and were sometimes overpowered. The mobs were frenzied, and the soldiers all too often lacked heart to fight. In nothing perhaps was the weakness of the Old Regime more strikingly revealed than in its inability to maintain order in 1789. This failure was partly due to the reluctance of the officers to fire on the mobs, partly to a realization that if matters came to the worst the soldiers in the line might desert to the mobs. So helpless became the authorities that the city of Paris drove a compromise with its suburb Saint-Denis, whereby in return for nonmolestation of its grain convoys the city would guarantee to the suburb twenty sacks of flour daily.[81]

[79] *Op. cit.*, pp. 19-20.

[80] In this category are to be placed not only attacks on bakers' shops, but attacks on grain convoys, markets, and private storehouses. For accounts of some scores of these riots, see A. Tuetey (ed.), *Repertoire général des sources manuscrites de Paris pendant la Révolution*, I (Paris, 1890); Bailly, *op. cit.*, I; Lefebvre, *op. cit.*, chap. iii; and Gomel, *op. cit.*, pp. 556-561, 563-564.

[81] This agreement was reached on July 24, 1789 (Tuetey, *op. cit.*, I, No. 3162).

In certain of the riots of 1789, as indeed in those of earlier famines, women were ringleaders, and there was little to which these females did not stoop. Several victims of the bread riots of 1789 lost their lives, and others were threatened. Government grain agents were hated so furiously that in some instances they fled for their lives, the people not wanting to see their grain taken for use elsewhere. Sometimes the troops would shoot into the mob. At Orléans on April 26 the mounted police shot and killed eight or ten of the rioters who were pillaging magazines belonging to the state, but this action by the police was rare.[82] If earlier there had been shooting, there might have been less rioting and less revolution. It was in Provence, the home of Mirabeau and the chief early *foyer* of the Revolution, that the riots had their biggest impetus in early 1789.[83]

Bailly recorded in his *Memoirs* that officials earnestly attended to the matter of providing grain. He himself regarded the work as so important that he absented himself from the National Assembly, of which he was president, in order to assume charge of the committee of subsistences for the city of Paris, considering that his role as mayor of Paris was at this time the more essential. For three months during 1789 he and the other members of the committee worked and worried over the details of provisioning the capital. Frequently the city had stocks of flour for no more than one or two days ahead, and once or twice the timely arrival of a convoy found the city with provisions for only a few hours.[84] To his amazement no riots occurred at this time in Paris, and he attributed their absence to his own popularity with the masses resulting from his known attachment to the Revolution.

No figures have been found for the remissions in taxes accorded the various provinces because of this severe famine. According to certain authorities, the French government experienced a loss of more than 40,000,000 livres through its importation and subsidy of grain.[85]

[82] Gomel, *op. cit.*, p. 563.   [83] *Ibid.*, pp. 556-560.
[84] Bailly, *op. cit.*, II, 290, 291, 294.
[85] Statement by Boilandry, deputy of the Third Estate from Paris-hors-des-murs, before the national Assembly, *Archives parlementaires de 1787 à 1860*, série 1, XXI (Paris, 1885), 146. He asserted that the French government had spent from August, 1788, until November, 1790, around 74,000,000 livres on the importation of grain, and that the losses had been more than 40,000,000 livres, chiefly, in his opinion, because of Necker's imprudent, noisy buying. For, in common with Arthur Young and Gomel, he regarded the famine of 1788-89 as largely a psychological one. See also Bord, *op. cit.*, p. 104.

Approximately two thirds of the grain purchased came from foreign countries, such as the Barbary States, Belgium, Holland, Germany, and the United States; the rest came from certain of the more fortunate provinces of France, such as Burgundy, Picardy, Soissonnais, Aunis, and Poitou.

The famine did not completely end in 1789. In 1790 and 1791 grain was still being convoyed, though apparently purchased within France, and mob violence was feared. Much unemployment continued, and rice and soup were fed to the needy.

The Famine of 1792-95

When the Revolution came with its frenzied excitement, its humanitarian ideals, its legislative panaceas, the Revolutionists designed to prevent such calamities as famines. But the famine of 1792-95 was in no small degree a by-product of the Revolution. War, overthrow of the monarchy, sweeping changes in personnel and taxation, and, above all, inflation in currency were as much responsible as any shortage in the grain crop.[86] In fact, it is doubtful that the grain crop was really short, save possibly in the year 1792.[87] According to censuses taken by the government in the summers of 1793, 1794, and 1795, the prospects were bright for abundant harvests.[88] The Jacobins insisted that the famine was fictitious, resting not upon a shortage of grain but upon speculation and attempts of counter-Revolutionists to overthrow the Revolution.[89] Saint-Just in late November, 1792, insisted that the actual cause of

[86] Albert Mathiez, La vie chère et le mouvement social sous le Terreur (Paris, 1927), pp. 50-59.

[87] Eugène Creveaux, in a careful study based on archival material (op. cit.), shows that Soissonnais, one of the principal grain regions supplying Paris, enjoyed bountiful harvests during this whole period (1792-95) and sent extraordinary quantities to Paris, to other districts (even to the Hautes-Pyrenées), and to the army. He inclines toward the opinion that bungling and mismanagement played a large part in creating a fictitious famine.

[88] Mathiez, op. cit., pp. 166, 310, 322, 460; E. Brossard and Joseph de Freminville, Histoire de département de la Loire pendant la Révolution française (1789-1799), II (Paris and Saint-Etienne, 1907), 327; Département de Seine-et-Oise, Les subsistances dans le district de Versailles de 1788 à l'an V, documents collected and published by A. Defresne and F. Evrard, II (Rennes, 1922), 329-330.

[89] Mathiez, op. cit., p. 178. Throughout this famine, and more particularly during the Reign of Terror, there were constant accusations of a famine plot, just as there had been under the Old Regime, save that the royal family was no longer regarded as being mixed in it. Gustave Bord shows in his Le pacte de famine that the rumors before the Revolution were baseless, and it is possible that those of the Terror were equally ridiculous.

the famine was the inflation of paper money, and not a shortage of grains.[90] It is difficult, however, to see how the famine could have lasted so long had there not been a shortage in the grain crops in some parts of the country. The cheap price of money might well have encouraged a tendency to hoard commodities, but the country in the end would have smothered in wheat. This did not happen.

The famine of 1792-95 was similar to the famines of the Old Regime. In 1792 and 1793 bread riots occurred throughout France, as they had in 1709, the 1770's, and 1789. Grain was commonly sent by armed convoys, and even these were sometimes attacked by the irate citizenry of the grain-growing regions.[91] In several instances the National Guards, who were called out to put down the rioters, joined cause with them. Only on regular troops could reliance be placed. In the early half of 1793, at a time when the fortunes of war were not going favorably for the French, the country was almost paralyzed by these riots. Happily, the calling up of three hundred thousand young men for the army, in the *levée en masse* in the summer of 1793, had a wholesome effect in reducing greatly the number of riots. As time went on, other levies were taken, and gradually a large portion of the unemployed[92] and restless man power was absorbed. The beginning of the Terror, shortly following the *levée en masse*, operated in the same direction, with perhaps greater effect, and thenceforth bread riots tended to disappear.

As in the days of the Old Regime, agents were sent abroad to purchase supplies of grain. Others were sent from the needy regions of France to the more prosperous ones.[93] A committee left for the United States in late November, 1793, to buy grain and other commodities. Other agents were sent to Germany, Italy, and Switzerland.[94] In the United States larger purchases were made than

[90] Mathiez, *op. cit.*, p. 107. Mathiez inclines toward this view: "De tous les orateurs, Saint-Just fut celui qui approfondit le mieux les causes de la crise économique."

[91] Creveaux, *op. cit.*, pp. 112-115, 124, 126, 130-132, 148.

[92] The city of Lyons alone had thirty thousand unemployed silk workers in September, 1792, and March, 1793 (Mathiez, *op. cit.*, pp. 100, 164).

[93] Many agents were sent from Paris into Soissonnais. See Creveaux, *op. cit.*, pp. 122, 123, 127, 130-131, 183, 216.

The army also sent its agents; between them and those representing the city there was some competition (*ibid.*, pp. 123, 168, 227-228).

[94] Mathiez, *op. cit.*, pp. 428, 458.

during any previous famine. Since the French were hard pressed to find coin for these purchases, they resorted as much as possible to barter, employing for payment various articles of French production, such as wines, silks, and other items of luxury. The government was successful in negotiating a loan from a group of bankers for 50,000,000 livres. To the United States in particular large cash payments had to be made, and the French government resorted to melting down vessels and ornaments of gold and silver from the confiscated churches. Moreover, it took possession of the Compagnie d'Afrique, through which it made some grain importations from the Barbary States.[95]

But the purchases of grain abroad were disappointing in size, largely because of the British and Dutch blockade. On February 1, 1793, France declared war on Great Britain and the United Provinces, and at once the latter countries intercepted cargo vessels bound from neutral German states for French ports. Moreover, the enemy so frightened the north German neutrals that they were reluctant to undertake further shipments.[96] The Austrian and Prussian armies in the field no doubt rendered it impossible for the French to obtain grain from Poland and Germany by land.[97] The conquest of Belgium in November, 1792, and of the German Rhineland and a part of Holland in early 1793, did not help France replenish her grain stores. Partly on account of the treachery of Dumouriez, these conquests were lost shortly afterwards. In 1794 Belgium and Holland were reconquered. Evidently the French derived some material benefits from their occupation, but no record has been found of food supplies. Certainly for France the famine continued. Possibly an important factor was a misjudgment of the size of the harvest, based on inaccuracies in the census.[98] It will be recalled that officials under the Old Regime had inaccurately estimated the crops of 1708, 1748 (in Guyenne), and 1788.

[95] *Ibid.*, pp. 459-460.
[96] Meandre de Lapoulaye, "Le blocus des côtes de France et la disette à Bordeaux en 1793-95," *Revue historique de Bordeaux*, VIII (Bordeaux, 1915), 47.
[97] These troops had overrun a part of northern France in 1792 and bled it of food supplies. Though later expelled from France, they lay along the Rhine throughout the period of the famine.
[98] During the Revolutionary regime, as formerly, annual summer forecasts of the forthcoming harvest were made. In addition, censuses of the stocks of grain on hand were taken. Twice in 1793 (March and August) censuses of this type were ordered. Fraudulent reporting almost everywhere, however, made them of little value (Mathiez, *op. cit.*, pp. 166, 379-380).

One of the most interesting features of this famine was the requisitioning of grain and fodder from the more prosperous regions for those less fortunate. It was not a new idea. Throughout the eighteenth century the government of the Old Regime had maintained its armies by the requisitioning of supplies. Each year a generality was assigned a certain quota of grain that it must furnish to a particular army quartered in its vicinity. Much of this was taken from the taxes in kind *(en nature)* that the French farmers paid.[99] Every year, moreover, the council of finances, through the controller-general, assigned to each of the large grain-growing generalities an estimate of the amount of wheat, barley, rye, etc., that it would be expected to furnish neighboring generalities producing insufficient grain for their needs. Thus Champagne, Picardy, and Flanders were commonly asked to furnish Paris and Ile-de-France; Brittany, Aunis, and Poitou, Guyenne; Languedoc, Provence; and Burgundy, Lyonnais, and Dauphiné. Even force, if necessary, was applied to extract the required grain. The requisitioning that began in 1793 was, accordingly, not new, but perhaps it was applied with more thoroughness than under the Old Regime. It provided that every farmer, whether proprietor or renter, who raised more grain than was necessary to care for himself and his dependents must sell this surplus in the open market.

The first of these laws requisitioning grain went into effect on May 4, 1793, after insistence by Jacobin leaders that this action was imperative in order to weather the crisis and prevent counterrevolution. One of the chief features of this statute, called the Law of the Maximum, was the establishment in each department (the Revolutionists had divided France into eighty-three departments) of a maximum, or "ceiling," price for the sale of grain. Any transaction at a higher price, whether by farmer, merchant, baker, or miller, would be punished by confiscation of the grain and by a fine of 300 to 1,000 livres for both seller and buyer.[100] The measure

---

[99] As in the *dîme* (*ibid.*, p. 291).

[100] "Citizens convicted of having lost or hidden grains and flour would be punished with death; and 1,000 livres would be given to informers" (Madeleine Deries, *Le district de Saint-Lo pendant la Révolution, 1787-an IV*, Paris, 1922, p. 272). Creveaux (*op. cit.*, pp. 164, 213, 216) relates some instances of violation of this law and of fines. The widow Lefranc was fined nine sacks for submitting defective grain, which also was confiscated. Two farmers, Massiet and Louis, were condemned as violators, and their grain taken. The charge was made in early 1795 that farmers and grain dealers avoided with studied care the turning over of their

also provided that requisitions in grain would be made in house-to-house visits by the municipal and district officials. The minister of the interior, moreover, was empowered to requisition grain from one department in favor of another, less favored, department.[101]

The law turned out to be a failure. Its chief weakness lay in the fact that it permitted each department to fix its own maximum and that it did not provide uniform prices throughout France. The grain not requisitioned might be sold by farmers where they wished. Since the maximum was higher in some departments than in others, grain was taken (by farmers and speculators) to markets where higher prices prevailed.[102] Competition even developed between districts and communes within the same department. The city of Paris was slow to establish its maximum, so that the prices offered on its market were higher than those in the near-by district of Versailles, and farmers from the Versailles distirct carried their grain to Paris. In self-defense the department of Seine-et-Oise (of which Versailles is a part) took the step, on June 1, 1793, of prohibiting owners of grains from offering them for sale in markets outside the department. The bureaux entrusted with provisioning Paris protested on June 12 to Minister of the Interior Garat against this action. At the end of June, Paris complained again when flour destined for it was arbitrarily confiscated and sold at two places in Seine-et-Oise.[103] Within a few weeks from the time of its enactment, the law was regarded with contempt or indifference in much of France,[104] and little attempt was made to enforce it.

But instead of revoking it, the Jacobins decided in August that they must patch up its weakness and keep it. Accordingly, after several weeks of planning and discussion, they had the Convention on September 11 adopt a second Law of the Maximum. This second measure provided that a uniform maximum price for grains should be established throughout France, with a supercharge added for

grain for provisioning Paris. The present writer has found no record of the death penalty or of a heavy fine for infraction of the law. A boatload of grain was shipwrecked in the Marne on 12 nivôse an II (January 1, 1795), and all but twenty sacks in 819 (each weighing 200 livres or more) were spoiled, and seemingly no penalty was inflicted (*ibid.*, p. 174).

[101] Deries, *op. cit.*, p. 271.

[102] Mathiez (*op. cit.*, pp. 189-190) cites several instances where competition between departments resulted.

[103] Defresne and Evraud, *op. cit.*, I, 286.

[104] Mathiez, *op. cit.*, p. 190.

transportation, at a prescribed rate per kilometer. Thus the maximum for wheat of the first quality throughout France was set at 14 livres a quintal, with the price of transportation to be added.[105]

Before this second Law of the Maximum was passed, however, the food situation in Paris had become so severe that it was considered necessary, on August 15, to requisition the surplus grain from all farmers in the surrounding departments.[106] About the same time or shortly thereafter, it was found necessary to make heavy requisitions for the army.[107] On August 14 the Convention authorized the requisitioning of laborers for the harvest. Apparently this was an innovation. The Old Regime had seen the requisitioning of labor for the roads, under the *corvée;* but this service, ironically enough, had been suppressed by the Revolutionaries as unfair and cruel. In the summer of 1793 the government increased the number of youths aged eighteen to twenty-five necessary for the army under the *levée en masse* from 300,000 to 500,000, creating thereby a serious problem for the farms.[108] In certain regions youths lately called to the colors had to be released for harvest duty. In 1794 and 1795 deserters and prisoners of war were also sent to aid in this work.[109] In the Haute-Marne the procurer-general-syndic set an example by working and called upon all good citizens to aid by voluntary work in the harvest.[110]

Throughout the hungry summer of 1793 sentiment had been growing for the revival of the *greniers d'abondance*[111] (grain storage houses) which many generalities, cities, and even hospitals had maintained under the Old Regime, so that, as in ancient Egypt, surplus grain might be stored in the "fat" years for the "lean" years that lay ahead. Under the Old Regime, too, the army and navy had similar warehouses; and sometimes, in periods of famine, cities and provinces were allowed by the government to draw on these stores. Unfortunately, the number of them under the Old Regime was

[105] *Ibid.,* pp. 304-315.

[106] *Ibid.,* p. 314; cf. Creveaux, *op. cit.,* pp. 137 ff.

[107] In 1792 grain was requisitioned for the army (Creveaux, *op. cit.,* pp. 226-227), but the amounts taken, in grain, hay, and straw, appear to have been considerably increased in September and October, 1793 (*ibid.,* pp. 146, 149, 152, 156-158, 168-169).

[108] Mathiez, *op. cit.,* pp. 314, 380-381.

[109] *Ibid.,* p. 443; Creveaux, *op. cit.,* p. 216.

[110] Mathiez, *op. cit.,* p. 380.

[111] Also called *chambres d'abondance.*

always inadequate; and whereas they often rendered excellent service, they sometimes were a liability when their surpluses were eaten by rats and weevils, for French chemists had not yet solved the problem of exterminating rodents and insects, and of rendering warehouses capable of storage for indefinite periods. On August 9, 1793, the Convention decreed that *greniers d'abondance* should be set up in all the departments, one or more for each, depending on the need; and the sum of 100,000,000 livres was voted for their erection and maintenance.[112] Apparently, however, the *greniers d'abondance* were slow in being erected and operated, for on 27 brumaire an II (October 17, 1793) the appropriation was still untouched in the treasury, and in many districts the *greniers* did not exist as late as March, 1794.[113] The districts complained that they did not have the grain to fill them.

Perhaps the most interesting feature employed in fighting this famine was the use of the ration card. As early as May, 1789, the ration card had been used at Toulouse to enable the poor to obtain bread at sub-market prices;[114] but it perhaps was not employed elsewhere until the late summer and early autumn of 1793, when it was adopted almost simultaneously at Paris and Bordeaux.[115] Beauvais, Auxerre, Mamers, Besançon, Toulouse, and doubtless many other cities followed Paris and Bordeaux by making use of the bread card during the winter of 1793-94. According to the late Professor Mathiez,[116] Besançon and doubtless other cities did not make use of the cards compulsory for all their citizens, "but only indigents and

---

[112] *Ibid.*, pp. 182, 314, 378 n.

[113] *Ibid.*, pp. 378 n., 462, 464. As late as 6 frimaire an II (Dec. 26, 1794) none had been established in a portion of Soissonnais (Creveaux, *op. cit.*, p. 171).

[114] Félix Pasquier, *Notes et réflexions d'un bourgeois de Toulouse au début de la Révolution*, p. 25, quoted by J. Adher (ed.), *Recueil de documents sur l'assistance publique dans le district de Toulouse de 1789 à 1800* (Toulouse, 1918), p. 508.

[115] In August, 1793, it was adopted by one of the forty-eight sections of Paris (that of Gros-Caillou); on October 29, by all of Paris. At Bordeaux it was instituted about the same time, one of the twenty-eight sections adopting it on September 6, and the city as a whole adopting it on October 15.

[116] See his interesting account of these ration cards in his book, *La vie chère et le mouvement social sous le Terreur*, pp. 487-507. For information concerning the cards at Bordeaux, see G. Ducaunnès-Duval, "Les cartes de pain à Bordeaux en 1793," *Revue historique de Bordeaux*, X (Bordeaux, 1917), 164-169. An attractive feature of his article is a photographic reproduction of the two sides of the early card at Bordeaux.

At Toulouse the cards were distributed every ten days (Adher, *op. cit.*, pp. 456, 458).

the needy." At Besançon most of the bourgeois baked their own bread, from grain grown on their own land, and they did not patronize the bakers. Only the poor, who patronized the bakers, needed the bread card.[117]

Not only bread but other commodities rose tremendously in price during this famine (and war). In 1792, partly as a result of revolutionary disorders in Santo Domingo and partly from speculation, there was a short-lived sugar famine in Paris.[118] In 1793, as France increased her paper money and moved into the Terror, commodities of all sorts became dear. Price-fixing for all of them was adopted.[119] Moreover, ration cards for commodities other than bread came into existence. Thus in February, 1794, the meat card came into use in several sections of Paris, and lasted many months. A sugar card was used in certain sections of Paris and Besançon. Besançon, too, had its salt cards. Bergues had its cards for candles and soap. Dunkirk used cards for rationing soap, meat, butter, eggs, and liquors. Senlis rationed eggs and butter. Vienne rationed oil and soap. Alençon, Poitiers, and other places passed various regulations curtailing the use of necessary commodities. Without question, this rationing of necessities by means of the card marked a tremendous step forward in curbing hoarding and providing for an equitable distribution that Revolutionaries made toward the better handling of famines.[120]

Other interesting features of this famine were the Convention's concern with increasing the number of public ovens (for use by the poor), its proposal to tax the rich for the support of the poor,[121] its

---

[117] Besançon adopted the bread card on October 17, 1793.

[118] For an account of these disorders, see below, pp. 396-398. The sugar famine produced riots at Paris, and a boycott of sugar and coffee was advocated (Mathiez, *op. cit.*, pp. 37-38, 46-47).

[119] Later, in prairial and messidor an II (May and June, 1795), a maximum was established for wages and salaries in certain fields (*ibid.*, p. 598).

[120] The late Professors Mathiez and Marion, both notable scholars in eighteenth-century French history, disagreed concerning the question of the value of the drastic measures, more particularly those of requisitioning, adopted by the Jacobins in 1793-95. Mathiez, who revealed a sympathy for the Jacobins and lower classes, admitted that graft crept in everywhere, but contended that they did tide France through the crisis, at least the crisis of 1793-94. Marion, on the other hand, insisted that the regimentation merely increased the confusion and made the famine worse than it otherwise would have been. See Mathiez, *op. cit.*, pp. 481-483.

[121] *Ibid.*, p. 138; cf. *Inv.-som . . . Isère*, L 61, f 903v.

allotments of money to the departments for the purchase of grain,[122] its huge distributions of rice, its subsidies of bakers, its award of prizes for grain deliveries,[123] its permission for all who would to cultivate unused lands.[124] There was regimentation of planting. In some regions vines were ordered pulled up, and in others refusal was given to plant any new ones, in order that the space might be devoted to cereals.[125] Tobacco on land was to be replaced by oats, barley, and potatoes.[126] To lessen the drain on food stocks, a war was declared on cats and dogs.[127] Strict measures were taken to prevent the slaughter of females and the young among cattle, sheep, and hogs, lest the nation's supply of these animals be dangerously reduced.[128] Circulars, or bulletins of information, of various sorts, on fertilizers, on the sowing of crops, on the culture of the potato, on other vegetables, on animal breeding and diseases, were distributed by the government in the hope of obtaining through them greater food resources for the country.[129] Free seed for the planting of potatoes, carrots, cabbage, beets, and turnips were furnished by the commission of subsistences and the committee of public safety.[130] In several regions prizes were offered to cultivators who brought in the first samples of these vegetables.[131]

These efforts indicated a great outburst of national enthusiasm. And yet it must not be assumed that they met universal response from the French people. On the contrary, some reluctantly parted with their grain.[132] There were widespread bitterness, sulkiness, and attempts at hoarding by the farmers of Soissonnais, who felt that they were being deprived and exploited because of speculation and mismanagement. Some gave vent to counterrevolutionary senti-

[122] The department of Bouches-du-Rhône obtained the loan of 1,000,000 livres (*Inv.-som* . . . *Bouches-du-Rhône*, L III, 11, t. I, p. 238). The department of Doubs obtained the loan of 500,000 livres (Mathiez, *op. cit.*, p. 195). Several million livres were placed at the disposal of Paris (*ibid.*, p. 299 n.).

[123] Creveaux, *op. cit.*, p. 136; Mathiez, *op. cit.*, pp. 291, 388.

[124] *Ibid.*, pp. 439-441.

[125] *Ibid.*, pp. 444-445.

[126] *Ibid.*, p. 446.

[127] *Ibid.*, p. 455.

[128] *Loc. cit.*

[129] *Ibid.*, pp. 446-455. Grégoire proposed this campaign of propaganda. Among the circulars sent out were extracts from the writings of Arthur Young.

[130] *Ibid.*, pp. 447-448.

[131] *Ibid.*, 449-450.

[132] Creveaux, *op. cit.*, pp. 145, 146-147, 151-152, 158, 159, 164, 183, and *passim*. On the hoarding in Paris, see Mathiez, *op. cit.*, pp. 392-393.

ments;[133] others tried to defraud.[134] Abuses marked the administration of both Laws of the Maximum.[135] According to Géorgel, an estimated twenty thousand persons died of hunger during this famine.[136]

No summary figures are available for government expenditures toward aid during this famine. That they must have been large can be deduced from certain appropriations. In early 1792, 10,000,000 livres were set aside, and on September 4, an additional 12,000,0000 livres, for the purchase of grain abroad.[137] In August, 1794, in response to a request by Barère, the Convention appropriated 100,000,-000 livres for the purchase of grain and the creation of *greniers d'abondance*.[138] How much of these and of other appropriations was actually spent, it is not easy to ascertain. But large amounts were placed at the disposal of cities and departments by the government for subsidy of grain purchases. To the city of Besançon permission was granted to use the military stores.[139] While much of the money appropriated was slowly used, doubtless in large part because of the very trying circumstances, careful study would probably reveal that more money was spent by the government to meet this famine than had been spent to meet any previous famine in eighteenth-century France. In other respects, too, as in requisitioning and production-propaganda, the government probably made greater exertions on this occasion than during earlier famines.

[133] Creveaux, *op. cit.*, p. 144.
[134] *Ibid.*, pp. 164, 213. On fraud by Paris merchants, see Mathiez, *op. cit.*, pp. 396, 524-525.
[135] *Ibid.*, pp. 384-385, 574.
[136] *Mémoires pour servir à l'histoire des événements de la fin du dix-huitième siècle depuis 1760 jusqu'en 1806-1810* (Paris, 1820), IV, 331. He places the blame on the National Convention. Cf. Mathiez, *op. cit.*, p. 482.
[137] *Ibid.*, pp. 69, 80. Importations continued through 1793 and 1794; in fact, it was during 1794 that most of the imported grain arrived (*ibid.*, p. 482).
[138] *Ibid.*, pp. 297-298.
[139] *Ibid.*, pp. 194-195.

CHAPTER III

EFFORTS AT FAMINE PREVENTION

WITH GREAT credit to her government and civilization, eighteenth-century France made serious efforts to prevent famines. France's eventual success in solving the problem stands as "the record of an extraordinary mastery of the physical and social environment by the resolution and acumen of many relatively obscure individuals, lawyers, administrators, and statesmen."[1] In the first half of the eighteenth century government attempts at solution were relatively few and small, but in the second half they became considerable both in number and in size. This ever-enlarging interest and activity was not halted by the Revolution, but even gained momentum despite the Revolutionary government's preoccupation with war and other problems.

Before these attempts by the government at eradicating famines are considered, it seems well to examine their causes. First and foremost, in the opinion of the physiocrats and of later economic liberals, was the weakness of the mercantile system of the French government, with its elaborate, cramping police regulations concerning agriculture in general and the grain trade in particular. Sharing this view, in the later eighteenth century, were, strange as it might seem, the nobles, the large landowners, and the churchmen, who stood for freedom of trade in grains. Opposed to them were the masses and some of the officials, who insisted on maintaining the old system of government regulation and who declared that freedom of import and export, adopted by France from time to time in crises, merely led to grain shortage and misery.[2] When the Revolutionary leaders found it imperative to adopt the maximum in 1793, the masses still favored government control.[3]

Under the governmental regulation of the Old Regime, not only agricultural rents and certain taxes, such as the *dîme* and feudal dues,

---

[1] Usher, *History of the Grain Trade in France, 1400-1710*, pp. 361-362.

[2] Letaconnoux, "Les subsistances et le commerce des grains en Bretagne, au XVIIIᵉ siècle," *Annales de Bretagne*, XX (Rennes and Paris, 1905), 134-135.

[3] Mathiez, *La vie chère* . . . , pp. 390-392. The merchants, on the other hand, were opposed to it.

were often paid in kind, but also annoying tolls were paid on grain sent from one district to another and at the limits of cities. Even more exasperating was the government's frequent and sometimes arbitrary prohibition of exporting grain from France, or even of selling it to a district other than that to which it was destined by regulation. In a year of ample harvest, there might be no opportunity to sell the grain at a profit because of the hard and fast regulations of the government. No wonder that strong government efforts to increase grain acreage and production had little success. Farmers were reluctant to raise large amounts of grain for which they might get small return. They preferred vineyards, from which the return was better; and their sons all too frequently left the farm to seek opportunities in the cities. All through the eighteenth century this migration from the farm continued, some of the young rustics meeting success, others joining the horde of beggars and the unemployed.

Besides, there need have been no famines in 1709, 1747-48, 1788-89, and perhaps in many other years of the eighteenth century, if France had enjoyed full freedom of importation and circulation of grain. Under the mercantile system the misjudgment of a high official, the tardiness of the government in effecting the necessary purchases, and the haphazards of the transportation system often had tragic consequences. The government meant well and was convinced that its system was the best for France. Perhaps the mercantile system would have worked well enough to obviate famines in France had it not been for the major difficulty of slowness in communication and transportation. This weakness constituted the second great cause of famines.

Eighteenth-century France did not possess the radio, the telegraph, the telephone, the cable, or air-delivery mail; nor did she have the railway, the autotruck, the steamship, for transportation. Several days were necessary for letters from such far southern cities as Marseilles, Toulouse, and Montpellier to reach Paris.[4] Elaborate

---

[4] Lefebvre (*op. cit.*, p. 79) points out that in 1789 it took four days by ordinary post to go from Paris to the farthest points in the French Pyrenees, but that special couriers could go faster. The enormous improvement in roads during the course of the century had rapidly accelerated travel and communication.

Despite these possibilities, travel was not always fast. Arthur Young, traveling in Alsace, did not learn of the fall of the Bastille until he arrived in Strasbourg, on July 20, 1789; and he implies that the news had just reached the city (*Travels in*

correspondence, not only between the controller-general and the intendant of an afflicted province, but also between the controller-general and other intendants who might have a surplus of grain, was required to arrange for relief; thus two or three months might slip by in the process, even though during at least the latter half of the century France had the best highways in Europe.[5] Much of the grain of that period was transported by water, and, so far as ocean-going vessels were concerned, commerce was dependent upon the wind. Boats in the interior could, of course, travel downstream with the current or be pulled upstream or along canals[6] by horses from the bank, but in either case the process was exceedingly slow. It was too slow when incorrect estimates of the grain supply had been made and quick action was necessary.

A third cause was the general backwardness of agriculture and the failure of the French to plant enough grain to meet their needs. Crops in good years were sufficiently large to supply French needs, and even to permit some exportation. In "mediocre" (the French often use this adjective) years, the grain crop might suffice if proper shifts of supplies were made from the more fortunate to the less prosperous generalities. When the harvest was poor, only large importations could save the situation.[7] To repeat, the French simply did not plant enough wheat to meet their own needs, despite the most diligent efforts of their government to induce them to do so. The province of Guyenne, to cite an extreme case, did not raise enough grain to feed itself for more than one month in the year.[8] Even in the middle of the nineteenth century, when the famine problem had been conquered, or virtually conquered, France, according to V. Modeste, raised sufficient wheat for her needs in

---

France, ed. Betham-Edwards, London, 1889, p. 206). Mrs. C. C. Pinckney, in the 1790's, was eleven days en route from Bordeaux to Paris. David Garrick and his wife, in 1751, were four days en route from London to Paris (going via Dover and Boulogne).

[5] For a discussion of the French highway system, see C. P. Duclos, *Essai sur la voirie et les ponts et chaussées de France* (1759) (republished in Villeneuve's *Oeuvres complètes de Duclos*, Paris, 1821, III); Arthur Young, *op. cit., passim*.

[6] The very elaborate French system of canals is described by J. Dutens, *Histoire de la navigation intérieure de la France* . . . (Paris, 1829), Vol. I.

[7] Letaconnoux states that importation of grain was "without contradiction the best" relief measure available to the government in time of famine (*Les subsistances et le commerce des grains en Bretagne au XVIIIᵉ siècle*, p. 171).

[8] Ducaunnès-Duval, *op. cit.*, X, 164.

only one year out of three.[9]   Other countries without sufficient grain crops, of course, were able to avoid famines; but with slow transportation and a cumbersome system of governmental management, France could not.

Even the French lands sown in grain might have produced a sufficient yield under all circumstances had better methods of cultivation been employed.   Little was done by way of fertilization; there was no conscious rotation of crops, at least before the 1760's; and the usual method employed for the restoration of land was to let it lie fallow.   Relatively few types of crops were raised.   Vines, grains, nuts (chestnuts and walnuts), olives, various fruits, hemp, flax, and a few vegetables appear to have comprised the chief products of French agriculture.   There was a great need for more diversification, especially in vegetables, which might serve to some degree as grain substitutes.   It will be recalled that no foods were canned in the eighteenth century, and that not until approximately 1811 was canning in a rudimentary form originated by the Frenchman Appert.   It remained for Borden and Liebig, in the second half of the century, to perfect the process.[10]

The winter diet of Europeans in the 1700's was much limited. Little use was made of salted meats even during famines.   In the second half of the century the French government and the numerous agricultural societies which sprang suddenly into being everywhere, however, gave great encouragement to animal selection and breeding, and urged the use of salted meats.   Little use, too, was made of fish and oysters to meet the needs in famine periods.   According to Mercier, in his *Tableau de Paris* published in the 1780's, oyster-shops were common in Paris, and it was the vogue for Parisians to frequent them.   Sea fish also were sold in Paris; in fact, there was a sea-fish market.[11]   No doubt both forms of sea food were brought from the Breton and Norman coasts.   The question arises, Why were they not carried in sufficient quantities to meet famine needs?

[9] Quoted by Gustave Bord, *op. cit.*, p. 9 n.   Yet as late as 1817 and 1846-47 parts of France experienced famine, according to E. Ebrard (*Misère et charité dans une petite ville de France de 1560 à 1862* . . . , Bourg, 1866, pp. 115-118).
[10] Erick Ackhorn, *European Civilization and Politics since 1815* (New York, 1934), p. 50; Carlton J. H. Hayes, *A Political and Cultural History of Modern Europe*, II (New York, 1936), 29.
[11] M. Fregier, *Histoire de l'administration de la police depuis Philippe-Auguste jusqu'aux états généraux de 1789* . . . , II (Paris, 1850), 511.

And what excuse was there for famines in maritime provinces such as Brittany and Guyenne? [12]

A fourth cause of famine was the low standard of living in France as compared with that of other countries like England and Holland, which suffered no famines and had not the swarms of beggars and unemployed found in France. It was the marvel of French travelers to Holland that the Dutch had no beggars. Although England had her highwaymen and a numerous class of the poor, she had relatively few beggars. Arthur Young, whose *Travels in France* reveals the different scales of living in England and France, found that living in France was vastly cheaper, because of the much lower standard of living. No doubt famines and the standard of living are closely related. Famines are rare in a country where the standard of living is high, and frequent in such countries as Russia, India, and China, where the standard is low. Perhaps the laboring class in countries of low living standards have a much lower margin of safety. With little or no savings, they are unable to meet a crisis when it occurs. Certainly in the eighteenth-century famines the poor suffered the most, as indeed is always the case.

A fifth cause of famines lay in grain hoarding and speculation. During almost every eighteenth-century famine it was the cry of the populace, and sometimes of the leaders, that the distress was caused by the hoarding and speculation of those who wanted to profit financially from the rise in prices. In every famine censuses of grain stocks were made, and house-to-house inspection was undertaken. The hoardings of the few who were caught were seldom great. With so much accusation of speculation, some probably existed; but its extent was no doubt greatly exaggerated. That which did exist could hardly have taken place if France had followed a policy of free trade.

This fifth cause, therefore, may be considered as a fruit of the cumbersome mercantilist policy of the government. In short, only the first two causes were basal; the others, auxiliary. Thus, rapid communication and transportation, such as twentieth-century Europe enjoys, might have enabled the mercantile system to work without famines, and contrariwise the adoption of a system of complete free

---

[12] Certain of the worst famines occurred during periods of war with England or the United Provinces, or both, and fear of the fleets of these countries doubtless led to the curtailment of much fishing activity.

trade might have seen France move along, despite her slow communication system, without famines. The combination of these several factors caused the trouble.

The French government, however, tinkered and experimented a great deal with the framework of the mercantile system. Frequent shifts and changes were made.[13] It was not the French Revolution, or indeed Turgot, that initiated freedom of trade within France. Throughout the century France had short periods of interior free trade. In periods of widespread famine, and sometimes during other crises, as during the plague in the southeastern provinces in 1720-22, the French government removed all monetary restrictions in the way of tolls and established a policy of relatively free trade to aid the afflicted provinces.[14] The periods from 1703 to 1708; from September, 1708, to 1710; from 1715 to September, 1719; from October, 1719, to 1724; from 1730 to 1741; from 1741 to 1746; in 1748; in 1757; from 1759 to 1763 were moments of relatively free commerce of grains within France, at least for the great grain-growing province of Brittany.[15]

By a royal declaration of May 25, 1763, a new era in French commerce, with more liberal features than before, made itself felt as a result of the physiocratic influence; yet it was temporary and fell short of complete free trade. In 1774-76 Turgot went still further in the direction of free trade, only to see his measures later revoked. Again, early in the Revolution freedom of commerce in grains was adopted within France.[16] Both the National and Legislative assemblies proclaimed the liberty of internal commerce of grains, but, according to Letaconnoux, "before the popular passions exasperated by scarcity and misery, they were powerless to make it respected." In early 1793 the policy of free trade for interior commerce collapsed completely, under the crisis already described;

[13] Professor Letaconnoux, in his *Les subsistances et le commerce des grains en Bretagne au XVIIIe siècle* (Rennes, 1909) has chapters on importation and exportation admirably revealing them.

[14] Even then, however, it was considered proper, if not necessary, for the intendants to notify the controller-general of their plans for importation of provisions and to get his consent.

[15] Letaconnoux, *op. cit.*, pp. 176-180.

[16] A. Chéruel (*Dictionnaire historique des institutions, moeurs et coutumes de la France*, 4th ed., Paris, 1874, I, 501) writes: "The Constituent Assembly, by its laws of August 29, September 18, and October 3, 1789, of June 2 and September 15, 1790, and of September 26, 1791, proclaimed the liberty of commerce in grain within France. The assemblies which followed confirmed this disposition."

and until December 24, 1794, the laws of the maximum, with their return to the most rigid form of government control, prevailed.[17]

The policy concerning the exportation of grain during this period, had the same fluctuating history. For a brief while, even a period of years, it would be permitted; then suddenly it would be stopped by an order that might remain in force for several years. In two periods early in the century (from 1698 to 1702, and from 1709 to 1715) exportation of grain was prohibited under penalty of death.[18] In 1720 the government, adopting a more moderate policy, maintained free exportation for a while but tripled export duties *(droits de sortie)*; later it forbade exportation altogether.[19]

No one can therefore accuse the government of the Old Regime of absolute refusal to experiment with measures of free trade. The government of the Old Regime, in many ways conservative, did not have a closed mind. It was desirous of being progressive, and it was more progressive than the generality of its subjects. Why then were there no greater results from its experiments with free trade? Perhaps the reason is that its experiments were too timid or too brief. Perhaps it was difficult for the policy to succeed in a mercantilistic world. Certainly the populace and the officials did not regard the results of the experiments with free trade as justifying a permanent policy.

In agriculture, especially in the latter half of the century, the policy of the government was more generous. From 1753 onward it furnished seed, either gratuitously or on loans, to peasant farmers who had suffered heavily from famines. Thus, in 1752-53 it sent 100,000 livres to Guyenne to purchase seed for farmers who had suffered in the severe famine of 1751-53.[20] After 1770 the distribution of seed for sowing became more common.[21] In October, 1777, during a famine in Guyenne, Necker as director-general placed a large quantity of seed grain at the disposal of the province. It was to be loaned to needy farmers through municipal officers and the syndics of communities,[22] who were to be held personally responsible

---

[17] Chéruel, *op. cit.*, II, 758.   [18] Letaconnoux, *op. cit.*, p. 185.

[19] *Ibid.*, p. 186.

[20] *Inv.-som . . . Gironde*, C 1415. In addition, 300,000 livres were advanced the province during the famine, and 200,000 livres were given it for feeding the poor (*ibid.*, C 1410 and 1417).

[21] Letaconnoux, *op. cit.*, pp. 160-161.

[22] Local officials with duties resembling those of justices of the peace.

for the repayment. Repayment was to be made when the harvest was sold. Not all the money had been repaid in November, 1780.[23] In 1785 the government sold grain to the peasants of Brittany, during the famine of 1785-86, on the endorsement of the curés. Presumably this grain was to be used for planting. But the endorsement of the curés was no more effective than that of the municipal officers and syndics, for in December, 1787, most of the money had not been repaid, and certain wholesale dealers in Rennes and Messac, from whom the government had made the purchases, were trying to collect from the peasants.[24] Evidence that the practice continued into the Revolutionary period is found in the *Inventaire des archives départementales postérieures à 1789* for Seine-et-Marne,[25] which contains a request from the directory of that department, under date of vendémiaire and brumaire an V (September-October, 1796), to the minister of the interior for 3,500 quintals of wheat to be used in sowing lands in the canton of Sourdun, struck by storms.

Through this practice of furnishing grain for sowing, the government tried to assist the poorer farmers to re-establish themselves. It furnished them seed, not only for the sowing of grain, but also for the planting of other crops, some new, that it wished to encourage. Thus in 1785 the government, through its subdelegate at Nantes, ordered a grain merchant in that city to distribute gratuitously among the farmers of the region 2,000 pounds (livres) of turnip seed.[26] Again, in 1788, it gave a large quantity of turnip seed to farmers in the subdelegations of Rethel and Château-Porcien in Champagne.[27] Since the value of the turnip as a means of winter forage had been discovered a century earlier in England,[28] the

---

[23] E. Bourgouin, "Une disette en Guyenne à la fin de l'ancien régime (1777-78)," *Revue historique de Bordeaux*, XII (1919), 108, 115 with n. 1.

[24] Letaconnoux (*op. cit.*, p. 155) writes: "Some did not wish to pay under the pretext that the grains delivered to them were a 'benevolence of the king'; others refused to pay according to the agreed-upon rate. It was only a small number who filled their engagements without murmuring."

[25] L 77, f 49.

[26] Letaconnoux, *op. cit.*, pp. 157-158.

[27] *Inv.-som . . . Ardennes*, C 96. Arthur Young supported this movement to get turnips introduced in France. At a meeting of the Royal Society of Agriculture in Paris, June 12, 1789, he urged that a gift of 1,200 livres from the Abbé Raynal for premiums be used in this manner (*op. cit.*, p. 157).

[28] Introduced into England from Holland in the latter part of the seventeenth century as a winter-forage crop for cattle and sheep, the turnip grew rapidly popu-

French government hoped to see the turnip adopted widely among French farmers.

The culture of the Irish potato *(pomme de terre)* received more attention and encouragement from the French government than did any other "new" crop. In 1769 the government sent potatoes for planting in the Gironde, and with them printed directions for making bread from potatoes.[29] Clearly the government had in mind the value of the potato as a grain substitute. The intendant, in acknowledging receipt of the potatoes, wrote that the crop was already grown in certain parishes of his generality, and he believed that encouragement from the government would meet with much success. In 1771 the controller-general sent the intendant at Rennes, and doubtless other provincial intendants, a printed report by the faculty of medicine of Paris on the excellence of the potato as a food.[30] Writing to the controller-general from Rennes on March 8, 1772, Dupleix, intendant of Brittany, mentioned the successful experiments with the potato at Belle-Isle-en-mer, in his generality, and in Picardy. He proposed to employ, if the controller-general approved, a considerable part of the 40,000 livres allowed him by the government for famine aid in furnishing poor farmers with potatoes for planting purposes, and he believed that the potato crop would supplement the grain crop.[31] In 1774 Dupleix obtained 114 bushels of potatoes from Belle-Isle and distributed them through-

---

lar in eighteenth-century England. (J. C. Drummond and Anne Wilbraham, *The Englishman's Food: A History of Five Centuries of English Diet*, London, 1939, pp. 113, 213-214.

[29] *Inv.-som . . . Gironde*, C 3578. The potato had long been known on the European Continent. Introduced from Peru into Spain at the latest by 1573, it had rapidly made its way thence into several other countries. Brought into the French Pyrenees from Spain, and into the eastern provinces from Switzerland by the end of the 1500's, it slowly made its way for the next century and a half. Already by the early eighteenth century, according to Ernest Roze, who has written an excellent history of this tuber (*Histoire de la pomme de terre*, Paris, 1898), it had come into wide use among the poor in France's eastern provinces (notably Alsace, Lorraine, Burgundy, Dauphiné, and Auvergne). By the French upper classes it was little used until the second half of the century, when it gained popularity with them too, perhaps because Parmentier devised new recipes for cooking it. He even devised a recipe (not very successful) for making bread from it (Roze, *op. cit.*, pp. 117, 121, 128-129, 142-143, 158; E. Parmelee Prentice, *Hunger and History: The Influence of Hunger on Human History*, New York and London, 1939, pp. 130-135).

[30] *Inv.-som . . . Ille-et-Vilaine*, C 81.

[31] Arch. Nat., H 565.

out his generality, at the rate of 2 to 6 bushels a parish, for seed.[32]
Throughout the seventies and the eighties, as controller-general succeeded controller-general and intendant succeeded intendant, the
government's encouragement of the Irish potato continued. In May,
1789, the government paid 1,200 livres to the Abbé Le Fevre, the
general agent of the Royal Society of Agriculture, for the purpose
of introducing the potato along the coast of Normandy, and ships
of the admiralty were sent to Ireland for the potatoes.[33] In that
part of Dauphiné which today forms the department of Hautes-
Alpes potatoes were widely cultivated in 1789, and were an important item in the food of the rural classes and the villagers.[34]

The Revolutionists also encouraged the cultivation of the potato. In 1793 and in early 1794 they sent out much printed matter
on its planting, and on January 12, 1794, the Convention passed a
decree ordering the authorities "to use all the means in their power,
in the communes where the *pomme de terre* should not yet be established, for bringing all the cultivators composing them to plant
according to their capacity a portion of their land in *pommes de
terre*." It also offered to furnish potatoes for planting through its
commission of subsistences.[35] On 1 ventose an II (February 19,
1794) the committee of public safety ordered that the ministry of
the interior have the flower beds in the gardens of the Tuileries and
the Luxemburg planted with the potato, in order to destroy public
prejudice against it. The grounds of many confiscated châteaux and
the gardens of the *émigrés* in several departments likewise were
planted in potatoes. The results did not always correspond to the
great efforts made by the Revolutionary authorities to increase agricultural production, especially with the potato.[36] In certain portions
of France, however, notably in the north and east, the potato was
well established. The directory of the department of Seine-et-Oise
reported to the committee of public safety in mid-thermidor an III
(early August, 1795) that an immense crop of Irish potatoes had
been planted in the district of Versailles and was making a splendid

---

[32] H. Sée, "Les classes rurales en Bretagne du XVIe siècle à la Révolution,"
Annales de Bretagne, XXIV (Rennes and Paris, 1909), 195-196.
[33] Bibl. Nat., Fonds français 6793, ff 158-159.
[34] *Inv.-som . . . Hautes-Alpes*, C 5, 6, 16.
[35] Mathiez, *op. cit.*, pp. 446-447; *Inv.-som . . . Isère*, L 80, p. 685.
[36] Mathiez, *op. cit.*, pp. 449-450.

showing.[37] The potato has never since lost its hold on the French people; its use has greatly increased with the passing of the years, thanks in part to these efforts of the governments of the Old Regime and the Revolution.

Other crops that the government attempted to encourage were only indirectly beneficial in preventing famines. For cultivating the beetroot, destined chiefly for the feeding of animals, the government imported seed from Bavaria and Franconia and distributed it among the people.[38] The government also attempted to encourage, by printed matter, the growth of several forms of grass, valuable for pasturage and hay, such as lucern, sainfoin, clover, and vetch.[39] As early as 1756 the council of state gave certain privileges to all persons who would grow madder-root,[40] and in 1767 the controller-general sent 60 pounds (livres), imported from Smyrna, to the intendant Du Cluzel for free distribution among the farmers of his generality.[41] The plantings were successful, particularly in Anjou. Considerable attention was given to the extension of hemp-growing. Much hemp was already grown in France, but not enough for times of war. The royal navy annually consumed hemp to the value of 11,000,000 or 12,000,000 livres; the merchant marine also required a large quantity; and the lower classes wore it for clothing during the summer.[42] The Estates of Brittany in 1757-58 tried to encourage this crop in their generality by distributing "foreign grain" which produced a type of hemp superior to that commonly grown.[43]

In 1746 Tourny attempted to revive the growing of tobacco in his generality, but the opposition of the tax-farmers being too great, he gave up the project.[44] Despite Tourny's failure, tobacco was again introduced in France and was grown during the Revolution.

[37] Defresne and Evrard, op. cit., II, 329.

[38] In the period 1766-83 (Dumas, op. cit., p. 284).

[39] In Brittany, 1786 (H. Sée, op. cit., XXIV, 195-196).

[40] Ibid. [41] Dumas, op. cit., pp. 284-285.

[42] Dumas (op. cit., pp. 285-287) states that two thirds of the inhabitants of the generality of Tours were clothed in it during the summer months. See his interesting account of this crop as it concerned Touraine. As early as 1745 Tourny, intendant of Guyenne, had attempted to encourage the growing of hemp in his generality by distributing prizes to those who would grow it (Lhéritier, op. cit., p. 373).

[43] Sée, op. cit., XXIV, 198.

[44] According to Lhéritier (op. cit., pp. 373-374), tobacco had been grown with much success until 1720. In that year the farmers-general (i.e., tax-farmers), who enjoyed the exclusive privilege of importing tobacco from Virginia, obtained a ruling that tobacco should no longer be grown in France.

In the autumn of 1793 the district of Hazebrouck was compelled to ask its communes to replace their tobacco crop with oats, barley, and potatoes.[45]

From 1744 to 1754 attempts were made, with government encouragement, to grow cotton in Languedoc. Johannis Altem, described as an Armenian, requested permission to experiment with cotton in the neighborhood of Castres by sowing seed from the Levant.[46] The controller-general sent him to Le Nain, who placed at his disposal a large tract of uncultivated land belonging to the commune of Castres; and the Estates of Languedoc gave him subsidies and exempted him from the *taille* on any lands which he might rent and reserved to him the right of monopoly in case of success.[47]

In 1739-40 the government granted support to a company that undertook to introduce the growing of rice in certain river valleys in the neighborhood of the Rhône, in southeastern France.[48] The design of the company was to imitate the rice culture of Piedmont and Lombardy, where it had been existent for two centuries and was widespread, and thereby bring profit to themselves and a bread substitute to France. Italians who were experienced in rice growing were imported despite the bitter opposition of their governments, and designed the dikes, sluice gates, mills, etc. A Frenchman who had lived in India and was familiar with rice growing there was placed in charge of one of the farms and quickly came to dominate the entire enterprise. For several years rice was grown with varying degrees of success. The grain was excellent, but in some instances the crop was small. It might well have become a permanent crop and have assumed significant proportions had it not been that epidemics of fever (evidently malaria) broke out in one locality after another, with a high rate of mortality. Violent protests against

---

[45] Mathiez, *op. cit.*, p. 446.

[46] Throughout the eighteenth century France imported most of her cotton from the Near East.

[47] *Histoire générale de Languedoc*, XIII, 1069; Léon Dutil, *L'état économique du Languedoc à la fin de l'ancien régime (1750-1789)* (Paris, 1911), pp. 501-02. After 1745 the experiment was transferred to Montpellier. The results were not satisfactory.

[48] Plantings were attempted in Forez, Bourbonnais, Dauphiné, and Auvergne. The story of this undertaking is described by Paul M. Bondois in an interesting article entitled "Un essai de culture exotique sous l'ancien regime: la 'Peste de Riz' de Thiers (1741)," published in the *Revue d'histoire économique et sociale*, XVI (Paris, 1928) 586-655. Location of the rice farms, with the aid of maps, is given on pages 592-593.

the rice farms were made to the intendant and the controller-general, so that one rice farm after another was abolished; and in 1748, with the suppression of the farm in Bourbonnais, the last vestige of the enterprise collapsed.[49]

From early in the century the government greatly encouraged the planting of all types of trees, and it maintained in each generality one or more large nurseries to supply plantings.[50] While the chief end of the nurseries was to provide saplings of oak, elm, and chestnut for ornamenting the highways in consequence of the famous road act of 1720,[51] the nurseries shortly came to furnish mulberry, walnut, and even fruit trees, in considerable number, either gratuitously or at a nominal charge. The government gave particular attention to the dissemination of mulberry trees over France,[52] in an attempt to develop its silk industry. Not only were the trees furnished free, but bonuses and privileges were accorded those who would grow the mulberry. In certain sections of France, more especially in the triangle formed by the cities Tours, Bordeaux, and Toulouse, chestnuts formed an important item in the diet of the people; and the offering of trees for a pittance or for nothing was of value to those who wished them.[53] Similarly at various places in central and southern France the walnut furnished food, and frequently in the crop reports of the century the state of the walnut crop is mentioned.[54] In the nursery at Villeneuve-d'Agen a section was devoted to plums;[55] and, interestingly enough, Tourny, the great intendant of the mid-century, gave attention to trying to improve their variety.[56]

[49] Bondois is prejudiced against the rice growers in discussing the controversy.
[50] The *Inventaires-sommaires des archives départementales antérieures à 1790* abound with references to them; F. Dumas devotes several pages to the subject (*op. cit.*, pp. 290-293), and Michel Lhéritier has a fairly extended account (*op. cit.*, pp. 383-384).
[51] Isambert, *op. cit.*, XXI, 182-184; J. B. J. Paillot (ed.), *Manuel complémentaire des codes françaises et de toutes collections des lois* . . . (Paris, 1845), I, 136-138).
[52] Of both white and red types.
[53] According to Dumas (*op. cit.*, p. 293), cultivators commonly received trees for the highways free, but paid at the rate of one sou a foot for the trees destined to their private use. On certain occasions, however, all types of trees were given free.
[54] In early 1747 the government offered 155,000 walnut saplings in the nursery at Tours free to citizens of the generality of Tours and of neighboring generalities (*ibid.*, p. 291).
[55] *Inv.-som* . . . *Gironde*, C 3169.   [56] Lhéritier, *op. cit.*, pp. 372-373.

In the second half of the century the government interested itself in the increase and improvement of livestock, and censuses of horses were taken from time to time.[57]   The government sent at its expense, from province to province, men expert in the knowledge of stock-breeding.   Thus Machault, about the mid-century, sent shepherds from Brie into Berry for the purpose of improving the breed of sheep.   Each controller-general, it is said, renewed the prohibition, existent since the days of Colbert, against seizing livestock for taxes.[58]

After 1770 animals were frequently imported from other countries to improve the breeds in France.   Turgot, it is reported, imported to Limoges 200 sheep from Spain.[59]   In 1786-87 the French government imported further from Spain 360 ewes and 60 rams, sending them to Rambouillet, for the purpose of "naturalizing in France a precious race of wool-bearing animals."[60]   Similarly horses of excellent breed were imported from Denmark and other countries,[61] and cattle were brought in after epizootics and famine.   Thus after the severe famine of 1785-86, the government imported a large number of cows and helped the farmers to buy them.   According to Albert Babeau, one of the first scholars to point out the favorable side of the Old Regime, the intendant of Paris sold the animals at this time to the peasants on small annual payments.[62]   To encourage domestic strains of a superior type, two large appropriations of 50,000 and 200,000 livres were made by the Estates of Brittany in 1754-55 "for the purchase of stallions and mares."[63]

The eighteenth century witnessed a growing awareness of the value of fertilizers, and in this particular, too, the provincial and national governments in France manifested an interest.   As early as 1701 ferns were used as fertilizer in the generality of Béarn, near Spain, and stable-manure (les fumiers) by the inhabitants of the Franco-Belgian frontier.[64]   By 1705 it was a practice for peasants to

[57] One was made in the generality of Rouen in 1753 (Inv.-som . . . Seine-Inférieure, C 120).

[58] Henri de Jouvencel, Le contrôleur général des finances sous l'ancien régime (Paris, 1901), pp. 121, 266.

[59] A mémoire gives the date as 1776.   The flock was still existent in 1786-87.

[60] Inv.-som . . . Gironde, C 3617.

[61] Inv.-som . . . Seine-Inférieure, C 119.

[62] Le village sous l'ancien régime (3d ed., rev. and enlarged, Paris, 1882), p. 345.   Cf. Dumas, op. cit., pp. 284-285, and H. Sée, op. cit., XXIV, 198-199.

[63] Inv.-som . . . Ille-et-Vilaine, C 1757.

[64] Boislisle, op. cit., II, 101, 610.   In a mémoire of 1704 Boisguillebert, lieu-

buy deposits from the Paris cesspools for their vineyards, which, according to Alfred Franklin, in his *La vie d'autrefois*, were sometimes stolen.[65] In 1709 chestnut leaves were used by the farmers around Bordeaux.[66] In the 1770's and 1780's the peasants of Brittany used seaweed on a rather large scale.[67] Tourny, intendant of Bordeaux, gave his protection to the author of a tract who claimed "to have the secret of a composition for procuring to lands a much more considerable fertility than that which results from ordinary cultures."[68] In December, 1793, the commission of subsistences sent from Paris to all the districts a circular on fertilizers."[69]

Throughout the latter half of the eighteenth century the French government was continually distributing printed matter on methods of farming, first through the intendants, and later through the directories and the prefects. Books, pamphlets, tracts, and circulars on scores of agricultural topics[70]—occasionally as many as two thousand copies—were sent.[71] These publications dealt with such subjects as the cultivation of crops, the breeding and care of animals, and the storage and conservation of grain.[72]

Grain storehouses *(greniers d'abondance)*, which were widely distributed in the eighteenth century, produced such excellent results that Fleury advised the dauphin to make these storehouses general throughout France. They were never so numerous, however, as they should have been. In some instances they were maintained at the

---

tenant general of the bailliage of Rouen, mentions the cost of fertilizing an *arpent* (1½ acres) of vineyards, presumably with manure, at 24 livres, but says that this and other heavy costs led many vinegrowers to neglect their vineyards *(ibid.*, II, 558). For the employment of manure in the mid-century, in Guyenne, see Lhéritier, *op. cit.*, pp. 272-273.

[65] Boislisle, *op. cit.*, II, No. 863; Franklin, *op. cit.*, VII, 156.

[66] Boislisle and Brotonne, *op. cit.*, III, No. 410 n. A letter by the intendant of Bordeaux implies that chestnut leaves were used as fertilizer for wheat growing.

[67] Henri Sée, *Remarques sur la Misère, la mendicité et l'assistance en Bretagne à la fin de l'ancien régime* (Extrait de *Mémoires de la Société d'Histoire et d'Archéologie de Bretagne*, VI) (Rennes and Paris, 1925), 109-110.

[68] Lhéritier, *op. cit.*, pp. 372-373.

[69] Mathiez, *op. cit.*, pp. 372-373.

[70] An idea of the variety of topics can be secured from Mathiez's work, pp. 446-455. Two agricultural journals were so treated.

[71] On a bill submitted to the government in 1763 by one Guillin, a bookdealer *(libraire)* in Paris, for printed matter sent out by the controller-general, are listed, among three items, 2,000 copies for a pamphlet on apple trees. Of another pamphlet, 1,230 copies had been sent (Bibl. Nat., Fonds Français 6793, f 127).

[72] Sée, *op. cit.*, XXIV, 195.

expense of the central government, and in others at the expense of the city.[73]

In 1725 the government limited the acreage of vines in a large number of generalities for two reasons, to increase the price of wine and to make more land available for growing grain.[74] In 1731 the law was extended to the whole country. Throughout the first half of the century its enforcement was strict, and many proprietors were compelled to pull up vines which they had planted illegally;[75] but in the second half it became less severe, the government consciously relaxing its enforcement.[76]

In the second half of the century the government attempted to clear land long since uncultivated and to drain marshy regions, in order to make more land available for grain.[77] An order of council (*arrêt du conseil*) of August 16, 1761, offered to any person clearing land an exemption for ten years from any increase in the *taille*, the *vingtième*, or other taxes (*impositions*) which might normally ensue from the increase in value of land and crops resulting from such improvement. This offer applied to seventeen generalities, and after 1764 to eighteen. The results were less favorable than expected. Undismayed, however, the government went further in its offers in 1766, exempting these persons from all direct taxes (*impôts*), including the *dîme*, for the duration of fifteen years.[78] The citizens of certain provinces not included in this declaration of 1766 profited rather than lost, since in 1767-68 by special legislation they obtained yet more favorable terms; namely, exemption from taxes for twenty years and afterwards limitation of the *dîme* to the fiftieth sheaf of grain.[79] In some provinces little resulted from the offer, but in others the advantages were considerable. In Languedoc, by 1789, 100,000 *arpents* (about 126,000 acres) had been cleared; and results obtained in that province were less favorable than those in Brittany

---

[73] Bord, *op. cit.*, p. 22.

[74] The generalities were Tours, Bordeaux, Auvergne, Châlons, Montauban, and Alsace.

[75] Permission of the intendant was necessary before planting vines.

[76] Dumas, *op. cit.*, pp. 309-310.

[77] A good article on this subject by Henri Sée, entitled "La mise en valeur des terres incultes défrichements et dessèchements à la fin de l'ancien régime," is found in the *Revue d'histoire économique et sociale*, XI (Paris, 1923), 62-81. F. Dumas (*op. cit.*, pp. 295-297) also has some interesting matter on the subject.

[78] Sée, *op. cit.*, XI, 64-65.

[79] *Ibid.*, XI, 65-67.

and Guyenne.[80]   In almost every region of France some uncleared land was opened to cultivation.[81]   France continued to produce an inadequate amount of wheat, save in prosperous years.

A royal declaration of June 14, 1764, encouraged the draining of swampy land by offering for a number of years tax exemptions on such lands as increased in value. Some lands were drained, but this measure met with many less favorable results than those providing for the clearing of land. The chief obstacle lay in the hostility of the lower classes, who were accustomed to pasture their animals on the marshes. While clearance of land met hostility, the draining of the swamps brought furious opposition. At one place it led to attack on the home of the man who was in charge of the work.[82]   In spite of this opposition, which led to the curtailment of some of the projects, much marshy land here and there in France was drained and opened for cultivation.

The state co-operated with the farmers in attempting to combat insects, destructive animals, and animal diseases.[83]   When in 1686 a scourge of locusts (*sauterelles*) visited Languedoc, various communities hired peasants to kill them and bring in their bodies. Seventeen thousand quintals were amassed. At the same time the neighborhood of Araman, in the diocese of Uzes, borrowed 4,000 livres for the purpose, and the provincial government did not co-operate. In 1722-23, however, at the time of another locust scourge, the provincial government offered assistance. In February, 1723, after the locusts had made their appearance in several communes dur-

---

[80] *Ibid.*, pp. 68-70. In the generality of Tours 60,000 *arpents* were cleared in the period 1766-84 (Dumas, *op. cit.*, p. 297).

[81] But Sée does not indicate whether a larger wheat acreage resulted. In various generalities, such as Guyenne, Tours, and Artois, attempts were made during the 1760's to encourage foreigners to participate in these *défrichements*. Citizenship was offered them after six years of residence, and exemption from various taxes for a period of fifteen years. In case of their death, their parents, children, or other relatives domiciled in France might succeed them in these benefits. Relatives living abroad, however, could fall heir only to the movable property.

It happened that at this particular time many foreigners, mostly Germans, were desirous of settling in France and her colonies (Dumas, *op. cit.*, pp. 295-296; Sée, *op. cit.*, XI, 66, 68).

Ernest Martin (*Les exiles Acadiens en France au XVIIIᵉ siècle et leur établissement en Poitou*, Paris, 1936, pp. 133 ff.) tells at some length of a German settlement on the lands of the Marquis de Pérusse in Poitou, in the 1760's.

[82] Sée, *op. cit.*, XI, 75, 79.

[83] Its efforts in combating animal diseases are discussed later in a chapter on epizootics.

ing the preceding summer, De Bernage, the intendant, issued a detailed ordinance designed to bring about the total destruction of the insect eggs deposited in the ground. Each commune was ordered to name several notable citizens to direct the fight. They were to find the locust nests, hire and direct peasants to dig them up with plow or spade, and take notes on the findings. Women and children were to collect the eggs in sacks or bed sheets, take them to the consulate, and burn them in the presence of municipal officers or bury them three or four feet underground in trenches. Workers with plows were to be paid 50 sous a day, those with spades 17 sous, and women and children 1 sou for each pound of eggs, weighed in the presence of the consuls.[84]

In 1730-32 caterpillars became a scourge over virtually all of France, partly in consequence of the mild winters. In 1730 they were numerous; in 1731 they stripped the foliage from all types of trees (fruit trees, oaks, elms, lindens, etc.) and shrubs.[85] Various local and provincial officials then felt that the situation demanded action, and here and there ordinances were issued requiring the extermination of the pest. Eventually on February 4, 1732, the parlement of Parris issued an *arrêt*, which was received as a law generally over France, requiring that all property-owners and renters clear their trees and hedges of caterpillar eggs[86] within a week; else they would be liable to a fine of 30 livres, and would be liable to court action for damage by their neighbors for criminal negligence. The eggs were to be collected, taken a great distance[87] from any houses, trees, or heather, and burned.[88] In March, 1738, and in March, 1744, this measure was renewed. On all three occasions some landowners did not co-operate, and the legislation, as was the case with most French legislation in the eighteenth century, was only moderately effective. Nevertheless, according to Paul M. Bondois, the local enactments of 1731 and the general measure of 1732 were the precursors of similar legislation on the subject in France today.[89]

[84] *Histoire générale de Languedoc*, XIII, 972-973.

[85] Paul M. Bondois, "La protection des jardins et des cultures au XVIIIe siècle: la première loi d'échenillage (1732)," *Revue d'histoire économique et sociale*, XIV (Paris, 1926), 448.

[86] These eggs were deposited in grey, velvety sacks, attached to the limbs of the trees or branches of the hedge.

[87] "More than a fourth of a league" (i.e., more than a half mile).

[88] Bondois, *op. cit.*, pp. 454-455.

[89] *Ibid.*, p. 457. Cf. Dumas (*op. cit.*, pp. 294-295) for interesting action by the intendant Du Cluzel on the matter in 1779.

In 1761 Trudaine, intendant-general of finance, sent to the provinces a tract on the extermination of moles. In 1786 the government sent another on the means of destroying grasshoppers, and in 1787 yet another on the eradication of caterpillars.[90] From time to time printed matter was distributed on the destruction of wolves, more particularly by means of poison, and prizes were offered for wolf scalps. The prize varied, dependent on whether the scalp was that of a whelp, a grown female, or a grown male.[91] Eighteenth-century France was greatly troubled by wolves. They were chiefly bothersome to those who kept sheep, but occasionally a wolf afflicted with hydrophobia *(loup enragé)* attacked dogs and human beings.[92] Sometimes community wolfhunts took place; occasionally a band of men would set out hurriedly after a notorious wolf, like a posse after a desperado.[93]

Last, and perhaps one of its most useful services in aiding agriculture and the rearing of livestock, was the encouragement given by the government of the Old Regime to the numerous agricultural societies that arose throughout France in the second half of the century. The formation and phenomenal growth of these societies are a tribute to the development and popularity of science in the eighteenth century. The French government welcomed them, en-

[90] H. Sée, *op. cit., Annales de Bretagne*, XXIV, 196-197.

[91] In Champagne 6 livres were given for a grown male, 10 for a grown female, and 3 livres for a whelp (*Inv.-som . . . Ardennes*, C 105). In Burgundy, prior to 1754, 5 livres were given for a grown wolf, 50 sous for a whelp; but in 1754 the sums were raised to 6 and 3 livres, respectively (*Inv.-som . . . Côte d'Or*, C 3005). In Dauphiné, during the 1780's, 12 livres were given for a wolf, 6 for a whelp (*Inv.-som . . . Hautes-Alpes*, C 22). On occasion larger sums were paid those killing an "enraged" wolf (i.e., one afflicted with hydrophobia). In 1740 a gratification of 50 livres was given to one Antoine Viard in Burgundy, who killed a mad wolf of enormous size (*Inv.-som . . . Côte d'Or*, C 3187 fol. 426); a gratification of 150 livres was paid one Rouxel, in Brittany, for a similar service (*Inv.-som . . . Ille-et-Vilaine*, C 155); and in 1716 a gratification of the amazing sum of 300 livres was given one C. Mignot, in Burgundy, for killing a wolf that had "committed many ravages" (*Inv.-som . . . Côte d'Or*, C 3162).

[92] In one community in the 1770's twenty persons were bitten by a single mad wolf, and six died. The physician Thiesset treated them (*Inv.-som . . . l'Aude*, C 1165).

[93] Ernest Roschach has an interesting account of wolves and wolfhunts in the *Histoire générale de Languedoc*, XIII, 1193-1195. The *Inventaires-sommaires des archives départementales*, série C, teem with references to wolf-eradication. Two weird stories about wolves appear in the *Inventaire-sommaire* for Seine-Inférieure, C 121, and in that for Isère, L 113.

couraged their formation, and co-operated with them financially and otherwise in undertaking many projects.[94]

In conclusion, it is fair to say that increasingly during the eighteenth century the French government manifested an active interest in the agricultural welfare of its subjects, and by small monetary aid, prizes, exemption from taxes, and other forms of encouragement, tried to assist them in escaping famine and misery. These activities were much more extensive in the second half of the century than earlier, and by the time of the Revolution reached widespread proportions. The Revolutionaries carried on the work. Some of these activities were destined to have more manifest effects in later times, but the foundations were laid in the eighteenth century.

[94] An interesting but too limited study of these agricultural societies of the eighteenth century has been made by Emile Justin, *Les sociétés royales d'agriculture au XVIII*^*e* *siècle (1757-1793)* (Saint-Lo, 1935).

CHAPTER IV

FLOOD RELIEF AND CONTROL

THE CHIEF rivers of France have their origins either in the Alps in the east or the Pyrenees in the south. In the Alps rise the Loire and the Seine river systems, which flow roughly in a westerly direction, and the Rhône, which flows southward. The Garonne and the Adour have their source in the Pyrenees and flow westerly or northwesterly. These rivers with their tributaries, easily connected by canals,[1] provide France with a magnificent network of water communication; but they create at times an extraordinary hazard. For the rivers of France, with their mountainous origins, are subject to floods, as rains and melting snows turn them into raging torrents.[2]

Floods in eighteenth-century France were so common that few years passed without a great or small one in some part of the country.[3] Periodically, like financial panics, came great floods that devastated a whole river system or, indeed, all the river systems of the country. On such occasions the damage was enormous, sometimes running into millions of livres: dikes, bridges, dams, boats, rafts, logs, and mills were washed away; highways were ruined; homes were destroyed; food supplies, merchandise, and perishables were spoiled. In a few instances boatmen took food and other articles of necessity to people who had sought refuge in their garrets or on the second floors of their homes. Livestock, and occasionally human

---

[1] The network of eighteenth-century canals is briefly described by E. Levasseur in his *Histoire du commerce*, Part I: *Avant 1789* (Paris, 1911), p. 450; more elaborately by J. Dutens, in his *Histoire de la navigation intérieure de la France* . . . (Paris, 1829), Vol. I.

[2] Also due in large part to these mountains were the multitudinous hailstorms of eighteenth-century France, the most famous being that of July 13, 1788. These hailstorms played havoc with crops of all types, and on occasion were so bad as to precipitate famines. Not infrequently they occurred in common with floods. Remission in taxes because of hail damage was a common form of government charity. See, for example, the *Histoire générale de Languedoc*, XIII, XIV, *passim*. After the hailstorm of July 13, 1788, provincial and royal expenditures for relief reached 1,274,073 livres (Thomas F. Power, Jr., "Emergency Relief in France, 1788," *Journal of Modern History*, XIII, June, 1941, 222-223).

[3] Maurice Champion (*Les inondations en France depuis le VIe siècle jusqu'à nos jours*, VI, Paris, 1864, 21-29) attempts a complete catalogue of eighteenth-century floods, by year, month, river, and place. Only eighteen years of the century are not listed, five of these falling in the last decade.

life, were lost. Gardens, farms, orchards, with their crops, were ruined, sometimes for a year, sometimes for longer periods. The orchardists and vinegrowers suffered even worse than did the farmers, since two years or more were required for the growth of new vines or new trees. Frequently unemployment, and sometimes financial depressions, accompanied the floods.

On such occasions the finest and the basest in man showed themselves. Some plundered, extorted, and asked for aid above their deserts; others performed deeds of heroism, of generosity, and of patient, helpful service. Individuals, municipalities, provinces, the church, and the state co-operated in rendering aid to the distressed and needy. Since its policy was not to send cash for distribution, the state generally gave aid by remitting taxes. Frequently, however, the controller-general ordered the intendant to provide food or workshops for the needy or to rebuild houses or to make compensation for losses suffered, the payment to come from certain tax funds reserved by the intendant for charitable needs ("the free funds of the *capitation*") or from government grants to the province. Individuals made subscriptions, and the church sometimes solicited offerings for the flood sufferers.

A better idea of what took place can be obtained by specific attention to certain of the major floods of the century. On September 11-12, 1727, in southern France, heavy rains were accompanied by a warm wind which melted the snow that covered the peaks of the Pyrenees.[4] Instantly rivers were turned into raging torrents, and floods became general in that region. In the basin of the Aude a dozen communities were flooded, many persons were drowned, and many others lost all their property. Everywhere houses, bridges, and mills were destroyed. The town of La Grasse was half-destroyed by the Orbieu, as houses, furniture, and grain, were devastated; dye-shops and manufacturing establishments were wrecked; great quantities of wool were lost; and olive groves were ruined by gravel and debris. At Toulouse the Garonne, already swollen by several days' rain, overflowed the *faubourg* Saint-Cyprian and covered roads leading out of the city. All boats and rafts were either carried away or submerged by the flood, and it was impossible to carry aid to the suffering. Many houses made of unbaked brick

---

[4] *Histoire générale de Languedoc*, XIII, 1005-1008.

and other weak material collapsed. The Refuge of the Good Shepherd, housing eighty-four penitent women, sank in the flood, carrying all but six or seven of them to their death. Among the dead was the Père Badou, a celebrated missionary. Great quantities of wood brought from the Pyrenees and piled on the docks at Toulouse were carried away by the floodwaters. One hundred and ninety houses were ruined, and a much larger number of others were partly wrecked and became a source of danger to passers-by.[5] It was necessary to call in haste all the master- and journeyman-carpenters to strengthen the supports of these houses. The Hospital of Saint-Joseph de la Grave, housing some orphans and destitute adults, suffered heavily and came near collapse. In desperation the priests of Toulouse obtained from the *capitouls* (city authorities) permission to carry the Black Virgin from the Church of the Daurade in procession on the banks of the flooded river. The *chambre des vacances* of the parlement of Toulouse at a special meeting on September 14 passed orders restraining plunderers who sought to gain possession of furniture, wood, grain, and other goods carried down by the current. The plunderers were warned that their right to ownership would be contested.

The havoc wrought by the flood was felt the more keenly because the region had experienced severe hailstorms in June, July, and August of that year. Bernage de Saint-Maurice, intendant of Montpellier, hastened to offer grain from the official granaries to the *capitouls* of the flooded city of Toulouse, and was later commended by the controller-general of finance. The itemized report of the losses to the province of Languedoc from the flood, sent by Bernage de Saint-Maurice and summarized by Roschach in the *Histoire générale de Languedoc*, amounted to 1,846,891 livres, of which 601,265 livres represented the losses to the city of Toulouse. Bernage de Saint-Maurice requested and obtained from the controller-general indemnities or remissions to the extent of 248,050 livres on that year's taxes from the province, but there was apparently little consistency in his award of damages. To the diocese of Albi, which

---

[5] In the "Memoire au roy" (*ibid.*, XIII, 1007 n. 1) drawn up by the *capitouls* of Toulouse, it is stated, possibly with exaggeration, that 939 houses in Toulouse and its suburban districts collapsed or were carried away by the floodwaters of the Garonne; 436 others were so damaged as to need rebuilding; and 200 additional houses were flooded. Damages to the city and its environs they reckoned at more than 600,000 livres.

had experienced an estimated loss of 507,787 livres, Bernage de Saint-Maurice allotted only 48,000 livres by way of remission; to the diocese of Lavaur, which had suffered an estimated loss of only 1,100 livres, he granted 500 livres. To one portion of the province the remission was equal to one tenth of the loss, to four others one eighth, to two one sixth, to one one fourth, and to another one half. Possibly the intendant considered certain estimates of loss as submitted by his subdelegates excessive; possibly, too, he considered some regions as being richer and better able to stand the loss.

Rarely did anyone complain to the government that the money allotted for assistance was excessive. That the province of Languedoc, however, had a tendency toward excessive allowances for charitable purposes was charged in an unusual letter sent to Cardinal Fleury on November 21, 1728, by a group of middle-class people who signed themselves as "Les rentiers de la province de Languedoc,"[6] who professed to complain on behalf of the peasants, and who claimed that they themselves had suffered heavily from successive reductions in revenue. They denounced the rule, and indeed the capacity to rule, of the nobles and clergy in the estates of the province, charging that money was squandered on charities, indemnities, gratifications, etc.

On May 28, 1733, the levees along the Loire broke at a number of places between Roanne and Orléans, a distance of perhaps 125 miles, as water rose in the river to a height of 20 feet above normal. Orléans was inundated, streets were like rivers, pavement was torn up by the swirling waters, houses were overturned, and their inhabitants took refuge in convents and churches.[7] Logs, barrels, loose boats, and mills were swept along by the current and broke a number of bridges. Conditions were worst above and below the city for about 7 leagues. Twenty-one parishes, occupying a stretch about 13 leagues in length and from 1 to 2 leagues in width, were inundated. Farther down the river the city of Tours was so flooded that water rose to the height of 8 feet in the Church of St. Martin, and for three days the citizens were without food. No doubt Tours would have been ruined, states Lecler du Brillet, had not someone

---

[6] *Ibid.*, XIII, 1011-1012.

[7] Lecler du Brillet, *Continuation du traité de la police* (constituting Vol. IV of Nicolas Delamare's *Traité de la police*) (Paris, 1738), pp. 537-538; Champion, *op. cit.*, III, 16-25, xviii-xxv.

with foresight opened the levee at another point to carry the waters away from the city.[8] But by this diversion the near-by village of Ville-aux-Dames was flooded and its inhabitants and animals were drowned. In the rural regions vineyards and gardens were ruined. Even trees were uprooted. Farms were covered with sand and mud, sometimes 3 or 4 feet deep;[9] 50 houses were torn from their foundations, and about 200 others were shaken up and damaged; much of the furniture and movable property was carried away by the water or damaged; and a large portion of the livestock was destroyed. In some parishes more than half of the animals perished in the water. Many persons were drowned, but the exact number could not be determined. The archbishop of Paris directed a campaign for aid to the afflicted.[10]

The flood of December, 1740, was general throughout much of Western Europe.[11] Many towns in Holland were completely submerged. In France there were overflows along the systems of the Seine, the Loire, and the Rhône, and at one point along the Charente.[12] The older part of Grenoble, along the rivers Isère and Drac, was so flooded that the ground floor of houses was covered, and the magistrates were obliged to carry food daily in boats to the needy. A large portion of Paris was inundated. The city furnished boats, paying the boatmen 40 sous a day and forbidding them to take more than a liard from any person whom they ferried. Some houses became dangerous and were destroyed by orders of the police. The police force was enlarged in order to cope with the situation.

[8] According to Champion (op. cit., III, 17), the engineer Lecreulx doubted that this breach was made by design.

[9] Ibid., III, xix.

[10] From his mandement, quoted by Lecler du Brillet, many of these details are derived.

[11] The fullest accounts of this flood are given by Champion, op. cit. VI, 23 (list of references to volumes and pages); Barbier, Chronique de la régence et du règne de Louis XV (1718-1763), ou Journal de Barbier, avocat au parlement de Paris, III (Paris, 1858), 236-252; and by Bonamy in his article, "Mémoire sur l'inondation de la Seine à Paris, au mois de décembre 1740, comparée aux l'inondations précédentes; avec des remarques sur l'élévation du sol de cette ville," in the Mémoires de littérature, tirés des registres de l'Académie Royale des Inscriptions et Belles-Lettres, depuis l'année M.DCCXLI, jusques & compris l'année M.DCCXLIII, XVII (Paris, 1751), 675-708. Bonamy (p. 708) gives a daily chart on the height of the Seine at Paris for the months of December and January. Briefer descriptions of this flood are given by Marcel Fosseyeux, L'Hôtel-Dieu de Paris au XVIIe et XVIIIe siècle (Paris and Nancy, 1912), pp. 195-197; and Gustave Bord, Les inondations du bassin de la Seine (1658-1910) (Paris, 1910), p. 48 n.

[12] Champion, op. cit., VI, 23.

People were moved from shops and dwellings over several of the bridges, and the police kept people away from points of danger. The crest of the high water was reached on December 26, when it was 24 feet 4 inches above normal. The flood lasted into January, 1741, six weeks elapsing from beginning to end of the high waters.

The severity of the winter of 1739 and the smallness of the grain crop of 1740 in most of the French provinces had created a shortage in grain even before the flood. The flood, therefore, aggravated an already distressing situation. That the parlement of Paris issued an order commanding all vagabonds and poor persons from the provinces to leave Paris within six weeks under the threat of severe penalties, the parliamentary advocate Barbier thought wise, since food was scare and the danger of contagion following the flood was great. At the same time Barbier realized that the poor would face severe difficulties in leaving the city. The *chambre des comptes*, however, rescued the poor by denying the legality of the order.

Orry, the controller-general, ordered wheat brought into the city from Poitou, Rouen, and other parts of France. A company of men was engaged to import wheat from the north and from Sicily. It was impossible to obtain grain from England, since that country was threatening war and had prohibited any shipments of food. The stoppage of the mills by the high waters diminished the already small supply of flour at Paris. Moreover, several boats from Rouen loaded with wheat and other provisions for Paris were lost. Bread riots in the city were feared. A severe riot arising over the shortage of bread had occurred at the Bicêtre in September, 1740, and the guard and *maréchaussée* had been compelled to fight to put it down.

Other cities also were badly hit. The government sent 15,000 livres to the city of Grenoble for its urgent needs following the flood.[13] At Nîmes the silk factories were closed, workmen suffered terribly, prices of silk rose to extreme heights, and France was afraid lest the workmen emigrate and take their knowledge of the silk industry to other countries. The bishop of Nîmes and the general hospital gave aid to the needed. The experiences of other affected cities, their sufferings, and their relief were similar to those of Nîmes.[14]

[13] An account sheet showing the manner in which the money was spent lists 1,336 livres for bread given to the poor (*ibid.*, IV, xli).

[14] *Ibid.*, II, 37-38; III, 26-27; V, 52-54, 185; *Inv.-som* . . . *Seine-Inférieure*, C 226.

The flood of early 1784 wrought more havoc by far than any other flood of the century.[15] Hardly a province in France escaped heavy damages. The reports of the intendants to the controller-general of finance indicate stupendous losses and make it clear that the country suffered a major catastrophe. Dupont, intendant of the generality of Metz, reckoned the losses of his province at 1,476,559 livres; Delaporte, intendant of Lorraine, reckoned his as 1,476,559 livres; De Crosne, intendant of Rouen, estimated his at 671,278 livres; Sénac de Meilhan, intendant of Hainaut, placed his at 500,-000 livres. These generalities were among the hardest hit, and part of the losses stipulated in these figures resulted from storms and snow preceding the flood. The total loss to France from these devastations by nature in early 1784 was perhaps 15,000,000 to 20,-000,0000 livres.

The winter of 1783-84 was one of intense cold and suffering. Great quantities of snow fell, and much unemployment resulted as manufactories and other forms of work closed down. February brought terrific rains and a spell of warm weather that suddenly melted the quantities of snow and sent the rivers dashing to the sea with swollen crests. Floods occurred along all the rivers.[16]

Damage of almost every conceivable form was wrought. On February 24-25 the Iton overflowed at Evreux, and water was six feet deep in some of the streets. The inhabitants were obliged to betake themselves to their garrets. Garden walls and huts collapsed, and the foundations of many homes were destroyed.[17] Flood damage to the coal mine of Crisborn in Lorraine, on which the owner had just spent 50,000 livres to put it in a state of operation, was estimated at 30,000 livres. Water covered the streets of Caen for eight days and ruined the pavement in about one fourth of the city. In Roussillon, fields were covered with rocks and sand, several bridges were destroyed, and the dike Orry, constructed since 1777, was washed out by the simultaneous rising of two rivers at Perpig-

[15] Information covering this flood is derived chiefly from manuscript material in Arch., Nat., H 1418, 1419. Not a few of these documents have been published by Champion, op. cit., II, lii-lxxxviii; III, lix-lx; IV, li-lvi; V, viii-xxii. Other sources are Bachaumont, *Mémoires secrets*, XXV (Londres, 1786), 28, 73-74, 84, 86-87, 104, 119, 172, and Gomel, op. cit., pp. 92-93.

[16] In southern France heavy rains and floods began in late January, but in northern France snow and ice continued into mid-February.

[17] The small election of Evreux alone suffered losses to the extent of 354,699 livres (De Crosne to Calonne, March 23, 1784, Arch. Nat., H 1418).

nan. Moreover, communications between Roussillon and the rest of France were severely disrupted. In Franche-Comté much damage was done to homes, highways, and bridges, and unemployment was severe. Alsace suffered heavy damages to houses, bridges, and grain crops. Fields in several communities were covered with sand. In Touraine, houses, mills, merchandise, bridges, and animals were carried away in the flood when levees along the Loire broke. In Orléanais the misery was distressing in the winegrowing regions and in the dairy region of the Sologne. Communications were cut. All work ceased. On January 31, at an early stage in the flood, a sudden rise in the Loire swept away from Orléans thirty or forty boats laden with wood, wine, and other commodities. The ice-floes in the river caused the sinking of boats; the shipping that remained afloat was carried against the bridge at Blois and endangered it. Several heads of families thus lost their lives. The commissioners of Blois, Orléans, and Tours estimated the losses of their cities at more than a million livres. The intendant at Bordeaux described the damage in Guyenne: "An infinite number of owners have lost mills, forges, buildings, either wholly or in part, together with the furnishings and goods placed in them." Many bridges, some important, were destroyed or badly damaged, and highways and levees considerably harmed. In Lorraine, where losses were estimated greater than in any other of the provinces, damage was done to lands, houses, furniture, and animals. In the generality of Châlons 103 bridges were either completely destroyed or badly damaged, and heavy losses were sustained in homes, barns, furniture, grains, hay, and animals, as 93 parishes were covered with waters from the Suippe, Aisne, and Retourne. The intendant reported that 2,279 families lost their homes. Similar damages were sustained in other provinces.

One of the most serious effects of the flood was the increase in unemployment. Floods and other calamities in the summer of 1783, followed by heavy rains and snows and frigid temperatures in the ensuing autumn and winter, brought industry and business virtually to a standstill. Unemployment already had been great in many provinces for two or three months before the flood. In some provinces, like Lorraine, charity workshops were established by the intendants to alleviate suffering among the poor. The intendant of Lorraine was opposed to a dole, which in his opinion merely encouraged indolence among the masses. The intendants who opened workshops were fortunate in still having charity funds from the taxes of their provinces at their disposal, for many of the intendants had already disposed of their funds and were unable to install workshops. Although the French upper classes believed that assistance through charity workshops was preferable to a dole, food was furnished free by the intendants to the needy in many of the provinces. Great quantities of rice were given away. In the generality of Paris alone rice worth 10,000 livres was so distributed.[18]

Throughout France individuals, as well as the church, the municipality, and the province, rushed to the assistance of sufferers. At Amiens, where unemployment was great, the bishop and the intendant co-operated during the winter months of 1783-84 in running a relief bureau for the needy. According to the intendant, notwithstanding astonishing gifts from the well-to-do, there was still not enough to meet the situation. The intendant of Roussillon wrote that the rich and the well-to-do, and even the laborers, had come liberally to the relief of the poor; that the curés had given what they could; that he himself had spent about 15,000 or 16,000 livres of tax money in public works to assist employment, and had distributed 4,000 or 5,000 livres among those without work. Bread, beans, and meat were given to those in need. The intendant of Caen placed 6,000 livres of tax funds at the disposal of the city of Caen, and private individuals in the city gave liberally. In the generality of Paris, 39,140 pounds (livres) of rice were distributed, 29,280 provided by government funds, 5,100 by gifts from generous individuals. In nearly all of the fifteen towns and cities in Hainaut stricken by the flood, food, clothing, wood, coal, and money were distributed among the needy, in some instances by the municipality, in others by generous individuals. Yet for obvious reasons, in this catastrophe of huge proportions, aid from these sources was inadequate to meet the situation properly.

It was essential that the state come to the rescue. Calonne, the controller-general of finance, notified the intendants in mid-January that the government planned to distribute among the provinces remissions to the extent of 3,000,000 livres because of the severity of

[18] Rice valued at 25,000 livres was distributed in France by the various intendants.

the winter. After the floods of January and February he decided to allow them four millions additional, three millions by way of remissions for losses incurred and one million for charity workshops and reparation of bridges and highways. The second grant was made by an order of council of March 14, 1784.[19] The intendants were then asked to forward reports of damage in their provinces. These reports, elaborate in nature, repose today in the Archives Nationales, where they fill two large boxes. With the reports and other correspondence is an account sheet stipulating how 2,660,000 livres were distributed in remissions. The remission to any given province was small in proportion to the damages incurred. Thus Dauphiné, which reported losses of 759,000 livres, received but 150,000 livres; Metz, which reported losses of 1,001,646 livres, received 180,000 livres; and Lorraine, which reported losses of 1,476,559 livres, received 100,000 livres. In allotting the remissions, the controller-general did not strictly follow any mathematical ratio between losses and indemnities but made indemnities according to his own judgment. Perhaps this method was as fair as any, since a few of the intendants' reports of losses were probably "padded." Calonne planned to pay for the four millions granted on March 14 by curtailments in the household expenses of the royal family and in pensions above 10,000 livres.[20]

Amid the papers of the Archives Nationales are the stories of certain deeds of heroism which the intendants felt should be brought to the attention of the national government. A certain Thuillier, who saved the life of the mail carrier en route from Amiens to Abbéville, was recommended by the intendant of Amiens for a reward, and it was given. The intendant of Châlons reported the story of S. Husson, curé of the village Boule-sur-Suippe, whose twenty parishioners had taken refuge with him in a church during the flood and had neither help nor food there. "Then," says the

[19] De Crosne to Calonne, March 23, 1784, acknowledging receipt of letter of March 17 from the latter, and of some copies of the *arrêt* of March 14 (Arch. Nat., H 1418); Bachaumont, *op. cit.*, XXV, 172-173.

[20] Mentioned by Bachaumont (*op. cit.*, XXV, 74), who gives the king credit for having originated in January the idea of aiding the needy by a state grant of three millions. Bertin, in a letter to the controller-general, March 12, 1784 (Arch. Nat., H 1418), makes a statement to the same effect. Bachaumont (*op. cit.*, XXV, 74, 84), moreover, mentions gifts of 500 louis in late January and 12,000 livres in early February by the Queen. The latter sum was placed in the hands of the archbishop of Paris for distribution.

official report, "S. Husson, curé, exposed his life to the greatest danger: he traversed sixteen times the bed of the river where the water was four feet high, carrying on his shoulders those of his parishioners who either by their age or their infirmities were menaced with death because of lack of food and aid." The intendant had interviewed the curé and had been captivated by his modesty, for the curé insisted that he had only done his duty toward his parishioners. Since the curé was receiving only 500 livres a year, he was recommended to the controller-general for a reward and to the bishop of Autun for an increase in salary. Another instance of heroism was reported by the intendant of Flanders. The city of Merville and several villages in its neighborhood were flooded by the river Lys, and the inhabitants were obliged to climb to their housetops. According to the intendant, they would have died there had not his subdelegate, Le Dien, furnished food at his own expense and taken it to these people in boats. Moreover, Le Dien refused to be reimbursed.[21]

The floods of the Revolutionary period brought a few minor changes in the administration of relief. In mid-November, 1791,[22] heavy rainfall, accompanied by the simultaneous melting of snow in the mountains of Auvergne (and possibly elsewhere), led to precipitous floods along much of the Loire and Rhône river systems. In the single night of November 11-12 the Loire reportedly rose 23 feet and flooded the city of Roanne, damaging much property, demolishing a number of houses, and taking several lives. At the same time the Allier, twin source of the Loire, flooded Moulins to such an extent that water stood 11 to 12 feet in the houses of the lower part of the city. Six hundred and fifty-four "houses or households" (maisons ou ménages) were allegedly affected, and damage to buildings, furniture, and merchandise was estimated at 300,000 livres. The town of Val likewise was submerged, and seventy-four

---

[21] The departmental archives reveal several other instances of heroism during this flood. In Champagne, one Sébastien Guillaume Blondet rescued forty-six persons from the floodwaters of the Marne and was awarded a gratification of 300 livres; Antoine Pavillon lost both legs by amputation as a result of remaining too long in the icy waters at rescue work, and he, too, was given a gratification of 300 livres; Jean Maillart suffered a broken arm while at rescue work and was given 100 livres; and Joseph Collin, a boatman, was cited for conspicuous bravery on this and other occasions (Inv.-som . . . Ardennes, C 83, 35).

[22] Described in Arch. parl., XX, 472, 512, 590-591, 689, 749; XXI, 325, 362; Champion, op. cit., III, 64-69, lxxiv-xcii; IV, 78-79; VI, 29.

rescue boats were pressed into service. At Val, Tours, and Blois, units of soldiery, national guards, and *maréchaussée* were employed at guarding and building up the levees.[23] Simultaneous with this *débâcle* along the Loire and its tributaries, floods occurred with much damage along the Rhône and its tributaries, the Isère and Durance. But both reports and relief awards indicate that damage along the system of the Rhône was small in comparison with that along the system of the Loire.

Damage along the Allier alone was reckoned at 2,406,520 livres, and in a single department along the Loire at 1,917,215 livres. While each department was supposed to care for its own charities and reparations, unless too onerous, deputies from the flooded areas were quick to raise on the floor of the National Assembly the question of government relief. In a generous mood, the Assembly voted grants, first to three, then to four, five, seven, and finally nine, departments along the upper reaches of the Loire and Allier. To each of the first seven, 30,000 livres were given;[24] to the eighth and ninth, 45,000 livres.[25] Other provinces were requested to present their claims to the committee of finances. One member disliked the idea of the Assembly stopping work to attend to these matters. The king and queen from their privy purse gave 6,000 livres to the needy in the department of Rhône-et-Loire (in which Roanne was situated).[26]

Thus in the eighteenth century the French customarily relieved the distress following these accidents of nature, and the government, the municipalities, the church, and generous individuals participated in the work of alleviation. But, one may ask, did the French have no long-range policies? Did they do nothing to control the courses of rivers and prevent floods? Did they have no foresight? The answer is that the French did take steps to control rivers against floods. In fact, their efforts at flood prevention remind one very

[23] *Arch. parl.*, XX, 472, 689; Champion, *op. cit.*, III, lxxviii. The two regiments of soldiers, the Royal Comptois and the Regiment of Anjou, were later praised on the floor of the National Assembly.

[24] Nièvre, Loiret, and Allier, by decree of Nov. 12; Rhône-et-Loire, by decree of Nov. 18; Indre-et-Loire, by decree of Nov. 21; Cher and Loire-et-Cher, by decree of Nov. 26.

[25] Haute-Loire and Puy-de-Dôme, by decree of Dec. 8.

[26] The damage to this department was reckoned at 1,917,215 livres (Champion, *op. cit.*, III, 65 n. 1). This department was dismembered in 1793. There is no record of private contributions.

much of those taken in the United States; perhaps in view of the relative size of the two countries, in territory, population, and wealth, the steps in eighteenth-century France were not disproportionate to those in twentieth-century America. The French of the eighteenth century used dredging and levees extensively and discussed at length, whether or not they put it into practice, the shortening of rivers by canals which would cut off dangerous bends that retarded the progress of the waters. In 1790 one engineer even suggested the idea of spillways.[27]

Hundreds of years before the French brought to North America the levees on the Mississippi (*ca.* 1720)[28] they had used them on the Loire. According to Lecler du Brillet,[29] Louis the *Débonnaire*, king from A.D. 814 to 840, gave orders for work on levees, and even he was probably not the originator of them. Succeeding kings so improved the levees that in Lecler du Brillet's day (*ca.* 1738) they extended on the Loire-Allier system from Port de Sorges, near Angers, to Vichy, a distance of 180 leagues (approximately 450 miles). In some places they were on one bank, in others on both banks, as need required. In height they rose 12-22 *pieds* (feet);[30] at their top they were 4-5 *toises* (25.5-32 feet) wide[31] if they carried a highway, or 3 *toises* (19.2 feet) if they did not. No parapets or guard-rails were placed along the crest;[32] and according to F. Dumas,[33] carriages occasionally fell into the Loire.

In the period of Du Cluzel's intendancy France spent 500,000 livres annually on the maintenance of the Loire levees, the expense falling upon the provinces bordering the river. In 1771 Touraine let a contract to the lowest bidder for six years' maintenance for the sum of 480,000 livres. A special tax, levied along with the *taille*, was imposed for the purpose of providing the funds.[34] In the second

---

[27] *Ibid.*, III, 69.

[28] "Levee," *Encyclopedia Americana* (New York, 1932), XVII, 291.

[29] See his account of levees along the Loire in the eighteenth century (*op. cit.*, pp. 531-549).

[30] The *pied*, divided into 12 *pouces*, was equivalent to 0.3248 meter (*Nouveau petit Larousse illustré*, Paris, 1938), or 12.787 inches.

[31] A *toise* was equivalent to 1.949 meters, or 6.39459 feet.

[32] Du Cluzel, intendant of Touraine, announced in 1771, however, that he intended placing guard-rails at the most dangerous places on the levees.

[33] See *op. cit.*, pp. 236-258, for an excellent description of these levees. In 1788 the royal council ordered hedges planted along the crest of the levees by the neighboring landowners (*ibid.*, pp. 241-242). One anticipated advantage was a lessening of accidents.

[34] Lecler du Brillet, *op. cit.*, p. 538.

half of the century the levees reached a perpendicular height of 22 feet above normal water-level; yet in 1783 water rose 2½ feet above the levees at Saumur. At their base the levees were 12 *toises* (76 feet) wide. Their sides were riprapped or protected with stones 18 inches thick; moreover, hedges, and sometimes trees, were planted on their slope toward the river in order to strengthen them. Two rows of piles were driven into the bank at the bottom of the slope in order to protect the rocks that were so frequently loosened or in need of replacement. It became customary in the latter part of the eighteenth century to use huge stones instead of piles.

The French laws for the protection of the levees were strict. No animals were allowed to graze on them. Rabbits and hogs found feeding on them were to be killed; other animals might be seized and sold. No person could plant crops on them, under heavy penalty. No one could throw dirt or stones from the levees without liability to a fine. No buildings were allowed to go up within 10 *toises* (64 feet) of the levees, under penalty of a fine of 300 livres and imprisonment. Hedges and trees were planted in the space between the levees and the river in order to break the violence of the water against the levees in times of flood. Once every year a careful examination of the levees was required, together with repair of all faulty places.

At the head of the administration of the levees was the director-general of bridges and highways. Under him served an intendant of dikes and levees, two controllers, two receivers-general, and an engineer. The duties of the engineer were to oversee and plan all repairs and to make personal visits to places of danger whenever occasion demanded. In 1772 a radical change was made in the administration of the levees: the intendants of provinces were charged with the upkeep of the levees, each in his own generality.

In 1747 the minister Trudaine established the famous Ecole des Ponts-et-Chaussées for the training of road, bridge, and harbor engineers, the first institution of its kind in the world and one that was to have enormous influence.[35] In the second half of the eighteenth

[35] The young but brilliant Jean Rodolphe Perronet (1708-1794), destined to become the most celebrated French engineer of his century, was placed in charge (*Biographie universelle*, XXXIII, 425). A brief description of the institution is given by Frederick B. Artz, *L'éducation technique en France au dix-huitième siècle (1700-1789)* (Paris, 1939), pp. 26-27; reprinted from *Revue de l'histoire moderne*, Sept.-Dec., 1938.

century France had the best roads and best engineers in Europe, and levees and dikes no doubt shared in the improvement. A notable example of French engineering was the building of a stone bridge over the Loire at Tours, in the years 1765-79, at a cost of 4,300,000 livres.[36] It was 439 meters (1,440 feet) long, 14.4 meters (47.9 feet) wide, and had fifteen arches of 25.4 meters (83.3 feet) each.

While most of the levees were built along the Loire, some were constructed on its tributaries, the Allier and the Cher,[37] and some on the Rhône and other rivers and even canals.[38] At Saumur on the Loire a breakwater was constructed for the entire length of the city to protect it against the current, the city bearing one third of the cost of 400,000 livres.[39] A similar breakwater to protect the city of Roanne was constructed in 1711 at an expense of 210,000 livres.[40]

Great care was taken to keep clean the banks and bed of the Loire and its tributaries, and doubtless those of the other rivers. All owners of riverside property, millers, fishermen, and others who might share responsibility were required to remove logs, trees, sunken boats, rocks, and other debris found in the river or on its banks. No one was allowed to throw into a river anything that might clutter up its channel. Islands and sandbanks that formed in the Loire (for the Loire, like the Mississippi, changes its bed occasionally) were to be removed if found dangerous to navigation or to the levees.[41]

Similar provisions prevailed at Paris for the maintenance of a

[36] Dumas, op. cit., pp. 219-225. Trouble and extra expense were encountered in its construction; moreover, in 1789 four arches collapsed as the result of a flood.

[37] Ibid., pp. 237-238; Lecler du Brillet, op. cit., pp. 536.

[38] Lecler du Brillet (op. cit., pp. 536-543) and Dumas (op. cit., p. 236) indicate that France had levees only on the Loire and its tributaries. While this was her only great levee system, France did have short stretches of levees on the Rhône (Histoire générale de Languedoc, XIII, 1136) and its tributaries, the Isère, the Drac (Inv.-som . . . Isère, L 54, pp. 385, 413), the Saône, and the Doubs (Inv.-som . . . Côte d'Or, C 1003, 3184 [ff 222, 244], 3188 [ff 237, 305]). There were also levees on the Arroux (ibid., C 3189 [f 675]) and the canal of the Loing (Inv.-som . . . Seine, L 69 f 148) in the upper Seine basin and on the Adour near Bayonne (Boislisle, Correspondance des contrôleurs généraux, II, Paris, 1883, No. 495). Besides the levees, France had a multitude of dikes, which were generally shorter in length and were often made of stone, to protect vulnerable spots along rivers and seacoast.

[39] Dumas, op. cit., p. 238.

[40] Auguste Pawloski and Albert Radoux, Les crues de Paris (VIe-XXe siècle) (Paris and Nancy, 1910), p. 127.

[41] Dumas, op. cit., pp. 255-257.

clean channel in the Seine and its tributaries.[42]   During the months of August and September of each year the banks and beds of these rivers were to be given a thorough cleaning, the expense to be defrayed by the owners of property along them.   All trees, houses, or other obstructions within a distance of six feet from the river were to be removed at the owner's expense.

From time to time the French considered the feasibility of cutting off menacing bends in rivers and making their courses straighter and swifter.   Shortening the course of the Seine at Paris, where a tremendous bend occurs, by a canal from the Porte Saint-Antoine to the Porte du Temple was discussed, and—a project suggested as early as 1512[43]—twice in the seventeenth century was almost adopted by the city.   The path followed by the canal would have been an old bed of the Seine, more direct than its channel; floodwaters in 1740-41 had actually followed that course.[44]

Just below the city of Tours a canal connecting the Loire and the Cher carried commerce between the two rivers and served somewhat as a safety-valve when the Loire was flooded.   In 1774 Du Cluzel closed the canal, in spite of protests from the inhabitants of Tours. Later, in 1787, after Du Cluzel's death, De la Millière, director-general of bridges and highways, agreed to reopen it.[45]

Early in the century much discussed was the building of a canal that would aid in carrying off the waters of the Rhône in its delta. Several plans were proposed, and on one occasion a contract was let; but whether the canal was actually constructed is not clear.[46]

In 1790 the inspector-general of embankments and levees published a proposal to create a system of spillways by making occasional openings in the levees so that floodwaters would be carried

[42] Lecler du Brillet, *op. cit.*, pp. 306-307.

[43] *Ibid.*, p. 298.

[44] See map of the city of Paris in the *Mémoires de littérature, tirés des registres de l'Académie Royale des Inscriptions et Belles-Lettres* . . . , XVII, opposite p. 675.

Engineers proposed the construction of a canal in a bend of the Isère at Grenoble, after 1740, to protect that city against floods; but on account of the expense involved, the idea was rejected (A. Prudhomme, *Histoire de Grenoble*, Grenoble, 1888, pp. 570-571).

To protect Fréjus, an alteration in the course of the Argens was ordered in 1756 (*Inv.-som . . . Bouches-du-Rhône*, C 78 [f 193]).

[45] Dumas, *op. cit.*, pp. 243-249.

[46] See the present writer's discussion in his article, "Flood Relief and Control in Eighteenth-Century France," *Journal of Modern History*, XIII (March, 1941), 17-18; also his source, *Histoire générale de Languedoc*, XIII, 892-893.

over lands where presumably they would do least damage. But so strong were the protests of local officials that no action was taken.[47] This engineer pointed out the weaknesses of the levee system, the chief of which was the continual need of increasing the height of the levees because of the accumulation of sand in the river bed. All through the eighteenth century, even as today, this problem was present. Dredging as a remedy for this condition was little practised in eighteenth-century France.[48]

Whether flood sufferers camped on the levees of eighteenth-century France as they do on those of the Mississippi in twentieth-century America is not indicated, nor is evidence available whether soldiers customarily stood guard on the levees. They were present at various points along the Loire in the flood of November, 1790. Moreover, in Paris extra police were added in times of flood; *archers* were stationed to guard the bridges over the Seine, and, if the situation was dangerous, no one was allowed to cross. All occupants of homes on the bridges or by the river were compelled to move, and the landlords were obliged to move renters' property to safety. These precautions protected both the renter and the landlord.[49]

Floods and flood control and relief have undergone many changes since the eighteenth century. The Red Cross, the airplane, and the radio have vastly improved the relief problem; suction dredging and better spillways have improved flood control; but floodwaters behave very much as they always did, and an inhabitant of the lower Mississippi Valley may see many strong similarities between eighteenth-century French floods and those of twentieth-century United States.

[47] Champion, *op. cit.*, III, 69, lxxxiii.
[48] One cynical reader, commenting on the engineer's remarks, observed that in accordance with the engineer's reasoning the bed of the Loire at Orléans had risen 5 feet in the period of forty-five years preceding 1790, and in eighteen centuries around 245 feet (*pieds*). Champion (*op. cit.*, III, lxxx-xxxi nn.), who shares his sentiment, says that the question of the rise of the bed of the Loire has been much debated, with the best authorities denying that much increase has occurred. Dumas (*op. cit.*, pp. 238-239) asserts that sand did fill the river bed.
[49] Lecler du Brillet, *op. cit.*, p. 299.

CHAPTER V

FIRE RELIEF AND PREVENTION

BECAUSE of their narrow streets, the wooden composition of their houses, and their thatched roofs, and because of their inadequate and poorly developed methods of combating fires, eighteenth-century Frenchmen had great difficulty in controlling the numerous and huge fires which swept their land, creating great damage and loss of life. Often a dozen, a score, or even fifty, houses were destroyed by a single fire. Some of the fires burned for two or three days, or even longer, before they were extinguished. Often the furniture was burned with the houses, the barns were destroyed with their contents, and men lost their lives and their livestock in the holocausts. Frequently the fire sufferer was left as naked and as impoverished as the boil-afflicted Job of biblical fame.

TABLE (see page 87)

Place	Date	Number of Houses Destroyed	Number of Families Left Homeless	Estimated Loss (livres)
Naones (Somme)	May 30, 1792	50	..	40,540
Mouchy-Humières (l'Oise)	August 23-4, 1792	50	..	66,260
Breuille-Sec (l'Oise)	August 21, 1792	40	..	88,000
Fampoux (Pas-de-Calais)	No date given	..	72	118,350
Offin (Pas-de-Calais)	No date given	..	13	39,950
Vitry (Pas-de-Calais)	No date given	..	22	16,950
Avesnes-le-Comte (Pas-de-Calais)	No date given	..	158	187,500
Gomelin (Nord)	July 23, 1791	..	33	187,500
Sauvigny-les-Augiray (Haute-Saone)	September 28, 1791	..	21	42,616
Coincy (l'Aisne)	No date given	..	44	40,372
Mazerolle (Besançon)	September 16, 1791	40	..	126,100
Mittelschauffelsheim (Bas-Rhin)	September 1, 1792	17	..	97,200
Pouilly (Haute-Marne)	1790	..	30	125,854

NOTE: No place is listed which had less than twelve houses or families affected. In fact, one which suffered a fire on October 14, 1791, with loss estimated at 303,091 livres has been omitted because there was no mention of the houses or families concerned.

Even though by 1792 methods of fire prevention had been improved and the number of fires and their losses had been reduced in some parts of France, the committee of public aid, on September 8, in a report to the Legislative Assembly, estimated fire losses, particularly in the villages of northern and eastern France, at 3,225, 480 livres during the period 1790-92.[1] This report revealed in some instances the number of homes destroyed and in other instances the number of families left homeless (see the preceding table for a list of the more important losses).

The most devastating fire of the century occurred at Rennes in late December, 1720, while the country was suffering from one of its most severe financial panics,[2] and while Provence was suffering from a terrible epidemic of the bubonic plague. The fire began at midnight on December 22 and continued without abatement for six days and nights, until 850 houses and 32 streets had been destroyed, at a loss of 8,854,877 livres, or the equivalent of at least 35,000,000 francs at their 1914 value.[3] A drunken carpenter who set fire to his home on the rue Tristin (now 3, rue de l'Horloge), in the center of the city, was responsible for starting the conflagration. A fierce wind fanned it. The narrowness of the streets of old Rennes and the architecture of her wooden houses, whose second and third floors jutted out successively over the street (in reverse fashion to the modern "set-back" style), facilitated the spread of the flames.[4] The frantic inhabitants removed their furniture and other belongings into the streets and attempted to get them carted away to points of safety, but the narrow streets were well-nigh impassable. The city had but two pumps for fighting fires, and the conduits did not function well despite the fact that the city had frequently repaired them at much expense.[5] The regiment of Auvergne, then

---

[1] *Archives parlementaires de 1787 à 1789*, First Ser., XLIX, 464-469.

[2] In the aftermath of the John Law Scheme.

[3] "Les pertes furent évaluées à 6,326,930 livres pour les maisons et 2,527,947 livres pour less meubles, en tout 8,854,877 livres, qui vaudraient au moins 35 millions de francs aujourd'hui" (Arthur Le Moyne de la Borderie, *Histoire de Bretagne*, continued by Barthélemy Pocquet, VI, Rennes, 1914, 170-172). Another modern writer places the destruction at 9,000,000 livres independently of the loss in public buildings and monuments (Banéat, "L'incendie de Rennes en 1720," *Bulletin historique et philolophique du comité des travaux historiques et scientifiques*, Paris, 1909, p. 259).

[4] Banéat (*op. cit.*, p. 262) quotes an old traveler on this description of Rennes.

[5] Dom H. Leclercq, *Histoire de la Règence pendant la minorité de Louis XV*, III (Paris, 1921), 103.

in winter quarters at Rennes, received orders from the intendant of that city, Feydeau de Brou, to aid in fighting the fire and promoting order; instead, according to several contemporary sources,[6] the soldiers turned to incendiarism and pillage. One of the soldiers was caught carrying off the holy ciborium (of gold) filled with wafers and was executed by burning.[7] According to Boisrouvray, he was the only soldier punished for his actions. But so outrageous were the soldiery that a body of bourgeois citizens of the town organized themselves, disarmed the soldiers, corralled them in a spot on one of the walls, and kept them there under the point of guns throughout the remainder of the conflagration.[8]

A large number of men of the working class followed the soldiers in sacking the city; others demanded extravagant prices for their assistance.[9] Without question the disorganization and lawlessness aggravated the situation. The intendant had designed things otherwise, but his plans collapsed. He had asked the soldiers and some entrepreneurs to take charge and destroy a dozen homes in the path of the fire. This plan, which had been adopted with success in the late stages of the fire of London in 1666, might well have halted the flames. But when the soldiers ran riot, the intendant and others failed to organize the citizenry for execution of the design. The intendant, the bishop, the first president of parlement, the councilors and aldermen did don leather jackets and wooden shoes, carry buckets of water, and try to encourage the workers to fight the fire, giving them liberal drafts of wine,[10] but all to no avail. It was necessary to resort to workers from the country. Some of the leading citizens of the town went to the country, hired groups of peasants, and by their aid, according to Boisrouvray, successfully blocked the paths of fire, which since the third day had proceeded in four directions.[11] Perhaps a third of the city was saved.

During the first three days of the *débâcle* no relief either in food

---

[6] François René Jacquelot de Boisrouvray, "Journal inédit d'un député de l'ordre de la noblesse aux Etats de Bretagne pendant la Règence (1717-1724)," *Annales de Bretagne*, XXV (Rennes, 1909-10), 280; Dupuy and Charvot, "Journal d'une curé de campagne (1712-1765)," *Annales de Bretagne*, V (Rennes, 1889-90), 413; *Journal de Barbier*, I (Paris, 1857), 95.

[7] So says Barbier. Barbier, Boisrouvray, and La Borderie disagree concerning whether the soldier stole the ciborium or the chalice, or both, and whether he was burned or hanged. Barbier rests his account upon two letters from Rennes.

[8] Boisrouvray, *op. cit.*, XXV, 281.   [9] *Ibid.*, XXV, 280-281.

[10] Leclercq, *op. cit.*, III, 103.   [11] *Op. cit.*, XXV, 282.

or in shelter was forthcoming except what was given by relatives and friends in the still unburned portions of the city. On the fourth day the monasteries and convents threw open their doors, and "the inhabitants took refuge there with the few pieces of furniture and other effects that they had saved. Men, women, children, all slept pell-mell in the cloisters, in the dormitories; there they were at safety from the robbers and the soldiers." Some camped in the city and in the fields about the city.[12]   On December 28 (at the termination of the fire) the intendant issued ordinances for provisioning the city with bread, meat, and other necessities.[13]   The controller-general of finance granted the use of government property in the city for the erection of temporary barracks to house the unfortunates.[14]   The Duke of Orléans, the Count of Toulouse, the Marshal D'Estrées, the intendant, and other officials made up a purse of 57,000 livres, which was distributed as alms among the fire victims.[15]

By order of the Regent, the ministers requested the bishops throughout France to make a collection (queste) in behalf of the fire sufferers. The sum, which perhaps amounted to 40,000 écus (or 120,000 livres), was small; it was badly distributed, and favoritism was shown.[16]   The royal and provincial governments also made considerable grants of aid:

As monetary aid, the king [or government] extended the city a sum of 667,633 livres, and caused the distribution of 40,000 écus to indigents. He also gave the wood from 1,000 arpents [1,260 acres] of his forests of Rennes and Gavre, exempted the victims from all direct taxes (impôts) during two years, and reduced by some two thirds the duties on money-borrowings made for the purpose of reconstructing the burned houses. The Estates of Brittany, on their part, voted a grant of 300,000 livres, but this aid was destined uniquely to some works of public interest, and the inhabitants did not touch anything by way of indemnity.[17]

[12] Barbier states that he had seen some letters with the inscription "Aux prés de Rennes." Quoted by La Borderie, op. cit., VI, 170.

[13] Banéat, op. cit., p. 264.

[14] Inv.-som . . . Ille-et-Vilaine, C 282. According to Banéat, certain of these barracks still existed when he wrote in 1909.

[15] Ibid., C 282, 284.

[16] Boisrouvray, op. cit., XXV, 282.

[17] Banéat, op. cit., p. 265. Cf. Inv.-som . . . Ille-et-Vilaine, C 283, 284, 291, 292, 1188. The latter source designates the grant of 150,000 livres for removal of the ruins, 20,000 livres toward rebuilding of the cathedral, and "some sums that it pleased the king to give for the rebuilding of the city." Lecler du Brillet, in

In addition, the king, in order to alleviate somewhat the desperate situation of the city, exempted Brittany for certain periods in 1721 and 1722 from the triple duties set up in 1720, and granted the great grain-growing province the privilege of exporting grain on the simple duty of 10 sous per sack of 200 pounds (livres).[18] He also granted the city exemption from navigation taxes on imported building materials, such as stone from Anjou, Nantes, and Taillebourg, used in the construction of important edifices.[19] Finally, he sent Robelin, an engineer, to realign the city's streets and the property of individuals, and Gabriel *père* to serve as director or architect in the rebuilding of the chief edifices.[20] Mosseux was appointed engineer-in-chief or construction agent, under Gabriel, and served until 1731, when he was succeeded by Abeille.[21] Moreover, the provincial government, in order to facilitate the rebuilding of the city, made loans to citizens to the extent of 150,000 livres, and to certain religious orders to the extent of 130,000 livres.[22]

Despite this aid, the work of reconstruction lagged. Writing his memoirs three years later, Boisrouvray reported that not one individual had yet undertaken to rebuild in the city. He complained of "the rarity and great price of materials"; he criticized Robelin for wanting to take half of the city property to make streets and for wanting to tear down certain handsome homes in order to make the streets straight, and declared that Robelin wished to make his salary of 4,000 livres a year continue as long as possible.[23] This churlish attitude no doubt was shared by other well-to-do citizens of Rennes, with whom all did not go well during the trying days of reconstruction. Perhaps governmental assistance often appeared small and vexatious to the communities devastated by fire. The city of Rennes

---

his *Continuation du traité de la police* [Delamare, *op. cit.*, IV] (Paris, 1738), pp. 351-352, indicates that the money for rebuilding was raised by an increase in the *taille* throughout the *pays d'élections*, as was also done for Châteaudun, burned June 20, 1723.

[18] *Inv.-som . . . Ille-et-Vilaine*, C 284; Letaconnoux, *op. cit.*, pp. 186-187.

[19] *Inv.-som . . . Ille-et-Vilaine*, C Introduction, pp. x-xi.

[20] *Ibid.*, C 287. Robelin was to receive 4,000 livres a year; Gabriel, who was to serve in a nonresident capacity, 3,000. Gabriel died after a few months and was succeeded in the work by his son, destined to achieve fame as one of France's greatest architects.

[21] Their salary was 4,000 livres a year (*ibid.*).

[22] *Ibid.*, C 306.

[23] *Op. cit.*, XXV, 283-284.

took decades to recover from this blow. In 1751, thirty-one years after the fire, the intendant reported: "Not only are the suburbs ruined, but even the pavements of the residential sections, the watering-places, the docks, and those of the squares (places). The locks of Joué and Saint-Hélier, necessary for the passage of boats descending [the river] to Rennes, fall into ruin." The streets were so badly maintained that carriages could not pass; even cavaliers could not venture forth without peril; and peasants would not enter the city to sell their cider and wood. Commodities brought exorbitant prices because transportation was paralyzed. Besides, the city was deeply in debt.[24]

The fire of Rennes was one of the greatest débâcles of eighteenth-century France. It would be a mistake to regard it in all respects typical of other great fires of the century. Every fire had its own peculiar features, and the aid rendered varied to some extent with each. Perhaps in only a few was the role of the soldiery so disgraceful, or were the largesses of the royal and provincial governments so bountiful. And yet many of the features of this fire were similar to those of other fires of the period.

Whenever a fire occurred, the tocsin was sounded and soldiers of the nightguard (if the community was large enough to have one) were rushed to the scene and commanded to form a cordon about the spot, maintain order, protect the piles of furniture and other effects from plunder, and with the general public, who were pressed into water-brigades, to lend what assistance they could in combating the fire. Monks were sometimes put to work in similar fashion. In the notable fire of the Petit-Pont of Paris, April 27-30, 1718, when the quaint old bridge with its twenty-two houses was destroyed, at an estimated loss of 8,000,000 livres,[25] all groups acquitted themselves well, and the occasion was marked by maintenance of discipline.[26] In a fire that destroyed three homes and several lives in the faubourg Saint-Antoine, Paris, in April, 1723, five hundred soldiers

[24] A. Dupuy, "La Bretagne au XVIIIᵉ siècle: l'affaire de la constitution municipale; épisode de l'histoire de la ville de Rennes (1757-1782)," Annales de Bretagne, I (Rennes, 1886), 12-14.

[25] See accounts by Barbier, op. cit., I, 1-7; Lecler du Brillet, op. cit., pp. 162-167; and Leclercq, op. cit., II, 230-232. The estimate of the loss appears fantastic for a dilapidated bridge and twenty-two houses.

[26] Unfortunately many persons, including soldiers, were killed fighting the fire. This was an accompaniment of many eighteenth-century fires. The fire at Rennes exacted a heavy toll of life.

who were rushed to the scene evidently acquitted themselves well.[27] Again in a fire that destroyed parts of the famous old hospital, the Hôtel-Dieu,[28] August 2, 1737, soldiers and monks were ordered out and worked effectively. The sick were transported from the hospital to points of safety, some being placed in the Cathedral of Nôtre-Dame, some in the streets, and others carted to the Hospital Saint-Louis. Twoscore soldiers, monks, and other workers were injured by falling floors and beams, and other accidents.[29] Later in the same year (October 26-28) the Chamber of Accounts in Paris burned, and most of its valuable records were lost. Again soldiers, monks, and workers were pressed into duty, but there was much blundering, both in combating the fire and in handling the documents that were saved.[30] At Dinan, Brittany, a fire during the night of March 15, 1781, consumed forty-five houses and would have burned the entire city had it not been for the valiant efforts of the Royal Corsican Regiment.[31]

In at least one instance troops were used in fighting a forest fire. On the night of September 13, 1726, two regiments of troops and all the prisoners in Paris were rushed to check a fire in the heath at Fontainebleau, where the Great Forest was endangered. By digging trenches in front of the oncoming fire, they managed to save the forest.[32]

The aid rendered by soldiers and others was to some extent encouraged by the policy of the French government and cities, which provided occasional gratifications to those who displayed meritorious action in fighting fires or in other lines of public service. Thus about 1770 the intendant of Brittany donated 150 livres to workers who had fought a fire at the home of Pillet, director of the letterpost.[33] A few years later the city of Redon distributed 100 livres among workers who had taken part in fighting several fires, particularly one at the Benedictine monastery.[34]

---

[27] Barbier (op. cit., I, 227) states that the city contributed toward the maintenance of the soldiers in order to enjoy this service.

[28] The bakery, the linen-room, and perhaps other parts. Linen worth 700,000 or 800,000 livres also was destroyed.

[29] Ibid., III, 93-94.

[30] Some of those assisting were killed; others were crippled. Barbier suspected that Voltaire's brother was responsible for the fire (op. cit., III, 103-105).

[31] Inv.-som . . . Ille-et-Vilaine, C 490.

[32] Barbier, op. cit., I, 443-444. This beautiful forest of giant beeches still stands.

[33] Inv.-som . . . Ille-et-Vilaine, C 630.   [34] Ibid., C 419.

The government through its intendant made it a practice to render "first aid" in the way of food, clothing, and tools to fire victims. The expense was paid from the "free funds of the *capitation*," a reserve fund that the government allowed to each intendant for meeting urgent cases of need.[35] The government also permitted, upon request, the collection of alms for the victims, either through church or community channels. In certain large fires early in the century, such as those of Rennes and the Petit-Pont, the government not only permitted, but also took the initiative in requesting, the collection of alms, either locally (as in the latter instance) or throughout France (as in the former).[36] The contribution for the victims of the Petit-Pont amounted to 111,898 livres, which were distributed according to directions from the parlement of Paris,[37] after an inventory of all the losses had been ordered.[38]

No doubt abuses occasionally took place in connection with the collection and distribution of alms, and perhaps as much pilfering occurred when the public was allowed, and even asked, to take part in the rescue of movable property from burning homes. Certain unauthorized (and unscrupulous) parties, for example, participated in the collection of alms in Paris for the fire sufferers of the Petit-Pont. On the other hand, says Lecler du Brillet, a contributor donated a worthless note for 200 livres. According to Boisrouvray, favoritism played a part in the allocation of alms at Rennes, the money being "badly distributed"; and Rennes, he adds, was not an isolated case. The government through its courts and police did what it could to assist rightful owners in the recovery of stolen or lost property. Lecler du Brillet points out that this assistance was given after the burning of the Petit-Pont.

Relief from *impositions* (direct taxes), either wholly or in part, was commonly given for a period of time, usually for a year; and occasionally a grant of money was made toward rebuilding. The procedure called for the victims to ask aid of the intendant, perhaps through the subdelegate in charge in their locality; then the intend-

[35] A clear statement of this policy, concerning fire sufferers, is set forth in a letter from Harival to the Comte de Pontual, May 30, 1785 (Arch. Nat., H 565).

[36] Boisrouvray, *op. cit.*, XXV, 282; Lecler du Brillet, *op. cit.*, pp. 162-163. There was never any conflict between church and state in raising money for fire sufferers, but only close co-operation.

[37] By its *arrêt* of Aug. 19, 1718 (Barbier, *op. cit.*, I, 6 n. 3).

[38] Lecler du Brillet, *op. cit.*, pp. 162-163.

ant took up the matter through correspondence with the controller-general at Paris, who, with the council of finance, controlled all economic matters pertaining to the generalities, charitable or otherwise. It was customary for the intendant to indicate the extent of the loss and what amount of relief in tax exemption he thought just; but the controller-general made his own decisions. These were commonly approved by the council; afterwards the controller-general informed the intendant of the final decision and of the manner in which the aid was to be administered by the latter's subdelegates.

This practice continued until 1790-91, when the Revolution swept away the positions of controller-general, council of finances, intendants, and subdelegates, and substituted, with some relatively inconsiderable changes, those of minister of the interior,[39] the committee of mendicity,[40] and the departmental and district directories, commonly called administrations. In the place of the king stood the national parliament. At length under the Consulate, at the close of the century, the functions of intendant and subdelegate were revived by the creation of the prefects and subprefects. Throughout the period after 1789 requests for fire aid continued to be made, but direct grants instead of tax remissions were given. Thus on 18 thermidor an VIII (August 6, 1800) the minister of the interior informed Quinette, prefect of the department of the Somme, that he would allow 3,000 francs by way of indemnity to fire sufferers at Moislains, the distribution to be made by the prefect.[41]

Such was the order of things throughout the century in the *pays d'élections*, or provinces ruled directly by the government at Paris. In the *pays d'états*,[42] with their provincial assemblies which met once a year, as in the case of Provence, or once every two years, as happened in Brittany, there was a small degree of self-government,

---

[39] During the latter part of the period of the National Convention this portfolio was discarded, and its work, in charities, was administered by the commission of public aid. With the Directory the ministry was revived and continued through the century.

[40] Called the committee of public aid during the periods of the Legislative Assembly and the Convention.

[41] Arch. Nat., F 15, 103.

[42] Both *pays d'élections* and *pays d'états* were abolished in 1790-91, being supplanted by departments.

A list of the *pays d'états* is given by Chéruel, *op. cit.*, II, 960. The leading ones were Languedoc, Brittany, Burgundy, and Provence. As a general thing, the *pays d'états* had been added to France since the late Middle Ages, and constituted her border provinces.

and most charity problems were handled by the provincial government, using provincial funds.[43] The remission of taxes to fire sufferers was one of the items of expenditure normally supposed to be handled in this way, but in some instances this custom was not followed. For example, remissions were made to Rennes in the 1720's; and, after a fire of September 11, 1751, the council of state (at Paris)[44] allowed to Brittany remissions on the *capitation* for a period of ten years. On this occasion the provincial estates also granted aid. A third instance occurred in Languedoc, August 9, 1744, when the farmhouse *(métairie)* of a certain De la Redorte burned. Then the government granted him remissions in taxes for two successive years.[45] But in the 1770's and 1780's the government clearly stated its policy as having been over a long period that of leaving the *pays d'états*, save in the matter of first aid, to handle their own problem of assistance to fire victims. The case that evoked the declaration was one of Count de Pontual in Brittany. He asked aid of the government in 1771, and again in 1785, because of a fire which had occurred on his estate, in the diocese of St. Malo, October 28, 1771, destroying his houses, furnishings, barns, crops (garnered) and the animals of his renters. The count reckoned his loss at 30,000 livres and asked the government to give him 10,000 livres toward the rebuilding of the houses. The government refused, in a reply of November 13, 1771, explaining "that the situation of the finances did not permit his Majesty to grant any indemnities in a *pays d'état* for individual losses such as that which he came to experience; that it was for the province to provide it." The count was advised to

[43] An excellent description of the government of a *pays d'état*, in eighteenth-century Brittany, is given in the *Inv.-som . . . Ille-et-Vilaine*, C III, Introduction by Henri Bourde de la Rogerie, iii-v. The intendant resided in the province to counsel and coerce in all questions of policy and legislation. In matters of administration he was supreme. Over some of the problems of charity, such as provisioning during famines and administration of first aid in various disasters, he retained or assumed complete charge; others he turned over in part to the provincial government, or more particularly to an intermediary commission of thirty-six members, chosen from the most assiduous workers in the Estates, who formed a permanent committee, seated at Rennes, for collaboration with the intendant on various matters of a provincial nature. In the other *pays d'états* there were some faint shades of difference in governmental machinery, but in all of them the intendant counseled and guided and administered, using compulsion when necessary, chiefly in curtailment of tax remissions and other royal privileges.

[44] By *arrêt* of Dec. 26, 1752 (*Inv.-som . . . Ille-et-Vilaine*, C 3910).

[45] Le Nain to the controller-general, Oct. 4, 1745 (Arch. Nat., H 832).

present his petition to the Estates of Brittany.   In a second letter of refusal (for the count applied anew), the controller-general wrote by way of "Observations" to the intendant:

Down to the present the ministers, [my] predecessors, have refused to allot any indemnities in the *pays d'états* for individual losses such as this, and it can be said that there are only three or four old *(anciens)* instances in which one has extended any in Brittany, [and then] to some entire communities, such as a fire where total privation of their harvests has reduced [them] to the most frightful misery.   Their attitude in this matter has been that it was up to the province, which enjoys the benefit of some revenues *(abonnemens)*, to find in the economy of its own administration the necessary resources to care for it, and it is after these principles that M. the controller-general has replied to M. the Count de Pontual.[46]

The grants made both by the royal government and the provincial governments were commonly small.   Neither government desired to lend encouragement to the burning of old homes, barns, or other buildings, and they commonly took with a grain of salt the estimate of losses.   Down to the time of the Revolution there appears to have been no ratio of reimbursement for losses suffered.   In a report of the committee of public aid to the Legislative Assembly, September 8, 1792, the recommended reimbursement was one tenth in every instance, and this recommendation was followed in the appropriation.[47]   This was not necessarily, however, a fair distribution of aid, for on the very face of the report some of the departments had sent in higher figures for their losses than other departments. Moreover, the Revolutionary government did not render uniform aid on the basis of one tenth of the loss.   Thus in 1790 the town of Crèvecoeur suffered damages of 2,000,000 livres by a fire; by June 6, 1791, it had received in aid, from both royal and private sources, only 50,000 livres.[48]   The town of Selincourt had great difficulty

[46] Arch. Nat., H 565.   The irrepressible count, like many other applicants for aid in eighteenth-century France, made a third application in 1785 (doubtless after failure to obtain any relief from the provincial government).   A third time the government rejected his application, with similar remarks about the jurisdiction of his application (Harivel to the Count de Pontual, May 30, 1785, *ibid.*).
[47] It amounted to 322,548 livres (*Arch. parl.*, XLIX, 468).
[48] No less a person than Liancourt, chairman of the committee of mendicity, had witnessed the fire.   On June 6, 1791, he endorsed a petition from the inhabitants to Tarbé, minister of public contributions, that the government do more for them (Arch. Nat., F15, 101).

in getting aid from the government after a fire in 1789. Necker, who had pledged assistance, apparently fell from office before he was able to carry out his promise, for in June, 1791, and March, 1792, the receiver of the district was still writing from Amiens to Paris, in an attempt to obtain aid for the victims. This second letter roused to action Tarbé, who recommended to the Legislative Assembly small sums for relief.[49] In making a grant of 3,000 livres to the fire sufferers of Moislains in 1800, the minister of the interior, with much regret, employed the hackneyed apology, used throughout the eighteenth century, that the smallness of the sum was due to the straitened circumstances of the treasury.[50]

These grants were perhaps no worse or better than those commonly made under the Old Regime. Whole villages were sacked and burned by the Camisards in the first years of the century, and yet the Estates of Languedoc voted only 6,000 livres by way of relief for the sufferers in 1704, and 3,974 livres in 1706.[51] When on August 21, 1779, a fire in the industrial town of Vire, in the generality of Caen, did damage to the extent of 1,015,277 livres, the relief consisted of first aid in the form of food and clothing; the grant of 3,600 livres by the intendant, taken from the free funds of the *capitation*, for the purchase of tools and other instruments for the unfortunates; and exemption from the *vingtième* for a period of twenty years, to be reckoned from the time when the houses were rebuilt.[52]

The government of the Old Regime was occasionally more generous. To the unfortunate town of Châteaudun, burned in 1723, it granted 600,000 livres, wood for rebuilding, and exemption from all direct taxes for a period of ten years.[53] Toward the rebuilding of the Hôtel-Dieu of Paris, burned anew in 1772, with losses estimated at the time at 2,000,000 livres, but reduced by the modern scholar Fosseyeux to 600,000, the government had given 689,646

[49] The grant of 1,873 livres, and the abolition of 908 livres in uncollected taxes of 1789, inasmuch as the tax records of the town had been consumed by the fire (*ibid.*).

[50] Arch. Nat., F15, 103.

[51] *Histoire générale de Languedoc*, XIII, 36-42.

[52] *Inv.-som . . . Calvados*, C 978. This mode of tax exemption was to encourage each citizen to rebuild as quickly as possible.

[53] Lecler du Brillet, *op. cit.*, pp. 351-352; G. Cerise, "La lutte contre l'incendie avant 1789," *La controverse et le contemporain*, N. S ., IV (Paris and Lyon, 1885), 384-385.

livres by 1789.[54]   To certain glassmakers who experienced disastrous fires, timber (probably from the royal forests) was given for the rebuilding of their establishments.[55]   One of the most liberal gifts was made to Leberthon, first president of the parlement of Bordeaux, who, having lost his home by fire in 1740, was given, by agreement between the intendant and the controller-general, an indemnity of 100,000 livres and the temporary use of the hôtel-de-ville.[56]

Similar grants afforded a basis for the accusation made by Saint-Martin on the floor of the Convention, October 10, 1793, that under the Old Regime relief was rendered not in proportion to the need, but in proportion to "the fortune" of the applicant.[57]   There was a marked tendency in this direction under the Old Regime; yet in multitudinous instances ill-founded applications from the rich of the aristocracy were rejected.   Although Count de Pontual was a man of means,[58] an aristocrat, an old soldier, and a member of the distinguished Order of Saint-Louis, he applied in vain for aid to both the national and the provincial governments.   Nor was the government of the Old Regime insensible to real suffering.

The Revolutionaries had their own weaknesses in the administration of charity.   If they did not favor rank and wealth, they did rush first and always to the aid of those who were proved or alleged to be true Revolutionaries at heart.   In the realm of fire assistance, apparently there was not a great deal of difference in methods and liberality between the Old Regime and the Revolutionists: in fact, aside from employing monetary grants wholly, and dropping tax exemptions, the Revolutionists introduced no new methods; and the Old Regime was occasionally more generous.

[54] Marcel Fosseyeux, L'Hôtel-Dieu de Paris au XVIIe et au XVIIIe siècle (Paris and Nancy, 1912), pp. 261-262, 269 with n. 2.

[55] In addition to liberal loans and outright grants that had previously been made in the infancy of the establishments (Warren C. Scoville, "State Policy and the French Glass Industry, 1640-1789," Quarterly Journal of Economics, LVI, May, 1942, 443).

[56] Inv.-som . . . Gironde, C 3585.

[57] Saint-Martin declared that the "beneficent law" of February 20, 1793, had corrected "the principal abuses" in this respect: "Cette loi bienfaisante a fait disparaître les principaux abus que le régime intendential avait introduits dans la répartition de ce genre de secours. Le plus intolérable de tous était celui qui proportionnait l'indemnité non aux besoins, mais à la fortune du reclamant: plus abondants étaient les secours; en sorte que le riche avait tout, et le pauvre rien ou presque rien. C'est à quoi la loi a efficacement remédié en adoptant l'inverse de la méthode jusqu'alors usitée" (Arch. parl., LXXVI, 305).

[58] The intendant stated so in his first letter to the controller-general, and refused to recommend him for aid.

A curious form of aid was rendered in 1716, when the opera in Bordeaux burned with all its furnishings, and the proprietor, Barbarin, was allowed an indemnity of 25,000 livres, to be taken "on the future benefits of the royal lottery."[59] After the fire of the Hôtel-Dieu of Paris in 1772, someone suggested that the rebuilding be done by means of a royal lottery (for lotteries were not infrequently used in eighteenth-century France to raise charity funds), but the idea seems not to have been followed.[60]

Equally interesting as the monetary aid was the increasing attention given to modes of fire prevention. Throughout the *Inventaires-sommaires des archives départementales antérieures à 1789* one reads of increasing numbers of fire pumps and of the organization of fire companies. The city of Rennes in 1721, "after the horse had been stolen," so to speak, adopted elaborate fire regulations. It bought forks *(fourches)*, iron hooks *(crochets de fer)*, cables, and ladders *(échelles)*, as well as three new pumps from Holland. It required the proprietor of every house to furnish himself with a hatchet and a leather bucket. The carriage-drivers were held responsible for getting the pumps to the scene of a fire; ten men were assigned to handle each pump; and all the inhabitants, male and female, old and young, were ordered to transport water for the supply of the pumps. A large quota of carpenters and roofers, each aided by six workers, were ordered to be at hand with their hatchets. To detachments of the bourgeois militia was assigned the role of maintaining order. To make certain that the pumps remained in good condition, particular men were given the responsibility of exercising them at least every three months. Rennes did not wish to experience another fire.[61]

As the century wore on, almost every town of any size acquired at least one pump. The larger places had several. Paris acquired thirty. Bands of firemen who gave part or all of their time to fire service and wore uniforms were organized.[62] By the end of the century the professional fire brigades had been definitely formed.

[59] *Inv.-som . . . Gironde*, C 3585.
[60] Fosseyeux, *op. cit.*, p. 264.
[61] Banéat, *op. cit.*, pp. 363-264.
[62] A description of the fire corps at Brest in 1784-85 may be found in *Inv.-som . . . Ille-et-Vilaine*, C 587; one of the fire corps at Paris in the 1770's, in Cerise, *op. cit.*, IV, 297.

It was not the work of the national government but of the municipalities, yet the intendants encouraged the development.

Even more important was the attention given to the construction of houses. Throughout the century the royal and provincial governments aided in the rebuilding of burned houses. But increasingly, as the century advanced, it was the practice (at least during the Old Regime) to make remissions and gifts on the condition that the rebuilt houses be roofed with tile or slate. In 1724 the royal government extended aid for rebuilding the small town of Saint-Bonnet-en-Champsaur in Dauphiné, destroyed by fire in 1722, but stipulated that the buildings must be roofed with tile or slate, and no longer with thatch. This law did not remain a paper enactment, for at a later date in the century all of the houses in the town, where existed 314 families, had slate or tile roofs save eight;[63] four had straw, and four, boards. Similar demands were made by the government (1) after a fire at Fougères, in Brittany, in 1767;[64] (2) after fires at Château-Porcien, Rethel, and Aire, in Champagne, in 1776 and 1779;[65] and (3) after a fire of 1788 at Beurey, a village in Champagne, in which twenty-two houses were destroyed.[66] In Fougères, it was prescribed that no person in rebuilding his home should employ any wood in the front (façade) of his house, "under penalty of demolition at his own expense and a 500-livre fine"; and it was ordered that all porches to houses on two specified streets be demolished.[67] In the late eighteenth century, according to Louis Legrand, biographer of Sénac de Meilhan, intendant at Valenciennes, the government extended aid to homeowners who wished to replace thatch with tiles,[68] apparently regardless of whether or not they were fire sufferers.

The government also took an interest in embellishing cities after large fires by sending them engineers, architects, and construction experts and by ordering that the streets be made as broad and straight

---

[63] *Inv.-som . . . Haute-Alpes,* C 10.

[64] This little city suffered many fires in the eighteenth century, as an examination of the *Inv.-som . . . Ille-et-Vilaine,* série C, reveals. The government stipulated certain requirements for the rebuilding of the houses burned there in a fire of 1751 (C 389), but it is not clear what type of roofing was prescribed (C 384).

[65] *Inv.-som . . . Ardennes,* C 80.   [66] *Inv.-som . . . l'Aube,* C 394.

[67] The rues du Bourg-Vieil and de la Pinterie (*Inv.-som . . . Ille-et-Vilaine,* C 384).

[68] *Sénac de Meilhan et l'intendance du Hainaut & du Cambrésis sous Louis XVI* (Valenciennes, 1868), p. 178.

as possible. The city of Rennes was slowly rebuilt since it was necessary to destroy several handsome homes left standing after the fire if the engineer's plan for straightening and beautifying the principal street was carried out; and the owners of the homes very naturally offered strenuous objection. Architects were asked to design the new buildings and to prescribe the construction materials. This attention to the rebuilding of burned cities was but part of a larger scheme of municipal beautification which was a governmental policy throughout the century. In Bordeaux, with its magnificent Allées de Tourny, opera, and *jardin de ville,* all of mid-eighteenth-century construction, there was much local opposition, as Lhéritier (Tourny's biographer) indicates, but the great Tourny won out. When a large portion of Paris was rebuilt in the last few decades before the Revolution, the government had a considerable part in it.[69] It was customary for the government to order the demolition of dilapidated and unsteady houses that were a menace to passersby.[70] And in order to broaden and straighten the highways, it frequently ordered the destruction of houses that stood in the way, and reimbursed the owners. [71] So well done was the embellishment of Rennes after its great fire that Banéat was able to write in 1909:

Travelers who visit Rennes are generally struck by the regularity of her central streets, parallel and perpendicular the one to the other, and bordered by houses which present some great similarities among them, and all dating from the same epoch. It is easy to recognize there a plan of the whole, executed simultaneously; and one would be tempted to attribute to the city a very recent origin, if certain old quarters, certain rare monuments, did not recall its antiquity, and if one did not know [it to have been] the ancient capital of Brittany.

This transformation of our central quarters took place, in reality, at one stroke, in the first half of the XVIIIth century, following a terrible fire whose recollection the Rennaise still hold.

. . . .

It is thus that the fire of 1720, having been a disaster for the city, contributed grandly to give it the beautiful aspect that it presents today.[72]

[69] Mercier, *Tableau de Paris,* VIII (new ed., Paris, 1783), 190-194.

[70] To cite one instance, see S. Lacroix, *Actes de la commune de Paris pendant la Révolution,* VII (Paris, 1898), 454-455.

[71] For a few examples, see *Inv.-som* . . . *Ardennes,* C 296, 413; *Inv.-som* . . . *Côte d'Or,* C 3190; and *Inv.-som* . . . *Bouches-du-Rhône,* C 1019.

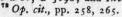

[72] *Op. cit.,* pp. 258, 265.

UNIVERSITY
COLLEGE
LIBRARY
NOTTINGHAM

Among the other cities that were embellished, according to plans drawn by royal or provincial engineers and architects, were Troyes[73] and Fougères.[74]

For a brief while in the 1780's and 1790's the governments of the Old Regime and the Revolution displayed passing interest in the experiments of François Cointeraux in building fireproof houses, stables, and walls for villagers and farmers out of *pisé*, or tightly compressed blocks of dried earth.[75] Not every form of dirt was suitable for the making of *pisé*, but Cointeraux insisted that the proper type or types could easily be found throughout France, and in his letters to the Revolutionary governments in 1790-92[76] he emphasized the inexpensiveness of the procedure as well as the material's immunity to fire. The claims for *pisé* by Cointeraux are well borne out by articles in *La grande encyclopédie* and *Larousse du XXᵉ siècle*. A writer in the latter publication declares: "The structures of *pisé*, which are perfectly satisfactory for buildings of little importance in countries where stone is rare, are able to last a very long time if they are protected against the humidity of the soil by a small basement in stone or brick, and if the exterior surfaces are from time to time whitewashed with lime." The one great weakness of *pisé*, of course, is its inability to withstand prolonged dampness.

Cointeraux did not claim to be the inventor of *pisé*,[77] but only a perfecter of the process. He had had experience with it in his youth, but his interest in it as a panacea for the fire problem in the villages and countryside of France dated from the year 1784, when he was gainfully occupied with other work in Grenoble. Somewhat

---

[73] After a fire of Jan. 19, 1729 (*Inv.-som . . . l'Aube*, C 1792, 1888).

[74] After fires of 1734, 1751, 1762, and 1767 (*Inv.-som . . . Ille-et-Vilaine*, C 384, 388, 390, and 3910). After the fires of 1734, Gabriel and Huguet drew plans for realigning the streets and otherwise adorning the city.

[75] Preliminary to making *pisé*, rocks and pebbles were removed by means of a sieve. The loose dirt was then moistened and pressed into molds.

[76] Found in Arch. Nat., F15, 101.

[77] Thirty houses of *pisé* reinforced with chopped heather (*brande hachée*) were constructed in Poitou for an Acadian colony in 1773-74 (Ernest Martin, *op. cit.*, p. 172). Nor were these the first buildings of *pisé*. According to a long and enthusiastic article on *pisé* in the New York *Sun* of December 28, 1940, the reader is told that *pisé* is "nothing new": "The writings of Pliny refer to the rammed earth towers built by Hannibal that were in use 250 years. In Normandy pisé de terre construction, so called, dates from Neolithic times—3,000 to 10,000 years B.C. In France on the Rhône River rammed earth houses from 600 to 900 years old are still occupied and in good condition."

after the manner of Jean Jacques Rousseau, he was inspired by a question set forth by the Academy of Amiens, How prevent the fires that were the scourge of the villages? In his efforts he was encouraged by the Comte de Vergennes, the Duc de Charost, the intendant of Dauphiné, and academicians. He brought a small tract of land in or near Grenoble and began his experiments; afterwards he engaged in travel through fourteen provinces of France in order to observe at first hand the different materials and the different modes of construction of homes in villages, and to find which ones were the most inexpensive and immune to fire. In 1787 he went to Picardy and carried off the prize (a gold medal valued at 600 livres) against forty-eight competitors. The intendants of Picardy and Dauphiné sought to have him rebuild certain villages burned in their generalities in 1787-88, but the council of state did not approve. In 1789 he carried off the prize (a medal of 300 livres) given by the Royal Society of Agriculture, on "the means of rendering farmhouses safer, healthier, more economical, and more immune to fire." In 1790 his experiments in Paris received encouragement from the Royal Society of Agriculture and the committee of agriculture and commerce of the National Assembly.[78] Later he was placed in charge of a charity workshop on the site of the old Coliseum, and was permitted to instruct the workers assigned him in the methods of constructing houses of *pisé*. He called it his School of Rural Architecture, and himself a professor of Rural Architecture. The National Assembly supported him for a while, but in March, 1790, withdrew this support after expending 2,768 livres on the project, since some inspector or inspectors made an unfavorable report on his work, claiming that the houses built of *pisé* would not stand rigorous weather more than three years, and that Cointeraux's methods were in no way superior to those employed by others in the region of Chartres and elsewhere.[79] Undismayed by the withdrawal of financial support, Cointeraux continued to maintain his School of Rural Architecture, or charity workshop, even paying the workers from his own purse. From 1790 well into 1792, however, he ad-

[78] In Arch. Nat., F15, 101, are two long transcripts from the Registers of the Royal Society of Agriculture, the one for June 21, 1790, and the other for May 5, 1791, both commending Cointeraux's work and signed by A. Broussonnet, *secrétaire perpétuel*.

[79] Alexandre Tuetey (ed.), *L'administration des ateliers de charité: Rapport de J. B. Edme Plaisant* (Paris, 1906), pp. 152-153.

dressed a series of letters to the National and Legislative Assemblies requesting what he considered his legitimate "back pay," and urging the government, as he had done since 1787, to embark on an adventure of widespread wooden-house clearance in France and of reconstruction in *pisé*, directed by him and his pupils.

Supporting him in his several petitions were the Academy of Amiens, the Royal Society of Agriculture, army officials, the minister of the interior, the minister of foreign affairs, two intendants, and Paoli, all praising his methods of building from *pisé* above those of others and recommending that France launch such a housing program as he advocated. At length in September, 1792, Cointeraux received a government grant of 6,000 livres.[80] What happened to him and his housing program afterwards, however, is not related.

Under the Old Regime the government occasionally rebuilt houses for the victims of floods, and in 1773 it set out on a program of constructing 150 houses for Acadian refugees in Poitou.[81] Throughout the century the government sometimes gave timber from royal forests and church lands for the rebuilding of structures after fires and floods. After the middle of the century, however, the government, at least in regard to rebuilding after fires, resorted more and more to monetary grants, payable in installments after the construction was undertaken, rather than to the grant of timber. In December, 1790, the National Assembly refused a request from some eight families of the parish of Erehes, department of the Somme, for 150 or 160 elm trees, after a fire of November 8 had destroyed their homes, barns, and harvests.[82] The governments of both the Old Regime and the Revolution were committed to the idea of better housing, housing that was safer, more attractive, and more sanitary; but they moved slowly, lacking the funds for an extensive program. For a moment at the beginning of the Revolution[83] the

[80] Tuetey, *Répertoire général*, VII, No. 1597. Ernest Martin, in his recent book on the Acadians (*op. cit.*, p. 173), points out that houses of *pisé* constructed for them in 1773-74 on the estate of the Marquis de Perusse are still standing and in good condition. In fact, some were strong enough to permit the recent addition of a second story. In his appendix Martin illustrates one of the original Acadian homes in Poitou made from *pisé*. It is similar to the well-known Burns home of Ayr.

[81] Martin, *op. cit.*, p. 173; article by the present writer in *Social Forces* of May, 1938, entitled "Some Eighteenth Century Housing Projects in France."

[82] Arch. Nat., F15, 101. The National Assembly was willing to give monetary aid on this occasion, but not timber.

[83] Judging from the report on the hospitals by the committee of mendicity.

government seemed ready to launch upon a gigantic building program, at least in the reconstruction of hospitals, but internal strife and foreign war shortly absorbed the government's attention.

In our own day government aid to fire sufferers is not needed inasmuch as fire insurance at low rates is available to most individuals. In France insurance companies were not established until 1754, when the government permitted a maritime insurance society to issue fire policies. In 1786 two new companies were authorized by the council of state; but they did not long engage in the business, being suppressed, in common with other financial institutions, during the Revolution by decrees of 17 ventôse and 26 germinal an II (March 5 and April 15, 1794). Simultaneously with these commercial insurance companies were created the philanthropic insurance societies, or bureaux, founded by certain bishops. One at Troyes, founded in 1769, flourished until 1790.[84] It received voluntary contributions and gave aid to fire sufferers in the parishes of that city as need arose. In 1786 it distributed 21,915 livres. About 1785 another society, founded at Autun, drew up an elaborate set of regulations to govern the giving of alms.[85] In 1787 it received gifts amounting to 18,798 livres, 4,000 livres being given by the provincial government of Burgundy; and it expended during the year, for fire relief, 14,091 livres.[86] All in all, fire insurance in eighteenth-century France was in an embryonic state.

[84] Babeau, *op. cit.*, p. 334 n. 5.

[85] Described at length by Montarlot in his article, "Un bureau de secours aux incendiés du diocèse d'Autun en 1787," *Mémoires de la Société Eduenne*, N. S., XXV (Autun, 1897), 333-335.

[86] An extended account of these companies is given by Cerise, *op. cit.*, IV, 390-412.

CHAPTER VI

RELIEF FOR EPIZOOTICS

Numerous epizootics or animal plagues swept France during the eighteenth century, some local, others national in importance. The three most severe fell upon the cattle in the years 1714-15, 1742-48, and 1773-76, and were identified by later authorities as outbreaks of one and the same malady known to veterinarians under the various names of cattle plague, cattle typhus, and rinderpest.[1] The rinderpest had afflicted Europe on many occasions in earlier ages. Its real home was perhaps Asia, where for centuries it had been prevalent. From Asia it emerged early in the eighteenth century to overrun Europe. In 1709 it began to appear along the Don and the Volga rivers in Russia and even in the region of Moscow. In 1710 it spread further into European Russia, and in 1711 made its way into Poland, Brandenburg, Silesia, Hungary, Moldavia, Wallachia, Austria, Bavaria, Swabia, Dalmatia, Italy, and Switzerland.[2] Everywhere it worked havoc. In Silesia alone 100,000 cattle died of it.[3] Paulet, writing later in the century, estimated that in Europe 1,500,-000 cattle died of this plague in the years 1711-14.[4] In 1713 it entered Holland; in 1714, England, France, Belgium, and Ireland.[5] Few parts of Europe escaped, and not until 1717, if indeed then, did

[1] Franz Hutyra and Josef Marek, *Special Pathology and Therapeutics of the Diseases of Domestic Animals*, ed. John R. Mohler and Adolph Eichhorn (3d authorized American ed., Chicago, 1926), I, 292, 315; George Fleming, *Animal Plagues: Their History, Nature, and Prevention* (London, 1871), pp. 209, 377-381, 466-471; and [J. J.]Paulet, *Recherches historiques et physiques sur les maladies épizootiques, avec les moyens d'y remedier, dans tous les cas* (Paris, 1775), I, 402-403, II, 49, 135. Hutyra and Marek were professors at the Royal Veterinary College of Budapest, Fleming was an English veterinarian of high distinction, and Paulet was a doctor of the medical faculties of Paris and Montpellier. Paulet identified the three epizootics as outbreaks of the same malady, but he hesitated to name it.

Mr. John R. Mohler, Chief of the Bureau of Animal Industry of the United States Department of Agriculture, very kindly assisted the present writer in identifying this malady and brought to his attention the treatment by Hutyra and Marek.

[2] Fleming, *op. cit.*, pp. 181-185.
[3] *Ibid.*, pp. 195-196.
[4] *Op. cit.*, II, 229.
[5] It reached Ireland in December.

the disease cease its depredations.[6] In 1726 it was still existent in European Russia, and in 1728 it started another march into the countries of Western and Southern Europe, not to be completely exterminated throughout the remainder of the century.[7]

It moved intermittently from country to country, making its greatest advances during wartimes, when large movements of cattle were necessary for the provisioning of armies.[8] During the War of the Austrian Succession, in the 1740's, when it had its second most active recurrence in the century, it swept away approximately three million cattle in "Western central Europe."[9] In fact, so widespread and severe was the cattle plague in Europe that, according to Fleming, "from 1711 to 1769, this awful scourge could not have destroyed less than 200,000,000 head of cattle in the various countries to which it had been carried."[10] Since cattle were valuable not only as sources of meat and milk, but also as beasts of burden used in the cultivation of the fields in many parts of Europe, and particularly in France, these losses were a staggering blow to the economic life of the affected countries.[11]

[6] *Ibid.*, II, 229. Fleming (*op. cit.*, p. 198) writes: "The Cattle Plague ceased its ravages in this year as a general epizooty, its cruel effects being only displayed here and there at irregular intervals. It may be said to have terminated its devastating career in Hungary, Prussia, Silesia, and Bavaria." Elsewhere he says that it continued in Holland until 1723.

[7] *Ibid.*, pp. 260 *et seq.*

[8] *Ibid.*, pp. 260, 269 n. 3.

[9] *Ibid.*, p. 359.

[10] *Ibid.*, p. 381. In another work (*A Manual of Veterinary Sanitary Science and Police* . . . , London, 1875, I, 370-371 n.) Fleming gives the same figure of 200,000,000, but for the period 1711-96. His "competent authority" is one Faust. The present writer regards the mortality figure as ridiculous. To him, one tenth of that number would seem more reasonable. Certainly if only one and a half millions died in the intense period of 1711-14, and only three millions during some eight years in the active period of the 1740's, the figure of 200,000,000 is fantastic.

[11] Since this disease has never visited North America (which seems almost a miracle in view of its highly contagious nature), a brief description of its external symptoms may prove of interest. The disease is carried by infection. The incubation period extends from three to nine days. The earliest symptom is a high temperature. The sick animals at first manifest great excitement and restlessness, but shortly fall into deep depression, with head drooped, eyes closed and often watery, back arched, appetite gone, little or no rumination, heavy breathing, and often in the early stages of the disease frequent coughing. A heavy discharge of mucous covers the nose and mouth. The tongue and gums of the animal become covered with ulcers and small gray or grayish-white nodules. These cause great pain, and the animal grinds its gums and shakes its head from side to side or up and down. The ulcerous condition extends down the gullet, so much so as to make swallowing difficult. In some instances nodules occur along the back and on the feet. These

Despite the fact that many distinguished physicians of the eighteenth century and many scientists of the nineteenth century, including the great Koch, labored to discover the cause of the malady, success was not attained until 1902, when two Turkish scientists, Nicolle and Adil Bey, proved that it was a virus filterable through porcelain filters.[12]   Earlier, in 1711 or 1712, Lancisi, physician to the pope, suggested that the disease was transmitted by corpuscles,[13] while Cogrossi, physician of Cremona, believed that it was carried by, and consisted of, "an infinity of invisible worms."[14]   Physicians of eighteenth-century Europe apparently made no attempt to apply the use of the microscope, then recently perfected and popularized by Leeuwenhoek, to the study of this disease, but they labored strenuously at investigating the malady.   If they obtained only negative results for the most part, it must be acknowledged that scientists today know little more about it.   In 1926, when the third American edition of Hutyra's and Marek's book was published, it was still impossible to cultivate the virus.   Nor has any effective method of healing a sick animal yet been found.[15]

This most terrible of cattle diseases made its way into parts of eastern and southeastern France from Germany and Italy, about March, 1714,[16] and quickly spread over the provinces of Lorraine,[17]

---

were looked upon as a healthy sign by the eighteenth-century doctors, who thought that they improved the animal's chances of recovery. After several days these places dry up or scar over, and the hair falls off. At the outset the animals are constipated, but this changes after some time into profuse diarrhea; in fact, animals lose control over both bowels and bladder. With the appearance of diarrhea, however, the fever begins to drop, and in some instances it goes below normal. This is usually about the fifth or sixth day of the sickness. The disease does not commonly last beyond a week. If the animals survive, they are usually immune for life. The disease has many external characteristics in common with glossanthrax and the foot-and-mouth disease, yet it is more contagious than the former and vastly more dangerous than the latter (at least as it is commonly known). This description, borrowed from Hutyra and Marek, op. cit., I, 305-315, tallies with the description of the outbreaks in France in 1711-14, 1742-48, and 1773-76, as given by Paulet and others.

[12] Ibid., I, 292.

[13] Fleming, Animal Plagues, p. 199. Hereinafter, unless special designation is made, all citations to Fleming will apply to this work.

[14] Cogrossi based his opinion on the observations of Redi and Cestoni on the itch and of Kircher on the bubonic plague. Vallisnieri shared Cogrossi's view (Paulet, op. cit., I, 123).

[15] Hutyra and Marek, op. cit., I, 314. One French scientist denies the claims of the Turkish scientists regarding the filterable nature of the virus.

[16] Fleming, op. cit., p. 209; Paulet, op. cit., I, 129-130.

[17] The whole of Lorraine was not in French possession until 1766.

Champagne, Burgundy, Franche-Comté, Dauphiné, Lyonnais, Auvergne, Languedoc, Bourbonnais, Berry, Nivernais, Orléanais, and Ile-de-France (in which province Paris was seated). Thus it overran virtually all of eastern France and penetrated heavily into north central France. A rumor that it had entered Brittany proved to be false. Bernières, intendant of Flanders, was fearful of its spread into his generality when it appeared near Mons, in Belgian territory, just across his borders; but apparently Flanders also escaped. The regions of heaviest attack were perhaps Lorraine,[18] Champagne, Burgundy, and Bourbonnais.

Throughout the summer and early autumn of 1714 the disease wrought havoc, but during the winter it almost ceased, and was not very active thereafter. In certain provinces it lingered until spring or summer, with only a few sporadic cases. In February a faint recurrence in Bourbonnais, and in July and August another in Dauphiné and Auvergne, were of short duration.[19]

For the most part the disease was limited to cattle, but in a few places sheep also were affected. Moreover, in Lorraine and Dauphiné horses were attacked.[20] Horses were affected not only in parts of France in 1714, but in 1712 the horses in most parts of Europe (both those invaded by the cattle plague and others) were affected from time to time in a manner closely resembling that of the cattle.[21] This question whether the malady affecting the cattle was really the cattle plague, or rinderpest, puzzled Lancisi and Paulet; but the eighteenth-century physicians, after weighing all the evidence, decided that they were faced not by one but two diseases. Fleming also reached the same conclusion. Paulet claimed that the horses had glossanthrax; Fleming was positive that they had influenza.[22]

[18] The generality of Metz.

[19] This account is based upon the reports of the intendants and other government officials (Arch. Nat., G7, 1667).

[20] Revealed in the statistics submitted by the intendants (Arch. Nat., G7, 1667). The intendants had been ordered in October, 1714, to keep statistics for later presentation to the government. The heavy loss of horses in Lorraine throws an interesting side light upon the epizootic of 1714-15, for horses and other solipeds are not subject to infection by the rinderpest.

[21] Fleming, op. cit., pp. 192-195.

[22] In strong support of their opinion that there were two diseases, one of horses and the other of cows, is the elaborate official correspondence preserved in the Archives Nationales, in which the malady is described as the "cattle epizootic." According to the statistics submitted from several of the provinces no horses (or

The government first attempted to cope with the situation by sending considerable quantities of a "remedy" or drug concocted by one Giraudly. Before the end of March, 1714, the drug had been sent to Provins for use in Champagne, where it was given to the poor, but sold to those in comfortable circumstances.[23] Other provinces came to use this drug, and for a time it was very much sought, though on the whole the results were disappointing, save in Berry.[24] Remedies by Helvétius, Chomel, Bieb, Bailly, Manger, De la Salle, De la Brettonière, Azenedot, and possibly others, also were used.[24a] The government, moreover, printed and distributed the directions for several remedies and modes of treatment.

A large number of physicians, surgeons, and apothecaries were sent into the infected regions at state expense, some by the central government, others by the intendants. Among them were Herment,[25] a physician at the Hôtel-Dieu in Paris; Renault, a surgeon at the same institution; Drouin, surgeon-major of the king's bodyguards; Bailly, a Parisian physician; and De la Rue, a physician of Sens. The royal government paid their traveling expenses and gave them ample compensation. Thus Herment was paid a total of 3,500 livres, 1,342 for traveling expenses and 2,158 as an honorarium.[26] Drouin was paid 1,500 livres for three months' expenses.[27] De la Rue was promised payment of his expenses and a fee of 500 livres. Bailly was accorded 758 livres, part for expenses and part for drugs.[28] Renault was paid 1,037 livres for expenses and was given a fee of 2,500 livres.[29]

In the summer of 1714 the government sent Daguesseau, the procurer-general, and Bignon de Blanzy, the intendant of Paris, into

---

even sheep for that matter) are listed as having been struck by it. This immunity would have been almost impossible under glossanthrax, which falls heavily on all types of animals.

[23] Letter from Daguesseau, March 29, 1714 (Arch. Nat., G7, 1667).

[24] Letter from Daguesseau, Aug. 31, 1714 (*ibid*).

[24a] That by Manger, a physician of Rouen, was credited in October by the government as having had more success than any of the others ("Résultat de l'assemblée du 11ᵉ October 1714," *ibid.*).

[25] Name often spelled "Hermant" in the documents.

[26] "Résultat de l'assemblée du 8 mars 1715. 30ᵉ assemblée" (*ibid.*).

[27] His very interesting *mémoire* of expenses is found in Bibl. Nat., Fonds français, 6793, ff 91-94.

[28] Memorandum of the controller-general's office, of late August, 1714 (Arch. Nat., G7, 1667).

[29] "Résultat de l'assemblée du 4 janvier 1715" (*ibid.*).

the provinces with an advance of 4,000 livres to make a study of the situation and to suggest plans for better combating it.[30] In mid-December it even decided to send a certain peasant of Maine, who had been studying animal diseases for twenty-five years, on a grant of 50 livres, to some of the afflicted regions to observe the malady and make suggestions to the government.[31]

A fraction of the sick animals recovered from the malady, possibly in spite of the remedies and the royal physicians and surgeons, rather than by virtue of them. Many were the modes of treatment. Bleeding and purging of the sick animal were common. Setons were frequently applied to induce the formation of pus, regarded as an avenue of escape for the sickness. Quicksilver was sometimes injected. Various chemical and herbal compounds were given to the animal to chew or swallow, so as to increase the saliva and the nasal discharge. The farmers and the physicians early observed that the animals with the least marked outward manifestations of the malady were prone to die first; therefore they worked hard to get discharges from the nose, the mouth, the skin, and the bowels.[32] Many of the methods were excessively crude. In August, 1714, one Chamblay described to the controller-general's office the following treatment which he claimed had met with success: the tumors or pustules under the animal's tongue had been opened with a sharp instrument; then a handful of ashes had been thrown into the animal's mouth to induce slobbering; to make the slobbering a long process, a muzzle had been placed over the mouth; after an interval the ashes had been washed out with a solution of vinegar and salt. The same treatment was used in Savoy in July, except that the Savoyards added pepper to the solution.[33]

The government early prescribed certain sanitary requirements. Sick cattle were to be kept separate from animals that were well. None of the infected and none from infected herds were to be moved from one place to another, or to be put on sale at fairs or markets. No sick animal was to be butchered, and none of its meat was to be placed on sale. All persons owning livestock were to report their number and condition; sick animals were to be reported at once to

[30] Report of Aug. 14, 1714 (*ibid.*).
[31] Report of the nineteenth assembly, Dec., 1714 (*ibid.*).
[32] Diarrhea, however, was regarded as a bad sign.
[33] *Ibid.*

local officials. All animals dying of the disease were to be buried three feet underground. Until late 1714, moreover, it was forbidden to skin any animal dead of the epizootic, lest the skin preserve and convey the elements of infection. Late in 1714, however, for fear of a shortage in leather, the government rescinded its action on hides. Penalties were provided to enforce these requirements, and a large number of inspectors were sent at state expense to observe the markets, fairs, and farmers' barn lots.[34] Nevertheless, according to Drouin, who traveled widely in fighting the malady, all of the government regulations were poorly executed, whether the orders of the council, orders of the parlements, or ordinances of the intendants, and the injunction to bury the cattle without skinning them was flagrantly disobeyed. Almost everywhere the peasants removed the skins and sold them.[35]

During the late summer and early autumn of 1714,[36] Dangervilliers, the intendant of Dauphiné, took it upon himself to order the slaughter of all sick animals and to reimburse their owners in full. Whether he was influenced by the advice of Lancisi to the Roman state in 1713 is not indicated; but Lancisi had early despaired of finding a remedy and had suggested the axe. The Sacred College, however, considered his suggestion too cruel and costly, and put into effect policies that had been followed by France in 1714. Since Lancisi's book did not appear until 1715, Dangervilliers may have followed the English precedent. The rinderpest invaded England in mid-July, 1714, according to Bates (in September according to Kanold and Iberville), and the government quickly ordered the extermination of all infected animals. On the advice of Bates, surgeon to George I, who was sent to work with the cattle and suggest a remedy, and who came independently to the same opinion held by Lancisi, the government ordered that all owners of infected cattle be reimbursed 40 shillings (or half the market value) for each animal that was killed and burned within twenty-four hours from the first appearance of the sickness. For animals destroyed

[34] In 1715 the government refunded to the province of Burgundy alone 9,386 livres which the subdelegates had advanced to inspectors and visitors during the epizootic of 1714 (ibid.). Another payment of 2,300 livres was made to inspectors, evidently sent from Paris (Bibl. Nat., Fonds français, 6793, ff 89, 99-101).

[35] Report of the fifteenth assembly, Nov. 16, 1714 (Arch. Nat., G7, 1667).

[36] The malady did not hit Dauphiné until July or August, and never worked great havoc there.

after the first day the owners would be reimbursed only for the hides and horns. This remedy, it is said, worked remarkably well for England; and by Christmas, 1714, according to Bates, England was completely free of the disease.[37] Thenceforward throughout the century the example of England was pointed to as the ideal mode of handling this particular epizootic.[38] Thus Dauphiné was applying the same method that was used in England, at the same time, with more liberal compensation to owners.[39]

Even Paulet, who advocated this mode of treatment, praised the English for having set the example, apparently unaware of Dangervilliers' action in Dauphiné. It should be noted that during the autumn the French government had a representative in London, Iberville, with special instruction to report regularly on the progress of the cattle plague there, that he made about twenty reports,[40] and that he mentioned the English process of extermination. News of this type was quickly relayed among the cultured and officials of that day, and no doubt Dangervilliers was soon acquainted with the English procedure. But apparently official Paris did not learn of the epizootic in England until the last of September or early in October,[41] and since Dangervilliers would almost certainly have been slower in learning of it, it is unlikely that he got his idea from England.

On October 7, 1714, at its twelfth meeting the assembly of politicians and physicians, which met weekly at the home of Daguesseau in Paris to discuss ways and means of combating the epizootic,[42]

[37] Fleming, op. cit., pp. 209-212, 221. According to Iberville's letters in Arch. Nat., G7, 1667, it continued in England past mid-January.

[38] Indeed, it is still regarded as the best solution. See Hutyra and Marek, op. cit., I, 314, 320. It was so exterminated in Belgium after a flurry in 1920 (ibid., I, 293).

[39] No one has observed the fact that Neuchâtel, Switzerland, in February, 1702, offered a bounty of 25 livres for every animal killed, in order to rid itself of an unnamed and undescribed cattle malady, which had troubled it since August, 1701 (Dr. [C. A. E.] Cornaz, Une épizootie aux joux de la ville en 1701 et 1702, Neuchâtel, 1864, pp. 5-6). Perhaps it was a dropsy of the chest. Cf. Fleming, op. cit., p. 176.

[40] Found in Arch. Nat., G7, 1667.

[41] Report of the ninth assembly, Oct. 4, 1714 (ibid.). It was announced at this meeting that the epizootic had reached England in mid-September. The letter describing the epizootic had been written from London on September 24.

[42] There were thirty-five meetings first and last. The thirty-fifth occurred in March, 1715. Thenceforth meetings evidently were considered unnecessary. The assembly was given the full jurisdiction of a general staff in mapping out measures for exterminating the disease, and its recommendations for monetary expenditures and for other matters were always approved by Desmaretz, the controller-general. See its reports in Arch. Nat., G7, 1667.

decided to disapprove of Dangervilliers' action, fearing that it would be too costly and that it would enrage the peasants. This step met the hearty approval of the controller-general, if indeed he was not responsible for it,[43] and Dangervilliers was thereafter restricted in his method to regions where the epizootic had not yet been. In those regions he might kill any animals that became infected, if he deemed it wise for precautionary purposes, paying the entire value of the animals to their owners. The assembly at its twenty-sixth meeting, on February 8, 1715, hearing of the success that had attended the English in their mode of extermination, recommended that it be used in French Flanders, at least in two or three localities and up to the destruction of fifty animals, if the malady should come across the border from Austrian Flanders. To this the controller-general agreed. But apparently French Flanders escaped the epizootic.

On the whole the French mode of attack may be said to have been precautionary and remedial. It relied chiefly upon segregation of the sick animals and upon sanitary measures. It was a cautious, compromising policy. The expense turned out to be less for the government than extermination would probably have been. On the other hand, the losses of its subjects were much greater. Possibly the French government, after the long War of the Spanish Succession and the "Great Winter of 1709" did not feel that its treasury was equal to the strain of the more expensive policy. It is more probable that the real reason for the pursuance of the French policy was the reluctant, vacillating disposition of Desmaretz, the controller-general. He commented on the margin of the report of the twelfth assembly of October 25, 1714, that the disease was still making great headway in England (despite the method of extermination). Moreover, he was not niggardly in meeting the expenses incurred under his cautious plan.

What the epizootic cost the government is unknown, but at least 50,000 livres, irrespective of remissions allowed to the provinces because of the losses and expenditures that they had undergone, and irrespective of concessions made to individuals in lieu of losses, were spent. Two cattle importers, Rosnay of Rouen and Lobel of Paris,

[43] See marginal comment; also the report of the twenty-sixth assembly, of Feb. 8, 1715.

claimed losses of 37,330 and 37,225 livres, respectively, suffered in their business because of the quarantine restrictions imposed by the government on cattle importations from England and Ireland. The controller-general agreed to reimburse Rosnay in part by exempting him from duties in imports of glass bottles and lead to the extent of 15,000 livres.[44] Lobel obtained a reimbursement of 24,000 livres through exemption of import duties on lead and grindstones.[45] As for diminutions, Dauphiné, whose losses were small in comparison with those of Burgundy or Lorraine, was allowed a diminution of 60,000 livres on the *taille* for 1715, 24,000 livres on the *dixième*, because of the epizootic.[46] Inasmuch as similar diminutions almost certainly were granted the other generalities which suffered, the indirect losses to the state through cancellation of taxes must have been considerable. As for direct costs, Giraudly was paid 31,131 livres for remedies, and Chomel 9,160 livres; other apothecaries received at least 1,000 livres; physicians and surgeons, at least 8,000 livres; and inspectors, 2,300 livres. The generalities also had large expenses in fighting the malady, paid in part by the royal government through reductions in taxes.

The heaviest losses were borne by those whose animals were victims of the disease. Up to March 20, 1715, Lorraine (or more definitely the generality of Metz) had lost a total of 75,709 animals, of which 32,747 were cattle, 24,929 were sheep, and 18,033 were horses.[47] By November 16, 1714, Burgundy had already lost, in sixteen *bailliages*, a total of 72,475 cattle, and the epizootic was still raging throughout the generality.[48] In Bourbonnais 26,768 cattle had died up to the end of December, 1714,[49] and 6,922 in Auvergne;[50] in Dauphiné, 3,052 animals of all types (175 of them

---

[44] "Résultat de l'assemblée du 22 mars 1715," with marginal note (*ibid.*).

[45] "Résultat de l'assemblée du 18 may 1715," with marginal note (*ibid.*). These two cunning importers played fast-and-loose with the government. The government questioned their honor, but they were always able to prove their case sufficiently.

[46] "Résultat de l'assemblée du 8 mars 1715. 30e assemblée" (*ibid.*).

[47] "Résultat de l'assemblée du 5 avril 1715. 34e assemblée" (*ibid.*).

[48] "Résultat de l'assemblée du 16 novembre 1714. 15e assemblée" (*ibid.*). An idea of the high rate of mortality in these sixteen *bailliages* is given in the following records: 13,616 oxen died out of a total of 26,920 existing prior to the epizootic, 1,522 bulls out of 3,023, 44,785 cows out of 57,417, 12,552 veals and heifers out of an undesignated larger number.

[49] "Résultat de l'assemblée du 16e février 1715" (*ibid.*). In a letter dated October 3, 1714, Michel Dumont mentioned that sheep as well as cattle were attacked, but no mention of them was made in this report of February 16, 1715.

[50] *Ibid.*

horses) in the same period.[51]   In the election of Paris 1,371 cattle died, according to a statement of D'Argenson on February 1, 1715.[52] Coming so shortly after the terrible winter of 1709, which itself played havoc with French livestock,[53] this epizootic was a severe disaster to the country.

During the months of August, September, and October, 1714, the assembly intrusted the controller-general with oversight of combating the epizootic, and the intendants gave much attention to the problem of replenishing the devastated regions with sufficient animals for cultivating the next year's crops.   It was pointed out that the plowing would be done in January and February, and it was suggested that horses and mules be obtained to take the place of the dead oxen.   The government even considered the imposition of a special tax for three years to raise the necessary money, and asked terms of certain wealthy entrepreneurs of Lyons.   What its final action was, does not appear.[54]

In 1742 and 1743 the soil was prepared for a second epizootic when germs of the disease were introduced into Lorraine, Alsace, Franche-Comté, and Dauphiné, seemingly in connection with the movements of armies in the War of the Austrian Succession.[55]   At first its progress was slow.   In 1744 it invaded Lyonnais and Provence, but not until 1745 did it take on the aspects of a plague. During that year and 1746 it spread over perhaps two thirds of France, attacking not only Lyonnais and Provence but also Champagne, Burgundy, Bourbonnais, Auvergne, Limousin, Poitou, Saintogne, Angoumois, Ile-de-France, Normandy, Picardy, and French Flanders.   After 1746 it virtually disappeared from France, although a few traces lingered in Burgundy in 1747 and 1748.[56]   In extent and severity this second outbreak of the rinderpest in eighteenth-century France was much greater than the first.

Its symptoms and the measures taken against it, which Paulet described at length, were practically the same.   No horses were at-

---

[51] "Résultat de l'assemblée du mars 1715.   30e assemblée" (ibid.).

[52] "Résultat de la 25e assemblée" (ibid.).   Figures for the other generalities are lacking.

[53] Bramard, La dernière famine, pp. 51 ff.

[54] It did grant a subsidy of 15 sous per sheep, or a total of 14,925 livres, on 19,900 sheep imported from Germany by two entrepreneurs following the epizootic (Bibl. Nat., Fonds français, 6793, ff 87-88).

[55] Fleming, op. cit., p. 267.   [56] Paulet, op. cit., I, 230-231.

tacked, and the number of sheep was small.[57] Bleedings and purgings continued to be employed. Setons of various types were used much more than in the former epizootic, and such substances as black hellebore root and black currant bark were inserted under the skin of the animal, with claims of success. Some persons cruelly used hot irons on the back of the legs of the animals. Others drenched them with wine. The French frantically tried dozens of treatments. They opened carcasses (as, indeed, they had done in 1714-15) in an effort to discover what organ or organs the disease principally attacked, and how to combat it. No one, in the light of the information collected by Paulet, can accuse the eighteenth-century French physicians of failure to experiment and investigate. But, despite successes claimed in certain localities, all remedies and modes of treatment availed little.

The faculty of medicine at Montpellier drew up suggestions for fighting the malady, and at least one of its members, De Sauvages, went into the Vivarais to observe it and wrote a book setting forth his findings and suggestions. Of the several members of the faculty of medicine at Paris who were sent into the field, evidently by the government,[58] one, Chomel, likewise published a book on the subject.

Greater attention was given to disinfection and segregation than in the earlier epizootic. In some regions lines of soldiers *(cordons sanitaires)* were drawn up to prevent any suspected cattle being led across the borders; in others vigilantes, employed and posted on guard with arms to prevent such movements, saved certain communities in Lorraine and Languedoc,[59] and Guyenne.[60] Stables were submitted to *parfums,* or supposed disinfectants.[61] The parlement

---

[57] Languedoc seemingly was the only province which lost sheep. In 1745 its diocese of Mende lost 2,162 cattle, 22,479 sheep, and 1,189 hogs from "la maladie contagieux" (Arch. Nat., H 834).

The mention of hogs dying from the disease is odd. Whether hogs can have the rinderpest is still a matter of dispute. Yet certain twentieth-century scientists claim that they have succeeded in infecting hogs with it. See Hutyra and Marek, *op. cit.,* I, 300.

[58] Paulet (*op. cit.,* I, 200) names De l'Epine (the dean), Bouvart, Cochu, Malouin, Bertin, Chomel, Le Moine, Le Monnier, Le Thuillier, Ferrein, and Procope.

[59] *Ibid.,* I, 214-217.

[60] Lhéritier, *op. cit.,* p. 375.

[61] "The stables were fumigated with burning junipers, sage leaves, and rosemary and absinthe" (Fleming, *op. cit.,* 370). Paulet (*op. cit.,* I, 198) mentions other substances : "On purifie en même temps la demeure de ces animaux avec une once d'assa-foetida, une once de camphre, deux têtes d'ail, le tout bien pilé & mêlé ensemble."

of Rouen recommended,[62] "for preventing the evil," that the tongues of well cattle be scraped almost to the blood with a silver spoon, and that this be followed by giving the animals a concoction of crushed garlic, pepper, and vinegar. In England, Holland, Germany, and Denmark, where the epizootic was likewise experienced, greater attention was given to sanitary measures than formerly.

The most significant development of this epizootic for veterinary science was the discovery by certain Englishmen that the principle of inoculation, which since the second decade of the century had been known to Western Europe, could be applied also to the cattle plague. Dobson, a Yorkshire gentleman, acting on the suggestion of an unnamed Yorkshire physician, experimented in 1754.[63] In 1755 Malcolm Fleming and in 1757 Layard published pamphlets advocating the extensive usage of inoculation as a preventive, and in doing so paved the way for what is at present a widely used expedient for saving the well cattle in an area infected with the rinderpest.[64] Strangely enough, a French marquis, De Courtivron, stumbled on this process in Burgundy in July, 1745, and published a paper in the *Mémoires de l'Académie des Sciences* of that year on his findings, but did not recognize the significance of his experiment.[65] In order to settle the question whether the disease was carried by contagion or through the air (a big issue regarding all diseases in the eighteenth century), he placed infected hides on two well cows, which experienced a very mild form of the disease and recovered; but since the common characteristics of the malady did not show themselves, the marquis fallaciously concluded that the disease was not carried by contact. In 1748 he made further experiments and reached the same conclusion. Evidently French physicians and other scientists were no more clever than De Courtivron, for they were silent after reading of his experiments. In consequence, credit for the discovery of the process of inoculation for the rinderpest goes to the English.

---

[62] In its *arrêt* of March 13, 1745 (*ibid.*, I, 205).

[63] Fleming, *op. cit.*, p. 283. The plague lasted in England from 1745 through 1757, and this despite the fact that the English used the same mode of extermination and bounties that proved successful in 1714. But the English government delayed several months in 1745 before having recourse to this method, and the malady got well entrenched.

[64] Hutyra and Marek (*op. cit.*, I, 315-320) describe several forms of serum with which the inoculation is made.

[65] See Paulet, *op. cit.*, I, 217-227; II, 134-142. He made some further experiments in 1748.

Not much information has been found covering this epizootic. Presumably the government rendered aid similar to that given in 1714-15. The council of state on May 27, 1746, for example, extended to the province of Languedoc an advance of 300,000 livres in the form of temporary remissions, to be repaid in 1747, because of losses in 1745 amounting to 12,016,698 livres from the epizootic and from floods.[66] According to Babeau,[67] the government sent veterinarians to try to heal the sick cattle, and workers to bury the dead ones and give indemnities to the owners. Since no evidence concerning these workers or indemnities has been found elsewhere, it is possible that Babeau confused this epizootic with that of 1773-76.

In the 1770's occurred the third great outbreak of the rinderpest in eighteenth-century France, the disease being introduced momentarily into the provinces of Artois and Picardy in 1771 by way of Belgium and Holland.[68] In 1773 it reappeared in northern France, again coming from Holland, which perhaps because of its marshy nature had harbored the disease more than any other country of Western Europe. French Flanders, Hainault, Soissonnais, Picardy, and Champagne were attacked, as was Artois in 1774, with great severity. Either from this point or from Holland it was introduced through hides into the port and region of Bayonne, near the Spanish border. Thenceforth the malady attacked the country like an invading army with two giant pincers, one in the north and the other in the southwest. The southern movement exhibited much the greater force. The provinces Gascony, Guyenne, Saintonge, Limousin, Orléanais, and Languedoc were heavily attacked in 1774 and remained under attack well into 1776. Béarn and Rousillon, in the extreme south, were hit in 1775, and thence the malady made its way into Spain. In February, 1775, the generality of Rouen, in upper Normandy, was severely attacked. Indeed, according to Fleming,[69] all of the western provinces save La Vendée, Brittany, and part of Normandy were overrun. In the east Franche-Comté and in the Mediterranean Corsica were invaded.

[66] Total losses as a result of the epizootic were reckoned at 1,023,547 livres; the rest of the above sum was due to floods ("Recapitulation des dommages causés par les inondations à un grand nombre des diocèses de le province de Languedoc, et par la mortalité des Bestiaux," Arch. Nat., H 834).

[67] *Le village sous l'ancien régime* (3d ed. rev. and enlarged, Paris, 1882), p. 347.

[68] Fleming, *op. cit.*, p. 436.

[69] *Ibid.*, p. 466.

From 1773 to 1776 the malady raged in ever-increasing intensity, save for the fact that it generally experienced a check during the winter months. Eventually in 1776 it disappeared, probably as a result of the carefully laid measures of the government against it.

Seemingly it did not extend over as much French territory as did the epizootic in the 1740's, and possibly the loss in cattle was no greater; but beyond all doubt it was the most expensive for the French treasury which the country had ever undergone. According to Fleming, it was estimated that the epizootic of 1773-76 in France took a toll of 150,000 cattle, with a value of 152,000,000 livres.[70] The cost to the French government is nowhere stated, but since the government adopted a policy in late 1774 of reimbursing the owners of sick animals killed by direction of the officers to the extent of one third of their value, and later made this retroactive in practical application, the cost was certainly many millions. In his treatise published in the spring of 1775 Paulet estimated that the malady had already cost France more than fifteen millions.[71]

A chorus of voices in late 1774 and early 1775 urged the government to adopt the practice of exterminating the sick cattle in the earliest stages of the disease—Doazen,[72] Esmangart (intendant of Bordeaux),[73] Bourgelat,[74] Vicq d'Azyr,[75] and Paulet.[76] It was the policy which Lancisi had advised in 1712, which the English had employed with success in 1714, and which more recently, in 1771, had been followed in Austrian Flanders. Since the best medical opinion of France despaired of finding any remedy that would cure the malady, Turgot as controller-general adopted the method of

[70] *Ibid.*, p. 466. The evaluation is excessive, since cows were commonly valued at 60 to 90 livres, and not 1,000 livres, in the contemporary account sheets.

[71] He evidently included both government and citizens (*op. cit.*, II, 230).

[72] Physician of Bordeaux, engaged by the *jurats* and physicians of that city to study the malady and offer suggestions. His report was published in late 1774. (P. Foncin, *Essai sur le ministère de Turgot*, Paris, 1877, p. 137).

[73] In a letter dated November 5, 1774, to Turgot he recommended the slaughter and burial of sick animals, and the reimbursement of those owners who could not afford the loss (*ibid.*, p. 138). Esmangart's letter stirred Turgot to action.

[74] Director of the veterinary school at Alfort (F. Dumas, *op. cit.*, pp. 307-308).

[75] Paris physician and member of the Academy of Sciences. He was sent on a commission to study the malady in the south in late 1774. He recommended killing the animals and paying the owners in full: 150 francs for each ox, 90 francs for each cow, and 48 francs for the younger animals (Foncin, *op. cit.*, pp. 138-139).

[76] In his treatise published in the spring of 1775. The government had already adopted the policy, but Paulet's advice reassured the government and bolstered its firmness to continue it.

extermination. An order of council of December 18, 1774, required that all animals sick of the epizootic, to the extent of ten in a herd, be killed at the orders of the veterinarians or the local officers, and be buried in quicklime with their hides, to the depth of six or eight feet. If these conditions were fulfilled, the owner would be reimbursed by the government, through its intendant, to the extent of one third the value placed on the animal by the veterinarians.[77]

Since Turgot did not feel that the treasury could stand the expense of full reimbursement and of slaughter of all sick animals, as Vicq d'Azyr had recommended, he adopted the less expensive plan followed by Austrian Flanders in 1771, hoping that it might succeed. On January 30, 1775, however, another order of council prescribed the killing and burying of all sick cattle in a herd, whatever their number, and the payment of one-third value to the owners. The hides were to be cut in such a manner as to be rendered unfit for use, and a fine of 500 livres was placed on anyone who removed a hide, transported it, sold it, or bought it.[78] Later in 1775 the government prescribed that the dead animals should be buried in quicklime, since this would aid not only in sanitation but would supposedly render the hides unfit for use even should the animals be disinterred and skinned.

At the outset of the epizootic the government called upon Bourgelat and the newly formed veterinary school at Alfort, near Paris, for students and graduates to be sent into the afflicted regions and to assume charge of directing the attack on the disease. Sometimes two were sent together. They received orders and pay from the intendant and his subdelegates, who in turn got them from Paris. The veterinarians were accompanied when they desired by the local syndic and soldiers or members of the mounted police (maréchaussée). If permission to examine a cow or a herd was denied them, they were empowered to use force. These veterinarians were really the key men in the undertaking; they had to move fast and inspect all suspected barns and pastures, decide if any sick animal was afflicted with the malady, render the decision for killing and burial (despite the protests and entreaties of the owners), place an estimate of value, order the disinfection of the premises, and make

[77] Ibid., p. 140.
[78] "Arrest du Conseil d'État du Roi" (Arch. de la Seine-Inférieure, C 101).

almost daily reports by letter to the subdelegate or the intendant. Sometimes they worked into the night. Often they met bitter opposition from the inhabitants among whom they were sent, and on occasion they were even denied places to sleep. Malicious reports were spread against them. Theirs was anything but an easy task. Coquet, *médecin-vétérinaire*, a graduate of Alfort, who was assigned to the subdelegation of Eu, in the generality of Rouen, in February, 1775, and served throughout that year, exhibited tact, firmness, and kindness in all these difficulties and came gradually to acquire the confidence of the people.[79]

Another important feature in the government's attack on this epizootic was the placing of military cordons around the infected areas to prevent by force any movements of animals between infected and uninfected areas. Throughout the century the government, realizing the part that contact plays in the dissemination of disease, hastened to proclaim on the outbreak of epizootics the need of separating the sick from the well animals, but this order far too commonly went unheeded. The eighteenth-century Frenchman, who was very much an individualist, and not a lawabiding person, commonly ignored the law when it seemed to his advantage to do so, regardless of the severe penalties. In all three epizootics which have been described the law was flagrantly violated, not merely by one or two, but by multitudes of Frenchmen. The government used troops in 1745-46 in a half-hearted attempt to secure enforcement. In 1775-76 it sent a large army into the field, which provoked the wits in Paris to remark that the government was sending its soldiers to fight sick cows. But so widespread was the epizootic that all the many regiments of troops were not enough; companies of the *maréchaussée* were added, and bands of vigilantes were organized.[80]

Besides forming a cordon around the infected area, the troops gave other assistance to the veterinarians in charge. Thus in February, 1775, the troops in upper Normandy were ordered: (1) to visit the stables daily, look for sick cattle, and report to their officer; (2) to see that cattle were confined to their stables and on no condition allowed to go into the pastures;[81] (3) to see that all dogs were

---

[79] His letters are in Arch. de la Seine-Inférieure, C 101.

[80] Foncin *(op. cit.)* perhaps best describes these cordons. See also the *Oeuvres de Turgot*, II, 484, 487, and the *Histoire générale de Languedoc*, XIII, 1238, 1248.

[81] The veterinarian Coquet shortly opposed this regulation and got it altered.

confined, and to kill any that were not;[82] (4) to report all sick cattle to the veterinarians, and together with the syndics to get peasants to clean the stables; (5) to pay 24 sous for each clean stable, and the same amount for each pit *(fosse)* dug for burial of a cow;[83] and (7) to see to the cleaning of the stables, removal of the humid matter, burning of the straw, and the application of disinfectants.[84]

In December, 1774, when the epizootic assumed large proportions both in the north and in the south, Turgot called upon the Academy of Sciences in Paris to appoint several of its members on a commission to study this disease and make a report to him. One of the commissioners was Vicq d'Azyr, a prominent physician. He and certain others were sent into the infected regions of the south to observe the disease and make recommendations preliminary to the report of the commission. Vicq d'Azyr, a man of much personality, quickly came to dominate the commission. Following the recommendation of the great Haller (in 1773) and other physicians of the time, he urged upon the government the extermination of the sick cattle. His bold, unhesitating recommendations led Turgot to place him, at least nominally, in charge of the campaign against the disease by naming him the government's official adviser. From time to time he undertook trips into the infected areas to observe conditions, to experiment, and to formulate plans. He published a hastily composed but suggestive book on the disease, entitled *Exposé des moyens curatifs & préservatifs qui peuvent être employés contre les maladies pestilentielles des bêtes à cornes,* in which he offered "a collection of memoirs brought together without any order."[85]

A more scholarly work, published at the same time, was that of the physician, Jean Jacques Paulet, on whom Fleming relied for much of his information. The government asked Paulet, apparently early in 1774, to make a study of the relation of this epizootic to that of 1745, concerning both its nature and remedies.[86] Although

---

[82] As dogs were carriers of the disease.

[83] The pits were to be eight feet deep ("fosses ayant huit pieds de profondeur"), and care was to be taken that the blood of the massacred animals be buried with them.

[84] "Observations sur les órdres qu'il convient de donner aux différents détachemens qui seront distribués dans les villages pour la préservation et désinfection de la paroisses" (Arch. de la Seine-Inférieure, C 101).

[85] *Encyclopédie méthodique,* Médecine, IX, 467.

[86] This is mentioned in a letter by one Belbeuf, written from Paris, February 8, 1775, to De Crosne, intendant of Rouen: "Mr. Paulet médecin chargé de rassem-

Paulet made a careful historical survey of the epizootics of all past history, with especial attention to those which had afflicted France and Europe in the eighteenth century, he was not able to make use of government documents. He did, however, make an exhaustive study of the multitudinous pamphlets and articles which the cattle plague had provoked from eighteenth-century physicians and other writers, examining them with a critical and philosophic mind. The result, his two-volume treatise entitled *Recherches historiques et physiques sur les maladies épizootiques, avec les moyens d'y remédier dans tous les cas,* at once a storehouse of historical information, still useful to the student of eighteenth-century epizootics and veterinary medicine, and filled with suggestions similar to those of Vicq d'Azyr and Haller,[87] must have proved valuable to the government in 1775. He was granted 1,800 livres by the government to meet the expenses of publication, and he won the prize of 1,200 livres which the Society of Agriculture of Paris had offered for the best memoir on this subject. The government distributed the work gratuitously through the provinces.[88]

The work of another physician, Dufau of Dax, was twice denied the right of publication by Turgot, because his suggestions for meeting the epizootic ran counter to the policy that the government was pursuing.[89] Turgot also rode roughshod over the parlement of Toulouse, which in September, 1775, opposed the method employed.[90] Everywhere opposition was generally more or less unexpressed. The owners of animals and the local farriers all too commonly tried to cure the animals in barns or near-by forests. In Condomois, Guyenne, so violent was the opposition of the peasants to the prescribed measures that the government left that region pretty much alone, merely relying on the cordon of troops around it to prevent the spread of the malady. This cordon was contracted as rapidly as possible to diminish the *foyer* of infection. In Nor-

---

bler tout ce qui avoit été fait en 1745 pour guérir les animaux malades et pour arrêter la communication de cette maladie de proche en proche m'a demande le mars dernier le remède que fut alors regardé comme le meilleur. Ce je luy ay envoyé. Mais on m'a dit que les symptômes de la maladie actuelle n'étoient pas les mêmes, celles qui desole la bretagne et le normandie en 1745" (Arch. de la Seine-Inférieure, C 101).

[87] See Fleming, *op. cit.,* pp. 456-457.
[88] Foncin, *op. cit.,* pp. 164-165.
[89] *Ibid.,* p. 324. [90] *Ibid.,* p. 322.

mandy also the opposition was widespread, but passive rather than violent.

All the government's efforts to aid the peasants appear to have gone relatively unappreciated. The veterinarians, the soldiers, the printed matter, the huge quantities of drugs and disinfectants, the interment of the dead animals, the remuneration of one third the value, all at a great cost to the state, meant little to the farmer who saw only his own loss.

In some regions indeed the owner suffered no loss, since church and provincial authorities paid him the other two thirds of the value of his dead animals.[91] This was true in parts of Languedoc and in the generality of Rouen,[92] at least for short periods. In Languedoc only necessitous owners were repaid the extra two thirds, while in the generality of Rouen all owners were reimbursed. In practical application doubtless little difference was made between the two regions, for in Languedoc 100,000 livres were paid out by the diocesan treasurer for this cause, despite the fact that there, as in most parts of France, the epizootic virtually subsided during the first six months of 1775.

In Guyenne, where the malady seemed to be more stubborn than elsewhere, a radical plan for breaking its grip on the province was suggested in late 1775 by Clugny, the new intendant, and was approved by Turgot. In December all of the cattle of the infected provinces on the right bank of the Garonne River were transported to the left bank, and the region on the right bank was left void of animals. The plan was to confine the disease to a smaller territory and thus protect the regions to the north and east. It called for much added expense, especially to provide food and shelter for the beasts. Turgot was not overly pleased with the results, for in February, 1776, he ordered the abandonment of the plan and a return to his former policy of cordons and extermination.[93]

But Clugny, who possessed fertile ideas, had already conceived a new plan. (Incidentally he had not closely followed Turgot's original policy and had been reprimanded for his neglect.) Clugny now suggested that on the outbreak of the malady in any stable all

---

[91] *Histoire générale de Languedoc*, XIII, 1237, 1247-1248, 1250.

[92] Letters by Vicq d'Azyr and Charles, subdelegate at Eu, on Feb. 12 and 13, 1775, respectively (Arch. de la Seine-Inférieure, C 101).

[93] Foncin, *op. cit.*, pp. 323-324.

the cows sheltered in it, well and sick alike, be killed. Clearly this proposal would be expensive, but Turgot, who was willing to be venturesome, gave the nod to it.[94]

The government officials and the veterinarians tried to protect the peasants against charlatans who peddled remedies among them and extracted their small savings. De Crosne, intendant of Rouen, wrote in a long *Instruction* in early 1775 to his subdelegates: "The most reliable experiences demonstrate how curative methods are useless. These charlatans, in running from village to village, carrying the malady in their garments, bring about very considerable expense to the people without any utility, and destroy all the precautions taken by the government, which are the only ones that are able to bring success."[95] In the same year the government published at Versailles a thirteen-page *Mémoire instructif* severely attacking the charlatans who treated the cattle of the peasants of Condomois, in Guyenne:

There are some other cantons where the peasants, deceived by false hopes given them by charlatans, persist in guarding their sick beasts until they die, leaving them mixed with well beasts in the same stables where the disease has been before placing other animals there. Nothing has been able to conquer the stubbornness of the peasants of Condomois on all these points; and it is chiefly to this cause that one must attribute the violence with which the malady has ravaged this portion of Guyenne.[96]

Historians have frequently criticized the government of the Old Regime as stupid and cruel, but in numerous matters, and in particular in the fight against epizootics, the government sought the advice of its best experts, tried to carry through their recommendations, made modifications when necessary, and dealt with violators far more often in leniency than in severity. And certainly in connection with the eighteenth-century epizootics the peasants and others behaved in a manner both stupid and exasperating.

Utilizing improved methods of sanitation and disinfection, the government, as it did throughout the eighteenth century, prescribed careful sanitary measures to bring the plague to an end and to protect

[94] *Ibid.*, pp. 484, 486. This was in January, 1776. There is no report concerning its success, but the epizootic disappeared in 1776.
[95] Arch. de la Seine-Inférieure, C 101. This intendant was put to death during the Reign of Terror as an "enemy of the people."
[96] *Ibid.*

its citizenry. It ordered that all the diseased cattle be buried in pits with quicklime; that the stables be thoroughly cleaned, disinfected with *parfums* or "antiseptics" to kill the "germs,"[97] and preferably whitewashed; that all well cattle be isolated from the sick; that all dogs be chained at home or killed, lest they carry the disease from one barn or pasture to another; that no vagabonds be allowed to sleep in barns, lest they, too, carry the disease; that only soldiers and veterinarians approach sick cattle and that they remain at a distance from those that were well; that veterinarians wear a linen overgarment when they entered a stable to inspect sick cattle, lest they carry infection from one barn to another; that all meat offered for sale by the butchers be inspected, and none from an infected cow be sold; and that hides be buried with the dead animals. This last clause was modified in 1775, when Vicq d'Azyr, after some experiments, asserted that the disease was not carried by the hides of diseased cattle if dipped in limewater.[98]

Paulet and Vicq d'Azyr, who opposed inoculation, might have rendered great service had they espoused the opposite view. Vicq d'Azyr claimed that he had tried many experiments with it and that nearly all of the inoculated animals had died.[99] Evidently there was something wrong in the way Vicq d'Azyr had performed his inoculation, for Coquet, the veterinarian, had obtained entirely different results in upper Normandy. In a memoir of nine pages written to the intendant in late December, 1775, he expressed to De Crosne his belief that he had found a preventive which, if used on the well cattle at the onset of the malady in a region, would render them immune. In his own experiments with fifteen or eighteen cattle, every one of which underwent a mild form of the disease, all had survived.[100] After making the inoculation, he had fed the cows acid foods and drinks for a time.[101] Later he had put the cows to graze again, and had rubbed their backs with solutions. He had employed no filthy or severe remedies such as many of the peasants and charlatans used. Coquet thought that some others had met

---

[97] These terms are found in Paulet's work. Turgot also used the word "germes."

[98] *Histoire générale de Languedoc*, XIII, 1260, 1262.

[99] Fleming, *op. cit.*, p. 468.

[100] He mentioned that the subdelegate Charles, of Eu, had often accompanied him and had encouraged him in his experiments.

[101] According to various writers, the cows sick with the rinderpest would not touch foods save those of an acid nature.

failure in their experiments with inoculation because they had waited until the cows contracted the disease before inoculating.[102]

According to a document[103] signed by Espagnoû, clerk (greffier) of the parlement of Toulouse, on November 12, 1775, 116 cattle had been saved in certain vicinities of Languedoc since May by means of a remedy composed chiefly of brandy (eau-de-vie) and olive oil. On a farm near Castelmauron, of 30 cattle that had been infected, not a single one was lost. At Garidach 9 cattle had been attacked, and all were healed save one. At Fossat 28 were attacked, and 22 recovered. In the county of Novital seven were sick, and five recovered (the other two being killed). Out of 141 cattle taken with the malady, 116 recovered under the administration of this remedy and only 25 were lost. Considering the fact that according to De Sauvages nineteen out of every twenty cattle attacked died during the epizootics of 1714-15 and 1745, and according to others the same proportion died in 1775 (a proportion undoubtedly too high), the low mortality in these particular places is remarkable. There is apparently no reason to doubt the accuracy of these remarkable healings, but it is possible that the epizootic had reached a less virulent stage, or there might possibly have been life in brandy and olive oil.

The epizootic of 1773-76 caused tremendous devastation. A writer stated that in Guyenne

. . . cultivation has experienced an irreparable loss. The consequences of the epizootic are manifold. Almost all the cattle of the generality are dead or slaughtered, above all in the election of Lannes and Condomois, where cattle are the principal source of wealth. Furthermore the cultivation of the soil suffers because one lacks the animals necessary for plowing. At length there is not enough manure for fertilizing the fields. . . .

In October, 1776, after a tour of his generality, the intendant Dupré de Saint-Maur was able to write the controller-general D'Ormesson: "It

---

[102] His interesting paper was tucked in the intendant's files, where it has since reposed: "Observations importantes sur la Maladie Epizootique des Bêtes à cornes que a Regnée L'année 1775 dans Le Comté d'Eu" (Arch. de la Seine-Inférieure, C 101).

[103] An interesting memoir of twenty pages entitled "Certificat du Sr. Trebose du nombre des Bêtes à cornes attaquées de la Maladie Epizootique et qui sont gueries" (Arch. Nat., H 1644). Accompanying this memoir are several sworn testimonials by local officials, all witnessed by Espagnoû, giving precise figures for each region where the epizootic had been; in nearly every instance most of the animals had recovered.

is difficult to draw an idea of the desolation that the epizootic has spread in the countryside. It is only in seeing cultivation almost entirely abandoned, some inhabitants in misery and discouragement, some populations exhausted by the losses that many have experienced twice and by the aid that they have been obliged to give to their tenants (*colons*), that one is able to judge the sad results that this scourge had produced."

In 1777, appreciating the ravages committed, he estimates that "the regions which have experienced the scourge of the epizootic have as yet only been able to procure for themselves a third of the animals necessary for cultivation," and that, in consequence, "many fields are left fallow."[104]

This same writer estimated that the total cost of the epizootic to the generality of Bordeaux by June, 1775, was 6,000,000 livres.[105] In the generalities of Auch and Bayonne, in Gascony, the government had spent 2,435,000 livres by December, 1775.[106] Languedoc spent 3,000,000 livres.[107] These were merely three in a large number of provinces that experienced the epizootic. In the generality of Bordeaux the government expended 721,273 livres for the single item of reimbursement to owners for one third the value of their slaughtered cows.[108] Some of the provinces had to borrow heavily to meet expenses resulting from this plague. On December 30, 1777, the

[104] E. Bourgouin, *op. cit.*, XI (Bordeaux, 1918), 157-158.

[105] *Ibid.*, XI, 157. Foncin (*op. cit.*, p. 321) reports that 335,000 livres had been spent in this generality up to the end of September, 1775. Foncin's figure seems entirely too low.

[106] Foncin, *op. cit.*, p. 326. Foncin is wrong in speaking of them as a "single generality."

Douglas Dakin (*Turgot and the Ancien Régime in France*, London, 1939, pp. 197-199), relates a scandal in connection with the payment of animal-owners in the generality of Auch. False estimates of the value of the cattle were submitted, and payments were made for animals never slain. The result was that the intendant "distributed 2,000,000 *livres* in indemnities and had promised another 5,000,000." Journet, the intendant, was called to appear in the royal council to explain the situation, but the day before his appearance he committed suicide. Dakin exonerates him, saying that "Journet's personal honesty was never suspect," but lays the blame on his inexperience and on some corrupt subordinates. "In paying indemnities Journet had established officials whose remuneration amounted to half the fund he proposed to disemburse. These subordinates were thoroughly corrupt; they made false estimates of the value of cattle slain and granted indemnities for animals which had never been destroyed." After Journet's suicide, a commission was set up at Auch to revise the payments, and as a result "the indemnities actually paid were reduced to 500,000 *livres*, legal action being taken against those who had made fraudulent claims—a course which followed also in other *généralités*."

[107] Babeau, *op. cit.*, pp. 347-348.

[108] "Extrait des Etats fournis par les subdelegués de la Généralité de Bordeaux les plus pauvres habitants des Paroisses de leurs subdélégations qui ont perdu des bestiaux par la maladie épizootique" (Arch. de la Gironde, C 79).

estates of Languedoc borrowed the sum of 1,316,012 livres for that purpose.[109]

In addition to reimbursing owners of slaughtered cattle one third of their assessed value, the government rendered diminutions in taxes where the losses had been very great. Thus the inhabitants of three towns in Guyenne were released from one third or one half of their *vingtièmes* for 1776 and the two following years.[110] The government also by an order of council of January 8, 1775, offered bounties for every horse or mule fit for plowing which should be imported and sold in the markets of Guyenne, Auch, Navarre, Béarn, and Bayonne prior to April 20 of that year. Thirty livres was offered for each horse or mule sold before February 20 in certain specified markets, 24 livres for each animal sold in certain other designated markets in this same interval, 20 livres and 16 livres respectively for each animal sold in these same markets between February 20 and March 20, and 15 livres and 10 livres respectively for each animal sold in the two groups of markets between March 20 and April 20.[111] Later, by an order of council of October 29, 1775, these terms were extended into 1776.[112]

This was a queer way to encourage the restocking of farm animals in a region. The buyer rather than the seller needed aid. The "enlightened" Turgot nodded in this instance, one reasons; perhaps this explains why Guyenne was slow in replenishing her farm animals. Turgot, however, was judicious in preferring horses and mules to oxen for plowing both for speed and for greater immunity to epizootics. Moreover, he supported a request from the parlement of Toulouse that royal loans be placed at the disposal of farmers who wished to restock their farm animals.[113]

As a final step, Turgot, by an order of council of April 26, 1776, set up what was intended to be a permanent commission of six physicians in Paris, to be named by De Lassonne, first physician to the king, to carry on correspondence with the provincial physicians and those of foreign countries for the purpose of learning the best meas-

[109] *Histoire générale de Languedoc*, XIII, 116.
[110] Letter from Clugny to D'Ormesson, Feb. 21, 1776 (Arch. de la Gironde, C 79).
[111] *Oeuvres de Turgot*, II, 479.
[112] *Ibid.*, II, 489.
[113] Letter to Miromenil, Nov. 16, 1775 (Foncin, *op. cit.*, pp. 609-610). Whether anything came of this request is not known.

ures for combating epidemics and epizootics.[114] Occasionally its members were to visit the provinces for study of particular problems at first hand. Moreover, other physicians and students of medicine might be admitted to meetings of the commission, in order to popularize its findings. Animal ailments were to be studied along with human needs, and the history of epidemics and epizootics was also to be investigated.[115]

Later epizootics, of various forms, in the eighteenth century saw a revival of certain of the measures already employed, such as the placing of Vicq d'Azyr in charge, the use of cordons, and the killing of dogs (during a cattle malady of 1779 similar in many respects to the rinderpest),[116] and the forced killing of horses sick of the glanders, with reimbursement to their owners (during an epizootic on horses in the region of Caen, Normandy, in the 1780's).[117] Nothing novel was done.

Not only the rinderpest or cattle plague, but also other types of epizootics took a heavy toll of French livestock, with consequent government concern and indemnities to owners. Foremost among them was the anthrax, which appeared in several forms. The most common and dangerous was glossanthrax, a malady with certain external similarities to the rinderpest but also certain marked differences. It developed faster than the rinderpest and frequently ate through the tongue and caused death within twenty-four hours;[118] it attacked all types of animals, even human beings; and its outbreaks were much more frequent in France. In fact, according to Fleming, the mountains of Auvergne and Dauphiné, in southeast France, were throughout the eighteenth century the central *foyer* of glossanthrax in Europe.[119] From France this disease was imported during the eighteenth century into Louisiana, where it has since remained endemic, and whence it has frequently spread to other areas of the United States.

[114] *Oeuvres de Turgot*, II, 474-476.
[115] Out of this commission developed the Royal Society of Medicine (Dakin, *op. cit.*, p. 199).
[116] Fleming, *op. cit.*, pp. 490-504.
[117] Apparently 1784 or 1785 (*Inv.-som . . . Calvados*, C 1033-36, 1039, 1043).
[118] Rinderpest usually killed its victim between the fifth and eighth days.
[119] "History shows that all the great invasions of the malady [glossanthrax] have originated in sub-alpine France—in Dauphiné or Auvergne, and have spread from thence as a centre, sometimes but a short distance, at other times a long way in every direction, and generally by Germany into Poland, though never reaching England" (*op. cit.*, p. 526 n. 3).

Certain outbreaks of this malady in eighteenth-century France were almost as severe as the outbreaks of the cattle plague. One occurred in 1763.[120] Occasional outbreaks of the glanders in horses and the rot (clavelée) in sheep also occurred. Throughout the century it was customary for the royal government to grant diminutions in taxes to those who had experienced losses because of epizootics.

Government aid in epizootics in eighteenth-century France has- tened and encouraged the development of veterinary schools devoted to a scientific study of animal diseases. France, and more particu- larly Claude Bourgelat, founded in 1762 the first veterinary school in the world. Prior to that time animals were cared for by farriers, who were commonly uneducated and who acquired their knowledge by experience and from older farriers. Some physicians gave the diseases of animals passing attention, as is evident from the volum- inous amount of printed matter on epizootics; but there was as yet little study of comparative medicine. Bourgelat, a native of Lyons and a graduate in law of the University of Montpellier, was a lawyer at Grenoble who gave up his profession to enter the army and then became more interested in treating horses than in military tactics and maneuvers. At length he asked and obtained the headship of the Royal Riding Academy (Académie royale d'équitation) of Lyons, which he made famous and which drew its students from France, Piedmont, Switzerland, and Germany. In addition to his interest in horsemanship, he made dissections of horses to study their anat- omy and he read all that he could find in print on veterinary sub- jects. Later he wrote treatises on the nature of the horse. On re- quest, he contributed several articles on the horse to Diderot's en- cyclopedia. He asked and obtained, through influence of his devoted friend, Bertin, former intendant of Lyons, the headship of the royal stables (haras). In 1760 he petitioned the controller-general for the privilege of founding a veterinary school at Lyons, and thanks again to the support of Bertin, was enabled on January 1, 1762, to open this school,[121] which was supported in part by the government.

From the very outset Bourgelat, a skilled advertiser, drew the

[120] Described at some length in an article by Paul M. Bondois, "La protection du troupeau français au XVIIIe siècle: l'épizootie de 1763," Revue d'histoire éco- nomique et sociale, XX (Paris, 1932), 352-375.

[121] Monfalcon, op. cit., III, 55-56.

attention of all France and even of Europe to his newly founded institution. Pupils came not only from all parts of France but from foreign countries. Almost immediately schools modeled on his were established in other countries. In 1763 he offered the assistance of his pupils to the government in the severe epidemic of anthrax of that year, and 120 pupils were sent into the provinces of Bourbonnais, Limousin, Auvergne, and Forez, where they won the applause of the controller-general and were credited with saving 5,000 cattle.[122]

Realizing the value of trained veterinarians to the state, the government decided to create a second institution of the same type at Alfort, near Paris, which was opened on July 8, 1767.[123] Bourgelat was brought to Paris, made director of both institutions, and placed in immediate charge of the one at Alfort. The school at Lyons was committed for a while to the hands of the Abbé Rozier, another misfit in life who became a distinguished scientist.

Soon there was a rage for founding veterinary schools in France and in other parts of Europe as well. In France one was created at Limoges in January, 1766, for the immediate needs of Limousin, and lasted three years.[124] About the same time Du Cluzel, intendant of Tours, gave careful consideration to the establishment of a school to serve his territories, but Turgot discouraged him.[125] In 1777 the Estates of Provence promised one Guyot 1,200 livres annually toward the establishment of a veterinary school in their province or region,[126] but the plans evidently fell through. Nevertheless, in 1788 these same Estates accorded Guyot 400 livres for instructing two pupils in the veterinary art.[127]

The two institutions at Lyons and Alfort flourished throughout the rest of the century except for one brief interruption, 1793-95, first with partial and later total state support. The provincial governments, in turn, paid the expenses of all or virtually all of the French students who attended them. Almost every province was represented at one of these schools by one, two, or three students,

---

[122] Bondois, *op. cit.*, XX, 371-372. [123] *Inv.-som . . . Calvados*, C 2503.

[124] Dumas, *op. cit.*, p. 302. A special study of this institution has been made by L. Moulé and A. Raillet, entitled *Turgot et l'école vétérinaire de Limoges (26 févr. 1766—5 nov. 1768)* (Paris, 1902), 60 pp. It appears both separately and in the *Recueil de médicine vétérinaire d'Alfort*.

[125] Dumas, *op. cit.*, p. 302.

[126] *Inv.-som . . . Bouches-du-Rhône*, C 93.

[127] *Ibid.*, C 100.

officially appointed and supported, with a definite allowance.[128] Prior
to the Revolution the sums allowed *(pensions)* varied from 200 to
600 livres, according to the generosity of the intendants and the
provincial estates. When the pupils had completed the course of
training, commonly three years, they were almost always able to
obtain positions with the provincial government that had supported
them as students, on salaries that compared well with those paid by
the provinces to the physicians sent into the country districts.[129] That
they were bitterly opposed by the old farriers *(maréchaux)* mattered
little since they enjoyed government support. They served their
country faithfully and well.[130] It is chiefly due to their efforts and
those of later trained veterinarians that the world of today is freer
of epizootic scourges than was France in the eighteenth century.

[128] It is revealed by an examination of the *Inventaires-sommaires des archives
départementales,* série C. See also Dumas, *op. cit.,* pp. 303-304.

[129] Dumas writes: "En venant exercer dans la généralité ils recurent une uni-
forme, 600 livres, et 900 livres en trois ans, 200 livres la première année, 300 la
seconde et 400 la troisième. On leur fournit tous les instruments nécessaires pour
l'exercise de leur art" *(op. cit.,* p. 305). The annual salary of the country physician was also 300 livres a year. In some respects the veterinarian fared better.

[130] During Bourgelat's lifetime, and even afterwards, the attention of the two
schools, it is said, was directed almost entirely to the diseases of horses despite the
fact that, according to estimates, France lost three times as many cattle from epizootics as horses in the eighteenth century *(Encyclopédie méthodique,* Médecine, IX,
464, 468).

CHAPTER VII

THE PLAGUE OF 1720-22

IN 1720-22 a dire scourge commonly known as the "Plague of Marseilles" struck southeastern France and necessitated government aid of diverse types. The most extensive outbreak of bubonic plague in France since the notorious Black Death of the fourteenth century, this epidemic would have been a national calamity under any circumstances, but coming in concurrence with the financial panic resulting from the collapse of John Law's Scheme, it was doubly so.[1]

The epidemic had its origin in Marseilles in the spring of 1720, when several persons were taken sick with a malady resembling and later diagnosed as the plague.[2] Perchance it had been brought from the Near East by way of Austria and other Continental countries; possibly it was to some extent endemic in Marseilles.[3] Be that as it may, there was a second and more important source of the plague in 1720. On May 25 a pest-laden ship, the *Great Saint Anthony*, docked at Marseilles on her return voyage from Saida and other Syrian ports, where she had acquired a number of passengers and a

---

[1] Law's System began its decline in May and collapsed in December, 1720 (Earl J. Hamilton, "Prices and Wages in Southern France under John Law's System," *Economic History (Supplement)*, Feb., 1937, pp. 454-455; J. B. Perkins, *France under the Regency . . .* , Boston and New York, 1892, pp. 498-508). Law insisted that the Marseilles plague precipitated the crash of his System, and that without it he might have succeeded. His own words are: "J'ai dit que, si la France eust exemptée de la maladie [de Marseille], la système de M. Law auroit pu estre soustenu" (John Law, *Oeuvres complètes*, ed. Paul Harsin, Paris, 1934, III, 172).

[2] Professor Hamilton (*op. cit.*, p. 456) dates the plague in Provence from the late spring of 1720.

[3] Paul Gaffarel and the Marquis de Duranty, *La peste de 1720 à Marseille & en France, d'après des documents inédits* (Paris, 1911), pp. 45-48.

W. G. Bell, author of *The Great Plague in London in 1665*, asserts that the plague remained endemic in London throughout the seventeenth century, or at least throughout 1679, occasionally bursting forth in epidemic proportions.

London had epidemics in 1603, 1625, 1640-47, and 1665. Bell (*op. cit.*, pp. 5-7, 9, 252-253) disagrees with the common opinion that the Great Fire of 1666 killed the germs of the plague entirely, pointing out that sporadic cases continued in the city until 1679. He insists that London's riddance of the germ was due to better housing conditions and the disappearance of the black rat in the years following the Great Fire.

Marseilles suffered fourteen outbreaks of the plague in the 1500's, and two in the 1600's (1630 and 1649) (Gaffarel and Duranty, *op. cit.*, pp. 5-7).

cargo consisting chiefly of silks. En route from Saida, where the plague was existent, to Marseilles, nine sailors died; and although the ship's officers attributed the deaths more to a malignant fever than to the plague, iron hooks were used to cast the bodies overboard.[4] Apparently no buboes, the distinctive characteristic of the plague, were to be found on the victims. Furthermore, the ship carried certificates of good health from all the ports which she had touched save the last, Leghorn.

Harbor authorities at Marseilles permitted the passengers to disembark and go their way. The crew and a large part of the cargo were ordered ashore to the infirmary and lazaret, respectively, for quarantine and disinfection. One of the longshoremen engaged in transporting the goods was quick to contract the malady and die. Other cases of the sickness quickly broke out in homes of the poor where persons from aboard the ship had gone.

The city authorities of Marseilles manifested concern, and not being satisfied with the declaration of their own physicians and surgeons that the malady was only a malignant fever, they asked the government to send health officers to make a more thorough examination. Chicoyneau and Verny, members of the medical faculty of Montpellier (one of the two most famous medical schools in France), who were sent by the regent to Marseilles, reached the same conclusion.

But deaths from the ailment continued to mount. Alarm spread, and a few of the wealthier inhabitants evacuated the city. Eventually, on August 17, physicians pronounced that the epidemic was in truth the *peste*. Like wildfire, the word spread over the city, and so great was the exodus of people of all walks of life that, according to Pichatty de Croissainte, a municipal official, it seemed as if the crowd in its mad flight would take off the very gates of the city walls.[5] Although the city authorities passed regulations prohibiting, under heavy penalties, the departure of persons from the city, they were more or less powerless to enforce them.

The precaution of setting aside certain hospitals as pest infirmaries and certain buildings as places for the quarantine of persons exposed

---

[4] Leclercq, *op. cit.*, III, 76.

[5] See his vivid eyewitness account of the epidemic, *Piéces historiques sur la peste de 1720* (n. p., n. d.), I, 56-58. According to Pére Feuillée (*ibid.*, II, 13), forty thousand persons (doubtless an exaggeration) left the city.

to the plague quickly proved inadequate. By the first of September the epidemic was reaching its peak; nearly a thousand persons were dying daily. This high death rate continued throughout September and into early October.[6]

A chief characteristic of the plague was a high temperature which made it well-nigh impossible for the sufferer to bear clothing. Many persons who were ill betook themselves to the streets, and great numbers of others reportedly were deposited there by their cowardly, terror-stricken families.[7] The streets, accordingly, became filled with the dead and the dying, and for a while it was impossible for the city to bury the dead. This problem was solved by the government's permitting the use of convicts from Toulon, the convicts being promised their freedom if they survived. Of a total of 692 convicts (forçats) and 6 Turks assigned to the city from August 10, 1720, to January 4, 1721, for the purpose of burying the dead,[8] only a few survived. Gigantic trenches were dug by beggars and peasants impressed into service and were filled with quicklime for receiving the corpses.[9] Two towers or dungeons were used for the same purpose. But so great was the problem of the disposal of the dead that many decomposed bodies lay on the streets for weeks.[10]

To escape the contagion some of the citizens locked themselves in their homes, and the monks of Saint Victor and nearly all the nuns shut themselves in their monastic institutions.[11] Other French cities and provinces passed ordinances forbidding the entry of persons or goods from Marseilles. One by one all the governments

---

[6] Ibid., I, 77, 80.

[7] The summer was hot and dry at Marseilles, even as was the plague year of 1665 at London.

[8] Ibid., II, 191-192.

[9] One of them was 22 toises long, 8 toises wide, and 14 pieds deep (ibid., I, 104). Since a toise was 6.39459 feet and a pied 12.787 inches, this made the trench 140 feet long, 51 feet wide, and 14.9 feet deep (ibid., I, 104).

[10] On September 6, 1720, 15,000 corpses were lying on the streets of Marseilles, according to Pichatty de Croissainte (ibid., I, 86-88). For his initiative in removing these disintegrated bodies from the most congested region and burying them (at his own expense) on September 16, the Chevalier Roze was hailed as one of the heroes of the time. Several portraits of him at this task have been drawn, and a tablet to his memory stands in Marseilles. Nearly all of the workers who assisted him that day died; Roze himself fell sick and narrowly escaped death. Gaffarel and Duranty (op. cit., p. 208) call him and his men "the Saviors of Marseilles." Cf. Pièces historiques, I, 95-98. Roze also provided personally the funds for the maintenance of a hospital (ibid., I, 53).

[11] Ibid., I, 233-234.

of Europe save the Turkish quarantined themselves against communication with the doomed city and with Provence generally.[12]

The plague, however, did not remain confined to Marseilles. From the first of August to the first of October, 1720, according to an official report from Cardin Lebret, intendant of Provence, to the controller-general, dated June 1, 1721, it made its way into twenty-five communities in southern Provence; before January 1, 1721, it had spread into a total of forty-nine communities in that province.[13] Aix, Toulon, and Arles were severely hit.

During the spring and summer of 1721 the epidemic spread from Provence into isolated communities in Languedoc, Auvergne, Dauphiné, and the Comtat. Correjac and La Canourgue, villages in the Gévaudan and the first two communities in Languedoc to be attacked, became infected in May. An attempt to isolate the sickness utterly failed. In August the disease spread to the more populous centers, Mende and Marvejols, and by October 10 was present in fourteen or fifteen parishes of the Gévaudan. Montpellier and the greater portion of Languedoc succeeded in escaping the epidemic, and the winter of 1721 virtually brought it to an end in that province. In Auvergne the community of St. Flour, in Dauphiné the city of Orange, and in the Comtat, Avignon, were struck heavily by the plague; but fortunately it did not go beyond their walls, and the remainder of these provinces appear to have escaped harm. In 1722 the epidemic disappeared save for sporadic cases. The numerous quarantines and disinfections were followed by a gradual restoration of trade, first within the provinces themselves, and afterwards with the rest of France and the world. Such in outline was the plague of 1720-22, in which, according to an official report sent by Lebret to the controller-general in January, 1722, Provence alone experienced 122,469 cases of sickness and lost 93,290 victims from an original population (in these places) of 292,165[14]

[12] Gaffarel and Duranty, *op. cit.*, pp. 424-429.

[13] By July 31, 1721, 7,534 persons had died in Aix, according to an elaborate report to the controller-general (Arch. Nat., G7, 1731). In a letter of April 3, 1721, Vauvenargues, first consul at Aix, stated that about 11,000 persons were left in the city, and that 6,000 of them were destitute (Arch. Nat., G7, 1729). été obligés de faire à l'occasion de la maladie contagieuse, et des secours qu'elles to this report, Marseilles alone had lost 39,115 inhabitants. ont reçus, soit de S. A. R., soit de la province" (Arch. Nat., G7, 1736). According

[14] "Etat général des dépenses que les communautés contaminées de Provence ont

What part did private, church, and state assistance play in alleviating the sufferings of the people during this trying time? Although Bertrand, one of the resident physicians of Marseilles, reported in his account of the epidemic that charity was stifled in all hearts,[15] such was not the case. Almost immediately upon receipt of the news that Marseilles was afflicted with the *peste*, several physicians and surgeons of neighboring regions, and even of Paris, volunteered their services. Neighboring towns and cities proffered their aid.[16] Rural people and others played host to the thousands who fled the city. Vauvenargues, first consul and later commandant at Aix, and Chancellor Roze at Marseilles gave liberally of their fortunes to aid their unfortunate communities. The gallant service of the consuls, the aldermen, the military leaders, the physicians, the surgeons, the hospital attendants, and others should not go unmentioned. Although a few who were able to render service fled, the vast proportion remained and acquitted themselves heroically at their post of duty.

Contemporaries paid high tribute to the Catholic clergy for their courage and service. Here and there a priest fled and a colony of monks locked their doors, but for everyone who shunned his duties perhaps a dozen moved courageously among the sick and dying, especially attentive to administer the Last Sacrament. A number of Jesuits from other sections came to the afflicted regions and labored; and the Oratorians, forbidden by Belsunce, bishop of Marseilles, to administer the Last Sacrament, because of his grudge toward them, undertook to nurse the sick.[17] Great numbers of Jesuits, Oratorians, and others in orders died at their post throughout the plague area, and perhaps no other profession, unless that of the surgeons, lost so large a percentage of men.[18]

The chief hero of the plague in the eyes of his contemporaries (for he acquired an international reputation) was Belsunce, bishop of Marseilles, and a Jesuit, who was constantly on the streets ab-

[15] Quoted by Gaffarel and Duranty, *op. cit.*, p. 91.

[16] *Pièces historiques*, I, 43 ff.

[17] J. Michelet, *Oeuvres* (Paris, 1887), XVII, 313. The Oratorians were enemies of the bull *Unigenitus*. The bitterness between the Jesuits and the Oratorians at the time of the plague is to be seen also in a number of acrimonious narratives of the plague, in which each group (and more especially the Jesuit) belittles the courage and service shown by the other.

[18] Gaffarel and Duranty, *op. cit.*, pp. 105, 155.

solving the dying and dispensing charities among the poor. A more obscure hero was the Père Millay, likewise a Jesuit, who administered soup to the sick on the streets of Marseilles, and who himself later died from the plague.[19] The bishop of Toulon and the archbishop of Aix won the plaudits of Lebret, who wrote to the controller-general of their charities and heroic work in confessing the dying. In Paris the curé of Saint-Sulpice collected 100,000 livres in the winter of 1720-21 for the plague sufferers of Provence;[20] and the Pope, on the suggestion of the bishop of Avignon, sent in the autumn of 1720 three vessels laden with grain.[21]

Nevertheless, the church and the public, despite their praiseworthy efforts, failed dismally to provide the needed assistance. The Last Sacrament no doubt proved a great consolation to the sick and the dying, but the stricken communities needed food, medicine, nursing, and other necessities of life, of which the church and the public gave but a pittance in comparison to the need. Accordingly, it was necessary for the state to intervene.

Each town and city spent the funds in its treasury, and then proceeded, after obtaining permission from the controller-general, to borrow heavily from financiers or from the province.[22] The Estates of Provence in their turn borrowed heavily.[23] The government in

[19] The latter (Vintimille) distributed 150,000 livres which had been placed in his hands for charities (*Pièces historiques*, I, 71). Some years afterwards he was translated to the archbishopric of Paris.

[20] Letter from Beaumont, agent of Provence at Paris, to the controller-general, Jan. 3, 1721 (Arch. Nat., G7, 1667).

[21] Two of these vessels fell into the hands of the Turks (Barbary pirates?), who, when they learned their mission, promptly released them (Gaffarel and Duranty, *op. cit.*, p. 293).

[22] In a letter dated July 20, 1721, Lebret stated that Marseilles had already paid out 178,403 livres in provincial funds, was in debt to the province for more than 400,000 livres additional, and was "infinitely" in debt to certain citizens of Provence and Languedoc. In the same letter he mentioned that Aix had borrowed 56,028 livres of provincial funds for purchasing cattle from Languedoc (Arch. Nat., G7, 1731). Mende, in Languedoc, borrowed 30,000 livres in August, 1721 "for aid to the plague-stricken" (Ville de Mende, *Inventaire-sommaire des archives communales antérieures à 1790*, drafted by M. Ferdinand André, Mende, 1885, BB 10). Toulouse, likewise in Languedoc, was granted permission to borrow 300,000 livres to make preparations for an attack of the plague which did not come (De Bernage to the controller-general, Jan. 6, 1721, with marginal note of approval, Arch. Nat., G7, 1729). These are but a few instances. The provinces not only loaned but gave great sums to the cities, towns, and villages visited by the plague. For many illustrations, see *Inv.-som . . . Bouches-du-Rhône*, C 65.

[23] More strictly, the borrowing was done by the *procureurs nés et joints*, represented by their agent in Paris, the syndic De Beaumont. Numerous expenditures by the province in meeting the emergency are listed (*ibid.*, C 65, ff. 198-370v; 911).

late August or early September came to the aid of the afflicted region with 200,000 livres in gold and 500,000 livres in banknotes.[24] Beginning in December, 1720, the government sent monthly gifts of 60,000 livres, as repeated appeals for aid came from Lebret, Vauvenargues, the Marquis de Caylus, certain bishops, and others.[25]

Requests for aid became greater in the spring of 1721, when the plague (after slackening during the winter) renewed its virulence and began to rage in Aix, Arles, Toulon, and many smaller places.[26] The government, realizing the gravity of the situation, took more adequate steps to meet it. In early March it sent 400,000 livres (apparently as a loan) to the province;[27] on April 1 it granted the province permission (by royal declaration) for the floating of a second loan of 1,000,000 livres;[28] and in June it established a fund of 3,000,000, borrowed from the tax farmers (*receveurs généraux des finances des généralités des pais d'élections*) for provisioning Provence. This last, news of which brought instant joy to Lebret and to all France, was to be financed by an increase of 3 deniers in the *capitation* of 1722 throughout all the *pays d'élections* and in such *pays d'états* as would agree to collect it.[29] The money was to go

[24] *Ibid.*, C 65, f 210.

[25] The record of these payments through April, 1721, is found in Arch. Nat., G7, 1729. Gaffarel and Duranty (*op. cit.*, p. 387) record one of 60,000 livres made in the late summer of 1722.

[26] If Barbier is to be believed (see entry in his *Journal* for May 26, 1721), the government experienced a case of the jitters in late May. The king considered leaving Paris, and preparations were made for turning the Hôpital Saint-Louis into a *peste* lazaretto.

[27] Letters from Lebret and Vauvenargues, respectively, to the controller-general, March 9 and 16, 1721 (Arch. Nat., G7, 1729). Lebret in his letter mentioned the receipt of 214,000 livres in December, 1720, which, he said, had served to meet expenses until two days previous.

[28] Permission for floating the first million had been granted by the council of state on October 17, 1720. The money was to be borrowed in the open market, at Paris or elsewhere. Such difficulty did De Beaumont meet, however, that late in the year he had obtained only 100,000 livres. Whether the money market subsequently became more fluid and De Beaumont was able to obtain from it the 214,000 livres sent to Provence in December and the 400,000 livres sent in March, or whether this money had to be advanced by the government, is not clear. Of the two millions, oddly enough, it seems that the government spent only 1,361,250 livres (*Inv.-som . . . Bouches-du-Rhône*, C 1451; "Extrait du Memoire remis par Sr. de Beaumont sindic de Provence, sur la maladie contagieuse qui regne dans une partie de cette province, Et sur les secours de bled, de Bestiaux et d'argent qu'il est necessaire d'y faire passer," n.d., Arch. Nat., G7, 1729).

[29] Copy of unsigned letter, apparently by one De Brou, dated June 1, 1721 (*ibid.*, G7, 1730); J. P. Papon, *Relation de la peste de Marseille . . .* (Montpellier,

for the purchase of foodstuffs (meats, grains, and vegetables), and to be placed at the disposal of the province, evidently as a gift,[30] at the rate of 300,000 livres a month. The plan went into effect in June, and thenceforward economic conditions in the province were distinctly better.[31] It so happened that shortly afterwards the plague subsided in Provence, and much of the fund went to Languedoc and the cities of Orange and Avignon.

Both national and provincial governments sent large numbers of physicians and surgeons, and some apothecaries, into the epidemic areas. The royal government sent several members of the medical faculties of Montpellier and Paris, as well as other physicians, at the rate of 1,000 livres a month and the surgeons at 300 livres.[32] The intendant of Provence and the officials of the afflicted cities made arrangements directly with many physicians and surgeons in southeastern France at the time of the greatest emergency. The contracts varied in price. Some of the physicians demanded prodigious sums,[33]

1820), p. 55; Pierre Gaxotte, *Louis the Fifteenth and his Times,* tr. J. Lewis May (London, 1934), p. 51; Leclercq, *op. cit.,* III, 90.

Languedoc refused to give the 150,000 livres requested of it (memorandum of the controller-general's office, dated June 9, 1721, Arch. Nat., G7, 1730), despite the fact that it had profited from sales of provisions to Provence; and the intendant of Auvergne *(a pays d'élection),* another province that had profited, replied that his province would not be able to give any aid if attacked (Brunet d'Evry to the controller-general, June 12, 1721, *ibid.*).

The controller-general called upon not only the *pays d'états,* but also upon the bishops and archbishops of the kingdom for contributions toward this end. They were asked to collect alms in their dioceses for stricken Provence. Some replied that they had long been taking alms for this purpose; others, that they had sent their alms to the fire sufferers of Rennes, or that their dioceses had been ruined by the collapse of Law's System *(ibid.,* G7, 1730, 1731).

[30] Most of the correspondence implies that it was a gift, but the present writer is not certain of this interpretation. If it was a gift, it was consonant with the French practice, as of 1709, of levying a tax on the affluent classes for the support of the poor.

[31] The controller-general announced the inauguration of the plan by sending to each of the intendants, bishops, and archbishops a bulky, printed *Instruction* of sixty or more pages, compiled evidently by the council of health, with elaborate details for meeting all problems arising from the plague.

[32] "Extrait des deliberations prises sous le bon plaisir de S. A. R. au conseil de santé tenu à Paris le 26 Janvier 1722" *(ibid.,* G7, 1736); "Etat des Medicins, Apoticaires, Chirugiens majors Et garcons chirugiens, qui sont servi dans la Ville de Marseille pendant la contagion, et qui sont envoyés par ordre de S. A. R. ou sur les affiches des Eschevins" *(ibid.,* G7, 1738-1745).

[33] Pons, a member of the medical faculty of Montpellier, demanded 200 livres a day while serving at Marseilles, and a pension of 3,000 livres a year. *Mirabile dictu!* he was engaged. His case is mentioned in the *états* sent on October 6, 1721, to the controller-general by the *échevins* of Marseilles *(ibid.,* G7, 1734). These

and because of the desperate situation the provincial government had to accede to their demands. Later, toward the conclusion of the epidemic, the controller-general, on the request of Lebret and the recommendation of the council of health, revised all the agreements made directly by physicians with provincial and municipal officials, and specified uniform payment to physicians, surgeons and surgeon apprentices.[34] A small allowance was made for travel.

Among the physicians who rendered magnificent service were Chicoyneau, Verny, and Deydier, of the medical faculty of Montpellier, and Bailly, Lemoine, and the Abbé Quintrandy, of the medical faculty of Paris—all sent by the royal government. Bailly and Lemoine labored faithfully at Marvejols and La Canourgue, in the Gévaudàn, despite the fact that each was stricken, Lemoine twice, with the plague. They took to their beds only under compulsion and were up serving the public within a few days.[35] The Abbé Quintrandy, sent by the government to Aix to experiment with the remedy of Garrus, which he used with success, served gallantly and requested nothing in the end for his services.

The Abbé aroused the animosity of local physicians at Aix because he failed to charge for his services, and there was fear of a riot.[36] Nowhere, however, did the physicians and surgeons sent by

états, four in number, give an account of the financial arrangements made with each physician and surgeon who aided in combating the plague at Marseilles, an account of his services both as to time and quality, and in some instances recommendations of changes. One contract recommended for revision was that of Pons.)

At the opposite extreme, one Vigne, physician, and Faure, apothecary, of Mazères, near Perpignan in the French Pyrenees, made application to serve without mention of financial recompense, and were sent to Arles (memorandum of the controller-general's office, dated June 22, 1721, ibid., G7, 1730). The German physician Antoine Mulshenoge ("alias Melchisédech") came to Aix and served for 40 livres a month (Inv.-som . . . Bouches-du-Rhône, C 66, f 109).

[34] "Copie de la lettre de M. le Contrôleur général à M. Le Bret le 31 janvier 1722" (Arch. Nat., G7, 1736). The prescribed method of payment was that recommended by the council of health at its meeting of January 26.

[35] Thirty of forty letters from these two physicians, reporting on the progress of the epidemic, are in Arch. Nat., G7, 1729 ff. In the same cartons of documents are several letters from various officials in southeastern France praising the work of the two men. De Bernage included them in the list of those recommended for graces because of meritorious service during the epidemic.

[36] So stated both Vauvenargues and Lebret in letters of February 5 and 10, 1721, to the controller-general (ibid., G7, 1729). Lebret added, however, that the Montpellier physicians, Chicoyneau and Verny, had encouraged the animosity, because, as he explained, of their dislike for the spagiriques, or those who used chemical remedies. The well-known rivalry between the medical schools of Paris and Montpellier might have been a factor.

the government or the province charge their patients for medical attention, and it was natural that much hostility resulted between them and the local physicians. Moreover, the imported physicians, according to Bertrand of Marseilles, displayed an unbearable haughtiness; in his opinion they were less capable than the native physicians. Furthermore, a number of the imported physicians remained after the plague had ceased in the towns and cities whither they had been sent,[37] and insisted upon payment before departure. Meanwhile their salary continued, though they performed no further service. Only after correspondence between Lebret and the controller-general and after the latter's consent that from a stipulated date the monthly salary of the idle doctors should be decreased in amount were some driven away.[38]

The total bill for the physicians, surgeons, surgeon apprentices, and apothecaries who served in Provence and Languedoc for the period of the contagion was at least 666,362 livres, with some unsettled claims outstanding. Of this sum, the expenditures and indebtedness of Marseilles amounted to 259,440 livres, that of the rest of Provence to 168,280 livres, and that of Languedoc to 238,642 livres.[39]

Of the seventeen physicians sent by the king or engaged by the province to serve at Marseilles, three died; of ninety-seven surgeons and one surgeon apprentice, thirty-one died; and four apothecaries and seven apothecary apprentices. To other places in Provence the royal or the provincial government sent eighteen physicians, forty-five surgeons, two surgeon apprentices, six apothecaries, and one apothecary apprentice. One of the physicians, five of the surgeons, one of the surgeon apprentices, and two of the apothecaries died

[37] E. Rochach (*Histoire générale de Languedoc*, XIII, 966 n. 2) cites the instance of a physician from Paris named Loyron, sent to Languedoc to combat the plague, who allegedly sent false information to Paris on several occasions in order to hold his tenure. On one occasion he reported as deaths from the plague three persons who died from mushrooms. Later he reported that persons dead of other causes had been suspected of having the plague.

[38] The physicians who served at Marseilles were reduced in pay February 1, 1722, from 1,000 livres a month to 300, the surgeons from 500 to 150, the surgeon and apothecary apprentices from 300 to 90. Five physicians, twenty surgeons, and seven surgeon or apothecary apprentices remained after this date ("Etat des Médicins, Apoticaires," etc., Arch. Nat., G7, 1738-1745).

[39] *Ibid.* Of the bill for the city of Marseilles, 215,595 livres represented the expense for medical service during the period of the plague (or, rather, up to February 1, 1722), and 43,845 livres for medical service after that date.

during the epidemic.[40]   Certain of the physicians and surgeons served for a period in Marseilles, afterwards in the province, and later in Languedoc.   The figures for Languedoc may be incomplete, but from Paris six physicians, seven surgeons, and twelve surgeon apprentices were sent there.   From other parts of Languedoc came eight physicians (four of them from Montpellier), six surgeons, and eleven surgeon apprentices.[41]   Most if not all of the physicians and surgeons sent to the plague-stricken areas were men of ability.   To be selected for the duty was regarded as an honor.

Both national and provincial governments sent large quantities of drugs into the plague regions.   Among the drugs were certain "remedies," or patent medicines, sent for free distribution among the poor by physicians, curés, and heads of hospitals.   Certain of the remedies sent at this time into southeastern France were prepared by Helvétius,[42] grandfather of the well-known eighteenth-century farmer-general and philosopher.[43]

A much more considerable item than the remedies was the drugs for disinfectant purposes.   Various solutions known as *parfums*, powerful in strength, were concocted and used upon hands, noses, and foreheads of persons as well as furniture, letters,[44] coins, and clothing. The most famous was known as the "Four Robbers."[45]   The physicians, some of the Marseilles aldermen, and even Belsunce commonly carried with them flasks of *parfum*, which they used for disinfectant purposes.   According to Pichatty de Croissainte, an alderman of Marseilles, while directing the removal of the dead from the streets,

[40] *Ibid.*   The same rate of payment prevailed for those who worked in the province as for those who served in Marseilles.   In both instances it was very high, but the work was exceedingly dangerous.

[41] "Etat des médecins Et Chirugiens qui ont été Envoyés au Soulagement des pestifferés en Languedoc," dated Jan. 9, 1723 *(ibid.).*   Bailly and Lemoine were each paid 19,000 livres for their services and 400 livres for travel expenses, and given a gratification of 3,000 livres.

[42] De Bernage to the controller general, June 24, 1721 *(ibid.,* G7, 1730).

[43] He was the author of a pamphlet, *Remèdes contre la peste* (Paris, 1721). See *Biographie universelle, ancien et moderne,* XX (Paris, 1817), 25.

[44] A large portion of the documents in the ten boxes of material relative to the *peste* in the Archives Nationales bear stains left by the disinfectant fluids.   For an account of the manner in which the *parfums* were applied, see Edme de la Poix de Freminville, *Dictionnaire ou traité de la police générale* (new ed., rev. and corrected, Paris, 1771), pp. 247, 252.

[45] *Ibid.,* pp. 262-263.   An elaborate account is given of the ingredients and mode of application.   Its base was vinegar; as a result, the *parfum* is frequently styled *vinaigre* in the documents of the time.

was hit in the face with some bandages thrown from a window. Immediately he washed his face with the disinfectant from his flask and proceeded with his work without mishap. The galley slaves engaged in burying the dead made a practice of dipping their handkerchiefs in disinfectants and tying them over their noses to purify the air, which they regarded as contaminated.[46] In homes the windows and doors were closed, and sulphur was burned as a disinfectant. Other germicides and preventives were wine, garlic, soap, and boiling water.[47]

At the conclusion of the epidemic a period of forced quarantine followed in every community, lasting forty days, in which careful fumigation was made of all houses and furniture. Physicians and surgeons and all other travelers were required for a similar period to be subjected to certain fumigating odors before being allowed to leave the plague-stricken territory. So strong were the odors that some of the physicians nearly succumbed.[48] Their clothes and the clothes of all other persons who had been sick with the *peste* were ordered to be burned, the city or regional government undertaking

[46] There was lively discussion during the plague on its cause and mode of transmission. The physicians from Montpellier, who apparently wore the elaborate, time-honored, freakish costume for plague service (see illustration, Gaffarel and Duranty, *op. cit.*, p. 96), created amazement by sitting beside their patients and feeling their swellings. It was universal belief that the malady was transmitted by direct contact, and most persons held that it was also transmitted by the air. Accordingly, an attempt was made in early August, 1720, to stamp it out in Marseilles by creating, on preconcerted notice and after the examples of ancient Greece and seventeenth-century London, a circle of fire around and through the city (*Pièces historiques*, I, 43-44). The ecclesiastics insisted that it was sent by God because of the people's sins; the pope declared that it was a visitation because of the Jansenist heresy (*ibid.*, I, 84, 110, 165-171; *Hist. gén. de Languedoc*, XIII, 947; Leclercq, *op. cit.*, III, 90-92); as a result, Belsunce marched barefoot through the streets and celebrated the mass in public (*Pièces historiques*, I, 112-113, 116-117).

Of more merit, several physicians in Marseilles, of whom Bertrand was the most vocal (he expressed his opinions in a pamphlet), asserted that the plague was caused by germs. Such an attitude was repellent to the medical fraternity of the city (Gaffarel and Duranty, *op. cit.*, pp. 111-113). But the heresy was not confined to Marseilles: it made its way into the Gévaudan, or at least found expression there in 1721 in Bailly and Lemoine (J. B. J. Goiffron, *Relations et dissertation sur la peste du Gévaudan . . .*, Lyon, 1722, "Au Lecteur" or Preface); and in 1722 it provoked a book, with favorable discussion, by Goiffron, a prominent physician of Lyons (see pp. 42, 44-45, 60, 62-65).

[47] On this last, see *Hist. gén. de Languedoc*, XIII, 964; XIV, 2115-2119.

Wine, vitriol (sulphuric acid), and *stiptique* water were used by Bailly and Lemoine in cleasing and disinfecting wounds which had been probed for pus (Goiffron, *op. cit.*, p. 13).

[48] Certain other persons, in fact, did succumb (*Pièces historiques*, II, 2-6).

to provide fresh clothing.[49]   Bedding of all persons ill with the plague was burned.   Prior to the burning a careful inventory was made of destroyed articles and kept by the government as the basis of indemnification.   The government undertook to reimburse the owners of the *Great Saint Anthony* (whose cargo was eventually ordered to be burned)[50] and also the property owners in Correjac.[51]

Perhaps the most substantial aid rendered by the national and provincial governments to the afflicted areas came in the form of provisions.   At least this aid caused the most concern and expenditure and necessitated the largest volume of correspondence between the intendants and the controller-general.

The situation was complicated by the fact that for several months prior to the outbreak of the plague Provence had experienced a famine.   Lebret, the intendant, had been obliged to resort to much correspondence and to make arrangements with various parties, within and without France, in order to provide food for that emergency,[52] which had been handled satisfactorily.   Although the harvest of 1720 in Provence was expected to provide sufficient grain for the forthcoming year, the hot, dry summer of 1720 brought a second successive crop failure.

[49] Individuals were fed by the state during the quarantine (*Hist. gén. de Languedoc*, XIII, 917; XIV, 2115-2119).

[50] Gaffarel and Duranty, *op. cit.*, p. 42.   Chataud, the captain of this ill-fated vessel, escaped the plague through imprisonment in the Château d'If.   On March 14, 1722, he petitioned for his release, insisting that he had complied with regulations and that the epidemic was not his fault (Arch. Nat. G7, 1736).

[51] The entire hamlet was burned to the ground, on official orders, even to the clothes of the people (letter from De Bernage to the Marquis de la Vrillière, Oct. 27, 1721, *ibid.*, G7, 1734).

A vast quantity of merchandise and other property was burned in France at this time as suspect of the plague.   The council of health at Paris, at its meeting of January 19, 1722, ordered the burning of twenty-eight bales (*ballots*) of English and Indian cloths "because they came from Jersey, where they might have come in contact with merchandise shipped from suspect lands" (*ibid.*, G7, 1736).   On October 14-15, 1721, the plague having spread to the lodging of the monks of Chambon at Bes, this building was burnt ("fut livré aux flammes"), together with 300 sheep, 30 cattle, and 10 horses (*Hist. gén. de Languedoc*, XIII, 962).   It seems incredible that such vast quantities of material were burned; on the other hand, the people in many places found ways of keeping material that was designated for destruction.

[52] Ever since December, 1719, it had been felt keenly both in and beyond Marseilles; the peasants were forced to live on herbs; riots were feared in Marseilles; and as late as July 6, 1720, the Duke of Orléans sent 8,000 livres in banknotes to Lebret for aid in meeting the crisis (Bibliothèque Nationale, Fonds français, 6950, 8956, 8960).

In the eighteenth century, as has been noted, it was the duty of the intendant each summer and autumn to see that his province was sufficiently provided with stores of grain and meat for the ensuing winter and spring; if food stores were insufficient, he entered into correspondence with intendants of regions where abundance prevailed, or (if there was a shortage throughout France) with the rulers of foreign states, seeking permission to purchase for his province a designated quantity of provisions. Thereupon the intendant asked of the controller-general, or rather of the council of state through him, permission to make the tentative importation, the word of the controller-general being final. Usually he merely ratified the decisions and plans of the intendants, but he was the source of great power:[53] Lebret, a veteran intendant of nearly two decades, stated on one occasion that he never dared to take action about provisioning his province without the controller-general's consent.[54]

John Law was the controller-general at the outset of the plague; from December 12, 1720, until early in 1722, Le Peletier de la Houssaye held the office; and in the closing period, Dodun, Marquis d'Herbault. All were sympathetic toward the plague-stricken regions. Law and De la Houssaye contributed personal gifts of 100,000 livres each.[55] De la Houssaye was responsible for the huge government gift or loan of 3,000,000 livres, arranged in June, 1721. Dodun continued the arrangements of De la Houssaye.[56]

In those days of slow communication much time was frequently lost in provisioning a province; the intendant had to guard against getting an oversupply as well as an undersupply. At the height of the epidemic 1,720 people in Marseilles starved for lack of food, and for most people fear of famine was even greater than that of the plague.[57] Yet, according to a report by De Beaumont, syndic and agent of Provence at Paris:

[53] Marcel Marion, *Dictionnaire des institutions de la France au XVIIe et XVIIIe siècles* (Paris, 1923), p. 143.

[54] Letter to the controller-general, Nov. 9, 1721 (Arch. Nat., G7, 1735). On this particular occasion Lebret was seeking permission to import provisions (meat and grain) from Italy.

[55] Leclercq, *op. cit.*, III, 90; *Pièces historiques*, I, 104-105.

[56] According to Leclercq (*op. cit.*, III, 89-90), the Duke of Orléans gave 600,000 livres, and the Count of Toulouse (an illegitimate son of Louis XIV by Mme de Montespan), 200,000.

[57] *Pièces historiques*, I, 114-115; Gaffarel and Duranty, *op. cit.*, p. 261.

M. Lebret gave at once all the aid that he was able to, whether in grain, or in meat, or in cash. At the same time the government, having been informed of the epidemic, gave orders for the establishment of some quarantine lines to be guarded by troops in order to prevent communication; and sent medicine, surgeons, coin, and grain.[58]

Some of the grain was purchased in the countryside of Provence, some in Languedoc, but the greater portion in the province of Guyenne, of which Bordeaux was the port.

On November 4, 1720, the Parisian government ordered Boucher, intendant of Guyenne, to purchase 6,000 *quintaux* (hundredweight) of grain for shipment to Provence, and to pay for it out of future taxes from his province. The grain was bought immediately at the prevailing high prices for a total of 79,050 livres,[59] and shipped by installments via water to Toulouse, and thence to Provence. At one moment during this trying period an ordinance by the aldermen of Marseilles compelled the bakers of that city to distribute free bread to the people.[60] By November 26, however, the food situation was alleviated; on that day Lebret wrote to De Bernage, intendant of Languedoc, that Provence was adequately supplied with grain.[61]

The shortage of meat was not great if we may believe an official report made in January, 1721, by De Beaumont, who wrote: "Meat has not been lacking in Provence during the last four months, M. Lebret having obtained some from the neighboring provinces. . . ."[62] He observed further that Lebret had made engagements with certain entrepreneurs, chief of whom was one Fulque, to send 3,881 sheep and 101 cattle each week. In fact, since September, Fulque, who was stationed in Auvergne, had sent large numbers of animals from that province. The 60,000 livres which the king's government gave monthly, beginning with December, 1720, were spent in obtaining each week (through Fulque) 2,000 sheep and 96 cattle. By January, 1721, food conditions in Marseilles had improved suffi-

[58] Arch. Nat., G7, 1729.
[59] Boucher to the controller-general, April 6, 1721 (*ibid.*).
[60] *Pièces historiques*, I, 291.
[61] Bernage to the controller-general, Dec. 8, 1720 (Arch. Nat., G7, 1729).
[62] *Ibid.* A windfall to the city of Marseilles had been the arrival of a shipload of codfish, under Captain Ponantois, at the height of the plague. Lebret stated that it was of great aid. In March, 1721, after seven or eight months of quarantine in the harbor, Ponantois was restless to go back to his fishing grounds off Isle Royale (Cape Breton Island), and Lebret wrote in his behalf to the government (Lebret to the controller-general, March 23, 1721, *ibid.*).

ciently for a marked decline in prices.[63]   Notwithstanding the improvement, some apprehension lingered.

In January, 1721, Lebret wrote to the controller-general that Fulque was holding up shipment of animals until he was paid for past shipments and that a meat shortage threatened Provence.   The Marquis de Caylus wrote on January 24 that the provincial treasury was exhausted after heavy borrowings, and that the government shipments of grain and meat had kept up the people.[64]   He expressed alarm, since the plague had spread to Arles and was threatening Toulon.   A letter written from Vauvenargues on the same day described to the controller-general the critical situation prevailing at Aix.   All the city's funds as well as heavy loans had been spent; virtually every source of taxation had dried up; all commerce had ceased; and fifty quintals of flour, in the form of bread, were distributed weekly among the poor at city expense.

In early March, 1721, the royal government, finding the epidemic spreading, sent an additional 400,000 livres to Lebret to be used in meeting the situation.[65]   Apparently this was part of a loan negotiated through De Beaumont.   The same letter from Lebret acknowledging receipt of this sum also acknowledged 214,000 livres more in December, 1720, perhaps a further part of the loan.

Throughout the spring months of 1721 Lebret was kept busy sending supplies to various communities in Provence, where the plague was raging.   In a letter of April 7 he reported to the controller-general that he had sent 2,959 sacks of wheat from Burgundy to seventeen towns and cities, 2,237 to Aix alone.[66]   Thirty-five hundred sacks had come from Guyenne and had been distributed to Martigues, Toulon, and Arles.   Other places still lacked food.   As a rule, the smaller places, according to Lebret, had sufficient wheat, while the larger places were most in need.

In early June the government's fund of 3,000,000 **livres for** Provence was announced.   Lebret, in a letter of June 10 thanking the controller-general, requested that animals to the value of 300,000

[63] See chart and table of index numbers of commodity prices, Hamilton, *op. cit.*, pp. 444-445.   With prices of 1716-17 as a base, prices in Marseilles rose from 149.6 in January, 1720, to 229.1 in December; in January, 1721, they fell to 181.4, and in February, to 175.4; in March they rose again to 191.4.

[64] Arch. Nat., G7, 1729.

[65] Lebret to the controller-general, March 9, 1721 (*ibid.*).

[66] *Ibid.*

livres be sent to Provence for the months of June and July and wheat to the value of 200,000 livres. He added that, if necessity compelled, the expenditure for wheat could be foregone, since the province had stocks of grain that would suffice for the time being.[67]

In connection with the aid of 3,000,000 livres the government agreed to issue passports to those who transported the wheat and grain into Provence, in order to avoid the duties ordinarily levied upon these shipments. Accordingly, the Marquis de la Vrillière, secretary of the regency, was asked to prepare the passports at once and place them in appropriate hands.[68]

De Bernage, intendant of Languedoc, in a letter to the controller-general, July 22, 1721, alleged that an unfortunate result of the government fund was a tremendous rise in food prices. Not only was there a rise in prices, but in Auvergne, where Fulque was stationed, the failure to obtain good animals for the provisioning of Provence caused widespread complaint. Consequently, from late July into the autumn of 1721 Lebret sent a number of requests to the controller-general that the contracts with Auvergne be terminated[69] and that meat be imported from the Barbary coast and Italy.[70] Apparently the chief result was to replace Fulque with an unscrupulous agent, who proceeded to ask exorbitant prices in order to fill his own pockets and those of his friends who had secured him the post.

If the meat-dealers of Auvergne were grafters, the citizens of Arles were supine. The generous provisioning of that city led the consuls to request that Lebret supply it with 60 quintals of wheat and 40 sheep daily, in addition to cash. When he reported the request to the controller-general, Lebret commented that it would be tantamount to furnishing the city free meat and would cost over half a million livres a month. Accordingly, he had written the consuls that Arles must pay for its meat.[71]

In a report to the controller-general on August 13 Lebret listed

[67] *Ibid.*, G7, 1730.

[68] Memorandum of a letter sent by the controller-general to the marquis, June 5, 1721 (*ibid.*).

[69] Letters of Sept. 4 and Nov. 9, 1721 (*ibid.*, G7, 1733 and 1735 respectively); also letters of complaint from the Marquis de Caylus, Aug. 14, and from one Guireine, Oct. 14 (*ibid.*, G7, 1732 and 1724, respectively).

[70] Letter of Sept. 20, 1721 (*ibid.*, G7, 1733).

[71] Letter of Aug. 2, 1721 (*ibid.*, G7, 1732).

twenty-four items, involving a total expenditure of 77,811 livres, recently given or advanced to various communities.[72] Among the items were 50 quintals of wheat to mariners from Arles living aboard vessels on the Rhône; 2 quintals of sulphur (for disinfectant purposes) and 30 pieces of waxed cloth (worn by physicians and surgeons); 120 quintals of quicklime (for burial of the dead) to Maillane and St. Remy; 2 quintals of *parfum* (disinfectants) for Pertuis; 70 sheep, 50 loads *(charges)* of wheat, and 2 *minots* (78 liters) of salt to St. Remy, in addition to numerous grants and loans to towns and cities afflicted with the plague.

After the plague subsided in Provence there was still need of assistance. To the controller-general on October 13 Lebret wrote that large numbers of the poor would have to be fed during the forthcoming winter because of the interruptions of commerce occasioned by the plague. Hospitals, he observed, would provide for the care of these people, but he named communities where the need was especially great. Marseilles, Aix, and Toulon, though entirely free of the *peste*, still had to be supplied with meat. He had no idea how much the government had sent, or how much the province. All the cities had made heavy expenditures. They had been compelled to pay in cash (their credit having been severely curtailed by the plague), and now coin was no longer obtainable. Accordingly, it was essential that the government continue its aid.[73]

Beginning with September, 1721, De Bernage, intendant of Languedoc, made appeals to the controller-general for assistance as the plague reached epidemic proportions in his province. Languedoc was a fertile agricultural region that ordinarily grew much more grain of all types than was needed. There had been heavy sales to Provence during the first twelve months of the plague. In June, 1721, the approval of Paris was asked for a conditional contract to ship a large consignment of oats, barley, rye, and wheat to Italy. Permission was asked again in August. Although he showed himself cautious at times, De Bernage did not seem to realize the ravages that an outbreak of the plague would make on his resources. The controller-general, who was more level-headed, advised him in April and August to guard his stores and make no further shipments of wheat abroad.[74]

[72] *Ibid.*   [73] *Ibid.*, G7, 1734.
[74] Letters from De Bernage to the controller-general, April 11 (acknowledging

To Languedoc the government diverted a considerable portion[75] of the three million livres originally destined entirely for Provence without arousing protests from Lebret or anyone else in Provence. Indeed, a better spirit was shown in Provence than in most of the other provinces of southeastern France during this epidemic. Certain of her neighbors, Auvergne and Languedoc, as well as the more distant provinces of Burgundy and Guyenne, derived large profits from the plague there. The wholesale dealers of these regions, instead of offering wares at reduced prices to Provence, asked the normal price or more, and in the case of Auvergne, as already mentioned, sent goods of poor quality. Most of the neighboring provinces, including Lyonnais and Dauphiné, manifested little or no spirit of generosity. Even in Provence the merchants tried to exploit the buying public by charging exorbitant prices;[76] and the people in those regions untouched by the plague (incidentally seventeen out of twenty-two were untouched)[77] refused to pay taxes, obliging Lebret to make collection by threat of force.[78] Had Lebret not made these collections, the provincial treasury would have been even more handicapped than it was.

The national government was slow to realize the seriousness of the situation. The aid rendered in 1720 was relatively small. Not until December of that year did it begin sending its grants of 60,000 livres a month. It was an established principle in the eighteenth century that the provinces should do all that they could to handle

the order of April 1), June 16 and Aug. 11, 1721 (Arch. Nat., G7, 1729, 1730, 1732). In his letter of April 11, De Bernage applauded the order as a wise act; in that of June 16, he reported that Languedoc still had a surplus of wheat from the harvest of 1720; in that of August 11, he acknowledged the new government order of August 1, forbidding exportation, against which he mildly protested. At length on September 1 he described the poor harvest of 1721 in Languedoc and suggested that Provence thenceforth be allowed to draw her grain supplies from the Levant. He even thought that Languedoc should import some grain, to drive down prices, feed the troops maintaining the blockade barriers (about the infected district), and provide against extension of the plague (ibid., G7, 1733).

[75] From December, 1721, 100,000 livres were sent monthly for aid in the way of food to the poor in the plague-infested regions of Languedoc (memorandum on the back of De Bernage's letter of Nov. 24, 1721, ibid., G7, 1735; Hist. gén. de Languedoc, XIII, 965-966).

[76] Gaffarel and Duranty, op. cit., pp. 262-266.

[77] Six hundred and thirty communities in Provence escaped the plague; some sixty-nine others were attacked.

[78] The archbishop of Aix to the controller-general, Feb. 21, 1721; and Lebret to the controller-general, April 3 (Arch. Nat., G7, 1729).

their own charities before calling upon the central government to render assistance. Thus the failure of the government in 1720 to do all that it should was not without extenuation. When the government realized the helplessness of the afflicted regions, it did a creditable job of rendering aid. According to an official "Account of the Receipt and Expense Made by Sr. Geoffrey for the Contagion, from the first of June, 1721, to January 23, 1723," the government advanced to the stricken communities 3,278,571 livres, and collected in taxes for this purpose only 2,362,545 livres; in other words, it sustained a deficit of 916,026 livres in this work.[79]

Possibly as a result of a suggestion by De Bernage in August, 1721, an order was issued by the controller-general in the autumn of that year removing duties on all grains, vegetables, and flour shipped from one part of France to another.[80] Here was a temporary and partial establishment of internal freedom of commerce on foodstuffs in France.

No account has been given of the plague at Orange in Dauphiné, Saint-Flour in Auvergne, and Avignon in the Comtat, though all three suffered therefrom and received bounteous charities from the national and provincial governments. It is noteworthy that this was true of Avignon, though situated in papal territory.[81] The city of Orange was so well treated that its citizens wrote a letter of appreciation to the controller-general[82]—one of few towns that did so. Marring the otherwise excellent demeanor of this city was the practice of its board of health, fifty in number, to dine daily at the city's expense in the Hôtel de Ville. One taxpayer protested to the national government against this abuse, but for his pains received a reprimand from the council of health, at Paris, and an order to mind his own affairs.[83]

If the government was kindly in assisting the plague-stricken regions, it was also strict in its insistence that the health of the rest

---

[79] *Ibid.*, G7, 1738-1745.

[80] Bernage de St. Maurice (son of De Bernage in Languedoc) intendant of Montauban, to the controller-general, Oct. 15, 1721 (*ibid.*, G7, 1734). Duties on meat had been removed by the *Instruction* of June, 1721.

[81] "Extrait des délibérations prises sous le bon plaisir de S. A. R. au conseil de santé le 20e 8bre 1721" (*ibid.*, G7, 1735).

[82] Letter from the consuls, Nov. 12, 1721 (*ibid.*).

[83] "Extrait des délibérations prises sous le bon plaisir de S. A. R. au conseil de santé tenu à Paris le 26 Janvier 1722" (*ibid.*, G7, 1736).

of France be safeguarded. A series of elaborate quarantine measures for southeastern France was issued during August and September, 1720, by the parlement of Toulouse.[84] A pamphlet entitled *Instruction*, issued in June, 1721, carried information on sanitation and disinfection. The council of health that met twice weekly in Paris, composed largely of eminent physicians, was concerned not only with the infected areas, but also with guarding the noninfected ones. Among the measures taken were the forced disinfection of all persons and houses and a quarantine of forty days in every city or community following the cessation of the plague within its bounds.[85] Commerce within the provinces of Languedoc and Provence was gradually restored during 1722 and early 1723. From early January, 1722, a degree of freedom of trade within the province was allowed to Languedoc (between the communities recovered from the plague and those that had escaped it).[86] On February 23 the council of health at Paris granted similar privilege of internal free trade to Provence.[87] Even at the last of March, however, no commodities could be shipped from Provence to the rest of France.[88] Not until December 1, 1722, were full privileges of commerce restored between the two provinces, since a few sporadic cases of the plague occurred in each province.[89] And to enforce these regulations many battalions of soldiers (twenty in Languedoc alone) stood guard around the infected areas, as they had done since the beginning of

[84] Several "Extraits des Registres du Parlement" for these two months, containing interesting ideas on sanitation and disinfection, are found in Arch. Nat., H 1644.

[85] *Hist. gén. de Languedoc*, XIII, 967; Gaffarel and Duranty, *op. cit.*, pp. 332, 467, 515, 583.

[86] "Extrait des délibérations prises . . . au Conseil de Santé tenu à Paris le 5 Janvier 1722" (Arch. Nat., G7, 1736). De Bernage was dissatisfied, wishing greater freedom; Lebret was equally so, asking the same privileges for Provence (letters of Jan. 22 and Feb. 9, respectively, to the controller-general, *ibid.*).

[87] "Extrait des délibérations . . . le 23 fever 1722" (*ibid.*).

[88] "Extrait des délibérations . . . le 30 mars 1722" (*ibid.*, G7, 1736).

[89] Even then, and until January 15, 1723, Mende and Avignon were isolated (*Hist. gén. de Languedoc*, XIII, 969).

The city of Marseilles had a few spasmodic cases of the plague during 1722 and 1723 (*Inv.-som . . . Bouches-du-Rhône*, C 908; Gaffarel and Duranty, *op. cit.*, pp. 375-429).

The reopening of trade between the two provinces was marked by a jubilant celebration. Dances, dinners, fireworks displays, illuminations, and parades were held (*Hist. gén. de Languedoc*, XIII, 969-970).

the plague, in an effort to isolate the epidemic.[90] The last quarantine measures on trade were not removed until early 1723.[91]

Something did stay the epidemic and confine it to narrow limits in southeastern France. But for these sanitary measures the plague might have been vastly worse. It is interesting to note that this outbreak of the bubonic plague was the last in France, although it continued endemic in the Near East, and several large outbreaks occurred in other European countries in the eighteenth century.[92] French ports on several occasions were obliged to take strong quarantine measures against it.[93] No doubt the memory of this plague and of the *Great Saint Anthony* lingered.

It is perhaps impossible to ascertain the total expenditures—municipal, provincial, and national—in fighting the plague of 1720-22. Lebret submitted to the controller-general on February 10, 1722, an elaborate account sheet for Provence, showing the national and provincial expenditures (which he lumped together) up to that date. They amounted to 5,878,292 livres, and he noted that this statement of expenditures in his province was not complete, since he had not yet received the information about expenditures in five communities: namely, Noves, Maillane, St. Anastasie, Toulon, and Apt. The expenses in these communities, he thought, would perhaps increase the total bill by 360,658 livres.[94] Nor was the expense yet ended, for among other items the province still had on its hands many physicians and surgeons to be paid, and some lines of blockade to be maintained, at a combined expenditure of 30,000 or more écus (about 90,000 livres) a month.

On all the regions of southeastern France which experienced the plague the expenses were great, and a burden of debt weighed for years, especially on Provence. According to Gaffarel and Duranty, authors of an excellent history of this plague, the national govern-

[90] Memorandum of the controller-general's office, dated May 25, 1722 (Arch. Nat., G7, 1737).

[91] Gaffarel and Duranty, *op. cit.*, pp. 424, 427-428.

[92] Arturo Castigliono, *A History of Medicine*, tr. from the Italian and ed. E. B. Krumbhaar (New York, 1940). p. 638.

[93] Gaffarel and Duranty, *op. cit.*, pp. 433-434.

[94] The account sheet itself is dated January 19, 1722, but the letter accompanying it is dated February 10 (Arch. Nat., G7, 1736).

The parlement of Provence in September, 1722, estimated that Provence had lost more than 100,000 persons from the plague, and 15,000,000 livres (*Pièces historiques*, II, 134).

ment, by a decision of November 1, 1723, remitted a total of 4,500,-
000 livres in taxes, in Provence to spread out over fifteen years
(1723-37).[95]

In the aftermath of the epidemic the government bestowed a
large number of pensions and gratifications (about 170 in Provence
alone) upon citizens who had rendered distinguished service during
the period of the plague. These graces were recommended by the
intendants. On the list sent by Lebret the particular service of each
individual was given, and also the award was recommended.[96] Most
of those honored were provincial and municipal officials who had
remained and worked valiantly at their posts; others were military
figures who had maintained the cordons; a few were physicians,
Jesuits, or men in smaller stations. To a few of the most distinguished personages, Lebret recommended decorations (of an order)
rather than monetary awards. Among those on his recommended
list were the intendant De Bernage and the first consul Vauvenargues.
For himself Lebret asked and received nothing. Yet the record reveals him as perhaps the greatest hero of the plague. On him depended the welfare of a province, and he performed his duties with
the untiring industry, calmness, and sober judgment of a veteran intendant. He represented the intendancy system at its best, even
as did his father before him; and he was in turn followed by a son
as intendant, and a grandson as a leading French official at the outbreak of the Revolution.

Very clearly the French government of the early eighteenth
century handled the situation differently from the manner in which
a great nation today would handle it. It was slow and close-fisted;
but communication was slow, and money was worth at least five
times what it is today. Moreover, a great deal more was expected
of local regions in caring for their own needs than is the case today.
Though the government was slow and bungling, with its creaky,
"red-tape" mercantilism, its intentions and its efforts were paternalistic. It was without question interested in the welfare of its
subjects.

[95] *Op. cit.*, p. 550; *Inv.-som . . . Bouches-du-Rhône*, C 66 (f 188v),2277.

[96] The gratifications given for service in Provence amounted to 106,600 livres,
and the pensions (annual expenditures) to 22,450 livres (Arch. Nat., G7, 1738-
1745).

CHAPTER VIII

MEDICAL AID BEYOND HOSPITAL WALLS

Before 1789

THE EPIDEMIC of 1720-22 was by far the greatest, but not the only one, in eighteenth-century France. Epidemics were common.[1] There was perhaps not a year in which the single province of Brittany did not suffer an epidemic of some type.[2] The most severe were those of dysentery and typhoid, which after 1757 were more or less endemic in the province.[3] Other epidemics were smallpox, scarlet fever, and possibly malaria. The mortality was staggering; of those attacked, one fourth often died. For the eighteen years 1770-87 deaths exceeded births in Brittany by 80,128,[4] and the references to epidemics in the *Collection des inventaires sommaires des archives départementales antérieures à 1790* and in other documents reveal that many provinces suffered the bitter experience of Brittany.[5]

In most epidemics, from the beginning to the end of the century, government aid was similar to that rendered in the great bubonic plague of 1720-22. The intendant received frequent reports from his subdelegate on the scene and transmitted them to the office of the controller-general of finance at Paris. Only in the larger epidemics, however, was it necessary for the government to send money or medical aid from outside the province. Usually the generality was able to care for itself. In an emergency the intendant sent to the stricken community physicians and surgeons, as well as "remedies" (patent medicines) and often money to be distributed among the needy by curés, judges, city officials, or other citizens of

---

[1] See A. Dupuy's excellent study, *Les épidémies en Bretagne au XVIIIe siècle*, which appeared as an extended article, in four installments, in *Annales de Bretagne*, Vols. I-III (Rennes, 1886-88), and also separately in book form. It is based on archival study.

[2] *Ibid.*, II, 30.

[3] *Ibid.*, II, 41. Dupuy's diagnoses of disease, however, were challenged by the eminent physician Mauricet. See below, pp. 159, 160 n.

[4] Dupuy's figures for deaths are 972,242, and those for births 892,119, based upon statistical reports of the intendants of Brittany (*ibid.*, II, 49).

[5] See, for instance, *Inv.-som . . . Côte d'Or*, C 369-72; *Inv.-som . . . l'Aube*, C 1166; F. Dumas, *op. cit.*, pp. 367-370.

integrity; and for just such an occasion he was expected always to keep on hand a small percentage of the tax money from the province, called the "free funds of the *capitation*." After an epidemic the government often made grants for the economic recovery of the afflicted communities. Thus in 1775 the controller-general extended to Brittany 10,000 livres to enable the poorer farmers in parishes hit by epidemics to sow their farms;[6] in 1779 he granted the generality of Tours 80,000 livres because of an epidemic;[7] and in 1784 he set aside 80,000 livres for those in Poitou who had suffered from the epidemic of 1783.[8]

As early as 1717 the royal government sent remedies for distribution in the town of Le Mans,[9] which was suffering from an epidemic of dysentery and fever.[10] In 1710, when several regions in what later became the department of Yonne experienced epidemics, possibly as a result of privation during the famine of 1709-10, the government sent skilled physicians to combat them.[11] In September, 1722, an epidemic of dysentery reigned in several localities of Auvergne, and the intendant sent a surgeon, some remedies, and 1,000 livres by way of relief.[12] In 1741-42 approximately 80,000 died in Brittany in a very severe epidemic, diagnosed as dysentery by Dupuy and as typhus by the physician Mauricet.[13] The government, the province, and individuals contributed their respective shares of aid.[14] During the same period there was also an epidemic at Thiers, in Auvergne, where a private company, with government consent, was making experiments with rice-growing. When the fever, evidently malaria, took a heavy toll, so much local opposition to the rice plantation was aroused that the council of state withdrew

[6] Dossier: "Bretagne. Secours demandés pour les cas fortuits, 1724 et 1757 et 1779" (Arch. Nat., H 565).

[7] Babeau, *op. cit.*, p. 331.

[8] "Généralité de Poitiers. État de distribution en masse de la somme de 150,000 livres accordée par sa Majesté en la Généralité de Poitiers" (Arch. Nat., H 1419).

[9] In the generality of Tours.

[10] Boislisle and Brotonne, *op. cit.*, II, No. 1325.

[11] Abbé Bouvier, *Histoire de l'assistance publique dans le département de l'Yonne jusqu'en 1789* (Paris, 1901), p. 115.

[12] Brunet d'Evry to the controller-general, Sept. 7, 1722 (Arch. Nat., G7, 1737). He intended to replace the 1,000 livres by a slight increase in the taxes of a neighboring election.

[13] Dr. Alph. Mauricet, *Histoire des épidémies de maladies fébriles de 1792 à 1851* . . . (Vannes, 1883), Introduction, p. iii.

[14] Dupuy, *op. cit.*, II, 30-34. Dupuy is not very specific in describing this aid.

its concession and the rice company was forced to abandon its experiments. During this epidemic the government and church generously contributed aid: the intendant sent a physician to the scene to assist those of Thiers; Fleury, from Paris, sent 2,000 livres; and Massillon, bishop of the diocese, and the intendant provided the 200 livres a day required to feed the poor.[15]

In 1757-58 there occurred in Brittany the great epidemic, known then and since as the *Maladie de Brest*, second in notoriety among the French epidemics of the century, and identified by Dupuy variously as typhoid fever[16] and typhus.[17] The disease was introduced by two French naval vessels coming from Louisburg, Canada, and docking at Brest on November 4, 1757. When nearly all of the more than 4,000 sailors on the ships were taken ill, they were quickly transported to the hospitals of the city, where they were placed pell-mell.[18] Physicians, surgeons, and drugs were then rushed to the scene, and the government sent 150,000 livres by way of aid. But the malady defied efforts to combat it, made its way from the hospitals to the homes of the city, and thence spread throughout most of Brittany.[19] No complete statistics, or even estimates, of the mortality, the costs, and the aid rendered are available; but approximately 10,000 died in the hospitals at Brest alone, and more than 3,483 died in the city outside hospital walls.[20] The mad excitement of the epidemic, the helplessness of the people, and the aid rendered suggested a repetition of the famous *Peste de Marseille* on a smaller scale. Once again galley slaves were put to work, and when 850 of them fell sick, other persons were impressed into service, and carts were commandeered for burying the dead and cleaning

[15] Paul M. Bondois, "Un essai de culture exotique sous l'ancien régime: La 'Peste de Riz' de Thiers (1741)," *Revue d'histoire économique et sociale*, XVI, 611-638.

[16] *Op. cit.*, II, 20, 41, 47.

[17] *Op. cit.*, II, 36, 39. Mauricet, while hesitant at identifying it, criticizes Dupuy's blunder in confounding typhoid and typhus as one disease. He himself regards it as military fever (*op. cit.*, Introduction, pp. iii-iv).

[18] At the first physicians diagnosed the disease as the scurvy. This error led to its spread (*ibid.*).

[19] Dupuy describes its ravages outside Brest (*op. cit.*, II, 36-40).

[20] Gilbert Cuzent, *L'hospice civile et les hôpitaux de Brest* (Brest, 1889), pp. 49-50. Cuzent devotes several pages (42-50) to this epidemic. A more extended account is given by P. Levot, *Histoire de ville et du port de Brest* (Paris, 1865), Vols. II and III.

the streets.[21]   Five of the fifteen physicians, 150 of the surgeons
(many of whom had been sent from other points in the province
and from Paris), and more than 200 nurses *(infirmiers)* perished in
Brest alone.[22]   Again, as in the *Peste de Marseille*, came the sanitary provisions, such as the removal of the *abattoirs* outside the city
limits[23] and the burning of the mattresses used by the sailors, the
government bearing the expense in the latter case.[24]   Finally came
the government pensions and gratifications to the families of physicians, surgeons, and apothecaries who died in service during the
epidemic.[25]

These were but a few of the multitude of epidemics in eighteenth-
century France.   After 1760 a steady increase of interest on the
part of government, province, and city in meeting the menace of
recurring epidemics brought larger appropriations, better medical
organization, and speedier attention.   One of the functions of the
Royal Society of Medicine, founded in 1776, was to keep in correspondence through its secretary, Vicq d'Azyr, with the physicians
of the provinces, to learn of maladies that afflicted provincial localities, and to dispatch directions and the means for combating them.
In times of epidemic the government sent to it the reports of the
intendants and physicians.   The Society itself founded a journal,
arranged meetings and discussions among the physicians and surgeons,
printed memoirs on medical matters, and promoted medical essay
contests, with prizes to the winning papers.[26]

In the decade following the birth of this Society at least four
generalities (those of Paris, Grenoble, Poitiers, and Rennes), with
government permission, set up establishments or organizations for
meeting epidemics.[27]   At Rennes, Bertrand de Molleville set up an

[21] Cuzent, *op. cit.*, p. 47.

[22] *Ibid.*, p. 49.

[23] *Ibid.*

[24] *Inv.-som . . . Ille-et-Vilaine*, C 2532.

[25] "Extrait de l'État des pensions et gratifications extraordinaires accordées aux
familles des Chirurgiens, Médecins et apothicaires de Rennes et de Quimper morts
à Brest de la maladie Épidémique.   300 livres de gratification extraordre au sr
Le Roy fils du chirugien de Rennes mort de Brest" (Arch. Nat., F15, 396).

[26] Dupuy, *op. cit.*, II, 218.

[27] Mention of the first three establishments is made by De la Millière in a letter
of May 2, 1785, to De la Cypierre, who also had applied for one in the generality
of Orléans (Arch. Nat., F15, 230).   The request was in all likelihood granted to
the generality of Orléans.   As for the organization in the generality of Rennes (or
Brittany), see H. Sée, *op. cit., Annales de Bretagne*, XXIV, 657.

inspector-general of epidemics for the province of Brittany with whom the physicians and surgeons working with epidemics were to correspond. Thus the provinces copied features of the government's plan of medical organization. The expense of this service was paid from the "free funds of the *capitation*," always at the disposal of the intendants for meeting charities of an emergency nature.[28]

It is doubtful that these attempts at organization against epidemics achieved much success prior to the Revolution. Indeed, what was most needed was the development of bacteriology through the use of the microscope. Although this instrument performed wonders in the late seventeenth and early eighteenth centuries under Leeuwenhoek, it was not applied with success to the study of germs until the later nineteenth century. Several French and certain Italian physicians in the early eighteenth century, however, attracted attention by their advocacy of a germ theory of certain diseases.

In May, 1776, a royal ordinance directed that all cemeteries (many of which emitted offensive odors and were considered sources of contagion) be removed outside of the precincts of cities and villages throughout France.[29] In most instances nothing came of this regulation, but in some places action followed. In Paris repeated complaints and government consideration since 1737 finally led in the 1780's to the removal of the bones from the Cemetery of the Innocents to a spot outside the city walls.[30] Another royal ordinance in the same month forbade future burials in the walls or floors of churches, save in rare instances, since they frequently produced unbearable conditions.[31]

In some places local action preceded this decree by the central government. In 1758 the parlement of Brittany, for example, issued an order for the exhuming of all bodies in churches and for their transportation to cemeteries. Then little apparently was done.[32] In 1742 the bishop of Grenoble ordered the closing of a church

---

[28] Letter from Millière to Cypierre, cited above.

[29] Dupuy, *op. cit.*, I (Rennes, 1886), 121-122. Dupuy has several pages on the cemeteries of Brittany as an evident source of contagion.

[30] For an account of the affair, see Alfred Franklin, *La vie privée d'autrefois* . . ., VII (Paris, 1890), 195-200. This cemetery, one of eighteen in the city, was the oldest, dating from 1186, and was estimated to contain the remains of some 1,200,000 corpses.

[31] *Ibid.*, VII, 200-203; Dupuy, *op. cit.*, I, 126.

[32] Dupuy, *op. cit.*, I, 126.

cemetery in Grenoble because of unsanitary conditions.[33]   These ordinances and orders were designed by the government to remove the *foyers* of infection.[34]

A feature of government aid during epidemics was the tendency on the part of many physicians, surgeons, and nurses to profit at the government's expense.   Moreover, sometimes great lords, with residence at court, obtained aid for distribution to their vassals and took the credit for themselves.[35]   More exasperating was the frequent reluctance of the peasants to receive the physicians and surgeons sent by the government, or to follow the prescribed remedies.   Instead, they followed the advice of quacks and submitted to superstitious or otherwise absurd treatments.   In 1758, when the *Maladie de Brest* was ravaging Brittany, the intendant recalled the surgeons from certain parishes because no one would receive them.[36]

Medical aid was by no means limited to times of epidemic.   From the beginning to the end of the century the government attempted in various ways to improve the health of its people, and in the case of the poor or the military its services were gratuitous.   One of its chief expedients, a practice begun by Louis XIV in the late seventeenth century, was the annual sending of remedies to the provinces for free distribution among the needy.   By inventing and popularizing some of these remedies, the first and second Helvétius made their family fortune.   Several times during the century the quantity of drugs dispatched was increased.   For example, on March 1, 1769, the council of state ordered that the quantity of remedies annually distributed be increased thenceforth from 126,910 to 932,136 doses.[37]

These drugs were destined specifically for distribution in rural regions, and not in cities or hospitals.   On February 9, 1776, the allotment was increased still further by the council of state.[38]   In

---

[33] Prudhomme, *Histoire de Grenoble*, pp. 571-572.

[34] For instance, in the early 1780's the government contributed 150,000 livres toward the draining of swamps near the town of Fréjus, in Provence (*Inv.-som . . . Bouches-du-Rhône*, C 1114).

[35] Dupuy, *op. cit.*, II, 221, 224-225.

[36] *Ibid.*, II, 212-214.

[37] *Inv.-som . . . Seine-Inférieure*, C 89.

[38] Instead of the 32 large boxes and 742 small boxes of remedies specified by the order of March 1, 1769, there were to be sent out thenceforth 32 large boxes and 2,226 small boxes.   This represented a tripling of the number of small boxes (Isambert, *Recueil général des anciennes lois françaises*, XXIII, 348-349).

1789 their cost to the government was 60,000 livres.[39]   They were selected under the direction of the first physician to the king, with special attention to the needs of each province.   Thus in 1777 into the generality of Caen, in Normandy, where malarial fevers were prevalent because of swamps, seventy-three boxes of remedies were used to meet this need.[40]   In all instances the drugs were sent in custody of the intendant, to be distributed by his subdelegates, with the assistance of curés, judges, aldermen, and other persons of integrity.   There was little if any complaint concerning the distribution of the remedies.   Apparently they were doled out in the conservative fashion of all eighteenth-century charities.   The intendant generally held in reserve a sufficient amount for emergencies.

In 1776 Turgot, who was responsible for an increase in the annual quantity of these drugs, also succeeded in obtaining a royal ordinance that "for the good of humanity" there should be deposited with the government thenceforth two copies of the prescription of each remedy sold to it or approved by it, and further that the government might at any time publish these prescriptions and pension the inventor either temporarily or for life.[41]   This measure, of course, was intended to promote the public health.   By publishing the formulae, the government would make the remedies known more widely and thus facilitate the war against various ailments.   Among the formulae bought and published by Louis XV was one to make blood coagulate, devised or possessed by one Brassard.   A remedy for treating the tapeworm was bought and published by Louis XVI.[42] A remedy for puerperal fever, discovered by the physician Doulcet of the Hôtel-Dieu of Paris and tried with marked success, was published by the government in 1782.   Since puerperal fever had been endemic in the Hôtel-Dieu, Doulcet's remedy was hailed as a medical discovery of outstanding value.   Accordingly, Doulcet and his family were pensioned, and the midwife, his assistant in the experiments, was awarded a gratification of 600 livres.[43]

[39] Martin-Doisy, *Dictionnaire d'économie charitable* . . . , ed. Abbé Migne, II (Paris, 1855), 431.

[40] *Inv.-som* . . . *Calvados*, C 248.

[41] *Oeuvres de Turgot*, II(Paris, 1844), 473-474.

[42] P. Théod. Legras, *Notice historique sur les deux hôpitaux et l'asile des aliénés de Rouen* (Rouen, 1827), pp. 47-48.

[43] Michel Möring and Charles Quentin, *Collection des documents pour servir à l'histoire des hôpitaux de Paris*, ed. M. Brièle, II (Paris, 1883), 127, 130, 133-134,

Sometimes the government published medical pamphlets or books of a popular nature. One of the most popular of the many medical books published by the government in the late eighteenth century was Tissot's *Notice to the People on Health* (1761), which went through numerous editions. Sometimes the provincial governments published or bought for distribution a large number of copies of a medical work. Thus in 1785 the general assembly of Provence bought for distribution 150 copies of *Instructions on Accouchements* by Verguin, naval surgeon-major at Toulon.[44]

The government was plagued by persons who claimed to have possession of secret cures and who wanted to sell them. Obviously most of the remedies were valueless. To prove their merits, the government submitted each to the medical authorities at Paris for an opinion, and sometimes resorted to tests on patients. For example, in 1782 the government asked the administrators of the Hôtel-Dieu of Paris to try out a proposed treatment of epileptics by electricity, but the administrators refused, asserting that the hospital never permitted experimentation on its patients.[45] Later the controller-general, Calonne, corresponded with the intendant of Burgundy over an alleged remedy by a physician, Mittié, for the treatment of syphilitics by common vegetables, without mercury. Mittié was later permitted to demonstrate his treatment before the Academy of Dijon.[46]

One of the most common drugs sponsored by the government from the early 1760's was the pill by the physician Keyser for the treatment of venereal patients, which was sent in considerable quantities for the treatment of soldiers, prostitutes, and other victims in the hospitals. Venereal disease was especially prevalent in the army and among prostitutes. The government, as well as the provinces, for at least two or three decades prior to the Revolution made it a practice to render free service to all venereal patients who came to

---

140, 147. According to these records of the Hôtel-Dieu, the remedy had been tried on two hundred cases, with cures in every instance, before the government sponsored it. There were also three instances in which deaths resulted, but they were regarded as unfair test cases inasmuch as the patients were brought late to the hospital of the experiment.

[44] *Inv.-som . . . Bouches-du-Rhône*, C 98, f 194v.

[45] Möring and Quentin, *op. cit.*, II, 128-129. This was not altogether true, as the instance of Doulcet above reveals.

[46] *Inv.-som . . . Côte d'Or*, Introduction, p. xix; C 363. No mention is made of the outcome.

the hospitals for treatment.[47]   Choiseul, minister of war, wrote in 1767 to Fontette, intendant at Caen, that the remedy had been tried with very favorable results in many parts of France.   Since the soldiers in the hospitals of the generality of Caen had a repugnance to it and would spit out pills after the physicians departed, Choiseul insisted that the physicians and surgeons remain long enough to make certain that the pills were swallowed.[48]

Special remedies were also sent to the provinces for the use of nurses who were caring for indigent children from Paris.   In 1777 the council of state ordered that thenceforth one hundred boxes of drugs be sent annually for the use of children under the care of nurses in several of the northern provinces of France.[49]

On the eve of the Revolution the government tried to encourage the practice of inoculation for smallpox, and here and there hospitals permitted their *enfants trouvés* to receive it.   A physician named Jauberthon was sent, at government expense, on a tour of hospitals, and in the hospitals of La Rochelle the children were required to be inoculated by him.[50]   The intendant of Provence desired to invite Jauberthon into that province in October, 1786, for inoculating the *enfants trouvés* and others in the hospitals.[51]   Several communities in Champagne practised inoculation, and the intendant at Troyes distributed instructions on inoculation to his subdelegates.[52]

The slowness of the French government in encouraging inoculation was almost certainly due to physicians and others of influence who frowned upon this treatment at late as the 1770's.   When in 1770 the administrators of the Hôtel-Dieu of Paris heard a rumor that many persons had been inoculated in the two wards allotted to smallpox cases, they ordered an investigation.   Although the physicians and surgeons of the hospital denied the charges, the adminis-

[47] During one year in the late 1780's the generality of Caen spent 640 livres in free venereal treatment, and during another 978 livres (*Inv.-som . . . Calvados*, C 233).

[48] *Ibid.*, C 840; *Inv.-som . . . l'hôpital de Grenoble*, E 145, 148; *Inv.-som . . . Ille-et-Vilaine*, C 1336, 1337; *Inv.-som . . . Bouches-du-Rhône*, C 2610; Tenon, *op. cit.*, p. 82.

[49] Alfred Franklin, *op. cit.*, XX, 61-62 with n.

[50] *Inv.-som . . . Charente-Inférieure*, C 212.   The date is not given, but was presumably after 1785.

[51] *Inv.-som . . . Bouches-du-Rhône*, C 1132.   In all likelihood the invitation was extended (cf. C 2626).

[52] Mention of this literature is made in *Inv.-som . . . l'Aube*, C 297.

trators sharply admonished them and all employees of the hospital not to inoculate anyone or to procure pus for serum, on the pain of being expelled forever from the hospital. No outsiders who might do so were to be allowed in the halls.[53] In 1778 the College of Medicine in Lyons, adopting a similar attitude, declared that inoculation had increased the prevalence of smallpox in Lyons until there was a permanent epidemic. Consequently, it obtained a court order prohibiting the performance of inoculation within the city limits.[54]

The French government in the eighteenth century took an interest in extending the use of medicinal baths to soldiers, sailors, and indigents. Attendance at watering resorts, which had come into great popularity in the latter half of the seventeenth century, steadily increased throughout the eighteenth century. Among the earliest resorts were Vichy, Bourbon, and Veris, all established by Louis XIV "for receiving indigent bathers."[55] In the early 1730's the government repaired the baths at Barèges and ordered numerous additions, among them the construction of quarters for sick, wounded, or crippled officers and soldiers, who were to take the baths for their recovery.[56] The general assembly of Provence in 1764 granted a subsidy of 2,000 livres to Grevier, a preacher who owned and operated the resort of Gréoulx for the free treatment to the poor.[57] Sénac de Meilhan, while intendant at Valenciennes, erected a building for needy persons at the resort of Saint-Amand-les-Eaux, and provided free maintenance, baths, and thermal mud.[58] On June 28, 1787, a magnificent new bathhouse was constructed at Luchon in Languedoc by the estates of that province, and was equipped with individual cells or rooms, each with bath, a large common room, and two arcades for promenades.[59] The government encouraged the development of several other resorts and for these stations "created

[53] Möring and Quentin, op. cit., II, 10.

[54] Et. Dagier, Histoire chronologique de l'Hôpital Général et grand Hôtel-Dieu de Lyon II (Lyon, 1830), 277. Later, in 1801, vaccination, with cow's serum, was tried at the Charity Hospital in Lyons (ibid., II, 390-391).

[55] Martin-Doisy, op. cit., IV, 1216. During two periods a year at Vichy the indigent were to be received. Soldiers also were given free treatment.

[56] Paillet, op. cit., I, 207-208. Barèges later became a fashionable resort under Napoleon, being frequently visited by the Bonapartes (Walter Geer, Napoleon and His Family: The Story of a Corsican Clan, New York, 1927, I, 106, 107, 125).

[57] Inv.-som . . . Bouches-du-Rhône, C 83.

[58] Legrand, op. cit., p. 141.

[59] Young, op. cit., p. 37.

a service of inspection."[60] Often the government of the Old Regime sent officers and soldiers to the baths and paid their traveling expenses.[61]

Numerous persons were bitten in eighteenth-century France by "mad wolves" *(loups enragés)*. The community, or the province, or the state usually shouldered the expense of treating these persons, and in case of their death assisted their needy families. Of twenty-two persons bitten in several villages of Champagne in 1774 by a mad she-wolf, nine died; the others recovered. A physician and surgeon of Troyes cared for them, but many of the peasants went on pilgrimages to Saint-Hubert, in the Ardennes, where they inserted under the skin of their foreheads, as protection, a small piece of the saint's stole. The government paid the complete expense of medical care for the victims, and aided their families, for a total of 2,366 livres.[62] In Provence the community or the province bore the expense.[63]

The government took an interest in the improvement of surgery and in the extension of medical and surgical attention, as far as possible, to all French subjects. Both Louis XIV and Louis XV were greatly interested in surgery and were active in improving it and in elevating the status of surgeons. According to Fielding H. Garrison, Louis XIV was grateful for the successful operation for the removal of a fistula by two royal surgeons, Félix and Mareschal.[64] In 1731 Louis XV created the Academy of Surgery, and he founded several chairs in the surgical College of Saint-Côme at Paris. In raising the quality of surgical instruction through this latter institution and in divorcing in 1743 the surgeons from the barbers, he did much to elevate the profession. Steadily throughout the century surgery made advances. Of course, not all surgeons were well trained, or were yet regarded as being on a level of respectability with the physicians. Most of those in France throughout the century continued to attain their *maîtrise* through apprenticeship rather than a surgical school, and the greater portion of those in Brittany

[60] Boissonnade, *op. cit.*, II, 531-532.

[61] *Inv.-som . . . Calvados*, C 839; *Inv.-som . . . Ardennes*, C 145. The resorts of Barèges, Bourbonne, Digne, and Saint-Amand-les-Eaux are specified.

[62] Babeau, *Le village sous l'ancien régime*, p. 331.

[63] *Inv.-som . . . Bouches-du-Rhône*, C 88 (f 102v), 1054.

[64] *An Introduction to the History of Medicine* (Philadelphia and London, 1922), pp. 409-410.

were poorly trained. Even so, chiefly under the patronage of the
government, surgery made considerable advances. The province of
Brittany, following the lead of the royal government, established
and maintained colleges of surgery, with free instruction, at Nantes
and Rennes.[65]

Down to the end of the Old Regime France suffered a great
shortage of physicians and, to a lesser degree, of surgeons. Many
communities had neither. The problem was made more acute by
the fact that rural inhabitants often were unable to obtain admittance
to the hospitals of the neighboring cities and towns. The committee
of mendicity in its report of August 6, 1790, declared that the rural
people had been badly neglected and needed better attention. It
therefore recommended for each canton the employment of a physician, to be paid 500 livres a year by the state, and the establishment
of free dispensaries for drugs.[66]

As a matter of fact, there was, as Dupuy observes, a considerable
increase in the number of physicians in the villages and the countryside for a period before the Revolution.[67] In scores, perhaps hundreds, of instances towns and communities engaged themselves to
pay a certain annual sum to a physician or a surgeon (generally the
former) in return for his free services to the poor of the community.
The salary might be merely 200 or 300 livres a year, as in Brittany,[68] or more, as in some other province. Sometimes a town en-

[65] Dupuy, op. cit., II, 195-199; Oeuvres de Turgot, II, 468-469. The instruction in the College of Saint-Côme in Paris was also gratuitous. Under Louis XVI
and Turgot, another professor was added to this college, and plans were made to
obtain more spacious quarters and to add a hospice with a small number of beds
for poor patients afflicted with rare maladies of especial interest for surgical observation.

[66] Cited by Camille Ferdinand-Dreyfus, Un philanthrope d'autrefois: La Roche-
foucauld-Liancourt, 1747-1827 (Paris, 1903), pp. 176-177. See Dupuy, op. cit.,
II, 192-193; Joseph Coiffier, L'assistance publique dans la généralité de Riom (au
XVIIIe siècle) (Clermont-Ferrand, 1905), p. 272.

[67] Dupuy speaks of the period as "the ten years which preceded the Revolution,"
but the number had actually increased much earlier, as a perusal of the Collection
des inventaires-sommaires des archives départementales antérieures à 1790, série C,
will reveal.

[68] Dupuy, "L'enseignement supérieur en Bretagne avant et après la Revolution,"
Annales de Bretagne, IV (Rennes, 1888-89), 371; Inv.-som . . . Ille-et-Vilaine,
C 511, 512, 580, 672. It appears to have been generally 300 livres a year for physicians in the 1780's, and 200 livres for surgeons, unless the latter taught courses
in midwifery, when they would be paid perhaps an additional 100 livres. In 1779
a surgeon dentist was employed by the intendant of Bordeaux to serve the poor of the
generality, for 200 livres annually (minute of May 30, 1780, Archives de la Gironde,
C 2510).

gaged a physician for particular service. Thus, according to Lallemand, the town of Bar-le-Duc engaged "a practician" to treat the eyes of indigents and paid him for his service 53 livres a year.[69] The intendants encouraged the practice of placing physicians and surgeons in the smaller places in their generalities, but in all or nearly all instances the responsibility and the expense were borne by the local communities.

The medical care of the military was vastly better in the eighteenth century than it had been in the seventeenth. Credit for this improvement is attributed chiefly to Louis XIV. Before his day army surgeons were few, and it was the practice to carry wounded soldiers to near-by homes for treatment, where they usually died. Louis XIV provided his armies with hospitals and ambulances and increased the number of surgeons.[70] Scores of hospitals in France throughout the eighteenth century were devoted wholly or in part to the care of sick or wounded soldiers or sailors at government expense, since the government wanted them to have adequate medical attention.

In accordance with the policy of increasing the number of physicians and surgeons in their generalities, the intendants also encouraged the training of competent midwives and in some cases the importation of nurses. In 1742 the intendant of Brittany interested himself in the matter of seeing that the small towns of his generality were adequately equipped with nurses who could assist or assume charge at the delivery of children. In his letter to the controller-general on December 30, 1742, he observed that the fee of 12 livres charged by the surgeons for deliveries was too high for the poor, and that consequently the surgeons were shunned.[71] In fact, Brittany imported nurses on certain occasions.

This lack of a sufficient number of trained midwives was one of the most glaring needs that France had to face. The better-trained surgeons who were qualified to handle the cases were seldom consulted by the poor because of their high fees and because of female reluctance to have male midwives. Not until the latter half of the

[69] Léon Lallemand, L'assistance médicale au XVIIIe siècle (Extrait du Bulletin des sciences économiques et sociales du Comité des travaux historiques et scientifiques) (Paris, 1895), p. 7.

[70] L'Abbé Petetot, "Des hôpitaux," Annales de la charité (1846), pp. 2-22.

[71] Inv.-som . . . Ille-et-Vilaine, C 1249.

seventeenth century did male midwifery originate in Europe, and throughout the eighteenth century it made its way slowly because of the reticence of women. Some of the midwives in eighteenth-century France obtained their *maîtrise* after training by surgeons; but, according to Dupuy, they, too, were little sought, at least in Brittany, because their fees, though smaller than those of the surgeons, were deemed high by the peasants. Most of the midwives were women of little or no training, and little better than quacks. Their charge was a pittance, and the poor probably paid in food or drink. Most of the poor paid absolutely nothing for the service,[72] and in return they got service that deserved little or no payment. The mortality of children and mothers in childbirth was enormous. Bertrand de Molleville, intendant of Brittany, wrote to the controller-general in 1786 that the midwives created more havoc in his province than did the epidemics.[73] From all parts of France for some time prior to the Revolution came complaints of the incompetence of the midwives and a demand for better trained ones.[74]

In the early 1760's the government turned its attention to the problem. Gratuitous courses in midwifery, often taught by surgeons, came to be given, sometimes at municipal, sometimes at provincial, expense. Such a course was given at Rennes in 1762; another at Saint-Pol-de-Léon in 1767 and several subsequent years; a third at Morlaix, in the 1770's, for a period of six years; all at the expense of Brittany.[75] These courses, running often no longer than a month, came rapidly into popularity in the 1760's, and in the 1770's and 1780's were given in perhaps every generality in France.[76] A course at Cambrai in 1778-79 lasted for thirty days, and was conducted by a surgeon at a military hospital. The students (young women se-

---

[72] Dupuy, *op. cit.*, IV, 184.

[73] *Ibid.*, IV, 179. See also *Inv.-som . . . Ille-et-Vilaine*, C 1329.

[74] The *cahier* of the clergy of the *sénéchaussée* of Limoux in 1789, revealing that the incompetency of the midwives took a heavy toll of deaths in France daily, demanded that courses of instruction for midwives be instituted in all the leading towns and cities of the nation (*Hist. gén. de Languedoc*, XIV, 2617).

[75] Dupuy, *op. cit.*, III (Rennes, 1888), 187-188. The intendant of Auvergne claimed to have instituted the first course in 1760 (Léon Lallemand, *Histoire de la charité*, IV, Part II, Paris, 1912, 395).

[76] The *Collection des inventaires-sommaires des archives départementales antérieures à 1790* abounds in references to them. See, for example, *Inv.-som . . . l'Aube*, C 1167; Babeau, *op. cit.*, p. 333 with n. 2; *Hist. gén. de Languedoc*, XIII, 123, 124, 127; Legrand, *Sénac de Meilhan . . .*, pp. 177-178.

lected by the mayors and curés of towns) were each paid by the government 20 sous (1 livre) a day during the period.

To assist in this program of training midwives, there came forward about 1765 an extraordinary woman, Madame du Coudray, a trained midwife of the school of Paris, an inventor, and a clever teacher.[77] She was introduced to the work by De Thiers, a wealthy landowner, who engaged her to instruct the matrons on his lands. Struck with dismay at their ignorance, she decided that she must teach them by some ocular means. Accordingly, she constructed a machine to represent the body of a woman. In it she placed a dummy infant in all conceivable positions, and showed her audience how delivery should be made in each instance. De Thiers recommended her to the intendant of Auvergne, who proceeded to engage her to give her course to various groups in his generality and who bought from her samples of her machine for use in all his towns and cities. The intendant recommended her to the controller-general, Laverdy, and to other intendants. Laverdy engaged her at government expense to visit the various provinces with her machine and give lessons to prospective midwives. For twenty years this gifted, enthusiastic woman went from province to province, city to city, greeted everywhere by large crowds upon which she made a remarkable impression. Her audiences, composed of approximately eighty women and girls, and even some surgeons, were drawn from city and country. Her course lasted two months. By 1777 she had given the courses for twelve years, had labored throughout thirteen generalities, and had taught more than four thousand pupils. Cities felt honored to secure her services and provided her maintenance; often she was paid 300 livres or more for a stay of two months. On occasion she was asked to repeat the course to accommodate those who could not gain admittance to the first class. Sometimes the intendant furnished her and her needy pupils expense money. Her lectures in Champagne, it is said, cost the cities of that province 8,000 livres.[78] As a rule, the provinces, and sometimes the cities, bought samples of her machine, at a cost of 280 livres each.[79] It is not clear whether the government paid her during the entire twenty years of her teaching,

[77] For brief accounts of her and her work, see Dupuy, op. cit., III, 189-192, 197-200; Lallemand, op. cit., IV, Part 2, 395-396 with nn.

[78] Dupuy, op. cit., III, 192.

[79] Ibid., III, 190.

but according to an entry in the *Livre rouge* she was paid 4,000 livres in salary for the first six months of 1783.[80]

Historians have little remembered the work that Madame du Coudray performed. Nevertheless, she charmed her contemporaries, and many an intendant wrote eulogistically of her work. That there were still a large number of quack midwives on the eve of the Revolution reveals the magnitude of the task that she faced.

After 1789

The policies of the Old Regime in regard to public health were continued by the Revolutionary governments as best they could with the limited financial resources available. Free courses in midwifery were occasionally given. The physician-in-chief of the marine, Pierre Duret, offered one in 1790 at the hospital in Brest, but the pupils were chiefly young men students of the naval medical school rather than women.[81] The physician Paris and the surgeon Potrier were permitted by the directory of Bouches-du-Rhône to give a similar course at Marseilles in 1791.[82] At Grenoble a three months' course was planned for 1793. Twenty-four women were to be instructed, a definite number coming from each of the several districts composing the department. Each pupil was to receive 5 sous a league as travel pay to Grenoble and the same amount on her return at the end of the course. In Grenoble she was to be allowed 40 livres a month for living expenses. The surgeon giving the course was to receive 500 livres. To encourage good work, three prizes "not to exceed the sum of 100 livres" were to be offered. At the end of the course "each pupil-midwife judged sufficiently instructed" was to be given a case containing the instruments necessary for her profession. The total expense was estimated at 4,000 livres, and, to raise it, a small tax, payable for one year only, was ordered placed on the taxpayers of the department.[83] At Angers a free course of *accouchement* was taught from the years V through VII. The 4,000 francs a year requisite for expenses were voted by the directory of the department

---

[80] *Arch. parl.*, XIII, 250. There appears to be no biography of her, not even an article in a learned journal.

[81] Cuzent, *op. cit.*, p. 330.

[82] *Inv.-som . . . Bouches-du-Rhône*, L IV, 5 (II, 94).

[83] *Inv.-som . . . Isère*, L 58 (p. 314).

in germinal an IV (March-April 1796).[84] The total number of these courses was not large, and they were vastly fewer in the 1790's than in the 1780's. The *cahiers* on the subject went unheeded. In fact, the Hôtel-Dieu of Paris in 1792 required 180 livres, payable in advance, of each pupil who wished to pursue its three months' course in midwifery.[85]

When epidemics broke out here and there during the Revolutionary period, the provincial governments, now ruling over departments and not generalities, sent physicians to the scene on request. Thus in October and December, 1790, Michel, a physician engaged by the department of Isère, was directed to centers of epidemics within his department.[86] Later, in December, 1795, and March, 1796, two "health officers"[87] were sent to cope with epidemics in parts of Isère.[88] Still later, in December, 1799, another epidemic in Isère, in the city of Grenoble, broke out in its five hospitals packed with soldiers. Physicians, hospital attendants, and others also were attacked. A great many persons were stricken with the malady, and a few died. At this time the city had an ample supply of physicians and medicines and did not summon outside aid. A report on the situation, however, was sent to the minister of the interior, and the Society of Health of Grenoble (evidently composed of the physicians and surgeons or "health officers") drew up sanitary regulations for arresting the epidemic.[89]

Similar situations no doubt arose in many of the departments and were handled in like fashion. In the summer of 1795 an epidemic

[84] B. Bois, *La vie scolaire* . . . (Paris, 1929), pp. 422-425. One thousand francs were to be paid to the instructor, and 3,000 to the pupils, who would come from all parts of the department.

[85] Tuetey, *Répertoire général*, VI, 181-182, No. 1501.

[86] On one occasion he was sent by the directory of the department, which commonly had jurisdiction over matters of charity and the public welfare, and on a second he was dispatched by the procurer-general-syndic, who later reported his action to the departmental-assembly or legislature and was commended for it (*Inv.-som* . . . *Isère*, L 54, p. 277; 63, pp. 396, 622). Accompanying one of the requests for a physician came also a request for medicines.

[87] Designation of physicians and surgeons during the Revolution.

[88] One of the epidemics is specified as malaria; the other is unnamed (*ibid.*, L 83, pp. 80, 301).

[89] These were: (1) separation of beds so that they would be two thirds of a meter apart; (2) permission for only three rows of beds in the halls; (3) removal of all trash or filth, and washing of the courts and corridors with lime water; and (4) renewal of straw and bed linen. Further, it ordered a printed report posted in all the communes of the department (*ibid.*, L 128, frimaire).

of typhus, known variously as the *Maladie de Quiberon*, the *Maladie des Chouans*, and the *Maladie des Prisonniers*, swept the prisons of several cities and towns in Brittany, wherein were heaped with little regard for comfort or sanitation great numbers of British soldiers, French *émigrés*, and Chouan reactionaries awaiting execution. The malady had been brought from England by an ill-fated expedition of 17,000 or 18,000 British troops and French *émigrés*, which landed on the peninsula of Quiberon in an attempt to assist the Chouans. The greater portion of the invaders (possibly as many as 10,000), including several hundred of the *émigrés*, were captured and thrust into prison at Quiberon, Vannes, and Auray.[90] In all three cities the epidemic broke out during the month of thermidor (July-August) with severe results. Among the prisoners at Vannes, 324 died. From these places the disease spread throughout the countryside when numerous peasants taken prisoner by the Revolutionaries were released. Apparently the state took no part in meeting this situation.[91]

In ventôse and germinal an III (February and March, 1795) an epidemic in the French-occupied city of Antwerp affected the soldiers and the bourgeois families with whom they were billeted. When a report was made to Paris, the committee of public safety ordered the French political officials at Brussels to go to Antwerp, accompanied by an experienced army physician and a general or military commander, and to take all the necessary steps for meeting the situation. The magistrate at Antwerp, whose report was acknowledged, was then informed of their action.[92]

The Revolutionists, even as the government of the Old Regime, tried to increase the number of physicians and surgeons in the villages and rural regions. Realizing that the physicians themselves were chiefly at fault in limiting the number of trained men, the Convention struck home by abolishing the distinction between physician and surgeon. Thenceforth both were to be known as "officers of health."

---

[90] Appalling conditions prevailed in respect to food, sanitation, and terrorism. Many, if not most, of the several hundred *émigrés* and Chouans were courtmartialed and shot by firing squads. A contemporary writer reported that 500 were shot in the single town of Vannes by 21 thermidor (Aug. 9) (Mauricet, *op. cit.*, Introduction, pp. xxiv-xxviii).

[91] *Ibid.*, pp. xxviii-xxix. See also a review of the book by Dupuy in *Annales de Bretagne*, III (Rennes, 1888), 643-645.

[92] Two letters of 4 germinal, an III, by committee of public safety ("Correspondance Général. Cahier des Lettres Écrites par la Section des Secours de comité de Salut Public," Arch. Nat., F15, 102).

In itself this step was doubtless commendable, since the French physicians had frequently been as conceited and insolent as they were narrow and pedantic, and there was little excuse for their desire to lord it over the surgeons. The Convention, however, went farther and abolished all the medical schools; in fact, it closed all faculties of the universities (1792); and thence until 1803 only "schools of health" existed. The Convention also offered the opportunity to practise medicine to all who could pay for a license, in the hope of removing discrimination and of enlarging the medical profession. But in making no adequate provision for medical training the Convention pursued a confused course.[93]   Barère, one of the members of the committee of public safety, succeeded in getting an act adopted in May, 1794, to establish in each district (subdivision of a department), three "health officers," paid 1,000 livres apiece to provide each district with eight boxes of drugs valued at 30 livres; and to furnish each poor person who was sick with a pension of 10 sous a day, with an additional allowance of 6 sous for each dependent child under ten years of age. This law was formally adopted, but whether any attempt was made to enforce it is not clear.[94]

From time to time during the 1790's boxes of remedies were sent to the departments for distribution among the poor, as formerly. Thus on 17 fructidor an II (September 3, 1794) the commission of public works wrote that it was sending to the administrators of the department of Haute-Garonne, at Toulouse, twenty-four boxes of drugs (*médicaments*) for distribution to the rural inhabitants.[95]   Similarly twenty-one boxes were sent shortly afterwards to Bourges, for distribution in the department of Cher, as a letter and receipt of 18 brumaire an III (November 9, 1794) reveal.[96]   Both shipments were made in execution of the law of 22 floréal an II (the law sponsored by Barère) although, instead of each district receiving eight boxes as specified by the law, the directory at Bourges complained

[93] Chéruel, *op. cit.*, II, 1241, 1243; Garrison, *op. cit.*, p. 410; Bois, *op. cit.*, pp. 110, 421-422; Francis R. Packard, *Guy Patin and the Medical Profession in Paris in the XVIIth Century* (Oxford, 1925), pp. 243-244. The Royal Society of Medicine and the Academy of Surgery were abolished at the same time as the eighteen medical faculties and fifteen medical colleges. The "schools of health" were set up in 1795. Positions in hospitals were made competitive, a practice that continued until 1821.

[94] Ferdinand-Dreyfus, *L'assistance sous la Législative et la Convention (1791-1795)*, pp. 73-74.

[95] Adher, *op. cit.*, pp. 468-469.

[96] "Le President de Directoire du Departement du Cher, aux Citoyens Composant la Commission des Secours Publics" (Arch. Nat., F15, 102).

that that district had received only three.[97]   On 27 thermidor an II
(August 14, 1794) the committee of public works approved a request
for 8,000 livres to be used for the purchase of medicines for the poor
in three sections of Paris and to come from a large appropriation of
480,000 livres made for assistance to the poor of the city.[98]   A scarcity of funds made for few shipments of drugs for the poor in the
1790's.   On 26 messidor an VIII (July 13, 1800) the bureau of
beneficence of one of the sections of Paris informed the minister of
the interior that the sums at its disposal were so small that it could
give only the most meager aid to indigents, and requested a special
grant for the free distribution of medicines among the needy.[99]

In 1791 gratuitous treatment was still rendered to all afflicted
with venereal disease in the depot of mendicity at Grenoble.[100]
Medicinal baths also were given without charge to the poor in Paris
in the period 1791-95.   Save in one instance, where a private owner
treated wounded and sick soldiers, sailors, and indigents,[101] the baths
were maintained by the city out of funds evidently set aside by the
government for charities.   Rheumatism was one of the ailments
treated in this manner.   Two "health officers" of the prisons of Paris
recommended to the government as an absolute necessity the bath
treatment for Antoine Estadens, an incarcerated deputy of Haute-
Garonne, suffering from rheumatism, headaches, insomnia, and lack
of appetite.[102]   Over a period of several months in 1790-91 the
privilege of free baths was much abused, since many of the poor
sold their tickets instead of using them.   The city officials, learning
of this practice in the autumn of 1790, took no action against it until

[97] For terms of the law of 22 floréal an II, on drugs, see Ad. de Watteville,
Législation charitable . . . (2d ed., Paris, 1847), pp. 30-31.   Apparently this distribution of drugs was to be made annually, since other matters treated in the law,
such as salaries, are described on an annual basis.

[98] Alexandre Tuetey (ed.), *L'assistance publique à Paris pendant la Révolution,
documents inédits*, IV (Paris, 1897), 516.

[99] "Bureau de Bienfaisance de la Division des Lombards, Au Ministre de l'Intérieur" (Arch. Nat., F15, 103).

[100] *Inv.-som* . . . *Isère*, L 103 (f 52).

[101] Albert to the commission of public aid, 2 messidor an III; also the commission
of public aid to the commission of subsistence, 4 messidor an III (Arch. Nat., F15,
102).   Albert asserted that he would be obliged to close his "hospice" unless he
received government aid.   A memorandum shows that the government allowed him
six cords of wood and two *foyers* of coal.

[102] Tuetey, *Répertoire générale*, IX, No. 121.   Entry for 5 vendémiaire an III.
Another deputy, Faure, suffering likewise in prison from rheumatism, asked permission to be allowed to go to the sea for baths, declaring that the government need
fear no plotting from him (*ibid.*, IX, 23).

July or August, 1791. Then their prohibition, however, was not enforced by October, 1791, when the committee of public aid urged the mayor to put it in operation.[103]

On May 18, 1799, free baths and douches at the water resorts were still furnished gratuitously to sick indigents who presented themselves.[104] The travel expenses en route were paid by the communes sending them from charity funds placed by the government at their disposal.[105] "Health officers" as before were named each year for the inspection and oversight of the resorts. In addition to seeing that sanitary conditions prevailed, they were to have surveillance of the baths and the shipments of bottled water, and were to make annual statistical reports to the minister of the interior, giving accounts of their patients and the outcome of each treatment.[106] Anyone who discovered on his land a source of mineral water was ordered to inform the government, so that the latter in turn might examine its properties and regulate it.[107]

On 11 messidor an VIII (June 30, 1800) Orens Jean Baptiste Agras, a patient in the Grand Hospice d'Humanité (the Revolutionary name for the Hôtel-Dieu), requested aid from the government for travel expenses. In his application to the minister of the interior he described his army service[108] and his affliction with a lung trouble and mentioned the recommendation of physicians that he go from Paris to his home in the Pyrenees, where the air would be much better for him. Whether or not his request was granted by the government is not indicated.[109] Under the Old Regime travel pay was commonly allotted to sick officers and men in the king's service.

In the closing months of the eighteenth century the practice of vaccination was introduced from England into France.[110] Knowl-

---

[103] "Note. Bains gratis pour les pauvres" (Arch. Nat., F15, 102). Cf. Tuetey, *L'assistance publique*, IV, 522, 523.

[104] A. A. Carette, *Lois annotées ou lois, décrets, ordonnances, avis du conseil d'état, etc. (1789-1830)* (Paris, n. d.), pp. 498-499.

[105] *Ibid.*, art. 6.

[106] *Ibid.*, arts. 1-4, 11-13. The reports were to be sent by the "health officers" to the municipal administration of the canton, and thence to the minister of the interior.

[107] *Ibid.*, art. 17.

[108] He had been for several years a "health officer" in the marine, with the rank of lieutenant.

[109] Arch. Nat., F15, 103.

[110] See Professor Robert G. Dunbar's interesting article, based in part on archival study, "The Introduction of the Practice of Vaccination into Napoleonic France," *Bulletin of the History of Medicine*, X (Dec., 1941), 635-650.

edge of Jenner's work, however, was first brought to France and to Western Europe by the October, November, and December, 1798, issues of the *Bibliothèque britannique*, a Genevan journal, established in 1796 to acquaint French-reading Continentals with current English literature.[111]

With cowpox virus obtained from London, the physicians Pinel and Aubert attempted vaccinations in Paris on August 16-17, 1799, and April 14, 1800, but failed because of the faultiness of the virus. Immediately the physician Woodville, "the most experienced vaccinator in England," decided (doubtless under the persuasion of Aubert, who had come to London to study his methods) to go to Paris and demonstrate the new practice before the French physicians. Although Britain and France were at war, the French government issued a passport, and Woodville went to France. At Boulogne he successfully vaccinated several children, and moved on to Paris, where he arrived July 25, 1800. The serum which he had brought from London was dead by this time, and his first vaccinations in Paris were failures; but from the patients in Boulogne he was able to obtain virus "less than twenty-four hours old," and thus attained success in Paris. From Paris the serum and practice were spread in all directions. Other French points of entry for the practice were Nancy, Rheims, Toulouse, Bordeaux, and Rennes, in all of which it was introduced in late 1800.[112] With amazing rapidity vaccination spread throughout France, making its way into numerous departments by 1801. Many of the early vaccinations were performed gratuitously.[113] Physicians deserve the most credit for introducing this great scientific advance, even though the government smiled on it by granting Aubert the privilege of going to England and Woodville the privilege of coming to France in time of war.

Finally the government interested itself in improving sanitary conditions of the prisons. An order was issued in 1717 that clean straw must be provided in the dungeons once every fifteen days and

[111] Only a short notice appeared in the October issue, but the November and December issues carried "a nearly complete translation" of Jenner's book. "This translation," writes Dunbar, "was continental Europe's first extensive introduction to the contents of Jenner's treatise" (*ibid.*, X, 638).

[112] But after Paris, Geneva was the chief focal point for dissemination, cowpox virus being sent thence to physicians throughout eastern and southern France (*ibid.*, X, 646-647).

[113] *Ibid.*, X, 639, 648.

in the cells with light once a month. No payments were forced from prisoners on entering, and they were to be fed daily one and one-half pounds (livres) of bread of good quality. In 1724 a royal declaration stipulated that the system of farming out jails to jailers should cease. Necker, as much an enthusiast for prison reform as he was for hospital reform, was largely responsible for a royal declaration ordering better conditions in several of the Paris prisons and *maisons de force*. In his *Compte rendu* of 1781 were published the government's plans to improve not only the prisons of Paris, but also those of other cities. Despite the war then existing, he thought it wise to propose to his Majesty the advancement of aid from the royal treasury for these improvements.[114] A royal declaration of August 30, 1789, announced that improvements had been made in the Conciergerie and the Grand Châtelet, that the Petit Châtelet had been demolished, and Fort l'Évêque sold. No mention was made of the Bastille, which had recently been destroyed.[115]

Under the Revolutionary governments interest in prison reform rarely got beyond the stage of discussion, for the governments of the 1790's were too poor to devote money to remodeling the prisons or building new ones.[116] Under both the Old Regime and the Revolution sick prisoners occasionally were sent to hospitals for treatment.[117] Much no doubt depended upon both the character of the prisoner and of the officials concerned. Not a great deal was done by the government or by municipalities for prison reform during the eighteenth century, yet the governments of the two regimes were not entirely oblivious of the need.

[114] *Op. cit.*, pp. 101-102. Necker's action was due in part to the remarkable impression made on Europe by Howard's book of 1776, in part to interest already shown in such work by Turgot, who as controller-general made a liberal grant (50,000 livres) in December, 1775, to the city of Tours for prison reform (Dumas, *op. cit.*, p. 334).

[115] For a discussion of French prison reform, see Marcel Marion, *Dictionnaire des institutions*, pp. 457-458.

[116] See much discussion on making the prisons more sanitary, in *Inv.-som . . . Isère*, L, Vol. I.

[117] Möring and Quentin (*op. cit.*, II, 2-3, 81) record instances in 1767 and 1780 when the government asked the Hôtel-Dieu of Paris to admit some for treatment; but, since the Hôtel-Dieu had no rooms with barred windows in which they could be locked, certain other hospitals in Paris more commonly treated them.

A royal ordinance of December 12, 1775, stipulated, among conditions governing and protecting galley slaves, that the sick prisoners were to be treated in the hospitals (Isambert, *op. cit.*, XXIII, 278). For an instance of a prisoner sent to a hospital in Grenoble 1 floréal an IV (April 20,1796), see *Inv.-som . . . Isère*, L 84, 783.

CHAPTER IX

AID TO HOSPITALS

Before 1789

The number of hospitals of various types in France in the late eighteenth century probably exceeded two thousand. The committee of mendicity in its sixth report to the National Assembly, January 31, 1791, declared that a questionnaire sent to 2,185 hospitals had brought forth replies from 1,438.[1] Paris had fifty-one; other cities and towns had a proportionately large number. Only in rural regions and hamlets were hospitals lacking. Inhabitants of these neglected regions, however, generally obtained admittance to the hôtel-Dieu (municipal hospital) in the nearest city.[2]

Though France was abundantly supplied with hospitals, in places they were too small or too few, and conditions within them were far from ideal. Many of the hospitals were very old; the number had been increasing for hundreds of years.[3] In the sixth century there were a few at Paris and Lyons. Slowly through the Middle Ages they appeared at other cities. Modern times saw a great acceleration in the movement; during the seventeenth and eighteenth centuries, as French wealth grew and the humanitarian spirit quickened, hospitals sprang up everywhere.

Among the French of the eighteenth century, however, the word "hospital" had a broader meaning than it has with Americans in the twentieth century. It was a state-recognized charitable institution existing for the benefit of the needy, whether sick, disabled, or dependent. Thus it might be either a hospital in our present sense of the word or it might be an asylum. Of the 2,185 "hospitals" in

[1] *Arch. parl.*, XXII, 607, 618.

[2] According to Coiffier (*op. cit.*, p. 272), however, the hospitals of Riom were reluctant to receive nonresidents as patients. On the similar situation at Toulouse, see Buchalet, *op. cit.*, pp. 33-34.

[3] There is difference of opinion as to the time of the origin of hospitals. According to Professor C. J. Singer (*A Short History of Medicine*, Oxford, 1928, pp. 149-150), hospitals originated among the Romans about the first century A.D.

France in 1790, a large proportion were asylums that housed unfortunates of one type or another.[4]

Hospitals varied in size from the Hôtel-Dieu of Paris, which could accommodate approximately 2,500 patients, to the Hôpital des Ecoles de Charité in Paris, founded by the French government in 1774 with six beds for unusual cases of illness, to serve as an experimental institution for the surgeons of the Ecoles de Charité. Most of the hospitals maintained by religious orders, such as the Brothers of Charity, the members of St. John of God, and the Lazarists, were small. The largest hospital in each city was commonly the Hôtel-Dieu,[5] which was regarded as a municipal establishment, and received more financial assistance from the city and the provincial and national governments than did the private hospitals. Moreover, whereas some hospitals were restricted to the treatment of one or more diseases, the hôtels-Dieu treated almost all types of diseases. Even mental patients were confined and treated at the Hôtel-Dieu of Paris. Almost the only patients not treated at this hospital were sufferers with the itch, who were sent to certain other institutions,[6] known as "pest" hospitals, affiliated with the Hôtel-Dieu.

On the eve of the Revolution France had seventy or more military and naval hospitals.[7] Seventeen military hospitals were located in the single generality of Caen, in Normandy.[8] There were naturally more military hospitals in times of war than in times of peace; the government commandeered part or all of the space in various hospitals near the military encampments for the care of the soldiery. Even in the periods of peace the government habitually commandeered wards in the civil hospitals near the camps for the care of sick soldiers, and was responsible for the expense entailed, paying a certain amount each day for a soldier's maintenance. The sum, which varied from place to place and increased considerably as the century

[4] Asylums will be treated later; the present chapter is restricted to institutions devoted to the care of the sick and wounded.

[5] Hostel-Dieu or Maison-Dieu. Originally the word "hospital" meant a place of hospitality, as affecting the sick and unfortunate. The word "hôtel" is a modern contraction of the older word "hostel."

[6] The Bicêtre and the Hôpital Saint-Louis.

[7] Albert Babeau, La ville sous l'ancien régime, II (2d ed. rev. and enlarged, Paris, 1884), 211-212. Cf. a report on the French military hospitals by Louis de Noailles, July 25, 1791 (Arch. parl., XXVIII, 609-636); also account by Martin-Doisy, op. cit., IV, 1266-1296.

[8] Inv.-som . . . Calvados, C 836.

progressed, was agreed upon by the government and the particular hospital. Although the hospitals usually set their demands high, and sometimes asserted that it would be impossible for them to continue in existence if their demands were not met, they commonly yielded when the government replied with offers of perhaps two thirds or three fourths of the sums proposed. Thus, in 1723 the bureau of the Hospital of the Recovery at Brest insisted that the government must increase its allowance for soldiers to 16 sous a day, but accepted an offer of 12.[9] In the first quarter of the century the captains paid a portion of the hospital expenses for the soldiers, as they had done in the seventeenth century; but this practice was probably discarded entirely in the 1720's, when the government assumed responsibility for all such expenses.[10] Similarly the government made arrangements with certain hospitals for the treatment of sailors, but the number of naval hospitals was far less than the number of military hospitals.[11]

As regards administration, the hospitals of the various religious orders were governed entirely by those orders To be sure, the government could make requests and even demands of them, but this action was seldom taken. The hôtels-Dieu were administered by bureaux or committees of the leading citizens, ecclesiastical, political, judicial, and economic, chosen either on account of their position or their influence in the community. They served gratuitously. Generally they were glad to serve and they considered election to this service an honor.[12] In some cities they were elected for periods of two years, in others for life.[13] The groups held frequent meetings; members served on various committees and performed real duties.[14]

[9] Cuzent, *op. cit.*, p. 78. Buchalet (*op. cit.*, p. 37) reports that in 1747 the government allowed the Hôtel-Dieu of Toulouse 8 sous a day for each soldier, but that the cost to the hospital was at least 25. In 1781 the allowance was raised to 12 sous, and in 1787 to 14.

[10] *Idem.*

[11] See, for instance Viaud and Fleury, *op. cit.*, I, 328-329.

[12] Those at Poitiers usually made, on election, a donation of money to the hospital known as a "gift of welcome" (Pierre Rambaud, *L'assistance publique à Poitiers jusqu'à l'an V*, II, Paris, 1914, 69). Those at Lyons, elected for two years, deposited with the institution, as a guaranty of good management and as aid to the institution, some large sums without interest (Le Baron Dupin, *Histoire de l'administration des secours publics*, Paris, 1821, pp. 34-35).

[13] Cf. Trélat, "Des hôpitaux," *Annales de la charité* for 1845 (2d ed., Paris, 1846), p. 23.

[14] See, for instance, Fosseyeux, *L'Hôtel-Dieu de Paris au XVIIe au XVIIIe siècle*, pp. 66-70.

Generally the bishop or archbishop of the city served as a permanent chairman.

Nurses were customarily members of a religious order, the most famous, for the women, being the Sisters of Charity, founded in the seventeenth century by Saint Vincent de Paul, and, for the men, the Brothers of Charity. In a few instances, even before the Revolution, the nurses were lay.[15] They were usually girls or widows, of high character with a spirit of service, and were called "sisters," even as were the nuns. The nurses left the menial duties to servants of various grades and types. They were also assisted by bookkeepers, who kept the financial records of the institution, collected the revenues, and made disbursements. In addition, chaplains confessed the sick, buried the dead, performed mass in the chapel,[16] and rendered any other spiritual services that might be needed. All in all, several hundred persons constituted the corps of nurses, bookkeepers, servants, and other personnel for a large hospital like the Hôtel-Dieu of Paris.[17] They were engaged at so much a year, the rate of payment varying from the salary of 200 to 400 livres paid the chaplain to the wage of 30 to 45 livres paid an *archer* for policing the hospital grounds.[18] From time to time during the century the wages of nurses and other hospital attendants were raised to meet the ever-rising scale of living costs.

In the larger and more crowded hospitals patients were fre-

---

[15] Coiffier, *op. cit.*, pp. 81-82; Viaud and Fleury, *op. cit.*, I, 336-337.

[16] No matter how crowded the hospital, a chapel in it had to be reserved for mass.

[17] Seven hundred persons were employed at the Hôtel-Dieu of Paris in 1790 (*Arch. parl.*, XXII, 379), and five hundred at the English naval hospital at Portsmouth (Tenon, *Mémoires sur les hôpitaux de Paris*, Paris, 1788, p. 181).

[18] At the Hôtel-Dieu of Poitiers, valets were paid 20 livres a year from 1681 to 1789, save in 1721, when one received 38 livres 5 sols. *Infirmiers* and other servants received 20 livres annually until 1750, and 50 livres thereafter. Washerwomen were paid 6 livres a year after 1727, with lodging, food, and clothing furnished, until their jobs were suppressed in 1757. Water carriers fared better, receiving 60 livres in 1700, 75 livres in 1750, and 80 livres in 1757. These last also received gratifications of 5 to 10 livres a year. The *chasse-coquins*, who did police work, dug graves, and carried the sick home, received 48 livres in 1700, with occasional gratuities, but in 1787 their wages were reduced to 12 livres. The barber, who shaved the sick gratis, received in 1792 the pittance of 26 sous (1 livre 6 sous) a month. The nurses received 80 livres a year, in addition to all living expenses and free care in case of sickness. An apothecary received 50 livres in 1740. The almoner Picoron received 500 livres in 1789, and allegedly could scarcely live on it! The surgeon Maury received only 100 livres, and each of two physicians 200 livres a year (Rambaud, *op. cit.*, II, 87-92, 113, 178, 180, 183, 197-198).

quently placed three and four in a bed.[19]   The most notorious hospital in France in this respect was the Hôtel-Dieu of Paris, whose unfortunate conditions were publicized to the world and posterity by Tenon in his *Mémoires sur les hôpitaux de Paris* (Paris, 1788). He found many instances of four persons confined to a bed of fifty-two inches. This crowding allowed only thirteen inches to each person. Once or twice he noted as many as six persons on a bed. They probably were small children. Bru, a late nineteenth-century writer, observed that thirteen persons were found in a bed at the grim prison and hospital, the Bicêtre, just outside Paris. Both Tenon and Bru probably exaggerated, though conditions were no doubt very bad. It should be noted on the other hand that in many French hospitals, even prior to the Revolution, patients had individual beds, and that a nation-wide movement was gaining momentum after 1770 to place all hospital patients on single beds. A phase of this movement was the desire to install iron beds to avoid the vermin bred in those made of wood.

David Garrick, who visited the Hôtel-Dieu of Paris on May 31, 1751, found the institution "a most stinking place & very disagreeable." The same could have been said of many other hospitals with equal accuracy. Bedding was changed infrequently, possibly not more than once a month,[20] and patients were probably never bathed.[21] The toilet facilities of the hospitals were grossly inadequate in comparison to present equipment. The urinals for the men and "chambers of ease" (i.e., privies) for the two sexes in wings of the building were filthy. The menial servants, and sometimes prisoners, were kept constantly at work cleaning them. Patients who could not walk from their bed were obliged to use bedpans and "chairs of ease." The latter could be covered, and, being on wheels, were rolled from the room by servants. But their contents were not in-

[19] The patients were so placed that the feet of every alternate person were under the noses of his neighbors.

[20] Buchalet (*op. cit.*, p. 84) asserts that bed sheets were changed every Saturday at the Hôtel-Dieu of Toulouse.

[21] The government sponsored a number of bathing resorts for treating sick and disabled soldiers, but the present writer has found no reference to baths being administered to ordinary patients in the hospitals. On 21 frimaire an IV (December 12, 1795) a request was made of the minister of the interior to install twelve bathtubs (*baignoires*) for the sick at Val-de-Grace, Paris ("Le ministre de la Guerre au Ministre de L'Intérieur," Arch. Nat., F15, 102). No indication is given of the action taken.

frequently spilled, and the chairs and pans were not kept clean. In consequence, the air in many hospitals was foul. The greater use of drugs and the infrequent resort to surgery added to the odors, as did inadequate ventilation. Finally, disinfectants, though no doubt abundantly used, were as a whole much less powerful than those of today.

Toward the close of the century, accompanying the movement for individual beds, came a movement for better aeration of hospitals. Architects were employed to compute the number of cubic feet of air at the disposal of individual patients in the various hospitals, and normal standards were set. Attention was also given to ventilation. In most of the hospitals built or remodeled in the last two or three decades of the century proper ventilation and sufficient air space were emphasized. In fact, one of the arguments advanced in 1755 in favor of constructing the handsome and very expensive dome of the Hôtel-Dieu of Lyons, costing 1,456,956 livres, was the need "of rendering the air there salubrious."[22] At the Easter, 1777, séance of the Académie des Sciences in Paris a paper was read on the construction of hospitals with better ventilation and separation of patients.[23] Thenceforward the hospital records of the century were filled with discussion of methods of improving ventilation.

Another movement in the eighteenth century was toward the separation of patients with different diseases. Some steps had already been taken. In all save a few hospitals women were placed in different wards from men. Pregnant women awaiting delivery, smallpox cases, venereal cases, and insane patients were usually isolated in separate wards. Surgical cases, too, were usually segregated. But patients of other types were apt to be thrown together promiscuously. In some instances the *accouchement* ward might be adjacent to the smallpox ward, or the surgical ward next to the insane ward. Convalescents, in most hospitals, had no special wards and no places for receiving exercise or warm sunshine.[24] The few con-

---

[22] Dagier, *op. cit.*, II, 124, 166. Citing the records of the year 1755, he writes in part: "The air is so infected in the new buildings that, despite all the precautions taken to purify it, many sick who could be healed there find death; the men of the medical art unanimously consider that the elevation of the projected dome alone is able to render the air healthy. Humanity then does not permit us to postpone this means. . . ."

[23] "Precis d'un Ouvrage sur les hôpitaux" (Arch. Nat., F15, 101).

[24] Tenon (*op. cit.*, pp. xxvi, xxviii-xxix, xxxv, 290-291) criticized these conditions.

valescent hospitals in France at the time—two in Paris, one in Marseilles, and those established by the government in connection with military hospitals—were perhaps the best.[25]

Almost all of the patients in the hospitals, whatever the ailment, were treated gratuitously. There were a few with means from whom reimbursement was expected, but they usually were treated at home, and not in the hospitals, which were for the poor and thus were much more exclusively charitable institutions than they are today.

Hospitals of the twentieth century have frequently been used by physicians and surgeons to exploit their patients, or rather their paying patients. Such was not the case in the hospitals of eighteenth-century France, where patients were almost exclusively from the poor. Many physicians and surgeons (possibly one fourth of the whole) rendered their service without remuneration;[26] others received very modest salaries. Many, like the Sisters of Charity, did not receive more than the 100 or 200 livres a year;[27] the greater number, however, received 250, 300, or 400 livres.[28] A few of the better paid received 900 or 1,000 livres.[29] At the Hôtel-Dieu of

[25] *Ibid.*, pp. xxxvi, 41-42, 109, 285-286. Cf. *Arch. parl.*, XXII, 384-385.

[26] For some instances, see Coiffier, *op. cit.*, pp. 76-79; Bouvier, *op. cit.*, pp. 293-294; Viaud and Fleury, *op. cit.*, I, 338; and *Inv.-som* . . . *Isère*, E 9, p. 80. According to *Inv.-som* . . . *Isère*, a physician named Antoine Patras served the Hôpital Général (an asylum, to be sure, and not a hospital in our present meaning of the word) gratuitously for a period of thirty years, carrying out "his duties with great zeal and extreme care, visiting the poor almost every day." In 1787 one hundred young surgeons, other than those interned, gave free service at the Hôtel-Dieu of Paris (Möring and Quentin, *op. cit.*, II, 201).

[27] The nurses at Libourne received 150 livres a year (J. B. J. Eugène Burgade, *Histoire de l'hôpital de Libourne*, Bordeaux, 1867, p. 139). The Hôtel-Dieu of Poitiers employed a surgeon from 1718 to 1730 at 40 livres a year, in 1730 and 1731 at 60 livres, in 1748 at 50 livres, and from 1784 to 1793 at 100 livres (Rambaud, *op. cit.*, II, 108-109, 183). The Hospital of the Incurables at Paris paid its physicians 200 livres a year from 1705 to 1754 (Département de la Seine, *Supplément à l'inventaire sommaire des archives hospitalières antérieures à 1790*, written by M. Brièle, Paris, 1889, pp. 280, 284, 289). The Hôtel-Dieu at Thiers in 1729 paid its surgeon 150 livres a year (Coiffier, *op. cit.*, p. 77). The Hôtel-Dieu of Paris for a period in the 1700's paid its "expectant" physicians, or interns, 200 livres a year (Möring and Quentin, *op. cit.*, II, 18).

[28] Coiffier, *op. cit.*, pp. 76-79; Möring and Quentin, *op. cit.*, II, 49; *Inventaire des archives anciennes de l'hôpital Saint-Jean d'Angers* (Paris and Angers, 1870), E 374, 378, 387.

[29] The seven "ordinary" (regular) physicians of the Hôtel-Dieu of Paris were raised in salary from 800 livres a year to 900 in 1771. In 1777 they were reduced to 400 livres (Möring and Quentin, *op. cit.*, II, 15, 18, 49). In 1754 the Hospital of the Incurables at Paris paid its surgeon 1,000 livres (Département de la Seine,

Paris in 1750 one physician was given 1,500 livres; the first surgeon in 1786, 2,400 livres.[30]   There were, however, other returns to the physicians and surgeons who served the hospitals, such as the esteem of the public, occasional exemption from certain taxes, and, in the case of some surgeons, advancement toward the position of master in their guild or corporation.[31]   It should be noted, however, that many complaints were made by the hospital bureaux against physicians for negligence in visiting their patients,[32] and the movement toward increasing the salaries of physicians and surgeons was partly inspired by a desire to get better service from them.

The hospitals did more than care for the sick confined to beds within their walls; the hôtels-Dieu at least gave free medical and surgical consultations daily to the poor who called for advice; and from their pharmacy shops (in the eighteenth century almost every large hospital had its own pharmacy) they dispensed large quantities of free drugs.   From 1763 to 1790 the Hôtel-Dieu of Lyons maintained an extension nursing service, sending out nurses into the homes of the people for tending the sick.   For the protection of the nurses, however, it was provided that they could be sent on cases only after permission in each instance was granted by three of the hospital rectors (officials) or by the bureau of administrators.   Eventually, after almost thirty years of trial, this service was abandoned because of alleged abuses.[33]

In view of the crowded conditions in many of the hospitals, it is surprising that this service did not become more widespread in cities. There seemed to be no lack of nurses.   Scores of nursing orders were established; a strong spirit toward social service pervaded the Roman Catholic Church; and nurses were held in public esteem.   There was ample opportunity for a new Saint Vincent de Paul to inspire nursing

---

op. cit., p. 289).   In 1789 the Hôtel-Dieu of Angers paid its chief physician 1,000 livres, and in 1740 its lithotomist (appointed and paid by the king) 1,500 livres (*Inventaire des archives anciennes de l'hôpital Saint-Jean d'Angers* . . . , p. xxvii, E 387).

[30] Möring and Quentin, op. cit., II, 18, 171.   Louis Boucher (*La Salpêtrière, son histoire de 1656 à 1790, son origine et son fonctionnement au XVIIIᵉ siècle,* Paris, 1883, p. 89) states that a physician and a surgeon at the Salpêtrière about the 1770's received salaries of 9,000 livres a year.   The present writer has seen no such figures elsewhere, and distrusts their accuracy.

[31] Coiffier, op. cit., p. 76.

[32] Möring and Quentin, op. cit., II, 15, 219; *Inv.-som* . . . *Isère,* E 21, pp.98-99.

[33] Dagier, op. cit., II, 150, 336.

orders to go into the homes of the people. On the eve of the Revolution this plan was discussed; in fact, "some wished to see the hospitals abandoned entirely and the poor treated only in their homes," but nothing came of it.[34]

The hospitals, especially the large hôtels-Dieu, rendered many services. They had their own laundries, their own seamstresses (who provided the bed linen, the shirts and caps for the sick, and garments for the children), their own kitchens and bakeries, their own grain storages. Sometimes grain was stored in the hospital attics, sometimes in unused buildings belonging to the hospitals (for the hospitals owned much real estate, and drew no small portion of their revenue from the rental). In 1736 Louis XV ordered the hospitals of Paris to keep at all times a supply of grain on hand for at least two years in order to forestall famine.[35] The hospitals, moreover, had their own slaughterhouses and made their own candles. All in all, the eighteenth-century hospitals were to a considerable degree self-sustaining, complex institutions.

Even so, the hospitals (and asylums) of France on the eve of the Revolution were spending more than they received, though their annual receipts amounted at least to 29,000,000 livres.[36] The revenues of the Hôtel-Dieu of Paris in 1788 were 924,106 livres, and the expenditures 906,799 livres.[37]

Whence came the hospital revenues? From legacies and other large gifts, from alms, from rentals on real estate belonging to the institutions, from state and municipal grants (on special occasions of

[34] Emily Greene Balch, *Public Assistance of the Poor in France* (Publications of the American Economic Association, VIII, Baltimore, 1893), p. 63.

[35] Freminville, *op. cit.*, p. 360. Not only hospitals but also seminaries, colleges, and religious communities within forty leagues, or sixty miles, of Paris had to do likewise. They must always have on hand on January 1 of each year a three years' supply of grain, and never during the year let their stock dwindle below a two years' supply.

[36] According to the sixth report of the committee of mendicity, rendered to the National Assembly on January 31, 1791 (*Arch. parl.*, XXII, 607). The 1,438 hospitals that replied to the questionnaire of the committee reported revenues normally totaling 20,874,664 livres, while 747 hospitals did not reply. The amount of their revenues was not known, but the committee estimated them at more than eight millions. In 1790, at the depth of the economic depression attending the Revolution, the revenues of the 1,438 hospitals of the committee's report had fallen to 13,987,787 livres.

[37] In 1770, when they reached the highest point for the century, the revenues of this institution were 2,800,225 livres, and expenditures 2,740,084 livres (Département de la Seine, *op. cit.*, p. 320).

need), from taxes, fines, lotteries , balls (until 1715), and from the privilege of selling fish, game, and other meat during Lent.[38]

It is frequently assumed that the charities of the Old Regime, more especially those of the hospitals, were the work of the church. The church, it is true, played a larger part in the hospitals than in other forms of charity under the Old Regime, but even in them it had a lesser share than might be expected. For one thing, the larger hospitals or hôtels-Dieu were municipally owned and were controlled, not by the church, but by large private boards (bureaux) of administrators, composed of the leading citizens of each community. Ecclesiastics seldom if ever constituted above one fourth of the number. More surprising is the fact that the church furnished only a small part of the hospital revenues. Alms collected for the hospitals were trivial in amount. The chief revenue of most hospitals came from other sources, including the revenues from real estate and other hospital property, almost all of which had been bestowed on the hospitals as legacies or gifts. Each year gifts and legacies swelled the hospital endowments. Some institutions, to be sure, more particularly the large hôtels-Dieu in cities like Paris, Lyons, Bordeaux, Lille, and Marseilles, derived more from these sources than the smaller hospitals. The large bequests made annually to the Hôtel-Dieu of Lyons, as recorded in Dagier's *Histoire chronologique de l'Hôpital Général et grand Hôtel-Dieu de Lyon*, reveal that a humanitarian spirit was prevalent. Not a few exceeded 100,000 livres, and many were above 50,000 livres. The Hôtel-Dieu of Paris was still more fortunate.[39] One writer reports that it was fashionable, in fact almost universal, for testators to insert a clause in their wills in favor of a local hospital. Judging from examples of itemized hospital revenues, it would appear that possibly 40 to 50 per cent of the income came from endowment, legacies, and gifts; 5 to 10 per cent came from church sources; and the remainder came from state, provincial, or municipal sources.[40]

The chief governmental aid came in the form of taxes. Most of

[38] Meat sold during Lent by the Hôtel-Dieu of Paris was until 1770 commonly 2 sous a livre higher than the normal market price. In 1770 it was raised to 3 sous above market price. The estimated revenue was placed at 100,000 to 150,000 livres (Möring and Quentin, *op. cit.*, II, 10-11).

[39] In 1789 it received a legacy of 320,000 livres from an estate of 1,200,000 livres left by one Goudon (*ibid.*, II, 252).

[40] Some itemized accounts of hospital revenues are given by the following: Fos-

the taxes in question were municipal, others provincial or national; but all were levied with government approval and formed a part of the national tax system. Of these taxes, the *octroi* commonly yielded the most money.[41] They were duties levied on goods entering the city, more especially on wines, cider, and *poiré* (fermented pear juice), and almost everywhere in France a portion or all of their receipts (depending on the place) were given to the local hôtel-Dieu and general hospital.[42] Widespread also was a tax on meat sold in the markets.[43] In many cities the hôtel-Dieu or the general hospital, or both, enjoyed the privilege of selling meat during Lent.[44] In 1724, 1727, 1747, and 1776 the government imposed a surtax of 3 deniers per livre in connection with the *taille* in certain generalities for the benefit of the hospitals.[45] After 1776 it became a permanent tax. The hôtels-Dieu of many cities enjoyed the right to a percentage of the receipts from theatricals and other public entertain-

---

seyeux, *L'Hôtel-Dieu de Paris au XVIIᵉ et au XVIIIᵉ siècle*, pp. 167-168, 171-173; Martin-Doisy, *Dictionnaire d'économie charitable*, IV, 897-898; G. Gross-Mayrevieille, "L'assistance publique à Narbonne au XVIIIᵉ siècle et les mémoires de Charles de Bellainvilliers," *Bulletin de la commission archéologique de Narbonne*, VIII (Narbonne, 1904), 290-291; Cuzent, *op. cit.*, pp. 105-106; Tenon, *op. cit.*, pp. 331-338.

[41] Out of the hospital revenues of 1,500,000 livres at Lyons in 1789, 560,000 livres were furnished by the *octroi* (*Exposition universelle de 1900: l'économie sociale et l'histoire de travail à Lyon*, Lyon, 1900, pp. 263-264). To the Hôtel-Dieu of Paris around 1780 the *octroi* were worth 274,000 livres (Möring and Quentin, *op. cit.*, II, 88, 233-234). In 1788 the *octroi* at Paris were converted to the fixed sums of 212,000 livres for the Hôtel-Dieu and 36,000 livres for the Hospital of the Incurables (*ibid.*, II, 233-234). To one of the hospitals at Rennes the *octroi* furnished 10,000 livres out of total revenues of 32,144 livres (*Inv.-som . . . Ille-et-Vilaine*, C 1267).

[42] Thus at Vannes, until 1730, there was an *octroi* on drinks, two thirds of which went to the Hôtel-Dieu and the other third to the Hospital Saint Louis (*Inv.-som . . . Ille-et-Vilaine*, C 1278). In 1721 the council of state ordered an *octroi* on wine, cider, and *poiré* in all places in the generality of Caen where there were hospitals, in favor of them (*Inv.-som . . . Calvados*, C 590).

[43] At Narbonne a tax of 2 sous per livre (weight) was levied for this purpose (Gross-Mayrevieille, *op. cit.*, p. 284).

[44] The Hôtel-Dieu of Paris long enjoyed this monopoly (Möring and Quentin, *op. cit.*, II, 10-11, 125). Turgot in 1774-75 called it a nuisance and abrogated it, giving the Hôtel-Dieu in its stead 50,000 livres a year, to come from a tax on animals brought to Paris and on the sale of meat in the markets (*Oeuvres de Turgot*, II, 225-226). The General Hospital of Grenoble was allowed the privilege in 1751, but in 1758 leased it to a butcher for 1,560 livres (*Inv.-som . . . Isère*, B 12).

[45] *Inv.-som . . . Gironde*, C 3064, 3992; *Inv.-som . . . Côte d'Or*, C 1727, f 12; *Inv.-som . . . Calvados*, C 237.

ments.[46] In the generality of Caen, and also at Clermont-Ferrand, a professional tax, to aid the hospitals, was levied upon legal officials and upon those in the guilds receiving the maîtrise.[47] The Hôtel-Dieu of Paris drew a considerable revenue from tolls on a bridge over the Seine, which in 1765 amounted to 12,159 livres.[48] The city of Brest in 1787 agreed to turn over to its hospital the money arising from the sale of manure taken from its streets, which provided 13,000 livres out of a total revenue of 55,945.[49] The same hospital drew a revenue of 900 livres from the concession of cleaning the streets: in 1791 it was given the right to sell debris in the harbor and the ballast of ships, estimated to bring in 12,000 livres a year. The city of Brest also placed a small tax on young men who refused to go to sea, and in certain instances on those who contracted marriage.[50] The hospital at Antibes, in Provence, enjoyed a tax on the salt franchise.[51] The hospitals of Rennes enjoyed the right of selling coffins and funeral hangings.[52] The hospitals of Grenoble had the proceeds of a small tax placed upon flour and upon bakeries.[53] At Riom merchants paid a tax to the hospitals whenever they rented a shop.[54] No doubt a large number of these taxes, some municipal, others provincial or national, were levied here and there in the various towns and cities of France, with little or no uniformity. Perhaps no two hospitals enjoyed quite the same tax revenues.

Not only did the hospitals derive revenues from certain taxes, but they were also exempt from others. Thus all hospitals were exempt from taxes on the wine and meat consumed by their patients.[55] In Dauphiné, if not also in other provinces, hospital property, at least for periods in the eighteenth century, was exempt from payment of

---

[46] The Hôtel-Dieu of Paris was one. During the last two decades before the Revolution it had much difficulty in collection, and frequently had to be content with a smaller share than was its right by law (Möring and Quentin, *op. cit.*, II, 32, 70, 146, 268-269, 274-275).

[47] *Inv.-som* . . . *Calvados*, C 590; Coiffier, *op. cit.*, pp. 189-190.

[48] Tenon, *op. cit.*, p. 333.

[49] Cuzent, *op. cit.*, pp. 105-106.

[50] *Ibid.*, p. 104.

[51] *Inv.-som* . . . *Bouches-du-Rhône*, C 1002.

[52] *Inv.-som* . . . *Ille-et-Vilaine*, C 1267. On the similar privilege enjoyed by the Hôtel-Dieu of Toulouse, see Buchalet, *op. cit.*, pp. 70-71.

[53] *Inv.-som* . . . *Isère*, B 16.

[54] Coiffier, *op. cit.*, p. 190.

[55] *Inv.-som* . . . *Isère*, B 10; *Inv.-som* . . . *Calvados*, H Suppl. 73, B 70; Cuzent, *op. cit.*, p. 104; Dumas, *op. cit.*, p. 87.

the *dixième* and the *taille*.[56] Furthermore, it was apparently a pre-
rogative of all the hospitals to bring lawsuits in behalf of their property and rights exempt from court charges and lawyers' fees.[57]

Small sums accrued to the hospitals from fines. A multitude of
French laws and ordinances carried penal clauses inflicting on violators fines large and small, one third, one half, or even all of which
was to go to the nearest hôtel-Dieu or general hospital. Thus an
arrêt of the parlement of Paris, dated February 8, 1708, forbade the
operation of any gambling games or devices at fairs, in the markets,
or elsewhere, on penalty of confiscation of the devices and of the
money on hand, and liability to a fine of 100 livres, all of which was
to go to the nearest hôtel-Dieu.[58] An *arrêt* of the parlement of
Dijon, April 21, 1701, provided that persons who taught children
games of chance were to be fined 3,000 livres, of which one third was
to go to the informer, one third to the king (i.e., the government),
and one third to the General Hospital of Dijon.[59] Merchants selling
merchandise on credit to minors without legitimate reason were to
be fined 500 livres, payable to the hospitals of the region.[60] A fine
of 1,500 livres (later in the century increased to 3,000 livres) was to
be inflicted upon anyone who imported, sold, or printed contraband
books in France, one third of it to go to the Hôtel-Dieu of Paris.[61]
Most of the fines imposed for violation of the rules of the bourse at
Paris were large in amount and were to go in part or exclusively to
the General Hospital of that city.[62] Half of a fine of 300 livres
imposed on iron-workers throughout France who abandoned their
work, according to an *arrêt du conseil* of December 27, 1729, was to
go to the profit of the nearest hospitals, the other half to the master
of the furnace or forge abandoned by the worker.[63] By an ordinance
of Louis XV, dated August 4, 1731, robbers and receivers of stolen
material for road-paving were to be fined 1,000 livres each, one third
of it to go to Hôtel-Dieu of Paris if the crime was committed in

---

[56] *Inv.-som* . . . *Isère*, B 20, 21. The Hôtel-Dieu of Poitiers regularly paid
taxes, but they were commonly remitted at the end of the year (Rambaud, *op. cit.*,
II, 130).

[57] Coiffier, *op. cit.*, p. 191.　　　　　[58] Freminville, *op. cit.*, p. 386.

[59] *Ibid.*, p. 322.　　　　　[60] *Idem.*

[61] *Ibid.*, "Privilege du roi"; *Etat général des unions faites des biens et revenues
des maladeries, leproseries, aumôneries & autres lieux pieux, aux hôpitaux des pauvres
malades* (Paris, 1705), "Privilège du roy."

[62] By an *arrêt du conseil* of Sept. 24, 1724 (Paillot, *op. cit.*, I, 150-155).

[63] *Ibid.*, I, 195.

Paris, otherwise to go to the nearest hospital.[64] These were a few of the vast number of the ordinances and *arrêts* that imposed fines which went, at least in part, toward the support of the hospitals. According to Marcel Fosseyeux, all fines and confiscations in eighteenth-century Paris went exclusively to the Hôtel-Dieu and the General Hospital.[65]

Occasionally the government permitted lotteries for raising money in behalf of the hospitals. Three lotteries to raise funds for the Hôtel-Dieu of Lyons were held in 1700.[66] In Provence Lebret *père* (1686-1704) had recourse to lotteries for the creation of hospitals in various cities. In 1787 the council of state authorized the city of Paris to borrow 12,000,000 livres to aid the hospitals and to employ lotteries for repaying the money.[67]

More commonly the national or the provincial government made outright grants of money when hospitals found themselves in dire need. In the case of cities in the *pays d'élections*, in which category were most of the French provinces, the national government made the grants; but in the *pays d'états*, the provincial government generally made them. Instances of the latter were the appropriation of 150 livres by the general assembly of Provence for the House of Refuge at Aix in 1728 and the appropriations of 30,000 livres to two hospitals in Marseilles in 1783.[68] An example of the former was a government grant of 3,000 livres in 1713 to three Parisian hospitals which had suffered severe monetary losses as a result of the famine of 1709.[69] On occasion during the eighteenth century the government made grants to the Hôtel-Dieu of Paris, certain of them large.[70] To the hospital at Brest the government in 1788

[64] *Ibid.*, I, 202.

[65] *Le budget de la charité à Paris au XVIIIe siècle*, p. 7. Not the whole of the fines went to the hospitals, however; Fosseyeux makes a careless statement.

[66] Dagier, *op. cit.*, II, 25-27.

[67] Léon Lallemand, *Histoire de la charité*, IV, Part I (Paris, 1910), 353 with n. 26. The sum of 1,200,000 livres was raised for this purpose by lottery in 1788-89, but the money was applied by the Revolutionary government to other ends (*Arch. parl.*, XXII, 382). Other lotteries took place in the early period of the Revolution. See Tuetey, *Répertoire général* . . . , III, 28, 52, Nos. 310 and 580.

[68] *Inv.-som* . . . *Bouches-du-Rhône*, C 68 (f 206), 2501.

[69] These hospitals had suffered a total loss of 434,302 livres for the period 1707-13 (Bibl. Nat., Fonds français 6802, ff 220-221).

[70] Thus by 1786 the government had appropriated 1,200,000 livres toward the reconstruction of its buildings after the fire of 1772 (Möring and Quentin, *op. cit.*, II, 167). In the 1780's it provided the Hôtel-Dieu with 1,000 single beds (*ibid.*,

granted 30,000 livres toward the construction of two new halls.[71] In 1725 it allotted 12,488 livres to the hospitals of Troyes.[72] These were but a few instances in which the royal and provincial governments aided the hospitals. When Roland in his report to the Convention as minister of the interior on January 9, 1793, stated, "I ought to set forth that the public treasury has hitherto paid to different hospitals some annual sums under the category of relief, and that the extent of this aid reached 806,226 livres [in 1791]," he was not describing a Revolutionary practice alone, but also one which had existed under the Old Regime.[73]

The city governments also made frequent appropriations to assist their local hospitals. Thus the city officials of Rochefort in 1761 voted a sum of 205 livres for their institution.[74]

These gifts by the government were separate from the subsidies to the hospitals for the care of foundlings and soldiers, for which large sums were paid annually. To the hospitals of Lisieux alone, the government in 1779 paid 10,412 livres for the treatment of soldiers and 5,416 livres for the maintenance of foundlings. These sums constituted more than one fourth of the hospital revenues of 57,825 livres that year in Lisieux[75] The government regularly made similar subsidies to scores of hospitals.[76] The committee on pensions set forth three government subsidy grants to hospitals in 1789 amounting to 1,817,106 livres.[77]

Sometimes the government was called upon to make a trivial grant of miscellaneous nature to the hospitals. For example, it paid 50 livres a year for the right of placing and maintaining cannon and

---

p. 168), at a cost of 600,000 livres (Martin-Doisy, op. cit., IV, 900). In 1786 the government offered to give the Hôtel-Dieu 212,000 livres a year in lieu of revenues on objects of consumption (Möring and Quentin, op. cit., II, 171).

[71] Cuzent, op. cit., p. 390.

[72] Inv.-som . . . l'Aube, C 1896.

[73] Arch. parl., LVI, 642.

[74] Inv.-som . . . Ville de Rochefort, 707.

[75] Inv.-som . . . Calvados, H Suppl. 418 E 257, arts. 104-107.

[76] The Livre rouge, published in 1790, lists a large number of these payments (Arch. parl., XIII, 205-259).

[77] Ibid., XVI, 654. Nor does this figure include a gift of 32,000 livres for soldiers' orphans or one of 49,500 livres for "gratifications and aid in favor of [charitable] establishments" (idem). Miss Balch (op. cit., p. 66) states that of the estimated 38,000,000 livres spent on charities in France under the Old Regime, 7,500,000 were contributed by the government. These estimates she attributes to the committee of mendicity of the National Assembly.

ammunition on hospital property at Grenoble.[78] In 1786 it was called upon to indemnify certain hospitals because a highway to Caen was run through their property.[79] In 1758 the city officials of Dinan requested the king to give them, for use as a hospital, the local convent of the Benedictine nuns as soon as it should be unused.[80]

In the 1770's and 1780's the government took a belated but prominent part in a movement to render the hospitals more sanitary and comfortable. The early 1700's had seen an occasional advocate of fresh air and single beds, as evidenced by a legacy for the latter at Riom in 1710.[81] Later in the century, apparently in the 1770's, when the movement began to attract attention, the intendant of Riom took an interest in seeing that the new buildings for the General Hospital of that city were constructed with high ceilings and numerous windows, so that the inmates would have plenty of light and air.[82]

In 1779 the royal government joined in the movement led by Madame Necker, a woman of strong Christian and charitable sentiments, who, when she visited the hospitals of Paris and observed their insanitary condition, urged her husband, the director-general of finance, to alleviate the situation. In 1779 the government accordingly presented the Hospital of Saint-Sulpice and the Large Rock (today the Hospital Necker) with 120 single beds at a cost of 42,000 livres.[83] Necker also planned to introduce 2,500 single beds two and a half feet wide, and 500 double beds, with partitions, four and a half feet wide, the latter for convalescents and pregnant women, in the Hôtel-Dieu of Paris The measure was to be an experiment. New buildings were to be constructed, and the men and women placed on different banks of the Seine. The government offered to bear the entire expense.[84] The hospital administrators preferred

---

[78] *Inv.-som . . . Isère*, B 22.

[79] *Inv.-som . . . Calvados*, H Suppl. 171 E 10.

[80] All of the nuns there were old, and no new ones were being received; hence it would soon become unoccupied (Remoras to the Duc d'Aiguillon, Arch. Nat., F15, 396).

[81] Coiffier, *op. cit.*, p. 75. The hospital apparently took the money but did not install the beds.

[82] *Idem.*

[83] *Arch. parl.*, XXII, 386; A. Cretin, *Organisation de l'assistance hospitalière libre et libérale* (Paris, 1886), p. 20; Jacques Necker, *Compte rendu au roi* (Paris, 1781), pp. 100-101.

[84] Möring and Quentin, *op. cit.*, II, 94-97.

single beds three feet wide and double beds (with partitions) five feet two inches wide.[85] By 1787 the government had installed these beds, or most of them.[86] It would thus appear that Tenon's criticism of the crowding of patients at the Hôtel-Dieu was based on his visit there in 1786, before all of the new beds were installed. The government also provided more sanitary mattresses (in lieu of the old feather beds), bedclothes, and new pillows. In every instance the government consulted the hospital administrators and its physicians and surgeons before making the changes.[87] Moreover, it introduced baths for the patients in the new hall.[88]

The only opposition to these innovations came from an unexpected quarter. The nuns who served the hospital as nurses and internal administrators showed a sullen resentment toward the installation of the single beds. In the 1780's there was much animosity in the Hôtel-Dieu of Paris and apparently in other hospitals between them and the physicians and surgeons. The government consulted the physicians and surgeons and ignored them on matters that they felt keenly concerned them. Jealous and piqued, they fought the new measures and brought unfounded charges against certain of the physicians and surgeons.[89]

The partial destruction of the Hôtel-Dieu of Paris by fire in 1772 was followed by an important, extended controversy over the matter of its rebuilding. Some advocated abandoning the Hôtel-Dieu entirely and enlarging certain other Parisian hospitals. The government manifested interest in the proposal. Administrators and friends of the Hôtel-Dieu, however, came forward with such plausible arguments for its retention that the proposal was allowed to drop. About 1786 the proposal was again brought forward, this time by the architect Poyet and the Academy of Sciences. The latter appointed a committee of its members to investigate the proposal. One of the committee was Bailly, later first mayor of Paris. Another was Tenon, a physician at the Hospital of Charity at Saint-Germain-des-Près, who visited hospitals in England, collected statistics on them (especially on their sanitary condition), and in 1788 published his

---

[85] *Ibid.*, pp. 108, 111.

[86] *Ibid.*, pp. 168, 219, 225-228.

[87] *Ibid.*, pp. 100-102, 105, 107, 108, 111.

[88] *Ibid.*, p. 109.

[89] *Ibid.*, pp. 215-219, 225, 229-230, 236-243, 249, 250-251. Cf. *Arch. parl.*, XXII, 379.

findings in a notable volume, under the title *Mémoires sur les hôpitaux de Paris*.[90] He and the Academy of Sciences had more influence with the government than did the administrators of the Hôtel-Dieu, most of whom were in favor of the *status quo*, and in 1788 the government issued orders that the Hôtel-Dieu should in time be abandoned and its patients moved to four hospitals in widely separated suburbs of the city.[91] A popular subscription for funds was started and resulted in the raising of over 2,000,000 livres. The government promised its aid. The aim was to improve the sanitary conditions of the Parisian hospitals and to put the stamp of government disapproval on conditions at the Hôtel-Dieu, where one patient in six on an average had died throughout the eighteenth century. But amid the turmoil and lack of money in France during the Revolution the project was abandoned for the second time.[92]

A further instance of government aid to hospitals came in connection with the founding and endowment of the Hospital of the Schools of Surgery. In an effort to promote surgical science in France, the government in 1774 established this institution with six beds and a professorship in chemistry and authorized a grant of 7,000 livres for annual expenses. The institution would serve the function of a laboratory, where the faculty and students of surgery at Paris might keep for special observation patients of both sexes who had rare ailments. In 1782 Pichault de la Martinière, first surgeon at the time, endowed the institution with ten additional beds. The next year the government added six more beds and a professorship in botany, setting aside an additional 7,000 livres for their annual maintenance.[93] During the eighteenth century surgery in France made notable advances, and Louis XIV, Louis XV, and Louis XVI had some part in its encouragement.

The Period 1789-1800

The Revolution was not a boon to French hospitals. On the con-

---

[90] This work exerted tremendous influence in France for the next decade and has ever since been consulted by scholars as the leading contemporary study of eighteenth-century French hospitals. It is a large repository of interesting data, but Tenon was partisan.

[91] Möring and Quentin, *op. cit.*, II, iv-v, 26-28, 35-38, 63, 114, 125, 163-164, 172-173, 190-191, 195, 199-205, 232.

[92] The Hôtel-Dieu still occupies its time-honored site and renders its service to humanity.

[93] Tuetey, *L'assistance publique*, IV, 77, 81, 93-94; *Arch. parl.*, XXII, 388.

trary, it ushered in a period of severe financial hardships. The economic crisis which had been gradually gathering momentum since 1786 broke with full intensity in 1789 and 1790, and in each of these two years hospital revenues fell heavily. According to the committee of mendicity, the income of 1,438 hospitals (747 others did not report) fell from 20,874,665 livres in 1788 to 13,987,778 livres in 1790.[94] In Paris the revenues dropped from 7,958,799 livres to 4,129,206 livres. Only a small part of this decline was due to legislation by the National Assembly. Some taxes and dues that had brought income to the hospitals were suppressed in 1789, but the *octroi* (the chief tax for hospital revenue) was not abolished until May 1, 1791.[95] Others taxes, such as that on public entertainments, from which the hospitals drew revenues, were retained. In brief, the fall in hospital revenues in 1789-90 was due not so much to suppression of taxes as to certain other factors: the inability and unwillingness of the French at that particular time to pay taxes, the drop in revenues from investments held by the hospitals, and the drying up of private charities.

A law in March, 1791, which suppressed all indirect taxes, was followed shortly by the abolition of the *octrois*.[96] By these two acts hospital revenue from taxes disappeared, and the hospitals, already suffering acutely from their diminshed income, were rendered helpless and dependent upon the state. Occasional grants or "advances" followed. A "loan" of 3,000,000 livres was made to the hospitals by a decree of July 25, 1791, to supply temporary needs, and another of 1,500,000 livres by a decree of September 12 On January 22, 1792, 1,500,000 livres also were placed at the disposal of the minister of the interior to be loaned the hospitals on terms similar to those of 1791.[97] Apparently these "loans" or "advances" were never repaid; indeed, they could not have been, for in the 1700's the hospitals were never in a position to repay advances. Altogether

[94] *Arch. parl.*, XXII, 607, 618. Martin-Doisy (*Dictionnaire d'économie charitable*, IV, 1045) states that in 1789 the hospital revenues had fallen, according to some authorities, to about 17 millions, according to others to 13 millions.

[95] According to Roland, minister of the interior, the *octrois* brought in a total of 10 to 12 millions; but he does not indicate how much of this sum went to the hospitals (*Arch. parl.*, LVI, 642).

[96] Louis Parturier, *L'assistance à Paris sous l'ancien régime & pendant la Révolution* (Paris, 1897), p. 212.

[97] *Ibid.*, pp. 213-214; *Arch. parl.*, LVI, 642-643.

the government advanced or granted 9,000,000 livres to hospitals in 1791-92, 4,670,000 going to the hospitals of Paris alone.[98] And yet this sum was insufficient; as one writer has observed, twenty-six millions should have been voted in 1789-90.[99] In 1793 the government accorded eight millions and in 1794, ten millions.[100] By this time, however, inflation had considerably reduced the value of the livre, and the larger grants did not represent greater generosity on the part of the Revolutionary government.

Not only did the state strike at the sources of hospital revenue, but after January 1, 1791, the hospitals were obliged to pay a tax to the government on landed property. This was something new in French hospital history,[101] and so heavy was the new tax that according to Roland, in his report to the Convention on January 9, 1793, it reduced the hospital income by a fifth.[102] It is almost incredible that the Revolutionary government should have taxed its hospitals.

But the government was desperate for money to carry out its ends. In November, 1789, it had confiscated the property of the church and the religious orders, including the hospital property of the latter. In February, 1790, the religious orders, save those devoted to nursing and teaching, were abolished; and on August 18, 1792, these last were suppressed, though their members were ordered to continue their work in the hospitals.[103]

These actions by the government brought confusion. Some of the hospitals of the religious orders were closed or united to others that were in operation, but according to a document of 29 germinal an II (April 18, 1794) most of the hospitals that had belonged to the orders were still existent and enjoying their revenues.[104] The nurses had been encouraged to remain at their posts in the hospitals, despite the dissolution of their orders. Until pressure was brought

[98] An itemized account of its distribution is given in Roland's report (*Arch. parl.*, LVI, 644).

[99] Ferdinand-Dreyfus, *L'assistance*, p. 20 with n. 5.

[100] Decrees of July 14, 1793, and Feb. 1, 1794 (Parturier, *op. cit.*, p. 214 n.).

[101] "Avant 1789, les hôpitaux ne supportent aucune imposition . . ." (Léon Lallemand, *La Révolution et les pauvres*, Paris, 1898, p. 158).

[102] *Arch. parl.*, LVI, 642. In 1796 the Hôtel-Dieu of Beaune, renamed the Hospice d'Humanité, was not able to pay all of its taxes (Etienne Bavard, *Hôtel-Dieu de Beaune, 1445-1800*, Beaune, 1881, p. 293).

[103] Dagier, *op. cit.*, II, 347-348.

[104] Tuetey, *L'assistance publique*, IV, 81.

to have them take the oath of allegiance (after January 1, 1792) and until they were forbidden to wear their religious garb (1794), virtually all appear to have remained. These orders brought widespread, if not unanimous, defiance from the Sisters, some of whom left their work. Others remained and flouted the regulations. At Beaune three were incarcerated in 1794, until the death of Robespierre.[105]

In some places lay women assumed the posts vacated by the nurses, and at Poitiers they did their work with zeal and efficiency.[106] But what became of the Brothers of Charity, the Brothers of St. John of God, and other nursing orders of monks is not clear. The priests that had served the hospitals, however, were chased from them without ado in all instances where they refused to take the oath to the state, being replaced by clergy who were willing to swear loyalty.[107] In some instances the number and duties of these priests were then reduced. During the Terror all religious services in the hospitals were prohibited and the hospital chapels closed; the priests were evidently dismissed.[108]

The confiscation of the property of the secular (or municipal) hospitals was destined to follow that of the religious orders. The matter was broached early in 1791 and was debated in a session of the National Assembly of January 21. Andrieu, Bouche, De Folleville, and the Abbé Bourdon fought the measure and succeeded in getting it defeated. Liancourt, replying in behalf of the committee of mendicity, which sponsored the idea, replied that hospital aid was

[105] Bavard, *op. cit.*, pp. 286-289. Revolutionary bitterness toward the Church showed itself at Beaune in January, 1794, by much vandalism at the hospital. The burial vaults of the dead Sisters were destroyed; all emblems of Catholic worship, including cross, seven-branched candlestick, fount, images of Christ and the Virgin, were thrown out or otherwise removed; some copper tombs were taken from the chapel and the bones tossed aside; and paintings in the chapel by Flemish masters were mutilated and ruined (*ibid.*, pp. 284-285).

[106] Rambaud, *op. cit.*, II, 199, 221. On the lay nurses at Libourne, see Burgade, *op. cit.*, pp. 177-179, 189.

[107] Bavard, *op. cit.*, pp. 279-280.

[108] If the hospital clergy suffered severely during the Revolution, they had often battened at their work under the Old Regime. Twenty-four priests (besides seventy-two monks and nuns) were employed at the Hôtel-Dieu de Paris in 1790 (*Arch. parl.*, XXII, 379). Until 1788, when their salary was lowered to 800 livres, the clergy serving the Hôtel-Dieu of Angers received each 1,000 livres (*Inventaire des archives anciennes de l'hôpital Saint-Jean d'Angers* . . ., p. xxxi). The chaplain of the General Hospital of Bayeux received 500 livres in 1784 (*Inv.-som* . . . *Calvados*, H Suppl. 1137. II E 13).

UNIVERSITY
COLLEGE
LIBRARY
NOTTINGHAM

a very pressing matter, that in nine tenths of the rural districts no aid whatever was forthcoming, and that most of the hospitals were in debt. He added that confiscation of hospital property and state control did not necessarily mean that the property would be sold at once.[109]

Though the measure was defeated, its eventual passage was certain; and on July 11, 1794, a law transferred hospital property to the state. The government at the same time assumed responsibility for hospital indebtedness and maintenance.[110] The law stipulated that some of the property would be sold to clear up indebtedness. In consequence, much hospital property was sold, but those in charge of the hospitals in some places were successful in staving off the sale.[111] The minister of finance in 1794, who proposed the law of July 14 to the Convention, declared that it was necessary to pay the expenses occasioned by the war in which France was then engaged.[112] But it might have been adopted in any case, since it was the logical end of the philosophy of relief then prevalent. After 1789 it was the almost unanimous opinion in France that the problem of relief was one for the state to handle. Beginning with the question of unemployment, this view quickly was extended to charities of all types. State ownership of hospital property and state administration of hospital needs and services were but the logical conclusion of events that had been shaping themselves since 1789—if, indeed, they were not the logical conclusion of events that had been developing since the 1500's and 1600's.

How did this interesting experiment in state ownership of hospital property turn out? It was not a success, and by laws of October 25, 1795, and April 17, 1796, the decree of July 11 was suspended, the sales were stopped, and the revenues of hospital property temporarily returned to the hospitals. Finally, a law of 16 vendémiaire an V (October 7, 1796) returned to the civil hospitals their unsold property and investments, with the right of enjoying all proceeds from them. The hospitals were to be compensated for the sold property, but this law remained an empty promise.[113] The hospital revenues had now fallen. Instead of the thirty millions before the Revolution, there were in the year V (1796-97) only three or four

---

[109] *Arch. parl.*, XXII, 592-593. [110] Dagier, *op. cit.*, p. 364.
[111] Lallemand, *op. cit.*, pp. 162-164. [112] Ferdinand-Dreyfus, *op. cit.*, p. 86.
[113] A detailed résumé of the law is given by Burgade, *op. cit.*, p. 192.

millions.[114] The government supplemented this revenue with subsidies. The hospitals of Paris were granted 500,000 livres in late December, 1796, and 300,000 livres on March 17, 1797, but figures for the total sum allotted at this time to French hospitals are not available.

The grants were small in view of the needs of the hospitals and of the depreciation of French money, for from 1796 through the year 1800 distressing appeals for aid were made to the government. The French of the eighteenth century were quite adept at making piteous appeals when requesting aid, and sometimes their exaggeration is manifest. There was doubtless, however, little exaggeration in the reports of suffering sent by the hospitals to the minister of the interior in these years.[115] In October, 1798, the administrators of the department of Haute-Garonne wrote to the minister that the two civil hospitals of Toulouse were in distress, no funds having been received for a long time; that there was a dearth of supplies, especially bedclothes; that there was no linen, and the poor were in rags; that winter was approaching, and that no woolen goods of any kind were to be had.[116] On December 13 the same administrators again begged aid and reported that the hospital had no wheat, no flour, no wine in its storerooms; that it had no woolen cloth or cover, that the poor were still dressed in summer material; and that unless aid came within ten days Toulouse would be without hospitals.[117] Happily for the hospitals of Toulouse aid did come within ten days, in a grant of 39,500 livres.[118] But the relief was temporary and partial, for on April 25, 1799, another letter to the minister of the interior in behalf of the same hospitals represented them as still being in need.[119]

In their desperation for funds the hospitals of Toulouse in early 1798 asked Destrem, the city's representative to the Council of the Five Hundred in Paris, to represent their situation to the minister of

[114] Ferdinand-Dreyfus (op. cit., p. 87) says that they were four; Parturier, only three, and that much of this was needed for repairs on houses rented. In 1790, Parturier adds (op. cit., p. 239 with nn.), the hospitals had drawn from their investments 6,699,525 livres.

[115] Lallemand (La Révolution et les pauvres, pp. 177-180, 189-210, 280-384) sets forth, by documentary quotation, the frightful misery of scores of hospitals and asylums throughout France. Cf. Bavard, op. cit., p. 293.

[116] Adher, op. cit., p. 199. [117] Ibid., p. 201.

[118] Ibid., p. 202. [119] Ibid., pp. 211-212.

the interior and the Corps Legislatif.[120]   In June he replied that other hospitals in France were in the same distress as those at Toulouse.[121]

The minister of the interior of this period, François de Neufchâteau, pretended to Destrem in March that he did not know that the hospitals at Toulouse were experiencing difficulties,[122] alleging that the hospitals at Toulouse had not sent to his office the reports required by law.   He could promise, however, no relief.   One who reads the correspondence between Toulouse and Paris at this time, as reproduced by Adher, is convinced that funds available for the needs of the hospitals were sadly inadequate.   Occasionally a check was sent, but the aid was a pittance, and the hospitals of Toulouse would have been forced to close had it not been for loans to cover the heavy deficits.[123]   In 1800 the state of the two hospitals in Toulouse was "extremely alarming."   The government still owed them for the years IV, V, VI, and VII a total of 751,131 francs.[124]

Following the law of October 7, 1796, which returned the unsold hospital property and its revenues to the hospitals, the government proceeded to re-establish certain of the pre-Revolutionary taxes in favor of the hospitals in an attempt to help them meet their expenses.   The first of the taxes thus revived was that on shows, provided by the law of 5 frimaire an V (November 27, 1796), under the terms of which one tenth of the return on tickets to plays and other public performances was to be set aside in every city for the use of its hospitals.   But the revenue from this source was small.[125] Another tax restored was the *octroi*.   From the beginning of the year VII (September 22, 1798) the government permitted one city after another to establish *octrois* on wine and other commodities entering their gates, part of the proceeds to go to the maintenance of their hospitals.[126]   The *octroi* was restored in Paris, October 18, 1798;[127]

---

[120] *Ibid.*, pp. 174, 194.   [121] *Ibid.*, p. 194.
[122] *Ibid.*, pp. 187-188.   [123] *Ibid.*, pp. 202, 204-205.
[124] *Ibid.*, p. 226. From 1795 the term "franc" replaced that of "livre" in the documents as the unit of French money. The franc had a slightly higher value. One livre, it is said, was worth 0.9877 franc (Madeleine Deries, *op. cit.*, p. 501).
[125] Burgade, *op. cit.*, pp. 193, 198, 202; Dupin, *op. cit.*, pp. 295-296. According to Parturier (*op. cit.*, p. 240), this tax was made applicable to hospitals by a law of July 26, 1797.
[126] Lallemand, *op. cit.*, p. 180; Dupin, *op. cit.*, pp. 87, 193. According to Dupin, the re-establishment of *octrois* by cities became optional after December 1, 1798, and after February 24, 1800, mandatory for all cities not having sufficient hospital revenues.
[127] Parturier, *op. cit.*, p. 240.

in Lyons and Toulouse, September, 1799;[128] in other cities, by a law of February 24, 1800.[129] At Lyons the portion of the *octroi* applicable to the hospitals amounted annually to 270,000 francs;[130] at Toulouse, to 240,000 francs.[131] But these sums provided for only a fraction of the expenses of the two cities' hospitals. A law of May 15, 1800, restored to the hospitals once again, after a lapse of several years, a portion of the municipal police fines.[132] On March 30, 1800, a general alms was ordered taken throughout France for the benefit of the hospitals.[133] Thus the close of the century saw the hospitals drawing revenues again from rents, certain taxes, fines, and alms. It was a lame and inadequate return to the conditions of 1789.

The attempt of the state to take over the hospitals and their property and to manage them was thus badly bungled. In no similar period of years in the eighteenth century did the hospitals suffer to the degree that they did in the years 1789-1800. The Revolutionists were guilty not only of neglect but also of the more serious fault of having employed hospital revenues and holdings for military and political expenses. They had robbed the poor and needy, as well as the church, to maintain their regime. Their aims no doubt were laudable, but the result was tragic.

The increased measure of state support during this period brought increased state management. Even for a time prior to the Revolution the civil hospitals had been loosely under the financial oversight of the controller-general of finance, who in turn had delegated it to a subordinate, De la Millière, an intendant of finances. To a far greater extent the hospitals had been under the control and supervision of the provincial intendants, the provincial assemblies, and the subdelegates. When the National Assembly and later legislative bodies took over the power of the king, or rather that of the controller-general and the council of finances, as the final voice of authority concerning the hospitals, Millière's place was taken, more or less, by the minister of the interior. Throughout the decade 1790-1800 the minister of the interior had a varying degree of jurisdiction over the hospitals. He received their reports and heard

---

[128] Dagier, *op. cit.*, pp. 386-387, and Adher, *op. cit.*, p. 224.
[129] Martin-Doisy, *op. cit.*, IV, 803.   [130] Dagier, *op. cit.*, p. 386.
[131] Adher, *op. cit.*, p. 226.   [132] Dupin, *op. cit.*, p. 194.
[133] Martin-Doisy, *op. cit.*, IV, 803.

their requests for money, acting as chief intermediary between the hospitals and the legislative bodies. There was, indeed, one brief period, from April 1, 1794, to October 2, 1795, when all the ministries were abolished, and their work was undertaken by twelve national commissions. During this interim the role of supervision of the hospitals was placed in the hands of the sixth commission.[134] The place of the intendant, in regional control, was taken over in large measure by the departmental directory. A decree of the National Assembly of September 22, 1789, provided that the work of the intendant would be assumed by two committees, elected by popular vote and serving terms of four years, a council of the department and a directory of the department, the one body deliberative and seldom meeting, the other administrative and constantly in service. In actual practice it appears that control over the hospitals fell almost exclusively to the directory.[135] Below the departmental directories in jurisdiction and power came the municipal administrations, also elected. They filled the role roughly analogous to that of the former subdelegates. Finally came the administration of the individual hospital, similar to the bureau of administration during the Old Regime, except that the members were selected in a different manner, and no clergy or aristocrats were to be found in them, at least after 1792.

This general description of the administration of the hospitals during the Revolution is probably too simple. In Paris Jussieu, the lieutenant mayor, assumed charge of the hospitals in 1789, and the old bureau of the Hôtel-Dieu (which governed not only this hospital but also certain subsidiary establishments) offered its resignation at the same time; but the bureau was asked to continue in service and complied, holding its last session on April 2, 1791. Thenceforward the hospitals of Paris had a fluctuating history, passing through a total of seven administrative regimes.[136] To be sure, Paris had a special hospital administration, varying somewhat from that of the rest of France; nevertheless, other cities too, no doubt, had their administrative changes. During the period of the Convention, when hospital property was confiscated and in part sold,

---

[134] Ferdinand-Dreyfus, op. cit., pp. 108-109; Chéruel, op. cit., II, 799.
[135] On the establishment of these bodies, see Georges Bonnefoy, Histoire de l'administration civile dans la province d'Auvergne . . . , I (Paris, 1895), 351-353.
[136] Ferdinand-Dreyfus, op. cit., pp. 107-109.

the hospitals were supposedly regulated in a more direct manner by the government; and the same law of October 7, 1796, which returned to the hospitals their unsold property and its revenues, provided also for the return of hospital administration to local authorities. Theoretically this act was to make hospitals self-sustaining and independent of the national government, but in actual fact it did not, as can be seen in the instance of the two hospitals of Toulouse, already cited.

Government control made itself felt to some extent in the selection of physicians and surgeons, and even more in laicizing the hospitals. Nonjuring priests were expelled and replaced by others loyal to the Revolution; in time the mass was prohibited in the hospitals, and the chapels were closed; and by the law of August 18, 1792, the religious orders were suppressed. Their members, however, were ordered to continue in the hospitals.[137] The wearing of religious costume was forbidden, and the nuns were directed to take secular garb. In some places the nuns refused to serve longer and walked out, their places being taken by lay nurses;[138] in others they remained, but refused to take the oath. Thus at Beaune the Sisters of Charity refused stubbornly to take the oath, despite the incarceration of three of their number; and so badly was the government in need of experienced nurses that it had no other choice but to let the nuns have their way.[139]

Amid the vicissitudes just described the project of abolishing the Hôtel-Dieu in Paris and establishing in its place four hospitals in various parts of the city came to naught. Occasionally the project was mentioned until about 1793, when disasters in war and the outbreak of the Reign of Terror caused the subject to be permanently shelved. This was perhaps as it should have been. The arguments set forth several times by the hospital bureau for the maintenance of the Hôtel-Dieu in its time-honored, central position in the city were very strong.[140]

The agitation for single beds and for better ventilation in the

[137] Dagier, op. cit., II, 347-348.
[138] See, for instance, Burgade, op. cit., pp. 177-179, 189, 212. The chapel in this hospital was converted into a hall for the sick.
[139] Bavard, op. cit., pp. 280-289. The incarcerated nuns were freed on the death of Robespierre. The hospital went through terrible financial stress in the years 1796-99.
[140] Möring and Quentin, op. cit., II, 24, 26.

hospitals likewise was continued for a time. The committee of mendicity appointed by the National Assembly to study all the forms of state charity, especially the hospitals, presented several elaborate reports in 1790-91. In its third report much emphasis was laid upon the need of single beds and ample ventilation.[141] Papion *le jeune,* one of its members, pointed out the example of Spain, where each patient had his own bed, and charged that the failure to follow a similar policy had cost France many human lives.[142] Condemning conditions in French hospitals, he asserted: "There are sometimes even 8 children with smallpox in the same bed; when one places 4 or 6 sick persons in a bed of 52 inches width, one places two or three of them at the head, and as many at the foot of the bed, so that the feet of the ones come to the shoulders of the others, and vice versa."[143]

The Convention passed a decree on November 15, 1793, that every hospital patient should have his own bed and that the beds should be separated from each other by a distance of three feet.[144] This decree had little effect, however. The cramped financial conditions of the hospitals made it more or less impossible for them to invest in a large number of new beds. Hospital records reveal that institutions were crowded throughout the century. Improvements in ventilation, however, were made. Oddly enough, though the hospitals were cramped for funds in 1792-94, the government opened a number of new hospitals by converting deserted ecclesiastical buildings and added new wings to hospitals already in operation.[145] In the construction of these new wings and buildings care was taken to provide good ventilation, as indeed appears to have been the practice throughout France during the latter half of the century.

It is a detail worthy of note that during the period of the Convention the Revolutionaries changed the names of the hospitals, adopting the word "hospice"; for the names of the individual insti-

[141] See its criticism of conditions at the Hôtel-Dieu of Paris (*Arch. parl.,* XXII. 379-381).

[142] *Ibid.,* XXII, 631 with n.

[143] *Ibid.,* XXII, 632 n. It is odd that the hospice de la rue Mouffetard had a single bed for each patient, and yet a mortality of 1 in 3 (*ibid.,* XXII, 390-391).

[144] Martin-Doisy, *op. cit.,* IV, 927.

[145] Thus a wing was added to the hospital at Beaune. In Paris the hospital De l'Evêché was one of two or three new ones to arise. See Tuetey, *L'assistance publique,* IV, 98-101, 102, 104, 107 *et seq.* Many hospitals, especially hospitals run by religious orders, were closed as needless.

tutions, which commonly were religious in tone, they substituted philosophical or sociological designations which appealed to the minds of the Enlightenment. The name "hôtel-Dieu" was commonly changed to that of "hospice d'humanité," but sometimes the designation "hospice de bienfaisance" was chosen. Physicians and surgeons became "health officers."

The Revolutionaries deserve credit for calling attention to the need of hospital services in rural and other neglected regions. To be sure, the government of the Old Regime had maintained a number of physicians in out-of-the-way places for gratuitous treatment of the sick, and annually had sent out quantities of "remedies"; it had also attempted to develop a better type of midwife. But it had done little or nothing to sponsor hospitals in the smaller places, or to extend nursing service outside the hospitals. The Revolutionaries encouraged both. Roland, in his report of January 9, 1793, urged the establishment of hôtels-Dieu in rural regions. He pointed out that, among other values, their establishment would help in the extirpation of mendicity, since (as he said) almost all of the beggars of the city were persons from the country who had come to city hospitals with sickness and who, after being healed, had not enough money to return home.[146] The committee of mendicity in January, 1791, and the committee of public aid in March, 1793, recommended the supplanting of large hospitals as much as possible by regional hospitals and home treatment.[147] In certain cities an extramural hospital service during the 1790's provided without charge for physicians, nurses, and drugs in the homes of the sick.[148]

During the period of Revolutionary control there were also abuses in some hospitals, even as there had been under the Old Regime. Abuses of a new type appeared, however, in the form of graft. In his "Memoir on Mendicity," rendered to the National Assembly in 1791, Papion le jeune charged that there was much

[146] Arch. parl., LVI, 646.
[147] Ibid., XXII, 380; LX, 321.
[148] The hospice de Saint-Merri in Paris rendered this service in 1791. The eight Sisters of Charity served not only as nurses in the hospital but taught young girls and visited the sick in the parish. They placed hospital linen and utensils at the disposal of the sick and the poor (Arch. parl., XXII, 387-388). In 1790 the General Hospital of Mercy at Marseilles cared for 1,200 sick in their homes; and in 1799 city authorities billeted invalids in the homes of the rich (Augustin Fabre, Histoire des hôpitaux et des institutions de bienfaisance de Marseille, II, Marseilles, 1856, 361, 460).

graft in hospital funds, and that the sick and needy were plundered through the sale of drinks and beds.[149] At the Hospice de l'Evêché, an institution with three hundred or more beds, created out of the old archbishop's palace in Paris in 1794, such scandals and internal turmoil occurred that the institution was suppressed in early January, 1795, and its patients were moved elsewhere. Among the particular grievances were charges of quackery and brutal treatment of the patients by one physician named Enguchard, the extraction of gratuities from patients for various types of service which should have been rendered free, and the sale of the patient's clothes and pocketing of the money by hospital officials.[150] Probably this was a rare incident, and in no way typical. Though there were abuses in the hospitals, they were perhaps for the most part of petty nature. The worst abuse of the hospitals was the starving of them financially by the Revolutionary governments.

[149] *Arch. parl.*, XXII, 632 with n.
[150] Tuetey, *op. cit.*, IV, 154-158, 172-173, 175.

CHAPTER X

AID TO ASYLUMS

A GREAT NUMBER of institutions in eighteenth-century France afforded asylum to various classes of unfortunates, such as foundlings, orphans, the aged, the infirm, the blind, the insane, the prostitute, though these institutions were seldom called "asylums." They were commonly referred to as "hospitals," "hospices," or "houses." Many of these institutions were set apart for a particular type of work, such as care of foundlings, or prostitutes, or aged and disabled war veterans. A larger number cared for several types of unfortunates, such as foundlings, prostitutes, war veterans, the aged, the insane, and even prisoners. One asylum which had greater heterogeneity than most of its class in 1788 was the Salpêtrière:

The Salpêtrière is the largest hospital in Paris and perhaps in Europe: this hospital is both a house for women and a prison *(maison de force)*; it admits pregnant women and girls, wet nurses with their charges; male children from seven or eight months to four or five years of age; young girls of all ages; old women and aged married men; raving madmen, imbeciles, epileptics, paralytics, blind persons, cripples, ringworm sufferers, incurables of every sort, children with scrofula, etc.

At the center of this hospital is a detention house *(maison de force)* for women, consisting of four different prisons: *le commun*, for the most dissolute girls; *la correction*, for those not hopelessly depraved; *la prison*, reserved for persons held by order of the king; and the *grande force*, for women branded by [courts of] justice.

I have seen at the Salpêtrière as many as eight thousand persons; all this crowd is distributed by dormitories [i.e., wards] in the buildings, which have three floors in addition to the ground-floor *(rez-de-chaussée)*.[1]

Manifestly this system, differing from anything that is familiar today, was complicated. It had grown up through generations and centuries. Yet beneath all the confusion there was some uniformity. The chief asylum in a city, commonly known as the General Hospital, might consist of a single building or of several. The General Hospital of Paris in 1786 included eight subsidiary institutions, scattered

---

[1] Tenon, *Mémoires sur les hôpitaux de Paris*, pp. 85-86.

over the city and caring for 12,000 persons in residence. In addition, it had the oversight of 15,000 foundlings placed in the custody of nurses in the country.[2] In some cities, like Grenoble and Narbonne, the same institution served both as hôtel-Dieu and general hospital. In the general hospitals were commonly found various classes of unfortunates, for whose maintenance the institution was usually responsible.[3] Sometimes one or more classes of unfortunates, other than the sick, were cared for in the hôtels-Dieu. Frequently special institutions were set aside for certain types of unfortunates, such as orphans, war veterans, destitute families of sailors, the aged, and the blind. These institutions, some of which were maintained by religious orders and financed and managed by the church, almost invariably were small in size, and cared for only a fraction of the asylum inmates in France. In fact, the failure of church charities to care for these unfortunates was largely responsible for the establishment of general hospitals by Louis XIV in 1656 and subsequent years. Thenceforward throughout the seventeenth and eighteenth centuries the story of French charities evinces the inadequacy of church and private charities and the increasing need of government assistance.

At the outset the flood of beggars in France provoked the establishment of the general hospital. The first important unit so created was the General Hospital of Paris in 1656, by order of Louis XIV. The idea is credited to Pomponne de Bellièvre, first president of the parlement of Paris.[4] The institution was intended to furnish work for deserving indigents and to care for all who were unable by physical infirmity to care for themselves. Distinction was made between deserving and nondeserving indigents. Indeed, throughout the seventeenth and eighteenth centuries French officials charged with the supervision of charities tried to distinguish between the deserving needy and those who were not, perhaps no more successfully than others trying to make that distinction and thus sometimes subjecting themselves to criticism from the public.

[2] *Ibid.*, pp. 20, 84, and 89.

[3] The paying patients (*pensionnaires*) will be discussed later in the chapter.

[4] Christian Paultre, *De la répression de la mendicité et du vagabondage en France sous l'ancien régime* (Paris, 1906), p. 155. The institution at Paris, however, was not the first, being anticipated by several elsewhere (*ibid.*, p. 209). The General Hospital at Toulouse dated from 1647, that of Béziers from 1654, that at Caen from 1655. By 1658 there were sixteen in Languedoc, according to Gross-Mayre-vieille (*L'assistance publique et privée en Languedoc*, Montpellier, 1914, p. 83).

In 1662, at Colbert's request, Louis XIV ordered that a general hospital be created in every province of France, to put an end to begging and vagabondage "by obliging the worthy poor to work and the others to let themselves be maintained in hospices which would be regulated under a severe discipline."[5] The money was not immediately available, however, and in many places the order was not carried out. Accordingly, in 1676 Louis XIV renewed the edict of 1662, asking for a general hospital in every city and large town in the kingdom. The intendants lacked power to impose taxes for this purpose, being empowered merely to collect taxes for the support of hospitals already in existence. But they did have the power of persuasion, and it behooved them to persuade local civic leaders to unite for the establishment of such an institution. In some instances these hospitals were created by municipal or regional funds, in others by private contributions. Slowly but steadily general hospitals came into existence throughout France, each decade witnessing new establishments, until by 1789 most French cities were provided. In their care or custody were perhaps two thirds of the asylum inmates of France in the latter half of the eighteenth century.

The most numerous class of inmates were foundlings and orphans. Of the eight institutions in Paris constituting parts of the General Hospital in 1786, four were devoted exclusively to their care, and a fifth, the Salpêtrière, received them along with unfortunates of other types.[6] Children were brought to the General Hospital of Paris from all parts of France, a curious fact inasmuch as all the general hospitals received foundlings and assumed responsibility for their upkeep. In the last decades of the eighteenth century it was customary to farm out the children to nurses in country districts at approximately 40 livres a year per child, at government expense.[7] The General Hospital at Paris in 1786 cared for fewer than 2,000 foundlings and orphans within its walls, but had custody of approximately 15,000 farmed out to nurses or for service in the rural districts. The practice was to farm the children out for the first seven or eight years of life; afterwards they could either be retained for work on the farms or returned to the institution for continued upkeep

[5] Charles Godard, *Les pouvoirs des intendants sous Louis XIV* (Paris, 1901), p. 357; Bloch, *op. cit.*, p. 48. A lengthy account of the establishment of the general hospitals is given by Paultre, *op. cit.*, pp. 137-310.

[6] Tenon, *op. cit.*, pp. 17-19, 84-85.   [7] *Ibid.*, pp. 18-19.

and training. The General Hospital assumed responsibility for the children until they were able to make their way in the world. For the girls, this might be until they reached the age of twenty; for the boys, until fifteen or sixteen. The girls were usually taught spinning, sewing, and possibly a little cooking in order that they might become maidservants. A few got married and were given dowries. The boys were apprenticed if they had any ability. An agreement for that purpose was forced from the various guilds and corporations in Paris in 1656, when the General Hospital was established. At that time these organizations offered stiff opposition, but finally acceded. In afteryears they discharged apprentices who proved to be undesirable. Very few foundlings ever attained the rank of master.[8]

Similar conditions prevailed in other French cities. General hospitals assumed responsibility for training the children for life. Almost all of them had rooms for spinning, weaving, lacemaking, or sewing, for the girls; and a trained person was in charge to instruct them. Their products were sold, and the proceeds, sometimes reaching respectable sums, were devoted to the maintenance of the institution. Often there were also workshops for the boys for making shoes, tools, and other articles. But the boys' workshops were not so numerous as the girls', nor so remunerative. More commonly the boys were put to work in the garden. At the general hospitals, too, the children were given elementary instruction in the "three R's" and religion.

As already indicated, the general hospitals were not the only institutions that cared for foundlings and orphans. They merely took the children not placed in more fortunate institutions. At Paris, for example, in 1786, of eleven institutions for foundlings and orphans, not all belonged to the General Hospital.[9] Several of the private institutions, like the Trinity, the Mercy, and the Holy Spirit, dressed the children in uniforms. The Trinity, apparently the most select of the institutions for orphans in Paris, gave preference to orphans of masters or companions (journeymen) of "good quality." It cared for children between the ages of nine and twelve born in

---

[8] Many, in fact, turned into criminals and remained a burden to the state (Ferdinand-Dreyfus, *Une philanthrope d'autrefois*, pp. 155, 156).

[9] Fifteen thousand of their 16,197 children, however, were in the care of the General Hospital (*ibid.*, pp. 17-19, 83-89).

Paris of legitimate marriage, who had lost one or both parents. Inmates of the institution wore a blue uniform, received instruction, and spent some time each day marching in funeral processions. The boys were given a chance to learn a trade under the tutelage of artisans engaged by the institution. The government gave to all the boys completing the course the same special privileges as the sons of masters.[10] The corporations protested in vain. Although parents who placed their children in this institution were required to renounce all authority over them, the Trinity was extremely popular, and so many were the applications that seldom could two members of the same family be admitted.[11]

The Mercy also received only children who were natives of Paris or its suburbs, born of a legitimate marriage, and destitute of money. An extract of the baptismal record of the child or of the mortuary record of her parents had to be submitted by way of evidence. Only girls were admitted, and they not before the age of six or seven. They lived in dormitories or halls of twenty-five beds, each girl having her own bed. They wore as a uniform a violet serge dress and a white bonnet. All of the linen was made in the house, the older girls doing the sewing. A third of the proceeds from their sewing or embroidery went to the girls as a remuneration. In the event of death whatever property they possessed went to the institution. The incorrigibles could be sent to the Salpêtrière and replaced by other orphans of the same age. Otherwise they could remain at the institution until twenty-five years old unless previously they married or entered a convent or other service. Ordinarily they might expect a dowry of 100 livres in case of marriage, but misconduct might lead to its loss. Those who became ill were treated at the Mercy rather than at the Hôtel-Dieu, lest their morals become corrupted by association with coarse women there. A nurse, chosen with the greatest care for her exemplary character, was engaged to tend them.[12]

During the Revolution, when all asylums came under government control, even as did hospitals for the sick, some of the homes

<hr>

[10] To this there were added economic advantages.

[11] Léon Cahen, Le grand bureau des pauvres en Paris au milieu du XVIIIe siècle (Paris, 1904), pp. 54-61.

[12] Marcel Fosseyeux, La maison des Cents-Filles ou de la Miséricorde au faubourg Saint-Marceau (1623-1795) (Paris, 1925), pp. 6-8.

for foundlings and orphans were consolidated. Thus on 2 thermidor an III (July 20, 1795) five such establishments in Paris were united, and their children were placed in the buildings of the Maison de l'Enfant Jésus, deserted since early in the Revolution. Twenty-nine persons, among whom were two "health officers" and eleven teachers, served the new institution as officials and servants.[13] The general hospitals were continued with few changes, save that chaplains were dropped, as at the hospitals for the sick; and because of the penurious conditions fewer children were cared for.

Sanitary and sleeping conditions were only a trifle better in the general hospitals than at the hôtels-Dieu. According to Garrick, who visited the General Hospital at Paris in 1751, all the children had itch, and "tho ye smell is not so intolerable as ye Hotel Dieu yet it is scarcely bearable." It was "worth seeing for once,"[14] he added. The committee of mendicity of the National Assembly in 1790, headed by Liancourt, found overcrowded and unhealthy conditions at the Pitié, one of the subdivisions of the General Hospital. Of 1,396 children between the ages of four and twelve, 100 had itch and 136 ringworm. Nevertheless, there were 1,100 beds, so that almost all children had individual beds.[15] At the Salpêtrière the 200 to 300 children slept in small cradles, apparently one to each cradle, in a large, well-aired hall. There was however, a foul smell about the place from a near-by sewer and a hog-pen. Moreover, a large percentage of the children had either itch or ringworm.[16]

One of the number of institutions, some private and others state or municipal, that cared for both destitute children and adults was the Marine Orphans' Hospital at Rochefort, founded in the closing years of the seventeenth century by the famous Bégon, intendant of the marine there. Maintained by the government, it received the orphans of marine officers, master marine workers, and even port workers. The institution also cared for a number of poor women and older girls, and seamen and arsenal workers who were ill. It

[13] Tuetey, *L'assistance publique*, IV, 23-25.

[14] Garrick, *op. cit.*, p. 16.

[15] Ferdinand-Dreyfus, *Un philanthrope d'autrefois*, p. 155.

[16] Boucher, *La Salpêtrière* pp. 53-54. In the General Hospital at Narbonne the children slept on straw, the ventilation was bad, and the children were "pale and puffed" (G. Gross-Mayreville, *op. cit., Bulletin de la commission archéologique de Narbonne*, VIII, 295).

was at once an orphan asylum and a hospital for adults.[17] At Brest was a house of correction for prostitutes, the Royal Refuge, in a part of which also were maintained wives, widows, and daughters of state employees, "who, during the absence or after the death of their fathers or of their husbands, found themselves deprived of all means of livelihood."[18] The Salpêtrière not only cared for 200 to 300 foundlings, but gave asylum to 628 women of all ages and types— 15 blind, 22 insane, 124 crippled or invalid, 34 sick, 9 prisoners, and 424 who were able to work in the institution, either at overseeing the children or at other tasks.[19]

Numerous persons were cared for in the general hospitals and other asylums. Three small asylums for widows in Paris, with a total capacity of thirty-six, gave their inmates lodging but not meals.[20] The Petites-Maisons, a larger institution at Paris, accepted old persons of both sexes;[21] in 1790 it received 538 poor of all types —some aged, some 40 or 50 insane persons, some venereal cases, and commonly 20 to 25 children needing treatment for ringworm.[22] The most numerous class was the aged. To gain admittance, applicants had to be over seventy or afflicted with infirmities that made future work impossible, and in the eighteenth century preference was more and more shown to members of the bourgeois class.[23] Some inmates were destitute; others established pensions of 500 to 600 livres for their own upkeep when entering the institution.[24] The destitute in the institution were assisted in Paris by a private charitable organi-

---

[17] The city paid 100 livres a year to the hospital for the care of the sick women (Viaud and Fleury, *op. cit.*, I, 271, 328-329; *Inv.-som . . . Charente-Inférieure*, H 93).

[18] Cuzent, *op. cit.*, pp. 317-318.

[19] Boucher, *op. cit.*, p. 39. The Salpêtrière gave dowries of 300 livres to its girls who married.

[20] Tenon, *op. cit.*, pp. 22-23.

[21] This institution was not under the control of the Hôtel-Dieu or of the General Hospital, but under that of the Grand Bureau des Pauvres, which represented a third division of city charities of Paris late in the Old Regime (Bonde, *op. cit.*, p. 9).

[22] *Arch. parl.*, XXII, 395-396.

[23] Cahen, *op. cit.*, p. 43.

[24] This was a fairly common practice throughout eighteenth-century France. Many priests, widows, spinsters, and others without a relative or friend on whom they could rely for support in their old age gave a portion or all of their property to the hospital on the understanding that they might reside within its walls for the remainder of their days on the interest from this property. In the late years of the Old Regime and during the Revolution this practice was also followed by certain old soldiers, who made over to the hospitals their pensions from the ministry of war. Cf. Rambaud, *op. cit.*, I, 507-508, 527, 563.

zation known as the Great Bureau of the Poor. They had to be sound in body and mind and to provide their own food. The Petites-Maisons gave them only lodging, salt, and wood. They were placed in wards, whereas those who paid their own expenses were placed two in a room. The institution made the small allowance of an écu (3 livres) a week to all for the purchase of food.[25]

Other institutions for the aged at Paris were the Hôpital du Nom-de-Jésus and one at Saint-Mande, in the suburbs. Both were small. The former in 1793 cared for forty-one persons of both sexes and suffered financial distress. The chores were performed by four aged Sisters of Charity and other inmates, since the younger Sisters had deserted in April, 1790.[26] The institution at Sainte-Mande, established in 1705, cared for twenty-seven aged and infirm women, eleven of them gratuitously. Thirty nuns resided there and served the institution, which in 1790 was described as "vast and beautiful" and having ample resources.[27]

During the Revolution certain additional institutions were established for the care of old persons. The Hospice des Vieillards, in October, 1794, cared for sixty-five aged individuals, five of whom paid part or all of their expenses; the rest were charity patients. Four were insane. A few months later, on 11 floréal an III (April 30, 1795), more than a hundred old persons of both sexes were inmates. Cost of operating the institution was 18,300 livres a year, or 15 sous 5 deniers a person daily.[28] Plans were shortly afterwards drawn up to increase the institution to 600 beds.[29] Bordeaux had a similar institution founded in 1794 and called the Hospice de Bienfaisance, which maintained two hundred old persons.[30]

Earlier at Bordeaux an establishment, founded in 1768, provided a retreat for aged and infirm employees in the taxing system. For its maintenance a portion of the salaries of those in the taxing corps

[25] *Arch. parl.*, XXII, 395; Cahen, *op. cit.*, pp. 42-46 Apparently the inmates prepared their own food in the building. The ill were placed in the infirmary. The aged were disciplined if they engaged in begging, the men forced to stand in the pillory, and the women scourged. Nor could they leave the grounds on Sundays and fete days without permission.

[26] Tuetey, *L'assistance publique*, IV, 27-35. The government's aid was inadequate.

[27] *Arch. parl.*, XXII, 390.

[28] Tuetey, *op. cit.*, IV, 66-72.

[29] *Ibid.*, IV, 74.

[30] Bernadau, *Histoire de Bordeaux*, pp. 397-398.

was set aside and was matched by an equal fund from the government. Crippled, disabled, and superannuated members were admitted to the home and received aid in proportion to their investments. No inmate was permitted to work toward his living, and all were freed from taxes.[31]

The committee of mendicity of the National Assembly reported January 31, 1791, that the infirm and aged among the poor in France numbered 804,775, or approximately one fourth of the total number of all types in the country needing aid. Destitute children below the age of fourteen needing aid numbered 1,866,935, slightly more than half of the 3,207,073 needy persons in France. The destitute sick (at any one time) numbered only 42,519, or about one-seventy-fifth of the poor needing aid.[32]

One group of the aged and infirm cared for by the state were old and crippled soldiers, *les invalides*, of whom in 1764 and 1789 there were 30,000. Ever since the late Middle Ages, if not earlier, the French kings had cared for their old and crippled veterans by placing them as *oblats* in monasteries of royal foundation or control.[33] So much inconvenience resulted, however, that after 1600 the practice gradually gave way to support by pensions.[34] Henry IV conceived the idea of an establishment for maintaining such officers and soldiers, and by an act of 1600 set apart for them a building in the *faubourg* Saint-Marceau, called the Royal House of Christian Charity. By a later act of 1604 he endowed it and appointed a bureau of administrators, but the establishment lasted only a short while. After this institution was suppressed, the inmates were again placed as *oblats* in monasteries.[35] Around 1734 Louis XIII began to rebuild the famous (or infamous) hospital and prison called the Bicêtre, just outside Paris, partly for the purpose of providing an asylum

---

[31] Terray to Esmangart, March 2, 1774 (Arch. de la Gironde, C 61).

[32] *Arch. parl.*, XXII, 619-620. The committee estimated the total population of France and Corsica at 26,288,887, and the number of the "worthy poor" at 515,363, about one sixth of those in need of assistance.

[33] The question of the date when this practice began is discussed at some length by F. Danjou, *Archives curieuses de l'histoire de France depuis Louis XI jusqu'à Louis XVIII . . .* , 2d ser., II (Paris, 1840), 82-83. An uncertain tradition held that it existed even under Charlemagne.

[34] *Ibid.*, II, 84, 86, 88-89.

[35] *Ibid.*, II, 85. On this story of origins, see also Paul Léon, *Les Invalides, les fastes de l'hôtel, ses musées, ses églises, le tombeau de l'empereur* (Paris [1929]), pp. 8-12.

for old soldiers. At length Louis XIV and Louvois undertook to build the celebrated Hôtel des Invalides, which was begun in 1670 and completed in 1674. Louis gave it considerable revenues, of which 300,000 livres formerly had gone to the monasteries for maintaining lay monks (old soldiers and others), and a tax of 3 deniers per livre on war expenditures, amounting in 1714 to 1,250,000 livres.[36]

Throughout the Old Regime and the Revolution the Hôtel des Invalides continued to serve as a home and hospital for soldiers whose age or wounds or health rendered them incapable of earning their own livelihood. The number who found asylum there varied from 1,500 to 3,000. Abuses of different types were pointed out from time to time, and attempts were made at reform. At the beginning of the eighteenth century neither Protestants nor artillerymen were admitted. Moreover, to be admitted, a soldier, unless incapacitated by a wound or an accident, must have had twenty years of continuous service in the army. These regulations were shortly modified, so that after the middle of the century soldiers from the Swiss, German, Irish, and Italian regiments in the French Army were eligible on the same terms as native French soldiers.[37] On several occasions (notably in 1764 and 1776) it was felt that too many had gained access to the institution, some by favor, and attempts were made at reform. Nevertheless, at the outset of the Revolution there were again 3,000 inmates, who seemingly were well cared for.[38]

Those who found asylum at the Hôtel des Invalides were but a fraction (the most favored fraction) of the 30,000 *invalides* in France cared for by the government. The remainder were maintained either at provincial asylums or on pensions at their own homes. In the provincial asylum at Dijon a single company was kept;[39] in

[36] Marion, *Dictionnaire des institutions*, p. 301; Danjou, *op. cit.*, II, 90.

[37] Léon, *op. cit.*, pp. 24-25. According to Danjou (*op. cit.*, II, 99), Swiss Catholic soldiers were eligible for admission even in the early years of the century. Louis XIV refused admission to the Swiss Protestants, but in 1710 ordered the annual setting aside of 6,000 livres from the revenues of the Hôtel for pensions to ten officers and fifty soldiers. The officers were given pensions of 100 livres. In 1711 the number of pensioned soldiers was reduced to sixty-nine, and their pension raised to 72 livres 9 sous each.

Danjou's account of the Hôtel des Invalides ends with the Regency, but it has much of interest on the institution's early history.

[38] Tenon, *op. cit.*, p. 12. Tenon did not criticize their condition.

[39] *Inv.-som . . . Côte d'Or*, C 121, 122.

another at Dieppe a company of invalid canoneers was stationed;[40] and in a third at Rouen in the early 1750's were ten companies of *invalides*.[41] Five companies were employed as guards at the Tuilleries, at Vincennes, at the Bastille, at the Arsenal, and at the Military School in Paris.[42] The government sent officers to inspect the conditions of veterans.[43]

The government also rendered aid to old and invalid sailors, at Rochefort and at Toulon, giving each invalid sailor a pension *(solde)*.[44] At Port-Louis homes were established for them, and they were freed from the *capitation*. Some were provided with mattresses; others were forced to sleep on straw.[45]

Veterans at the Hôtel des Invalides cheered the Revolution. By permitting the rabble of Paris to seize guns and ammunition from the arsenal of the Hôtel on the day before the taking of the Bastille, they contributed toward the downfall of the Old Regime. They entertained rosy expectations of benefits from the Revolutionary government and submitted to the National Assembly petition after petition for the betterment of conditions at the Hôtel and for relaxation of discipline. The Assembly thereupon created a military committee, under the direction of Dubois-Crancé, charged with studying the problem of the veterans. This committee reported that the maintenance of three thousand retired soldiers at the Hôtel des Invalides was costing the nation around 2,800,000 livres a year, a sum out of all proportion to the benefits received, and declared that it would be much better to suppress the institution and employ the money spent on it for pensions, thus placing all the old veterans in France on the same footing. It reckoned that thereby pensions varying from 1,200 livres for each lieutenant colonel to 237 livres for each soldier could be paid. It proposed also to abolish the homes for companies of veterans in the provinces. In February and March, 1791, the Assembly seriously debated the question and was about to abolish the Hôtel, when the old veterans in asylum there were struck

[40] *Inv.-som . . . Seine-Inférieure*, C 734. Some *invalides* were kept also at the châteaux of Auxonne, Bourg, Bellay, Seyssel, the citadel of Chalon, at Versoix, and at Gex (*Inv.-som . . . Côte d'Or*, C 129, 133-134).

[41] *Ibid.*, C 673.

[42] *Inv.-som . . . Ille-et-Vilaine*, C 1094.

[43] *Ibid.*, C 734.

[44] Paillot, *op. cit.*, I (Paris, 1845), 47.

[45] *Inv.-som . . . Ille-et-Vilaine*, C 1095; *Inv.-som . . . Seine-Inférieure*, C 444.

with remorse and begged that it be retained. Groups of them and their friends appeared in the Assembly. Petitions for retention were sent. In a stormy session the Assembly was divided. Through the influence of Clermont-Tonneau the institution was saved, but some specified reforms were ordered.[46]

That this decision was not satisfactory to all is revealed by the fact that on November 27, 1791, a petition was presented to the Legislative Assembly by the war veterans of Paris nonresident at the Hôtel, asking that they be placed on the same financial footing as those at the Hôtel. They declared that those in residence at the Hôtel received 50 to 60 livres every two months, while those outside received only 9 to 12 livres.[47]

In 1792 the government confiscated the endowment of the Hôtel, as later it did of all charitable institutions in France, and made itself responsible for all expenses. In the same year the Legislative Assembly ordered a reorganization of the Hôtel, limited its occupany to 300 officers and 1,700 under-officers and soldiers, and created pensions for all who preferred to retire to their families. The slowness with which this plan was put into effect, however, aroused many protests.[48] The wars of the Revolution soon created a new and considerable class of cripples and invalids eligible for entrance to the institution who were not welcomed by the veterans already there. During the periods of the Convention and the Directory the lot of the veterans throughout France grew steadily worse as funds diminished. At length the Directory afforded some relief by creating homes for old soldiers in Paris, Versailles, and Saint-Cyr, as branches of the Hôtel des Invalides, and by improving living conditions. Even so, the veterans of the Hôtel were delighted with Napoleon's coup d'état in 1799. This time their faith was not misplaced, for Napoleon quickly manifested an interest in them and considerably improved their condition, and the condition of all other veterans in France.[49]

Next to the foundlings and the aged, the most numerous class cared for in asylums was composed of prostitutes and venereal patients. Occasionally these were admitted to the hôtels-Dieu, but they were more often received in the general hospitals or in special insti-

[46] Léon, *op. cit.*, pp. 28-31.
[47] Tuetey, *Répertoire général*, VI, No. 1597.
[48] *Ibid.*, VI, 194; *Arch. parl.*, XLII, 555.
[49] Léon, *op. cit.*, pp. 34-37.

tutions. There must have been constantly between 10,000 and 20,000 such patients, for every city of consequence had at least one institution for them. Paris had a dozen: the Salpêtrière, where 500 to 600 prostitutes were confined;[50] the Bicêtre and the Saint-Louis, where several hundred venereal cases were sent each year from the Hôtel-Dieu;[51] the Vaugiraud, where children as well as women were treated for venereal disease;[52] the Pitié, which had a quarter for "debauched girls and women";[53] the Hôtel des Invalides, which had a hall given over to venereal patients among the war veterans;[54] four private establishments for repentent women, the Good Shepherd, the Saviour, the Saint-Pelagius, and the Sainte-Valère;[55] and the Petites-Maisons, where a few venereal cases were treated.[56]

Private institutions furnishing asylum to "penitent women" were numerous throughout the kingdom. Women entered these institutions of their own accord. Once admitted, however, they could not leave until they had been given a certain amount of religious and moral instruction. In these institutions an attempt was made to reform the inmates and to teach them a means of earning a livelihood.[57] Their residence was thus for an indefinite period; some remained permanently.

The prostitutes cared for in the general hospitals were commonly committed by force and held behind barred windows and doors.[58] Those condemned to the Salpêtrière were placed in a cart with straw and escorted through the streets by *archers* (police), while crowds

[50] Ferdinand-Dreyfus, *Une philanthrope d'autrefois*, pp. 157-158; Mercier, *Tableau de Paris*, XI, 83-89.

[51] In the single year of 1781, 431 women and 432 men with venereal troubles registered at the Bicêtre (Paul Bru, *Histoire de Bicêtre*, Paris, 1890, p. 37). The Hôtel-Dieu of Paris refused to treat venereal, skin, or other contagious troubles.

[52] Tenon, *op. cit.*, p. 82; Tuetey, *L'assistance publique*, IV, 51-65; and Martin-Doisy, *op. cit.*, IV, 953. Martin-Doisy writes that infants were treated by medicines administered to their mothers or nurses. Evidently the medicines were placed on the breast.

[53] Lallemand, *Histoire de la charité*, IV, Part 1, 452.

[54] Most of the military hospitals in France had wards for the treatment of soldiers with venereal disease. The *Collection des inventaires-sommaires des archives départmentales antérieures à 1790*, série C, reveals this fact.

[55] Lallemand, *op. cit.*, IV, Part 1, 453.

[56] Cahen, *op. cit.*, p. 38.

[57] *Ibid.*, with n. 87.

[58] *Inv.-som* . . . *Isère*, E 9, 24. Buchalet (*op. cit.*, pp. 34-35) reports that at Toulouse syphilitic women betook themselves to prostitution or paid *archers* to arrest them, in order that they might receive the antisyphilitic treatment given in the city hospitals.

looked on and jeered.[59]   In these municipal asylums prostitutes, as well as venereal patients, were commonly kept in wards, although in some instances the young were kept apart from the older and more hardened offenders.[60]   All except possibly the few confined for unruliness[61] were put to work, partly that they might be occupied and partly, it seems, that they might learn a means of livelihood, and were subjected to certain religious requirements: the compulsion of joining in morning and evening prayers, of learning the catechism, and of attending mass on Sundays and feast days.[62]   Frequent cases of unruliness appear in the history of these institutions. Sometimes the girls would call from their windows to men, and occasionally the two sexes arranged clandestine meetings in the buildings. Sometimes the girls would plot an insurrection, or would scream and hurl missiles.[63]   They were not an attractive crowd. Even the French Revolutionists, who displayed sympathy toward virtually all other classes of unfortunates, killed a large number of prostitutes at the Salpêtrière and the Bicêtre in the September Massacres of 1792.[64]

The prostitutes, however, did not lack cause for complaint. Sanitary conditions were not good at either the Salpêtrière or the Bicêtre. In each institution several persons were forced to sleep on the same bed; indeed, at the Bicêtre many were forced to sleep on the floor. The air was foul, and the court of the Bicêtre was strewn with dung. Both institutions were prisons, and were filled to overflowing with the miserable of every type.

Venereal patients were commonly treated free in hospitals and asylums of eighteenth-century France. In the second half of the eighteenth century the government took great interest in this form of hospitalization and contributed much toward it.[65]   The usual treatment was that invented by Keyser. It consisted of gradual

[59] Boucher, *op. cit.*, p. 47.

[60] *Inv.-som* . . . *Isère*, 24, 25. Mercier (*op. cit.*, XI, 83-89) was of the opinion that this segregation availed nothing, and that the young offenders were not made worse by association with the older prostitutes.

[61] Some of the prostitutes were so defiant and troublesome that they had to be locked in cells until tractable.

[62] Boucher, *op. cit.*, pp. 48-49.

[63] *Ibid.*; Tuetey, *Répertoire générale*, II, No. 3321.

[64] Bru, *op. cit.*, pp. 405-409.

[65] See, for example, *Inv.-som* . . . *l'hôpital de Grenoble*, E 145, 148; *Inv.-som* . . . *Isère*, L 103, fol. 52; *Inv.-som* . . . *Calvados*, H Suppl. 1137-II, E 13, p. 332; Tenon, *op. cit.*, p. 82; Cuzent, *op. cit.*, pp. 51-52, 317-320.

application of a mercurial salve to one part of the body after another according to a definite schedule, and of occasional baths.[66]

Another large class maintained in asylums were the insane, of whom there were an estimated 18,000 to 20,000 in 1789.[67] If any institutions were devoted exclusively to them, they were rare. In the 1780's Dupré de Saint-Maur, intendant of Bordeaux, appeared as an innovator when he recommended to the government the creation of special institutions for the insane.[68] Throughout France the insane were placed in general hospitals, in hôtels-Dieu, in hospitals of the religious orders, in prisons, and in "depots of mendicity" (compulsory workhouses), along with a motley collection of the poor of other types—foundlings, prostitutes, prisoners, and the aged. Indeed, they were commonly placed in separate wards to protect other inmates of the institutions. Epileptics and victims of hydrophobia were sometimes placed with them.[69] They were allowed the freedom of the hospital during the day but were confined at night. The dangerous were kept locked day and night, generally shackled with chains. Sometimes they were placed in dungeons, and slept on straw.[70] In one instance they were reported to have been kept twenty-five to thirty feet underground.[71]

The provision of comfort, food, and sanitation varied among institutions, and sometimes even within the same institution. The committee of mendicity in a report to the National Assembly in 1791 praised the conditions of the hospital at Charenton, in the Paris suburbs, where eighty-seven insane persons were kept; it severely criticized the conditions at the Bicêtre, which housed nearly two hundred; and it gave the Petites-Maisons, which cared for forty or fifty, a rating between the two.[72]

The Cordeliers had five institutions in the generality of Riom[73]

[66] See the numerous references in the *Inventaires-sommaires*, série C. A full description of the treatment is given by Louis Boucher, *op. cit.*, p. 131.

[67] Martin-Doisy, *op. cit.*, I, 474.

[68] *Inv.-som* . . . *Gironde*, C 3595.

[69] The General Hospital of Grenoble, however, segregated the epileptics in a hall to themselves (*Inv.-som* . . . *l'hôpital de Grenoble*, E 25). Those at the Bicêtre were also isolated (Bru, *op. cit.*, p. 157).

[70] Martin-Doisy, *op. cit.*, I, 478-479; Dagier, *op. cit.*, II, 327; Boucher, *op. cit.*, pp. 54-55, 125-126.

[71] Boucher, *op. cit.*, pp. 125-126.

[72] *Arch. parl.*, XXII, 385-386, 395.

[73] At Montferrand, Riom, St. Pourcin, La Cellette, and Vic-le-Comte.

for the care of the insane, and conditions in them were so much better than in others in that part of France that families and friends from other provinces tried to place patients in them.[74] In general, conditions were worse in the municipal institutions caring for the insane than in the private institutions, because most of the inmates of the private institutions were maintained on "pensions," varying from 100 to 600 livres, paid by their relatives or friends. On the other hand, a large portion, doubtless a majority, of those cared for in the general hospitals, hôtels-Dieu, and depots of mendicity were indigents and paid nothing whatever toward their upkeep. Their expense thus fell upon the public, and the tendency of public charities in that day was toward the minimum allowance for keeping soul and body together.

Not all the mental patients in the municipal institutions, however, were charitable cases. Many were maintained in part by "pensions" paid by relatives or friends. Even a large portion of those cared for at the Bicêtre enjoyed this status. The institution accorded these patients better sleeping accommodations, better food, and no doubt better service than those dependent entirely on charity.[75] The pensioners were allowed to sleep in single beds; the others were forced to sleep several in a bed. Twenty-three institutions in Paris in 1786 received *pensionnaire* mental cases.[76] No small percentage of the cases in Parisian hospitals came from other parts of France.

Three institutions in France rendered medical treatment to "maniacs" considered curable: the hôtels-Dieu of Paris and Lyons and the General Hospital of Rouen.[77] Those who entered the Hôtel-Dieu of Paris were treated for three months; if then they were not cured, they were transferred to the General Hospital.[78] The treatment at the Hôtel-Dieu consisted of "douches, cold baths, repeated bleedings," purgatives, cold drinks, and blistering of the legs.[79]

---

[74] Coiffier, *op. cit.*, pp. 170-171.   [75] Bru, *op. cit.*, pp. 160-162.

[76] Tenon, *op. cit.*, pp. 118-119. His chart shows the distribution, by institutions, of the insane and epileptics in Paris.

[77] *Ibid.*

[78] Möring and Quentin, *op. cit.*, II, 90; Fosseyeux, *L'Hôtel-Dieu de Paris*, p. 278. The Hôtel-Dieu had a financial arrangement with the General Hospital whereby it paid a certain sum for the upkeep of each "incurable" mental patient that it sent (Bru, *op. cit.*, p. 181).

[79] Lallemand, *op. cit.*, IV, Part II, 29; Tenon, *op. cit.*, p. 215; Adher, *op. cit.*, p. 301. Adher's elaborate description apparently includes not only the treatment at Paris, but also that at Toulon, in 1795.

Tenon objected to this treatment, pointing out that the patients were not given enough liberty, fresh air, and exercise, and that some features of the treatment weakened them, whereas they needed to be built up both in flesh and in buoyancy of spirit.[80]

A physician named Martin was engaged by the General Hospital of Clermont-Ferrand (apparently in the 1770's or 1780's), at the price of 100 livres, to attempt to cure the "fools" in it. Four were placed at his disposal for experimentation.[81] Later in brumaire an III (October 22-November 20, 1794) a "health officer" named Valentin wrote to the commission of public aid offering to demonstrate a secret cure on insane patients. He asked that he be allowed to work it on a number of patients in a small institution for a period of two months, and that he be paid by the government 500 livres a patient for the medicine. His extravagant fee suggests that he was a charlatan, and he was so regarded by the commission. The commission did discuss the matter with the committee of public aid, and a subcommittee was appointed to learn more about the proposal. Neither commission nor committee, however, was inclined to grant permission until full details about the secret remedy were known. This hesitant attitude about new remedies characterized the policy of governments both of the Old Regime and the Revolution, and protected the poor from quackery.[82]

The remarkable work of Philippe Pinel was beginning at the very moment Valentin made his application. On October 11, 1793, Pinel was appointed chief physician at the Bicêtre, and almost immediately he went before the Commune of Paris with the request that he be allowed to employ a different policy in regard to the treatment of the insane. He proposed, in short, to unlock the doors and give them the freedom of the hall. Couthon, one of the members of the Commune, made a visit to the Bicêtre the next day to investigate whether conditions were as bad as Pinel reported. He found them to be worse. Astounded by what he saw and experienced

---

[80] *Op. cit.*, pp. xxv-xxvi.

[81] Coiffier, *op. cit.*, p. 169 n. 2. Without describing the outcome or giving other details, Coiffier asserts that this was "an isolated attempt" at curing them.

[82] Valentin was not allowed to demonstrate his remedy. The committee of public aid did not think that his request merited any more consideration than that of a certain Dorez, evidently along the same line. Several letters and a "Rapport au Comité des Secours Publiques," this last dated 17 frimaire, deal with the matter (Arch. Nat., F15, 102).

(for he tried in vain to engage in conversation some of the insane), Couthon turned to Pinel and asked, "Citizen, are you yourself crazy in wishing to unchain such animals?" He then bade Pinel do with them as he liked, and expressed the hope that he would not become their victim. Pinel proceeded to unlock the doors to the cells of some of the most dangerous inmates: an English captain, who had been imprisoned in a lunatic cell for forty years; a French officer, who had been in chains for thirty-six years; a littérateur, who had long lost his reason and for twelve years had been chained; a French soldier, victim of delusions of grandeur and terror, who sometimes broke the chains in which he had now been shackled for ten years; three Prussian soldiers, who objected greatly to his removing their chains and would not even leave their cell when they were liberated; and, finally, an old ecclesiastic, grave and solemn, who had the delusion that he was Christ. To all these Pinel gave the freedom of the prison without untoward result. Thenceforward, according to Pinel's son, the patients improved.[83] During a long career of useful service among the aliénés Pinel revolutionized their treatment.[84]

Another distinct group of asylum inmates were the blind. A committee of the Legislative Assembly in 1792 estimated that then France had more than three thousand blind persons,[85] of whom a large portion were in no charitable institution. The Bicêtre and the Salpêtrière[86] and evidently numerous other institutions in the general hospital system throughout the country cared for small groups. In France, seemingly, only two institutions were devoted

---

[83] Account by Scipio Pinel, quoted by Bru, op. cit., pp. 454-458.

[84] Without wishing to detract from the glory that has so long been attributed to Pinel, candor compels mention of the fact that he was anticipated in this mode of kindly treatment of the insane by the Scotch physician Alexander Hunter (1733-1809), and possibly others. Hunter's work in an asylum at York, England, was known abroad in early 1790, when the Duc de la Rochefoucauld-Liancourt wrote him at the behest of the committee of mendicity, inquiring for particulars of his methods. See Camille Bloch and Alexander Tuetey (eds.), Procés-verbaux et rapports du comité de mendicité de le Constituante, 1790-1791 (Paris, 1911), pp. 19, 163-164; and praise of Hunter's methods by Papion le jeune in his "Mémoire sur la mendicité," presented to the National Assembly in 1791 (Arch. parl., XXII, 631). If Augustin Fabre (Histoire des hôpitaux, II, 67-69) is accurate, the French government had manifested an interest in treatment of the insane since 1785, and in 1787 the chains had been removed from the insane in the Hôpital Saint-Lazare at Marseilles.

[85] Tuetey, op. cit., IV, 207.

[86] Ibid., IV, 317; Boucher, op. cit., p. 39.

exclusively to the blind: the Hospital of the Blind at Chartres[87] and the Hôpital des Quinze-Vingts at Paris. The institution at Chartres, founded by Renaud Barbou in 1292, had been designed to receive one hundred and twenty patients, but never, even in its palmiest days, had received more than seventy; and at the time of the Revolution had only fifteen. It was a private institution entirely, without any support from the government, save that its inmates were permitted, as were those of the Quinze-Vingts, to wear the *fleur-de-lis* on their garments and to beg in public. During the Revolution it became, in common with all other charitable institutions, the ward of the government.

The Quinze-Vingts had closer connections with the government from the outset, having been founded by Saint Louis in 1254.[88] In 1746 the government accorded it one half of the lottery of Saint-Sulpice for building purposes, and it participated in drawings of this lottery down to its suppression in 1766. Thereupon the government set aside a building fund of 40,000 livres annually for the Quinze-Vingts, and in 1780 turned over the accumulated amount of 450,000 livres to the institution.[89] The government further took an active interest in effecting a change in location for the institution in the 1770's and 1780's, which worked greatly for its financial betterment. In other respects, however, down to the time of the Revolution it was a private institution, in finances, management, and regulation.

From the point of view of the twentieth century the Quinze-Vingts was perhaps the most peculiar charitable institution of eighteenth-century France. It was a semimedieval institution with resident membership traditionally limited to 300. Since many of the members had families, the total number of individuals living in the hospital at Paris in 1791 was approximately 800. In addition, in 1791, 483 nonresident members who received pensions totaling 63,900 livres annually were scattered through the provinces.[90]

[87] Also called the Hospice des Six-Vingts and the Hospital of Saint Julian and Saint Gatian. Some fragmentary information on it can be found in the *Inventaire-sommaire des archives hospitalières antérieures à 1790, rédigé par Lucian Merlet. Hospices de Chartres* (Chartres, 1890), pp. vi, xvii-xviii, 163-178.

[88] Chéruel, *op. cit.*, II, 1041.

[89] Léon LeGrand, *Les Quinze-Vingts depuis leur fondation* (Paris, 1863), I, 185-190.

[90] *Arch. parl.*, XXII, 392-393. These nonresident members, it appears, were

Admittance to membership was difficult on account of the heavy competition. In 1794 there were reputedly 800 to 900 applicants for every vacancy.[91] All applicants had to be native French and Catholics. The administrators made it their practice to select applicants on the bases of their place on the list, their age, and the size of their families.[92] Charges of favoritism in the selection of members were frequent during the Revolution.[93] Whether they were justifiable is difficult, perhaps impossible, to determine. More than one governmental investigation was made. On April 9, 1792, the Legislative Assembly summoned before it 102 members of the Quinze-Vingts and asked if they were satisfied with the institution's management. They replied that they were satisfied in every way, stating that the grievances which had led to the immediate investigation had come from a few turbulent ones wishing to create trouble. The Assembly thereupon declared itself satisfied with the management.[94] Of course this investigation was not thorough. Whether other inquiries were more careful is not clear.

Once a person was elected to membership, he (or she) was required to make over to the institution all of his earthly possessions, which presumably were kept intact during his lifetime, lest he later be expelled from membership or lest there be children to claim half of it as their inheritance upon his death. Even jewelry had to be transferred. This abjuration of property was made in the presence of a notary. Thenceforward the inmate had to live under the discipline of the institution, as created by the administrators and by the confraternity itself. Thus he entered upon a communistic state, but oddly enough a degree of private ownership existed within the institution. Each member received a certain monetary allowance a day for expenses. The sum varied from time to time according to

created in the 1780's. See Géorgel, *Mémoires*, I, 486, 495; LeGrand, *op. cit.*, I, 193. According to Géorgel and LeGrand, the number of resident memberships was raised in 1781 to 325 or 333, to accommodate certain blind gentlemen and ecclesiastics who were indigent.

[91] This claim was set forth in a letter by the secretary of the institution, written in answer to a complaint from an old woman of seventy who had been an "aspirant" (on the waiting-list) for twelve years.

[92] Bricard, the secretary, stated that several score candidates were older than the woman in question (Tuetey, *op. cit.*, IV, 355).

[93] *Ibid.*, IV, 179, 185, 192-193, 239, 293-294.

[94] *Ibid.*, IV, 194. See denial of favoritism by the administrators, *ibid.*, IV, 226-228.

the needs of the members and their families.[95] Members might, with the administration's approval, marry after entering the institution provided they would marry wives or husbands with eyesight. No marriage between two blind members was permitted.[96] The seeing members were regarded as a great asset to the community. During the day they led their husbands, or wives, or other members to the churches and other public places for begging.[97] Reading to the blind members was another important service performed by certain of the seeing members. It was an old custom, continued during the Revolution, for the men to gather in one group and the women in another group for two hours each day, to listen to two readers who were paid for their efforts.[98] Many of the seeing sisters when left widows married again within the institution,[99] and the same was possibly true of the widowers. In 1787 there were 73 seeing members (25 men and 48 women), and a policy of replacing them by blind members was introduced. As a result, in 1794 the Quinze-Vingts had only 43 seeing members, 15 men and 28 women.[100]

For the children of the institution gratuitous education was supplied from at least the year 1671 through the eighteenth century. A school for boys and another for girls with well-paid teachers were established.[101] The studies, however, were elementary, with apparently no attempt to teach a craft. Prior to 1752 blind infants and

[95] Thus in 1791 an unmarried member received 24 sous a day; a married member 40 sous; children and youths below sixteen 3 sous; widows resident in the institution who had lived five years with their husbands, 12 sous; nonresident widows who had lived five years with their husbands, 15 sous (*Arch. parl.*, XXII, 392-393).

[96] In 1792 a blind "sister" married without permission and became pregnant. She was dismissed. Twenty-four members protested (Tuetey, *op. cit.*, IV, 191).

[97] Each blind member carried a wallet for the bread that was given, a leather box for the coins, and a printed card granting him the permission to beg at church doors. Throughout the eighteenth century begging was permitted only one other group in France (Martin-Doisy, *op. cit.*, IV, 1391-1392). In 1780, following the institution's change of location and greatly increased financial status, begging for members of the Quinze-Vingts also came to be forbidden.

[98] The institution paid a certain amount and the individual members a certain amount to these readers (Lallemand, *Histoire de la charité*, IV, Part II, 46).

[99] *Arch. parl.*, XXII, 391-392.

[100] Tuetey, *op. cit.*, IV, 301. The committee of mendicity in 1791 observed that inasmuch as begging had come to be forbidden and the Quinze-Vingts possessed an infirmary (since 1780), there was no longer need of so many seeing sisters (*Arch. parl.*, XXII, 392).

[101] In 1671 the master received 200 livres a year, and the mistress 150; in 1755 the master received 700 livres, and the mistress 300 (LeGrand, *op. cit.*, II, 130-131). On pages 180-183 LeGrand reproduces the school regulations for 1784.

children were received into the Quinze-Vingts and cared for, and in time were made members. In 1752 this custom was abolished as too expensive.[102]

This, in brief, was the quaint and intricate society known to history by the odd name of the Fifteen-Twenties. Down to 1780 the institution, like most other French charitable institutions, struggled along on a lean income; but the change effected through the sale in 1777 of its valuable property on the fashionable rue Saint-Honoré (for 6,000,000 livres) and the removal of the cheaper district of Saint-Antoine brought from 1780 until the Revolution an increase in the stipends of members and a considerable extension of the number of recipients. The government contributed an annual income of 250,000 livres. Thus by 1789 this organization had become one of the most fortunate charitable institutions in France.[103] The Revolution brought a change for the worse. The Revolutionary government continued to pay the members at the rate that they had received under the Old Regime, but the depreciation in value of the assignats made the situation within the institution critical after 1793, and much suffering was experienced,[104] despite the increase in stipends in 1794 and 1795.[105]

So much complaint was made by petitioners for membership in the Quinze-Vingts during the Revolutionary period that on April 21, 1794, the Convention appropriated 40,000 livres to be distributed among them at the rate of 15 sous a day. This sum being insufficient, an additional appropriation of 20,000 livres was made some months later, and on January 21, 1795, the rate was raised to 20 sous a day.[106]

Throughout the period of the Revolution complaint and recrim-

[102] *Ibid.*, II, 120.

[103] Tuetey, *op. cit.*, II, 13-14, 39; LeGrand, *op. cit.*, I, 189-204.

[104] *Arch. parl.*, LX, 524; Lallemand, *Histoire de la charité*, IV, Part II, 45-46.

[105] By order of 26 pluviôse an II (February 14, 1794), an increase of 5 sous a day was made in the income of all resident blind members above the age of sixteen. Thenceforth the scale of income ran: for single members, whether blind or seeing, 29 sous a day; for married members (both belonging to the society), 20 sous each a day; for blind members married to seeing nonmembers, 30 sous a day. The allowance for children under sixteen continued at 3 sous a day, and that for members resident in the provinces remained at 250 livres per annum (Tuetey, *op. cit.*, IV, 301-302). On June 20, 1795, the committee of public works ordered a yet more substantial increase (at least in figures) of one-third the stipend granted by the order of 1794 (*ibid.*, IV, 345).

[106] *Ibid.*, IV, 290, 325.

ination were constant. That the charges of abuse covered a wide field is surprising since the blind were receiving more liberal benefits from the government than were most other recipients of charity.

Some within and without the institution demanded that the institition be done away with entirely, its oaths suppressed, and all the blind in France treated on a parity. This of course was the rational solution. Whether, however, it was possible in April, 1792, with a war beginning, is debatable. The Revolutionary government was almost always embarrassed for lack of money, and possibly for practical reasons it decided to let this semimedieval, outmoded institution pass into the nineteenth century.

Certain other groups hospitalized in asylums were the "incurables"—paralytics, tubercular and cancer cases, and others confined to their bed with little or no hope of cure. Apparently all of the general hospitals might have inmates of this type; there were also some special institutions for them. The Hospital of the Incurables (now the Hôpital Laennec) at Paris,[107] privately founded and endowed, had revenues in 1790 valued close to 400,000 livres. This special institution was provided with 446 beds, of which 199 were for men and 247 for women, and it cared for approximately 528 persons a year.[108] The men were housed in one building and the women in another. The committee of mendicity, inspecting it along with the other institutions at Paris in 1790, spoke well of its sanitation and accommodations. Each patient, or virtually each patient, enjoyed a room to himself (in certain instances a block of space curtained off), a table, chair, small stove, and other necessary furniture. The better rooms were rented to patients at a high price. The committee of mendicity, however, recommended to the National Assembly that the institution be discontinued, its property sold, and its revenues (which would then be carried above 450,000 livres a year) paid in pensions for the care of the incurables in their homes.[109] This recommendation was not adopted.[110]

Here and there in various institutions, usually in *maisons de*

[107] According to Amedée Bonde (*op. cit.*, p. 9 n. 1), the Hospice des Incurables at Paris was under the control of the Hôtel-Dieu rather than the Hôpital Général. Similarly one at Toulouse, with thirty to forty patients, was controlled by the Hôtel-Dieu of that city (Buchalet, *op. cit.*, pp. 38-39).

[108] The annual mortality was forty, or one in thirteen.

[109] *Arch. parl.*, XXII, 382-383.

[110] Bonde, *op. cit.*, p. 9 n. 1.

force of the general hospitals, were found small numbers of epileptics. According to Tenon,[111] there were in 1786 322 in Parisian charitable institutions: 300 (women) in the Salpêtrière, 15 (men) in the Bicêtre, and 7 (men) scattered elsewhere. Those at the Salpêtrière were segregated in a special building by themselves, and after the manner of criminals and the insane were fettered with irons.[112] Tenon, who professed to represent the most advanced ideas of medicine and hospitalization in his day, classified them in a chart alongside "furious fools" and "imbeciles." In June, 1792, the government manifested an interest in a proposal by one Ledru to attempt the cure of epileptics by electrical treatments. Philip, the dean of the faculty of medicine in Paris, considered treatment by this method within the realm of possibility. The administrators of the Hôtel-Dieu were officially requested to place a room in the Hospital Saint-Louis at Ledru's disposal for this purpose. But the stubborn administrators flatly refused to do so, saying that it was a traditional policy with them not to permit experimentation with untried remedies on the poor under their care. They concluded their reply by suggesting that since the patients were already confined at the Bicêtre and the Salpêtrière the experiment be conducted in those institutions.[113] It is not clear whether the experiment was made, but later in 1781 a physician at the General Hospital at Toulouse treated paralytics, reportedly with success, and the Society of Medicine at Paris at once asked for details. In 1790 or 1791 a certain Mauduyt read a paper before this Society "on the value of installing electrical treatments in the hospitals."[114]

Finally, there were the transients. Formerly innumerable guesthouses, as well as monasteries and convents, opened their doors freely to indigent transients. But the severe laws against mendicancy of the seventeenth and eighteenth centuries, and more particularly the rise of the general hospitals and the depots of mendicity (i.e., workhouses), resulted in the closing of most doors of such hospitality.

[111] *Mémoires*, p. 228.

[112] Boucher, *op. cit.*, p. 52. Those cared for in the General Hospital of Grenoble were also segregated in a special ward (*Inv.-som . . . l'hôpital de Grenoble*, E 25, 104).

[113] Möring and Quentin, *Collection de documents*, II, 128-129.

[114] Buchalet, *op. cit.*, p. 86; Tuetey, *Répertoire général*, III, No. 296. The charlatans Mesmer and Saint-Germain had done much to attract attention in Paris by attempted cures through electricity.

Nevertheless, in 1745 numerous hospitals and convents in Burgundy still gave hospitality to the transient poor of the province, the hospitals being directed to do so; both hospitals and convents were aided financially for this purpose by the cities and the provinces.[115] Briançon in 1764 and Marseilles in the 1750's and 1760's gave one night's free lodging to needy transients.[116] Paris in 1786 had two houses of hospitality, one for men and another for women, which gave indigents lodging and food for three days. The institution for women was the Hospital Saint-Catherine; that for men the Hospital Saint-Anastasius and Saint-Gervais. The former had sixteen large beds, on each of which sometimes as many as four persons were placed, and five small beds. Tenon considered its average capacity sixty-nine persons. The hospital for male transients had seventeen large and thirteen small beds. Tenon reckoned its average number of occupants at one hundred. Since the number fluctuated from thirty to two hundred, many must have slept on straw or on the bare floor.[117]

The administration and finances of the general hospitals were similar to those of the hôtels-Dieu. All general hospitals, like hôtels-Dieu and other charitable institutions not run exclusively by religious orders, had their bureaux of administrators composed of local citizens of prominence from the clergy, the politicians, the lawyers, the merchants, the financiers. The bureau of administrators of the General Hospital of Paris, in the mid-century, consisted of twelve men, chosen by the parlement of Paris;[118] in the 1780's there were seventeen.[119] The General Hospital of Grenoble had thirty-eight.[120] In Paris the administrators were chosen for life, or until they saw fit to resign; at Lyons they were elected for periods of two years. They held frequent meetings (at Grenoble and Poitiers once a week), and exercised almost complete jurisdiction over the institution.[121] Their service was free. Theoretically their seats were posts

---

[115] *Inv.-som* . . . *Côte d'Or*, C 3004, f 195.

[116] *Inv.-som* . . . *Hautes-Alpes*, C 152; Fabre, *op. cit.*, II, 23-25.

[117] Tenon, *op. cit.*, pp. 21-22. The two Parisian institutions were closed during the Revolution (Louis Rivière, *Les oeuvres d'hospitalité de nuit en France: leur développement, leur état actuel, leur avenir* [Extrait de la *Revue Philanthropique* of Aug. 10, Sept. 10, and Nov. 10, 1898]).

[118] Martin-Doisy (*op. cit.*, I, 241) gives the names and professions of the administrators of this institution for the years 1741 and 1751.

[119] *Encyclopédie méthodique*, Finances, II (Paris, 1785), 501.

[120] Nine were administrators because of positions that they held; the other twenty-nine were elected (*Inv.-som* . . . *Isère*, B 155, pp. 37-38).

[121] Their work could be reviewed by parlement and the council of state.

of distinction. Criticism, however, was sometimes leveled at their work.

In 1790 all hospitals were placed under departmental (provincial) supervision. Those at Paris were entrusted to a commission of five members. As the Revolution advanced, other groups temporarily gained control. Finally, on January 17, 1801, a consul-general of hospices, assisted by an administrative commission, which lasted until 1849, was created.[122]

The chief revenues came from monetary or landed investments. Next in importance in most instances came the *octroi*, which fluctuated much in size between cities. Finally came alms, inheritances, fines, feudal dues, part of the tax on entertainments, part of a tax to combat mendicity, a tax on the installation of ecclesiastical, judicial, and financial officials, the monopoly of the sale of meats during Lent, a portion of the taxes on tobacco and salt, revenues from the hides of butchered animals, rental from chairs in public places, an occasional benefit from lotteries, profits from the sale of mortuary cloth, property confiscated from duelists, proceeds from sales of products made in the workshops of the institutions,[123] occasionally the property of some defunct private hospital or other charitable institution, and not infrequently outright monetary gifts from the city, the province, or the state (made to the institutions in distress).[124]

Government aid to these institutions, considering both the direct and the indirect forms, was far from small. Much of their endowment was due to government grants in property, a policy begun by Louis XIV, their founder, in the late seventeenth century.[125] Much

[122] Bonde, *op. cit.*, pp. 11-12.

[123] Revenues from this source constituted about a fourth of the total receipts of the General Hospital of Riom in 1752 (Martin-Doisy, *op. cit.*, IV, 802). The income from manufactures at the General Hospital at Poitiers netted in 1747 a profit of 8,118 livres, constituting 20 to 25 per cent of its income (Rambaud, *op. cit.*, I, 530, 537).

[124] *Ibid.*, II, 431, 461-590; IV, 802, 954-956; Bonde, *op. cit.*, pp. 10, 15, n. 2; *Histoire de Grenoble*, p. 614; G. Cross-Mayrevielle, *op. cit.*, VIII, 284; Rambaud, *op. cit.*, I, chaps. x, xii; *Inv.-som . . . Isère*, H, Introduction, pp. xiv-xv, E 9; *Inv.-som . . . l'hôpital de Grenoble*, E 15, B 13; *Inv.-som . . . Calvados*, H Suppl. 1137-II E 13, p. 332; *Inv.-som . . . Côte d'Or*, C 3005-3007; Département de la Seine, *Supplément à l'inventaire sommaire des archives hôspitalières antérieures à 1790*, compiled by M. Brièle (Paris, 1889), p. 259.

[125] Rivière, *op. cit.*, p. 7.

property confiscated from the Huguenots was turned over to these institutions, as was also much property of decadent or abandoned private hospitals. Government appropriations sometimes formed a considerable portion of the revenues. For instance, the government grant of 4,000 livres formed almost one third of the revenues (13,312 livres) of the General Hospital of Riom in 1752, and in 1789 the government grant to the General Hospital of Paris amounted to 180,000 livres.[126] Finally, of indirect assistance, was the exemption of the general hospitals, like other charitable institutions, from most forms of taxes.[127]

During the Revolution the general hospitals suffered as much as the hôtels-Dieu and other charitable institutions from the lack of adequate finances. From 1787 until approximately the end of the century the financial condition of all these establishments became progressively worse. First the severe economic depression (1786-91), and then war (1792-1802), diverted funds from charities. But worse blows came in the suppression of the taxes and feudal dues (1789-92), and finally (by act of 23 messidor an II [July 11, 1794]) in the confiscation of their property, landed and otherwise. The state took over their maintenance, but the provision was inadequate. By September, 1798, the hospitals and asylums of Paris had lost, according to one writer, three fifths, according to another, approximately five sevenths, of their pre-Revolutionary revenue.[128]

[126] Doisy-Martin, *op. cit.*, IV, 802; II, 431. Scores of grants to hospitals and asylums in the late 1780's are recorded in the *Livre rouge*, published by the National Assembly.

[127] *Ibid.*, II, 497. They were not wholly exempt, however. In 1793 the General Hospital of Grenoble was paying annual taxes *(impositions)* of 6,000 livres (*Inv.-som . . . Isère*, série H, Introduction, p. xv).

[128] Bonde, *op. cit.*, p. 15 n. 2.

CHAPTER XI

CARE OF FOUNDLING CHILDREN

Before 1789

ONE OF THE saddest features of eighteenth-century French history was the wholesale abandonment of infants by their parents. According to the Oratorian scholar Léon Lallemand,[1] a total of 388,817 abandoned children were received in charitable institutions in Paris alone during the years 1701-1800. From the beginning of the century the number of exposures steadily increased down to 1772, in which year 7,676 were received, according to hospital records; after that the numbers fluctuated between 5,444 and 6,705 annually through the year 1786.[2] In this last year, according to Tenon,[3] 15,000 were cared for in the provinces under the auspices of two houses of the Foundlings' Hospital at Paris, a dependency of the General Hospital of that city. Altogether eleven Parisian institutions assumed custody of foundlings and orphans; the largest were parts of the General Hospital, and the others (several in number) were private establishments.[4]

According to Sebastien Mercier, a propagandist not always reliable for his figures, almost half of the children born each year in Paris were exposed.[5] The large number of exposed children in Paris included children of legitimate as well as illegitimate birth.[6] A *proces-verbal* of 1760 stated that out of 5,032 admissions at Paris, 4,297 were illegitimate and 735 legitimate infants.[7] Accordingly,

---

[1] *Histoire des enfants abandonnés et délaissés* (Paris, 1885), pp. 161, 741. Chronological charts are given. Tenon (*op. cit.*, pp. 91-92) also gives a chart covering the period 1670-1786, during which time 250,304 had been exposed at Paris. All but 2,806 had been exposed since 1700.

The committee of mendicity in 1791 estimated the number of foundlings in France at that time at 40,000 (*Arch. parl.*, XXII, 612).

[2] Tenon, *op. cit.*, p. 91.   [3] *Ibid.*, p. 89.

[4] For a description of them, see Tenon, *op. cit.*, pp. 17-19, and Lallemand, *op. cit.*, chap. vi.

[5] *Tableau de Paris*, XII, 84-88. This number seems incredible.

[6] Alfred Franklin (*op. cit.*, XX, 59-60) says that approximately 21,000 children were born each year in Paris. If 6,000 were exposed, they would accordingly constitute less than one third.

[7] Lallemand, *op. cit.*, p. 163. A report of the *Société philanthropique* for 1790 stated that every year 1,200 to 1,400 legitimate children were exposed at the Foundlings' Hospital in Paris (*Arch. parl.*, XXII, 397-401).

the children of legitimate birth constituted approximately one seventh of those exposed. Throughout France the exposure of legitimate children was large, and the practice of exposure was not greater in Paris than in other parts of France. Every city had its own institution, or institutions, to care for the *enfants trouvés* exposed within its walls or within the province. Marseilles, it is said, had 2,000 in its charitable institutions. Throughout France several hundred hospitals and "houses" cared for these children. Moreover, a large number of children from the provinces were annually brought to Paris. According to an order of council of January 10, 1779, this number reached 2,000 a year.[8]

Nine tenths of the provincial children brought to Paris died before they reached the age of three months as a result of the terrible privations to which they were subjected. Those who transported them from such distant generalities as Auvergne, Alsace, Lorraine, Brittany, and Flanders were usually persons of little capacity and often illiterate. Consequently, the children were poorly fed, many were given wine, and a large number died on the way or shortly after their arrival.

Those who reached Paris were taken to the Foundlings' Hospital and registered on the books. Then identification marks in lead were securely placed about their necks. After a day or so in residence, they were commonly farmed out to nurses, who, generally from the country districts, might take them to Picardy, Burgundy, Champagne, or Artois, for rearing till they reached the age of six or seven. In this fashion all the general hospitals farmed out children, and as the eighteenth century advanced, the custom became more widespread. The hospital administrators, the enlightened public, and the government enthusiastically endorsed the rearing of children in the country rather than in the crowded hospitals, claiming for it economy and a great reduction in mortality.[9] In years of scarcity the mountain women of Auvergne sometimes took advantage of the custom by

[8] Cited by Lallemand, *op. cit.*, p. 162. Necker, in his *Compte rendu au roi* (Paris, 1781), pp. 99-100, gives the same figure.

[9] President De Brosses calculated that whereas 100 children cared for at the hospital cost annually 6,037 livres, the same could be cared for in the country for only 3,600 livres (Martin-Doisy, *op. cit.*, IV, 571-572; Coiffier, *op. cit.*, pp. 151-152; Lallemand, *op. cit.*, pp. 188-192). Lallemand gives a history of the development of this practice from the late seventeenth century to 1790.

exposing their children and later obtaining custody of them as nurses at the general hospital.[10]

The nurses were paid a monthly rate by the hospitals from which they received the infants, most of the wages coming from government donations to the hospitals. Stipends to nurses varied from place to place throughout France, and from time to time. In general, a stipend ran from 3 to 7 livres a month. The hospitals at Rennes, in Brittany, paid 4 livres a month during the period 1778-86,[11] while the intendant fixed the compensation in the generality of Guyenne during the same period at 6 livres.[12] The generality of Auvergne had no uniform rate, and in 1777 some places paid 3, others 4, 5, 6, and even 7, livres a month.[13]

Nurses were allowed only one infant at a time, out of consideration for the welfare of the child; but there were evidently some violators of this regulation.[14] Inspection of the children was required twice a year.[15] Inspectors were usually nuns from the hospitals. The Hôtel-Dieu of Lyons sent out a monk as inspector until 1763, when, upon the discovery of many abuses, it decided to send out one of the rectors (or administrators) instead.[16] The General Hospital of Grenoble required two inspections each year in the nurses' homes, one by a woman and the other by an *archer* (policeman), besides an inspection at the hospital itself. For this last inspection, which was made annually until the child was five years old, the nurse was obliged to accompany the child, and a travel allowance of 3 sous per league was made.[17] As a further means of

[10] Coiffier, *op. cit.*, 136-137.

[11] *Inv.-som . . . Ille-et-Vilaine*, C 1287.

[12] *Inv.-som . . . Gironde*, C 3458. This action brought much complaint. Some sections of the province claimed that they could not rear children on the small allowance. In the early 1770's nurses in Guyenne received the high rates of 10 and 12 livres a month (*ibid.*, C 3454).

Sometimes it was difficult to get nurses. In 1770 and 1773 the General Hospital at Paris had difficulty and was compelled to raise their allowances (Martin-Doisy, *op. cit.*, IV, 554).

[13] Coiffier, *op. cit.*, p. 149.

[14] Alfred Franklin (*op. cit.*, XX, 54), describing the Paris nursing bureau for children not abandoned, reports that some nurses managed to get custody of two and even three children and farmed out the second and third children to other nurses for lesser rates. This practice was condemned by a royal declaration of May 1, 1727.

[15] Bloch, *op. cit.*, p. 107.

[16] Dagier, *op. cit.*, II, 149-150. The monk and the rector also paid the nurses.

[17] Regulation of May 15, 1769 (*Inv.-som . . . l'hôpital de Grenoble*, E 22, p. 99).

protecting the child, the hospitals required that nurses present cer-
tifications of their good health and character from their local
curés.[18]

The contacts between the hospitals and the nurses were not as
close as they should have been. Communication and financial arrangements between the two were quite commonly made by an in-
terloper, often an illiterate, who, like the nurse, was required to
present to the hospital from his curé a testimonial of character.[19]
He transported most of the children from the hospitals to the nurses
and periodically paid the nurses. His pay consisted of small commissions and travel allowances given by the hospitals. Sometimes,
too, he perhaps "beat down" the nurses' allowances to his own advantage. He was in part a parasite, yet a necessity when nurses
lived (as most of them did) at a distance from the hospital.

Children who were ill in the homes of their nurses were attended
by a local surgeon or physician, who, if he did not perform the
service without a fee, sent the bill through the local curé to the
hospital that had oversight of the child.[20] Children ill at a general
hospital were sent to its infirmary or to the hôtel-Dieu. Apparently
children afflicted with disease were commonly retained at the general hospital; but at Dijon they were farmed out to nurses just as
other children, and the hospital (the Hospital of the Holy Spirit)
underwrote such expenses as their care necessitated. Thus, children
with venereal or scrofulous tendencies were confided to women to
be nourished on cow's milk.[21] Children who were frail, epileptic,
cancerous, or otherwise invalid, were left with their nurses beyond
the limit of twelve years set for normal children by this hospital,
which agreed to meet their expenses for life if necessary. Occasionally the hospital admitted the children into the wards of the
old men and women, according to their sex, the government paying
60 livres a year for their upkeep.[22]

[18] *Inv.-som . . . Ille-et-Vilaine*, C 1287.

[19] Bloch, *op. cit.*, p. 107.   [20] *Ibid.*, p. 106.

[21] This was to protect the nurses against catching venereal germs from the child.
Oddly enough, infant mortality from syphilis was large (*ibid.*, p. 111), and nurses
frequently caught the disease from nursing them. In 1736, 1750, and 1769 the
spread of venereal disease by nursing children in the Hospital of the Holy Spirit
occasioned an expense of 3,000 livres (Martin-Doisy, *op. cit.*, IV, 570).

[22] *Ibid.*, IV, 572-574. For a nine-year-old child, "weak in mind and body," the
Hôtel-Dieu at Bayeux paid the sum of 6 livres 10 sous a month, or 80 livres a year,
in 1789 (*Inv.-som . . . Calvados*, H Suppl. 1090-G 8, p. 278).

In the earlier half of the century the hospitals did not fix the length of the early nursing period, which varied from two to seven years. In 1761 the government encouraged the retention of the children in the country as long as possible. Exemption from military service was promised to the head of the home, or to a son, brother, or nephew, for each male foundling reared to the age of sixteen. At that age the foundling would enter the ranks in the place of the member of the family normally to be drafted.[23] The government also agreed to pay a yearly pension to those rearing children above six years of age. For boys, the pension of 40 livres a year would be paid until they reached the age of twelve, when a pension of 30 livres would follow until they were fourteen. For girls, the pension of 40 livres a year would be paid until they were sixteen. It was assumed that the boys at fourteen and the girls at sixteen would become useful to those keeping them and worthy of their maintenance, or else would be able to make their way in the world.[24] Some kept youths past these age limits without recompense,[25] and in 1772 the government decreed that henceforth, if kept past the age of twenty, youths must be accorded wages of 40 livres a year in addition to maintenance. As amended, the system worked well and was commended by the committee of mendicity in 1790.[26] In Provence and in Touraine, if not in other provinces, those who reared *enfants trouvés* were exempt from the *capitation*.[27]

Throughout the latter half of the eighteenth century the royal and the provincial governments in France gave much attention to the establishment and development of nurseries for the production of fruit trees, mulberry trees, and of larger trees, like elms, for ornamentation of the highways. In 1765 the government set up a central nursery at La Rochette, near Melun, some thirty or forty miles above Paris on the Seine, with twenty-four *enfants trouvés* placed in it to work and to study trees and shrubs. It planned to establish

[23] Martin-Doisy (*op. cit.*, IV, 541) quotes at length the letter from Choiseul to the intendants explaining the matter.

[24] Lallemand, *op. cit.*, p. 190. Later by orders of 1765 and 1772 the pension for both sexes was fixed uniformly at 40 livres a year, and the period was prolonged until the youths were twenty (Bloch, *op. cit.*, p. 112 n. 3).

[25] Others sent back youths who were indolent and unwilling to work (Lallemand, *op. cit.*, pp. 197-198).

[26] *Ibid.*, pp. 191-192.

[27] *Inv.-som . . . Bouches-du-Rhône*, C 88; Dumas, *op. cit.*, pp. 365-366.

further nurseries in the different provinces and to use *enfants trouvés* to tend them.[28] In 1771 the government ordered that a certain number of *enfants trouvés* be chosen in the generality of Guyenne for cultivating nurseries.[29] None of these government enterprises, however, turned out well.[30]

Foundlings were also employed in at least two private nurseries. One, consisting of thirty *arpents* (about forty-five acres), stocked in part with fruit trees, situated at Rosay in Brie, and owned by a man named Cassin, employed eight foundlings and instructed them in the art of nursery culture. Cassin asked no pensions for them from the government, but in the flood of 1784 he suffered heavy loss and requested flood relief. Officials in considering his application commented that another man, Morceau de la Rochette, had likewise apprenticed foundlings at the nursery business and for it had received from the government "some considerable sums."[31] The committee of mendicity in 1790 reported that most of the children reared in the country turned out to be good citizens.[32]

Many of the youths were apprenticed in the cities. Here, too, the government came to their aid. The guilds and corporations of the various cities of France were required to accept a certain number of foundlings and orphans for apprenticeship, and after approximately six years of training to admit them to the *maîtrise* without charge. Girls were apprenticed at the hosiery and linen trade, and likewise acquired the *maîtrise*.[33] On completing their apprenticeship, girls received from their patrons "a trousseau, a furnished bed, a sum of 200 to 300 livres, [and] annual wages of 75 livres."[34] Ordinarily a master trained only one apprentice at a time, but in some instances masters were allowed the privilege of apprenticing several foundlings or orphans from the hospitals.[35] Some foundlings, moreover, were sent to sea. The government by letters patent of 1760

[28] An account of this establishment, and of others later founded, is given by Emile Justin, *op. cit.*, pp. 233-234. Cf. Martin-Doisy, *op. cit.*, III, 1226-1228; IV, 547. Some differences exist between the two accounts.

[29] *Inv.-som . . . Gironde*, C 3238. [30] Justin, *op. cit.*, p. 234.

[31] Petition from Cassin (Arch. Nat., H 1419).

[32] Quoted by Lallemand, *op. cit.*, p. 192.

[33] For an account of the terms at Paris, see Marcel Lecoq, *L'assistance par le travail en France* (Paris, 1900), pp. 79-81.

[34] Bloch, *op. cit.*, p. 113 n. 5.

[35] *Ibid.*, p. 113, n. 4; E. Levasseur, *Histoire des classes ouvrières . . .* , II (2d ed., Paris, 1901), 382.

extended the General Hospital of Nantes the right to send them to sea at the age of ten, in the role of cabin boys, and they were given precedence at Nantes over all other applicants.[36] According to various authorities the youths apprenticed in the cities turned out badly. For example, the *Register of the Deliberations* of the bureau of the General Hospital of Paris, dated January 2, 1761, noted: "The boys when they reach the age of men find themselves without trade and without usefulness; a part run away. Those that the bureau places in trades regard themselves as free and independent, and scatter either in Paris or in the provinces, while misery turns them into vagabonds and libertines. Abandoned to themselves, they become subject to all sorts of vices, and often come to a tragic end."[37] Actually few of the apprentices acquired the *maîtrise*. Many ran away from their masters, and others lacked ability to learn and were dropped.[38]

The hospitals themselves cared for a considerable number of the children. Seldom if ever were all of the children farmed out to nurses, and when the period of nursing was ended (customarily at six, after 1761) some of those farmed out were returned by the nurses or called in by the hospitals. The hospitals had need of a certain number to do the rough work, such as washing and gardening, and serving in their workshops at beating hemp, spinning thread, weaving cloth, and (sometimes) making thread. Most of the material produced in the workshops was sold, and the proceeds went to the support of the hospitals. In some instances this income constituted an important percentage of the hospital revenues. The children received nothing for their work, save perhaps an occasional fancy handkerchief, perfume, or some sweets. In some instances, it appears, the regimen of work for the children was severe;[39] in others,

[36] *Inv.-som . . . Ille-et-Vilaine*, C 1281. Since 1681 *enfants-trouvés* at Marseilles had been apprenticed as cabin boys. Commonly 100 to 150 went to sea each year from the Hôtel-Dieu of Marseilles. For a discussion of their training and pay, see Gaston Valran, *Assistance et éducation en Provence aux XVIIIᵉ et XIXᵉ siècles* (Paris, 1900), pp. 25-28, 56-68.

[37] Quoted by Martin-Doisy, *op. cit.*, IV, 538. The bureau, dismayed at this state of things, appointed a commission to study ways of improvement. Out of the study came the recommendation (and government policy) to let the children grow up in the country.

[38] The Revolution brought little change. See, for instance, Tuetey, *L'assistance publique*, III, 545.

[39] See Bloch, *op. cit.*, p. 115.

so lax that little was accomplished. The younger children frequently served in funeral convoys of the well-to-do, for which service the hospital received a small fee, at so much per dozen children taking part. Eight dozen children marched in the funeral procession of Cochin, a Parisian curé. Since it was fashionable in the eighteenth century for families to have convoys, the hospitals took advantage of the vogue to add to their revenues, even to the extent of exploiting the youth in their charge. The children were often rushed from one convoy to another, subjected to irregular meal hours, and inadequately clothed. Many contracted illness; others became habituated to idleness.[40]

For their children the hospitals had schools, in which were taught one or more of the "three R's" and always the catechism. The children were forced to rise early each morning (5:00 A.M. in summer, and 5:30 A.M. in winter), as indeed was customary for children throughout Europe, and for many hours each day they were subjected to long drills, especially in the catechism. Of secular knowledge they learned next to nothing. Of the eight hundred girls at the Salpêtrière (in 1790), only twenty-four knew how to read.[41] Punishments were very severe,[42] and favors almost unknown. Since the hospitals failed to give their charges adequate experience and training for life beyond the hospital walls, a large portion of their youth failed to make a success in the world, the boys going into vagabondage or crime, the girls into vagabondage or prostitution.

Some of the girls, however, got married. Then the general hospitals gave them dowries, generally of 300 livres apiece, on which they could start their household. Dowries sometimes came from other quarters. Since their hearts were kind and they wished the girls to succeed, the French were anxious that every girl getting married, no matter how poor, have a dowry. A larger number of the girls became household maids. Others remained at the general hospitals or with farmers' families until they were twenty-five. The state contributed financial support and supervision until they reached that age. That many did remain at the general hospitals until twenty-five suggests that, severe and penurious and insanitary as

[40] *Ibid.*, pp. 114-115.
[41] *Ibid.*, p. 115.
[42] Martin-Doisy, *op. cit.*, IV, 573.

the hospitals were, they still presented a kindlier aspect to their inmates than did the large, alluring, but all too commonly unkind world outside.

Several times during the eighteenth century men of foresight suggested that their government send *enfants trouvés* to the colonies. Twice in October, 1714, the farseeing Pontchartrain, secretary of state for the marine, made this proposal to Desmaretz, the controller-general of finance.[43]   In his second letter Pontchartrain pointed out that if French colonies in the New World were to survive against the hostility of the ever-increasing English, it was imperative, indeed a military necessity, that the French increase the numbers of their colonists; else, he declared, the English in some future contest would rob the French of all their possessions, even as they had just done in the instance of Acadia, and he feared that the French might even be expelled from them entirely.   He suggested that France send for the peopling of her colonies large numbers of vagrants, poor families not able to support themselves, *enfants trouvés* (of both sexes), and some Flemish war refugees that were at the moment requesting to be allowed to proceed to French colonies. Since Desmaretz, who had bungled the provisioning of France in 1709, showed slight interest in the proposal,[44] little action was taken. Later in the century Malouet, another minister of the marine, and Chamousset, noted philanthropic writer, likewise suggested colonization with *enfant trouvés*. . Malouet proposed that twenty chosen girls from the hospitals be sent each year to Guiana and placed with "the most honest inhabitants," to learn household duties, the tending of fowls and animals, the spinning of cotton, and afterwards to be married.[45]   Chamousset, who would give the boys useful work as orderlies, sailors, and soldiers for the colonies,[46] suggested the sending of foundling youths to Louisiana.

On a small scale colonization with the youths was actually under-

[43] They are given by Boislisle and Brotonne, *Correspondance des contrôleurs généraux*, III, No. 1721.

[44] Boislisle and Brotonne *(ibid.)* summarize his letter of October 8, 1714, in reply to Pontchartrain's first letter, saying that the population of France was declining and that it would be dangerous to favor emigration.

[45] P. V. Malouet, *Collection de mémoires et correspondances officielles* (Paris, 1802) I, 88-89, 92.

[46] This was in 1756 (Bloch, *op. cit.*, p. 119 n. 5; Lallemand, *op. cit.*, pp. 244-245).

taken. In executing the John Law scheme, the government in 1719 permitted the sending to Louisiana of several hundred youths of both sexes from the foundlings at the different institutions of the General Hospital of Paris.[47] Later at intervals during the century girls were sent from the hospital at Rouen to Louisiana.[48]

The declaration of the order of council of 1779 that of the two thousand foundlings born in the provinces and transported to Paris every year nine tenths perished within the first three months because of improper food, irregular feeding hours, and other hardships incident in part to the rigor of travel,[49] was often repeated later in the eighteenth century by writers and speakers. Of course the percentage was not as high among children not transported. Of 320 children brought to the Hôtel-Dieu of Bayeux in the period 1779-1785, 236 were dead by 1786, 5 had been adopted by charitable individuals, and 16 had been returned to their mothers.[50] At Angoulême, in the last three months of 1782, 27 children were admitted and 28 died (out of a total enrollment of 281 children); during the first nine months of 1783, 91 were admitted and 54 died; in 1784, 125 were received, 71 died, and 39 were withdrawn; in 1785, 123 were received, 99 died, and 18 were withdrawn; in 1786, 132 were admitted, 104 died, and 19 were withdrawn; in 1787, 104 were received, 59 died, and none were withdrawn.[51]

At Aix in Provence, 4,844 children were exposed between January 1, 1722, and December 31, 1767, of which number 2,224 died during their first year of existence. Moreover, during the period 1768-78, of 2,490 children exposed, 1,817 died during their first year.[52] At Tours, 11,682 children were admitted in the period 1742-1801, and 7,788 died (but not necessarily in their first year);[53] at Paris, where the highest rate seemed to prevail, partly because of

[47] Five hundred were sent from the port of La Rochelle in August and September, 1719, not without some resistance from the girls. Leclercq (*op. cit.*, II, 418-420) relates that 125 girls from the Salpêtrière were married at one time to 125 young men in Paris, preparatory to transportation to Louisiana, but does not indicate whether they were a portion of the 500.

[48] Boys from the same institution were sent to Le Havre, for service in the marine (Bloch, *op. cit.*, p. 119 n. 6).

[49] Martin-Doisy, *op. cit.*, IV, 567-569. An important cause of mortality, oddly enough, was syphilis. See Lallemand, *op. cit.*, pp. 246-247; Martin-Doisy, *op. cit.*, IV, 570, 574.

[50] *Inv.-som . . . Calvados*, H Suppl. 1089-G 7, pp. 277-278.

[51] *Inv.-som . . . Charente*, C 82.   [52] Lallemand, *op. cit.*, p. 246.

[53] Giraudet, *op. cit.*, p. 109.

the importation of one fourth or one third of its foundlings from the provinces, 25,476 (or 80 per cent) of the 31,951 children admitted at the Foundlings' Hospital in the years 1771-77 died during their first year. The percentage of children dying at the various hospitals in France probably varied at the frightful rate of 50 to 80 per cent, by cities. According to Rousseau[54] and Jonas Hanway,[55] 50 per cent of all children born, however, usually died before they were eight years old.[56]

Conditions in France were universally admitted to be bad throughout the second half of the century, and various measures were taken by hospital boards and the government to improve them. For instance, on solicitation from the General Hospital of Paris, the government in 1779 forbade for the future the transportation of foundlings outside the provinces of their birth, with the severe penalty of 1,000 livres against all persons, even drivers, transporting them. Again, for a time after 1773 an attempt was made to provide a more careful inspection of the children by surgeons, but it was given up because of the expense.[57]

Several cities in France maintained private nursing bureaux, necessitated by the reluctance of French mothers during the eighteenth century to nurse their own children. According to Alfred Franklin,[58] of approximately 21,000 children born each year in Paris, only about 700 were nursed by their mothers; the rest, by hired nurses, either in Paris or in the provinces. In Paris four private nursing bureaux combined into one in 1769, under police and governmental supervision, made an effort to protect the health and life of children.

A small number of parents voluntarily paid to have their children nursed by the general hospitals. A much greater number were apprehended after exposing their children and were compelled to pay. Indeed, if the parents were married, they were usually compelled to take the child back and care for it themselves; but if they

---

[54] *Oeuvres*, V (Paris, 1791), 32.

[55] *Observations* (London, 1772), p. 39.

[56] Even down to 1870 one child out of every four born in New York City died before the passing of the first year (*The New York Times*, Sec. 2, p. 1, Aug. 25, 1935).

[57] Bloch, *op. cit.*, p. 111.

[58] See his interesting and scholarly *La vie privée d'autrefois*, XX (Paris, 1896), 59-60.

were unmarried, efforts were made to have the mother (commonly a domestic servant) disclose the father's name. The apprehended father was then compelled to pay for the child's upkeep, which was commonly designated in language of the day as the "month of nursing" because the father was required to pay so much a month or go to jail. The records of the latter half of the century reveal that many men were placed in prison for inability or refusal to pay this fee. In 1786, 755 of this class of fathers were arrested in Paris, marched in public procession, and made to wear a particular costume for the occasion.[59] Many tears were shed over this class of prisoners by eighteenth-century humanitarians, and at length in 1791 the French Revolutionists opened the prison doors for them.

The government of the Old Regime was actuated partly by a desire to shift the burden to the individual, who, it thought, should pay it, and partly by a wish to repress illegitimacy. It required the unmarried mother to declare her pregnancy, and her failure to do so by an edict of 1556 incurred the death penalty. This penalty was probably not inflicted in the eighteenth century, as was the case with many regulations, but the edict had the effect of driving unmarried mothers to midwives who were willing to treat them in secrecy. Since the government feared to make exposure of infants a capital crime lest it lead to infanticide, there thus prevailed, strangely enough, a more severe penalty for hiding pregnancy than for the exposure of the newborn infant. Only if the exposed child met death did capital punishment ensue. One mother was condemned to hanging because her exposed child was devoured by dogs.[60] Ordinarily the mother was subject to whipping and possibly banishment; this last penalty, however, was probably never administered. Indeed, very little was done to the mother except to try to persuade her to confess the name of the father of the child. The law on its face presented a cruel picture, but it is erroneous to judge eighteenth-century conditions too much by the laws. The design of the government was to prevent bastardy and child-exposure. It feared that a different policy would lead to an increase of the evil.

A few hospitals by rendering occasional aid to needy parents enabled them to rear their children. The practice, however, was

[59] Mercier, *Tableau de Paris*, XII, 84-88.
[60] Bloch, *op. cit.*, pp. 99-101 with n. 3 on last page.

open to abuse.[61] The General Hospital of Grenoble in 1788 decided not to receive any legitimate children, but to give assistance to needy parents for rearing their children, at least till the children were weaned. The amount of aid, which depended upon the actual needs of the family, might extend to 3 livres a month, and even to the gift of bread, if the mother nursed her own child, or it might cover the full cost of having the child nursed up to eighteen months in case the mother was unable to do the nursing herself.[62] Necker believed that all abandoned children, including those whose parents were known, should be reared at government expense.[63]

One factor which tended to increase the number of *enfants trouvés* at the hospitals was the tendency of the lords high justices to dump on the hospitals a burden which was rightfully theirs. Under a feudal law valid to the end of the Old Regime in France, children exposed on the lands of the lords high justices were to be cared for at the expense of these landowners. In the eighteenth century a few continued to fulfil this obligation, but most of them sought to avoid the obligation by taking the child either to a near-by hospital or to the Foundlings' Hospital in Paris. The king himself owned land in Auvergne and elsewhere which came under the category of the high justices and was liable to the expense of rearing the found-lings left on it. The lords high justices encouraged the placing of the *enfants trouvés* on the king's lands. The king passed them on to the hospitals but underwrote the expense.[64]

Not all of the foundlings were reared by the general hospitals and the hôtels-Dieu. A few were adopted or otherwise cared for privately. Many others were reared by religious orders or philan-thropic societies in private institutions, designated under the names

---

[61] Martin-Doisy, *op. cit.*, IV, 571.

[62] *Inv.-som . . . l'hôpital de Grenoble*, E 28, pp. 111-112.

[63] *Inv.-som . . . Gironde*, C 3457.

[64] A long discussion of the matter is given by Coiffier, *op. cit.*, pp. 129-138. See also Martin-Doisy, *op. cit.*, IV, 580-581. The latter cites a statement by Necker that there were 40,000 foundlings in France at the expense of the lords high jus-tices, but these figures are preposterous. The committee of mendicity in 1791 esti-mated the total number of foundlings in all France at only 40,000 (*Arch. parl.*, XXII, 612). Also Martin-Doisy's statement that Paris hospitals had custody over 40,000 foundlings in 1789 is on the same basis preposterous. Ordinarily he appears very reliable, but he is almost certainly in error here. More acceptable is his state-ment that a law of November 29, 1790, discharged the *seigneurs* from the obligation of paying the expense for the care of *enfants trouvés* found on their lands, and placed it to the charge of the state.

of "hospitals" and "houses." But the great majority, perhaps two thirds or five sixths of the whole, were reared in the municipal institutions, at the expense of city, province, and government. The committee of mendicity in 1790 estimated the annual sum spent on foundlings in France at 3,148,184 livres.[65] A large portion of this expense was borne by the government either directly or indirectly, in subsidies, in grants from the *octrois*, the *vingtiéme*, other taxes and services, and by gifts from lotteries. The direct subsidies were large, and were sometimes based on a ratio per child.[66] After the 1730's the government in some instances adopted the policy of giving hospitals definite annual allowances, without regard to the number of children in their custody.[67] In 1767 the government granted two subsidies, one of 150,000 and another of 120,000 livres, to the Foundlings' Hospital of Paris, and established the policy of giving each year 120,000 livres (with other occasional subsidies) to this institution.[68] A grant of 4,000 livres by the government to the hospital of Riom in 1787 constituted one third of the expenses for foundlings there that year.[69] A grant of 10,267 livres in the same year to the General Hospital of Grenoble was equal to at least one third, and possibly one half, of that hospital's expense for foundlings.[70]

In the *pays d'états*, as was indicated earlier, the provincial assemblies (rather than the government in Paris) commonly cared for their own provincial charities. Thus the General Assembly of Provence in 1764 allotted 40,000 livres to its hospitals for the care of foundlings. This allowance was reckoned at the generous rate of 150 livres per year a child.[71] In 1783 its rate was 175 livres a child. The amount given is not indicated, but in 1772 it was already

[65] Martin-Doisy, *op. cit.*, IV, 581.

[66] The General Hospital at Grenoble was granted subsidies from 1724 to 1733 on the following basis: 2 sous a day for children up to four years of age; 4 sous for children from four to eight; 5 sous for children from eight to twelve; and 6 sous for those above twelve. *Inv.-som . . . l'hôpital de Grenoble*, F 2, pp. 135-136. Cf. Coiffier, *op. cit.*, pp. 138-139.

[67] Coiffier (*op. cit.*, pp. 139-145) gives considerable discussion to this evolution of policy with regard to the hospitals in the generality of Riom. For some decades it worked great hardship on the hospitals there, since the new subsidies proved less generous than the former.

[68] Lallemand, *op. cit.*, 140-141.

[69] Martin-Doisy, *op. cit.*, IV, 802.

[70] *Inv.-som . . . l'hôpital de Grenoble*, E 28.

[71] *Inv.-som . . . Bouches-du-Rhône*, C 83, f 372.

100,000 livres.[72] At their triennial assembly the Estates of Burgundy gave regularly 8,000 livres to the hospital at Dijon for this purpose from 1757 to 1781, when the sum was raised to 10,000 livres.[73] Sometimes a *pays d'état* might find the burden of relief greater than it could bear, and might call upon the royal government for aid, as did Provence in 1788, when it needed additional funds for paying the children's nurses.[74]

Revenues from lotteries and the *octrois* were large. With government permission, a few hospitals were able occasionally to run lotteries for the acquisition of revenues. The most notable was the Foundlings' Hospital of Paris, which from 1717 to the time of the Revolution acquired its largest single source of revenue from the lottery.[75] For a time its lottery produced 240,000 livres annually. From 1695 to the end of the Old Regime the Foundlings' Hospital likewise enjoyed, in common with the Hôtel-Dieu and the General Hospital (of which it was a part), a portion of the *octroi* on wines and liqueurs entering Paris, which amounted to the huge sum of 156,670 livres during the 1770's.[76] Since the hospitals throughout France rather generally participated in the receipts of their cities' *octrois*, the *octrois* were an important revenue for the support of the foundlings. Other taxes from which, in isolated cases, the hospitals drew money for this cause were the *vingtième* (half of which at Paris went for the purpose),[77] the *pied fourché* (at Paris),[78] and a tax on the upper classes (at Tours).[79]

At Bordeaux the *enfants trouvés* were accorded revenues from a most unusual source. Some Jews from Avignon were naturalized there in 1776 on condition that they contribute 60,000 livres for the construction of a new building for the *enfants trouvés*.[80]

---

[72] *Ibid.*, C 91, f 142v; 98, f 60v. [73] Martin-Doisy, *op. cit.*, IV, 570.

[74] *Inv.-som . . . Bouches-du-Rhône*, C 100.

[75] In 1755 and 1776 changes were made whereby other institutions shared in the lottery. After 1776 it was known as the Royal Lottery of France (Lallemand, *op. cit.*, pp. 142-144).

[76] The Hôtel-Dieu got fourteen times this amount (Möring and Quentin, *op. cit.*, II, 87).

[77] Martin-Doisy, *op. cit.*, IV, 558, 569.

[78] Chéruel (*op. cit.*, II, 978) describes it as a municipal tax placed on cloven-hoofed animals entering the city, such as cattle, hogs, sheep. In the 1770's revenue from this tax to the extent of 8,158 livres went to the foundlings (Möring and Quentin, *op. cit.*, II, 87).

[79] Martin-Doisy, *op. cit.*, IV, 530.

[80] Five Jews are named (*Inv.-som . . . Gironde*, C 3869).

After 1789

The changes effected in the treatment of foundlings and orphans during the Revolutionary period (1789-1801) were trivial in character, although a severe curtailment in funds increased distress. The Revolutionaries, it is true, by their laws of September 15, 1791, and August 25, 1792, abolished first the practice of imprisoning, and later of arresting, the fathers of illegitimate infants who could not or would not pay the small hospital fee for their children's nursing. They gloried in this action as the liberation of an oppressed segment of the French population, but the benefit accrued solely to the fathers. The state assumed the expense of nursing their children, as indeed had been the case hitherto. Periodically grants were made for paying the "month of nursing." Thus on December 11, 1791, the government allocated 225,788 livres for this purpose; on August 15, 1792, it granted another 140,000 livres; on January 19, 1793, it gave yet another 62,102 livres.[81] Nevertheless, the administrators of the department of the Haute-Garonne in 1796 insisted that parents of foundlings, when identified, should bear the expense of upkeep; otherwise they determined to refuse to maintain the children.[82]

Throughout the period the hospitals continued to place the infants with nurses for rearing, preferably in the rural districts, and paid for their care at a specified monthly rate. The rapid depreciation of French currency during much of the period necessitated repeated increases in the wages given for nursing. Sometimes the nurses gathered as a group and threatened to "strike" (despite the law of the French Revolutionaries against striking) unless their rate of pay was increased. Thus on May 13, 1795, eight of the sixteen wet nurses employed at the Hôtel-Dieu of Toulouse came before the bureau of administrators with the complaint that their wages of 25 livres a month were not sufficient to buy a handkerchief, and that two months' wages were required to buy a pair of shoes. They complained that they worked day and night, and that their health was impaired by nursing several children each. They threatened to quit unless they were given a raise. Despite the fact that only a

---

[81] Lallemand, op. cit., p. 255 with nn. Hitherto the state had not made grants for this designated end, but in actual fact it did pay most of the expense of the foundlings when the fathers failed to pay.

[82] Adher, op. cit., pp. 140-141.

short time before they had been allowed an increase from 15 to 25 livres, they were now promised 40 livres a month.[83]

Sometimes, as in 1796, the country nurses were paid in grain because of the scarcity of money.[84] Only one child could be placed with a rural nurse, and the municipalities were urged to exercise a strict surveillance over the welfare of the child. In the case of bad care, they were to report at once to the directory of their district, which had immediate custody of the hospitals.[85] State inspection of nurses was continued during the Revolution;[86] but this inspection was evidently lax, since it was difficult to get the needed number of nurses. With their wages low and often in arrears, some nurses cared for the children gratuitously; others neglected or deserted their charges.[87]

A few institutions experimented with the feeding of infants with goat's or cow's milk in a bottle provided with a rubber nipple. One experiment was begun at Grenoble in March, 1792.[88] Another was projected in 1798 by the Hospice d'Humanité (the former Hôtel-Dieu) of Toulouse. Two goats were to be bought, pap was to be made of the milk, and children were to be fed thereby.[89] In the mid-eighteenth century it was the custom among French mothers to feed their children on pap, a practice which Rousseau denounced in his *Emile* because of the heavy fatality attending it.

The terrific mortality of foundling children continued throughout the Revolutionary period. According to Lallemand, leading authority on the history of the *enfants trouvés*, 95 per cent of the infants left with the Foundlings' Hospital (Paris) in 1797 died, and not more than 3 or 4 per cent of them lived beyond several years.[90] At Marseilles in the year X (1801-02) the death rate was

---

[83] Adher, *op. cit.*, pp. 100-101. In 1793 the rate had been 6 livres a month (*ibid.*, p. 67). Cf. *ibid.*, pp. 98, 120-121.

[84] *Ibid.*, p. 138. "Les nourrices de la campagne ont été payées au taux de 15 livres, 25 livres, 40 livres, 120 livres par mois en méteil." The nurses preferred their payment in grain, since the grain, unlike the paper money, did not fluctuate in value.

[85] Deries, *op. cit.*, p. 398. The hospitals were required to send periodic reports to the departmental directory, and the directory in turn made reports to Paris.

[86] Ferdinand-Dreyfus, *L'assistance*, p. 107.

[87] *Ibid.*, pp. 90-91, 102; Adher, *op. cit.*, p. 228.

[88] *Inv.-som . . . Isère*, H, Introduction by A. Prudhomme, p. xvi.

[89] Adher, *op. cit.*, pp. 195-196. The results of the two experiments are not given.

[90] *Op. cit.*, p. 261.

nineteen-twentieths, or 95 per cent.[91] These figures, representing the two most congested cities, were probably higher than the average throughout the France of that period; nevertheless, the mortality rate everywhere was severe. In all the hospitals of the south children slept four in a bed.[92] At Nancy, in Lorraine, in the year IV (1795-96) they suffered from hunger, lack of clothing and bedding; at Douai, in French Flanders, they were given coarse food, and many died through negligence; and at Tarbes, near the Spanish frontier, 250 children were near starvation.[93] From all parts of France came reports of privations and heavy mortality of the children. The privations of course were chiefly due to the fact that after 1792 France was continually at war, and had even less money for charities than hitherto. It is not surprising, therefore, that the death rate was even higher than before 1789.

Probably the wisest action concerning foundlings taken by the government during this era was the decision, in 1793, to give monetary aid to needy unmarried mothers. By the law of June 28 of that year it was provided that pregnant girls might go to hospitals at state expense for the period of their delivery. If they wished to nurse their children, the state would extend monetary aid; in one instance, according to Martin-Doisy, a mother and child were given temporary aid of 150 livres. Finally, in the event that health or other reasons rendered it impossible after a time for the mother to continue nursing her child, and she desired to place it in a hospital or with a nurse, the state would make the arrangements for this care. All that was necessary to obtain any of these forms of aid was that the mother inform the municipal authorities of her needs and wishes. This was perhaps the first French law to set forth the principle of aid to unmarried mothers (filles-mères).[94]

Moreover, the Revolutionary government tried to soften the term "foundlings." The law of June 28, 1793, provided that thenceforth they should be known as "orphans." A week later the Convention, by its decree of July 4, ordered that for the future they

---

[91] Ferdinand-Dreyfus, op. cit., p. 102.

[92] Ibid., p. 102.

[93] Ibid., pp. 90-91.

[94] Martin-Doisy, op. cit., IV, 581-582. In the year VIII (1799-1800) the government was 18,000 francs in arrears to unmarried mothers in the city of Paris alone ("Ministère de l'Intérieur, 1ère Division, 1ère Bureau. Proposition de fonds pour la 1ère décade de Germinal," Arch. Nat., F15, 103).

should be known as *enfants naturels de la patrie*.[95] Thenceforward they frequently appeared in the records under one or the other of these two designations, yet occasionally under the old designation of *enfants trouvés*. The government assumed (by law of June 28, 1793) the entire cost and responsibility of rearing all foundlings, and it desired that they be regarded in an honorable and patriotic light.

Still another change in the care of foundlings was made by the Revolutionary government. Except in extraordinary cases, the government assumed, through the hospitals, responsibility only to the completion of the twelfth year. This action was taken by the Convention on August 19, 1793.[96] Under the Old Regime the foundling was sometimes kept till his twentieth or twenty-fifth year. The foundling was given religious instruction, but shielded and permitted to receive little actual knowledge of the outside world. As a result, the matured male foundling frequently ended in vagabondage, and the matured female in prostitution. Compelled doubtless by economic necessity, the Revolutionary government, on the other hand, probably went too far in laxity. Little or no religion was taught, and at the age of thirteen the children were cast adrift in the world.[97]

The government did provide apprenticeship for those wishing it. It issued a general appeal to manufacturers, tradesmen, artists, and farmers to take apprentices from the *enfants de la patrie* of the hospitals, and thus help relieve the crowded conditions at these institutions. Many were taken[98] and apprenticed for a period of three years. No longer did the guilds exist. No longer was it possible for a farmer to avoid military service for himself or his son by adopting a foundling. There were evident advantages from these changes, yet, in the opinion of the minister of the interior in 1797, the new system did not work smoothly. Especially disappointed

[95] Martin-Doisy, *op. cit.*, IV, 581-582.

[96] Families undertaking to rear these children were to be paid sums proportional to local wages, but not to exceed 80 livres a year for children below the age of ten; thenceforth the allotment was to be decreased one third, as the children's labor had some value. The government was not to support children after their twelfth year. This age limit lasted down to the time of Lallemand (1884) (Lallemand, *op. cit.*, p. 258).

[97] By the law of 27 frimaire an V (Dec. 17, 1796), children could be left on the farms after they were twelve (Martin-Doisy, *op. cit.*, IV, 719-720).

[98] They could also be apprenticed to ship captains for sea duty, if the youths desired. This permission was given by the law of December 17, 1796.

were the youths apprenticed to manufacturers. Many ran away before their apprenticeships were completed. The training was long and arduous, and the manufacturers found little profit from it for themselves.[99]

In April, 1793, the Convention considered a proposal to make foundling youths from twelve to twenty-one work in an arms manufacture in Paris, but apparently nothing resulted.[100]

The ministry of the interior, which had jurisdiction over most of the institutions and works of charity of the Revolutionary period, estimated that, "after some very exact returns," a total of 60,687 *enfants abandonnés* were cared for by the hospitals in 1800, at a cost of not less than 6,780,000 francs a year.[101] Four hundred thousand francs were needed "for appeasing the nurses who clamor loudly from all regions," and more than 18,000 francs were already due to unmarried mothers in Paris alone.

The decree of March 19, 1793, inspired by the financial distress of the charitable institutions, made the state responsible for all charitable institutions, confiscated their property, ordered it sold for the benefit of the state, and declared that thenceforth public assistance would be a governmental obligation.[102] In the severe economic and political crisis since 1788, private contributions had dwindled, hospital property and other investments brought greatly diminished returns, and one by one the feudal dues, taxes,[103] fines, and the lottery,[104] which had contributed substantially to the support of these institutions, were abolished by the National and Legislative Assem-

---

[99] "Le Ministre de l'intérieur au Tribunal Civil de Départment de Seine et Oise. Paris le 25 frimaire an VI de la république" (Arch. Nat., F15, 103).

[100] Tuetey, *Repertoire générale*, VIII, 313, No. 2087.

[101] "Ministère de L'Intérieur, 1ère Division, 1ère Bureau. Proposition de fonds pour la 1ère décade de Germinal" (Arch. Nat., F15, 103). The preamble of the law of 25 ventôse an IX (March 14, 1800) pointed out that within the last decade the number of *enfants trouvés* in hospices had doubled, the current number being 63,000 (De Watteville, *op. cit.*, p. 73).

[102] Lallemand, *op. cit.*, p. 256. For a time it permitted the Society of Maternal Charity, a noted Parisian institution formed by the wealthy in May, 1788, to continue its work of assisting poor mothers in the delivery and nursing of their children; and during 1793 it even made several large benefactions to it (as it was in dire straits); but in 1795 this and all other charitable societies were abolished (Ferdinand-Dreyfus, *op. cit.*, pp. 49-52).

[103] The *octrois*, the chief tax supporting these institutions, had been abolished May 1, 1791 (*Arch. parl.*, LVI, 616-617).

[104] Abolished 25 frimaire an II; restored 25 vendémiare an VI (*The Cambridge Modern History*, VIII, 709).

blies and the Convention; and only temporary state grants for current expenses were made to take their place. Nationalization of charitable institutions, including care of the *enfants trouvés*, was thus the sensible policy for the government in 1793.

Since 1789 the state had made some large allocations of money for the support of foundlings. Two such grants were made in 1791: one of 100,000 livres, January 24, and a second, April 3, of 1,969,000 livres.[105] On January 9, 1793, another appropriation provided 1,500,000 livres.[106]

After the nationalization of charities on March 19, 1793, the appropriations became larger in amount, not because of greater state benevolence, but because of inflation. On May 5, 1793, the Convention found it necessary to make a new subsidy of 3,500,000 livres, and on 7 germinal an II (March 28, 1794) still another of 4,600,000 livres, for the care of foundlings.[107] Thereafter the figures reached astronomical proportions. The care of foundlings in the custody of the Hospice d'Humanité (the former Hôtel-Dieu) of Toulouse for the period from September 23, 1795, to March 21, 1796, cost 1,298,483 francs; on May 3, 1796, the government extended the hospital 2,000,000 francs for all its various needs.[108] During the year 1796 this hospital was granted a total, for all purposes, of 9,500,000 francs; and the Hospice de Bienfaisance (the old General Hospital) was allotted a total of 3,000,000 francs.[109] The cost of maintenance for the foundlings at the Hospice d'Humanité during the first half of 1796 amounted to 1,266,226 francs in paper or 4,498 francs in specie.[110] In March, 1797, Bénezech, minister of the interior, placed at the disposal of this hospital 40,000 francs in metallic money, which at the rate of exchange of October 30, 1796, would have amounted to 11,210,000 paper francs.[111]

Thenceforth the French money had higher valuation, since the

---

[105] The expense for the care of the *enfants trouvés* in 1791, however, was estimated at 2,500,000 livres; for 1792, 3,000,000 livres ("Enfants trouvés. Mémoire," Arch. Nat., F15, 101).

[106] *Arch. parl.*, LVI, 616-617.

[107] Lallemand, *op. cit.*, pp. 256, 258.

[108] Adher, *op. cit.*, pp. 128, 138. The Revolutionary governments seldom, if ever, made it a practice to give the full amount necessary to cover expenses. The result was that there were always deficits.

[109] *Ibid.*, pp. 143-145.

[110] *Ibid.*, p. 149.

[111] *Ibid.*, p. 150.

government on May 21, 1797, demonetized all currency (assignats and mandats) held by the public. But this action, though it restored financial credit, did not place more money at the disposal of the government. In fact, it became even more difficult to get money from the government for the care of foundlings or for other charitable needs. From 1798 to 1800 the hospitals and the *enfants trouvés* of Toulouse suffered as perhaps they never before had suffered during the eighteenth century.[112] Nor was this distress limited to Toulouse; it was experienced throughout France.[113]

[112] See the various documents quoted or summarized by Adher, *op. cit.*, pp. 198-234.

[113] Lallemand, *op. cit.*, pp. 234-236, 243-245, 246-252; Ferdinand-Dreyfus, *op. cit.*, p. 102; *Inv.-som . . . Isère*, L 128, fructidor.

CHAPTER XII

TREATMENT OF BEGGARS, VAGABONDS, AND THE NEEDY

Before 1789

IN FRANCE and the other Latin countries of Europe in the eighteenth century perennial begging and vagabondage ate like a cancer at the economic and social vitals of the state. The number of beggars and vagabonds, varying from time to time, was greatly swelled during, and sometimes after, wars, famines, severe winters, and periods of economic crisis. The historian Duclos (1704-72) estimated that there were normally in Paris from 20,000 to 30,000 beggars.[1] The Revolutionary deputy, Papion *le jeune,* a member of the celebrated committee of mendicity, informed the National Assembly in 1791 that under the Old Regime there had habitually been, and that there still existed, 100,000 scattered throughout France, "troubling security in all the kingdom."[2] In times of crisis the number no doubt increased to 200,000 or more. Vauban in his *Dixme royale* (1706) stated that from observations extending over more than forty years of travel in all parts of France he had found one tenth of the French people reduced to beggary, and five additional tenths living in a state of misery little removed from beggary.[3] It is well to

---

[1] *Oeuvres complètes de Duclos, précédés d'une notice sur sa vie et ses écrits, par M. Auger, de l'Académie française* (Paris, new ed., 1821), VII, 183; IX, 237.

[2] *Arch. parl.,* XXII, 638 with n.

[3] "By all the investigations that I have been able to make during the several years that I have devoted myself to it, I have become strongly convinced that in these last times almost the tenth part of the people is reduced to mendicity, and exists by begging; that of the other nine parts five are not in condition to render alms to it, because they themselves are reduced to very nearly the same condition; that of the four other parts remaining, three are very ill-provided, and encumbered with debts and lawsuits; and that in the tenth, where I place all the men of the sword, the robe, ecclesiastics and laymen, all the high nobility, the distinguished nobility, and men in charge, military and civil, the good merchants, the most secure bourgeois living from investments, one is not able to count above one hundred thousand families; and I do not believe that I lie when I say that there are not ten thousand, small or great, that one is able to say are decidedly at their ease . . ." (*op. cit.,* p. 4. Cf. pp. 2-3).

For forty years France had been at war, and conditions had become increasingly severe. Nevertheless, this classic passage from Vauban is probably too pessimistic. Accepting the picture fully, it is difficult to explain the prosperity and greatness of the Age of Louis XIV.

observe, however, that statistics are not available, and that the historian is obliged to rely heavily upon the estimates of eighteenth-century writers.

Many begged from necessity; others from choice. Some were professionals who had learned various tricks-in-trade for eliciting pity and alms. Frequently they were organized in bands, with leaders, headquarters, laws, and an argot of their own. Apprentices were trained by veteran members. In Paris the headquarters of various bands were the notorious Cours des Miracles,[4] where they had "an organized society, an independent horde, recognizing neither law, nor superior, nor police." When the compassion of passers-by was not sufficiently aroused, they sometimes drew arms to extract gifts. And to their lair, the Cours des Miracles, "never did an honest man penetrate." Other bands, of course, operated in the provinces.[5] That of Charles Hulin (1767-90), known as "The Blond," was "the most considerable of all by the number of its affiliates and its crimes," containing 166 members, of whom 45 were women. Four of the members, one a woman, committed eighty-nine crimes. In the band were former members of various trades and professions, including a jeweler and a surgeon. Orléannais, Touraine, Beauce, Berry, Brie, Burgundy, Champagne, Franche-Comté, Normandy, Morvan, Sologne, Gatinais, and possibly other regions, were scourged by them. They wandered over the countryside, begging food and gifts and sleeping in barns. They threatened, and if they were denied, they took by force. The peasantry found it more prudent to yield to them than to oppose their many deeds of vandalism, and few dared to inform against them. In times of famine and distress these bands multiplied in numbers and increased in insolence, the most famous occasion being that of "The Great Fear" in the summer of 1789.[6]

The beggars and vagabonds, however, were but a small fraction of the misfits and needy in eighteenth-century French society. They were the lazy, the indifferent, the churlish—the unsocial and the antisocial. The vastly greater portion of the poor, on the other

[4] Bru, *op. cit.*, pp. 15-17, 351-353. Paultre (*op. cit.*, p. 310) states that, because of the creation of the General Hospital, the Court of the Miracles had disappeared prior to the eighteenth century; but Bloch (*op. cit.*, p. 31) asserts that it was still existent.

[5] Bloch, *op. cit.*, pp. 32-35.

[6] See also the sixth report of the committee of mendicity (*Arch. parl.*, XXII, 559).

hand, were industrious, self-respecting, socially minded, and desired nothing more than to earn their food by work. The committee of mendicity, reporting to the National Assembly in 1791, estimated that about one twentieth of the French population, even in normal times, remained destitute and in need of aid in one form or another, whereas in times of adversity and crisis this figure rose to one tenth or one ninth of the total population. Some needed partial, others total, support. Some needed food and medical attention; others asylum for afflictions or old age. In times of distress the percentage of the needy in some districts rose very much higher than one tenth or one ninth. For instance, an estimate of 1788 reveals that, aside from beggars, Paris had 120,000 indigents, and another of 1787 that it had 200,000 indigents working on state- and city-supported relief projects.[7] Since pre-Revolutionary Paris had a population of only 600,000, the first estimate (1778) would place one fifth, the second (1787), one third, of its inhabitants on relief. Moreover, it is commonly agreed that distress in eighteenth-century France was more acute in the agricultural districts than in the cities.[8]

What were the causes of these conditions? First, there were the social and natural catastrophes, such as wars, famines, economic depressions, floods, hailstorms, and severe winters. A flood or a hailstorm in a fruit- or a vine-growing region might damage or ruin an ungathered harvest and throw the whole population into desperate circumstances. An economic depression, brought on by war or the glutting of the market or a change in fashion of dress, might throw hordes of industrial workers out of employment and on the mercy of the public. Depressions in the silk trade in 1749, 1754, 1778-79, and 1787-89 created unemployment at Lyons, and the city and state came to the aid of the victims.[9] Secondly, the planting and marketing system in agriculture was fundamentally defective. Permission from the intendant was necessary before making any changes in the planting of crops, and harvested crops had to be disposed of at

[7] Bloch, *op. cit.*, p. 6. He cites a number of eighteenth-century writers on mendicity who give higher estimates of the needy, both for normal and abnormal times, than the committee of mendicity.

[8] See, for instance, Henri Sée, *Remarques sur la misère, la mendicité et l'assistance en Bretagne à la fin de l'ancien régime*, p. 116.

[9] Paul Lacroix, *XVIIIe siècle: lettres, sciences, et arts* (Paris, 1878), pp. 531-532; Thomas F. Power, Jr., "Emergency Relief in France in 1788," *Journal of Modern History*, XIII (June, 1941), 222.

stated times and in stated places. Throughout the eighteenth century French agriculture remained in a bad plight. Small farmer, share-cropper, hired worker, all suffered. There was a steady drift of population away from the farm to the city. The government deplored this drift and, increasingly as the century advanced, endeavored to rehabilitate the farms, with little or no success.[10] Thirdly, the industrial system was too inelastic.[11] The guilds, still numerous and powerful, controlled the greater part of French production. The best opportunity for a poor boy was to obtain entrance as apprentice in one of them. But what of the boys who could not gain this opportunity? In most instances they were doomed to be manual laborers, at low wages, dependent on the whims of the market. It is true that the domestic and the factory systems were making their way in eighteenth-century France. In the glass industry[12] the factory system had made no small progress; but the two systems had not arrived at the point of laissez faire and were as yet minor movements. Fourthly, wages throughout the eighteenth century lagged sadly behind prices.[13] This was in part due to the fact that the French government (as also the British government) set wage schedules for workers, and the labor market was far from free.[14]

[10] The Abbé Montlinot, who was director of the "model" dépôt de mendicité at Soissons in the 1780's (see Bloch, op. cit., p. 221), states in his several Etats (reports) on that institution that agricultural distress sent most of the several hundred inmates to him every year, and he considers as the fundamental cause the failure of every farm worker to own his own tract of land, of every city worker to own his own machine and shop.

[11] See Earl J. Hamilton, "Growth of Rigidity in Business during the Eighteenth Century," American Economic Review Supplement, XXX (March, 1940), 305.

[12] Professor Warren C. Scoville, the author of four able articles on the French glass industry of the eighteenth century, based on elaborate archival study, reveals in the third, entitled "Large-scale Production in the French Plate-Glass Industry, 1665-1789" (Journal of Political Economy, I, Oct., 1942, 669-698) that in the Royal Plate Glass Company the factory system made considerable development. From 200 in 1765, its factory personnel swelled to "at least 450 skilled, semi-skilled, and unskilled workers" in 1700; to 1,000 in the decade 1741-50; to "probably as many as 1,200 or 1,400 in 1775" (pp. 679-680). Its capital and dividends were correspondingly great. In 1776 its assets amounted to 12,154,217 livres, and its dividends to 690,000 livres. See charts, pp. 680, 683. "In all other industries, apparently only the coal-mining company of Anzin was larger," with its "4,000 work-people and 600 horses, its assets of approximately 23,000,000 livres, and its annual income of about 3,500,000 livres" (p. 681).

[13] Earl J. Hamilton, "Profit Inflation and the Industrial Revolution, 1751-1800," Quarterly Journal of Economics, LVI (Feb., 1942), 270. "According to M. Labrousse, commodity prices were 63.7 per cent higher in 1785-89 than in 1726-41. But in the same period wages rose only 22 per cent."

[14] Calonne, controller-general of finance, was responsible for an arrêt in 1786

Workers were forbidden by law either to organize or strike, or in some instances to resign.[15] Fifthly, many regiments in the French army were composed of Swiss, Germans, Scots, Irish, Belgians, Hungarians, Turks, Italians, Poles, and Swedes.[16] The expense of these regiments fell upon the French government, and it might well have employed its own subjects. In place of the foreign troops, some of whom were very costly, possibly forty thousand Frenchmen might have been hired.[17] Sixthly, the failure of the French to follow a more active policy of colonization prevented them from getting the trade that might have been theirs and from disposing of some of their "surplus" population abroad. Indeed, attempts were made, but they were too spasmodic and shortlived to have much effect.

Several devices were used by the government to eradicate the evil. As for the beggars and vagabonds, outright repression, with temporary imprisonment for the first offense and severe penalties for repetitions, was pursued down to the Revolution, even as it had been for centuries previously, perhaps even from the days of Charle-

---

placing labor "on a capitalistic basis by abolishing all wage schedules established by government authority and providing for freedom of contract between worker and employer. It also forbade the exclusion of women workers and placed them on the same legal footing as men. The purpose was to free workers from wage scales which could not be kept in line with the cost of living. Since [however] they were not permitted to strike, this legislation was of doubtful benefit to the laborers" (Wilma J. Pugh, "Calonne's 'New Deal,'" *Journal of Modern History*, XI, Sept., 1939, 303).

[15] "On January 2, 1749, Louis XV issued a general order forbidding workers in any French industry to organize against their employers; and in January, 1762, a special order threatened their workers at the Sèvres bottle factory with fines, corporal punishment, and imprisonment, if they did not work peaceably. Glass workers were forbidden to wander more than a league's distance from the furnace at which they worked without written permission from their employers, and under no circumstances could they resign from their position without having demanded *two years in advance* a written discharge" (Warren C. Scoville, "State Policy and the French Glass Industry, 1640-1789," *Quarterly Journal of Economics*, LVI, May, 1942, 446-447). Like other French laws, this law, however, was not always observed, for French workers did sometimes organize, though clandestinely, and force their will on their employers (Maxime Kovalewaky, *La France économique & sociale à la veille de la Révolution*, II, Paris, 1911, 24-27, 31 with nn.).

[16] Alfred Rambaud, *Histoire de la civilisation française* (Paris, 1887), II, 214-216, 229-231; Eugène Fyffé, *Histoire des troupes étrangères au service de France* ... (Paris, 1854), I, chap. iii. There was one brigade of Negroes (*ibid.*, I, 281).

[17] Rambaud writes that the eleven or more Swiss regiments cost excessively. According to F. C. Montague (*The Cambridge Modern History*, VIII, 51), the French army in the reign of Louis XVI consisted of "about 170,000 regular troops, of whom perhaps one-sixth were foreigners."

magne.[18] Every few decades, as was French custom, these laws were proclaimed anew in a royal edict or proclamation. Several times in the eighteenth century, notably in 1701, 1724, 1750, and 1764, royal declarations were issued.[19] Occasionally they were reissued in intervening years by parlement, intendant, municipal authorities, or hospital. Although slight differences appeared in these various declarations, in general they demanded that all beggars and vagabonds obtain work at once or return to the place of their nativity and warned that failure to do so would render them subject to arrest by *archers* of the *marechaussée* (national mounted police) or by *archers* specially employed by municipalities or hospitals. First offenders might be released after a month or two with a warning; those repeating the offense within a period of years would be branded with the letters *V* (for *voleur*) or *M* (for *mendiant*) or with the *fleur de lis*. The men would then be sent to the galleys for several years or for life; the women, to a general hospital for scourging and imprisonment. The declaration of 1764, which, Bloch says, was "the last solemn expression of the ideas of the ancient monarchy,"[20] was but slightly less severe than those that preceded it.

This policy of severity met the disapproval of most of the contemporary writers on mendicity,[21] and it had little success. Several thousands were arrested every year,[22] but a much larger number escaped, perhaps on account of the negligence of the police or the difficulty of apprehending them, or both. Vagabonds and beggars were on the lookout for the police quite as much as the police were

[18] Bernard, a member of the committee of public aid, declared in a speech before the Legislative Assembly on June 13, 1792, that France had been making severe laws against mendicity, without success (*Arch. parl.*, XLV, 155). He is borne out by Paultre (*op. cit.*, pp. 381, 589) and Lecoq (*op. cit.*, pp. 67-68).

[19] Description of these declarations is given by Bloch, *op. cit.*, pp. 52-53, 159, 161-162. See also Paultre, *op. cit.*, pp. 311-424; *Inv.-som . . . Calvados*, C 591, 593, 594; and *Inv.-som . . . l'hôpital de Grenoble*, F 2.

[20] Banishment (or sending a beggar from one province to another) was given up; a vagabond was defined as a wanderer who had been out of work for six months; and mention of branding was omitted.

[21] Paultre, *op. cit.*, p. 590.

[22] Levasseur (*La population française . . .*, III, Paris, 1892, 119) quotes Necker as saying that there were probably 50,000 arrested in 1767. The figure appears too high for the normal year. The committee of mendicity in its sixth report (1791) mentions that in approximately one sixth of France 1,656 vagabonds were arrested annually. This ratio would approximate 9,539 for the whole of the country (*Arch. parl.*, XXII, 599 n.). Papion *le jeune*, a member of this committee, however, set an estimate of 15,000 to 16,000 for all France (*ibid.*, XXII, 638 with n.). See further, Paultre, *op. cit.*, pp. 602-605; Bloch, *op. cit.*, pp. 164 n. 3, 171 n. 3.

for them, and they had ways of evasion. Some even took jobs temporarily when they suspected that they were being watched; others fled to Paris. In the second half of the century it came to be generally recognized that repression would never cure mendicancy, and that work must be provided.

An attempt at providing work had been made by the French kings of the sixteenth and seventeenth centuries. Francis I, it is said, offered the needy work in 1516.[23] In 1656 Louis XIV ordered the creation of the General Hospital of Paris, and in 1662 the creation of similar institutions in other French cities, for the purpose of offering employment and asylum to all the deserving poor. Decade by decade, down to the time of the Revolution, saw new general hospitals going up in one part or another of France.[24] But, as we have observed, the general hospitals were woefully too few or too small to provide for all who needed work or care; and most of those placed in them were sufferers of physical disabilities or prisoners incarcerated for petty infractions of the law.[25]

To supplement the general hospital, *dépôts de mendicité* (concentration camps with workhouses) were brought into existence through government encouragement. A few, established in 1724 and following years, lasted only a brief while.[26] Others, formed in 1764 and later,[27] led a checkered existence down to 1793 or later. Some died shortly after their establishment. Turgot disliked them and reduced their number to five, but later in answer to complaints re-established eleven. His successor, Clugny, restored the others.[28] Necker in 1785 counted thirty-three, and Roland in 1793, thirty-four.[29] They were scattered among the cities of France. The most famous was that formed by Necker at Soissons in 1781, and administered by the Abbé Montlinot, who published several elaborate reports on it.

---

[23] Lecoq, *op. cit.*, p. 68.

[24] Paultre (*op. cit.*, pp. 636-637), without claiming completeness, lists sixty-two general hospitals in France.

[25] All able-bodied persons in the hospitals were required to work. Often there was more pretense than work. On the other hand, the charge was sometimes made that they were exploited (Bloch, *op. cit.*, pp. 91-92).

[26] *Ibid.*, p. 163.

[27] In response to the declaration of 1764 on mendicity.

[28] Paultre, *op. cit.*, pp. 410-411; Bloch, *op. cit.*, pp. 168 n. 3, 193-194, 209.

[29] Paultre (*op. cit.*, pp. 634-635) lists seventy-one *dépôts de mendicité* that were in existence at one time or another. Paultre (pp. 425-514) has the most extensive treatment of the *dépôts de mendicité* that this writer has found.

The depots of mendicity were penal institutions, not only for beggars and vagabonds arrested and condemned by the *marechaussée*, but for prostitutes, libertines, idiots, and pregnant girls who could not be cared for in the general hospitals or hôtels-Dieu.[30] For the beggars, the period of confinement was commonly only a few weeks, but at Soissons it was six months. Clothing, food,[31] and bedding[32] were provided. Medical care was given when needed. All except the sick were forced to work at spinning, weaving, knitting, or polishing glass (at Soissons), and were given some small pay, with which they were able to buy such luxuries as wine or tobacco. Inmates could obtain release from the institution at any time by joining the army or by convincing those in charge that they would find employment. They were sometimes able to obtain employment through relatives or friends, with whom the depot tried to put them in touch.[33] Infants and older children were cared for as they would have been at the general hospitals. Of course conditions varied from depot to depot.

Whereas the work offered in the general hospitals and depots of mendicity was compulsory (penal in case of the arrested), it was voluntary in a third type of institution, the charity workshops, found in great numbers in the latter half of the eighteenth century. Occasionally in the first half of the century one was set up here or there, sometimes by a noble or bishop, but more commonly by a town or district. When an establishment served a district, the money was provided by the intendant or the provincial estates. In 1770 the Abbé Terray, controller-general of finance, became an enthusiast for these workshops, provided funds for their establishment in all the generalities, and urged the intendants to resort to them as temporary panaceas for unemployment. Thenceforward to the end of the Old Regime, indeed to 1794 or 1795, France had a mania for charity workshops. Appropriations, often large, were made for them almost every year by national, provincial, and city governments. A large number of seasonal workmen and of the unemployed availed themselves of the opportunity to work in the charity workshops; the

---

[30] Bloch, *op. cit.*, pp. 169-170, 172 n. 3; [Montlinot,] *Etat actuel de la maison de travail de la généralité de Soissons* (1781), p. 3.

[31] Consisting of bread, soup, vegetables, or meat.

[32] Straw mattresses, placed on the floor.

[33] Bloch, *op. cit.*, pp. 171-176.

general public was pleased with them; and the French government in the last decades of the eighteenth century definitely committed itself to the policy of attempting to solve the unemployment problem by offering temporary work at submarket wages.

The expedient of sending beggars and vagabonds to the colonies was many times suggested during the century.[34] Among those proposing it were John Law, Turgot, Montlinot, and the anonymous author of a pamphlet (1790) dedicated to Benjamin Franklin.[35] One interesting attempt was made in 1717-20, in connection with the John Law Scheme for the development of Louisiana. Appeals for voluntary colonists met with little response. Thereupon the government, from May 23, 1717, resorted to sending vagabonds, beggars, army deserters, contraband saltmakers, pickpockets, thieves, robbers, prostitutes, and youths of both sexes from the Bicêtre and the Salpêtrière. Porters were impressed into the police at Paris and paid 10 livres for every vagrant arrested for colonization. Large numbers of innocent people were arrested in Paris, Orléans,[36] and elsewhere; and the public raged in indignation. The arrested were chained and sent to La Rochelle, accompanied by *archers* of the *marechaussée*, for embarkation to New Orleans (founded 1717).[37]

According to Leclercq, most of the beggars had no knowledge of cultivation of the soil, yet the Abbé Montlinot, director of the depot of mendicity at Soissons (1781 *et seq.*), who had a penchant for statistics and critical observations in his several annual reports

[34] *Ibid.*, pp. 50-51.

[35] *Aperçu hazardé sur l'exportation dans les colonies* (Paris, 1790). The author cites the example of England, which had successfully colonized Botany Bay and St. Helena in this manner (p. 3). He would have colonists sent to Madagascar, Mozambique, Mahé, Senegal, Gorée, Abyssinia, Santo Domingo, and French Guiana (pp. 34-53). While to all he would send beggars and vagabonds, to parts of Africa he would send also criminals. He thinks that many workers from the charity workshops, if taken to the colonies, would become owners of estates after a few years (p. 36).

[36] Dorothy Mackay Quynn, "Recruiting in Old Orleans for New Orleans," *American Historical Review*, XLVI (July, 1941), 832-836.

[37] Dom H. Leclercq, *Histoire de la Règence*, II, chap. xxxvii. Besides the recruiting, Dom Leclercq describes the arrival and vicissitudes of the colonists in Louisiana.

The *Louisiana Historical Quarterly* for October, 1938 (XXI, 965-978), prints an article entitled "Ship Lists of Passengers leaving France for Louisiana, 1718-1724," translated by Albert Laplace Dart, wherein are listed many score vagabonds, tobacco and salt smugglers, army deserters, women and girls, with particular designation after each person's name. Some of the vagabonds came from Lyons, Orléans, and Rennes. Names of some persons exiled from Bayonne are included.

on that depot, remarked that most of the several hundred men and
women brought yearly to his depot were agricultural laborers. This
would imply that over half of the vagrants and beggars of France
had had farming experience. Moreover, the Abbé observed that
every woman from the agricultural regions knew how to spin thread.
Possibly they might have made successful colonists. The chief
objection came from the respectable, voluntary colonists already in
the field. Another difficulty was the heavy expense to the government which the scheme would have entailed; but France was the
wealthiest country of Europe and should have been able to meet it.
In short, it might well have paid France to have attempted vastly
more in the way of colonization with these social misfits; but, aside
from the possible instance of La Désirade,[38] this was evidently her
only experiment in the period 1700-89.[39]

The French of the eighteenth century had a laudable practice
of frequently giving dowries to poor girls, especially if orphaned, to
fit them for marriage. The benefactors were commonly charitable
individuals, general hospitals, and municipalities; sometimes provinces or the government. The birth or death of a member of the
royal family, the coronation of a king, the winning of a battle, stimu-
lated largesses of this type.[40] The dowries were not handsome in
scale or abundant in number, and usually in the later decades of the
century amounted to 300 livres, but hundreds of poor girls in France
were glad to receive them each year. Sometimes, too, on occasions
of public joy or mourning, purses of money, given by municipalities,
provinces, or the royal government, were distributed among the
poor, either through the curés or the general hospitals.[41]

A solution of greater significance was the government policy of
promoting industrial and agricultural progress by introducing new

[38] Fernand Mitton, *La férocité pénale: tortures et supplices en France* (Paris,
1909), p. 257. In 1763 the government designated La Désirade, near Guadeloupe,
"for the internment of young men of bad conduct"; but Mitton does not indicate
whether any were actually sent.

[39] Certain projects of transportation were discussed during the Revolution, but
only some "refractory clergy" (and not vagabonds) were actually sent.

[40] See, for instance, the grant of dowries for several girls by two towns in Brittany, in 1774, on the occasion of Louis XVI's coronation (*Inv.-som . . . Ille-et-
Vilaine*, C 690, 708).

[41] Thus several towns in Brittany distributed alms among their poor on Louis
XV's death in 1774: Lambelle, 300 livres; Vitre, 120; Moncontour, 200; Concar-
neau, 30; Saint-Pol-en-Léon, 200; and Ploërmel, 100 (*ibid.*, C 511, 451, 532, 683,
761).

crops and new industries, better types of animals, and, to some degree, better methods in industry. Measures to improve agriculture have already been discussed. Those designed to extend and improve industry, in their bearing upon pauperism, merit perhaps more attention than can be given here. From the days of Colbert to the Revolution, the government endeavored by direct subsidy, tax exemption, honors and distinctions to promote the economic welfare of the kingdom in establishing new industries or re-establishing old ones.[42] In the fifty years prior to 1789 the French government contributed 5,500,000 livres as aid to manufactures,[43] and it was not unmindful of its value in providing an antidote to indigence.[44] General national prosperity has been in all times the best cure of unemployment.

The government specifically had the needy in mind in its ever-increasing endeavors after 1723 to encourage the silk industry among the rank and file of the realm. It established nurseries of mulberry trees in virtually every generality, sometimes several in a generality.[45] From them it distributed trees among the people, either free or at slight expense. Each year quantities of silkworm eggs were distributed free, at the expense of the generality. The government, moreover, sent printed instructions on sericulture to those interested. It aided in the erection of silk factories.[46] In Burgundy (and doubtless elsewhere) it sent out an instructress to demonstrate to workers how to unravel cocoons and spin the silk;[47] in Touraine a school of demonstration was set up in 1750.[48]

The silk industry in France, though still dominated by guild

[42] For example, in the re-establishment of the silk industry at Tours, in 1730 and 1756, after it had been almost ruined, the government of Louis XV had an important share; and even as late as 1787, when decline again set in, at least 2,600 workers were employed (Giraudet, op. cit., pp. 114-115).

[43] Pugh, op. cit., XI, 301.

[44] "The king's advisers pointed out that the establishment of each new industry would help make France great. . . . Each new glass furnace would increase the demand for labor and create jobs for indigent people who could find no means of earning their living" (Warren C. Scoville, "State Policy and the French Glass Industry, 1640-1789," Quarterly Journal of Economics, LVI, May, 1942, 438, 442).

[45] An excellent account of the government's efforts in this matter in Poitou is given by P. Boissonnade, Essai sur l'organisation du travail en Poitou, depuis le XIe siècle jusqu'à la Révolution, II (Paris, 1900), 457-459, 516-520. Almost all the volumes in série C of the Collection des inventaires-sommaires des archives départementales antérieures à 1789 have material on the establishment of mulberry nurseries and the distribution of trees from them.

[46] Dumas, op. cit., pp. 144-149.

[47] Inv.-som . . . Côte d'Or, C 3220 (f 435).

[48] Dumas, op. cit., pp. 146-147.

features, had acquired marked aspects of the domestic and factory systems. At Lyons, for instance, where on the eve of the Revolution there were 800 master workers and 8,000 journeymen, there were 50,000 nonguild workers.[49] After the 1720's the government made increasing attempts at extending the domestic system by promoting the unwinding of silk, and the spinning of cotton, flax, and hemp, throughout the French countryside, so that families could be engaged during idle periods, particularly in the winter, at making extra money.[50] On occasion spinning-wheels were distributed among the poor.[51] In the second half of the century extensive efforts were made to encourage the growth of the madder-root, to be used as a red dye in manufacture. The intendants distributed the seed or shoots free, sent instruction on the mode of culture, and sometimes sent an agricultural specialist to demonstrate for the people.[52] That this form of government assistance increased greatly as the century advanced is evidence that the government was not oblivious of the problem of unemployment.

Few if any topics of public interest attracted more attention of writers in the second half of the century than pauperism. Scores of treatises on the subject were published;[53] a much larger number, however, went unpublished.[54] Many were called forth by prize contests sponsored by academies or scientific bodies. In a contest in 1777 sponsored by the Academy of Sciences, Belles-Lettres, and Arts of Châlons, more than one hundred competitors, from all parts of France and abroad, participated. The competitors represented a wide variety of professions. At length extracts from some of the papers were published in 1780. Similar contests had been numerous

[49] The manufactured goods were turned over to ninety merchants, who paid the workers for their labor and assumed all care of selling the goods (Monfalcon, *op. cit.*, III, 3).

This picture of the fusion of guild, factory, and domestic system is given also by F. Dumas, who presents a very informative account (*op. cit.*, pp. 133-156) of the silk industry in Touraine. See also Kovalewsky, *op. cit.*, II, 33.

[50] The domestic system for winding off silk in the homes of individuals was adopted to some extent in Touraine, but the quality of the work suffered (Dumas, *op. cit.*, pp. 147-148).

[51] *Inv.-som . . . Côte d'Or*, C 3219 (f 139).

[52] Boissonnade, *op. cit.*, II, 526-527.

[53] A partial list can be found in Camille Granier's *Essai de bibliographie charitable* (Paris, 1891), pp. 317-322.

[54] Some were sent in correspondence to the controller-general of finance and may be found today in the Archives Nationales.

in France in the twenty years before 1777.[55] In at least one, and perhaps others, of these contests government officials had a part. In November, 1776, the intendant of Orléans offered through the agricultural societies a prize on the subject. It was awarded, in April, 1778, to the Abbé Genty, professor of philosophy in the College of Orléans; he was honored by being named an associate of the Society of Agriculture of Orléans; and it was decided to publish his work.[56]

The government made annual contributions to the problem throughout the century. Indirect aid, in the form of subsidies to industry, was doubtless much larger, at least in the first half of the century, than the direct expenditures, but only the latter come within the scope of this treatise. Of the direct grants, some illustrations may be given. During the early years of the century, Louis XIV, until his death (1715), made an annual gift of 80,000 livres in four payments for distribution among the poor of Paris to provide them with the necessities of life. In 1716 the practice was renewed and continued under the Regency.[57] From 1724 to 1734 the government granted subsidies to various cities for the maintenance of beggars and vagabonds in depots of mendicity. The city of Troyes, one of the cities where a depot was situated, received 11,000 to 12,000 livres annually. In 1734 the government ceased its contributions, and the depots went out of existence.[58] In 1775 the royal treasury paid out 1,014,675 livres for combating mendicity in the provinces.[59] In 1789, according to Martin-Doisy, the government appropriated 1,200,000 livres for the purpose.[60]

These figures illustrate the ever-increasing interest of the government of the Old Regime in the problem of the unemployed. It is not altogether clear, however, whether these figures are entirely unrelated to those set forth in previous chapters on such topics as flood,

[55] Bloch, op. cit., pp. 211-212.

[56] Justin, op. cit., pp. 231-232.

[57] Bibl. Nat., Fonds français, 6801, f 229. See also Fosseyeux, Le budget de charité à Paris au XVIIIe siècle, p. 2.

[58] Babeau, La village sous l'ancien régime, p. 324 with n. 5. From 1724 to 1733 the city incarcerated 1,090 beggars.

[59] Bibl. Nat., Fonds français, 6801, ff 115-118. Some generalities received large grants, others small ones, all according to their need as the controller-general of finance and the council of finances envisioned it. Thus the generality of Paris received 479,000 livres, and that of Auch, 5,200; the generality of Orléans, 40,800 livres, that of Bordeaux, 8,800, and that of Caen, 2,000.

[60] Op. cit., II, 431.

famine, and hail relief. Evidently there is reduplication. For example, money appropriated for famine relief is frequently listed among the recorded appropriations for combating mendicity.[61]

Besides making direct grants, the government also authorized certain taxes for municipal and provincial relief. Most cities had charitable bureaux, which in some (if not most) instances were largely subsidized by municipal poor taxes authorized by the government. Thus Paris had a Grand Bureau of the Poor, a private organization with special privileges accorded it by the government, among them the collection of a poor tax, an *octroi* of 5 sous on wines, and an ecclesiastical tax to help fill its chest for charities. This poor tax, first ordered by the parlement of Paris in 1532, for a long time was voluntary, but in the eighteenth century it was obligatory. All citizens of Paris except paupers, monks, nuns, and domestic servants, paid it; and the paupers, to escape it, presented a certificate of poverty signed by the curé of their parish. Varying assessments were placed on individuals according to their trade or professional role: artisans, for instance, 13 sous; physicians and ordinary merchants, 26 sous; lawyers, architects, captains, and wine-merchants, 52 sous.[62] The sum collected was not large, and the work of the Grand Bureau was necessarily very limited. Only a fraction of the poor of Paris were cared for by it, and in the eighteenth century its funds were dispensed almost entirely to the poor of the bourgeois class.[63] In 1709 the government also authorized the doubling of a tax on street maintenance *(boues et lanternes)*, to help care for the poor.[64] In Amiens money received from the *capitation* went toward the support of the poor and was administered by the Hospital St. Charles. Until 1668 the money had been administered by the Bureau of the Poor.[65] In 1776 the government ordered that thenceforth there be an in-

---

[61] In the *pays d'états* the provincial assemblies made the appropriations at their annual, or in some cases biennial, or triennial, meetings. Thus in 1759 the Estates of Brittany allotted aid of 150,000 livres, and in 1760 and 1761 grants each of 200,000 livres, by way of exemptions to suffering taxpayers, the appropriations being designated also as poor relief *(Inv.-som . . . Ille-et-Vilaine, C 5057).*

[62] Cahen, *op. cit.*, pp. 63, 67. Those who refused to pay the tax were pursued by justice officials.

[63] *Ibid.*, p. 27.

[64] Bonnefroy, *Mémoire sur la mendicité* (Paris, 1791), p. 14.

[65] In 1784 a certain usher of Amiens named Bernard refused to pay this tax, and legal proceedings ensued (Hospital administrators to De la Millière, March 29, 1784, Arch. Nat., F15, 396).

crease of three *deniers* for every livre from the *taille* and other direct taxes for combating mendicity. It was to be assessed throughout all French provinces, *pays d'états* as well as *pays d'élections*. It was estimated that this new tax would bring 862,160 livres in 1776, and 1,386,493 livres in 1777.[66]

The poor benefited from the royal lotteries. By a lottery planned for January, 1741, 1,000,000 livres were to be raised for the care of the needy in Paris.[67] Another was held in 1789.[68] Presumably the first was a special lottery for a particular purpose, while the second was that run annually through most of the century for the benefit of the hospitals. From time to time special lotteries were permitted, doubtless some of them during times of great distress to relieve the needy.

After 1789

The Revolution did not reduce the number of beggars. Despite various measures of relief, Paris in December, 1791, according to Bailly, its mayor, was "inundated" with them;[69] in March, 1792, the city had 100,000 indigents; in November, 1793, 120,000; in 1794, 70,000.[70] Conditions in Paris were indicative of conditions elsewhere. Bo, reporting to the Convention in March, 1793, for the committee of public aid, declared that France was still afflicted with a swarm of beggars;[71] Delaporte, reporting for the same committee to the Council of the Five Hundred on 13 messidor an IV (July 1, 1796), estimated that there were over 500,000 beggars in France;[72] and in 1800 it was reported to the Consuls that there were 300,000 beggars.[73]

Even under Napoleon beggary and its allied evils of brigandage, murder, and plunder flourished to a frightful extent. Bands of brigands wandered over the countryside, as they had in days preceding the Revolution, creating terror. Sometimes they tortured those whom they thought rich by burning their feet. Beggars cooperated with these outlaws by furnishing them with information

---

[66] Bibl. Nat., Fonds français, 6801, ff 119, 121.
[67] Barbier, *op. cit.*, III, 256-258.
[68] Tuetey, *Répertoire général*, III, Introduction, ii.
[69] *Ibid.*, V, No. 3404.
[70] *Arch. parl.*, XXXIX, 521-522; Ferdinand-Dreyfus, *L'assistance*, pp. 136, 146.
[71] *Arch. parl.*, LX, 324-325.
[72] Lecoq, *op. cit.*, p. 129.
[73] Ferdinand-Dreyfus, *op. cit.*, p. 103 with n.

on the movements and character of travelers. Napoleon sent an army against them and within a period of six months shot several hundred. But still in early 1801, if certain writers are to be believed, a traveler was scarcely able to go from Paris to Rouen, or from Paris to Orléans, without danger of being slain.[74] The mighty Napoleon might conquer Europe, but he could not suppress begging in France.[75] Like "the old man of the sea," this scourge clung to the neck of the French nation.

Every available means was employed to get rid of it—soft words, threats, imprisonment, scourging, free food, a monetary dole, employment (with pay) in charity workshops. All in vain. Begging remained one of the most baffling problems Revolutionary France had to face. On every hand it was denounced; no one held a brief for it; but evidently there were much private compassion and charity, or it would not have persisted.

This is not to say that there were no grounds for begging in Revolutionary France. Far from it! Distress was bitter. Indeed, it is doubtful if any similar period in the eighteenth century saw more. Economic depression, revolution, war had brought a three-fold upheaval of society, which went terribly for the lower classes. The beggars were but a small portion of the needy. Papion *le jeune* told the National Assembly on January 31, 1791, that the greater portion of the miserable in France suffered in silence. Not over one in five of them became a beggar. He estimated at four millions the French destitute.[76] The government's steps to meet the situation, moreover, fell short of the need. The money appropriated was too small in amount, and was often distributed in irregular fashion.

The Revolutionists spent much time denouncing the Old Regime for its handling of the problem and making flowery promises to end all misery, but in actual fact they followed rather generally the avenues set up under the Old Regime. There were denunciatory laws, carrying arrest, imprisonment, and for repeated offenders scourging.[77] As under the Old Regime, foreign beggars were to be

---

[74] Martin-Doisy, *op. cit.*, IV, 1450-1451; Ferdinand-Dreyfus, *op. cit.*, p. 103.

[75] Ferdinand-Dreyfus, *Un philanthrope d'autrefois*, p. 547.

[76] *Arch. parl.*, XXII, 629-630. The total population at that time has been variously estimated at twenty-five or twenty-six millions.

[77] Branding and sending to the galleys, however, disappeared (1791) (*La grande encyclopédie*, XVIII, 371; XXIII, 286).

expelled, and provincial beggars in Paris and other large cities were to be sent home. A law of May 30, 1790, provided that all of these beggars and vagabonds be sent to the place of their birth with the payment of 3 sous per league for every ten leagues.[78] They had to follow a charted map provided by the police, else they were liable to arrest and could not collect their travel allowance. Foreigners (chiefly Italians) were extended the allowance of 3 sous per league to the nearest city in their country from the French frontier.[79] Scores, possibly hundreds, of Italians and thousands of French provincials were expelled from Paris by this law. Some of the French vagabonds were accused of returning to Paris after they had collected the travel allowance, and were sent home a second or a third time. The makers of the law had not foreseen this possibility. The object of the law was twofold: (1) to protect Paris against further riots, like that of Bastille Day, and (2) to make every community, as much as possible, care for its own unemployed. The Revolutionary governments, like that of the Old Regime, regarded the problem of relief as largely a local matter.

From the early days of the Revolution relief was declared to be a national obligation, a debt that the state owed to its citizens.[80] In words the Revolutionists probably went further than the Old Regime, but in deeds they merely followed policy that had long been established under the Old Regime. They moved gradually in seizing all sources of charity funds for the state (taking this action in steps from 1789 to 1793), and from first to last they placed the expenditure of state funds in the hands of provincial and local officials, even as had been the case in the days of the intendants and subdelegates.

Depots of mendicity were continued. In his report of January 9, Roland, minister of the interior, informed the Convention that there were then thirty-four depots in France. Not only were arrested beggars and vagrants placed in them, but also women charged with prostitution and persons afflicted with venereal disease, and persons without funds who might ask for this means of support. Medical

[78] Watteville, *op. cit.*, p. 1.

[79] The principle of giving 3 sous per league to foreign beggars was renewed in the law of 24 vendémiaire an II (October 15, 1793) for the suppression of mendicancy (*ibid.*, p. 25).

[80] Ferdinand-Dreyfus, *L'assistance*, p. 85.

attention was given to all, and an attempt was made to cure the venereal cases. Each depot had a staff of officials, paid by the state: a porter, a physician, a surgeon, an apothecary (suppressed in 1791), and others. The expense of the depots in 1792 was 1,315,500 livres.[81] Other houses of repression for vagrants were established, one in the chief city of each department, by the law of October 15, 1793,[82] but little came of them.

Charity workshops, both for men and for women, were also continued. At first great enthusiasm was expressed for them and they were tried on a large scale, but criticism quickly developed. After 1791 they were continued only in desultory fashion here and there, and there was never the same enthusiasm for them that had existed in the period from 1770 to 1791. The idea behind the workshops was to furnish work to the needy unemployed at wages slightly below those normally paid in the labor market. Work in them was voluntary. Therein lay the chief difference between them and the depots of mendicity.

The government also aided the unemployed by sponsoring public works projects, such as road construction, the erection of buildings, and demolition of others. Thus the Bastille was removed, stone by stone, and the magnificent new Church of Ste Geneviève (now the Panthéon), planned by the great Soufflot, was completed. Sometimes charity workshop workers were employed on these projects. Public works as an indirect aid to the working class were not new, but had been employed before 1789, chiefly in connection with road and canal construction.

From time to time, as local expedients, food and other items were accorded the needy. Thus on May 9, 1793, the Convention apportioned to the little city of Puy the sum of 6,730 livres for the provision of free soup to its poor.[83] On September 23, 1793, the city of Toulouse decided to subsidize the sale of bread to its poor at a submarket price, and to place printed bread cards in the hands of all those who were qualified to receive bread at this figure.[84] In early vendémiaire an III (September, 1794) the committee of be-

[81] *Arch. parl.*, LVI, 644-645; *Inv.-som* . . . *Isère*, L 54.
[82] Watteville, *op. cit.*, pp. 25-26.
[83] *Arch. parl.*, LXIV, 353.
[84] A forced loan from the rich, to the extent of 1,500,000 livres, was to finance the project (Adher, *op. cit.*, pp. 448-450, 459).

neficence in one of the forty-eight sections of Paris was distributing bread and meat (including fresh pork) to the needy on the first day of each *décade* (ten-day period).[85] Bread and meat were also given in another section of Paris in late messidor an VIII (July, 1800).[86] Free medicine, too, on a very limited scale, was given in this last instance. The committee of beneficence in charge requested funds of the minister of the interior with which they could buy more. An invalid soldier, in the district of Orange, was given two suits by the directory of that department on July 20, 1791.[87] These were but a few instances of the "aid in kind" that was administered.

By an order of the committee of public safety, 5 prairial an II (May 24, 1794), infirm persons among the needy in all the large communes of France were to receive a dole. This dole was a new feature, not found under the Old Regime. Invalid indigents were to receive 15 sous a day if single, 25 if married, and 5 additional for every child under the age of twelve. Indigents partially invalid, able to do some work, were eligible for only two thirds of this aid.[88] The law, however, had not been placed in execution in the department of Seine-and-Marne in late February, 1795, but the departmental directory, in lieu of it, accorded one old man temporary relief of 150 livres.[89] The steady decline in the value of French currency led the committee of public aid to order, on 24 floréal an III (May 13, 1795), an increase in the dole, since the sums hitherto given were insufficient to maintain the invalids and their families. The dole was therefore raised to 20 sous (one livre) for single persons, 30 for those with wife; the allowance of 5 sous for each child under twelve remained the same. The dole for partially infirm indigents was raised from 10 to 15 sous. These measures, however, did not prevent mendicancy in Paris, for complaints of much begging (and of insolence from beggars) still came to the government committees of public aid and public safety.[90]

After October, 1792, large numbers of indigent parents, wives, and families of soldiers and sailors (*défenseurs de la patrie*) were

[85] Tuetey, *L'assistance publique*, IV, 462.

[86] "Le Bureau de Bienfaisance de la Division des Lombards au Ministre de l'Intérieur" (Arch. Nat., F15, 103).

[87] *Inv.-som . . . Bouches-du-Rhône*, L 14, 6.

[88] Tuetey, *L'assistance publique*, IV, 533-534.

[89] *Inv.-som . . . Seine-et-Marne*, L 64, f 141.

[90] Tuetey, *op. cit.*, IV, 537-540.

aided.[91] A law of 22 floréal an II (May 11, 1794) provided aid for indigent farmers and artisans who were either past the age of sixty or unable to work, and for mothers and widows who had the problem of rearing a certain number of children below the age of ten.[92] For the farmers and artisans this aid was a form of old-age pension. The farmers were to receive 160 livres a year, payable in advance in two sums, six months apart. The artisans, oddly enough, were allowed only 120 livres a year, as though it were cheaper to live in the city than in the country. Mothers and widows were to receive only 60 livres a year, as though three or four could live on less than one; at the end of the year they were each to be provided a bonus of 20 livres if the government inspector found that the children were still living! Barère was the author of this bizarre law, which had many ridiculous features.[93] It called for the appropriation of 12,244,000 livres, of which 7,400,000 livres were to provide for invalid farmers and artisans, and 3,600,000 livres for the widows and mothers intrusted with the care of families.[94] In early May, 1795, 54 farmers of the district of Toulouse were receiving pensions of 160 livres each.[95]

The practice of giving dowries to a limited number of poor girls was continued. The Popular Society of Toulouse, a private charitable organization, had plans in March, 1794, for endowing fifteen girls with 1,000 livres each. A citizen named Castelpert contributed 3,000 livres to this endowment fund, and another named Bec 50 livres. In the district of Toulouse "frequent" gifts were made for the purpose.[96]

Other types of aid were occasionally given the needy. Thus the Popular Society of Toulouse made a gift of 48 livres in 1790 to Sernia, a carpenter, native of Clermont in Auvergne, wounded in Paris at the taking of the Bastille, in order that he might go to the waters of Barèges for treatment.[97]

A small degree of private aid continued through the period of

[91] Adher, op. cit., pp. 448, 473-474, 481.
[92] Three for mothers, and two for widows. In each instance, one child must be a babe in arms, being nursed with milk (Watteville, op. cit., pp. 29-30).
[93] Ferdinand-Dreyfus has criticized it severely in his L'assistance, p. 76.
[94] Ibid., p. 74.
[95] Adher, op. cit., p. 476. Eight of them were over eighty in age, the rest younger. Five were below fifty, and one was only twenty-five.
[96] Ibid., pp. 458-459. [97] Ibid., p. 445.

the Revolution. In July, 1794, for example, several private organizations, such as the *marmite* (soup kitchen) groups, the Philanthropic Society, and the Maternal Society, were doing relief work in Paris. In fact, private contributions toward charities were being renewed in the parishes of that city.[98] The Church as a charitable agency was rendered impotent through the seizure of its property early in the Revolution and through its position as a hated and persecuted institution. Municipalities, however, continued through parts of the Revolution to have some power to tax themselves and raise money in other ways for their relief needs. Thus in 1792 or 1793 Paris was able to hold a public lottery to provide funds of this nature.[99] In December, 1793, the tax for the benefit of the poor on entertainments was still collected in Toulouse.[100] In October, 1800, the city council of Marseilles appropriated 10,000 francs to its bureau of beneficence for distribution to the needy.[101] Had not municipalities shifted for themselves, at least to some degree, misery no doubt would have been even greater than it was.

Most of the money for charities came from the national government. Numerous were the appropriations, some large, others small. Some concerned the whole nation, others a single municipality or department. A decree of June 13, 1790, provided 30,000 livres to be spent in each of the eighty-three departments in establishing charity workshops; another for the same purpose, December 19, 1790, carried an appropriation of 15,000,000 livres. A decree of January 24, 1792, appropriated 2,350,000 livres for indigents.[102] On 2 prairial an II (May 21, 1794) an appropriation of 10,000,000 livres was made for relief at home (*secours à domicile*).[103] On 16 ventôse an II (March 6, 1794) the Convention made a grant of 500,000 livres to disabled indigents.[104] On June 5, 1793, an appropriation of 1,000,000 livres was made to provide for the depots of mendicity during 1794.[105] According to Roland's report of Jan-

---

[98] Tuetey, *op. cit.*, IV, 456-457.

[99] *Loterie patriotique, avances et vente publique* [Paris, 1792 or 1793] (Archives de l'Assistance Publique, D¹ 12, D).

[100] Adher, *op. cit.*, p. 456. A national tax on entertainments (theaters, balls, fireworks displays, concerts, horse races, and exhibitions) of 2 sous per livre on the price of tickets was ordered by a law of 7 frimaire an V (Nov. 27, 1796) (Watteville, *op. cit.*, p. 42).

[101] Fabre, *op. cit.*, II, 379.

[102] Tuetey, *op. cit.*, IV, 459, 483.

[105] *Arch. parl.*, LXVI, 67.

[102] Adher, *op. cit.*, p. 447 n. 1.

[104] *Ibid.*, IV, 508.

uary 9, 1793, to the Convention, a fund of 300,000 livres had been established for the purpose of caring for indigents and for assisting localities suffering from intemperate seasons.[106]

From September 1, 1793, to August 14, 1796, Paris alone spent 4,441,703 livres, furnished by the government, in caring for its needy. But, according to Ferdinand-Dreyfus, this seemingly large figure, in *assignats*, had an actual coin value of only 616,760 livres.[107] Sometimes in the large appropriations a definite sum was earmarked for the city of Paris; and the purposes for which the money was to be spent were usually designated within narrow limits. Sometimes the conditions were stated so specifically as to be a handicap, either slowing up the distribution of the money[108] or rendering the money allotted insufficient for the needs. On other occasions the terms were so vague that much correspondence between local and national authorities concerning the interpretation of clauses was necessary before the money was transmitted to those needing it.[109]

Among the bizarre features of the Revolution was the adoption on 24 brumaire an II (November 14, 1793) of a tax on the rich to supply the needs of the poor. The rich citizens in every canton were to be taxed to clothe, lodge, and feed the indigents within its bounds so that misery might disappear. The collection and disbursement of the funds were to be placed in the hands of each municipality, which was to be responsible in turn to the government. Any cities refusing or neglecting to make the collection were to be declared suspect of disloyalty. Only one type of bread, called "Bread of Equality," was henceforth to be made. In each municipality a census was made of citizens according to their wealth. The tax was graduated, falling chiefly on married citizens with a fortune above 100,000 livres and on single persons with a fortune above 50,000 livres. In the department of the Loire the method provided that the collector call at the home of the citizen with a squad of soldiers, take him to prison, and there extract the money from him in cash

[106] *Ibid.*, LVI, 642.   [107] *L'assistance*, p. 149.

[108] The Revolutionists had a mania for statistics, and repeatedly demanded of municipalities and departments a census of this and that need. These censuses commonly followed the passing of an appropriation measure by the government and were requisite to the receipt of funds. Weeks and months frequently elapsed before the funds reached their destination.

[109] The correspondence in Tuetey's four volumes of *L'assistance publique* makes this abundantly clear.

or pledge. But the collection went poorly. The tax to be collected from some sixty-nine persons in the department having a total wealth of 24,220,000 livres was 4,128,700 livres. After many delays, the collector finally extracted a total of only 459,150 livres. Additional pledges of approximately 480,000 livres were made but never collected. The collector thus managed to get slightly more than one tenth of what was expected. Of the 459,150 livres collected, very little went to aid the needy. Save for 70,000 livres given to this end, the rest went for other purposes, chiefly war industries.[110] The tax was collected only during the severe years 1793-94.

During the Revolution the idea of colonizing with beggars was revived. The committee of mendicity, in 1790 or 1791, recommended that beggars arrested for the third time be transported to a colony, preferably Corsica.[111] In 1793 the committee of public aid (the successor of the committee of mendicity) proposed to the Convention the sending of beggars to French Guiana.[112] At length in its laws of 24 vendémiaire and 11 brumaire an II (October 15 and November 1, 1793) the Convention adopted these suggestions, but fixed upon Madagascar rather than Corsica or Guiana as the place of colonization. Only beggars arrested and convicted for the third offense were to be transported, and then merely for eight years. For signal service to the colony the period might be shortened; for recalcitrancy it might be prolonged. The banished were to be put to work for the good of the colony. One sixth of the product of each individual's work was to belong to him, half of it to be paid at the end of each week, the rest at the end of his period of banishment. By paying half of this sum he could obtain land in the colony; if he married and children were born, monetary reductions were allowed.[113] But all this was paper legislation. According to Martin-Doisy, no beggars were sent to Madagascar.[114] On 2 pluviôse an IV (January 22, 1796) a citizen who called himself "a true republican" wrote from Namur to Merlin, French minister of the police, urging again the colonization of French lands in the New World

[110] Brossard and Freminville, *op. cit.*, II, 269-278. On the collection of the tax elsewhere, see Ferdinand-Dreyfus, *op. cit.*, p. 96. No indication of success is given.
[111] Martin-Doisy, *op. cit.*, IV, 1399-1400.
[112] Ferdinand-Dreyfus, *L'assistance*, p. 68.
[113] The text of this legislation, setting forth other details of interest, is given by Watteville, *op. cit.*, pp. 26-28.
[114] *Op. cit.*, IV, 1403-1404.

with beggars and vagabonds.[115] Merlin forwarded the letter to the minister of the interior, but nothing came of it.

As might be expected, abuses, delays, and weaknesses in the administration of relief were frequent during this period. The relief money was often irregularly paid. At no time were all cases of need adequately cared for, or was begging exterminated. Merlin, a member of the committee of public aid, in his letter to the Convention in June, 1794, charged that abuses had crept into the disbursement of relief in the city of Paris, and that some who were not indigent were receiving the dole.[116] Later, on 20 vendémiaire an V (September 11, 1796), the indignant minister of the interior wrote to the committees of beneficence of the sections of Paris pointing out that some of the members of these committees were themselves using the bread and meat cards placed in their hands for distribution to indigents.[117] Of course it was very advantageous, if not indeed essential, in obtaining aid for the applicant to declare himself a good republican, even as under the Old Regime it had been useful to profess to be a good member of the church.[118]

Sometimes funds appropriated for charity remained unspent for months, indeed for a year or two. For example, on September 26, 1792, 5,675,000 livres remained from funds appropriated in certain enactments of 1791 and of earlier months in 1792.[119] This reluctance to spend, a legacy of the Old Regime, was, however, not altogether a virtue, since throughout France this was a period of terrible need. In conclusion, it may be said that Revolutionary France indulged in interesting experiments, but that most of the policies were based upon practices of the Old Regime. The thorny problems of unemployment and mendicancy were handled with little if any more success than before 1789. Noble aspirations and legislation did not wipe out or even decrease misery.

[115] Arch. Nat., F15, 102.

[116] Tuetey, op. cit., IV, 512.

[117] Arch. Nat., F15, 103.

[118] When testimonials from curés were required, and when often the curés disbursed the aid.

[119] From the appropriation of June 19, 1791, there remained 435,000 livres; from that of October 9, 1791, 3,200,000 livres; from that of July 12, 1792, 1,980,-000 livres; and that of January 6, 1792 (toward the construction of the Burgundian canal), 60,000 livres ("Fonds de secours. 26, 7bre, 1792. Bordereau," Arch. Nat., F15, 102).

CHAPTER XIII

CHARITY WORKSHOPS

Outdoor Workshops

DURING periods of acute unemployment the French, as we have seen, maintained charity workshops, in which the needy, if they were able to work, might find temporary employment at light tasks with wages somewhat below those paid in the open market. There were two types of these institutions: (1) the *ateliers de charité* proper, or outdoor workshops, devoted to such projects as repairing roads, cleaning streets, removing city walls, and rebuilding sea dikes; and (2) the *ateliers de filature*, or indoor workshops, in which only women, girls, old men, and children were employed at cleaning and spinning hemp, cotton, or linen, or at sewing, knitting, or lace-making. The *ateliers de filature* (translated literally "spinning work-shops") resembled the modern "sewing-rooms." The *ateliers de charité*, on the other hand, were roughly similar to the Works Progress Administration projects of the Franklin D. Roosevelt administration.[1]

Both institutions long antedated the 1700's. As Martin-Doisy writes: "At all times some *ateliers de charité* have existed, under various forms; at all times also they have elicited protests from the side of the ordinary workers."[2] Edouard Cormouls-Houlès also points out that these institutions were established by the ancient Egyptians and Greeks.[3] In the 300's A.D. they were employed in connection with certain Christian hospitals at Caesarea in Palestine and at Constantinople, founded by St. Basil and St. John Chrysostom, respectively.[4] Occasionally in sixteenth-century France orders by parlement or royal declarations and decrees set up charity workshops for

---

[1] The French phrase, meaning "charity workshops," was a misnomer, for the workmen were not placed in buildings or given training, as was commonly done in noncharitable *ateliers*. That French historians, however, have continued to use these eighteenth-century terms is a sufficient reason for continuing to do so here. Accordingly, *ateliers de charité* will be referred to as "charity workshops" or "outdoor workshops," and *ateliers de filature* as "spinning or sewing workshops."

[2] *Op. cit.*, I, 1257.

[3] *L'assistance par le travail* (Paris, 1910), pp. 152, 154.

[4] Martin-Doisy, *op. cit.*, IV, 775, 777.

beggars, vagabonds, and the unemployed in Paris: namely, in 1516, 1524, 1545, 1547, 1551, 1582, 1586.[5] Other cities, too, such as Lyons (1523) and Reims (1573-74), experimented with them.[6] Several times in the seventeenth century, more especially in the "hard times" of the 1690's, they were employed at Paris.[7] In 1698-99 others were operating at Mantes, near Paris, and in the intendancies of Orléans, Alençon, and Bourges, with a total expense of 158,545 livres.[8]

Up to 1770 they slowly but steadily continued to increase throughout France. The "Great Winter" of 1709 occasioned their establishment in Paris and certain other French cities. In 1713, amid the misery that marked the close of the War of the Spanish Succession, a few were set up at Montauban, and a request was made by the intendant of Limoges for permission to establish them in his generality.[9] During the severe famine of 1739 the intendant of Poitiers set up workshops which employed workers on the roads at 10 sous a day and beggars and vagabonds at reconstructing quays at 3 sous a day with lodging and food.[10] For a while in 1739 the archbishop of Tours maintained his own charity workshop for nine hundred persons, reportedly out of spite toward the government, which in the preceding year had refused him a pension.[11] Workshops were established in the generality of Riom in 1741.[12] Tourny installed a number in Guyenne during the famines of 1747-48 and 1752, working not only men but also women and children above the age of twelve.[13] The famine of 1752 introduced others in the gen-

[5] *Ibid.*, I, 1240-1244; Lecoq, *op. cit.*, pp. 68 ff. Lecoq (pp. 68-69) disclaims the institutions among the ancients and medievalists as "charity workshops," and declares that the first charity workshop was set up by the *arrêt du parlement* of 1516. Yet somewhat inconsistently he points out (p. 70) that the work provided by the act of 1516 was by way of penalty and not of charitable assistance, and that it was not until later in the century that voluntary work was offered. Martin-Doisy and Cormouls-Houlès (*op. cit.*, pp. 171-173) indicate that voluntary work was offered in all the charity workshops after 1524, but that for beggars and vagabonds work was often compulsory.

[6] Cormouls-Houlès, *op. cit.*, p. 170; Bloch, *op. cit.*, p. 44 n. 1.

[7] Boislisle, *op. cit.*, *Revue des questions historiques*, N.S., XXIX, 498-499; Martin-Doisy, *op. cit.*, I, 1244-1251. The latter mentions also several *ateliers de filature* created in the 1600's.

[8] Boislisle, *op. cit.*, XXIX, 498-499; Boislisle and Brotonne, *Correspondance des contrôleurs généraux*, II, Nos. 39 and 55.

[9] Boislisle and Brotonne, *op. cit.*, III, Nos. 1441 and 1456.

[10] Boissonnade, *op. cit.*, II, 464.   [11] Barbier, *Journal*, III, 181.

[12] Coiffier, *op. cit.*, p. 250.   [13] Bourgoüin, *op. cit.*, XII, 101.

erality of Rouen, in Normandy.[14] During the cold winters of 1767-68 and 1768-69 some were created in Paris and Rouen, to assist unemployed workmen on projects useful to these cities. Among the several projects planned at Paris were the leveling of "the mountain of Etoile" and the completion of the bridge at Neuilly.[15] Government interest in the workshops was revealed when the controller-general allotted to those in Paris 50,000 livres during the winter of 1767-68, and promised tentatively in October, 1768, to allot 100,000 (at the rate of 20,000 a month for five months) during the winter of 1768-69.

Government interest in the workshops as an auxiliary to the general hospitals in providing aid to the "deserving poor" thus slowly but steadily increased. In 1770, with the Abbé Terray as controller-general of finance, the earlier policy was revolutionized. Instead of waiting for requests from intendants and then making appropriations for local projects, the government assumed the initiative, placed a sum regarded as sufficient at the disposal of every intendant,[16] and urged him to create outdoor workshops in which all the needy wishing work, men, women, and children, might find it. It will be recalled that the year 1770 was one of the most severe famine years for France in the eighteenth century, and that this famine continued, in parts of the country, to 1775. Throughout the period the government, first under Terray and later under Turgot, maintained this policy of emphasis upon the *ateliers de charité*.[17] Even after 1775 the government continued its interest in the work-

[14] *Inv.-som* . . . *Seine-Inférieure*, C 838, 2261.

[15] Bibl. Nat., Fonds français, 6801, f 133; *Inv.-som* . . . *Seine-Inférieure*, C 2263. This is by no means a complete list of the outdoor charity workshops in France prior to 1770. Careful research in the archives or the *Inventaires-sommaires* would probably swell the list to surprising proportions.

[16] At least those intendants in charge of the *pays d'élections*. The *pays d'états* were supposed to provide for their own charities. Often they, too, obtained government aid.

[17] Turgot was intendant of Limoges in 1770, and from that year he took great interest in the workshops. His published writings have provided students with a very interesting, and in fact the only elaborate, description of any charity workshops prior to the Revolution. For this reason there has been a tendency on the part of most historians to exaggerate Turgot's role in the history of the workshops, indeed in the whole history of state charities. Turgot was a great humanitarian, but it is unfair to the other intendants and controllers-general, most of whom also were humanitarian, to exaggerate his significance. Turgot's chief contribution to the workshop movement appears to have been his carefully studied ideas of workshop management and direction.

shops, and to the end of the Old Regime made generous grants year by year to all *pays d'élections* (and sometimes even to the *pays d'états*) in which there was need. In years of widespread disaster (such as 1783-84 and 1788-90) vast sums were appropriated. Thus in early 1784, following the severe winter and February-March floods, the government specifically allotted 1,000,000 livres for workshops, in addition to 3,000,000 livres for public works, such as the reconstruction of bridges, mills, and houses; in 1789 it made an appropriation of 1,500,000 livres.[18]

It would be fruitless to indicate the dates or the locations of *ateliers de charité* after 1770: they were far too numerous. No year after 1770 was without them in various parts of France. In certain regions, like Normandy and the election of Amiens, they continued almost without interruption.[19] Those in Paris, always the spoiled child, probably got larger funds than those of any other generality. It is doubtful if there was any region in France that did not establish outdoor workshops at this time. But "in Brittany these *ateliers de charité* did not really function,"[20] even though Necker promised her 50,000 livres on December 29, 1777. According to Sée, the workshops were never set up, since *cahiers* from Brittany on the eve of the Revolution had asked that they be introduced into the province. Brittany, it is true, was a *pays d'état*, with her own assembly, or legislature, with jealously guarded liberties in taxation and expenditure, and was supposed to provide her own charity funds. Nevertheless, Brittany and the other *pays d'états* did occasionally receive aid from the royal government, not only in remission of taxes (because of misfortunes experienced), but also in direct grants of aid.[21]

As for Brittany, the royal government in 1770, when the intendant D'Agai applied for remission of 28,000 livres to be used for the establishment of charity workshops to repair with rocks the roads between Nantes and Bourgneuf and between Machecoul and Port St. Méme, refused the grant on the ground that *pays d'états* must build and maintain their own roads. Moreover, it appears to have demanded that Brittany employ 28,000 livres from her own

---

[18] See above, p. 78; Martin-Doisy, *op. cit.*, I, 1266.
[19] Bloch, *op. cit.*, p. 207.
[20] Sée, *Remarques sur la misère*, pp. 121-122.
[21] Thus Languedoc in 1783 was allowed remission in taxes of 112,570 livres, and in 1784 of 206,285 livres, for the maintenance of *ateliers de charité* (*Hist. gén. de Languedoc*, XIII, 121, 123).

appropriations to this end before granting remission of 100,000 livres for which she asked.[22] Accordingly, the proposed charity workshops were probably put into operation in Brittany. In 1775 a series of charity workshops were set up by the bishop of Rennes in Rennes and other cities of his diocese, where thousands were unemployed. Then De la Bove, the intendant, asked the government to give 3,000 livres to the bishop's project; and the government, after some delay, decided to do so.[23] In August of the same year, De la Bove mentioned in his letter to Turgot that the Estates of Brittany had just voted a grant of 100,000 livres for charity workshops.[24] In 1785 at an *atelier de charité* at Rennes the workers were put to demolishing old ramparts of the city. Again, on the eve of the Revolution, Rennes borrowed money for workshops of charity.[25]

Perhaps intendants in other generalities were more alert than was De la Bove. Thus in the neighborhood of Troyes fourteen charity workshops were operating in 1781, and twenty-nine at the outbreak of the Revolution.[26] Berthier, intendant of Paris, hoped in December, 1788, soon to have 150 charity workshops, composed of fifteen to twenty men each, in the neighborhood of the capital grinding and transporting flour for the city's provisioning.[27] According to the *Inventaires-sommaires*, several hundred outdoor charity workshops were operating in France on the eve of the Revolution. Even so they were far from being numerous enough to provide work for all who needed and wished it. In fact, they had never been able to do so.

[22] Letter from Albert, intendant of commerce, to Mesnard de Conichard, Feb. 5, 1770, and other papers (Arch. Nat., H 565).

[23] An undated memorandum of the controller-general's office (Arch. Nat., H 565).

[24] De la Bove was afraid that the province would consider the sum sufficient for relief for several years.

Again, as in 1770, the fact of this appropriation does not establish that the workshops were actually set up.

[25] *Inv.-som . . . Ille-et-Vilaine*, C 337. Sée himself refers to a grant of 60,000 livres from the government in 1786 for an *atelier de charité*, to improve the navigation of the Vilaine (*Les classes rurales en Bretagne*, p. 481 n. 6).

It is doubtful, therefore, that Professor Sée's conclusion is accurate, but it appears likely that the number of workshops in Brittany was not large, that in fact it was near the bottom of the list of thirty-three generalities in this respect, not because Brittany was prosperous and did not need the workshops, but because, as Professor Sée makes clear, her needy population was too enormous.

[26] Emile Chaudron, *L'assistance publique à Troyes à la fin de l'ancien siècle et pendant la Révolution, 1770-1800* (Paris, 1923), pp. 41-43.

[27] Berthier to Joly, Dec. 16, 1788 (Bibl. Nat., Fonds français, 6793, f 29).

The enthusiasm for workshops continued during the earlier years of the Revolution; indeed, from 1789 through 1791 interest in them grew, and larger appropriations were made. In 1789 the government appropriated 1,500,000 livres;[28] in June, 1790, 2,490,000 livres;[29] in December, 1790, 15,000,000 livres;[30] and in January, 1792, 2,500,000 livres.[31] At first most of the departments rushed to get the money, but others were indifferent, and at the time of Roland's report to the Convention, January 9, 1793, 5,218,000 livres of these funds remained in the treasury.[32] Nevertheless, the greater portion of the money was spent. A total of 12,501,473 livres was spent on charitable workshops, outdoors and indoors, in the years 1789-91.[33] Hundreds, possibly thousands, of outdoor charity workshops were in operation during this period, with a variety of tasks. It was the heyday of the charity workshop.

The most famous, or notorious, workshops of this period were those of Paris.[34] They were begun in a small way on December 2,

[28] Martin-Doisy, op. cit., I, 1266.

[29] The law of June 13, 1790, placed 30,000 livres at the disposal of each of the eighty-three departments.

[30] The enactment of December 16, 1790, provided 15,000,000 livres to meet the unemployment problem by setting up public works of various sorts. The sum of 6,640,000 livres was to be divided immediately among the eighty-three departments, on the basis of 80,000 livres each; and the remaining 8,360,000 livres were to be distributed later, as need arose. Enactments of June 19 and October 9, 1791, regulated the distribution of this residue (Arch. parl., XXI, 516-517; XXXIX, 521; LVI, 641).

[31] Law of Jan. 17, 1792. A supplementary law of July 12, 1792, further regulated its expenditure (Arch. parl., XXXIX, 521-522; LVI, 641).

[32] Arch. parl., LVI, 641. Surprisingly enough, a new appropriation of 6,000,000 for public works was made February 6, 1793, inspired by the desire to provide work for the poor through charity workshops (ibid., LVIII, 278-279).

[33] Tuetey, Assistance publique, II, 215. The chart indicates that a trivial portion of this expenditure might have antedated 1789.

[34] With the exception of the workshops of Turgot in Limousin in the early 1770's, they are the only ones of the eighteenth century that have been describd at any length in print. The published sources are many: Tuetey, L'assistance publique, II, IV (the chief source); Tuetey, Répertoire général, I-II; Tuetey, L'administration des ateliers de charité: Rapport de J. B. Edme Plaisant (Paris, 1906); J. de Smith [Schmidt], Mémoire sur les ateliers de charité établis à Paris et aux environs (Paris, 1791); Bailly, Mémoires; Arch. parl.; Inventaire-sommaire des archives de la Seine. Partie municipale. Période révolutionnaire (1789-an VIII) (Paris, 1892); Maurice Tourneux, Bibliographie de l'histoire de Paris pendant la Révolution française (5 vols., Paris, 1890-1913); and various periodicals of the times, such as the Révolutions de Paris, the Journal de Paris, and La Chronique de Paris. The most elaborate modern account is a dissertation by Mme Yvonne Forado-Cunéo, entitled "Les ateliers de charité de Paris pendant la Révolution française, 1789-1791," published in La Révolution française, LXXXVI and LXXXVII (Paris, 1933-34). A shorter account, by the present author, entitled "Charity Workshops during the French Revolution," appeared in the South Atlantic Quarterly, XXXV (1936).

1788, amid a terrible economic depression and a growing famine. In the spring and summer of 1789, as conditions became critical, the number of workers increased. From 3,000 in some eight workshops in the spring, the number swelled to 17,000 in a single workshop on Montmartre in mid-August.[35] In the turbulent weeks following the destruction of the Bastille there was much discontent over an order from the National Assembly to diminish the pay of the workers, and disorders occurred.[36] Bailly and those responsible for law and order in the city feared further rioting, such as had marked Bastille Day,[37] and on August 17 ordered the workshops closed August 31.[38] New ones were instituted shortly afterward, with smaller units of men and more attention given to discipline.[39] Much improvement resulted; nevertheless, occasional acts of vandalism and signs of surliness continued.[40]

Nor was all the fault with the workers: numerous complaints were launched against the overseers (préposés) and the foremen (chefs), who were charged with injustices and other faults. Thirty-eight overseers and a number of foremen were discharged, some of them because of dishonesty and malversation of funds.[41] The result was that the Paris workshops lost the confidence of the public. Marat, who was favorable to the masses, distrusted the workshops and maintained in his issue of L'ami du peuple for April 7, 1791, that the royalists intended to use the workshop workers in a counterrevolution.[42] At the same time the distrust of Bailly and others revived,

[35] Mme Yvonne Forado-Cunéo, op. cit., LXXXVI, 322-323; Bailly, op. cit., II, 257-258.

[36] Ibid., II, 265; Plaisant, op. cit., pp. 39-43; Tuetey, Répertoire général, I, 95-96, Nos. 904 and 915; Tuetey, L'assistance publique, II, 92-97.

[37] Mme Grace M. Jaffé, in her Le mouvement ouvrier à Paris pendant la Révolution (1789-91) [Paris, 1924], p. 68, scoffs at these fears and insists that the men were peaceful. The documents do not bear her out.

[38] Tuetey, Répertoire général, I, No. 904. In actual fact, this was the second closing of the workshops in 1789, for the previous ones (eight in number) had been closed April 1. Mme Forado-Cunéo (op. cit., LXXXVI, 322-323) asserts that the Paris workshops were closed four times, and four times reopened, in the period 1789-91. Their first closing had not been because of turbulence.

[39] Tuetey, L'assistance publique, II, 106-119; Lecoq, op. cit., p. 110.

[40] Tuetey, L'assistance publique, II, 157-159; Tuetey, Répertoire général, II, 426, Nos. 4035 and 4036; Lacroix, op. cit., VII, 23-24; Plaisant, op. cit., pp. 39-43.

[41] Plaisant, op. cit., p. 43.

[42] In his issue of June 1, 1790, he declared that vagabonds, many of them foreigners, had been brought to Paris for the purpose of overthrowing the work of the Revolution at a favorable moment. For discussion of the matter, see Forado-Cunéo, op. cit., LXXXVII, 111-112.

and military protection was requested.[43] At length, June 16, 1791, the National Assembly, after hearing reports of various committees, ordered the closing of all outdoor charity workshops.[44]

The order for closing inspired several frantic appeals from the workers for continuation of the workshops. One of the petitions declared that the order threw twenty-five thousand men in Paris out of work, three fourths of them having dependent wives and children.[45] Failing to receive a favorable answer to their petition, the workers vented their spleen on Bailly, calling him "beggar, traitor, and scoundrel." One agitator wanted to hang him, as the person responsible for the closure.[46]

Thenceforward throughout the eighteenth century the charity workshop declined. As a substitute, the government relied upon public works, such as roads, canals, docks, and buildings, for which appropriations were increased. Some of these enterprises were undertaken by private contractors, and others by governmental agencies, such as the administration of bridges and highways. Indeed, the law of June 16, 1791, which closed the workshops, carried an appropriation of a million livres for specified public works, including the demolition of the gate St. Bernard and the jail, repairs to quays, new construction around the bridge of Louis XVI, the opening of a new canal to the Seine opposite Passy, and construction of a dry-dock at Charenton. The act, moreover, provided that the building

[43] Tuetey, *Répertoire général*, II, 426.

[44] Tuetey, *L'assistance publique*, II, 200-202. The workshops were to close on July 1. This decree marked the fifth and final closing of the Paris workshops since their establishment, December 2, 1789.

[45] *Ibid.*, II, 211-213. Even the foremen of the closed workshops presented a petition for their reopening.

[46] Mme Forado-Cunéo, *op. cit.*, LXXXVII, 118; cf. Tuetey, *Répertoire général*, II, No. 2567. Since July 15, 1789, Bailly had been mayor of Paris. In fact, he was the city's first mayor. Previously the position had been occupied by the provost of merchants. Bailly was not opposed to the workshops in principle, for he raised private funds and established a small but highly praised workshop in February, 1790, which ran for several months, and it was he who conceived the idea of having a workshop in spinning for needy women (Plaisant, *op. cit.*, p. 150). Bailly irritated the working classes a second time by suppressing with military force a disturbance that accompanied a gigantic celebration on July 14, 1791, at the Champs de Mars. Some lives were lost. The lower classes thenceforth regarded him with implacable hatred, and for these actions he was guillotined during the Reign of Terror. Bailly was a scholar and humanitarian. As a bourgeois, he approved of the destruction of the Bastille and of social change, but he was opposed to disorder, violence, and bloodshed.

of the Church of Ste Geneviève (now the Panthéon), which since April 10, 1791, had been supported by charity workshop funds, should be continued by a special appropriation for that purpose.[47] On August 4 a further appropriation of 300,000 livres was made for works of art.[48] In September, 1791, the National Assembly appropriated 2,760,000 livres for distribution among the departments for using the unemployed in draining swamps and clearing lands.[49] On February 22, 1793, the Convention set aside a fund of 20,000,000 livres for highway repairs and beautification.[50] In March, 1795, it appropriated a further 5,000,000 livres, to be spent in repairing local roads, as indirect aid to the unemployed.[51] Thus the sentiment toward outdoor charity workshops cooled, as it did again in 1848, though under somewhat different circumstances.

The charity workshop did not disappear after 1791. For example, on March 15, 1793, Garat, minister of the interior and Roland's successor, sent to the Convention a report on charity workshops then in operation.[52] In June, 1793, the directory of the department of Seine and Marne ordered four workshops established in the canton of Donnemarie for the benefit of the vinegrowers who had lost all hope of a harvest.[53] In January, 1794, charity workshops were operating in the Dordogne, and the workers were employed on the roads.[54] In 1794-95 there were also some in the department of Haute-Garonne.[55] According to Lecoq, Lyons worked 15,000 persons in *ateliers de charité* during the Revolution, at an expense of 400,000 livres a *décade* (a period of ten days), apparently

[47] Tuetey, *L'assistance publique*, II, 200-202; IV, 544-545. See report of December 13, 1791, on the progress made (*ibid.*, IV, 545-547).

[48] *Ibid.*, IV, 545.

[49] Ferdinand-Dreyfus, *Un philanthrope d'autrefois*, p. 189.

[50] *Inv.-som* . . . *Isère*, L 59, 69. One of the objects was the employment of those without work (*Arch. parl.*, LVI, 641).

[51] An act of 21 pluviôse an III (Feb. 9, 1795) had carried an appropriation of 10,000,000 livres to be divided among the departments for their charitable needs. Later, on 7 germinal an III (March 27, 1795), the Convention modified its provision, stipulating that half of the sum should go to indigents who were old or infirm, and the remaining half be used for "useful works, and principally for the repair of neighborhood roads" (Adher, *op. cit.*, p. 520).

These were by no means all of the appropriations for public works during the 1790's, but they suffice to reveal the trend of the day.

[52] *Arch. parl.*, LX, 216.

[53] *Inv.-som* . . . *Seine et Marne*, L 43, séance de 4 juin.

[54] Mathiez, *La vie chère*, p. 457.

[55] Adher, *op. cit.*, p. 519.

not earlier than 1792, since the new calendar was introduced that year.[56] A law of October 15, 1793, ordered, and one of 16 messidor an VII (July 4, 1799) recommended, the establishment of charity workshops in the departments.[57]

Doubtless a great many workshops after 1791 were supported by funds allotted to departments for public works, since considerable liberty was left in the hands of the departmental directories as to both the nature of the works and the means by which they were to be accomplished. The ends for both the charity workshops and the public works were frequently the same: namely, the construction of works of public utility and the lessening of unemployment. At the same time there were probably some differences of emphasis. In the case of the charity workshops, the primary end was the lessening of unemployment; in that of the public works, the emphasis was upon the work projected. In the charity workshops, too, most of the labor was unskilled, and simple projects had to be undertaken, whereas in the public works enterprises skilled workmen might be engaged. In short, the charity workshop benefited unskilled laborers; the public works program might benefit also skilled workers. That pay in the charity workshops was always at a level lower than that of the normal labor market often resulted in discontent and slovenliness. In the public works enterprises, workers were paid the normal labor wage, were more satisfied, and probably performed better work.

Of numerous forms of work undertaken through charity workshops, the most usual was the building or reconstruction of roads and highways. During the eighteenth century hundreds of miles of French roads received attention from these workshops. Thus, in his report on the planned expenditure of the 80,000 livres allotted to his generality after the snows and flood of early 1784, the intendant of Paris listed fifty-one roads to receive attention and designated the work to be done and the money to be spent in each instance.[58] Nine highways were named, and the work was admired by the intendant of Moulins, who on the same occasion outlined the

---

[56] *Op. cit.*, p. 129. [57] Martin-Doisy, *op. cit.*, I, 1267.

[58] "Etat de distribution des 80,000 livres accordées par Sa Majesté par supplément pour être employées en Travaux de Charité en l'année 1784" (Arch. Nat., H 1418). Frequently the documents and literature on the workshops indicate the roads and even the limits to be worked.

anticipated expenditure of 19,600 livres given his generality.[59] According to the *Inventaires-sommaires des archives départementales antérieures à 1790*,[60] Plaisant, and other authorities,[61] many roads, most of them highways, received attention. Occasionally the project was the construction of a new road,[62] but in most cases it was repair of an old one. It might take the form of resurfacing, the correction of drainage and removal of ruts, the reopening of the ditches along the sides of the road, or the replanting of trees along the sides. The French had elaborate regulations about roads, and their highways were excellent. All of this work by the charity workshop workers, at least in the second half of the century, was supervised by engineers of the administration of bridges and highways.

Among other types of projects, the most common was the cleaning and repairing of city streets. Often in winter this labor took the form of removing snow. Sometimes dump-heaps were removed, quays and riverbanks cleaned, streets re-covered with rock, or trees planted along the streets.[63] In January, 1789, workers were employed in Paris at breaking ice on the river in order that the mills might operate and in spreading sand on icy landings.[64] Canal-digging received some attention. Charity workshop workers were used in excavating the Center, Picardy, Burgundy, and Dieppe canals.[65] In 1786 Brittany received from the government 60,000 livres to be employed in charity workshops for improving the navigation of the Vilaine.[66] At Havre and Cherbourg sea-dikes were constructed.[67] St. Valery-en-Caux, in Normandy, applied in July, 1790, to Necker

[59] "Projet de distribution de la somme de 20,000 livres augmentation de fonds destinés pour entretenir les ateliers de charité dans la Généralité de Moulins pendant l'année 1784" (*ibid.*).

[60] See, for example, those for Charente, C 75; Aube, C 1140, 1141, 1142, 2310, 2327; Charente-Inférieure, C 231, 232; Seine-Inférieure, C 869, 2263; Ardennes, C 419-429; and Gironde, C 1915. This is far from being a complete list.

[61] See, e.g., Plaisant, *op. cit.*, pp. 148-149.

[62] See *Inv.-som . . . Seine-Inférieure*, C 2261.

[63] See, for instance, *Inv.-som . . . Ille-et-Vilaine*, C 337, a list of projects to be undertaken at Rennes, 1784; Plaisant, *op. cit.*, pp. 51, 57, 92-93, 150, dealing with Paris, 1789-90; Bibl. Nat., Fonds français, 6801, f 133.

[64] Bibl. Nat., Fonds français, 6801, ff 138-139.

[65] The first two in 1788-89, the latter two in 1790-91 (Lefebvre, *op. cit.*, p. 17; Plaisant, *op. cit.*, pp. 57, 145-147; Tuetey, *L'assistance publique*, II, 105 with n., 197-198; cf. *Arch. parl.*, XVI, 118). In the 1770's and 1780's work had been done on canals around Troyes (Chaudron, *op. cit.*, pp. 41-43).

[66] H. Sée, *Les classes rurales en Bretagne*, p. 481 n. 6. The *Inv.-som . . . Ille-et-Vilaine* (C 1711) gives the size of the allotment as 50,000 livres.

[67] *Inv.-som . . . Seine-Inférieure*, C 869; Lefebvre, *op. cit.*, p. 17.

for 40,000 livres, to establish a charity workshop to undertake excavations for the cleaning and enlargement of its port.[68] The draining of swamps was sometimes undertaken.[69] Occasionally the old ramparts of a city were removed, new ramparts were constructed, or a hill was leveled.[70]

In 1789-91 the Bastille in Paris was demolished by charity workshop workers, under the direction of Palloy, a great showman; and the workshop was so marked with turbulence that in May, 1791, it was suppressed.[71] Further work was done toward the completion of the Church of Ste Geneviève.[72] Immense excavations and levelings were undertaken in June and July, 1790, on the Champs de Mars, Paris, to fit it as a sort of natural amphitheater for the Fete of the Federation, July 14, 1790. When it became evident that the project would not be completed by that date, volunteers by the tens of thousands turned out to lend assistance.[73] Martineau, deputy of the Third Estate for Paris, made a short speech before the National Assembly on December 4, 1790, in which he suggested reforestation as a project that the *ateliers de charité* might undertake, but without apparent result.[74] At Lyons, after the ill-fated insurrection of 1793-94, the richer quarters of the city were condemned to be demolished; and 15,000 charity workshop workers, a motley and unorganized mass, gathered not only from Lyons but also from neighboring departments, were employed, though little was accomplished.[75] Nu-

[68] "Mémoire qui présente à Monsieur Necker, Premier Ministre des Finances, Le Conseil général de la Commune de St. Valery-en-Caux." Arch. Nat., F15, 101. A map of the harbor and project is included. At Morlaix, in Brittany, a workshop for the same purpose was ordered in 1770 (*Inv.-som . . . Ille-et-Vilaine*, C 667).

[69] Chaudron, *op. cit.*, pp. 41-43; Plaisant, *op. cit.*, p. 51; Adher, *op. cit.*, pp. 515-516.

[70] Bibl. Nat., Fonds français, 6801, f 133; Defresne and Evrard, *op. cit.*, I, lxxvi; *Inv.-som . . . Ille-et-Vilaine*, C 337.

[71] The demolition cost 524,426 livres (*Inventaire-sommaire des archives de la Seine. Partie municipale. Période révolutionnaire (1789-an VIII)*, D 222, pp. 16 and 19; Lacroix, *op. cit.*, III, 156; Tuetey, *L'assistance publique*, II, 109-110, 167, 191, 207, 288).

[72] *Gazette nationale ou le moniteur universel*, VIII, 681 (June 17, 1791), IX, 70 (July 9, 1791); Tuetey, *op. cit.*, II, 201-202, 209. This enterprise, strictly speaking, was not undertaken by charity workshops, but by some five hundred men released from the charity workshops of Paris on July 1, 1791. It was a public works project.

[73] Plaisant, *op. cit.*, pp. 61-64, 101, 107 n.; Lacroix, *op. cit.*, VII, 227-231; *Révolutions de Paris*, No. 52, pp. 753-754.

[74] *Arch. parl.*, XXI, 203.

[75] Lecoq, *op. cit.*, p. 129; E. D. Bradby, *A Short History of the French Revolution, 1789-1795* (Oxford, 1926), p. 228.

merous smaller tasks, such as the removal of stones from the Bois de Boulogne at Paris, were also undertaken.[76]

Before 1789 women and children also participated in charity workshops, performed lighter tasks than those assigned to the men, and drew less pay. Turgot, who employed his workers in small groups and made it a principle to keep the members of a family together, gave the children nothing beyond the meals that were furnished to all the workers, on the theory that the children did little work and consequently deserved little recompense.[77] Women were always paid less than men. In the Paris workshops of 1709 (no women participated), apparently the men received only food, a pound and a half of bread a day in small loaves.[78] In the workshops at Montauban in 1713 the men were given 2 sous a day, the women and children the still smaller sum of 18 deniers (1½ sous).[79] In 1739 men worked in *ateliers de charité* on the roads of Poitou for 10 sous (½ livre) a day; and beggars constrained to work at reconstructing quays were given lodging, food, and 3 sous a day.[80] In the workshops in Guyenne in 1752 the men were paid 7 sous, the women 5, and the children 4.[81] In early 1789, 12 sous a day were paid to men in Brittany,[82] 18 to those in Paris, and 10 and 5 sous, respectively, to women and children in the Paris workshops.[83] When the Paris workshops were reorganized in April, 1789, women and children were excluded, and the pay for the men was raised to a livre a day, this rate continuing into 1790.[84] Those working on the canals near Paris, some at work on the Champs de Mars, and those at the Ecole Militaire in 1790 were paid 30 sous a day.[85]

Thus the wages paid in the charity workshops rose steadily during the century along with wages in general and the cost of living. Likewise wages paid in the charity workshops varied even as wages and the cost of living varied from province to province and from city to

[76] See Forado-Cunéo, *op. cit.*, LXXXVII, 57-58.

[77] Lecoq, *op. cit.*, pp. 91-95.

[78] There were more than 2,500 workers (Boislisle, *op. cit.*, XXIX, 500).

[79] Boislisle and Brotonne, *op. cit.*, III, No. 487.

[80] Boissonnade, *op. cit.*, II, 464.

[81] Bourgoüin, *op. cit.*, XII, 101.

[82] *Inv.-som . . . Ille-et-Vilaine*, C 404.

[83] Forado-Cunéo, *op. cit.*, LXXXVI, 322-323. Lecoq (*op. cit.*, p. 105), however, reports that the women and children got 15 and 10 sous, respectively.

[84] Tuetey, *L'assistance publique*, II, 116-118.

[85] *Ibid.*; Plaisant, *op. cit.*, p. 101.

city. Wages paid in the workshops after 1791 doubtless rose in ratio to normal wages.

Many were the criticisms of the workshops, more particularly in 1789-91. Prior to that time the workshops were more local in nature, smaller in number of workers, and discipline (save in the workshop of 1709) was good. The public did not expect a great deal in the way of achievement, since unskilled men and women were employed, and some of them were frail. It realized that these people were unemployed because of circumstances over which they had no control, and must be given the means of relieving distress. There was a public obligation to take care of them. But to give money or food without anything in return would have a tendency to make beggars of many. It was better to put them to work, though the accomplishment was small. Like the American public in the 1930's, the French of the eighteenth century had no intention of making the workshops permanent. They were to serve during severe winters, economic depressions, or following a natural catastrophe, such as a flood, a drought, or famine. When they lasted longer, and they sometimes did, more especially after 1770, the reason was partly the fact that the disastrous circumstances lingered.[86] Labor in charity workshops was voluntary in almost all cases. Workshops were designed to serve local communities, and to enable most or all of the workers to stay in their own homes. In Poitou in 1739, however, the workshop authorities concerned themselves with providing lodging for the workers; then some beggars were constrained to work.

Each time its fear dictated, the royal government made large grants to support these workshops. Throughout the century it made appropriations for these institutions in the *pays d'élections*. The *pays d'états* (which had their own elective assemblies and what Americans would call "states rights") were supposed to provide their own funds, and they did make large appropriations. Occasionally in the 1770's and commonly in the 1780's, however, the royal government also made appropriations to the *pays d'états*. Cities were supposed to tax themselves and to encourage private donations toward the establishment of charity workshops. In the last two decades prior to the Revolution and even during the early days of the Revolution it continued

[86] It was also in part the surge of humanitarian sentiment after 1770.

to be the policy to some extent to see what funds could be raised provincially and locally, both by taxes and by private contributions, before the central government made appropriations. The aim was to make each region and community realize that in so far as possible it should provide for its own needs, in the hope of lessening the continual, and increasing demands made on the national treasury.

No perfect solution of the problems of unemployment and pauperism has ever been found. Many have offered suggestions, and some, panaceas. Religion, war, change of government, strikes, higher wages and lower wages, birth control and no control, scientific advance, and exploitation of weaker peoples have all been tried with never more than temporary success. The charity workshop was never intended to be more than a palliative. As applied in eighteenth-century France, it had many limitations: it never provided for all the unemployed, and it reached but few of the beggars; it paid a wage on which people could barely exist; and even then, as in 1789-90, there were those who complained that it drew men away from regular employment and lowered the wages paid in the normal labor market. Sometimes, as in 1789-90, the workers were accused of sloth and surliness, and the overseers of brutality and malversation of funds. Even so, humanitarian statesmen in eighteenth-century France like Turgot and Necker warmly supported the charity workshop movement and believed that it provided the best solution to their problem of aiding temporarily the needy unemployed.

Indoor Workshops

With few exceptions, the indoor workshops (generally called *ateliers de filature,* or spinning workshops) were confined to spinning, knitting, weaving, lacemaking, and sewing. On occasion beggars and vagabonds were arrested, placed in certain houses, and forced to work in the hospitals, the men at grinding grain (with handmills), brewing beer, sharpening axes, beating cement, and other tasks,[87] as in Paris in 1612. Again, during the famine of 1788-89, an *atelier de charité* was set up in a building in Versailles, and two hundred old men were put to work grinding grain, with handmills and horse-drawn mills, since no rain had fallen since August and water in the Seine was low.

[87] The women and girls over eight were required to work at spinning, knitting, or sewing. All were to be lodged and fed, and forced to work under penalty of scourging. No mention was made of pay (Martin-Doisy, *op. cit.,* I, 1244).

It was an unhappy experiment. The old men became dissatisfied when their pay was dropped from 30 to 24 sous a day; moreover, criticism was leveled at the high cost of operation. The workshop, accordingly, was closed in late November, 1789, and the men were put to work on an outdoor project.[88] Of course, *ateliers* of various sorts were established in the general hospitals throughout France for the training of youth toward their *maîtrise*. In the middle of the century training was given youths in the General Hospital at Paris for the guilds of glass-painters, wheelwrights, bakers, apothecaries, coopers, carpenters, and garmentmakers. These *ateliers*,[89] however, were not considered as coming under the designation of "charity workshops."

It is not clear when the institution of charity spinning workshops began. According to Cormouls-Houlès, "from time immemorial" curés and churchwardens at Paris had organized relief in famine periods through work at home by distributing material for spinning.[90] Certainly from the beginning of the seventeenth century needy women and girls were so employed in various hospitals. After 1612 spinning, weaving, sewing, and lacemaking at hospitals were common. The following cities were among those having these institutions in the 1600's: Troyes (1618),[91] Caen (1640),[92] Bordeaux (1659),[93] Paris (1666 and 1677),[94] and Bayeux (1667).[95] The eighteenth

[88] Defresne and Evard, *op. cit.*, I, Introduction, cxi-cxiv.

[89] Apparently also *ateliers* of watchmakers and goldsmiths (Martin-Doisy, *op. cit.*, I, 1256-1260).

[90] *Op. cit.*, p. 162.

[91] In the Hospital of St. Nicholas. Both sexes of the aged were employed at manufactures, chiefly of serge cloth (Martin-Doisy, *op. cit.*, IV, 811).

[92] At the Hôtel-Dieu children were employed at manufactures (*ibid.*, IV, 806, 807).

[93] At the Hôpital de la Manufacture, established as a general hospital in 1658. The work of the *atelier* included the spinning and weaving in cotton and silk, the bleaching of linen, the weaving of rugs, and the making of socks, hats, stockings, and coverlets (*Revue historique de Bordeaux*, IX, 1916, 368-369).

[94] In the 1660's the girls at the Miséricorde were employed at making rugs or hangings *(tapisserie)*. The proceeds were 1,260 livres in 1666, 1,500 livres in 1667, and 1,306 livres in 1668 (Marcel Fosseyeyx, *La Maison de Cents-Filles*, p. 10). In 1677 spinning, knitting, and sewing were done at the Salpêtrière (Brièle, *Supplément à l'inventaire-sommaire des archives hospitalières antérieures à 1790*, pp. 235, 237).

[95] *Inv.-som . . . Calvados*, H Suppl. 1096-IIA1. This volume has a large amount of material on this very interesting and profitable workshop which lasted down to the Revolution. The workshop was started as a school of instruction for the children resident in the General Hospital of Bayeux, whereby they would be taught the making of stockings, mittens, bonnets, and camisoles as a means of earning their

century witnessed a much larger number of hospitals providing work of this type. In addition to the cities mentioned, hospitals in the following other cities did so: Dijon (1720), Riom (1724), Nantes (1726), Avranches and Saint-Sauveur-la-Vicomte (1727), Libourne and Clermont (1730), Grenoble (1734), Vire (1736), Poitiers and Niort (1730's), Annonay (1757), Auxerre (1761), Lisieux (1765), Lorient (1766), Bar-sur-Aube (1776), Narbonne (1788), Nontron (1780's).[96]

Perhaps the hospitals would have continued the work of caring for unfortunates, though somewhat handicapped, had these sewing-rooms not existed. A lesser function of the *ateliers* was to occupy the time and minds of idle people, whose ennui otherwise might have been unbearable, a feature which would seem to qualify these sewing-rooms as charitable workshops. Those working in them were in-digents. Moreover, the profits from their work went toward the maintenance of their institution. At times an *atelier* provided as much as one fourth of the income of the institution. A leading fea-

---

living. In 1691 lacemaking was added, and in 1698 shoemaking (*ibid.*, pp. 309, 311). In 1691 there were 148 poor persons at work in this hospital, thirty of them at lacemaking. Evidently persons of all ages in the hospital were working. Certainly this was the case in 1725 (*ibid.*, pp. 366-367). In 1717 persons from out-side the hospital were coming there to work, and were given soup and cider for sustenance (*ibid.*, p. 367). Gratifications were given the best lacemakers (1744) (*ibid.*, p. 326). In the second half of the eighteenth century the profits from sales of goods made were several thousand livres a year, and appear (without, however, deducting the cost of raw material and the payment of instructors) to have covered about one fourth of the hospital's expenses (*ibid.*, pp. 359, 362-365).

[96] The dates do not in all cases mark the establishment of the *ateliers de filature* in the hospitals; in perhaps most of the institutions the *ateliers* were continued down to, or even through, the Revolution. Nor is this by any means a complete list of the cities in which there were hospitals with such *ateliers*. It is highly probable that every general hospital in eighteenth-century France (and there were scores on the eve of the Revolution), as well as many other hospitals in which children, in-valids, and old persons were maintained, had this feature. Far from being a rare institution, it appears to have been very common. Instead of being temporary, to relieve an emergency, as was the outdoor *atelier de charité*, it was more often than otherwise a permanent affair.

This suggests the question of whether or not the hospital sewing-rooms can really be regarded as charity workshops. Martin-Doisy so regards them, but other French writers appear not to do so.

Information on the majority of these can be found in the *Inventaires-sommaires des archives départementales antérieures à 1790*, sér. C, H, and E. Other sources are: Coiffier, *op. cit.*, pp. 102-104, 108-109; Cross-Mayrevieille, *op. cit.*, VIII, 291-296; Cross-Mayrevieille, *L'assistance publique et privée en Languedoc* (Montpellier, 1914), pp. 75-76; Burgade, *op. cit.*, pp. 116-117; Boissonnade, *op. cit.*, 459-461; Rambaud, *op. cit.*, II, 475; Lallemand, *La Révolution et les pauvres*, p. 157; and Martin-Doisy, *op. cit.*, I, 1255-1256, 1263, and IV, 795, 802.

ture of the hospital workshops, furthermore, was the training of youths, boys in some instances as well as girls, in the arts of spinning, weaving, knitting, lacemaking, and hatmaking, whereby they later might earn their living.[97]

In some instances the hospital workshops received workers from the outside, permitting them variously to work within the hospital during the day or to carry the raw material to their homes for work there. From 1693 to 1777 workers from the outside came daily to the *atelier*, or *ateliers*, of the General Hospital of Bayeux.[98] In 1710 fifty girls from the town and its suburbs came thither for lacemaking. The hospital fed them at the Christmas season. In 1717 the hospital provided the outside workers with soup and a pint of cider daily. Occasionally the receipts of the institution included items of sale of commodities made by outside workers. In 1762, however, the number of children from the town of Bayeux coming to the hospital was so small that the authorities decided to invite children from the rural regions. In 1784 two other charitable lacemaking institutions were operating in Bayeux.[99]

Repeatedly, perhaps continuously, during the period 1715-80 the hospital at Tulle, in south-central France, put out work to be done by the poor women of the town.[100] Balls of linen thread were given out for weaving. Some spinning was done also. The poor were charged small sums for the material when they took it, and were paid higher sums when they returned the completed work. In 1771-75 rabbit skins were put out to be fashioned into collars. The hospital at Monpazier, near Bordeaux, according to a pamphlet published in 1780, received poor girls and vagabond boys of the town for work in the Filature Royale de Coton and embarked on the policy of putting out small amounts of wool to country women for spinning. Twenty girls of the town worked at spinning in the *atelier*, in a building adjoining the hospital, and were given lodging and food. They were instructed not only in spinning but also in religion. The

[97] *Ateliers* existed also in various general hospitals for training youths in glass-painting, wheelmaking, barrelmaking, carpentry, baking, watchmaking, and the apothecary's and goldsmith's arts (Martin-Doisy, *op. cit.*, I, 1255-1278). Young girls were trained at typesetting in the General Hospital of Toulouse (Buchalet, *op. cit.*, p. 105).

[98] *Inv.-som . . . Calvados*, H Suppl. 1126, 1129, 1135, 1220, 1275, 1276, 1286.

[99] *Ibid.*, H Suppl. 1306.

[100] *Inv.-som . . . Hôpitaux de Tulle, Brive . . .*, G 12-15, pp. 252-255.

UNIVERSITY
COLLEGE
LIBRARY
NOTTINGHAM

boys were employed at various tasks, and sometimes assisted with the spinning of cotton and wool. Since the work performed outside the hospital by the country women proved of assistance to the poor, one writer (a traveler) enthusiastically anticipated that shortly two hundred poor women would be aided in this manner, and he recorded that the government was so pleased with the project that it had promised aid.[101]

At Clermont, Poitiers, Niort, Caen, and Avranches in the 1720's and 1730's, beggars were taken from the streets and forced to labor in hospital workshops at spinning, weaving, knitting, making hats, and other tasks.[102] In certain of the depots of mendicity, notably those at Tours, Montpazier, Beaulieu, Grenoble, and Bourges, spinning and weaving workshops were established, and beggars and vagabonds were forced to work.[103] A workshop capable of occupying six thousand beggars was created in the Château de Chambord.[104]

The French public regarded the hospital sewing-rooms with favor, and increasingly, as the eighteenth century wore on, pleas for their extension beyond the hospital walls as a means of aid to women, girls, and old men in times of crisis were heard. Advocates of this policy were Courson, intendant of Rouen (1709); Turgot (1770-75); De la Bove, intendant of Brittany (1775); Frederick Hildebrand, naturalized Frenchman and celebrated inventor (1789); Frier, Grenoble physician and pamphleteer (1789 and 1791); Bailly, mayor of Paris (1790); Dupré, pamphleteer and deputy to the National Assembly from Carcasonne (1790); Gerdret, Parisian judge (1790); Marat, famous journalist (1790); and numerous others, especially on the eve of the Revolution and in its early days.

As a matter of fact, charitable workshops in spinning and weaving having no connection with the hospitals had long been known in France, but previous to the 1770's they had been infrequent and sporadic. Some had been sponsored under private auspices, by

---

[101] Jean Mousson de Lestang, *Procès-verbal de la maison de charité et de l'hôpital y réuni de la ville royale de Monpasier en Périgord* [1780], pp. 4-12 (Arch. Nat., F15, 101).

[102] Coiffier, *op. cit.*, pp. 102-104, 108-109; Boissonnade, *op. cit.*, pp. 459-461; *Inv.-som . . . Calvados*, C 635, 639.

[103] Dumas, *op. cit.*, pp. 328-329; *Inventaire-sommaire . . . Gironde*, C 3591, 3592; *Inv.-som . . . Calvados*, C 684; Frier, *Analyse du plan qui fut publié en 1789 et 1791 . . .* (4th ed., Grenoble, 1817), p. 5 n.; Martin-Doisy, *op. cit.*, I, 1267-1268.

[104] Bloch, *op. cit.*, p. 213 n. 2.

churchmen, charity bureaux, or merchants. Others were established by municipalities, acting sometimes on their own initiative and sometimes on that of the intendants and subdelegates. It little mattered how they were started: there was no rivalry (save on a few rare occasions) between groups political, ecclesiastical, and private in the eighteenth century over the honor of originating or maintaining charitable enterprises. Rather there was commonly good will, and frequently cordial co-operation.

All three groups co-operated with a private charitable workshop at Bayeux in 1764. Private citizens, the bishop, and the city contributed funds in the hope of making it a success.[105] Similarly at Rouen in 1768 political, ecclesiastical, and private personages co-operated in establishing *ateliers de charité* and *ateliers de filature*.[106] In 1770 Turgot instituted charity spinning in Limoges and several small towns in Limousin, on funds furnished by the government, at the same time that he set up his more celebrated *ateliers de charité* and wrote his famous *Instruction* to guide his subordinates who were placed in immediate charge of them. Turgot showed a spirit of co-operation by sending copies of the *Instruction* to the curés, asking their assistance in promoting the workshops, and insisting that every poor person coming for aid must be provided with a certificate of indigence and good morals from his or her curé. Since Turgot did not mention the term *atelier* in connection with the spinning, perhaps the cotton or other matter to be spun was put out for work at home, rather than in a common assembly room.[107]

Later, when Turgot was controller-general of finance, he published a second pamphlet (1775), urging the intendants throughout France to inaugurate charity spinning and lacemaking, and to distribute the raw material to wives and children in homes where the

[105] *Inv.-som . . . Calvados*, H. Suppl. 1136. Some 13,000 to 14,000 livres were raised.

[106] According to Bloch (*op. cit.*, p. 202 n. 4), funds of 450,000 livres for the purpose were raised by subscription and loans. Cotton was passed out for spinning to the poor who came provided with certificate of indigence and good character from their curés.

[107] *Oeuvres de Turgot*, II, 15-16, 74. In his *Instruction* he suggested that spinning wheels, as well as material to be spun, should be put out for home spinning. This, of course, had long been a practice in France. Coiffier writes that Michaudière, while intendant of the generality of Riom, 1753-1757, distributed a large number of spinning wheels gratis among the country people (*op. cit.*, p. 253). Since the total expense of the charity spinning under Turgot in 1770 was only 1,691 livres, it is clear that he did not attempt this form of assistance on a large scale.

income for maintenance was not sufficient. The government was to provide the funds. Merchants and curés were asked to co-operate and to contribute their time.[108]

Other examples of charity spinning or weaving prior to the Revolution occurred during the "Great Winter" of 1709 in Rouen, where the women worked for 5 sous a day;[109] at Troyes in the famines of 1740 and 1770;[110] at Carcassonne, from 1768 to 1789;[111] at Lisieux, in 1783-84;[112] at Rennes, in 1775;[113] at Sassenage, in Dauphiné, in the 1780's;[114] at Rouen in 1768, 1777, and 1788;[115] at Vienne in 1790.[116] In Poitou and Saintogne several *ateliers de filature* were set up in the second half of the century,[117] and in 1778 certain bishops in Brittany, acting on suggestions from the government, urged that bureaux of charity and charity spinning be set up in all parishes.[118]

Paris had several *ateliers de filature*. One at the Maison de l'Enfant Jésus, an orphans' asylum for sixteen girls of the nobil-

---

[108] *Ibid.*, II, 452-454. An *arrêt du conseil d'état* of April 25, 1775, for which Turgot was responsible, reveals that charity knitting, spinning, and similar work were established in several parishes of Paris (*ibid.*, II, 186-187).

[109] Courson, the intendant, borrowed 50,000 livres from an individual, assuring him of government reimbursement, and set up both charity workshops for men and spinning workshops for women (Boislisle and Brotonne, *op. cit.*, III, No. 475).

[110] Material was given out for spinning and weaving; bread, rice, and wood also were distributed (Chaudron, *op. cit.*, p. 35).

[111] Dupré, *Moyens d'exciter l'industrie nationale, et de détruire la mendicité* (1790), pp. 17-22. Many details are given of this *atelier*, which the writer describes as the "first institution" of its kind in France. It was a municipal undertaking, and work was done in rooms provided for the purpose, not in the homes of the poor. Like the hospitals and other charitable undertakings, it had an administrative bureau of twenty-four citizens in charge; but immediate direction was in the hands of two persons hired for the purpose. The workers came and left at fixed hours, and received payment every day. On feast days they had to come for mass in the *atelier*, and were paid 2 sous and given a pound and a half of bread.

[112] Here master weavers took into their employ city outcasts and trained them at weaving. The curés and members of the charity bureaux made two weekly visits to see that all went well (*Inv.-som . . . Calvados*, H Suppl. 465).

[113] The government accorded 3,000 livres to reimburse a merchant for his advances (De la Bove to Turgot, Sept. 5, 1775, and Turgot to De la Bove, Sept. 18, 1775, Arch. Nat., H 565).

[114] This was a charity lace factory. In 1789 the royal treasury granted it 6,000 livres. It had then been in existence for some years (*Inv.-som . . . Isère*, L 54).

[115] Bloch, *op. cit.*, p. 202 n. 4, and Cormouls-Houlès, *op. cit.*, p. 181 n.

[116] It was proposed that the girls working in this workshop make clothes for the prisoners, who were greatly in need (*Inv.-som . . . Isère*, L 54, p. 89).

[117] Boissonnade, *op. cit.*, II, 523-526; *Inv.-som . . . Charente-Inférieure*, C 234.

[118] Sée, *Remarques sur la misère*, pp. 125-126.

ity,[119] was established in 1752 by Languet de Gergy, curé of Saint-Sulpice, and was fashioned closely after Madame de Maintenon's famous school of St. Cyr. This establishment, strangely enough, provided an *atelier de filature*, where poor girls and women from the city might come daily to spin cotton, hemp, flax, and wool; they were fed soup and bread and paid the pittance of 3 sous a day. This *atelier* continued in existence down to the eve of the Revolution, when the institution was closed, the furniture sold, and the nuns were arrested.[120]   Another establishment was set up in the 1770's under the direction of a M. and Mme Nau, with the financial support and interest of Lenoir, the lieutenant-general of police. Two thousand poor were aided by it each year. The government contributed 12,000 livres annually from the time of its origin to 1790; but this sum was far from sufficient, and the annual deficits of 30,000 to 40,000 livres were cared for by the police magistrates. Work was not done in an *atelier* but in the homes of the people. To get their raw material and to receive pay for their work, they resorted to the "general magazine" kept by the Naus.[121]   A third establishment in Paris in 1787 was housed in the *faubourg* Saint-Sulpice, where fifty-six poor girls, occupied at making black lace, were fed and were instructed in religion, reading, and writing.[122]   A fourth establishment was run for a year or longer in the 1780's by Frederick Hildebrand, the naturalized Swiss inventor, who trained at spinning on a machine of his own invention twelve blind persons brought to him by the Philanthropic Society, and freely gave his time, his chief object being to render these persons capable of earning a living.[123]

[119] Proof had to be shown that their families had enjoyed the rank of nobility for two hundred years.

[120] Tuetey, *op. cit.*, IV, 4-25; Alfred Franklin, *op. cit.*, XIV, 264-265; Tenon, *op. cit.*, pp. 17, 96. Tenon mentions that at the time of his writing twelve orphan boys were lodged and fed in the *atelier*, and that ninety-six others worked there during the day and were fed.

[121] The date of its origin is given variously as 1774, 1777, and 1779 (Tuetey, *op. cit.*, II, 351, 548, 550-552, 572-573, 617, 634-635; Bloch, *op. cit.*, p. 224). Lenoir had created a bureau, composed of some curés and merchants, to supervise it. Bloch mentions that there were existent in Paris in the 1770's several private *ateliers de filature* for charitable purposes.

[122] Tenon, *op. cit.*, p. 23.

[123] "Certificat de la Société philanthropique que prouve le S. Hildebran est l'auteur d'une machine pour la filature des aveugles et qu'il leur a donné ses soins avec zèle et gratuitement," dated June 13, 1786; also, "Exposé succinct des découvertes du S. Hildebran" (Arch. Nat., F15, 3596).

The "hard times" amid which the Revolution developed aroused as much interest in the *ateliers de filature* as in the outdoor charity workshops. In early 1789 many *cahiers* contained requests for them. In some places, at Nemours, for example,[124] the sewing-rooms, however, continued to function. In others, new workshops came into existence. The city of Toulouse in 1790 engaged one Cazals to change his own manufacturing enterprise into a charity workshop for the spinning of cotton, the profits to go thenceforth to the municipal hospital.[125] In Paris, Bailly, the mayor, with funds privately raised, opened in February, 1790, the *atelier* Sainte-Geneviève, with headquarters on the rue Bordet and with three branch establishments, a bleaching shop on the same street, a workshop at Chaillot, and a workshop at Picpus,[126] in which English machinery was used. Although the number of persons employed was not great, criticism of its expensiveness was soon made. For several months in 1790-91 Madame Bailly took an active part in this form of charity by receiving poor women at her home, giving out material for the knitting of socks and bonnets, and paying the women when they delivered their finished goods.[127] The *atelier* Sainte-Geneviève continued only until November, 1790, and closed with a deficit, which the government, on Bailly's request, assumed.[128] At its most flourishing period, during the summer of 1790, it accommodated only two hundred persons. It is doubtful if a much larger number of women were aided by the charity spinning provided by Madame Bailly, the Hospital of the Child Jesus, and other agencies. And yet the need was great, for adding to the local horde of unemployed in Paris came a multitude of hungry men and women from the provinces seeking work or relief. On May 30, 1790, the National Assembly decreed that both charity workshops for men and charity workshops in spin-

---

[124] *Inv.-som . . . Seine-et-Marne*, L 68, f 185.

[125] Hitherto Cazals had given out work to the poor to be done for his own profit. The new action was to help care for the great numbers who sought work in the outdoor charity workshops (Adher, *op. cit.*, p. 253).

[126] Lacroix, *op. cit.*, VII, 27-71; Tuetey, *L'assistance publique*, I, cxxx-cxxxii.

[127] Several letters on the matter are found in Arch. Nat., F15, 3596. She sent the knitted material to one Le Camus for sale. Her note of January 11, 1791, lists around 500 pairs of socks and 2 bonnets that she had sent him. Later in the month she severed her relations with the work. It was continued, however, by others.

[128] Tuetey, *op. cit.*, II, 350-351. It appears that the total expense had been 60,000 livres. The deficit was 5,600 livres. Cf. *ibid.*, IV, 639-640.

ning should be established to aid the needy, whether Parisian or provincial.[129]

Shortly afterwards two rather large workshops, accommodating twenty-five hundred women, came into being: one was established in a deserted monastery on the rue Saint-Jacques and was therefore called the Jacobin workshop; the second was housed in a deserted monastery of the Recollects, in a different part of the city, and called the Recollects' workshop. Later in the Revolution their names were changed to the North and South workshops, respectively. At the same time the government took over the establishment previously run by Madame Nau and her daughters and converted it into a General Magazine, or warehouse, for storing the raw material needed in the two workshops and also the finished products coming from them.

These were the best known of the eighteenth-century charity sewing-rooms,[130] and with some vicissitudes they lasted to 1795. In certain years, especially 1794-95, the pay was delinquent, and those in charge frantically besought the government for funds out of which the women could be paid. Then the workers became insolent, swore, fought and stole at times, and, more especially in the Jacobin workshop, kept the air surcharged with trouble.[131] In one instance a worker from the Jacobin workshop attacked with maniacal fury a woman on her way to mass in a near-by church.[132] A spirit of violence characteristic of the Montmartre outdoor workshop in 1789 was present also in these two women's workshops, and flamed anew from time to time at least through 1794; yet it did not provoke their closure, as it did that of the outdoor workshop, doubtless because the officials were less afraid of the women than of the men.

Hours in the workshops were long. The women assembled at 6:00 A.M. in summer and 7:00 A.M. in winter, and worked until 7:00 P.M., with two respites of an hour each during the day for

[129] *Ibid.*, II, 130-131; Watteville, *op. cit.*, p. 1. No foreigners were eligible; French beggars from the provinces, if they had not resided in Paris for six months and did not wish to take work, were to be given passports and sent home.

[130] See the documents published by Tuetey in his *L'assistance publique à Paris pendant la Révolution*. Cf. S. T. McCloy, "Charity Workshops for Women, Paris, 1790-95," *Social Service Review*, XI (June, 1937), 274-284.

[131] Numerous documents in Tuetey's *L'assistance publique* deal with this. Résumés of other documents are found in his *Répertoire générale*, VI, 163-168, 175-176; XI, 36-37.

[132] Tuetey, *Répertoire générale*, VII, Introduction, xi-ii; V, No. 3224.

food. Before March, 1791, they were fed vegetable soup or rice with vegetables; after that date the dispensing of soup and vegetables ceased, and the workers were allowed six pounds (livres) of bread a week.[133] Work consisted of spinning hemp and cotton. A small amount of weaving was attempted at first, but a ruling was soon made that it could be undertaken only in the homes of the workers. Spinning wheels were furnished by the government, and those who did not know how to spin were taught. Old men and children scutched the hemp. The pitifully small pay consisted of a few sous a day for an assiduous worker. No wonder youths below sixteen protested at being compelled to leave the outdoor workshops, where the labor was light and the pay a livre a day, to go into the spinning workshops at perhaps less than half that wage. The spinners were paid according to the quantity and quality of their work, but little of the work was of good quality. When the General Magazine had trouble disposing of the output, most of it was forced on the hospitals of Paris, which used it as shrouds or sacks for burying the dead. In 1795 the government ordered a large quantity for sailcloth.

The government expended on the workshops, according to a report of 15 floréal an III (May 5, 1795), a total of 3,940,583 livres, of which 3,478,507 livres were refunded from goods sold or were represented by finished goods and other assets. This left a relatively small deficit.[134] At the end of the year 1794, 9,031 persons had been aided, at an average daily cost, including food, of 7 sous 5 deniers, and the government had been reimbursed for most of the expense by the sale of the products.[135] Clearly these institutions did not care for all the women, old men, and children in need on the streets of Paris. Perhaps a greater number resorted to begging or plunder. Nevertheless, the project rendered considerable service.

At length in June, 1795, the two workshops were closed under the pretense of economy.[136] The General Magazine was ordered

[133] *Social Service Review*, XI, 279.
[134] Tuetey, *L'assistance publique*, II, 718-719.
[135] *Ibid.*, IV, 686-687.
[136] *Ibid.*, IV, 732-743. Berthollet and the committee of agriculture and the arts had tried to get the Convention to close them in late 1794, without success. During the five years of their existence these workshops were shifted about in political jurisdiction, and it appears that political favor had much to do with the appointments of workshop overseers, who were well remunerated. See the present writer's article, *Social Service Review*, XI, 282 n. 41.

continued, but henceforth raw material and spinning machines would be given out for work at home. On 21 fructidor an V (September 7, 1797), Cauchois,[137] director of the institution, reported, however, that at that time spinning was again being done within the workshop (the General Magazine) and that "around six hundred mothers of family and other very poor persons" were employed.[138] The workshop was then, and for some time had been, in dire distress, unable to get funds from the government for payment of the workers for weeks at a time. Moreover, the workshop experienced a shortage of raw material in 1797, after it had given thousands of pounds[139] of its stock of Levantine cotton to Dupeuty, an industrialist and farmer at Clairfontaine. In messidor an IV (June-July 1796) Dupeuty had attracted government support for his private enterprises in which he employed two hundred workers, many of them youths whom he trained as apprentices.[140] Perhaps the Paris institution did not survive these strenuous times, although in 1801 at a charity spinning establishment at the Hospital Andral material was put out to two thousand workers for spinning in their homes.[141]

The spinning workshops, as well as the outdoor charity workshops, suffered a decline after the early days of the Revolution. Many demands for spinning workshops were made in the *cahiers* sent from the provinces in early 1789, and during 1789 and 1790 a number of workshops of this type existed. After 1791 the workshops were seldom mentioned, although public opinion did not turn against them to any great extent, and they were continued in Paris, the pulse center of France, somewhat steadily down to 1848 with apparent public approval.[142] After 1795 the work was generally done in the homes of the workers, and not in an *atelier*, to avoid both expense and turmoil.

[137] A friend of Roland who for several years had held a high post in the workshops. See account of him by Mathiez, *La vie chère*, pp. 262-270. It is odd that he had been able to hold his post after Roland's execution.

[138] Arch. Nat., F15, 3602.

[139] Six thousand pounds by 8 thermidor an IV. Much was given after that.

[140] Arch. Nat., F15, 3602. On 7 frimaire an V (Nov. 27, 1796) Cauchois protested that he had made five large shipments of cotton, the last for 1,420 livres, to Dupeuty, on orders from the minister of the interior, and declared that the stocks for the workshop were getting low. Dupeuty claimed to be doing charitable work in training these youth, of whom he had fifty-two in late prairial an IV. It was not unusual, however, for Frenchmen to exploit youth in the last decades of the eighteenth century under the pretense of giving charitable training.

[141] Parturier, *op. cit.*, p. 250.   [142] Martin-Doisy, *op. cit.*, I, 1267-1269.

CHAPTER XIV

PENSIONS AND GRATIFICATIONS

Before 1789

EVER SINCE the publication of the *Livre rouge* in 1790 by the National Assembly, the pension system of the Old Regime has borne an unsavory reputation. Prior to that date it was common knowledge that many persons through favor enjoyed pensions and gratifications, but no one had more than a shadowy knowledge of the number or size of the pensions, since no list had ever been published. The scholar Forbonnais estimated that in 1700 they amounted to 3,122,890 livres.[1] The controller-general Silhouette in 1759 reckoned them at 8,000,000;[2] later, Turgot estimated them at 14,000,000 to 15,000,000;[3] in his *Compte rendu au roi* of 1781 Necker placed them at 28,000,000, of which less than 8,000,000 were for military pensions, and less than 1,800,000 for naval and marine pensions. He also gave amazingly high figures for pensions enjoyed by members and close relatives of the royal family, and he doubted that all the other countries of Europe combined paid more than half the sum of 28,000,000 livres. He therefore urged the king to reduce the sum.[4] Later, in 1788, he admitted that he had been at least 3,200,000 livres too high in his earlier estimate.[5] Fleury in 1783 and Calonne in 1785 estimated them at 25,000,000, and ministers in 1786-87 reported them as having reached approximately 27,000,000.[6] The rapid rise in the amount of the expenditure occasionally gave alarm to the controllers-general, and steps were taken to curb and even

---

[1] He estimated that gratifications to troops reached an additional 1,807,009 livres (*Arch. parl.*, XVI, 621).

Vauban, in his *Projet d'une dixme royale* of 1706 (pp. 80-81), estimated salaries, pensions, and gratifications paid from the royal treasury at 40,000,000 livres, but did not make a specific estimate for pensions.

[2] He placed total government receipts at 286,547,037 livres (*Arch. parl.*, XVI, 622).

[3] In addition to 1,200,000 livres paid out for pension purposes under other designations (*ibid.*, XVI, 624).

[4] *Op. cit.*, pp. 27-28, 110-111.

[5] According to the pensions committee of 1789-90, the pensions of 1781 were really not above 25,593,303 livres (*Arch. parl.*, XVI, 626).

[6] *Ibid.*, XVI, 626-627.

reduce them in 1717 (by the council of regency), in 1759 (by Silhouette), in 1770 (by Terray), in 1775 (by Turgot), in 1778 (by Necker), in 1785 (by Calonne), and in 1787 (by the Assembly of Notables). In every instance, however, restraint was only momentary, and possibly the greatest result was the excitement of public suspicion that here was an abuse that needed removal.[7]

It was accordingly natural that the National Assembly should raise the pension question on September 22, 1789, and order the publication of the pension list. Nothing having been done toward the compilation of the list by December 31, 1789, the Assembly belatedly appointed a pensions committee, headed by Camus, and directed it to publish the pension list and offer proposals of revision. This committee went to work with vigor and determination. By chance the director-general of finance was then none other than Necker, who in 1790 interposed obstacles in the way of the committee by acceding with reluctance to its demands for information, out of fear that more harm than good would come from the publication at such a moment. Since the government had no single pension list, the committee compiled one with the help of the departments of war, marine, the royal household, foreign affairs, and finances. Each of these departments was ordered by the committee to submit its list from its own records of pensioners and recipients of gratifications. For three months or more the committee and the several governmental departments worked furiously at the task, gathering information on 22,090 pensions, not to speak of gratifications and other government gifts; and in April, 1790, the committee submitted and published the famous *Livre rouge*.[8]

The work, which took its name from its red binding, was loosely constructed. It gave under several headings government expenditures from 1774 through 1787 for pensions, gratifications, hospitals, and divers charitable ends. It also bared the correspondence between the pensions committee and the obstructive ministers, thus assuming a bellicose and propagandistic character. Consequently, the report created a national sensation. An avid public gazed and gaped at the

---

[7] See the excellent historical sketch in the first report of the pensions committee (*ibid.*, XVI, 621-627).

[8] *Le livre rouge, ou liste des pensions secrètes sur le trésor royal, contenant les noms et qualités des pensionnaires, l'état de leurs services, et des observations sur les motifs qui leur ont merité leur traitment* went through two printings in 1790, and later was published in the *Archives parlementaires* (XIII, 177-299).

abuses exposed, abuses to which the pensions committee took pains to call attention.

Undoubtedly there were abuses. The king's two brothers, Monsieur and the Count of Artois, had received from the royal treasury between the years 1774 and 1787 a total of 28,364,211 livres.[9] Eleven members of the distinguished and rich family of Ségur, as well as the marshal of this name, were entered on the list; the family received pensions and gratifications totaling more than 500,000 livres. In addition, the Comte de Ségur, a son of the marshal, had enjoyed a salary of 20,000 livres for five years.[10] The names of numerous members of the nobility, men and women, in favor at court, appeared on the list, some as recipients of pensions, others of gratifications, in large amounts. A gratification of 24,078 livres as a birth present went in 1778 to the Duc de Berri, and another of 100,000 in 1774 to the Comte de Vergennes for his "establishment."[11] Most of the government functionaries, such as governors of provinces, had on retirement been allowed substantial pensions. In general the higher the social rank, the higher the pension or gratification. Pensions and gratifications ranging from 40,000 to 100,000 livres were common for functionaries of high social rank, and were probably accorded more willingly by the government than many of the small pensions or gratifications of less than 1,000 livres.

While the number of favorites was large and the sum spent on them vast, by far the greater number of the pensionaries were recipients of small sums (less than 1,200 livres a year), which they had earned by faithful service in the armed forces of the nation, in a political or civil post, in invention, in teaching, or in a similar manner. In the *Etat nominatif des pensions sur le trésor royal*, submitted separately by the pensions committee to the National Assembly at the same time as the *Livre rouge*, the state pensions were listed in seven groups: those in the first comprised sums of 20,000 livres and above; those in the second ran from 8,000 to 20,000; those in the third, from 2,400 to 8,000; those in the fourth, from 1,800 to 2,400; those in the fifth, from 1,200 to 1,800; those in the sixth, from 600

[9] *Arch. parl.*, XIII, 179.

[10] *Ibid.*, XIII, 190-193. The Marshal de Ségur protested that this account was a misrepresentation. His protest, including a relation of his military services, was published in the *Livre rouge* (*ibid.*, XIII, 193-195).

[11] *Ibid.*, XIII, 181.

to 1,200; and those in the seventh, from 600 to less. To those in the first (and highest) class, only 11 pages of the *Archives parlementaires* were devoted; to those of the second, 48; to those of the third, 175; to those of the fourth, 82; to those of the fifth, 142; to those of the sixth, 346; and to those of the seventh, 710. The names in the last two categories, comprising those receiving pensions lower than 1,200 livres, thus required 1,056 pages, as against 458 pages required by those receiving more. Unfortunately the sums received by those in the last two categories totaled only 9,268,035 livres, as against 24,231,098 livres by those in the first five.[12]

By far the most numerous class of pensioners had served honorably in the armed forces of the nation, and been accorded pensions either for invalidity arising from wounds or sickness while in the course of duty or superannuation. According to the *Etat nominatif des pensions sur le trésor royal,* at least four fifths of the *pensionnaires* belonged to this category. The government of the Old Regime, following the precedents of Henry IV and Louis XIV, had on the whole taken care of its old soldiers and sailors, but in most instances the sums had not been generous or the payments had not been made on time. The government of the Old Regime was not lavish in any of its charities, and it was not uncommon for it to be slow in making payment of the sums accorded. Even so, it was more generous in caring for the sick, invalid, and superannuated soldiers and their families than in any other form of charity. The figures for pensioned soldiers and sailors were large in comparison to the grants for all other forms of charity, including hospitals and asylums. It was the policy of the government to grant a pension— generally no more than maintenance—to soldiers and sailors disabled by wounds or sickness while in service, and also to those who had served honorably over a long period of years. The length of service was not fixed: it might be twenty years, or more. Necker, and later the National Assembly, thought that more uniform regu-

[12] The sums received by the various groups were as follows: (1) 3,032,665 livres; (2) 6,750,458; (3) 9,260,929; (4) 2,313,860; (5) 2,873,186; (6) 4,455,- 173; and (7) 4,790,862. A note by the editors of the *Archives parlementaires* (XIII, 301) states that the figures of the *Etat nominatif* are here corrected and allegedly completed. Originally the *Etat nominatif* embraced 22,090 names, and listed pensions for a total of 29,252,874 livres (*ibid.*, XVI, 630). As revised by the editors, the number of names was carried above 27,000 and the total of pension payments to 33,499,133 livres.

lations ought to govern these pensions. The government also pensioned widows and children of veterans, passing on to them part or all of pensions that had been extended their husbands, fathers, brothers, or sons. In some instances (the line of demarcation was not clear) pensions were given to soldiers by provincial and municipal governments.[13] Most of the pensioned sailors, or at least 14,000 of them, were recipients in 1789 not of government funds but of payments from the chest of the "Invalids of the Marine," a pool administered by the government but formed by forced contributions from the paychecks of the seamen. The payments from this fund reached approximately 1,800,000 livres, according to De la Luzerne, minister of the marine.[14]

In 1790 the minister of war pointed out in his correspondence with the pensions committee two forms of military pensions: (1) those paid directly from the royal treasury, and received only in Paris and Switzerland,[15] and (2) those, of a smaller nature, paid in the provinces from the funds of the ministry of war. The first, he stated, were paid only once every fifteen to eighteen months; the second, which he described as for maintenance only, were paid every two months.[16] The distinction, of course, was small. Before 1779 the pension funds for the *maréchaussée* had come under the administration of war, but in 1779 they had been removed and were payable directly from the royal treasury.[17]

The National Assembly in 1790 criticized the government of the Old Regime for its failure to have a regular scale of payments

[13] One of the eighteen categories of pensions for which the pensions committee asked a list from De la Tour-du-Pin, minister of war, on January 30, 1790, was an "état nominatif des pensions accordées sur les gouvernements des provinces, de villes, châteaux, etc." (*ibid.*, XIII, 269).

[14] *Ibid.*, XIII, 276. Léon Vignols, in an article entitled "La caisse des invalides et les dilapidations gouvernementales du XVIIᵉ au XXᵉ siècle," *Revue d'histoire économique et sociale*, XXIII (Paris, 1937), 143-176, describes how this fund was created, and also how it was frequently plundered and diverted by eighteenth-century politicians. The cases of graft in connection with the charities of the eighteenth century appear to have been surprisingly few; and this instance of scandal, if it was as bad as Vignols asserts, was much the worst that has come to the present writer's attention. It is surprising, however, that, if it was plundered and diverted as badly as Vignols says, it could provide pension payments aggregating 1,800,000 livres a year.

[15] A treaty had been made with the Swiss government providing for this.

[16] *Arch. parl.*, XIII, 269, 272.

[17] *Ibid.*, XIII, 271.

to pensioners.[18] Pensions for the various ranks of the military had no definite ratios. One lieutenant general in the 1780's drew 14,000 livres in pensions; another 6,360.[19] One brigadier general *(marechal de camp)* received 18,468 livres, a second 8,000, a third 5,600, a fourth 3,600, a fifth 2,600.[20] One brigadier of cavalry received 8,016 livres, another 2,000.[21] One colonel received 12,000 livres, and a second 4,800, and a third 3,400.[22] One captain received 13,080 livres, a second 10,040, a third 7,000, a fourth 3,600, a fifth 2,000, and a sixth 300.[23] One lieutenant enjoyed 12,000 livres, a second 9,400, and a third 150.[24] For other ranks, such as lieutenant colonel, major, and second lieutenant *(sous-lieutenant)*, the same wild fluctuation in figures prevailed. In fact, the amount of the pension to an officer depended upon the king and the minister of the department whose funds were affected, in most cases the minister of war. The king had the power, if he chose, to suspend a pension temporarily or permanently. Family prominence, and doubtless also personal acquaintance with the king and minister, were factors responsible for the higher pensions. There was probably no basic gradation according to rank; if so, the exceptions were too numerous.

There were similar fluctuations among the many noncommissioned officers and privates, whose names rarely appeared in the *Etat nominatif des pensions sur le trésor royal.* Apparently their names were kept on provincial, and not on the national, records. One bugler received 582 livres, a second 400, and a third 147.[25] In 1776 four retired sergeants in Champagne drew variously 15 and 18 livres a month.[26] In 1764-65 eighty-five invalid soldiers were re-

---

[18] The pensions committee charged that pensions had been bestowed under the Old Regime with "a blind and prodigal liberality" *(ibid.,* XVI, 617).

[19] Cases of Du Darut de Grand-Pré and Vaucresson de Commainville *(ibid.,* XIII, 336 and 539). Each enjoyed three pensions.

[20] Cases of Vintimille, Wimpffen, Basset, Ferrier du Châtelet, and Fumel *(ibid.,* XIII, 367, 368, 381, 438, and 443). Wimpffen was a member of the pensions committee.

[21] *Ibid.,* XIII, 348, 550.

[22] Cases of Lascaris, Belloy, and Fulques *(ibid.,* XIII, 348, 384, and 443).

[23] Cases of Baglion, Alsace, Fours de Fors, Bazin, Amabert, and Jean Stuart *(ibid.,* XIII, 323, 322, 442, 381, 550; XV, 192).

[24] Cases of Du Plessis-Richelieu, Hérissy de Vaussieux, and Tastes *(ibid.,* XIII, 337, 344; XV, 195).

[25] The names of the first two were Sturm and Tripoli *(ibid.,* XV, 192, 213). The third is unnamed, and his pension is dated 1776 *(Inv.-som . . . Ardennes,* C 185).

[26] *Ibid.,* C 185.

tired in their homes in Champagne on half pay *(demi-solde)* of 3 sous a day, and fourteen others on 4 sous a day.[27] All invalid soldiers retired on half pay, apparently whatever their rank, were given a uniform once every four years.[28] Of course it was not easy for invalid soldiers to live on 3 sous a day. Sergeants could have lived on their pensions; commissioned officers should have found it fairly comfortable, unless addicted to extravagance. Considering the multitudinous names of pensioners of all nationalities (apparently a fifth or sixth of the French army consisted of foreigners), one is impressed not by the abuses but by the paternalism of the French state, which on the whole cared faithfully, and often handsomely, for its old and crippled veterans. Here the government of the Old Regime displayed its greatest generosity.

Sometimes a single action of bravery or heroism won a soldier or officer a gratification or a pension. Thus Jean Marbotin, an army captain, was awarded a pension of 300 livres in 1783 because of his heroic conduct aboard the vessel *Scipio*.[29] A young lieutenant in the royal engineering corps, Florian de Plamcher, was given a pension of 300 livres for distinction in the battle of the Chesapeake, March 16, 1781, and for a wound received at the siege of Yorktown.[30]

Naval as well as military officers received pensions, but they were naturally fewer in numbers. According to the *Etat nominatif*, one naval pension was given for every twenty-five or thirty military pensions. The highest naval pensions went, unfortunately, to the naval political figures—the minister of the marine and the intendants of the marine, the latter stationed in the port cities of France. Sartine, the minister, drew a pension of 86,720 livres.[31] The marine intendants, of whom there were perhaps a dozen, drew pensions varying from 20,000 to 8,000 livres each.[32] Strangely enough, no

[27] These rates were equivalent to 54 and 73 livres a year, respectively (*ibid.*, C 174). In Guyenne the *demi-solde* was 72 livres; the full *solde*, 126 (*Inv.-som . . . Gironde*, C 3726).

[28] Mention is made of uniforms being given privates, noncommissioned officers, and lieutenants. They were given by the royal Hotel des Invalides (*Inv.-som . . . Ardennes*, C 172-176).

[29] *Ibid.*, XV, 12.

[30] *Ibid.*, XV, 103.

[31] This was even more than the pension of 83,300 livres accorded the Marechal de Ségur, former minister of war (*ibid.*, XIII, 316-317).

[32] One Aubenton drew 20,000, Bourgeois de Guedreville 12,000, Guillot 10,200, and Clouet 8,000 (*ibid.*, XIII, 307, 328, 343, and 333).

admirals appeared on the list; but there were a few commodores and many captains. The pensions for commodores ranged from 9,000 livres to 1,500,[33] those for captains from 12,000 to 1,200.[34] Naval lieutenants were pensioned variously from 1,500 livres to 300.[35] On the pension list also appeared the names of various captains, lieutenants, and ensigns of the East India Company service, whose pensions were smaller than those of the navy.[36] No enlisted men either for the navy or the merchant marine appeared on the government pension list. Perhaps no one was pensioned until he became invalid, and then he was pensioned not on government funds but on the government-controlled private funds of the Invalids of the Marine. On this fund were pensioned sailors of both the navy and the merchant marine.

Louis XIV had set up this fund and determined its direction. Having done much for military invalids, he wished to do something also for those of the navy. By an ordinance of April 15, 1670, he set up these pensions, ordering that 2 écus (6 livres) a month be paid to them for life. At first designed only for sailors of the navy, the fund was quickly extended to benefit sailors of the merchant marine, those of the corsairs, and around 1709 the intendants and other officers of ports and marine arsenals. Pensions at half pay were even extended to dockyard workers. Louis wished that all these services be provided for at one-half the highest pay received in the latest phase of service. Four deniers per livre of pay for the navy, six for the merchant marine, were paid into the fund during the eighteenth century by seamen, officers, and workers, from cabin boy

---

[33] To give an incomplete list, one Bory received 9,000, Boutier 6,000, Boscal de Réals 4,208, Aubert de Courserac 3,954, Beauharnois 3,708, Baraudin 3,600, Albert de St. Hypolite 2,154, and Faùtras 1,500 (*ibid.*, XIII, 327, 395, 393, 376, 382, 379, 550, and 682).

[34] Roux got 12,000 livres, Boisgelin de Kergomar 10,604, Fougeroux de Secval 6,600, Belleville l'Etendart 4,000, Bigot 3,600, Mine 3,000, Beaucaire 2,690, Bégon 2,072, and Darnaud 1,200 (*ibid.*, XIII, 329, 327, 441, 384, 389, 495, 382, 555, 666). The average pension for naval captains ranged from 3,000 to 3,600 livres.

[35] Duclos was pensioned at 1,500 livres, Ferron de Quengo (and certain others) at 1,200, Petersen at 300 (*ibid.*, XIII, 695, 683, 691, 693; XV, 92). Petersen was a young Swede, pensioned (in 1782) for his heroism and wounds in the siege of Pensacola.

[36] For instance, one Mazière, a captain, received only 500 livres; a widow Morphy, whose husband had been a captain, received 300 livres; the widow Mocheron, whose husband had been a lieutenant, received 200; Marion de Chenevert, a first ensign, received 150; Morphy, an ensign, received 150 (*ibid.*, XV, 28, 53, 17).

to captain. The fund was further augmented by the proceeds of wrecks and prizes taken at sea.

The pension fund looked well on paper, but, according to Léon Vignols, worked out poorly in practice. Down to 1722 very little was paid out because of lack of funds; and even afterwards, for considerable periods of the eighteenth century, there was a shortage of funds, because money was diverted from this fund to meet other financial demands faced by the government. According to Vignols, plundering was rife during the years 1726-43 and 1744-89. In spite of Turgot's attempt to restore order, the fund was short-lived. Besides the abuse of diverting the funds to other ends, large sums were granted to persons who in some instances had nothing to do with the navy or merchant marine. Prior to 1772 pensions amounting even to 6,000 or 10,000 livres were paid from this fund to courtesans and others not in the maritime service. In an attempt to stop the abuse an order of the council of state on February 28, 1772, stipulated that for the future no pensions exceeding 1,000 livres should be paid from this fund, and that when it was low the payment of pensions of sailors should take precedence over all other calls on it. Apparently even this attempt did not prevent abuse, for later, in the 1770's, Countess D'Amblimont and Mlle Dandeville, mistresses, were on the pension list. The *cahiers* from Marseilles, Dunkirk, and other ports in 1789 severely complained of the failure of the crippled and needy sailors to receive their pensions either entire or on time, and urged an improvement in the pension system.[37]

To the widows and children of naval officers and seamen the government gave pensions, just as it did to those of the military. The widow of Vice-Admiral Bauffremont, the Princess of Listenois, was recipient of a pension of 8,000 livres;[38] the widow of Captain Prépaud was given 400 livres.[39] Throughout the years 1779-82

[37] Vignols, *op. cit.*, XXIII, 143-181. Vignols does not give figures on the misappropriations or estimate how large they were. He does not cite manuscript sources. He does not hint that the funds were stolen: he merely charges that they were diverted to other government ends.

[38] *Arch. parl.*, XIII, 324.

[39] In 1753 Prépaud was killed by the dey of Algiers following a naval clash with the Algerians, an episode that produced a tense situation between France and Algeria (*Inventaire des archives historiques de la Chambre de Commerce de Marseille*, Marseilles, 1878, AA, arts. 65-66 with n.).

(during the war with Great Britain) the French government sent 200 livres or more monthly to three curés in Dieppe for distribution among the poor families of sailors in their parishes. In June, 1782, this appropriation was reduced to 100 livres a month.[40]

Sometimes pensions and gratifications were granted to naval men by provinces and cities. In the late 1750's the Estates of Brittany extended a pension of 1,000 livres to a naval ensign named Poulain, who in an encounter with the British in August, 1756, lost a leg and was carried prisoner to England.[41] In 1782 the city of Marseilles gave a bonus of 300,000 livres to the families of sailors from Provence who had lost their lives in the War for American Independence. Of this grant, 200,000 livres went to the families of Marseillais sailors, and 100,000 livres to the families of sailors from the rest of Provence. Other cities followed the example of Marseilles.[42] The Bordeaux chamber of commerce in 1782 voted a grant of 100,000 livres for distribution to the widows and orphans of seamen from Bordeaux and Guyenne who had lost their lives in the war. The sum of 280 livres 18 sous was given to each widow and orphan; but the distribution was slow, and not until 1789 were all the payments made.[43]

All retired or invalid officers and men of both army and navy, and their widows, were exempt from payment of the *taille* and the

[40] Much correspondence on the matter, between De Crosne, intendant of Rouen, and three curés of Dieppe (the curé du Pollet, the curé de St. Jacques, and the curé de St. Remy) is found in Arch. de la Seine-Inférieure, C 1007. See in particular letters of Nov. 9, 1779, June 3, 6, 11, and 12, 1782, and Dec. 22, 1782. In January, 1779, the government sent 300 livres to this end, in February 550, in April 200, in May 600, in June 200. Learning that the Cardinal de la Rochefoucauld had sent 600 livres, the government reduced its aid to 200 livres a month in order to extend the same form of aid to other cities in desperate circumstances. However, in a letter of June 12, 1782, De Crosne states that Dieppe was the only city in the generality receiving this form of aid, although St. Valery, Fécamp, and many other parishes along the coast had equal need of it. That the aid was rendered by the government, rather than by the province, is indicated by De Crosne's letters of June 11 and 12, 1782, to the curé du Pollet and the Abbé Perisse, respectively.

[41] *Inv.-som . . . Ille-et-Villaine*, C 3904.

[42] *Inv.-som . . . Bouches-du-Rhône*, C 1007, 1369, 2501; *Inventaire des archives départmentales postérieures à 1789 . . . Bouches-du-Rhône*, L III, 7. Whether the entire 100,000 voted to be distributed to the families in Provence was spent in entirety is not clear. Register C 1369 (p. 296) of the former work speaks of 85,064 livres having been sent, but says nothing of the rest.

[43] Arch. de la Gironde, C 2494-98. The General Assembly of the clergy in 1782 voted to give 1,000,000 livres to sailors wounded in the war, and to the widows and orphans of those killed (*Inv.-som . . . Calvados*, C 92).

capitation.[44] Since these taxes fell even upon the very poor, relief from them, as many applications for aid in the eighteenth century reveal, was always welcomed. Sometimes an old soldier was given a small job about a hospital or other civic institution.[45] Sometimes a soldier who had served in the army long enough to obtain government maintenance in a hospital because of invalidity was sent to the hospital of his native city, to be cared for at the expense of that institution. A grenadier of the Poitou regiment, for example, was returned by the intendant of Rouen to Lisieux, the soldier's home, to be cared for by the hospital there. Transportation was furnished by the intendant, but the expense of his maintenance in Lisieux was to fall upon the hospital.[46] A soldier or army officer might in distress apply to the nearest intendant for help. In the 1760's Lebret, intendant of Brittany, made a monetary advance to an invalid lieutenant, retired on a pension of 200 livres, who found himself without funds and was unable to support his wife and children.[47]

After the army and navy, the second largest group of pensioners included politicians and civil servants. In this large and heterogeneous group were ministers of state, governors and intendants of provinces, intendants of the ports, members of the parlements, retired subdelegates, royal councilors, procurer-syndics, consuls to foreign cities, dragomen, tax assistants, and others. Those most highly favored were naturally the ministers of state and the provincial governors, who commonly were of high birth and in many instances drew large pensions. Besides the ministers Sartine and Ségur, who received 86,720 and 83,300 livres respectively, there were many others: Amelot, secretary of state, who received 52,000 livres; Ber-

---

[44] *Inv.-som . . . Bouches-du-Rhône,* C 76 (f 37 v), 1017; *Inv.-som . . . Ardennes,* C 240; Arch. de la Gironde, C 61 (letter from Esmangart to the Duc D'Aiguillon, Feb. 26, 1774); A. Dupuy, "L'administration municipale en Bretagne au XVIIIᵉ siècle," *Annales de Bretagne,* IV (Rennes, 1888), 92; Isambert, *op. cit.,* XXIII, 484. A letter by Dausseville, subdelegate at Dieppe, to De Crosne, intendant at Rouen, April 18, 1779, reveals that sailors and their widows were exempted from the *taille,* that the parents of sailors were exempted from half the sum of their *taille,* and that consideration was also given to all former sailors. The letter indicates, furthermore, that persons other than sailors connected with the royal marine were to share in this remission (Arch. de la Seine-Inférieure, C 1005).

[45] Thus on April 17, 1775, the administrators of the General Hospital of Grenoble decided to employ an old soldier in the role of porter (*Inv.-som . . . l'hôpital de Grenoble,* E 24).

[46] *Inv.-som . . . Seine-Inférieure,* C 784.

[47] *Inv.-som . . . Ille-et-Vilaine,* C 1095.

tin, former secretary of state and controller-general of finance, 69,000 livres; Calonne, former controller-general of finance, 42,853 livres; Miromesnil, guard of the seals, 67,080 livres; and Le Tonnelier (Baron de Breteuil), minister of state and ambassador to various countries, 91,729 livres.[48] Not all ministers of state were so highly favored. Malesherbes and others, for example, received smaller sums. Governors of provinces, usually military men of high rank, were pensioned at sums often running from 24,000 to 33,000 livres.[49] Intendants of provinces, slightly less favored, commonly received pensions ranging from 4,000 livres to 29,000.[50] Governors of cities, who like the governors of provinces were aristocrats and military men of high rank, were often recipients of high pensions. Choiseul de Beaune, lieutenant general of Champagne and governor of Verdun, received 30,368 livres; Montmorin, lieutenant general and governor of Belle-Isle, 36,000; and Franquetot, lieutenant general and governor of the cities of Cambrai and Caen, 50,750.[51]

Officials of the parlements fell in the favored class and received pensions that commonly ran from 8,000 livres to 30,000.[52] So, too, did councilors of state, who generally held other government posts concurrently, and various types of intendants, other than those of the provinces, such as intendants of commerce, of finance, of the marine, of the colonies. Albert, councilor of state and lieutenant general of police at Paris, received the high pension of 27,000 livres, while Brunyer, another councilor of state and consultant physician of the French armies and the royal children, was given the modest sum of 4,000 livres.[53] Ambassadors were commonly well pensioned:

[48] *Arch. parl.*, XIII, 307-317.

[49] Beauvais, governor of Provence and Caillebot, and Marquis de la Salle, governor of La Marche, each received 24,000 livres; the Duc du Châtelet, governor-general of the region of Toul, received 28,500 livres; and the Marquis de Contades, governor-general of Lorraine, received 33,000 livres (*ibid.*, XIII, 307-309).

[50] Caze de la Bove, intendant of Brittany, for example, received only 4,000 livres; Agay, of Amiens, 8,000; Feydeau de Brou, of Caen, 12,480; Sénac de Meilhan, of Hainaut, 21,000; Des Gallois de la Tour, of Provence, 22,720; and Chaumont de la Galaizière, of Alsace, 29,000 (*ibid.*, XIII, 405, 321, 339, 316, 309, and 308).

[51] *Ibid.*, XIII, 309, 313, 310. Rohan, governor of Nîmes, however, received only 22,170 livres; and La Croix, governor of Montpellier, only 12,000 (*ibid.*, XIII, 315 and 311).

[52] Blondel and Barentin each 8,000 livres, Etienne 11,000, Du Mardy de Catuélan 18,000, and Aligre 30,000 (*ibid.*, XIII, 327, 324, 338, 337, and 307).

[53] *Ibid.*, XIII, 307 and 399. As for the various types of specialized intendants, Dubuq, intendant of colonies, received 20,000 livres; Thomassin, intendant of Mar-

Gravier, Marquis de Vergennes, ambassador to various countries, was rewarded with pensions amounting to 28,242 livres; Guignard, Comte de Saint-Priest, for his services as ambassador to the Porte and to Holland, was accorded 30,590 livres (although this pension was suspended while he held the portfolio and drew the salary of minister of state in the government); the Comte d'Adhemar de Montfalcon, formerly an ambassador, drew a pension of 16,000 livres; and the Baron de Choiseul, former ambassador to the court at Turin, was the recipient of a pension of 8,000 livres.[54]

Officials of lower rank, assistants, secretaries, bookkeepers, were commonly rewarded with pensions after long years of service. In this class, too, came consuls and dragomen. Brochier, French consul-general at Lisbon for twenty-seven years, was retired on a pension of 5,000 livres.[55] The widow Simian, whose husband had been French vice-consul at the Dardanelles, was pensioned in 1776 at 600 livres.[56] The widow and four children of Roustan, French dragoman at Constantinople who died of the plague, were allowed a pension of 12,000 livres.[57] The widow La Braze, whose husband had been dragoman at Salonika, was given, however, a pension of only 800 livres, which after her death was to be passed on to her daughter but diminished to 400 livres.[58] Brumauld de Beauregard, former subdelegate-general of the intendancy of Poitiers, was recipient of a pension of 3,160 livres.[59] Broucaret, former secretary to the intendants at Auch and Bordeaux, and later to the controller-general, drew 4,800 livres; Auzillon, former secretary to the keeper of seals, 6,000 livres.[60] Bourdin, head clerk under Bertin, was rewarded after forty-five years' service with a pension of 5,000 livres.[61]

---

tinique, 20,000; Aubenton, intendant of the marine and councilor of state, 20,000; Farges, intendant of finance and councilor of state, 15,000; and Chaumont de la Millière, intendant of the departments of bridges and highways and of hospitals, 8,000 (*ibid.*, XIII, 309, 317, 307, 338, and 331). Millière was in his forties when he was pensioned (1781 and 1786).

[54] *Ibid.*, XIII, 310, 321, 332.

[55] *Ibid.*, XIII, 397.

[56] *Ibid.*, XV, 183; *Inv.-som . . . Bouches-du-Rhône*, C 2498. This latter source records many pensions and gratifications, several of which were given to consuls and dragomen.

[57] *Inventaire des archives historiques de la Chambre de Commerce de Marseille*, AA art. 100.

[58] *Inv.-som . . . Bouches-du-Rhône*, C 2498.

[59] *Arch. parl.*, XIII, 398.   [60] *Ibid.*, XIII, 398, 394; XIV, 16.

[61] *Ibid.*, XIII, 395.

Collet, inspector of the royal buildings at Versailles, was accorded a pension of 2,000 livres; Dupuis, after thirty years' service as inspector of police at Paris, one of 1,200 livres; and Colombier, inspector-general of the hospitals and *maisons de force* of the kingdom, was given, as supplement to his salary, "in consideration of zeal and the distinction with which he fills the functions of this place," a pension of 5,000 livres.[62] For all those injured or grown gray in the service of the administration of bridges and highways, thanks to the efforts of Trudaine, pensions existed.[63] Widows also benefited. The eighty-three-year-old widow Vimar, whose husband had been an engineer in this administration,[64] drew a pension of 500 livres.

A third general group of pensioners, though very much smaller than either of the two already described, were ecclesiastics. Among the heterogeneous recipients were small groups of ex-Jesuits, priests, friars, nuns, and Jewish and Protestant converts to Catholicism. Since the Catholic church was the state church in France, at least until the period of the Revolution, it was supported financially by the state, both for its work within France and for its missions abroad. No other church or faith (until 1787) had legal recognition save in Alsace. The Catholic church therefore was in a very real sense a department of the state, and if pensions were given to civil servants it was but natural that they should be given also to faithful servants of the church who were superannuated or in need.[65]

[62] *Ibid.*, XIII, 568, 677, 413.   [63] *Oeuvres de Turgot*, II, 252 n.

[64] Indeed, every branch of government service apparently had a recognized, though perhaps vague, "system" of pensions for its employees, from ministers to porters, from first presidents to clerks. Hundreds, possibly thousands, of names occur on the pages of the *Etat nominatif des pensions*. Some of the entries for the smaller pensions are as interesting as those for the larger. Everyone having acquaintance with French history is aware that the courtiers and favorites received large pensions; it is not so well known that porters, secretaries, clerks, postmen, stagecoach assistants, and others of this level were given pensions as well. Perhaps the most impressive fact is not the scandal of large pensions but the vast number of public servants, military, naval, police, administrative, judicial, who were rewarded with pensions, some during, but a larger number at the termination of, their period of service.

[65] It is surprising, in fact, that more names in this category do not appear on the *Etat nominatif des pensions*; the list is far from complete. The explanation is that there was a special pension list for ecclesiastics, not included in the *Etat nominatif*, carrying a total of 2,500,000 livres, based on a portion of the *dîme*. See below, p. 342. According to Camus, chairman of the pensions committee, many insane, disabled, and aged clergymen were so pensioned (*Arch. parl.*, XXI, 120-121). The line of demarcation between those pensioned on this fund and those of the five other funds, however, is vague, for priests and members of religious orders were pensioned in both groups.

The Ursulines and the Brothers of the Christian Schools also received considerable pensions or benefactions from the government to support their teaching, yet only a few Ursulines, and no Brothers of the Christian Schools, were given pensions for themselves.[66] Once in a while a nun, often a Protestant convert to Catholicism, was benefited. There were still others, some superannuated, some teachers, some nurses or hospital officials. The awards varied from 100 livres, enjoyed by Marie Vatblé, a superannuated Carmelite nun at Abbéville, aged seventy-two, to 400 livres received by Marie Françoise Cassegrain, aged fifty-nine, for her excellent work at the Hospice de Charité in Paris.[67]

An occasional priest was a pension recipient, nor was he always aged. Fosserier, only thirty-three years old, drew a pension of 200 livres as chaplain of the Bastille;[68] and Jean Pompard, forty-seven, 571 livres as chaplain to Madame Sophie of the royal family.[69] Older pensioners were Mathieu Berthe, seventy-three, and Jean Gendre, seventy-two, pensioned at 180 and 240 livres, respectively, as retired almoners at the hospital for the galley slaves at Marseilles.[70]

A small number of ex-Jesuits in France and at missionary work in the French colonies were pensioned. In 1761 the work of the Jesuits in France was stopped and their assets were "frozen"; after a long court trial they were at length, in 1764, by royal order expelled from the country and their property was confiscated by the state.[71] The government then offered a pension to those who cared

---

[66] *Inv.-som . . . Ille-et-Vilaine*, C 596, records the fact that five Brothers of the Christian Schools received pensions of 400 livres each by the state's agreement with them in 1783.

[67] *Arch. parl.*, XV, 222; XIV, 473. Other recipients were: Madeline Viger, aged thirty-three, 150 livres; Catherine Vignial, forty-five, 200 livres; Marthe Aubie, twenty-nine, 150 livres; Suzanne Bienfait, seventy-six, 120 livres; Nicole de Bresson, sixty-six, 300 livres; Marie Chaussade de Jolimont, thirty-two, 200 livres; Marie Julie Cosette, sixty-six, 300 livres; Adelaide Esmangart de Beauval, fifty-eight, 250 livres; and Geneviève Henri, fifty-one, 250 livres (*ibid.*, XV, 231; XIV, 370, 415, 447, 491, 523, 598, 687). It is possible that the two or three youngest nuns were Protestant proselytes, as the government did not commonly endow Catholic-born girls entering upon their religious duties in a convent, whereas it did in the instance of Protestant-born girls and women.

[68] *Ibid.*, XIV, 621.

[69] *Ibid.*, XIV, 425.

[70] *Ibid.*, XIV, 408, 645.

[71] An interesting and unbiased account of the affair can be found by James Breck Perkins, *France under Louis XV* (Boston and New York, 1897), II, chap. xvii.

to remain in France if they would renounce their ties to the society. Of the four thousand Jesuits in France at the time of the expulsion, "hardly five submitted" to the offer, according to a Jesuit historian.[72] Six ex-Jesuits, all retired or engaged in missionary work in the French colonies of India or the New World, received pensions varying from 300 to 500 livres a year.[73] The ex-Jesuit Le Gué had formerly drawn a pension of 400 livres, and his family tried to get it re-established.[74] These, however, were but a few of those pensioned, if we may believe Goupil de Prefeln, who reported for the pensions committee on June 27, 1790, to the Assembly that the Jesuits were annually accorded pensions amounting to 206,000 livres.[75]

By far the most numerous recipients of religious pensions, as revealed by the *Etat nominatif,* were the "newly converted" to Catholicism. About nine in ten of these were women, and almost all of them came from Protestant ranks; rarely was there a Jew or Jewess. The pensions of the Catholic converts, of whom there were probably sixty or seventy,[76] varied widely. Jean de Chateauvieux, aged forty-one, received 500 livres.[77] Louis de Bourbers, aged eighty-four, received 500 livres, not because of his own conversion, but because of his mother's conversion and his need of money.[78] When Jean Jacques Denis, aged fifty-one, was converted, he received only 50 livres a year.[79] Thus while on the whole men were given

[72] Father Thomas J. Campbell, *The Jesuits, 1534-1921: A History of the Society of Jesus from its Foundation to the Present Time,* II (New York, 1921), 496. He says that the pension was offered by the parlement of Paris and consisted of only thirty cents a day, while in Languedoc this was cut down to twelve cents a day (*ibid.,* II, 485-486).

[73] *Etat nominatif des pensions* in 1790. Bonnecamp, aged eighty-three, 500 livres, for missions in Canada; Bourget, sixty-three, 400 livres, for missions in Martinique; Carpentier, sixty-nine, 300 livres, for missions at Cayenne; Ruel, seventy-four, 450 livres, for work at Cayenne; Schaack, sixty-two, 400 livres, for work in Martinique; and Vernet de Marqueysset, sixty-three, 500 livres, for work at Pondicherry (*ibid.,* XIV, 428, 439, 471; XV, 158, 173, 227).

[74] *Inv.-som . . . Ille-et-Vilaine,* C 86. Whether he, like the others, was engaged in missions is not indicated.

[75] *Arch. parl.,* XVI, 508.

[76] The present writer found close to forty names in little more than half of the list.

[77] *Arch. parl.,* XIV, 489.

[78] *Ibid.,* XIV, 432. He was perhaps the only pensioner who obtained aid on someone else's conversion. However, in the instance of widow Tessier de la Roche, a pension of 200 livres was given for changing her religion and "marrying a Catholic of long standing" (*ibid.,* XV, 198).

[79] *Ibid.,* XIV, 541.

the higher pensions on the ground of conversion, they were not so favored in every instance. Most of the pensions to women for this cause carried 150 livres, though in not a few only 120 livres. Occasionally they brought 200 livres;[80] in one instance, 300;[81] and in another, only 50.[82] One woman of eighty-three, Anne Boit de Crèvecour, was allowed a pension of 300 livres because her father, after coming to France from England and becoming a Catholic, had died without funds.[83] None of the *pensionnaires* of this type on the *Etat nominatif* were younger than twenty, while often they were quite old. Most of their pensions were drawn on the funds of the king's household *(maison du roi)*; some, on the funds of the department of finances; at least one on those of war; and one on those of foreign affairs.[84] As a matter of fact, the *Etat nominatif* perhaps included only half of those who drew pensions because of their conversion to Catholicism.[85]

[80] Instances of Marguerite Champeaux, Thérèse Deonnat, Marie Guillienne-Levy, Françoise Vassol, Catherine Vilhelmy.

[81] Case of Henriette de Berghan (*ibid.*, XIV, 405).

[82] Case of Marie Viol (*ibid.*, XIV, 230).

[83] *Ibid.*, XIV, 425.

[84] According to the *Arch. parl.*, XVI, 655, the *nouvelles convertis* were getting 70,000 livres in pensions in 1789, and the *nouveaux convertis* 104,359 livres. A spokesman for the committee, however, indicated a total of only 104,350 livres (*ibid.*, XVI, 508).

[85] This conclusion is supported by results derived from the list with the names of pensioners found in the *Inventaires-sommaires des archives départmentales antérieures à 1790* and in manuscripts of the Archives départmentales at Bordeaux. The pensions in question fall within the time limit of 1773-87 covered by the *Etat nominatif*. Less than half of the names checked appear on this published list. These are the names checked: Etienne Bonny, Lally de Boursel, Mlle de Charon, Anne Laurent Davignon, Lucie Guethin, Mlle Lecomte, widow Luguet and two daughters, Jeanne Monboucher, Jeanne and Marie Monnes, Thérèse Poisson de Coudreville, and Marie Villeponteux. Of these fourteen, only four appear on the published and supposedly completed list of the *Etat nominatif des pensions* in the *Archives parlementaires*. Of the others, it can be said that Etienne Bonny was accorded in 1779 an annual pension of 200 livres until completion of his education as a Catholic priest. A similar pension had been allowed his older brother, Pierre, who in 1779 was professor of philosophy at Périguex. Both had been Protestant-born (Bertin to Dupré de Saint-Maur, Sept. 5, 1779, Arch. de la Gironde, C 2512). Mlle de Charon was given an annual gratification in 1779 for her education in the convent of the Filles de la Foy at Périguex (Bertin to Dupré de Saint-Maur, Nov. 14, 1779, *ibid.*, C 2512). Mlle Lecomte was given a pension at first of 120, and later of 150 livres, in 1777 (*Inv.-som . . . Calvados*, C 1650). In 1783 the government promised pensions of 60 livres to the widow Luguet, and of 20 livres to each of her two daughters, beginning 1784, in view of their abjuration of Calvinism and espousal of Catholicism, and because of their financial need (Marville to Vergennes, Jan. 11, 1783, Arch. de la Gironde, C 2510). In 1786 Jeanne Monboucher was given a pension of 150 livres to support her in the convent of the Dames de la Foy of

According to various sources, the other half, although they received amounts similar to those listed in the *Etat nominatif*, were given pensions for a particular reason. In repressing Protestantism, the government allotted pensions to youths who carried on a zealous proselyting activity in behalf of its program.[86] On the complaint of any priest or neighbor, a *lettre de cachet* was issued for the arrest of a Protestant child, who was then taken from his parents and placed in a convent for rearing as a Catholic.[87] Employing persuasion and subtlety as well as force and zeal, the government thus effected conversions of Calvinists to Catholicism. In most instances, as a prerequisite for a pension, the "newly converted" was required to enter a convent or a theological school and after his training to go to work proselytizing other members of his family,[88] old friends, and children, since it was believed that he had a marked advantage over other Catholics in work with Protestants.

The zeal of the authorities to make converts was rivaled by the cupidity of the applicants for pensions. For every applicant given a pension probably two or three were rejected. Almost every applicant, whether accepted or rejected, made the plea of poverty. Probably the desire to get a "bread-ticket" was a large factor in many of the "conversions." The poor ninety-year-old widow Luguet, with six children, two of whom were daughters serving as domestics,[89] was so desperate that she was easily "converted." Strangely

Agenois (Vergennes to Dupré de Saint-Maur, May 11, 1786, *ibid.*, C 2515). Jeanne and Marie Monnes in 1779 were accorded a pension of 200 livres formerly enjoyed by their mother as a "newly-converted." They themselves entered a convent at Beaumont with the purpose of becoming Catholics (letters of March 16, April 7, and June 11, 1779, *ibid.*, C 2512). In 1779 one Marie Villepontoux, aged ninety, a recent convert to Catholicism, finding herself deserted by her family and in dire need, was granted a pension of 150 livres, payment to begin in August of that year. Feeling that this was not enough, Dupré de Saint-Maur, the intendant, wrote his subdelegate, Biram, at Bergerac, to give her an additional 75 livres because of her great need (letter of Sept. 8, 1779; also letter to Bertin, Sept. 23, 1779, *ibid.*, C 2512).

[86] The correspondence in the Archives départementales at Bordeaux made this very clear, but the great numbers of *liasses* and *cartons* on the subject in the *Inventaires-sommaires des archives départementales antérieures à 1790*, listed under "Newly-Converted" and "Lettres de Cachet," reveal the fact more clearly.

[87] Scores, doubtless hundreds, of such instances are to be found in the *Inventaires-sommaires*. This was only part of a policy of repression of Protestantism in general.

[88] In many cases sisters were converted.

[89] Her husband had been an army officer. It is surprising that she did not enjoy a pension on the funds of the department of war.

enough, many fathers besought this aid for their children.[90] Of course the intendants and the officials in charge of the king's household realized that many of the applications were fraudulent. Accordingly, they waited two or three years until the conversion was genuine and they had obtained evidence from a priest or mother superior who held the applicant under observation. Even then the "converted" sometimes lapsed, and the pension had to be revoked. The intendant De Crosne in Normandy wrote in 1777 that one pensioner had left the convent to get married but scandalously still drew her pension.[91] From the time of the Revocation of the Edict of Nantes to the eve of the Revolution, these pensions existed.[92]

In some instances gratifications rather than pensions were bestowed. Thus Marie Rocher, converted in 1773 at Caen, void of funds and deserted by her parents, was given in 1778 a gratification of 600 livres.[93]

In some cases Jews and Jewesses were beneficiaries. Bernard and Joseph Mendès, Jews, aged fifty and thirty respectively, and Jeanne Mezes, Jewess, aged fifty-nine, were recipients of pensions according to the *Etat nominatif*.[94] One "Jew" who pretended to be interested in conversion to Catholicism so aroused the suspicion of the intendant that he and the girl with whom he was touring France were jailed. Then it was discovered that he was neither a Frenchman nor a Jew, but a Hollander with an assumed name, and that his alleged wife and four children at Nantes did not exist.[95]

Louis XIV offered freedom to Algerian slaves in the French galleys who became genuine converts to Catholicism.[96] During the late sixteenth and the seventeenth centuries quite a few Turks and

[90] Several instances were found in the manuscript material examined at Bordeaux.

[91] *Inv.-som . . . Calvados*, C 1650.

[92] Boislisle, in his *Correspondance des contrôleurs généraux* (II, No. 780), reproduces some material on the subject. One letter of April 4, 1705, from D'Ormesson, intendant at Soissons, to the controller-general of finance, tells of a widow who had drawn a pension of 400 livres for twenty years on the grounds of conversion and blindness. At length it had been discovered that the woman was not blind but had been practising fraud.

[93] *Inv.-som . . . Calvados*, C 1642.

[94] *Arch. parl.*, XV, 31, 37. One Marie Anne Froment, Jewess, wife of Thomas Froment, applied for a pension as a "newly converted" in 1776 (*Inv.-som . . . Calvados*, C 1638), but her name does not appear on the *Etat nominatif des pensions;* accordingly, it is uncertain whether her request was approved.

[95] *Inv.-som . . . Calvados*, C 675.

[96] *Inv.-som . . . Charente-Inférieure*, C 154. They were called "Turcs d'Alger."

Algerians in France were converted to Christianity, some by Protestants, more by Catholics; one became a monk, another a priest.[97] Even in the eighteenth century there occurred some Turkish conversions.[98]   On the other hand, when in the eighteenth century Frenchmen turned Moslem, and others were suspected of doing so, their actions provoked the French government to anger.[99]

A fourth class of pensioners were favorites and servants of the royal household, ranging from aristocrats to the most humbly born. The Maréchale de Mirepoix, "lady of the queen's palace," drew a pension of 78,000 livres a year, and the Vicomtesse d'Aumale, under-governess of the royal children, 21,000 livres;[100] on the lower levels came a pension of 250 livres to *femme* Choquenot, aged sixty-nine, "in consideration of her services as laundress of the stockings of the king's wardrobe," and a pension of 182 livres to Gérard Warin, aged fifty-seven, "in consideration of his services in the capacity of goblet-boy to the princes before their marriage."[101]   In this group fell a large number of persons: minions, governesses, chamberlains, equerries, musicians, table-boys, cooks, goblet-boys, laundresses, stable-boys, and others of various classifications.   Among them were probably parasites, drawing sums out of proportion to their services; others, perhaps the greater number, received pensions that were little if any above their deserts.

A fifth class of pensioners were physicians and surgeons who had rendered service to France, for the most part in the hospitals of the kingdom.   Except in a few instances, their pensions were modest. Andouille, aged seventy, first surgeon to the king, and Heven, first surgeon to Madame, drew 9,900 and 10,233 livres, respectively.[102] Certain others drew relatively large sums, but apparently nine tenths or more of the medical and surgical pensioners fell in the three lowest pension groups.   In fact, at least half of them belonged to

[97] Some were converted to escape the galleys; some took the step as a requisite for French naturalization; some were bought as children in Constantinople and reared in France as Christians; and others adopted Christianity through persuasion. See a fascinating article by J. Mathorez, "Les éléments de population orientale en France," *Revue des études historiques*, année 83 (Paris, 1917), 194-201.

[98] Mathorez thinks that two of those converted were Jews rather than Turks, judging from their name of Abraham (*ibid.*, p. 201 with nn.).

[99] See the *Inventaire des archives historiques de la Chambre de Commerce de Marseille*, AA arts. 44, 81, and 251; Mathorez, *op. cit.*, p. 200.

[100] *Arch. parl.*, XIII, 312, 307.   [101] *Ibid.*, XIV, 498; XV, 240.

[102] *Ibid.*, XIII, 322, 345.

the lowest group. A large number of the pensioners had served the army or navy, and in some instances had lived in the French possessions of India, Corsica, or the New World. Many others had served in the civil hospitals at home and had received small yearly incomes between 400 and 500 livres.

A sixth class, not a large one, were inventors. Probably three or four dozen men were so favored. Philippe de la Salle, of Lyons, inventor of an ingenious mechanical loom, was granted, in consideration of this and certain other discoveries advantageous to commerce, a pension of 6,000 livres, and in addition was awarded the cordon of St. Michael.[103] Françoise Keyser, sister of the inventor of a celebrated antivenereal remedy, was the recipient of a pension of 500 livres, granted in 1762, out of funds of the department of war.[104] Michel Joseph Montgolfier, "in consideration of the discovery that he had made, conjointly with his brother, of the aerostatic machine" (the hot-air balloon), was awarded in 1784 a pension of 1,000 livres.[105] In 1783 J. A. C. Charles was given a pension of 2,000 livres for discovering the value of hydrogen gas in ballooning.[106] Claude François Berthelot, aged seventy-one, because of a discovery that he had made in the mounting of guns for coastal defense, was given a pension of 600 livres.[107] A pension of 400 livres was given to François Baud, aged thirty-two, in recognition of a machine that he had invented for splitting leather;[108] and a pension of 1,200 livres was given to the widow and daughter of one Grandville, of Burgundy, who had discovered a new means of cleaning hemp.[109] In some instances gratifications were bestowed instead of pensions. Thus, on Doulcet's request, a gratification of 600 livres went to the midwife who had assisted him in experiments leading to his discovery of a cure for puerperal fever. [110]

A seventh class of pensioners included several dozen professors

[103] *Ibid.*, XIII, 470; Foncin, *op. cit.*, pp. 290-291.

[104] *Arch. parl.*, XIV, 713.

[105] *Ibid.*, XIV, 242. The government also advanced in 1786, to aid him in his experiments, 40,000 livres for the construction of a balloon (*ibid.*, XIII, 182). Maurice Tourneux, in his *Bibliographie de l'histoire de Paris pendant la Révolution française*, III (Paris, 1900), No. 13478, cites the date as 1784.

[106] *Arch. parl.*, XIII, 566.

[107] *Ibid.*, XIV, 31.

[108] *Ibid.*, XIV, 390.

[109] Tuetey, *L'assistance publique*, II, 576-578.

[110] Möring and Quentin, *op. cit.*, II, 140.

and academicians. The academicians, as a rule, received the higher sums. Bailly, astronomer and member of the Academies of Sciences and Inscriptions and Belles-Lettres, drew 4,000 livres; Monge, of the former academy and professor of mathematics and physics at the royal engineering school at Mezières, 1,000.[111] La Harpe, of the French Academy, received 3,000 livres; Dacier, of the Academy of Inscriptions and Belles-Lettres, 1,200.[112] The highest pension to a professor or his family was one of 11,750 livres to the widow of Bourgelat, founder of the two veterinary schools at Lyons and Alfort, and commissioner-general of the king's stables.[113] Jean Digard de Kerguette, aged seventy-two, professor of hydrography and mathematics at Rochefort, received a pension of 1,400 livres.[114] But the average sums received by teachers, at least on government funds, were smaller.[115] Bouillet-Marjals, fifty-seven, royal professor of mathematics at Béziers, received 500 livres a year; Bertholet, after eighteen years of teaching in the royal college at Rouen, was retired on a pension of 800 livres.[116] Guillermet, another professor in the royal college at Rouen, retired in 1783, after twenty years of teaching, on an annual gratification of 500 livres. In 1791, probably because the gratification was no longer paid, he applied for reinstatement at his old job.[117]

There were other groups of pensioners, such as musicians, tax collectors, lottery directors, custodians of the king's stables, heads of large families,[118] and victims of accident or dire misfortune. Within this last group came the notorious Latude, of Bastille fame, pensioned at 400 livres in 1784 because of the injustice of his suf-

---

[111] *Arch. parl.*, XIII, 379; XIV, 239.

[112] *Ibid.*, XIII, 665.

[113] *Ibid.*, XIII, 328.

[114] *Ibid.*, XIII, 671.

[115] The University of Paris had a system of private pensions. Professors after twenty years of lecturing were able to renounce their duties and thenceforth draw a pension: 1,500 livres if they were among the younger members pensioned, or 1,700 livres if they were among the twenty oldest. The funds for these pensions were created by all the professors who lectured giving a part of their salaries every three months toward this end, in the hope of themselves being pensioned some day (Chéruel, *op. cit.*, II, 1028).

[116] *Ibid.*, XIV, 436; *Inv.-som . . . Seine-Inférieure*, D 551.

[117] *Idem.* These last two pensions are not recorded in the *Etat nominatif des pensions.*

[118] Consideration of the pensions to heads of large families will be found in another chapter.

ferings.[119] André Fabre, seventy-eight, shot by a soldier and unable to make a living, was allowed a pension of 100 livres from the funds of the war department.[120] A widow Blondel, whose husband had lost his life in a fire, June 8, 1781, was allowed a pension of 150 livres.[121] Women were pensioned because their husbands had lost their lives in fires, or by the explosion of guns, or by other means. Many persons pensioned by the government under the Old Regime were members of the middle and lower classes. Moreover, in addition to the pensions, there were multitudes of gratifications varying from thirty or forty to thousands of livres, bestowed for a particular act of service or in an immediate and temporary case of distress. The government, furthermore, in numerous instances published books by men like Doulcet, Paulet, and Tenon as a service to the French public.

The provincial governments, as well as the royal government, bestowed pensions and gratuities and financed the research and publication of books deemed of particular interest. The Estates of Provence, for example, subsidized the Oratorian Papon over a period of many years as he gathered material for his notable *Histoire de Provence;*[122] the Estates of Brittany voted in 1730 a sum of 1,200 livres to subsidize the publication of a French-Breton dictionary.[123] Pamphlets and books on matters legal, agricultural, economic, medical, were published by the provincial assemblies of the various *pays d'états*. The Estates of Brittany spent lavishly during the century large funds on elaborate maps of the province.[124] Even municipalities accorded gratifications,[125] and hospitals frequently gave both gratifications and pensions. In the latter instance, as already ob-

---

[119] In 1792 the Legislative Assembly extended him a supplementary grant of 3,000 livres (Ferdinand-Dreyfus, *L'assistance*, p. 19). The pension is not designated, however, in the *Etat nominatif*. The family of Jean Calas, while not pensioned, was given 36,000 livres by way of amends in 1765. See John Ray, *Life of Adam Smith* (London, 1895), p. 186.

[120] *Arch. parl.*, XIV, 602.   [121] *Ibid.*, XIV, 421.

[122] *Inv.-som . . . Bouches-du-Rhône*, C 91-100.

[123] *Inv.-som . . . Ille-et-Vilaine*, C 4921.

[124] *Ibid.*, C 4922-4925. Cf. Preserved Smith, *A History of Modern Culture*, II (New York, 1934), 87. Smith is correct in saying that Cassini did not undertake the cartography of Brittany, but François Le Roy, the provincial cartographer in 1749, was ordered by the Breton government to concert himself with Cassini in the latter's great work.

[125] *Inv.-som . . . Ille-et-Vilaine*, C 618, 718, 726; *Inv.-som . . . Bouches-du-Rhône*, C 2624.

served, they were given not only to physicians, surgeons, and nurses, but also to aged and faithful bookkeepers, police, and servants; indeed, various general hospitals of the kingdom made it a practice to pay life-annuities or pensions to aged priests and others who cared to bestow their savings on the hospital.[126]

Thus the system of pensions expanded greatly during the eighteenth century, as did other forms of charities, with the increase of French wealth and the growth of humanitarian feeling. Certainly by the latter half of the century the pension system was so elaborate that many people, whatever their profession, trade, or calling, could labor with the feeling that faithful and meritorious service might be rewarded with a pension for old age for themselves or with a gratification for those whom they might leave behind them. It was the one form of charity under the Old Regime in which allotments were relatively in due proportion to the needs.

After 1789

After publishing in the spring of 1790 the purported full list of pensioners of the royal government, with the sum and citation (or citations) in each instance, the National Assembly proceeded to revise drastically the whole pension scheme in France. Throughout 1790 and even to its termination in September, 1791, the Assembly was occupied with reform legislation proposed by its hard-working pensions committee, assisted in some instances by other committees, notably the military and naval.[127] The chief result was a reduction, by a decree of July 10-16, 1790, of annual pensions from the reported figure of 29,000,000 livres (actually 38,000,000 livres) to 10,000,000, and of gratifications from a reported 20,000,000 livres (actually 40,000,000) to 2,000,000. Camus, chairman of the pensions committee, estimated at "more than 80,000,000 livres" the amount of money spent "uselessly" on pensions and gratifications in France each year. The establishment of a maximum of 12,000,000 livres annually for pensions and gratifications was, in his opinion,

---

[126] The hospitals commonly allowed them 5 per cent interest on their money for expenses until death. There are many references to this practice in the *Inventaires-sommaires*.

[127] The complete record of this legislation can be found in the *Archives parlementaires*, which is certainly the best source of published material on pensions for both the Old Regime and the Revolution.

"sufficient to recompense all those who merited well of their country."[128]

Therefore in this period of economic crisis a great saving for the treasury was effected by a determined Assembly. Realizing that many of those who would be dispossessed of pensions might be in need, the Assembly provided that the most deserving cases should be cared for out of the sum of 2,000,000 livres allotted for gratifications. Of these, "the oldest in age and service" would have preference.[129] The sum of 12,000,000 livres for pensions and gratifications was not, however, to include the pensions to ecclesiastics, which would continue to be paid on "the funds allotted to them," or "the funds appropriated for the [Hôtel des] Invalides," or the part-time pay destined to soldiers and sailors.[130] Thus the Revolutionaries left hidden some fairly large sums actually expended for pensions and gratifications.

Not only did the Assembly reduce enormously the size of the bill for pensions and gratifications, but it also effected a thoroughgoing, much needed reform of the pensions by the notable statute of July 10-16, 1790, which was supplemented by several subsequent statutes. Definite age limits and periods of service were prescribed for those who claimed pensions on grounds other than wounds and physical disability, with sums dependent upon the form of service and previous salary. Thus, as article 17 of the decree of July 10-16 stipulated, no citizen might receive a pension unless he had per-

---

[128] Discussing the matter on the floor of the Assembly on July 16, 1790, Camus asserted: "Most of the departments have executed the decree enjoining them to furnish these *(états)*, but certain ones are delinquent. The pensions explained *(motivées se)* come to more than 30 millions; others whose object is less apparent come to more than 8 millions, and gratifications to 40. There was another sort of gifts which, by their nature, were incalculable, such as the remission of feudal rights and some portions of the [national] domains accorded under different pretexts. I estimate that these alienations add to more than 20 millions a year, and that the state pays more than 80 millions, uselessly. The intention of the Assembly not being to give to all those having [pensions at present], the sum of 12 millions will be sufficient to recompense those who have merited well of their country" *(Arch. parl.,* XVII, 134). Camus was perhaps in a better position to know the state of the pensions than anyone else of the eighteenth century; on the other hand, he was hostile toward the Old Regime. Earlier the pensions committee had given the figure for the listed pensions (with citations) variously as 29,252,874 and 29,460,460 livres, and it stated that beside these were pensions paid on funds other than those of the five departments, amounting to 3,749,241 livres *(ibid.,* XVI, 631, 654).

[129] Decree of July 10-16, 1790, art. 14 *(ibid.,* XVII, 135).

[130] Art. 16 *(ibid.,* XVII, 136).

formed thirty years of service to the state and attained the age of
fifty, or had received wounds or other infirmities while on duty that
rendered him incapable of continuing his service. Article 18 provided that in no instance was a pension to exceed 10,000 livres. As
a general policy, it was stipulated (articles 19 and 20) that the pension given after thirty years of service would be one fourth of the
pensioner's former salary, but never less than 150 livres. Thus a
minimal limit of 150 livres was set for pensions. For the pensioner
who had served the government longer than thirty years, it was
provided that for each year beyond the thirtieth he should receive
one twentieth of three fourths of the residue of his salary, so that
after fifty years of service he would receive the whole of his salary,
should it not be above 10,000 livres. As for those who were forced
because of wounds or disabilities to quit their duties prior to the
termination of thirty years, whether soldiers, sailors, or public officials, it was provided that they should receive pensions whose
amounts would be determined by the length and nature of their
services, and also by the nature of their wounds and disabilities.[131]

The king, who throughout the eighteenth century had hitherto
held, at least theoretically, absolute control over the pensions, now
lost it. Thenceforth he was to present each year to the Assembly
for approval a list of persons recommended for pensions. To it was
to be appended a second list giving the names of pensioners deceased
and of those still living.[132] The Assembly had to approve the list
of recommended pensions, and the king to give his sanction. In
January of every year the Assembly was to publish a list of the
changes in the pensions, and once every decade a complete list of
pensioners and their pensions.[133]

This act provided also that in no instance might a person receive
more than one pension, nor might a person receive a government
pension on any other than the funds of the treasury.[134] No person

---

[131] *Ibid.*, XVII, 136.

[132] No new names could be placed on the pension list until deaths had released
funds for the purpose. Here was a fundamental weakness of the pension law. It
was mechanical and static.

[133] *Ibid.*, XVII, 137.

[134] It will be recalled that under the Old Regime pensions had been largely based
on the funds of five departments; now they were to be based on those of the treasury
alone. Also under the Old Regime a pensioner frequently drew money from three
or four or five pensions. No longer might any such practice exist.

might receive a pension while yet drawing a salary, nor might a pensioner of the French government be at the same time the recipient of a pension from any foreign power. No pension might carry a clause of reversibility whereby a pension might be passed on after death to a relative, but the state would consider and grant pensions to widows and children according to the merits of each case.[135]

The giving of gratifications also was regulated. They were thenceforth to be rendered only for services to the nation or for dire needs, and in all instances must be approved by the Assembly. The king was granted the right of bestowing gratifications in emergency cases, but should it be found on later examination that the gratifications had been given "without motives and against the principles decreed," the minister who had countersigned the decisions was to reimburse the treasury from his own pocket. In no instance might a gratification be made for more than a single year without a new cause arising. Moreover, in January of each year the National Assembly was to publish a list of the gratifications accorded or approved, even as of pensions.[136]

Another decree of July 16, 1790, provided that every pension, gratification, salary, or other recompense from the public treasury, existent January 1, 1790, or accorded since that date, be suppressed; and the pensions committee was ordered to concert itself with the military and naval committees and draw up within eight days a new scale of pensions. Former pensioners were to be paid any arrears in their pensions for 1790, provided that they did not exceed 600 livres; to those having higher pensions, only 600 livres were to be paid.[137] By a later act of July 23, 1790, the Assembly provided that no municipal or other administration might grant a higher pension or gratification than 600 livres. Thus it reduced the municipal pensions to a scale commensurate with the new scheme for national pensions.[138]

On July 26 the three joint committees of pensions, war, and navy in their report to the National Assembly set forth a recom-

---

[135] *Ibid.*, XVII, 38-39. It was provided that when a pensioner died without leaving any money for his widow and children, the state would bestow on the widow an "alimentary pension," and rear and educate the children "at the expense of the nation," until the latter were able to earn their own living.

[136] *Ibid.*, XVII, 137.   [137] *Ibid.*, XVII, 139.

[138] *Ibid.*, XVII, 300. Camus pointed out that the city of Paris had paid a pension of 6,000 livres to its former treasurer, and a pension of 15,000 livres to a former procurer of the king.

mended statute in seventeen articles, dealing with reform of hitherto
existing pensions. After some debate and after consideration of the
articles one by one, they were adopted with only slight modification
in wording. For the history of the pensions in the Revolutionary
period this law was important, since it set forth the new scale of
figures for the revised pensions and gratifications. It provided (art.
2) that general officers of the army receive 2,000 livres if they had
been receiving pensions of that sum and had served through two
war campaigns. For each additional campaign they were to receive
500 livres, up to a maximum of 6,000 livres. Military or naval
officers pensioned prior to January 1, 1790, who had seen twenty
years of service and had served through two military or naval campaigns should enjoy a new pension created in their favor, not higher
than what they had been receiving (art. 3).[139] Article 4 provided
a new pension for other persons who had been pensioned prior to
January 1, 1790, for service rendered to the state, in whatever field,
but stipulated that this new pension might in no circumstances be
higher (and might be lower) than the old one. Article 5 stipulated
that widows and children of men who had rendered public service
to the state, especially the widows and children of officers killed
while on duty, should enjoy new pensions of the same amounts as
formerly, save that the combined sum of pensions to widow and children was not to exceed 3,000 livres. Nevertheless, the widows of
the marshals of France who enjoyed pensions would continue to
draw 6,000 livres. By article 7, former pensioners below seventy
years of age might not receive a re-established pension above 10,000
livres, nor those between seventy and eighty a new pension of more
than 15,000 livres, nor those above eighty-one over 20,000 livres.
Pensioners aged seventy-five or more who enjoyed a pension above
3,000 livres might continue to draw at least 3,000 livres. Those
aged seventy who held pensions for service in the navy or in the
colonies might continue to enjoy the same favor as octogenarians.
Furthermore, widows of the marshals of France who had attained
the age of seventy or eighty would enjoy this same scale of pensions.
(In short, a marshal's widow, aged eighty, might be awarded a pension of 20,000 livres.) Article 9 stipulated that those who had

[139] This was a modification of an article in the law of July 10-16 stipulating
thirty years as the minimum period of service prerequisite to a pension and the
minimum age limit fifty years.

rendered a service to the state and had not been recompensed, or had enjoyed a pension not to be re-established, should be recompensed from the fund of the 2,000,000 livres destined for gratifications.[140]

The pensions committee was ordered (art. 14) to draw up four lists of persons deserving pensions and gratifications, the first to comprise the new pensions based on the funds of the 10,000,000 livres created by the law of July 10-16; the second, the pensions re-established in accordance with the terms of articles 2, 3, 4, and 5 of the present decree; the third, the names of those who should be given gratifications in accordance with article 9 of the present law; and the fourth, the names of those who had performed deeds of valor and preferred to take pecuniary recompense, as provided by article 5 of the law of July 10-16.[141] These lists were to be published (art. 16), with the cause for pension or gratification cited in each instance. Finally, the pensions re-established by this law were to date from January 1, 1790 (art. 17).[142]

No sooner had this statute been enacted than Camus, chairman of the pensions committee, recommended that it not apply to the families of Assas[143] and Chambord, the widow and children of the late Marshal Lohendahl,[144] and General Luckner.[145] Lohendahl had formerly received in pensions 23,000 livres; Luckner, 36,000.[146]

[140] Article 12 provided for the establishment of this fund. Sums of 1,000, 500, and 150 livres were to be allowed to families and persons of various categories, based on needs.

[141] Article 5 of the law of July 10-16 reads: "Les marques d'honneur, décernées par la nation, seront personnelles, et mises au premier rang des récompenses publiques" (ibid., XVII, 38). This article as first recommended provided that a medal be bestowed in such instances, but Le Chapelier protested that "medals carry a preference which insensibly harks back to the nobility that you come to abolish"; in consequence, monetary recompense was made optional.

[142] For the terms of the law of July 26, 1790, see ibid., XVII, 350-354.

[143] The pension of the Assas family is described, ibid., XIV, 367. Because of the heroic death of Louis d'Assas, captain in the regiment of Auvergne, in the battle of Clostercamp, October 15-16, 1760, the government in 1777 made a pension of 1,000 livres to his family. His father, François, Baron d'Assas, was given 400 livres of this, and his brother, Jean François, 300. Another member, Jean Charles Marie, drew 300 livres. The pension was made for perpetuity to them and their eldest male descendants. The act of bravery which merited this pension is described by Jean Edmond Weelen in his Rochambeau, Father and Son . . . , tr. by Lawrence Lee (New York [1936]), pp. 54-55.

[144] Conqueror of Berg-op-Zoom and other places in the War of the Austrian Succession.

[145] A Bavarian general who had fought in the French Army during the Seven Years' War. He was guillotined on January 4, 1794, charged with treason.

[146] Ibid., XIII, 312.

The recommendation was adopted[147] although there was much discussion in the National Assembly during 1790 concerning the provision for the three sons of Marshal Lohendahl. On July 2 the pensions committee recommended that because of his unusual service to France (in capturing some ten places in the Low Countries in the mid-century wars) Lohendahl's three sons be rewarded with gratifications of 200,000 livres each.[148]

On July 31, 1790, the National Assembly adopted the recommendation of the joint committees of pensions, army, and marine governing the pensions that would be granted. Thirty years of service in the army or civil service, and twenty-five in the navy, were to be requisite for a pension, but a year of service in the colonies or on the sea would count as two for those in the civil service or the navy; a year abroad in time of war would count as two for soldiers; in time of peace it would count as eighteen months. The rule would apply to seamen and soldiers of all grades, including foreign officers and men serving in the French army. At retirement the pension would be based on the rank last held for two entire years. One forced from the service because of a wound would receive a pension conforming to the rank held at the time the wound was suffered. The four children of General Montcalm were specifically given continuance of the pension of 1,000 livres that they had been receiving, despite article 5 of the decree of July 26, stipulating that the maximum received by widows and children together might not exceed 3,000 livres.[149] Specific provision was made for continuance in their entirety of the pensions enjoyed by the families D'Assas, Chambord, Montcalm, and by General Luckner, despite any articles of preceding legislation to the contrary.[150]

On the same day the National Assembly adopted the proposal of the pensions committee concerning the pensions of artists, savants, and men of letters. It was recognized that for their services to society these men should enjoy national recompense. They were not in the future to receive gratifications while their work was in progress,

[147] *Ibid.*, XVII, 354.
[148] *Ibid.*, XVI, 613. It is curious that the pensions committee, apparently so desirous of economy, should in this case be so prodigal.
[149] *Ibid.*, XVII, 352.
[150] *Ibid.*, XVII, 444. For discussion of the claims of the children and sister of General Montcalm, see XVII, 443.

but only after its completion and after they had attained an age making it impossible for them to work. The amount of the pension would depend upon several factors; it might be as much as 10,000 livres, but not lower than 150. Thus the Revolutionary government placed literary men, artists, and savants on a level with military and naval men and political figures. The widow and children of a savant who lost his life on a perilous expedition or enterprise would enjoy the same right to a pension as those of any other man killed in the state's service. Similarly, the savant whose health was impaired as a result of travels or researches would be eligible for a gratification by the state. Annual gratifications were to be given as assistance to students of the arts and sciences or of other matters useful to the state for travel abroad in order that they might the better improve themselves.[151]

All of the legislation thus far described was re-enacted in a single general statute of August 3, 1790.[152] Other statutes concerning pensions enacted before the close of the Assembly in September, 1791, were minor in character, concerning such matters as the payment of arrears, the renewal of pensions for certain lesser groups, the granting of pensions to a few specific persons (like the widow of Jean Jacques Rousseau),[153] and the payment of pensions to Frenchmen living outside France.[154] This legislation left a surprising degree of discretion to the pensions committee. The National Assembly determined in a general way those who would be eligible for pensions and fixed maximum and minimum limits. The pensions committee, however, was free within these limits to determine what should be given to most of the pensioners. No limits were prescribed for pensions to the various military and naval ranks, or engineers, or civil

[151] Ibid., XVII, 445.

[152] Ibid., XVII, 572-577.

[153] She was granted a pension of 1,200 livres by the Assembly on December 21, 1790 (ibid., XXIII, 373).

[154] By its law of January 14, 1790, the Assembly ordered the cessation of pensions or gratifications to French functionaries living outside their country, unless on missions for their government (ibid., XXIII, 223). Later, on December 13, 1791, the Legislative Assembly ordered that every Frenchman having a pension, salary, or other income payable from the French treasury, must appear in person to get his payments or be represented by one whom he legally delegated to do this. (This was to prevent émigrés from obtaining pension payments) (ibid., XXXVI, 57).

servants. There were several specifications regarding three classes of savants and artists, but the pensions committee was free to determine who should come in these different classes. Apparently the Assembly, in its efforts to guard against future abuse, preferred to trust the judgment of the pensions committee rather than risk making the legislation too inflexible.

An examination of the pension lists as revised by the committee (and approved by the Assembly) reveals marked variations in sums paid to men of the same rank. One retired lieutenant general, Rouille de Coudray, was given a pension of 4,200 livres; another, Toustain d'Eseresnes, 5,980 livres.[155] Of four colonels, one received 6,000 livres, a second 5,000, a third 3,656, and a fourth 1,062.[156] The first of these colonels drew a larger pension than either of the two lieutenant generals. Of six lieutenant colonels on the revised list, one drew 5,800 livres, another 3,600, a third 2,790, a fourth 1,530, a fifth 1,475, and a sixth 1,020.[157] The variation in the case of captains was also considerable. Some got as high as 2,000 livres;[158] one got as little as 265 livres 10 sous;[159] others got intermediate sums such as 1,387, 680, 531, 442, and 355 livres. Of two lieutenants, one received a pension of 900 livres a year, the other only 400.[160] Two second lieutenants (*sous-lieutenants*) received 720 livres each.[161] Thus in some instances second lieutenants received larger pensions than lieutenants or captains, captains more than lieutenant colonels, lieutenant colonels more than colonels, and colonels more than lieutenant generals. In arriving at the new rate, the committee appears to have juggled three factors: the former pension, the last salary enjoyed by the pensioner, and the years of service. In a large number of cases the

[155] *Ibid.*, XXVIII, 284, 286. The former had served in thirteen campaigns, the latter in eleven; but the latter had served for 42 years, while the former had served only 28 years. The former had enjoyed a pension of 4,200 livres under the Old Regime; the latter, two pensions for a total of 7,718 livres.

[156] Instances of Dusauzay, Petel de Scallier, Gazeau de la Boissière, and Wiet d'Hegenet (*ibid.*, XXVIII, 282, 300, 286).

[157] *Ibid.*, XXVIII, 286, 289, 297, 298, 283, 287. Cases of Poulhariés, Bombar de Saint-Pierre, Geoffroy, D'Inguimbert, Dupille, and Trasegnies.

[158] Bonnel, Bonnet, and Manuel (*ibid.*, XXVIII, 289, 291).

[159] *Ibid.*, XXVIII, 283.

[160] Instances of Coupy and Lange de la Maltière (*ibid.*, XXVIII, 299, 284).

[161] *Ibid.*, XXVIII, 296, 300.

figure of the former pension was continued; in others it was lowered
or raised. Jean Bournol, a regimental surgeon *(chirurgien-major)*,
was reduced in pension from 531 to 370 livres, and Charles Roger,
a military engineer, was reduced in pension from 6,442 to 4,000
livres; on the other hand, Jerome Charles Gourdain, an old engineer and inspector of the administration of bridges and highways,
was raised in pension from 2,000 to 3,740 livres, and Pierre Taxier
de Lancey, former consul in Syria and Barbary for thirty-two years,
from 3,600 to 6,256 livres.[162] In the two latter instances the pensioners formerly had high salaries, which evidently were a determining factor in arriving at the pensions. Even with its variations
the new pension scale was an improvement on the old one, in which
variations were often of fantastic proportions.

The assumption of the French Revolutionaries that they had
reduced pensions and gratifications to a total of 12,000,000 livres
was illusory. This sum omitted the ecclesiastical pensions, which
under the Old Regime and in early 1790 were based on funds
arising from the *dîme,* and amounting approximately to 2,500,000
livres.[163] In early 1790 the sum necessary for ecclesiastical pensions
began to soar enormously, when, after abolishing all monastic orders
save those devoting their efforts to educational and hospital activities,
the National Assembly granted pensions to the disbanded monks
and nuns.[164] Treilhard, reporter of the ecclesiastical committee,
estimated the number of monks at 17,000 to 18,000 and the total

---

[162] *Ibid.,* XXVIII, 289, 300, 289, 291.

[163] The estimate of 2,500,000 livres for old curés and vicars was made by Mayet,
curé of Rochetaille and deputy to the National Assembly from Lyons, in a report of
March 19, 1790 (*ibid.,* XII, 245).

[164] The law abolishing the monastic orders was passed February 13, 1790. On
February 19-20 the Assembly voted to give pensions to the disbanded monks and
nuns, to lay brothers, and to those engaged in domestic service *(frères convers),* who
should choose to leave their monasteries (*ibid.,* XI, 592, 632, 650-651). Monks of
the begging orders, until fifty years of age, were to be given 700 livres; those of
other orders, 800 livres. Those over fifty received higher sums. Members of the
nonbegging orders, aged fifty to seventy, received 1,000 livres, and those over
seventy, 1,200 livres. The former Jesuits, who until this time had been receiving
400 livres in pensions annually, were by special amendment accorded the same sums
as the nonbegging monks. Lay and domestic brothers were accorded 300, 400, and
500 livres, depending upon their ages. Those under fifty received 300 livres, those
from fifty to seventy, 400 livres; and those over seventy, 500 livres (*ibid.,* XI, 623,
649). A statute of March 19, 1790, provided that monks who decided to continue
residence in the houses of their orders would be granted salaries. These salaries,
though the limits were not fixed, would be higher for the nonbegging than for the
begging monks (*ibid.,* XII, 238, 240).

of pensions to them, provided that each was given 800 livres a year, at 16,000,000 livres annually, and suggested that this amount could easily be raised from the sale of certain monastic property.[165] The pensions actually granted, however, averaged more than 800 livres a year. Moreover, Treilhard did not include an estimate of the nuns, of whom, as Martineau, a sober-headed critic, pointed out, there were 30,000. In March, 1791, certain abbesses in the department of Bouches-du-Rhône were drawing pensions of 1,500 livres, and many of the nuns 700 livres.[166] The secular clergy, too, were given pensions at generous rates. Thus Belloy, former bishop of Marseilles, was allowed in early 1791 a pension of 20,000 livres, and some twenty former canons of the chapter of Saint Victor in Marseilles, pensions ranging from 3,500 to 6,000 livres.[167] During 1792 the total cost of pensions to former monks and nuns alone, according to Roland, minister of the interior, was 56,000,000 livres.[168]

Roland expected this expense to rise to 60,000,000 livres in 1793, in consequence of legislation passed in August, 1792. On August 4 the Legislative Assembly confiscated the property of the monastic orders. On August 7 it extended pensions to monks and nuns not already receiving them, with the exception of monks and nuns engaged in care of the sick. These last would be paid the whole of their former income, but they might quit the monastic life when they chose. This law provided also that monks and nuns and former Catholic ecclesiastics, whether pensioned or salaried by the nation, might marry and conserve their salaries or pensions.[169] The king's refusal to sign this enactment irritated the public and was one of the factors leading to the fighting of August 10 and his abdication. On August 22 another pension law, more elaborate than that of August 7, was enacted, by which a large number of orders of both sexes, hitherto engaged in teaching or missions, were suppressed and pensioned.[170] Those members of orders engaged in hospitals and asylums, however, were directed to continue at their work and receive

[165] *Ibid.*, XI, 623.

[166] Other nuns got smaller sums, dependent upon their order and status (*Inventaire . . . Bouches-du-Rhône*, L IV, 5).

[167] *Ibid.*, L IV, 2 (II, 53, 57).

[168] *Arch. parl.*, LVI, 634.

[169] *Ibid.*, XLVII, 545-547.

[170] *Ibid.*, XLVIII, 350-356. Some of the pensioned were given as little as 100 livres; others as much as 1,200.

their full salary as hitherto; those who left their work would receive only half salary. With this legislation the state within the
space of three years saddled itself with a larger pension obligation
than had existed in the closing days of the Old Regime.[171]

Nor does this complete the story. There were some surreptitious
pensions and additional grants for special gratifications. In regard
to the pensions, Brissot de Warville charged on the floor of the
Legislative Assembly on August 4, 1792, that the ministry of foreign
affairs, besides making other reckless expenditures, had paid or set
aside 1,100,000 livres for secret pensions. He claimed that his information came from Dumouriez and Chambones, two former ministers of foreign affairs. When asked for at least a temporary
suspension of these pensions, the house went further, abolishing them
without debate and without delay.[172]

By bestowing pensions and gratifications on the wounded and
crippled "conquerors of the Bastille," and the widows and orphans
of those killed in taking it, the National Assembly, on December 19,
1790, built up a special pension list carrying 10,000 livres a year,
and a gratification list carrying at least 2,000 livres, and possibly as
much as 8,000 or 10,000 livres, a year. Twenty-six men and one
woman were specifically allowed pensions of 200 livres each because
of being crippled from the storming of the prison.[173] Eighteen
widows whose husbands were killed in the affair were each granted
pensions of 150 livres. The children of those killed, and in one
instance two grandchildren, were to receive a pension of 100 livres
until they should reach the age of twenty, and then or at the time

[171] La grande encyclopédie (XXVI, 304) states that in the year IV pensions
"reached 82 millions," and that in the year VI they were again reduced, to 15,704,
902 francs.

[172] Brissot charged that these pensions included, in part, the payment of approximately 400,000 livres to the house of Carignan, 130,000 to 140,000 livres to
nine clerks (commis) who had served under the Old Regime at deciphering letters,
and approximately 30,000 livres to one Dogny. That Brissot's charge had a sound
basis is to be seen in the fact that a list of the secret pensions was forthwith turned
over to the diplomatic committee by Bigot de Saint-Croix, the minister of foreign
affairs (Arch. parl., XLVII, 457).

[173] Marie Charpentier, veuve Haucerne, was cited also for her "great courage."
Two other instances have been found of women of the Revolutionary period cited for
courage as soldiers, and accorded gratifications. For one of them, the widow Aufrère, a cannoneer, see Tuetey, Répertoire générale, VIII, No. 2075; and for the
case of Françoise Imbert, a soldier successively in several regiments and later head of
the National Guard in Bergerac, Arch. parl., XXVII, 685.

of their marriage they were each to receive the sum of 1,000 livres.[174] Gratifications of 400 livres went to four men wounded in the events that day.[175] As time went on, certain others were extended aid for this enterprise.[176]

On the whole those who had stormed the Bastille, and many who claimed that they had had a part in storming it, came out well. They received many private gifts, including one of 45,000 livres from the thirty deputies representing the city of Paris in the National Assembly.[177] In February, 1790, they were released from the obligation of paying the *don patriotique*.[178] Feeling that they had not received enough, a group of the "conquerors" appeared before the Assembly June 19, 1790, and asked the country to show a little generosity. The Assembly acted that very day. Knowing that many of the "conquerors" were without jobs,[179] it voted that all able-bodied men among them should be incorporated into the National Guard of Paris, and that every one of the "conquerors" able to bear arms should at the expense of the National government be furnished a uniform, gun, and saber, in short, his complete military equipment.[180] To those not able to bear arms, and to the widows and orphans of those who had died in the undertaking, would be

---

[174] Since a complete list of the children is not given, it is impossible to determine how much in pensions or gratifications this would entail.

[175] The full terms are given in *Arch. parl.*, XXI, 566-567.

[176] Thus on March 20, 1793, the Convention gave 400 livres to the widow of Pierre Aufrère, whose husband had been killed in taking the Bastille and who had received no aid (*ibid.*, LX, 348). A pension of 2,000 livres was even accorded in April, 1793, to the Marquis de la Salle d'Offemont, commander of the Parisian militia on July 14, for acquiescence in the events of that day (Tuetey, *op. cit.*, I, Nos. 875, 881).

[177] According to the *Révolutions de Paris*, this sum was subscribed, not by the Parisian delegation, but by the whole Assembly (see *Mémoires de Bailly*, II, 78 n.), but the *Archives parlementaires* carries no record of it. Since the sum was not paid promptly, the workers complained and showed signs of an insurrection. Some notaries thereupon advanced the money, and the men were paid (*Mémoires de Bailly*, II, 94-95).

[178] Tuetey, *Répertoire général*, I, 39, No. 359.

[179] Most of them came from the poor section of Saint-Antoine in Paris, and many had been without jobs since the beginning of the Revolution.

[180] *Arch. parl.*, XVI, 371. The sabers alone for 263 men cost 2,630 livres. Tuetey, *op. cit.*, I, No. 405. A letter from Bailly indicated that 863 guns were given, costing 18 livres each (*ibid.*, I, No. 400). In his *Mémoires* (II, 249-250) Bailly scoffed at the idea that there could be as many as 800 placed in the category of "conquerors of the Bastille." He criticized the National Assembly for going too far. He thought that the real leaders should be recognized and rewarded, but not those merely present.

given "an honorable brevet" or diploma. One of those who received a diploma was Claude Fournier, called "The American," who rescued the papers of the Bastille and prevented the burning of the letters at the city post office (*Hôtel des Postes*).[181]

While the attackers of the Bastille were feted, praised, and rewarded, the defenders were not entirely ignored. On November 1, 1789, Louis XVI bestowed gratifications of 12,000 livres on the former officers and employees of the Bastille, by way of indemnity for losses, which in some instances had been great. Puget, a lieutenant, who claimed that he was robbed of 50,000 livres in coin and that his effects were pillaged, was given first and last 7,000 livres by way of indemnity.[182] On December 11, 1789, the minister of the king's household announced pensions to certain of the defenders and their widows: 4,000 livres to Puget, 3,000 to the Marquise de Launay (reversible after her death to her three daughters), 600 to Madame Miray, 500 to the Abbé Macanhou, 300 to the Abbé Faverly, and 200 to the Abbé Fosserier, these last three having been chaplains at the Bastille.[183]

Treated just as well as the "conquerors of the Bastille" were the soldier heroes of August 10, 1792.[184] From all parts of France, and even foreign countries,[185] donations came from responsive individuals to the National Assembly in behalf of the widows and orphans of that day. Many thousand livres were so contributed.[186] On August 12 the Legislative Assembly ordered the municipality of Paris to collect full information concerning those killed or wounded in that day's actions, and also the widows and children.[187] On August 20 it appropriated 20,000 livres to aid those widowed and

---

[181] Tuetey, *op. cit.*, I, Nos. 298 and 353.

[182] *Ibid.*, I, Nos. 292-295, 304.   [183] *Ibid.*, I, Nos. 296 and 328.

[184] They participated with a large mob in storming the Tuileries, cut to pieces the Swiss guard covering the retreat of the king's party, and forced the king's abdication. A vivid eyewitness account of the events of the day is given in François de la Rochefoucauld's *Souvenirs du 10 août 1792 et de l'armée de Bourbon*, published by Jean Marchand (Paris, 1929), pp. lix, 245. The writer, a son of the Duc de la Rochefoucauld-Liancourt, was in the presence of the king and queen throughout the events of August 9-10.

[185] An Englishman sent a gift of 160 livres.

[186] Some of these gifts are described in the following references: *Arch. parl.*, XLVIII, 279, 410, 431, 603, 617; XLIX, 198; Tuetey, *op. cit.*, IV, Nos. 2904, 2908, 2920, 2925, 2927, 2945. One man offered to rear one of the orphans. All in all, the event awakened intense feeling in the general public.

[187] Tuetey, *op. cit.*, IV, 334, No. 2626.

orphaned by the events of August 10, allotting 50 livres to each person.[188] On December 25, 1792, the National Convention, on the recommendation of the committee of public aid, placed a sum of 400,000 livres at the disposal of the minister of the interior for the relief of those who had been wounded, crippled, widowed, orphaned, or deprived of their financial support by the accidents of that day. In this last category came fathers and mothers who had lost sons. The crippled were to receive a life annuity of a livre a day, commencing August 10, 1792. Widows, indigent fathers, and mothers of citizens slain that day were to receive life annuities of 125 livres a year; children below eight, 25 livres, and those between eight and twelve, 40 livres. Those wounded short of crippling were to receive 30 sous a day until healed, and 6 sous additional for each of their children. The wounded needing treatment by thermal baths were to be sent to such places and cared for in hospitals at the nation's expense. Every person wounded who recovered and subsequently took his place in either the regular army or the national guard, for defense of the frontiers, would receive a bonus of 50 livres. Finally, the names of those killed August 10 were to be inscribed on a roll, printed at the expense of the Republic, and distributed among the eighty-four departments and the armies.[189] On September 13, 1793, the Convention decreed that fathers and mothers who had lost sons August 10, 1792, "in fighting against the tyrant," would be eligible to the same benefits as fathers and mothers whose sons had met death at the frontier.[190] The Convention also decreed, September 19, 1793, an indemnity of 120,097 livres to the many unfortunate citizens living in the Tuileries and its environs who had suffered losses from the fighting of August 10.[191]

While the national government extended aid to the sufferers of August 10, the municipal governments of Marseilles, Aix, and Avignon, and the departmental government of Bouches-du-Rhône, granted

---

[188] *Arch. parl.*, XLVIII, 425. The money was to come from the funds of the extraordinary, not from those normally set apart for pensions and gratifications.

[189] *Ibid.*, LV, 433-434. For a description of some of the grants that were made, see Tuetey, *op. cit.*, 354-355, 362, 368, Nos. 2789, 2848, and 2897. Pages 249-489 in this volume of Tuetey deal with the events of August 10, the wounded, and the relief accorded.

[190] *Arch. parl.*, LXXIV, 41-42. Laws of November 26, 1792, and May 4, 1793, had rendered aid to the families of soldiers serving at the frontiers.

[191] *Ibid.*, LXXIV, 414.

largesses to the soldiers who participated in the fighting and won laurels that day. The backbone of the rioters and victors over the Swiss Guard were troops from Marseilles and its neighborhood. Marseilles, Aix, and Avignon voted to give 600 livres to each of the soldiers of their respective towns who participated in the fighting.[192] Before the municipality of Marseilles paid this bonus, the Assembly of the department of Bouches-du-Rhône agreed, November 6, 1793, to bestow 600 livres to each soldier in the First Battalion who had been in Paris on August 10, 1792, and to pay the same sum to the parents or widows and children of those killed. "The Assembly expressed its wish that the parents of the victims and the invalids might receive a life annuity instead of an indemnity, that the children be aided until their majority, and that the soldiers of the Marseilles battalion even as their fathers or children be employed in preference to all others in the national *douanes*."[193] Finally the Assembly of Bouches-du-Rhône ordered that the names of the soldiers of the battalion be inscribed on a bronze plaque, to be placed in the departmental council chamber as a permanent memorial.[194] These measures, save in the instance of the municipal aid, did not remain empty statutes but were actually carried out. According to an account sheet, the department of Bouches-du-Rhône paid out a total of 263,185 livres by way of gratifications to soldiers and their families.[195] Apparently the grants to soldiers in the Revolutionary period were always paid faithfully, for the Revolutionists knew the value of the good will and support of the army, without which they could never have succeeded.

Every incident of importance in the downfall of the monarchy in which troops had any part was followed by liberal gratifications or pensions. Lavish gratifications were awarded officers and soldiers

[192] *Inventaire . . . Bouches-du-Rhône*, L III, 9, 11 (I, 149, 153, 167, 249). The Second Marseilles Battalion did not get to participate in the events of that day, as did the First, but was also, in 1793, voted the bonus of 600 livres for having been in Paris and seen the king executed, a culmination of the events of August 10. Soldiers from Orange, present in Paris on August 10, requested such a bonus, but no evidence has been found that it was granted.

[193] On September 19, 1792, the Legislative Assembly had adopted a statute to give preference to widows and daughters of soldiers killed in war for jobs in the service of the military hospitals and the infirmaries for the invalids (*Arch. parl.*, L, 146).

[194] *Inventaire . . . Bouches-du-Rhône*, L III, 11 (I, 239-241).

[195] *Ibid.*, L, III, 11. From this account sheet it appears that there were about 420 men of the battalion in Paris that day.

of the National Guards who had arrested the royal family at Varennes, June 21, 1791, in its attempted flight from France. Several National Guard officers were recipients of gratifications of 6,000 livres each;[196] Bayon, commandant of the battalion of Saint-Germain-des-Prés, was given 20,000 livres, for taking "measures necessary for preventing civil war"; and Lenieau, a gendarme at Clermont, was given 400 livres for his zeal in going from Varennes to Clermont to get the aid of its National Guards. Le Gay, a controller of *gabelles*, was allowed a gratification of 12,000 livres because of wounds that he received in the affair, and the widow Collet, whose son was killed at Sainte-Menehould, was awarded 3,000 livres. For heroism in saving sixteen horses on the night of October 5-6, 1790, a sergeant was given a gratification of 300 livres.[197]

After the outbreak of war in April, 1792, the French government had an ever-mounting bill for gratifications and aid to soldiers and their families. On September 15, 1793, the National Convention voted to place 5,000,000 livres at the disposal of the minister of the interior in addition to sums already appropriated for the purpose for aiding needy wives, widows, children, fathers, and mothers of "defenders of the country."[198] As early as November 27, 1792, the departmental Assembly of Bouches-du-Rhône ordered a census of the needy families of soldiers, with a view to aiding them, and throughout 1793 it granted them large sums.[199] The Assembly of Isère appropriated 120,000 livres toward this end in September,

---

[196] These included Colonel Carré of the National Guards of Clermont, who in the night of June 21-22 arrested 175 dragoons of the Thirteenth Regiment awaiting the king's arrival; Major Itam of the National Guards of Cheppy; Captain George of the National Guards of Varennes; Major Bedu of the National Guards of Clermont; and Nicolas Fenaux, of the National Guards of Sainte-Menehould and former quartermaster of the regiment of Limousin (Tuetey, *op. cit.*, I, 268). The National Guards of Cheppy protested against the award to their major, and those at Varennes protested against awards to several of their officers who had requested gratifications (*ibid.*, I, 261, 268). Captain George, of Varennes, tactfully gave half of his award for the maintenance of National Guards employed on the frontiers, and the other half to "some objects of public utility for the city of Varennes."

[197] *Ibid.*, I, Nos. 2382, 2307, 2257, 2301, 1008.

[198] The aid was to be administered by municipal and departmental administrations. Reports on the expenditure of this fund were to be made every eight days by the minister to the committee of finances, which in turn was to report monthly to the Convention (*Arch. parl.*, LXXIV, 212-213). See the former decrees of November 16, 1792, and May 4, 1793.

[199] On May 8 and July 22 the Assembly made two grants of 50,000 livres (*Inventaire . . . Bouches-du-Rhône*, L III, 10, 11, I, 199, 251).

1793.[200] The problem of war orphans became one of importance. On September 21, 1793, the National Convention set aside 18,202 livres as temporary aid for three months' maintenance of 104 war orphans at the military school in the section of Popincourt, Paris, providing for them at the rate of 700 livres a year per student.[201]

As if earlier legislation had not made the point sufficiently clear, the National Convention on 21 pluviôse an II (February 9, 1794) stated that fathers and mothers, brothers and sisters, as well as wives and children, of "defenders of the country" were eligible to monetary aid from the government upon declaring themselves to be wholly dependent for their living upon the labor of their soldier relatives. Under this law the figures for gratifications mounted. A letter from the commission of public aid to the committee of public safety, 14 fructidor an II (August 31, 1794), revealed the expenditure from those departments reporting for the last trimester as 11,652,656 livres.[202] This lavish expenditure was accompanied by many abuses, as various papers in the Archives Nationales make clear.[203] An old corporal at Colmar believed that he was eligible to receive aid under the terms of the law, since he had four sons in the service, and made application. The committee of public safety, however, decided that he was being well cared for in the army and that he would have to wait until he was in feeble health and discharged from the army before he could qualify for this aid.[204] Oddly enough, the committee of public safety did permit one parent having a pension of 194 livres a year, in violation of the pension law of 1791, to receive additional aid under the law of 21

[200] Another appropriation of 100,000 livres was passed on September 6, 1793, but evidently was rescinded by the grant of September 18, carrying 120,000 livres (*Inv.-som . . . Isère,* L 61, ff 650, 679).

[201] *Arch. parl.,* LXXIV, 574-576.

[202] Arch. Nat., F15, 102, dossier of papers on the law of 21 pluviôse an II.

[203] Many persons in good circumstances applied for aid, and officials negligently permitted them to receive it, knowing that the law was being abused. The committee of public safety placed credence in the reports and ordered investigation. Afterwards it revised the list of recipients ("Correspondance Generale. Cahier des Lettres Ecrittes par la Section des Secours du comité de Salut Public," pp. 2, 5, 14, 20. Arch. Nat., F15, 102). By a decision of 11 thermidor an II, the committee of public safety decided that young men drafted for work in the manufacture of sailcloth were not to be regarded as "defenders of the country," and that their dependents would not be eligible to obtain aid under the law (*ibid.,* p. 7).

[204] *Ibid.,* p. 17.

pluviôse an II.[205]   The widow Brun of Grenoble, aged ninety-four, grandmother of a numerous family, of whom several were in the armed services, was given 300 livres by the administration of the district of Grenoble.[206]

Necessarily, because of the character of the times, the chief recipients of pensions and gratifications were soldiers and their families, yet the range of other recipients was large.   Scientists, artists, savants, the *maréchaussée,* former government officials and assistants of various grades were among those restored to pension rolls in 1790-91 when revision was made.   Apparently it mattered little if under the Terror universities and academies were abolished: those with pensions still retained them.   Gratifications and indemnities were paid to people of every walk of life for a multitude of reasons, from losses by fire to deeds of heroism.   The government granted 10,000 francs to victims of a powder explosion at Nantes;[207] 1,100 francs were given the families of two men lost in an Alpine avalanche;[208] 1,200 livres were allowed twenty-five poor victims of a floor falling in a court of justice at Rogent-le-Rotrou;[209] 2,700 livres were allotted for distribution among the families of nine National Guardsmen drowned in the Rhône while putting down an uprising at Arles;[210] 4,000 livres were voted to the widow and children of a mayor *par interim* of Rouffac, in the department of Haute-Rhin, killed in a riot;[211] several citizens of Hazebrouck were allowed indemnities or gratifications of 200 livres, and a woodcutter of Rouen 100 livres, for false arrest and trial;[212] 1,200 livres were accorded to Le Blanc, discharged from his position as director of the Jacobin charity workshop for women in March, 1791, to tide him over until

[205] Sébastien Blain, father of two sons in the French army.   The committee thought his pension too meager to maintain him, but yielded the extra aid with reluctance, saying that actually his two sons ought to aid him (*ibid.,* p. 12).

[206] *Inv.-som . . . Isère,* L 184.

[207] In the year VIII (1800) (note of the ministry of the interior, dated 5 messidor an VIII, Arch. Nat., F15, 103).

[208] Letter from the minister of the interior to the administrators of the department of Mount Blanc, 12 pluviôse an VII (*ibid.*).

[209] De la Porte to De Lessart, Sept. 17, 1791 (Arch. Nat., F15, 101).

[210] In 1792 (*Arch. parl.,* XLV, 427).   The distribution was to be made at the rate of 300 livres to each family.

[211] In August, 1792 (*ibid.,* XLVII, 657-658).   The widow was to receive 1,000 livres, and each of the six children 500 livres.

[212] In 1793 (*ibid.,* LXXVI, 483).

he could find other employment;[213] the gendarmerie of Seine-et-Marne were allowed a gratification of 3,000 livres in August, 1791, because of "extraordinary service";[214] 100 livres were promised to the author of the arrest of any "refractory preacher," *émigré*, or accomplice in the rebellion of Lyons in 1793;[215] and for heroic work in a fire in August, 1798, a cleric was given 200 livres.[216] These were but a few of many similar grants.

Many requests for gratifications and pensions were refused. No doubt some were deserving, others farfetched. To have granted them all would have increased enormously the expense to the state. Without question many names were removed from the pension roll on its revision in 1790-91 which should have been left there. Later some of them were reinstated for a pension or a gratification. Politics entered the picture. Rarely was a pension or gratification originated during the Revolutionary period for those who had manifested royalist sympathies. On the contrary, in 1790-92 *émigrés* were deprived of their pensions, as later were refractory priests, at the time when the pensions and gratifications awarded those who had been active in Revolutionist activity or had suffered from the Vendeans, Chouans, or royalist insurrectionists at Lyons and Marseilles were almost legion. In short, in the same manner as the government of the Old Regime in no small degree had used pensions and gratifications to build up a loyal faction in the state, Revolutionist France now favored its partisans.

This is not to say that the primary end of the pensions under both regimes was not charitable. Apparently most of the pensions and gratifications under both regimes were well deserved, and paid for honorable service to the French nation. That there was probably more graft than has come to light was due to the absence of careful audits.

Payments of pensions and gratifications during the Revolutionary period were frequently delinquent. Throughout 1789 and 1790 pensions were often in arrears, and only the smaller pensions were paid in full. By the decree of January 4-5, 1790, persons with pensions or gratifications higher than 3,000 livres were to be allowed,

---

[213] Discharged because of inability (Tuetey, *L'assistance publique*, I, clxxvii).
[214] *Inventaire . . . Seine-et-Marne*, L 9.
[215] Brossard, *op. cit.*, 243.
[216] *Inv.-som . . . Isère*, L 54, p. 101.

for the time being, payments of only 3,000 livres, unless they were septuagenarians, in which case up to 12,000 might be paid.[217] In early 1791 some persons complained of not receiving their pensions for 1789, but Camus, chairman of the pensions committee, reported that he had been informed by the director of the treasury that all who had presented themselves in person had been paid.[218] Later, in April, 1792, the Acadians of Morlaix sent a petition to the Legislative Assembly asking for payment of the pensions allowed them by the decree of February 21, 1791. No payment had yet been made, and they claimed to be experiencing great hardship.[219] On September 2, 1792, the widow Mirabeau, who had been granted 200 livres because of her husband's long service in the army, presented herself for the third time before the Legislative Assembly and requested payment, but apparently got no satisfactory reply.[220] Roland, minister of the interior, in his report to the Convention, January 9, 1793, stated that the National Assembly on September 9, 1791, had set aside an annual grant of 300,000 livres for gratifications to artists; but thus far none of this money had been expended, partly because of a contradiction in the law, and partly for the reason that he could not find a satisfactory method of distributing the fund.[221] He called upon the Convention for direction. In July and August, 1794, complaint was made in letters to the committee of public safety that while some pensioners were being paid, others were not, and that in some instances trivialities stood in the way of payments.[222] During the period 1794-97 ecclesiastical pensions to nuns as well as retired clergymen were badly in arrears, and in the years 1796-97 great suffering was experienced, as documents of the department of the Hautes-Alpes reveal.[223]

[217] *Arch. parl.*, XVI, 617-618. The decree of June 27, 1790, dealing with the temporary payment of pensions, mentions (art. 1) that some pensions were still in arrears for 1789 (*ibid.*, XVI, 508-509).

[218] *Ibid.*, XXIII, 171.   [219] *Ibid.*, XLII, 325-326.

[220] *Ibid.*, XLIX, 198.

[221] *Ibid.*, LVI, 653. The decree of September 17, 1791, provided for the distribution of 100,000 livres annually in gratifications to artists (*ibid.*, XXXI, 58).

[222] "Correspondance Générale. Cahier des Lettres Ecrittes par la section des Secours du Comité du Salut Public," pp. 12-13, 20 (Arch. Nat., F15, 102). The committee ordered investigation and the payment of all *pensionnaires* promptly and at the same time.

[223] P. G., "Pensionnaires ecclésiastiques de 1790 à 1797: documents divers," *Annales des Alpes*, année 1903 (Gap, 1903), 267-272. Not only were the pensions delinquent, but the payments greatly depreciated in value.

Throughout the era of the Directory and into the Consulate came complaints of delinquent payments. On 7 germinal an VIII (March 29, 1800) Claude Arnoux, a *chasseur* in the infantry, wrote to the minister of the interior requesting arrears of a pension for the upkeep of a child which had not been paid him since 1 prairial an VII (May 20, 1799) because of technical difficulties.[224] Louis Antoine Caraccioli, an aged man of letters, wrote on 25 pluviôse an VIII (January 19, 1799) to the minister of the interior requesting payment of pension three months in arrears, since he was compelled to pay his room rent. Payment was immediately made.[225] As a general rule the Revolutionary governments were seldom more than a year in arrears on pensions, and often, as seen in these complaints, not more than a few months.

Thus the Revolutionary governments spent much more money for pensions and gratifications than for any other form of charity, not excepting hospitals, asylums, and schools, and their payments were made with much regularity. Perhaps the legislative bodies found it more pleasing to accord aid to men and women who deserved well of the state by service than to render it to beggars, "down-and-outs," foundling children, and other unfortunates who all too frequently are from the dregs of humanity. The *pensionnaires* and recipients of gratifications were commonly men and women of character, who by patriotic and social service had won the public's esteem. Furthermore, the Revolutionists were well aware that these people had influence, and that it was much more imperative to see that pensions and gratifications were paid than grants to other forms of charity. Finally, the fact that the state had always paid the bulk of the pensions, whereas it had not paid the greater portion of the expenses of many other charities, may have helped influence the Revolutionary assemblies to pay pensions and gratifications more liberally and promptly than other charities.

[224] His corps had moved in the interim, and the administrators of the new department would not pay the pension without specific authorization from the minister (Arnoust to the minister of the interior, 7 germinal an VIII, Arch. Nat., F15, 103).

[225] Letter with minute of the ministry of the interior, dated 27 pluviôse an VIII (*ibid.*).

CHAPTER XV

AID TO LARGE FAMILIES IN NEED

ANOTHER phase of eighteenth-century pensions and gratifications was the aid rendered to large families bordering on indigence. The policy had its origins in the sixteenth and seventeenth centuries. In 1573 in Burgundy an order of the parlement of Dijon exempted from the *impôt* (direct taxes) all fathers of twelve or more children.[1] By a royal edict of November, 1666, which applied to all of France, Louis XIV granted pensions to the heads of large families of the aristocracy and bourgeoisie under certain conditions. The father or widowed mother of an aristocratic family of twelve children was to receive 2,000 livres, provided all the children had been born of lawful wedlock and one or more had entered "the king's service" (i.e., the army or navy). It did not matter whether all of the children were still living, but no child could be counted in making the quota of twelve who had become priest, monk, or nun.[2] The heads of aristocratic families with ten children were eligible to receive 1,000 livres a year. Bourgeois families living in free cities were eligible to receive pensions of half the amount offered to noble families.[3] Bourgeois families, however, could not qualify unless at least one third of the children had borne arms in the king's service. In 1667 the terms affecting bourgeois families were extended to all subjects in France without distinction, and in 1669 to Canadians. By regulations of 1670 and 1680 non-Catholics and participants in mixed marriages were excluded.[4]

This legislation, whose object was to stimulate the growth of certain elements in the population, was revoked in so far as it applied to commoners by a royal declaration of January 13, 1683, because of the flood of applications and the abuses to which it gave rise.[5]

[1] Alfred Franklin, *La vie privée d'autrefois* . . . , XX (Paris, 1896), 123.

[2] This anticlerical touch, indeed the whole edict, is ascribed to Colbert.

[3] Heads of families of twelve children would be eligible for pensions of 1,000 livres; heads of families of ten children, pensions of 500 livres.

[4] "Extrait des registres de la cour du parlement," Archives de la Seine-Inférieure, C 1006; Lucien Schöne, *Histoire de la population française* (Paris, 1893), pp. 139-158; E. Levasseur, *La population française* . . . , III (Paris, 1892), 209; Joseph J. Spengler, *French Predecessors of Malthus* (Durham, 1942), pp. 24-26.

[5] Letters from D'Ormesson to De la Michaudière, Aug. 23, 1764, and De Crosne,

The part applying to the nobility was never revoked, but allowed after 1683 to drop into desuetude. The government, however, continued quietly to aid certain families, considering each case on its own merits, and emphasizing its charitable aspect. On September 17, 1764, D'Ormesson, intendant of finance, in a letter to the intendant of Bordeaux, wrote: "You doubtless are not ignorant that the privileges of fathers of families of commoners (*roturiers*) have been revoked, but the intention of the council in this has been to prevent the abuses made of it, and not to cease favoring the population. Thus it is the custom (*usage*) to write Messrs. the intendants when such demands have been made, that if these fathers of families appear to them to merit aid they might procure it for them."[6] A declaration of November 30, 1715, considered the parents of eight married children eligible for exemption from the *taille*.[7] In a case of charity in 1752-53, the government considered the possession of a large family and moderate means as contributing grounds for establishing a pension of 200 livres,[8] but instances of aid to large families in the period 1683 to 1760 were probably not numerous.[9]

Dec. 5, 1768 (Arch. de la Seine-Inférieure, C 1006). Cf. Spengler, *op. cit.*, p. 26; Levasseur, *op. cit.*, III, 209; Isambert, *op. cit.*, XIX, 413. Levasseur considers that the measure had little or no efficacy as a means of increasing the population.

[6] A letter written in regard to the application for aid by a lawyer and former city alderman (*jurat*) named Durantin, the father of twenty children, of whom twelve still lived (Arch. de la Gironde, C 33). A similar statement occurred in a letter written by D'Ormesson to De la Michaudière, intendant of Rouen, Aug. 23, 1764: "Although the privileges of fathers of aristocratic families have not been formally revoked as those of commoners' families have been, by declaration of the king of January 13, 1683, nevertheless they are fallen into desuetude and it is no longer customary to conform to the terms of the edict of November, 1666; however, as the intention of the council has never ceased to be to favor the population, it is for you to judge whether this gentleman [in question] is really in the position of deserving aid . . ." (Arch. de la Seine-Inférieure, C 1006).

Louis François de Paule Lefèvre d'Ormesson (1718-89), as intendant of finance, served in the office of the controller-general of finance. An account of him and his son (1751-1807), later intendant of finance and controller-general, is found in the *Biographie universelle, ancienne et moderne*.

[7] Age and "certain infirmities" were also set forth as grounds for exemption (Georges Bonnefoy, *Histoire de l'administration civile dans la province d'Auvergne et le départment du Puy-de-Dôme* . . . , I, Paris, 1895, 220).

Lorraine in 1729 (before its union to France) exempted the fathers of ten living children from direct taxes (Marcel Marion, *Dictionnaire des institutions de la France*, p. 444).

[8] The pension was granted Toustain (or Toustaing) de Richebourg, of the generality of Rouen, in order that he might be enabled to keep his dangerously insane brother in an institution. Another ground considered was the services that De Richebourg had rendered the crown. Several letters in Arch. de la Seine-Inférieure, C 1007, bear on the case.

[9] No mention of such aid has been found in published works on charities, popu-

Government aid to large families in need began to be more frequent in the period following the early 1760's, as various letters between D'Ormesson and the intendants of Rouen and Bordeaux in 1764 reveal. Perhaps it began earlier. Through the remaining years of the Old Regime it continued, possibly even to the beginning of the Revolutionary wars. During these three decades numerous cases were aided in one way or another, the policy of the government being primarily the provision of charity, and secondarily the encouragement of growth of population.[10] The intendant and his subdelegates carefully investigated each application to make sure that aid was needed.

The revival of state interest in the increase in population was coincident with, and no doubt proceeded in part from, the tremendous popular interest in the matter. La Chalotais observed that "everybody is disturbed over depopulation."[11] A number of French social theorists in published writings urged the state to offer families financial inducement in certain instances in order to encourage the increase of children.[12]

In its aid to large families, the state had no consistent policy.

---

lation, or even in the *Inventaires-sommaires des archives departementales*. One must not deduce too much from this, however. Cf. S. T. McCloy, "Government Aid to Large Families in Normandy, 1764-1786," *Social Forces*, XVIII (March, 1940), 418-424.

[10] See letters from the D'Ormessons to the intendants of Rouen and Bordeaux in the 1760's, 1770's, and 1780's. For instance, in a letter to Fargères, intendant of Bordeaux, D'Ormesson *père* wrote on February 5, 1770, saying in part, in regard to an application of this type: "I am only able to refer to what I have already remarked on this subject, in observing to you nevertheless that the intention of the king being not less to favor the population in his kingdom, his Majesty approves the assistance (*soulagemens*) that one is able to procure for large families" (Arch. de la Gironde, C 2478). On January 26, 1768, he wrote along a similar vein to De la Michaudière, intendant of Rouen: "You are not ignorant that the privileges of fathers of common families (*familles roturières*) have been revoked and that they may aspire only to graces that the council, after taking information on the state of their circumstances, judges proper to give them in consideration of the favor that the population always merits" (Arch. de la Seine-Inférieure, C 1006). Cf. letters from D'Ormesson to De la Michaudière, Aug. 23, 1764, and to De Crosne, Dec. 5, 1768, Jan. 18, 1776, April 18, 1776; and from Anson, chief of the department of *impositions*, to De Crosne, June 15, 1785 (*ibid.*). In one of these letters D'Ormesson refers to the population as "the true wealth of the state."

[11] Duruy, *L'Instruction publique et la Révolution* (Paris, 1882), p. 28.

[12] An elaborate, careful study of this movement by Professor Joseph J. Spengler, entitled *French Predecessors of Malthus*, appeared in 1942.

Some of the theorists proposed pensions, some reductions in taxes. Some urged higher taxes for celibates. See, in particular, *op. cit.*, pp. 85, 88-89, 96 n., 99, 104, 105, 108.

Ordinarily if the family was large (i.e., eight or more children) and in circumstances approaching destitution, some form of grant would be made, if no more than a temporary exemption from part or all of the *impôts*. If the provincial treasury was well filled and the applicant was well recommended (by the subdelegate or the intendant who made the investigation), he might receive, in addition to tax exemption, a monetary award varying from 50 to 300 livres. When an additional cause for charity existed, such as loss by fire or flood, the monetary award might be larger. In a few cases, notably where the person was of birth or prominence, pensions were bestowed. In at least one instance the intendant endeavored to assist the applicant to find a job.[13] In another, the father, an officer of dragoons, was given a deserted Acadian home and land on the estate of the Marquis de Pérusse in Poitou.[14] In a third, assistance was given toward the education of the children.[15] In a fourth, an Acadian, arrested for the contraband sale of tobacco, was shortly afterwards released, in consideration of his previous good conduct and his large family.[16] In some cases there was refusal to do anything; in others, the applicant could not later be found; in yet others, the government took little interest or procrastinated, and apparently no aid was given.

A common form of aid was the remission of taxes; this remission might be for part or all of the applicant's *impositions*. One recipient was Laignel, an advocate-consultant of Le Havre, father of ten children, the eldest of whom was not yet fourteen. Laignel's health had broken to such an extent that he had been compelled to quit the practice of his profession; moreover, according to the subdelegate, he was a man of mediocre ability. Nevertheless, he was "one of the most esteemed citizens of Havre," and merited "a recompense." De Crosne agreed to moderate his taxes. Since Laignel paid only

[13] Grisel, a jeweler of Rouen, was the father of sixteen children, of whom ten survived. When he went to Paris to seek employment with the *administration de la voirie et des messageries*, De Crosne urged D'Ormesson to do what he could to aid Grisel (Arch. de la Seine-Inférieure, C 1006).

[14] Ernest Martin, *op. cit.*, p. 238.

[15] The son of the widow Grandoit (one of four children) was maintained by government bounty at one of the royal military schools, in 1786 (Memoir, Arch. de la Seine-Inférieure, C 1007). Others made applications for aid toward education of their children, but it is not clear what disposition was made in most of the cases.

[16] Martin, *op. cit.*, p. 109.

10 livres on the *capitation,* his taxes were not heavy.[17] Ernoult, a master candlestick maker of Rouen and father of ten living children, was granted in 1785 merely some remissions in taxes.[18] Others given tax alleviation were an aged laborer named Bobée, father of fourteen children, who was in moderate economic circumstances;[19] a widow Manger, who had eleven children, three or four of whom yet lived with her;[20] a master shoemaker of Rouen, named Philippe Huray;[21] an innkeeper of Louviers, named Le Tellier;[22] a procurer of the king in the election of Lyons, named Denize, the progenitor of sixty-eight children, grandchildren, and great grandchildren;[23] and an inhabitant of Rouen, named Le Mire, father of eleven children.[24]

A large number of the applicants received a monetary gratification, sometimes accompanied by partial or total exemption from taxes. In this category fell most of the successful applicants in the generality of Guyenne. Among them were Favrion, a blind father of eleven young children, who was given a grant of 150 livres on the "free funds of the *capitation*";[25] Foucand, "a bourgeois of

[17] Letters from Oursel to De Crosne, July 26, 1786, and from De Crosne to De Vergennes, intendant of impositions, June 23, 1785 (Arch. de la Seine-Inférieure, C 1006). Laignel applied for a pension, but apparently was unsuccessful.

[18] Letters from Cauchet to De Crosne, July 17, 1785, and from De Vergennes to De Crosne, July 11, 1785 *(ibid.).* De Vergennes indicated that he could be aided only by exemption from his *capitation,* which amounted merely to 20 livres.

[19] According to his petition he paid 900 livres in taxes, but according to a note by De Crosne he was assessed 205 livres in 1772. The note states that his *impositions* in 1773 were reduced to 190 livres *(ibid.).*

[20] She was promised remissions, but their extent is not revealed (letters of July, 1786, between De Crosne and De Vergennes, *ibid.*).

[21] He was allowed only remission of his *capitation* (D'Ormesson to De Crosne, July 19, 1782, *ibid.*).

[22] Because of his large family and his inability to support it, he had already for several years been given a diminution in his *capitation.* De Crosne was told that he might extend the same aid again (Chevalier de Chastellux to De Crosne, May 24, 1777, and reply, June 5, 1777, *ibid.*).

[23] The old man earned only 114 livres in wages, and paid out 80 livres 8 sous in taxes. On De Crosne's recommendation, his taxes were reduced to 25 livres. The subdelegate, Framboisière, wrote that Denize was seventy-four years old, and that within the last two years he had paid out more than 3,000 livres on one of his sons-in-law who himself had a family of eleven children and was not able to care for them (letters of 1769, *ibid.*).

[24] He received exemption from the *vingtième* and reduction in the *capitation* for the years 1769 and 1770 (D'Ormesson to De Crosne, April 6, 1770, with marginal n., *ibid.*). Exemption from the *vingtième* was made only when losses had been sustained in goods subject to taxation.

[25] D'Ormesson to Esmangart, July 20, 1770 (Arch. de la Gironde, C 2478).

Marmande," father of eleven children, who was given a remission in taxes and a gratification of 100 livres on the same funds;[26] Jean François Espeut, a *perruquier* of Bordeaux, father of twenty-seven children (fourteen surviving), granted an award of 200 livres;[27] Sarpy of Fumel, father of twenty children (eleven living), given 300 livres;[28] the widow St. Signé, mother of a large family, allowed 100 livres;[29] Labarete of Marmande, accorded 200 livres;[30] Raymond de la Nauze, inhabitant of Lauzan, father of fifteen living children, granted 150 livres;[31] and Turpin of Bordeaux, aged father of fourteen children, given 300 livres.[32] In Rouen, Hamel, a baker with fifteen children, was given a grant of 300 livres on the free funds of the *capitation* in 1776,[33] but later (in 1782), when he had become the father of a sixteenth child and was encumbered with debt, he was given no further aid, not even the remission of his *capitation*.[34] Grisel, the father of a large family in poor circumstances, was granted 200 livres in 1776;[35] in the same year, Pain, father of eleven small children, was recommended for a grant of 160 livres;[36] and Jacques Pouchet and his wife, an aged couple of Rouen, with thirteen living children, were given 200 livres.[37]

[26] This same grant had been made to him the previous year (Esmangart to D'Ormesson, March 5, 1774, *ibid.*, C 61).

[27] This sum had been given for the two previous years; he applied again and was recommended by the intendant for a renewal, in 1775 (letter by the applicant of Sept., 1775, and report by the subdelegate Cojmartin, Nov., 1775, *ibid.*, C 2478). The applicant states in his letter that twenty-three of the children were by his second wife. He was first married in 1736.

[28] Receipt signed by Sarpy, May 2, 1776 *(ibid)*.

[29] Receipt signed on April 28, 1776 *(ibid.)*. Another widow, who had fifteen living children, was allotted 400 livres for the years 1773, 1774, and 1775. In 1776 she applied for continuation of the allowance.

[30] Letter from the subdelegate to the intendant *(ibid.)*.

[31] De Vergennes to the intendant *(ibid.)*.

[32] He asked that this aid be given for three years, but was refused, being told that he might apply again the next year for another grant. Gratifications were rarely given for more than one year at a time *(ibid.*, C 2510).

[33] De Crosne to D'Ormesson, March 26, 1776 (Arch. de la Seine-Inférieure, C 1006).

[34] Alexandre to De Crosne, April 29, 1782; D'Ormesson to De Crosne, July 5, 1782; and De Crosne to D'Ormesson, July 8, 1782. Earlier De Crosne had recommended a remission of the *capitation*, and D'Ormesson had approved, but De Crosne later changed his mind *(ibid.)*. As other letters of De Crosne in 1782 reveal (cf. Arch. de la Seine-Inférieure, C 1007), the war with England had produced heavy demands on his funds for charity, and he was obliged to refuse some applications which in normal circumstances he might have granted.

[35] De Crosne to D'Ormesson, July 24, 1776 *(ibid.*, C 1007).

[36] De Crosne to D'Ormesson, June 10, 1776 *(ibid.*, C 1006).

[37] Several letters between D'Ormesson and De Crosne in April and May, 1776 *(ibid.)*.

Pensions were also granted to the heads of large families in need. Two surgeons of Rouen, Le Cat and Pillore, qualifying on this basis, were granted pensions, that of Le Cat being based on the revenues of the *octroi* for the city of Rouen, and that of Pillore, on the free funds of the *capitation* of the generality. Le Cat was allowed a pension of 200 livres; Pillore was granted, for a period of only five years, 300 livres. Pillore was given, in addition, exemption from the *capitation*.[38] The widow of Pierre Caillé, who lived in the parish of St. Remy, near Nonancourt, and had given eight sons to the army (seven were in it at the moment), was in dire circumstances, and applied in 1782-83 for remission of her taxes. The king, hearing of the woman, was so deeply touched that he directed the Marquis de Ségur, minister of war, forthwith to accord her a pension.[39] Surprisingly for a case of royal interest, the pension provided only 100 livres a year.[40] After the pension was granted, the war office, apparently through carelessness, had much difficulty in finding the woman, and sent notification of the award to the intendants of Orléans and Rouen before learning that she dwelt in the generality of Alençon.[41]

According to the *Etat nominatif des pensions* (1790), a number of persons were pensioned because of their large and needy families. Thus Jean François Abadie, aged eighty-six, father of seven boys, was pensioned in 1756 in order to help him support them.[42] Henri Bazoche, aged forty-seven, was pensioned 200 livres in 1768, "to aid at his subsistence, that of his wife and his three children."[43] Pierre Antoine Bernelle, aged forty-one, in 1789 was pensioned 150 livres, partly because of his services and partly because of his "numerous family."[44] Pierre François Bony, aged sixty-seven, was

[38] D'Ormesson to De Crosne, April 30, 1777 (*ibid.*). Cf. McCloy, *op. cit.*, *Social Forces*, XVIII, 423. Pillore had rendered high service to his community and state.

[39] Several letters in Arch. de la Seine-Inférieure, C 1006, deal with the case, one from the curé de Chataincourt (Feb. 18, 1783), telling something of the history of the case. This curé took a great interest in the woman and sought a pension for her by writing to the intendant and visiting officials at Paris in her behalf.

[40] It is cited on the list of pensions published by the National Assembly in 1790 (*Arch. parl.*, XIV, 462).

[41] See a letter of the curé de Chataincourt to the intendant of Rouen. The present writer has come across several blunders of this kind made by the government of the Old Regime.

[42] *Arch. parl.*, XIV, 347.   [43] *Ibid.*, XIV, 393.

[44] *Ibid.*, XIV, 407.

granted a pension of 200 livres in 1781, for the same reasons.[45] Antoine Bernard Chaffner, aged fifty-eight, was in 1774 given a pension of 120 livres, partly for his services as doorkeeper in one of the royal buildings at Versailles and partly "to place him in a condition to raise his children."[46] René Trouvé, aged seventy-two, was in 1775 given a pension of 300 livres, "in consideration of his numerous family."[47] Christophe Benoît de la Grandière, aged fifty-six, in 1785 was pensioned 1,500 livres, "in consideration of his services in different places in the magistrature, and of his numerous family."[48]

Mademoiselle Salvet, one of seventeen children, and the third daughter in the family to devote herself to religious work, was pensioned 120 livres in April, 1779, when she entered the convent, since her family did not have the funds to help her, and the religious house of her choice was inadequately endowed.[49] Jean Dennel Clerc, an inhabitant of Montmarres, in Guyenne, was given in 1785 "an annual gratification" (tantamount to a pension), because of great age, large family, and "modicity of fortune." The intendant described him to De Vergennes as about a hundred years old, and having 107 living descendants out of 139 that had been born.[50]

Not infrequently the applicant for aid stated that an accident of nature or freak of fortune was largely responsible for his plight. Thus La Fitte de Pelleguignon, an aristocrat *(gentilhomme)* of Agen and father of twelve living children, asked aid in 1775 partly on the ground that for several years he had suffered from floods. He was given 300 livres on the free funds of the *capitation*.[51] When Claire Thomas, the father of nine sons, lost all his ten horses in a fire of August, 1786, and in consequence appealed to the intendant of Rouen for aid, the government granted him a diminution of 200 livres.[52] Pierre Philippe Samson, a farmer of Bray and father of fifteen chil-

---

[45] Bony had previously been allowed a pension of 200 livres because of his services as letter-bearer to the French ambassador in Switzerland (*ibid.*, XIV, 430).

[46] *Ibid.*, XIV, 479.

[47] *Ibid.*, XV, 213.

[48] *Ibid.*, XIII, 642.

[49] Letter from Bertin (Arch. de la Gironde, C 2512).

[50] De Neville to De Vergennes, Sept. 12, 1785, and reply of Oct. 15, 1785 (*ibid.*, C 2478).

[51] D'Ormesson to Esmangart, Jan. 8 and June 10, 1775 (*ibid.*).

[52] Letters by the Abbé D'Agoult, vicar-general, and the Curé D'Arthie, to the intendant, with marginal note on the latter (Arch. de la Seine-Inférieure, C 1006).

dren (twelve of them living), sought aid in 1779 largely on the ground that a hailstorm had damaged his harvest. What was done is not indicated, but the subdelegate Courtois wrote to the intendant that "never would charity be better placed."[53] When one Le Fortier wrote directly to the queen in 1780 for relief because of his large family and losses caused by a fire, his request was turned over to Necker and De Crosne, who decided that since a collection had already been made in his behalf in the diocese of Lisieux, diminution in his taxes was the only aid that the state could render him.[54] The widow Voustremer, of Aumale, whose husband, a physician, had died while combating an epidemic in the environs of his city, asked aid of the government in 1770 toward the rearing of her five little girls. Her husband, she stated, had been "taken in the flower of his age," and had not had time to accumulate savings for their future.[55] Jean Patin, a laborer, was crushed to death by a landslide while working on the road from Honfleur to Pont-Audemer in October, 1779, leaving a widow about sixty years of age and six children. The intendant asked aid for the unfortunate family because of this tragedy, and a gratification and reduction in taxes were made.[56] A chronic applicant of this type was Mousson de l'Etang, judge at the royal court at Montpassier and father of eleven living children, who in each of the three years 1772, 1773, and 1774, claimed heavy losses in animals and other property, and received for each of the first two years a gratification of 340 livres.[57]

In certain rare instances aid was requested toward the education of children, or complaint was made that destitute circumstances rendered the applicants unable to give their children an education. An interesting case of this type was that of François Varin de Bretteville, once a resident of Rouen, but at the time of his application for a pension, 1764, residing on his estate at Bretteville. He was the father of thirteen children, all living, five boys and eight girls.

[53] Necker to De Crosne, July 29, 1779; Courtois to De Crosne, Aug. 24, 1779; and D'Ormesson to De Crosne, April 10, 1783 (ibid.).

[54] Necker to De Crosne, June 9, 1780 (ibid., C 1007).

[55] No indication is given of the action taken by the council of state, but De Crosne recommended that aid be given (various letters of 1770, ibid.).

[56] Le Chevalier to De Crosne, Feb. 1, 1780, and reply of Feb. 5; other papers bear on the matter (ibid.).

[57] There is no indication what was done the third year (Terray to Esmangart, March 29, 1774, and other letters, Arch. de la Gironde, C 61).

Certain of the older children were in their twenties, and he was worried over the problem of establishing them; the younger ones needed education, and he was desirous of getting them placed in boys' and girls' schools maintained by the government. In his application for a pension, De Bretteville, as indeed did several other applicants,[58] appealed to the provisions of the pension law of 1666-67. The subdelegate and intendant recommended the placing of the younger sons in a military college and two of the younger girls in the school at St. Cyr by means of scholarships. D'Ormesson, however, scouted this idea, since De Bretteville was not in distressed circumstances; nevertheless, he indicated that it was agreeable to the government for the intendant to exempt him from certain of his taxes, and to give him a small grant on the free funds of the *capitation*.[59] The government granted 1,500 livres (date not given) to Mangos, councilor to the grand council, in order that he might live as his post demanded and "give a fitting education to his family, composed of nine children."[60] In 1778 it gave a pension of 500 livres to each of three adult sons of Esmangart de Bournonville, formerly head clerk of the bureau of foreign affairs, for them "to enjoy during the time of their education."[61] In granting aid to the widow Voustremer (also written Woutremer) and her five little children, in 1770, the office of the controller-general professed interest in seeing that the children were given an education. De Crosne's opinion was that the matter could be easily handled if only the five were boys, rather than girls, since they could be "placed gratuitously in colleges."[62] In his application for relief in 1766 because of his large family, Durantin, called by the intendant of Bordeaux "the leading lawyer in the province, and the most impartial," specified that he wished to be in a position to educate his twelve children.[63] The intendant stated that "the whole province would

[58] Bobée, Ernoult, and Le Mire were among this number.

[59] Several papers in Arch. de la Seine-Inférieure, C 1006. See also McCloy, *op. cit.*, Social Forces, XVIII, 420.

[60] Bibl. Nat., Fonds français 6802, f 73.

[61] *Arch. parl.*, XIV, 598. It is not clear in the latter case to what extent the family was large or in poor circumstances.

[62] Letter from the controller-general's office to De Crosne, Oct. 3, 1770, and reply, Dec. 25, 1770 (Arch. de la Seine-Inférieure, C 1007). No record has been found of action taken by the government.

[63] He was the father of twenty children, but only twelve were alive. Another was shortly expected.

applaud the grant that his Majesty might well wish to accord in favor of a citizen who has consecrated his talents and outlook with an impartiality too rare in this region to the defense of the widow and orphan, and in general to the public welfare."[64] Another "bourgeois of Bordeaux," Bernard, complained in his application for aid, in 1770, that "mediocrity of his faculties" rendered him unable to maintain and educate his "numerous family."[65] A physician of Marmande, Heraud, father of ten living children, complained that a hailstorm had so crippled his already small income that it was not sufficient for the maintenance and education of his family, and asked 200 livres and discharge from his direct taxes.[66]

Sometimes the intendant was requested by the controller-general or one of his subordinates to inform the applicant that the government could make no grant. This happened in instances when facts learned through investigation by the subdelegates did not match those stated in the applications, when the applicants were found to be in conditions better than they had described, and in cases where moral turpitude was discovered. Thus an applicant named Le Vaillant Dubuisson, dwelling near Lyons-la-Forêt in the generality of Rouen, was reported by the subdelegate to have squandered a fortune, deserted his children, turned away his servant with child, and to be undeserving of aid. The intendant thereupon told the applicant that he had no funds.[67] Investigation showed that Leglise de Lalande, of Guyenne, who had solicited aid because of his thirteen children, enjoyed an income of 10,000 livres. He, of course, was refused.[68] Sometimes the intendant was perhaps severe. Thus the *femme* Crespin, deserted by her husband and forced to support three children by teaching school, at which she earned 18 to 20 livres a month, made application for aid, and the subdelegate found conditions as reported. De Crosne, however, wrote to Paris: "After all these details, it appears to me that the *femme* Crespin is in the class of all persons born in poverty, and that there is no other ground

[64] Bontin to D'Ormesson, Jan. 11, 1766 (Arch. de la Gironde, C 33). No evidence has been found concerning the decision reached in Paris. It seems odd that a brilliant and popular lawyer was unable to earn enough to educate his children.

[65] D'Ormesson to Fargères, Feb. 5, 1770 (*ibid.*, C 2478). Again there is no indication of the decision reached.

[66] Heraud to Fargères, Jan. 11, 1770 (*ibid.*).

[67] Letters of 1786 (Arch. de la Seine-Inférieure, C 1007).

[68] Esmangart to D'Ormesson, Feb. 7, 1774 (Arch. de la Gironde, C 61).

for according her extraordinary aid."[69]   Some of the deserving applicants were turned away for lack of funds,[70] especially in the 1780's, during and after the war with England, when French finances were strained, and demands for charity were many.[71]

Thus the number of applicants was high.   In several of his letters to Paris, De Crosne described the number of large families in the generality of Rouen as considerable.[72]   In two letters he mentioned "a very great number"; in another, "a multitude."[73]   He was constantly uneasy lest the grants of aid to some heads of large families become noised abroad and lead to a deluge of requests.   According to the tax list of those paying the *taille* in the single election of Saint-Valery-en-Caux, in 1777, fifty-five families had ten or more children.[74]   By the same criterion there were eleven such families in the election of Andely, in 1778.[75]   In the generality of Caen the aid to large families amounted in 1785 to 20,470 livres, and in 1786 to 15,152 livres.[76]   There were naturally many other large families which did not apply for this aid.[77]   Doubtless families of the same

[69] De Vergennes to De Crosne, June 17, 1783, and reply by De Crosne, Aug. 19, 1783 (Arch. de la Seine-Inférieure, C 1007).

[70] Thus the widow Turpin, of Bordeaux, who appears to have deserved aid, was turned down in 1787 for this reason (Blondel to De Neville, Nov. 16, 1787, Arch. de la Gironde, C 2494).

[71] The cases mentioned in this chapter are but a small proportion of those that occurred in France during this period and are described in the manuscript papers of the departmental archives.   The *Inventaires-sommaires des archives départementales antérieurs à 1790* for certain departments, notably those for Seine-Inférieure, Calvados, and the Gironde (Rouen, Caen, and Bordeaux), list numerous *cartons* or *liasses* on the subject.   These cartons and liasses often treat as many as twenty-five or thirty cases.   The number is not fixed, and there is some overlapping, so that there is no way of determining the total number of applicants except by a study of all the records.

In the *Inventaire-sommaire* for Calvados liasses C 991-1018 deal exclusively with "Aid to Large Families," and the matter is further treated to some extent in C 233, 236, 238, 240, 250, 252, 253, 1006, and possibly elsewhere.   The *Inventaire-sommaire*, série C, for Gironde has perhaps an equal number of *cartons* or *liasses* on the matter; and that for Seine-Inférieure has some.

[72] Letters to D'Ormesson, March 12 and April 22, 1773.   In the former he writes: ". . . there are in the 14 elections of the generality of Rouen *un très grand nombre* of fathers of families which have from ten to 14 and 15 children, and which, like Sr. Bobée, have need of aid" (*ibid.*, C 1006).

[73] Letter to De Vergennes, June 25, 1785 *(ibid.)*.

[74] *Inv.-som . . . Seine-Inférieure*, C 275.

[75] *Ibid.*, C 276.

[76] *Inv.-som . . . Calvados*, C 233.   Assuming an average of 200 livres given to each of the heads of large families aided, this would indicate that 102 families were aided in 1785, and 75 in 1786.

[77] Messance, the eighteenth-century founder of French demography, reached the

prolific type existed in certain other generalities.[78]   Perhaps 40 per
cent of the large families investigated lived in Bordeaux, Rouen,
and other cities; large families were not overwhelmingly in the
rural regions.   Futhermore, all classes of society were represented
in the category of large families: nobles, professional men, merchants
large and small, farmers, and city workers.   Possibly the number
of families in each group was roughly proportional to the strength
in numbers of each group in the total population.   Applications for
aid came from each group, including the nobility.[79]

Not only was financial assistance employed to stimulate growth
of the French population, but also serious efforts were made toward
the same end by fostering prosperity in industry and commerce and
by improving the training of midwives so as to decrease infant mortality.[80]   The French government thus recognized the distinction
between stimulants and remedies, and did not neglect the latter.

During the Revolutionary period aid to large families was continued.[81]   Jean Martineau, father of twenty-five children, with his
wife and four daughters dependent on him, broken in health and
living in misery in 1791, was granted 300 livres by the National
Assembly.[82]   The Legislative Assembly in September, 1792, gave
400 livres to the widow Poissonneau, who had borne twenty-two

conclusion, following statistical compilations, that "families of six or more living
children comprised not over one-twenty-fifth of all families, and families with 10-12
children comprised not over one-thousandth of all families" (Joseph J. Spengler,
"Messance: Founder of French Demography," reprinted from *Human Biology*, XII,
Feb., 1940, 80-81).   One would be led to question the accuracy of Messance's con-
clusions with regard to the generalities of Bordeaux, Rouen, and Caen; but, according to Professor Spengler, Messance recognized that "family size varied by
place as well as in time."

[78] Messance stated that the fecundity of families was higher in Lyons and Auvergne than in Rouen *(idem)*.

Professor Georges Lefebvre in his book, *La grande peur de 1789* (Paris, 1932),
p. 9, cites the *cahier* of grievances of the village La Caure, in the *bailliage* of Châlons, as stating that the size of families made it hard for their heads to clothe and feed
them.

Only a portion of the *Inventaires-sommaires* have been searched for purposes
of this study.   Most of those examined have little material listed on the subject and
tend to support the conclusion of Messance, that the family size in France varied
from place to place.

[79] These last were from De Bretteville, Toustain de Richebourg, and Brecourt.

[80] Joseph J. Spengler, *France Faces Depopulation* (Durham, 1938), pp. 44, 107;
see above, pp. 171-173.

[81] To what extent is not known, since the published sources contain only scattered references.

[82] *Arch. parl.*, XXXI, 54.

children, five of whom at the moment were serving "under the flags."[83]   The administration of the district of Grenoble, on 24 prairial an II (June 13, 1794) extended 300 livres in aid and appreciation to the widow Brun, of the city of Grenoble, aged ninety-four, "grandmother of a numerous family, of which many members" were then "fighting for their country."[84]   Moreover, widows with several children living in destitution were made gifts varying from 150 to 300 livres, and three unmarried women, daughters of large families, were aided by the National Assembly in 1791 because of their poverty.[85]   The Revolutionists, as their speeches and their legislation indicate, were keenly interested in the family relationship and in relief of the destitute.[86]   Although no legislation was passed for the specific purpose of aiding large families, aid was given to these families, particularly to those in need.

[83] Cited by Ferdinand-Dreyfus, *L'Assistance*, p. 18.   A widow in Toulouse, mother of eleven children, had nine sons serving in the French infantry, and a tenth son was killed in the storming of the Bastille.   The Popular Society of Toulouse assisted her by a gift of 18 livres (Adher, *Recueil de documents*, p. 445 n.).

[84] *Inv.-som* . . . *Isère*, L 184, an II.

[85] The widow Martinet, with five children, was given 150 livres; the widow Desmoulins de Longchamps, also with five, was given 300; and several widows with smaller numbers of children were likewise aided.   The three unmarried women were Marguerite Lahaule de Compigny, Thérèse Lamorre, and the demoiselle Poirson de Bussy (*Arch. parl.*, XXXI, 53-54).

The meager list of cases found is not sufficient to support the conclusion that this form of assistance ceased during the Revolutionary period.   With the exception of the information in the *Inventaires-sommaires des archives départementales*, there has hitherto been virtually nothing in print concerning the aid rendered to large families prior to 1789.   Possibly in departmental archives may rest material for the Revolutionary period.

[86] See discussion before the Legislative Assembly on the matter of dividing communal goods and lands, Sept. 8, 1792 (*Arch. parl.*, XLIX, 469).   On the legislation, see Levasseur, *op. cit.*, III, 123-124, 210; Ferdinand-Dreyfus, *op. cit.*, pp. 73-74; Deries, *op. cit.*, p. 398; and *Arch. parl.*, LXXIV, 720-721.

CHAPTER XVI

ASSISTANCE TO REFUGEES, CAPTIVES, AND WAR SUFFERERS

Before 1789

THE ACADIANS, descendants of Frenchmen sent out as colonists for the most part by Richelieu in the early 1600's, settled in Nova Scotia, where they retained without adulteration their French blood, culture, and loyalty, despite the fact that since the Treaty of Utrecht in 1713 their territory had belonged to Britain. In their oaths of loyalty to the British crown they repeatedly refused to include a clause stipulating willingness to fight for Britain in a war with France. This refusal caused them to be looked upon with increasing distrust by both the British government and the British colonies to the south. The latter became alarmed, since shipping between New York and Boston on the one hand and London on the other, following the arc of a great circle, passed close to the shores of Nova Scotia and thus might be intercepted in time of war should the Acadians permit French privateers to operate from their coast. Consequently the divided loyalty of the Acadians brought on their fate.[1]

The crisis came to a head shortly after the appointment of Colonel Charles Lawrence as governor of Nova Scotia in 1753. A man of ambition and determination, realizing that war between Britain and France was approaching,[2] Lawrence acted on his own initiative (without orders from London), summoned leaders of the Acadians

---

[1] The most colorful story of eighteenth-century refugee life is that of the Acadians, immortalized by Longfellow's romantic poem *Evangeline*. Among the many works on the Acadians, see Ernest Martin, *Les exilés Acadiens en France au XVIIIᵉ siècle, et leur établissement en Poitou* (Paris, 1936); J. B. Brebner, *New England's Outpost: Acadia before the Conquest of Canada* (New York, 1927); Francis Parkman, *A Half-Century of Conflict* (Boston, 1899), I; Emile Lauvrière, *La tragédie d'un peuple: histoire du peuple acadien de ses origines à nos jours*, new ed., revised and corrected, II (Paris, 1924); James P. Baxter, "What Caused the Deportation of the Acadians?" *Proceedings of the American Antiquarian Society*, N.S., I (Worcester, 1901); and Herbert Ingram Priestley, *France Overseas through the Old Regime: A Study of European Expansion* (New York and London, 1939). Their story even yet has controversial aspects.

[2] Hostilities broke out between the colonies of the two countries in 1755, and war was formally declared between the two nations in 1756.

to a conference, and demanded that they take the oath of full allegiance to the crown, whereby they would agree to render military service if called upon to do so. Upon their refusal, he informed them that they had forfeited their British citizenship and could no longer expect to enjoy the right of living in the colony.[3] As a last step, he made a general appeal to the Acadian people, but without success. Thereupon, in August, 1755, he informed them that they would be imprisoned and dispersed among the British colonies to the south. In September came the expulsion. Most of the Acadians were crowded on British ships and transported, some to the British colonies to the south, some to England, while others escaped to French territories in Canada and the West Indies.

The population of Acadia proper at the time of the dispersion (1755-1764) was not great, probably from 8,000 to 10,000.[4] The deportation, however, affected New Brunswick, Maine, Isle Royale and Isle Saint-Jean (later renamed Cape Breton and Prince Edward islands) as well as Nova Scotia.[5] In short, the deportation of the Acadians was followed by that of French inhabitants of other portions of eastern Canada, as they were captured by the British during the Seven Years' War.[6] The total number of French in all the portions of Eastern Canada, including Quebec, was 70,000 or 75,000;[7] the population in the regions from which deportations were made was about 20,000.[8]

[3] By a clause in the Treaty of Utrecht Britain was to fix a year during which the Acadians might either emigrate to other French territories or remain and become British subjects. This option to leave had never been permitted (Ernest Martin, *op. cit.*, pp. 16-17). Parkman declares that they could have left at any time they wished, from 1713 to 1755 (*op. cit.*, I, 189).

[4] Brebner, *op. cit.*, p. 214. Martin (*op. cit.*, p. 18) estimates at 12,000 to 14,000 the French inhabitants of Nova Scotia, New Brunswick, and what is today Maine.

[5] *Ibid.*, pp. 21-22.

[6] An account of these later deportations is given by Martin, *op. cit.*, pp. 22-30. The present writer was not familiar with Martin's excellent work at the time he published his article in the *Louisiana Historical Review*, July, 1938. The book represents ten years of wide travel and exhaustive research in the archives and libraries of two continents, and its author has laudably succeeded in his aim to be candid and unbiased in his treatment of a very thorny subject.

[7] *Ibid.*, pp. 19, 30.

[8] In addition to the 12,000 or 14,000 of Nova Scotia, New Brunswick, and Maine, Isle Royale (Cape Breton Island) had about 5,000 and Isle Saint-Jean (Prince Edward Island), in 1752, had the exact population of 2,223. When the last-named was surrendered in 1757, however, its population had been swelled by some thousands of Acadians and stood at 4,000 to 6,000 (*ibid.*, pp. 23-24). A full account of the deportation from Isle Saint-Jean and Isle Royale, and of the events leading up to it, may be found in D. C. Harvey, *The French Regime in Prince Edward Island* (New Haven, 1926).

Perhaps all of these 20,000 were forcibly uprooted and transplanted. Some fled; others were made prisoners of war and deported. From Isle Saint-Jean alone 3,540 were taken to England and France. Of this number, 1,300 met their death from shipwreck and a smallpox epidemic.[9] During the war and immediately thereafter several thousand deportees were landed in England and France. Other thousands were dispersed among the English colonies from New England to Georgia. Some few took root, but the greater number were dissatisfied, restless, and roving. Many went to the French islands of the West Indies, and a large number found their way to Louisiana, which by the Treaty of 1763 was ceded by France to Spain.

Those who were taken to England were disembarked in early 1756, and numbered 1,226. During the next seven years they were kept in confinement in the cities of Liverpool, Bristol, Southampton, and Penryn, were treated as prisoners of war, and were given an allowance for maintenance from the British government. Those aged seven and above received 6 sous daily a person, those younger than seven, 3 sous, "more or less regularly until the peace, in February, 1763."[10] On the coming of peace the British government was disposed to permit them, on pledging their loyalty, to return to Acadia, but leaders among them prevailed on the Duc de Nivernais, French ambassador to London, to arrange their transportation to France. After negotiation between the two governments, it was arranged that the Acadians in England would be ceded to France on condition that the latter provide for their passage, pay their debts, reimburse the British government for a part of the allowance paid them, settle them on lands from which they could derive a living, and continue the allowance until they were settled.[11] Thereupon, in May and June, 1763, the 778 Acadians remaining in England (no doubt the rest had died) were brought in French vessels to the Breton ports of Saint-Malo and Morlaix.

They were not, however, the first Acadians to arrive in France. Since September, 1758, when 450 refugees from Isle Royale landed

---

[9] Martin, *op. cit.*, p. 25 with n. 2. Though documents in the Archives Nationales designate them as "Acadians and Canadians," these refugees came to be generally known as "Acadians."

[10] *Ibid.*, p. 38.

[11] *Ibid.*, p. 47; "Rapporte le 5 avril 1782," Arch. Nat., F 15, 3495.

at Rochefort, many other shiploads had come. The city of Saint-Malo alone in April, 1759, received 1,102 refugees from Isle Royale and Isle Saint-Jean.[12] From time to time lists were made public, including fifteen lists of officers and soldiers.[13] According to contemporary documents, a total of three to four thousand Acadians entered France first and last; according to Emile Lauvrière, in the summer of 1774 a total of 3,852 to 3,884 reached France.[14] In 1778, when Saint-Pierre and Miquelon were captured by the British, 115 more refugees joined the Acadians and Canadians who had sought refuge in France and remained there until after the Treaty of 1783.[15]

From the moment of their first arrival, in 1758, the French government agreed to pay a dole *(solde)* of 6 sous a day to refugee Acadians of ordinary rank *(basse condition)*, 12 sous to nuns, and 20 sous (a livre) to priests. In addition, gratifications ranging from 200 to 400 livres were paid to the priests. The Abbé Le Loutre, who, some historians report, encouraged the stubborn attitude of the Acadians under British rule and who certainly wielded tremendous influence over them as long as he lived, received "some yet larger sums." Pensions, based on the funds of the Marine, were bestowed on those of higher estate, such as the militia officers, the prominent citizens, and the noble family of D'Entremont.[16]

The Acadians were simple folk, with little or no education. Many could sign their names, but their penmanship and spelling were poor.[17] Most of them had been farmers before their uprooting from the New World; a few had been fishermen. To have left them in the growing and crowded French cities, where life was complicated, would have been to doom most of them to misery. The cities were already filled with an overflowing population.[18] It

---

[12] Martin, *op. cit.*, p. 26.　　　　[13] Lauvrière, *op. cit.*, II, 263.

[14] In 1772 there were in France 2,370 Acadians, of 626 families. These were increased by the arrival of 1,482 to 1,514 others, of every age, from October, 1773, to the spring of 1774 (*ibid.*, II, 174-175).

[15] Refugees from Miquelon had entered France during the years 1767-69. According to the Treaty of Versailles (1783), 120 former inhabitants of Miquelon were allowed to return to their fisheries (*ibid.*, II, 264).

[16] Martin, *op. cit.*, p. 32.

[17] Parkman (*op. cit.*, II, 190-191) has underestimated the number that could read and write, or at least sign their names.

[18] Throughout the eighteenth century there was a steady drift from the French countryside to the cities, with a resulting increase in mendicancy. According to

was thus more fitting that the Acadians be settled on the land. This the government planned to do; this the Acadians themselves at first wished.

All might have gone well had the French government acted promptly. But perhaps the chief weakness of the government in eighteenth-century France was indecision and slowness. By 1763 the Acadians proper had with a few exceptions[19] already been idle since 1755, satisfied with an allowance which enabled them to live in fair comfort.[20] The large numbers of refugees from Cape Breton and Prince Edward islands had lived in France on the pension list since 1758-59. The generation reaching maturity was little trained for work of any kind, and the older generations, whether or not they had ever been as industrious and prosperous in their New World homes as their partisans would have us believe,[21] were sinking into laziness and contentment.

Several colonizing projects, however, were evolved in time. The first was Choiseul's scheme in 1763 for colonizing Guiana by way of retrieving the loss of Canada. To get the necessary emigrants, Choiseul combed Europe, seeking volunteers not only in France but also, since the French lacked enthusiasm for the project, "in Germany, Belgium, Switzerland, and even Malta." "Religious freedom was guaranteed, and even military prisoners were accepted."[22]

Papion *le jeune*, of the National Assembly, France in the late eighteenth century had a permanent army of 100,000 vagabonds, of whom 15,000 to 16,000 were arrested every year. (*Arch. parl.*, XXII, 638 with n.).

[19] Some of the youths had worked as apprentices at Penryn, in England (Martin, *op. cit.*, p. 38).

[20] "One makes a mistake in imagining that this pension of six sous accorded to the Acadians was an insignificant sum. It was the pension that was given at the time to the invalids of the marine: 108 livres a year. But in each Acadian family all the members, including children in the cradle, received the *solde*. Even the old men and the infirm received, at the beginning, 8 and 9 sous a day. For an average Acadian family of eight persons, this made an annual pension of approximately 900 livres, or some 18,000 francs of our present money [1936]. The roll of pensions given to the 61 members of the noble family of the Entremonts, residing at Cherbourg, amounted exactly to 15,100 livres a year" (*ibid.*, p. 33). The cost to the French government at this period of maintaining the Acadians was more than 300,000 livres annually (*ibid.*, p. 58).

[21] Longfellow is their chief partisan. Lauvrière follows him at no great distance, and even Martin reproduces the picture of the Acadian New World thrift, prosperity, and happiness. On the other hand, Brebner (*op. cit.*, p. 95) quotes a Canadian writer to the effect that the Acadians had been lazy to an amazing degree even in the New World.

[22] Priestley (*op. cit.*, pp. 104-105) presents a good general account of this abortive enterprise, but says nothing of the part of the Acadians.

Among the heterogeneous crowds gathered in French ports for the undertaking were eight thousand Germans. Choiseul also attempted to enlist Acadian interest, even by sending agents to Nova Scotia and Miquelon to prevail on Acadians who had returned to those regions.[23] Only a few Acadians joined the expedition; and on May 1, 1765, only 138 Acadians were living in Guiana, and most of them were later repatriated in France.[24] This poorly managed enterprise turned out a fiasco. Most of the colonists died, partly because of their own inertia, and the remaining few soon returned to Europe.

Other Acadians, acting with the approval if not indeed at the instigation of the French government, sailed for the Falkland Islands (then called the Isles Malouines), Guadeloupe, Martinique, and Santo Domingo. Those who sailed for the Falklands embarked from Saint-Malo and Rochefort in the years 1763-66. When these islands were ceded to Spain in 1767, some of the Acadian families filtered back to France. Of those going to Guadeloupe, Martinique, and Santo Domingo, a few remained permanently. Many died, and most of the survivors departed for Louisiana, Miquelon, and other Canadian territories, or France.[25]

A scheme to settle at first seventy-seven, and afterwards seventy-eight, families on Belle-Isle, off the coast of Brittany, received much attention during the decade 1763-73 and the co-operation of the royal government and the Breton provincial government (the provincial assembly).[26] In 1761 the British had seized Belle-Isle and had held it until the conclusion of peace in 1763.[27] After the war the

[23] Martin, op. cit., pp. 54-55. Large numbers of Acadians who had taken refuge in the hinterland of French Canada returned to Nova Scotia after the peace of 1763. According to Brebner (op. cit., p. 226), approximately 25 per cent of the population of Canada's eastern maritime provinces today is of Acadian descent.

[24] Martin, op. cit., p. 35. The author of the official "Rapporte le 5 avril 1782" (Arch. Nat., F15, 3495) states that most of them perished in Guiana of misery.

[25] Martin, op. cit., pp. 55-56. Lauvrière writes that fifty to seventy Acadians embarked with Bougainville for the Falklands (1764) (op. cit., II, 253).

[26] The matter is discussed at length by Martin, op. cit., pp. 62-73, and in Vol. III of the Inv.-som . . . Ille-et-Vilaine, série C.

[27] During the war the British did much damage to the Breton coast, destroying Cherbourg, bombarding Le Havre, Croisic, Cancale, Saint-Servin, Saint-Malo, and capturing Belle-Isle (Inv.-som . . . Ille-et-Vilaine, C 694, 1085-1088; Doisy-Martin, op. cit., IV, 799). La Borderie gives a detailed account of it in his Histoire de Bretagne, VI, (Rennes, 1914), 261-277, and Lieutenant H. Binet has an article on the subject, entitled "La guerre des côtes de Bretagne au XVIIIe siècle: Saint-Malo et la region malouine après les descentes anglaises de 1758," in the Annales de

Breton government undertook the resettlement of the island by three groups: old colonists, *gourdiecs*, and Acadians. The inhabitants of Morlaix, who had already shown much kindness to the Acadians, were particularly interested in seeing some of them settle on Belle-Isle. Le Loutre, the spiritual father of the Acadians, now released from his eight years of imprisonment by the British, was engaged to foster interest among them in the project. His labors met with success, and in 1765 seventy-eight Acadian families, generously aided by national and provincial governments and even the city officials of Morlaix, proceeded from Morlaix and Saint-Malo to Belle-Isle. Each family was given a small tract of land, a house, a barn, a stable, a threshing-floor, a bakehouse, a horse, a carriage *(charette)*, harness, two oxen with yoke and straps, a plow and all necessary farm tools, a cow, some iron and coal. When they set out, they were advanced three months' rations. The mayor and city council of Morlaix reimbursed the fifty-six families that had lived among them the expenses that they had paid for lodging for the last two years. A boat was ordered built for their use in ferrying provisions from the Continent to the island. The Acadians were to continue drawing their pension until they had harvested one or two good crops. Finally, the farmers-general were asked to furnish them gratuitously every month 110 livres (weight) of tobacco.[28] To finance the enterprise of rehabilitating Belle-Isle, the royal government placed at the disposal of the Estates of Brittany 56,000 livres.[29]

Despite its auspicious beginning, this Acadian colony did not succeed. Le Loutre soon left to busy himself at the task of getting the other Acadians in France established. The crops were persistently bad from 1766 through 1772. The colonists complained that they had not obtained the amount of land which had been promised. Furthermore, they found themselves in unpleasant company, for the "old colonists" and the *gourdiecs* (a group of agriculturalists at the bottom of the feudal system) resented the Acadians. The old colonists, too, of whom there were 390 families, had lost everything

Bretagne for January, 1910. It is of interest that John Hunter, later to become one of the most celebrated surgeons of the eighteenth century, accompanied the expedition that took Belle-Isle, and there obtained, it appears, some of the material for his noted *Treatise on Blood, Inflammation, and Gunshot Wounds* (Harvey Graham [I. H. Flack], *The Story of Surgery*, New York, 1939, pp. 232-234).

[28] Martin, *op. cit.*, pp. 67-69.   [29] *Ibid.*, p. 62.

in the war, and though they were fitted up by the government in much the same manner as the Acadians, they did not receive the dole. *Gourdiec* animosity began or increased when in 1766 forty of their families were forced to abandon their homes, built or rebuilt after the siege, in favor of the Acadians. Thomas Martin, one such *gourdiec*, had served with distinction as cannoneer during the siege of Belle-Isle. Bitterness was natural. Another factor that evidently had some influence was the alleged inability of the Acadians to understand the language (Breton patois) of the old settlers.[30] As early as 1766 some of the Acadians, disgusted, began to leave.[31] They neglected to cultivate their fields and restricted their labors to small gardens, in which they grew potatoes and other vegetables.[32] With the almost total failure of crops in 1772 the greater portion of the remaining families abandoned their holdings and left. Only sixteen Acadian families then remained.[33]

In 1769-70 the Marquis de la Marche proposed a scheme to settle a large colony of Acadians in the recently acquired island of Corsica, after the manner of a Greek colony of one hundred and twenty families which had recently been planted there; but the Acadians refused to go, and the French government balked at the expense involved.[34]

The most important of the schemes of colonization, however, was the plan to settle fifteen hundred Acadians on a vast tract of land belonging to the Marquis de Pérusse in Poitou. This great estate, embracing 15,000 *arpents* (22,000 to 23,000 acres), had been acquired in part by inheritance and in part by purchase. It had long been uncultivated and was covered with scrub and a rank form of heather, difficult to exterminate, called *brande*. To initiate the clearance and cultivation of a portion of this land, the marquis imported in the years 1762 to 1764 a colony of 131 Germans, among whom were ten entire families. These people, completely subsidized by the marquis, cleared their portions of land and settled down in

[30] *Inv.-som . . . Ille-et-Vilaine,* C 5058, 5145, 5153.

[31] *Ibid.,* C 5136, 5145.   [32] *Ibid.,* C 5145.

[33] Martin, *op. cit.,* pp. 72-73. Numerous descendants of these sixteen families are still to be found on the island. Martin gives the principal names.

[34] Lauvrière, *op. cit.,* II, 175; report of April 25, 1784, Arch. Nat., F15, 3495. Eight families went to Jersey, received land, and had been dropped from the dole list by May, 1773 ("Copie de la lettre de M. le Contrôleur général à M. de Boynes du 14 May [*sic*] 1773," Arch. Nat., F15, 3495).

contentment to its cultivation.   The heavy expense entailed in equip-
ping them, however, left the marquis considerably in debt.   Instead
of trying to borrow from private sources, he conceived the idea that
the state should be interested enough in his project to advance the
money, and during the next several years he made one request for
aid after another, to little avail.   In 1768 he began to manifest an
interest in the Acadians, and in 1772 he approached the government
with a scheme whereby he would employ them at clearing and cultivating a portion of the estate.[35]   The government showed an interest.   Some delegates of the Acadians were sent to inspect the land
and came away satisfied.   Months were spent in negotiations and
ironing out details, and in 1773 the enterprise was begun.

Fifteen hundred Acadians were to be settled in five villages of
thirty houses each.   Ten Acadians were to reside in each house.
Each family would be given furniture, tools, and animals.   The
government agreed to advance to the Marquis de Pérusse, by installments, 600,000 livres with which to provide these things, and to continue the payment of the dole until the Acadians were well established.[36]

Not all the land to be settled belonged to the marquis.   The
Acadian delegates in their visit of 1772 had been accompanied by
Sarcy de Sutières, director of the Agricultural School of Compiègne,
and had selected for settlement 630 *arpents* of the marquis's lands,
2,400 *arpents* of lands belonging to the Bishop of Poitiers, and 980
arpents of the lands of nuns of Fontevrault.[37]   The government,
however, gave the Marquis de Pérusse custody of the whole enterprise.

The project was launched in 1773.   Houses were constructed
with walls of *pisé* (earth mixed with heather).[38]   Between the sum-

[35] Martin, *op. cit.*, chaps. vi-vii.

[36] "Rapporte le 5 avril 1782" (Arch. Nat., F15, 3495).   Later, in 1775, the
government agreed to extend the payment of the *solde* for six years (Martin, *op.
cit.*, p. 208).

[37] Lauvrière, *op. cit.*, II, 174.

[38] Martin (*op. cit.*, p. 173) states that "the most of the walls thus constructed on
the 'Acadian Line' are still standing, after 160 years, and [that] certain houses have
recently been raised above a single floor, with attractiveness and solidity, on the
earthen wall which had been judged sufficiently strong."   He adds (n. 2): "One
finds numerous constructions of this type in Brittany, notably along the route from
Rennes to Dinan.   In the Poitevan Swamp (in the old Isle de Bouin) many huts
(and above all [*batiments*] *de servitudes*) are still made out of earth mixed with
reeds or stable manure" (*funier*).   At the close of his book, Martin gives a picture

mers of 1773 and 1774 a total of 1,472 Acadians appeared on the scene. Since only fifty-eight houses were ever constructed for them, most of the would-be colonists were compelled to live at Châtellerault, Monthiron, and other near-by villages. For a while some of the younger Acadians, in company with the German colonists, worked at clearing land.[39] But delays in the building, difficulty in settling the feudal obligations of the new settlers to the marquis and neighboring lords, the hunger and suffering experienced during the hard winter of 1774-75, and finally the lure of Louisiana led most of the colonists to grow fainthearted and leave Poitou by the end of 1775. At government expense they went to Nantes and its vicinity. Only twenty-five families were residing on the estate in 1779; only twelve in 1785.[40]

The attempt to colonize the Acadians in Poitou was thus another fiasco. Government delay and feudal obligations had no doubt had some influence, but the chief deterrent to the Acadians was the prospect of hard work.[41] After well-nigh twenty years of living on pensions, most of the Acadians had forgotten what work was, and the younger generation had never learned it.[42] The experiment cost the government heavily. According to an official report in 1782, the outlay up to January 1, 1778, had been 1,730,000 livres. Of this amount, approximately one third was for the payment of the dole to Acadians who went to the estate either temporarily or permanently.[43] In the course of time government expenditures on the enterprise approached two millions.[44] As a part of the waste, quantities of wood, stone, and other materials were brought to the scene and not used. Some individuals plundered this material.[45]

---

of one of the Acadian houses in Poitou, resembling closely Burns's home at Ayr.

For a discussion of *pisé*, see above, pp. 102-104.

[39] *Ibid.*, pp. 185, 195.

[40] *Ibid.*, pp. 238, 248. Even so, there are still in the vicinity many descendants of the Acadian families, residing in some instances in the houses built at the time of colonization.

[41] This is Martin's view, and also the present writer's.

[42] The government, however, deprived of their pensions many of those who went to Poitou.

[43] "Rapporte le 5 avril 1782" (Arch. Nat., F15, 3495). Martin (*op. cit.*, p. 233) records that from 1773 to 1776 the government spent 1,072,409 livres on the project. This sum, he estimates, had a value of 22,000,000 to 25,000,000 francs of the 1930's.

[44] Lauvrière, *op. cit.*, II, 177.

[45] *Ibid.*, pp. 237-238; *Inv.-som . . . Ille-et-Vilaine*, C 5145.

From 1775, when the bulk of the Acadians who had ventured on the Pérusse undertaking turned back, the government began to moderate its interest in them. It had offered to assist in purchasing the *maîtrise* (master's position in the guilds) for any Acadian youths in the cities who showed themselves worthy.[46] It had endeavored to give agricultural land to any who would take it. Up to 1775 it had been rather punctual in paying the allowance of 6 sous a day. But from 1775 onwards it began to get in arrears with the payments. Moreover, those who had turned back from the Pérusse estate, and those who refused to go there after their engagement to do so, were removed from the dole-list, to their distress and lamentation.[47] At length the government reduced the allowance to half its former value, effective January 1, 1778. Thenceforth only 3 sous a day were to be paid to bona fide Acadian refugees who were fortunate enough to have their names on the list. This action reduced the load on the French treasury from 300,000 livres to 113,800.[48] It was, of course, never the intention of the French government to pension the Acadians for the duration of their lives, but merely to assist them until they should get settled in France.[49] The Acadians felt, however, that they had lost everything in the New World for France, and that the French government owed them a great deal.

As early as 1772 some of the Acadians in France had requested of the government that they be allowed to join hundreds of their compatriots who had drifted into Louisiana from the English colonies, more particularly from Georgia, the Carolinas, and Maryland, since 1758. In some instances members of their immediate families were in Louisiana, and correspondence or other communication was evidently maintained. The Acadians learned that the soil of Louisiana, like that of Acadia, was very fertile, and that existence there was easily supported. The chief obstacle to their going was the fact

[46] Memorandum of the controller-general's office, dated May 19, 1786 (Arch. Nat., F15, 3495).

[47] "Rapporte le 5 avril 1782" (Arch. Nat., F15, 3495); letter from Necker to Dupré de Saint-Maur, Aug. 22, 1779 (Arch. de la Gironde, C 2478); *Arch. parl.*, XXXV, 106-107.

[48] Report of April 25, 1784 (Arch. Nat., F15, 3495).

[49] Necker in a letter of Aug. 22, 1779, to Dupré de St.-Maur, intendant at Bordeaux, states this explicitly (Arch. de la Gironde, C 2478). In this letter Necker narrates the story of the government's policy toward the Acadians since 1775.

that in 1763 Louisiana was ceded to Spain,[50] and the French government did not relish the thought of its citizens becoming Spanish colonists. Accordingly, the request was ignored. In 1775, on the return of the large body of colonizers from the Pérusse estate, some of the Acadians at Nantes again took up the request.[51] Necker gave attention to it, but the war with Britain, beginning in 1778 and lasting through 1783, led to shelving the matter.

Meanwhile the Acadians of Nantes got into secret communication with the Count of Aranda, Spanish ambassador to France, and elicited his interest in the enterprise.[52] As late as 1783 the French government was opposed to their departure and ordered the arrest of certain Spanish agents working secretly among them.[53] But in 1784 it changed front, agreeing to let the Acadians leave for Louisiana, provided those emigrating would agree to swear allegiance to the king of Spain, and the Spanish government would transport them to Louisiana, give them land, tools, and animals for cultivation of crops, and continue the French payment of 3 sous a day until the immigrants should be able to care for themselves.[54] The Spanish government and the Acadians accepted these conditions, and the French government made ready to let the Acadians depart.

This agreement provided a moment of relief both for the Acadians and for the French government.[55] The government announced that the dole, which had fallen a year and a half in arrears for most of the Acadians, and longer for some, would be paid in full before their departure. To this end it requested from its intendants and subdelegates complete records concerning all Acadians who wished to go. It announced, however, that payment was not to be made until the moment of departure, and that all indebtedness of the Acadian emigrants to citizens in France must be cleared before the departure would be permitted.[56] The government announced ex-

---

[50] Some settlers had returned to France after the cession.

[51] All of those who left the Pérusse estate went to Nantes.

[52] Martin thinks that the Spanish government, rather than the Acadians, took the initiative and spread propaganda among them to this end.

[53] Martin, *op. cit.*, pp. 227-228.

[54] Lauvrière, *op. cit.*, II, 194-197; "Copie de la lettre de M. le Cte de Vergennes, Paris le 19 mars 1785" (Arch. Nat., F15, 3495).

[55] Report of April 25, 1784, and a memorandum of the controller-general's office, dated April 25, 1785 (Arch. Nat., F15, 3494). Both papers express pleasure over the saving to the French treasury.

[56] Letter from the controller-general to Bertrand de Molleville, intendant of

plicitly that no payment of arrears was to be made to any Acadian who did not indicate his intention of going, possibly an inducement to the Acadians to leave. The correspondence of the officials indicates that they were willing to dump into the lap of Spain the whole Acadian problem, which after nearly three decades was becoming tiresome.

The sailing, originally planned for the summer of 1784, took place in May and August, 1785, from Nantes and Saint-Malo.[57] Between fifteen and sixteen hundred Acadians embarked.[58] The subdelegate at Nantes wrote that the best of the Acadians had departed for Louisiana.[59] The remaining 652 Acadians in France, scattered chiefly in the towns and cities of Brittany and Normandy, were with few exceptions in wretched condition, dependent upon the government.[60]

The cost to the French government of paying arrearages to the departing Acadians was 430,000 livres.[61] Now that so many had gone, the annual expense of furnishing the 3 sous a day was lessened greatly from the former sum of 113,800 livres. Arrearages for the 652 for the years 1784-85 amounted to 83,000 or 84,000 livres,

Brittany, April 27, 1784 (copy) (Arch. Nat., F15, 3495). Through mistake the subdelegate at Nantes paid the arrears in the dole too early, before the Spanish were ready to transport the emigrants, and the government sternly called upon the subdelegate's superior, De Molleville, for the refund of the 227,981 livres. After much correspondence, the matter was corrected (ibid.). Cf. Shelby T. McCloy, "French Charities to the Acadians, 1755-1799," *Louisiana Historical Quarterly*, XXI, 662 nn. 32, 33.

[57] Martin, op. cit., p. 231.

[58] In a letter to Gojard, Oct. 8, 1785, Blondel cites De Molleville, intendant of Brittany, as saying that 1,599 Acadians left for Louisiana; but in a later letter of April 29, 1786, he says that less than 1,550 departed (Arch. Nat., F15, 3495). Martin says that a total of 1,560 embarked, 1,244 from Nantes on May 15, and 316 from Saint-Malo on August 1 (op. cit., p. 231).

[59] "Le Subdélégué dit, qu'aucun des Acadians de St. Malo, n'a la capacité nécessaire pour remplir le moindre emploi, les chefs les plus intelligens étant passés à la Louisiane" (from a report entitled "L'affair des Acadiens existans dans la Généralité de Bretagne depuis le passage d'une partie d'entr' eux à la Louisiane," Arch. Nat., F15, 3495). Among them were the D'Entremonts, to one of whom, Mius d'Entremont, the government made a special farewell gift of 150 livres (Lauvrière, op. cit., II, 251, 255). Most or all of those sailing from Nantes had turned back from the Poitou adventure (Martin, op. cit., p. 231).

[60] "Ces Acadiens ne pour remplir le moindre imploi, les plus intelligens étant passé à la Louisiane" (observations by Blondel, April 11, 1786, Arch. Nat., F15, 3495).

[61] Letter from Bertrand de Molleville to Blondel, Sept. 4, 1785 (Arch. Nat., F15, 3495).

according to Blondel, intendant of commerce.[62]   Blondel added[63]
that there were still, and had always been, about five hundred Acadians in France who were not recipients of the dole.   Many of this
last group, however, he added, had applied for the allowance several times a year without success.[64]   Beginning January 1, 1786,[65]
the payment was limited to old and infirm persons, unable to gain a
livelihood, and to minors.   Girls were to be assisted until they
reached the age of eighteen, and boys until they became twenty.
Thenceforth the annual expense of these payments to the Acadians
was reckoned at approximately 18,000 livres.[66]

Following the exodus to Louisiana, forty-two of the Acadians
remaining in Brittany requested that they be allowed to migrate to
the New England States of America.[67]   Written information was
furnished concerning those who wanted to go (their modes of livelihood, etc.),[68] but apparently the project fell through.   In 1786
there was an abortive attempt to organize a second expedition to
Louisiana, or one to Saint-Pierre and Miquelon.[69]   The Acadians
were ever restless and desirous of pursuing a new plan.

The French government was very patient and generous toward
them.[70]   The royal family (Louis XV and the Count of Artois in
particular) manifested especial interest in them.   Between the years

[62] Letter to the controller-general, April 11, 1786.   These arrearages had not
been paid by July 1, 1786, when it was estimated that they amounted to 102,000
livres.   The government still intended to pay them (Arch. Nat., F15, 3495).

[63] In another letter written about the same time.

[64] Numerous petitions for payment of the dole are to be found in Arch. Nat.,
F15, 3494 and 3495.

[65] Report on state aid to the Acadians, dated 19 août 1791, Arch. Nat., F15,
3495.   Martin, however, says 1788 (op. cit., p. 258).

[66] According to Martin, it dwindled in 1788 to 7,285 livres.

[67] "L'Affaire des Acadiens existans dans la Généralité de Bretagne depuis le
passage d'une partie d'entr' eux à la Louisiane" (Arch. Nat., F15, 3495).   These
forty-two were resident at Morlaix.   Martin (op. cit., p. 231) states that the 316
who went to Louisiana from Saint-Malo had previously requested permission to go to
Boston, where they had numerous compatriots (ibid., p. 51).

[68] Submitted by Blondel to the controller-general, April 11, 1786 (Arch. Nat.,
F15, 3495).   According to a marginal note, the advice of the intendant would be
followed.

[69] Blondel in his report of April 11, 1786, mentions that most of the 209
Acadians still resident on Belle-Isle wished to get up an expedition to go in 1787
to Louisiana or to the islands of Saint-Pierre and Miquelon (Arch. Nat., F15, 3495).

[70] This is also Martin's view.   Even Lauvrière, who at times is almost lachry-
mose in his sentiment for the Acadians, declares that no one can justly charge the
government of the Old Regime with lack of gratitude or generosity toward them
(op. cit., II, 233).

1763 and 1778 alone the government contributed toward their support and establishment a total of approximately 4,500,000 livres, which had a value of 90,000,000 to 100,000,000 francs of the 1930's.[71] Much was spent on them after 1778. Indeed, large numbers of Acadians continued on the pension list during the Revolution. Few forms of relief, and few groups in France, received under the Old Regime the generosity accorded to the Acadians.[72]

During the years 1745-48 the French government had as wards more than two thousand war refugees from Isle Royale as a result of that island's capture (1745) by the British. A French fleet which had gone to the aid of the island arrived "just in time to receive the garrison . . . , which had capitulated, and those of the inhabitants who fled English domination." The fleet returned to Rochefort, whence it had sailed. The two thousand colonists and the Louisburg garrison "were packed pell-mell" on the vessels, and their voyage was marked by a severe outbreak of smallpox and scurvy. Arriving at Rochefort in August, they found that city in the grip of a frightful epidemic of "a pestilential scurvy," weighing chiefly upon the sailors of a large fleet already anchored there. The city hospitals were filled, and the rate of mortality was high.[73] The hospitals of neighboring towns received what patients they could from the newly arrived fleet, and with great reluctance the citizens of Rochefort took the others into their homes. The epidemic continued for several months.[74] The colonists remained in Rochefort throughout their

[71] Martin, op. cit., p. 258.

[72] Many descendants of the Acadians are yet to be found in France. Martin expresses surprise at their number. He is acquainted with many and reports that some are in well-to-do circumstances. They have furnished an occasional person of prominence, such as an admiral in the French navy. Most of these descendants still live on the sites in Brittany, Normandy, and Poitou where their eighteenth-century ancestors settled, and they carry proud traditions with them. It is odd that in the 1700's only a few families (perhaps three or four) settled in Paris, only a few in Bordeaux, and only one in eastern France, at Dijon, whence the family had originally gone to Canada. Most of the families had originally come, in the late 1600's and early 1700's, from western France (a few from northern France), and to western France they returned.

[73] Two historians of Rochefort say that "one hundred and ten surgeons, twenty-two apothecaries, nineteen Sisters of Charity, five almoners, [and] a proportionate number of male nurses (infirmiers), succumbed to the first violence of this frightful calamity" (Viaud and Fleury, op. cit., I, 395-399).

[74] An interesting episode is the fact that Cochon Dupuy and his son, surgeons of Rochefort, treated thousands of scurvy cases on three French fleets during 1745-46 with a high degree of success in connection with the last two (ibid., II, 399,

stay in France, and apparently were maintained by the French government. Many of them wished to continue permanently at Rochefort, but the government in 1748 returned all to Isle Royale, which by the treaty of peace had been restored to France.

A large body of Dutch political refugees found asylum in France in 1787 and subsequent years and were cared for at the expense of the French government. In a clash in 1786-87 between the two famous political parties of the Netherlands, the Orangeists and their bourgeois opponents, the latter, supported by France, were on the point of deposing the House of Orange from its hereditary stadtholdership, when the king of Prussia, brother of the Princess of Orange, intervened in behalf of the Orange party. Britain was ready to assist Prussia and the House of Orange if necessary, and France found it discreet not to come to the aid of the "Patriot" party.[75] There was little or no bloodshed, but many leaders of the losing faction had their property seized and found it expedient to flee. The refugees went to Belgium, France, and parts of Germany. The French government, humiliated by its inability to render military aid, felt honor-bound to offer hospitality to the refugees who asked entry. Accordingly, it promised and gave them financial support for some years (evidently until French armies conquered Holland in 1794). In 1789, when the number of refugees was approximately the same as in 1788,[76] the appropriation was 829,448 livres.[77]

A unique form of French governmental charity was the ransoming of its subjects captured from time to time on the high seas by Algerian corsairs. Surprisingly, France, the greatest nation of Europe in the eighteenth century, permitted the pirates of Algiers or Tunis

---

404). This was before the publications by Huxham and Lind on the subject in England. See the *Dictionary of National Biography*, X, 363-364, XI, 1150-1151; and Castiglioni, *op. cit.*, p. 619.

[75] The moment was very propitious for Prussia's action, as Russia and Austria, the latter Prussia's inveterate enemy, were at war with Turkey. The incident proved a great humiliation to the French, and weakened the prestige of the French government in the eyes of its people (*Cam. Mod. Hist.*, VIII, 107, 286-289, 320-322).

A lengthy treatment of the quarrel that drove the "Patriots" from the United Provinces is given by C. M. Davies, *History of Holland . . .* , III (London, 1844), 499-554.

[76] Late in 1788 the French government announced that it would not give aid to further Dutch refugees that might come, evidently having in mind those who might come from Belgium and Germany (*Arch. parl.*, XVII, 374-378).

[77] *Ibid.*, XVI, 654.

to fall upon its ships upon the high seas and take as prizes its commerce and citizens. Rather than fight, France made periodic gifts to the Dey in order to forestall attacks, and occasionally contributed money for the ransom of the captives. In 1779 the government set aside 100,000 livres for the ransom of Corsicans held by the Algerians, and in 1784 it contributed the greater portion of a sum of 600,000 livres for the ransom of Frenchmen who had been made slaves.[78] On the other hand, the French took care of two hundred Algerians when their ship, a corsair, was shipwrecked on their shores in 1765;[79] and the Duc de Praslin (cousin of Choiseul, minister of war) bitterly criticized the Marseilles chamber of commerce in February, 1763, for contemplating reprisals on the Algerians because of raids made by an unknown corsair upon ships sailing from Marseilles.[80] In one instance, the ransom was paid, not to Algerians, but to "Greek bandits" who had seized the ship of Captain Bernard, a Frenchman; the French consul of the Morea was forced in June, 1776, to pay 7,000 piastres for its release.[81]

Throughout the century communities and individuals which had suffered from enemy invasion received indemnities from the government. French prisoners of war interned at Trent in 1702 received aid from their government.[82] During the War of the Spanish Suc-

---

[78] *Inventaire des archives historiques de la chambre de commerce de Marseille*, AA, arts. 100, 106. In connection with the latter grant, the religious orders in this work, with headquarters at Marseilles, were to furnish 130,000 livres; indeed, in the former instance the money was to be turned over to these orders, the Trinity and the Notre-Dame de la Merci. The ransoming of slaves had been their *raison d'être* since their founding in the late 1100's: they spent their time collecting alms for the ransom of Christian captives and in negotiations with the Dey. They had representatives in Algeria. They tried to insist on regular prices for the prisoners, but sometimes they had to pay increased prices for prisoners of rank. Sometimes large numbers of captives would be ransomed at one time. In 1720 one hundred were ransomed from Algiers and Tripoli; in 1723-24 seventy-four were ransomed from Algiers and Morocco; in 1750 one of the *pères* of the Trinity returned with 106 French slaves ransomed from Morocco; in 1767 two hundred Frenchmen were ransomed at Saffi, Morocco, at a cost of 1,000,000 livres (to which church and state contributed); and in 1785 the two orders ransomed 316 French slaves, who were brought to Marseilles on the frigate *Minerve*. An impressive ceremony, including a parade through the streets of Marseilles, always followed (Augustin Fabre, *op. cit.*, II, 315-322; Martin-Doisy, *op. cit.*, III, 1624-1632).

[79] *Inv. . . . de la chambre de commerce de Marseille*, AA, art. 82.

[80] *Ibid.*, AA, art. 80. This same book records the gifts, or bribes, made by the French government to the Dey to avert raids.

[81] *Inv.-som . . . Bouches-du-Rhône*, C 2570. At first the pirates demanded 40,000 piastres.

[82] The wives of Irish officers and soldiers serving with the French army in Italy

cession (1702-13) much damage by enemy invasion was done to portions of Provence and Dauphiné, in southeastern France, and a number of requests for tax exemption and other relief were made in the confident expectation that they would be granted. One request was made to the controller-general by Bouchu, intendant of Dauphiné, in a series of letters in the winter of 1704-05. After the communities of Briançonnais had been ravaged by the enemy and their resources depleted, Bouchu insisted that the controller-general ask the king for larger remission in taxes.[83] In 1707 the Duke of Savoy with an army reportedly composed of Prussians and Hessians, invaded a portion of Provence, and according to the bishop of Vence, who drew a heart-rending picture of the desolation to his own and neighboring dioceses, the troops had destroyed what they had not chosen to carry with them.[84] Lebret *fils,* who had lately succeeded his father as intendant of Provence, corroborated this picture of destruction in a letter to the controller-general, dated November 22, 1707, adding that some damage had been caused by French troops, and requested relief for these communities.[85] In December Lebret *père,* president of the parlement of Provence and former intendant, wrote to the controller-general, mentioning the remission of 200,000 livres in the *capitation* which had already been granted for 1708, and expressing the opinion that it would be necessary to remit 200,000 to 300,000 livres in the *don gratuit* for 1708, and perhaps also for 1709 and 1710. He asserted: "I do not speak of the *don gratuit* or of the *capitation* for the present year 1707, because I am persuaded that the intention of the king is to gratify as regards them the cities and communities which have been burned or pillaged, at least for the part and portion that each of them should have been able to support if the Duke of Savoy had not invaded Provence." He also described the excellent relief work rendered by his son at Toulon at the moment when it was besieged.[86] In March, 1709, the

---

received aid at the same time (France, Archives de la Guerre, Ministère de la Guerre, *Inventaire-sommaire des archives historiques (archives anciennes—correspondance),* I, Paris, 1898, 451, No. 1594).

[83] Boislisle, *Correspondance des contrôleurs généraux,* No. 198.

[84] *Ibid.,* II, No. 1315.

[85] *Ibid.,* II, No. 1351. In particular he asked for his province a diminution in the *don gratuit* (annual tax figure demanded as gift by royal government of a *pays d'état,* see Chéruel, *op. cit.,* II, 960).

[86] *Ibid.,* II, No. 1359.

archbishop of Embrun informed the controller-general of the frightful war damage to Briançon and to his own diocese, observing that there should be a general assembly of the clergy the next year but that he did not see how a new tax to support the expense could be imposed in these dioceses.[87] In 1714 six years' respite from direct taxes *(impositions)* was granted the community of Revest, which, according to the record, "has suffered much from the war."[88]

During the War of the Austrian Succession (1740-48) the provinces of Brittany and Provence suffered heavily from invasion. In Brittany, the English fell upon Quiberon in October, 1746, and through pillage and fire wrought destruction to an estimated value of 429,576 livres, aside from damage to commerce estimated at 205,000 livres.[89] In Provence, the provincial General Assembly granted aid to the communities which had suffered most and called upon the royal government for reimbursement.[90]

The Seven Years' War (1756-63), as already mentioned, saw a series of British attacks upon islands and coastal towns of Brittany. The damage from the two forays of Marlborough and Bligh in 1758 alone perhaps amounted to 3,913,474 livres.[91] Then the intendant ordered rice, flour, and buckwheat to be distributed free among the needy;[92] and the intermediary commission of the Estates of Brittany sent certain of its members to ascertain on the spot the extent of damage and the need of aid. According to Binet, neither the provincial Estates nor the royal government was able to offer much relief because of a dearth of funds.[93] The king's council, by order of October 30, 1760, did grant remissions on the *vingtième*, the *dixième*, and the *capitation* to the stricken communities to the extent of 41,560 livres 1 sous 1 denier, for each of the five years 1757-61. Fifty cities,

---

[87] *Ibid.*, III, No. 323.

[88] The *Inventaire-sommaire des archives départmentales* for *Bouches-du-Rhône*, C 63 (f 24).

[89] *Inv.-som* . . . *Ille-et-Vilaine*, C 1083.

[90] *Inv.-som* . . . *Bouches-du-Rhône*, C 76 (ff 165, 185v, 283v, 377), 78 (ff 2, 3, 42v).

[91] Lieutenant Binet reckons this to have had a value, in terms of French coinage of 1910, of 17,610,798 francs (*op. cit.*, XXV, 318). In addition, losses of more than 300,000 livres had been sustained in 1757, when many inhabitants, expecting a British attack, which did not develop that year, left their homes and took their movable property with them (*ibid.*, XXV, 310 n. 1).

[92] *Ibid.*, XXV, 308-310.

[93] At Saint-Malo, and apparently elsewhere, the people relied upon their own resources (*ibid.*, XXV, 321).

towns, and communities which had suffered from the two British assaults were to benefit from this remission.[94] By another order of January 20, 1761, the council gave Saint-Malo a remission of 27,804 livres. The Estates of Brittany granted 20,000 livres to the afflicted regions.[95] Doubtless from this last-mentioned grant were taken the gratifications of 100 livres each paid to two citizens who were among the war sufferers.[96]

Later in the same war the British seized Belle-Isle in April, 1761, and held it until May, 1763. There, too, much damage occurred, but the amount was small in comparison with that for the fifty cities and towns attacked in 1759. The inhabitants of Belle-Isle estimated their losses at 304,700 livres.[97] The council of state, by an order of November 26, 1762, granted the island a remission in taxes of 17,632 livres for each of the four years 1759-62.[98] The government agreed to pay the province 56,000 livres because of the lost income from the island during the British occupation.[99] Moreover, the government indemnified the inhabitants of Belle-Isle by the sum of 52,545 livres in 1766 for supplies furnished to the French troops during the siege (in 1761).[100]

The Norman city of Honfleurs solicited aid of the government in 1766, not because it had been invaded, but because in the late war the British had sunk "the great part" of its vessels and had brought its commerce to "complete cessation."[101] No record has been found of the government's action. The government did, however, aid the poorer artisans of Rouen by exempting them from the *vingtième* for a period.[102]

Finally, the Russian attack on the Morea (the Greek Peloponnesos) in 1770, during their war with Turkey, brought much damage to French property and some imprisonment and suffering to French-

[94] Arch. Nat., H565. This made a total remission of 207,800 livres for the five years (*Inv.-som . . . Ille-et-Vilaine*, C 4709).

[95] *Idem.*   [96] *Ibid.*, C 5057.

[97] In April, 1763 (*ibid.*, C 5127).

[98] *Ibid.*, C 4367.

[99] The British were to pay this sum to the French government (*ibid.*, C 5128).

[100] *Ibid.*, C 5058. It was common for the government to make indemnity for all animals or supplies that were requisitioned during a war. Cf. *Inv.-som . . . Bouches-du-Rhône*, C 78 (ff 195, 199v).

[101] *Inv.-som . . . Seine-Inférieure*, C 197.

[102] The artisans exempted were those whose tax quota was 3 livres or less, and who were out of work and not members of a trade corps (*ibid.*, C 478).

men resident there.[103]   Many requests were made for indemnity, and France, through the chamber of commerce of Marseilles (which had immediate jurisdiction over the commerce with the Near East), was generous in response. The "list of sums due to victims of this invasion" climbed to a total of 571,433 livres.[104] To liquidate this amount, the chamber of commerce of Marseilles was empowered to borrow 1,100,000 livres for the payment of debts in the Morea and in the Barbary States.[105]

Thus under the Old Regime, royal and provincial governments were definitely interested in war relief, and made appropriations when necessary, even though (save in the instance of the Acadians) the sums were negligible, and often late in coming.

After 1789

The Acadians hoped much from the Revolution. Despite the fact that they had been recipients of aid from the Old Regime for more than forty years, their sympathies lay almost wholly on the side of the Revolution.[106] The Revolutionists promised them much. In La Revellière-Lépeaux, deputy of the third estate of the séné-chaussée of Anjou, they found a passionate advocate. This deputy, presenting a report for the pensions committee to the National As-sembly on February 21, 1791, in behalf of greater aid to the Aca-dians, narrated in pathetic tones the sacrifice that these people had made for France, the repeated instances of cold and cruel treatment that they had received from the callous-hearted Old Regime, and their expulsion to Louisiana, where "almost all . . . found the last

---

[103] A brief but vivid account of the Russian attack, and of the savage Turkish massacre of the Greeks shortly afterwards, is given by Edouard Driault and Michel Lhéritier, *Histoire diplomatique de la Grèce, de 1821 à nos jours*, I (Paris, 1925), 21-23. The Russian attack and invasion was made by a naval expedition which sailed around Europe and into the Mediterranean by Gibraltar. Alexis Orloff was in charge. There was widespread revolt against Turkish rule among the Greeks, and 15,000 Greeks aided 400 Russians in attacking a Turkish garrison, at Tripo-litza, only to be routed. Brutal massacres of many hundred Greeks throughout the Morea followed. Navarino and all the islands of the Archipelago were taken by the Russians and held for a time.

[104] *Inv.-som . . . Bouches-du-Rhône*, C 2546.

[105] *Ibid.*, C 2545.

[106] Record of only one has been found whose loyalty to the Revolution was questioned—Claude Etienne Salignac Fénelon, an *émigré* (letter from the adminis-trators of the Charente to the minister of the interior, 7 frimaire, an VI, Arch. Nat., F15, 3494).

rung in their misery, Death!"[107] Men of the type of La Revellière-Lepeaux denounced the Old Regime and held out hope to distressed groups like the Acadians, who, they declared, had been the victims of injustice under it.[108] They hastened, moreover, to spread legislation upon the statute books.

Enactments to aid the Acadians were passed on September 10, 1790, February 21, 1791, and May 4, 1792. Of these the most important was that of February 21, 1791, which provided that sexagenarians should be given 8 sous a day; fathers and mothers of a family, and widows, 6 sous; and children and orphans (though born in France), 4 sous, until they reached the age of twenty, after which they should be ineligible for aid. These terms, giving the Acadians the most generous treatment that they had received since 1778, were to go into effect as of January 1, 1790. The same measure provided for the continuance of aid (pensions) to the military and civil officers of the Acadians and Canadians and to members of their families, though not as hitherto from the funds of the marine.[109]

It was easier, however, to enact legislation than to make payments. The Old Regime had made spasmodic payments to groups of Acadians even during the "hard years" of 1786, 1787, and 1788.[110] The New Regime, on the other hand, legislated, but paid little. No

---

[107] *Arch. parl.*, XXIII, 379. Cf. the present writer's article in the *Louisiana Historical Quarterly*, XXI, 11-12, where the most passionate, or demagogic, part of this speech is quoted, in English translation. That the speech abounds in inaccuracies, anyone who reads Martin's scholarly work will readily see.

[108] Deperet, reporting to the Legislative Assembly for the committee of public aid on November 17, 1791, spoke along the same line as La Revellière-Lepeaux (*Arch. parl.*, XXXV, 106-107).

[109] *Arch. parl.*, XXIII, 380. Accompanying this enactment is printed a descriptive list of 275 Acadians and Canadians, and the sum to which each was entitled, submitted by the intendant of the marine at Rochefort. It was far from embracing all the Acadians in France, of which there were probably between six hundred and a thousand. The list carried an expenditure of 45,696 livres. On the list were the names of Thérèse, a "savage by nation" (American redskin), and Valentin Vagnier, a German, who had gone blind at Cayenne in 1745 (*ibid.*, XXIII, 380-386).

[110] In 1786 the Acadians in France were paid arrearages in the dole for 1784 and 1785, amounting to 84,000 livres (report on government aid to the Acadians, Aug. 19, 1791, Arch. Nat., F15, 3495). Those in Poitou were given 15,581 livres (Memorandum entitled "1788, Acadians," *ibid.*).

In 1787 those in Brittany were accorded 1,428 livres (*ibid.*).

In 1788 only 136 Acadians were still eligible for the dole (report of Coster, Aug. 12, 1788, *ibid.*). The widow Hébert, who made numerous petitions to get payment of all arrearages in her dole, received 500 livres during the winter of 1788 (report to Necker, Feb. 17, 1790, *ibid.*).

payments whatever were made during the distressing years 1789, 1790, and 1791, save doubtless to the 275 on the pension list of the intendant of the marine at Rochefort.[111] Finally, on November 17, 1791, the Assembly decided that the minister of the interior should be requested to appear before it within three days and give reason why the Acadians were not receiving their money.[112] The minister appeared and explained that the reason lay in the fact that the departments had not complied with article four of the measure of February 21, 1791, which provided that lists of those eligible for aid, with data concerning these individuals, be sent to his office as a prerequisite.[113] Moreover, he added, the Legislative Corps had not authorized him to make the payments. The enactment of February 21, 1791, had ordered a census of all Acadians eligible for the payments, and there had been ample time to obtain the information, at least from a single department.[114] Apparently the minister was pleading technicalities.

Months passed without payments, and on March 13, 1792, a letter from Acadians and Canadians at La Rochelle was read to the Legislative Assembly, asking that the law of February 21, 1791, be enforced. This letter was turned over to the central commission with the direction that the commission inform the Assembly what the committee of public aid had to say on the subject.[115] Finally, on May 4, 1792, the Assembly, acting upon the recommendation of the committee of public aid, ordered that the Acadians be paid in full all that was owed them under the aforesaid law.[116] On the same date the Assembly decreed that the lands engaged by the government in the seventies from the Marquis de Pérusse, the bishop of Poitiers, the dames De la Paye, and the Abbey of Letrule be distributed among other Acadians wishing to settle there.[117] No directions, however, were given as to the manner in which the lands would be apportioned, or who would be eligible to receive them. Apparently

[111] Cf. Martin, *op. cit.*, p. 259.   [112] *Arch. parl.*, XXXV, 106-107.
[113] *Ibid.*, XXXV, 281.
[114] Martin (*op. cit.*, p. 260) records that a census of Acadians was made in 1791-92, and that 1,250 names appeared on the list. This number he considers impossible and indicative of fraud.
[115] *Arch. parl.*, XXXIX, 625-626.   [116] *Ibid.*, XLIII, 4.
[117] *Ibid.* Amid the "hard times" still existent in 1791 a large number of Acadians had attempted to get the government to revive its project of settling them on this land (report by the directory of the department of Vienne, summer of 1791; also report of state aid to the Acadians, Aug. 19, 1791, Arch. Nat., F15, 3495).

it remained an empty resolution, for according to numerous reports on the Acadians sent to the office of the minister of the interior during the next several years the Acadians were still in the cities of Brittany, Normandy, and other provinces, and still dissatisfied.[118]

Even in 1793 some groups of Acadians had as yet received nothing under the provisions of the act of February 21, 1791. In the department of Charente-Inférieure were twenty-four eligible for aid who had received nothing. All but five had been born in Canada. One had come to France in 1755, fourteen in 1758, one in 1768, and one in 1778.[119] During the next several years after 1793, at least through 1799 (when documents on Acadian charities dwindle away), payments were made carelessly and spasmodically, as they had been in the last two decades of the Old Regime.[120] The inflationary movement of the nineties naturally rendered the increase in allowance by the act of February 21, 1791, so insignificant that the plight of the Acadians was worse than before. In consequence, a large number of letters of distress were sent to the minister of the interior;[121] also, a large number of Acadians not on the list to receive payments endeavored to get on it. In 1796, 1798, and 1799 larger grants were made to the Acadians in order to enable them to meet the higher costs of living.[122] Despite this increase of aid during the

---

[118] Arch. Nat., F15, 3494.

[119] "Etat supplémentaire des Acadiens et Canadiens passés en France, residens dans le Département de la Charente-Inférieure, qui ont droit aux Secours accordés par l'art. 2 du décret du 21 février 1791" (ibid.).

[120] Arch. Nat., F15, 3494; Lauvrière, op. cit., II, 223. As late as April 24, 1793, the Acadians at Saint-Malo had not been paid under the law of February 21, 1791. Most of those signing a letter to the minister of the interior claimed arrearages for several years, one for twenty-three years.

[121] Among them was one from Cécile Hiriard, declaring that it was impossible to live on the 200 livres that she drew (her name was on the special list of families of Acadian military and civil officers receiving pensions), and protesting that the refugees from Santo Domingo drew 600 livres a year (letter in frimaire an IV, Nov.-Dec. 1795). She had made these complaints a month earlier, in a letter of October 25, 1795, to Belfontaine, maritime agent at Rochefort (Arch. Nat., F15, 3494).

[122] Lauvrière, op. cit., II, 239-240; Martin, op. cit., p. 261. The decree of December 7, 1796, according to Lauvrière, provided for the payment of 50 livres a month to Acadians and other war sufferers above the age of sixty, 35 for those between the ages of twenty-one and sixty, and smaller sums for women and children. Residues owed to them under former decrees were to be converted into payment at the rate of 6 francs for each 100 mandats. On October 8, 1796, and August 13, 1798, large sums were set aside for aid to the Acadians and other war sufferers. Finally, a law of 28 germinal an VII (April 17, 1799) provided for

Directory, the Revolutionary Regime had shown itself more dilatory toward the unfortunate Acadians than had the government of the Old Regime.

In justice to the Acadians, it should be stated that there was a fair minority who made a success in France and came to support themselves. Among them were those who remained permanently in Jersey, Belle-Isle, and Poitou. Eleven Acadians of Nantes in 1786 renounced their dole in order to acquire the position of master in a guild. No doubt others became guild masters at various times. Some Acadians eligible for the allowance scorned it. One Acadian acquitted himself so well that he was given by the king the distinction of "Gentleman of France."[123] Another became a member of the Legislative Assembly and participated in the discussion of the question of aid to the Acadians.[124] With the exception of four who entered the priesthood, none[125] in the eighteenth century entered the professions. On the other hand, there was only a single instance among them of crime or street-begging.[126] The numerous petitions for aid which they sent to the French government were frequently accompanied by high testimonials of character from their curés and local officials.[127] According to Martin, the post-eighteenth-century history of the Acadians, especially those in Louisiana and France, was marked by surprising success.[128]

An unknown number of Dutch "Patriots," who constituted the second group of refugees inherited by the Revolutionists from the Old Regime, drew uncertain amounts of aid. In 1789 the pensions committee listed an item of expenditure of 829,448 livres for them.[129] In the pension act of July 26, 1790, the National Assembly decreed that for the time being the same aid should be continued as in the

---

monthly payments of 30 francs to all colonial refugees above the age of twenty-one, 20 francs for youths from twelve to twenty-one, and 15 francs to children below the age of twelve.

[123] Case of Joseph Devau (letter from Blondel to Gojard, March 25, 1784, Arch. Nat., F15, 3495).

[124] *Arch. parl.*, XXXV, 106-107.

[125] Lauvrière, *op. cit.*, II, 253-254.   [126] Martin, *op. cit.*, pp. 109.

[127] Many are to be found in Arch. Nat., F15, 3494, 3495.

[128] *Op. cit.*, "Epilogue." They have become extremely numerous, more particularly in the United States and Canada. In Louisiana they number half a million, and cultivate the rich bayou lands given them in 1785 by the Spaniards.

[129] See under "Dons, aumônes et secours," constituting Part IV of "Suppléments de traitements, gratifications ordinaires et pensions attachées aux places" (*Arch. parl.*, XVI, 654).

past.[130] In 1791 this same body appropriated 816,000 livres for aid to the Dutch and Acadian refugees, according to a statement by La Revellière-Lépeaux.[131] In January, 1793, they were still resident in France, and Roland, the minister of the interior, inserted in his proposed budget for that year an item of 619,000 livres toward their maintenance.[132] After France declared war on the United Provinces on February 1, 1793, and after French troops overran them in 1794-95,[133] there was no longer any reason why Dutch refugees should remain in France. While the Dutch were in France, they eagerly supported the Revolution. In May and June, 1792, they sent three different offerings, totaling 5,660 livres, in support of the war,[134] and in August, 1793, fifty-seven of them, resident at Saint-Omer, sent a letter of loyalty to the French constitution.[135] The exiles expressed regret in the letter for conditions in their own "oppressed country" and hoped that one day the French constitution would be the basis of government there.

The Revolution brought into being first and last several groups of refugees of its own. Perhaps the first from the standpoint of time were two thousand or more Frenchmen who had been residents of Spain. According to Mr. G. P. Gooch, Spain alone of the countries of Europe had received from the outset news of the Revolution "with dislike."[136] Spanish distaste for the Revolution was largely due to the royal ties of the two countries, but attacks on the church

---

[130] *Ibid.*, XVII, 353.   [131] *Ibid.*, XXIII, 380.

[132] *Ibid.*, LVI, 633-634. An entry dated December 9, 1792, does not harmonize with those just recorded. According to this entry, the Convention on that date took action to continue the payment of pensions of Dutch refugees and of some old employees of the department of foreign affairs, allotting for the two groups the sole sum of 120,000 livres. Formerly, it is stated, the two groups had been cared for from secret funds of the department of foreign affairs. It was agreed that they would be so continued.

The sums previously granted the Dutch refugees had been for much larger amounts, and had not, apparently, been on secret funds of the department of foreign affairs. Possibly this reference applies to Belgian refugees, to be discussed later.

No further mention of the Dutch "Patriots" occurs in the *Archives parlementaires.*

[133] The campaign lasted from October, 1794, through January, 1795. The French leaders were Jourdan, Pichegru, and Moreau (*Cam. Mod. Hist.*, VIII, 436).

[134] *Arch. parl.*, XLIV, 21, 351-352; XLV, 688.

[135] *Ibid.*, LXX, 415. All of the Dutch exiles on French soil were stationed in Flanders, in the cities of Dunkirk, Saint-Omer, Gravelines, Calais, and Lille (*ibid.*, XLIV, 21).

[136] *Cam. Mod. Hist.*, VIII, 782.

shortly supplied a second reason. All news from France was rigidly excluded from the newspapers, and at length on July 20, 1791, doubtless as a further effort to immunize his country against French propaganda, the king of Spain, Charles IV, demanded of the French residents in his country an oath of allegiance to him, on penalty of expulsion from the country and loss of landed property. Of the estimated forty thousand Frenchmen living in Spain at the time, at least two thousand refused to take the oath and were expelled. They were aided in leaving the country by the French consul, at the expense of the French government. Ramond, reporting for the diplomatic committee to the National Assembly, declared that the committee would like to have the government grant 500 livres in aid to each of the refugees, but that the expense for forty thousand would amount to 20,000,000 livres.[137] He ended his speech by asking for only 1,000 livres, 600 of which were to go to Jean Kiguès, a master *perruquier* from Cadiz, and the remaining 400 to Hugues François Bernard, first controller and former director of hospitals at Cadiz, to enable them to get to their respective homes in Burgundy and at Pau.

Aid was by no means restricted to these two refugees. The French consul in Spain made advances to French residents desirous of returning home, and the cities of the department of Hérault gave them the 3 sous per league travel money which the law of June 13, 1790, extended vagabonds or transients returning to their homes. Ratification of this last step was asked of the Legislative Assembly.[188] Not until May 21, 1792, did the proposal reach the floor of the Assembly, and then it was immediately referred to the finance committee.[139] On March 26, 1793, this committee asked the Convention to appropriate 100,000 livres to aid temporarily Frenchmen "expelled by violence" from any foreign country and compelled to abandon their property and livelihood.[140]

[137] While he considered this too high for France at the moment, he commented that every *enfant trouvée* cost the country four times the amount of 500 livres (*Arch. parl.*, XXXVII, 728-729).

[188] The officials of Hérault considered the payment legitimate, and so did De la Millière, intendant-general, and De Lessart, minister of the interior; but De Lessart thought that it should be approved by the Assembly (two memoranda, one dated 7 janvier 1792, and a letter from the minister of the interior to the president of the National Assembly, Arch. Nat., F15, 101).

[189] *Arch. parl.*, LXIII, 617.

[140] Not only Spain, but according to Johannot, speaking for the finance commit-

The years 1791-93 saw the emergence of several groups of refugees which the Convention was called upon to assist.[141] The most numerous group came from the sugar islands, Santo Domingo, Martinique, and Guadeloupe. On the first two savage fighting had developed for the political domination of the islands, fostered by events, legislation, and propaganda in the home country.[142] On each of the islands were three racial groups: whites, mulattoes, and Negroes. The Negroes in each instance outnumbered by several times the total of whites and mulattoes; the mulattoes, according to Necker's figures in 1779, were roughly from one tenth to one fourth as many as the whites.[143]

In 1789 the whites of Santo Domingo were dismayed at the king's failure to ask them for representation in the Estates General, and proceeded on their own initiative to send delegates, certain of whom were received by the National Assembly on July 4.[144] In 1790 two regional assemblies came into being in Santo Domingo. One of them advocating separation from France was suppressed in October by the National Assembly, which then set about forming with force a new body in the island. The governor was expelled, new troops were installed to take the place of the old ones, and leg-

---

tee, Great Britain, Holland, Prussia, Austria, and the Papacy, had drawn up similar regulations for the expulsion of French citizens (*ibid.*, LX, 575-576). French residents of Lisbon, too, according to Mr. G. P. Gooch (*Cam. Mod. Hist.*, VIII, 784), were either imprisoned or expelled from the country. On the aid given those expelled from Rome, see *Inv.-som . . . Bouches-du-Rhône*, L III, 10.

[141] It is unnecessary to discuss the *émigrés* who since the destruction of the Bastille had left France by tens of thousands. They received no aid, at least no intended aid, from the Revolutionary governments. Their pensions (which many drew) were suspended, and their property, by the law of August 14, 1792, was seized.

[142] Priestley (*op. cit.*, chap. xxiv) presents an excellent summary, especially for Santo Domingo.

[143] Priestley (*op. cit.*, p. 267) cites population figures for the three islands as given by Necker and Ducoeurjoly. Necker's figures, for 1779, are as follows:

	Whites	Free Mulattoes	Slaves
Santo Domingo	32,650	7,055	249,098
Martinique	11,019	2,892	71,268
Guadeloupe	13,261	1,382	85,327
Ducoeurjoly's figures, for 1798:			
Santo Domingo	30,826	27,548	465,429
Martinique	10,634	5,779	83,965
Guadeloupe	13,712	3,058	89,523

There are, of course, considerable variations in these figures, as regards the mulattoes and slaves.

[144] Delegates from other islands were admitted later (*ibid.*, pp. 319-320).

islation to please the whites was passed. All the while the mulattoes resented their political exclusion. Encouraged by measures of the National Assembly in March and May, 1790, giving them partial political rights, they broke into a flurry of revolt in the autumn of 1790.[145] The mulatto ringleaders were shortly captured and savagely broken on the wheel."[146]

In August, 1791, the fighting broke out again; this time the mulattoes called in the aid of the Negroes. Apparently the whites had not foreseen that the slaves might rebel. The military forces were insufficient, and until aid came from Martinique the insurgent mulattoes and blacks spread fire and destruction. Before the end of October more than a thousand whites had been killed, and "two hundred sugar plantations and twelve hundred coffee plantations had been burned." Barbarities were practised by the Negroes. When they were put down, the whites in turn took vengeance. "Slaves taken in battle were hanged, burned, or broken on the wheel." In order to suppress the uprising, the whites made concessions to the mulattoes, who on their part did not wish political rights for the Negroes.[147]

A greater uprising occurred in the island in the summer of 1793. The Legislative Assembly, much influenced by the fanatical Society of the Friends of the Blacks, sent to Santo Domingo in the spring of 1792 three commissioners and six thousand troops.[148] The commissioners decided all questions at issue in favor of the mulattoes and against the whites, whom they described as "aristocrats of the skin." With the troops at their call they rode down all opposition. They quarreled with the newly arrived governor, General Galbaud, who was married to a Creole and accordingly well received by the whites. To strengthen themselves against the general's forces, with whom a battle developed,[149] they opened the gates of the city Le Cap to "several thousand revolted slaves," who ran amuck, mas-

[145] In Martinique a brief revolt occurred in late 1789 (*ibid.*, p. 321).

[146] *Ibid.*, p. 329.

[147] *Ibid.*, p. 331. The uprising developed out of white resentment at the measure of the National Assembly in France, May 13-15, 1791, giving the mulattoes the right of representation in "primary and colonial assemblies."

[148] *Ibid.*, p. 332.

[149] According to Frances Sargeant Childs, *op. cit.*, pp. 14-15, insults to white citizens by the mulatto soldiery provoked the fighting.

sacring the population, plundering and burning the city.[150] "Galbaud's forces retreated gradually to the fleet, which already held the Commissioner's deportees, while the destitute white refugees piled into both warships and merchant craft. The fleet, loaded to the gunwales, set sail on June 23 toward the American continent, and early in July dropped anchor in the Chesapeake." Ten thousand refugees were aboard.[151] Some of them remained in the United States; others returned to France. Martinique and Guadeloupe had similar troubles during the period 1789-93, with the greatest trouble apparently developing in 1793.[152] Refugees from them, too, went to the United States and France.

Of the French refugees who sought asylum in the United States, those from Santo Domingo came for the most part in destitute circumstances.[153] Many of the *émigrés* from France had sufficient funds to buy a farm or set up a business; others, artisans, were able to employ their skill as craftsmen. Not so those from Santo Domingo, who were dependent upon charity.[154] Private and state aid was readily given them by the Americans, as it was also given to *émigrés* from France.[155] The French legation and consulates in the United States gave financial aid to these colonial refugees, though with some reluctance, according to Miss Childs, since the refugees were regarded as "aristocrats" and "counterrevolutionaries," and later on returned them to France.[156]

According to Adher, "it was only about the beginning of the year III [September, 1794] that the Convention preoccupied itself" with the colonial refugees from America, who returned chiefly to Toulouse.[157] By this time the greater portion of them had long been

[150] Priestley, *op. cit.*, p. 333; T. Lothrop Stoddard, *The French Revolution in San Domingo* (Boston and New York, 1914), chap. xviii. Priestley speaks of the city as Port-au-Prince, but that city had been largely burned (by the mulattoes) in November, 1791. Cf. Stoddard, *op. cit.*, pp. 150-151.

[151] Childs, *op. cit.*, p. 15.   [152] Priestley, *op. cit.*, pp. 320-321, 338.

[153] This despite the fact that many had been wealthy in Santo Domingo. They had been forced to leave in precipitate haste.

[154] Some mulattoes and slaves were included in the group (Childs, *op. cit.*, pp. 56, 64).

[155] *Ibid.*, pp. 66-67. Congress early in 1794 appropriated $15,000 for aid to the Santo Dominicans, but wrote it off the debt of the United States to France. In actuality, therefore, the appropriation was forced from the French government.

[156] *Ibid.*, pp. 86, 177; Adher, *op. cit.*, pp. 488-489.

[157] The majority of the French inhabitants of the Antilles originally went from Toulouse and other places in southwest France.

in France.[158]   Until government aid came, they had been cared for by local funds, both municipal and private.[159]   On May 14, 1792, the Legislative Assembly allotted 100,000 livres for the education of refugee children from Santo Domingo residing in France, aged five to twenty.   The appropriation was to come from funds at the disposal of the minister of the marine, who was to supervise its expenditure.[160]

From the beginning of the year III (September 22, 1794), steadily into 1799, the French government disbursed aid to the refugees from Santo Domingo and other colonies.   At Toulouse there were 117 refugees in May, 1795; 146 in September, 1796; and 64 in April, 1799.[161]

The amount of aid usually varied "from 25 to 90 francs" a month, but occasionally for brief periods was higher.[162]   As illustrations, the widow Pigoreau, whose family had been massacred and her income of 30,000 livres or more lost, was given 600 livres a year; the widow Foust-Prévost, with nine children, living on 3 livres a day earned by her four oldest daughters, was given 1,000 livres.[163]   Elizabeth Nomand, a refugee from Martinique, was given an annual pension of 360 livres.[164]   Refugees from Martinique and

[158] Adher makes the statement that they had been in France "more than three years" ("Les colons réfugiés d'Amérique pendant la Révolution," *Bulletin de la Société de Géographie de Toulouse*, XXXIVe année, Toulouse, 1915, p. 154).

[159] *Idem.*

[160] Every month he was to render an account of the disbursements which he had made to this end.   The money was to be paid not to the children but to the "masters or mistresses of pension" (i.e., boarding-school teachers) for three months at a time (*Arch. parl.*, XLIII, 330-331).

[161] Adher, *op. cit.*, pp. 165-168.

[162] *Ibid.*, p. 166 n. 1.

[163] *Ibid.*, pp. 155-156 with n.   Both grants were made in December, 1794.   On an account sheet of relief expenditures by the French government for fructidor and the six complementary days of the year III (Aug. 18-Sept. 22, 1795), carrying a total expenditure of 6,390,531 livres(chiefly for hospitals and hospices), are to be found several items affecting the colonists: (1) a grant of 75 livres to refugees from New Orleans, on 5 fructidor; (2) a grant of 75 livres to refugees from Points-à-Pitze, on 17 fructidor; (3) a grant of 52 livres 10 sous to refugees from Martinique, on 19 fructidor; (4) a grant of 75 livres to refugees from Guadeloupe, on 8 fructidor; (5) a grant of 725 livres to refugees from the colonies *(sic)*, on 25 fructidor; and (6) a grant or expenditure in *mandats d'urgence* of 150 livres for refugees from Martinique, on 4 fructidor ("Commission des Secours Publics. Etat des sommes payées sur mandats, tant d'urgence qu'autres, compris dans les feuilles de distribution du mois de Fructidor et les six jo[rs] compléme[s] de L'an 3," Arch. Nat., F15, 102).

[164] In the year VIII she complained that she had not received her allowance for

Guadeloupe were given the same aid as those from Santo Domingo.[165]

Marie Françoise Carabasse, a refugee from Santo Domingo, offered in 1799 to the hospices of Toulouse the sum of 2,000 livres a month for a concession to conduct a gambling booth on the hospital grounds for a year. When her proposal was referred in turn to the minister of the interior and the minister of general police, the latter turned it down.[166]

On 18 pluviôse an VIII (February 7, 1800) there were still resident in the department of the Seine alone 1,189 colonial refugees who had not been paid for four years. The government owed them a total of 1,436,000 livres. The ministry of the interior estimated that throughout France there were "more than 3,000" such refugees. Since none had been paid, the total arrears were considerable. The ministry realized that an appropriation of three or four millions was necessary and was intent on trying to get it.[167]

In the years 1793-94, Corsica, under the control of Paoli and the British, expelled a large number of pro-French families, including the Bonapartes. From the outset of the Revolution Corsica had been split into two factions, those supporting the Revolution and those supporting the king. Paoli, exiled from the island since 1769, returned as lieutenant general in 1790, and by means of secret British aid made himself dictator there in 1793. Forthwith in May of that year he began to expel prominent families friendly to France. The exodus from Corsica became even greater in July and August, 1794, after the British captured the ports of Bastia and Calvi.

All or virtually all of the refugees went to Provence, and the greater number stopped at Marseilles. Others went to Nice, Toulon, Antibes, and perhaps other smaller places. The 1,003 who went first or last to Marseilles were placed by the municipal officers

---

more than a year or two and pressed for the arrears that she might go to visit her parents (apparently sick) at Grenoble (letter from the administrators of Seine-et-Oise to the minister of the interior and memorandum by the latter, Arch. Nat., F15, 103).

[165] Adher, *Recueil de documents,* pp. 474, 489-492.

[166] Adher comments that "it is remarkable that the author of this petition, who, according to the context, must not have been in absolute destitution, figures on the lists of aid granted to refugees from America" (*op. cit.,* pp. 216-217 with n.).

[167] "Ministère de l'Intérieur. 2ème Division. Bur. des Colons. Observations; Nombre des colons inscrits au Département de la Seine, au 18 Pluviôse an 8; Proposition de fonds pour la 1ère décade de Germinal" (Arch. Nat. F15, 103).

in former convents and in the confiscated homes of *émigrés*, sometimes two or three families together.[168]

The refugees found themselves in a bad plight on their arrival, but the Convention came to their aid with decrees of July 1 and 11, 1793; August 14, 1794; 17 and 27 vendémiaire an III (October 8 and 18, 1794). The first two of these decrees provided temporary aid of 50,000 and 600,000 livres, respectively; but those who remained in Corsica and suffered were to be cared for along with the refugees.[169] The third and fourth decrees were set forth in only general terms; the fifth made the terms of aid more definitive. This last decree, incidentally, authorized aid not only to the Corsicans but to refugees of every type in France, whether expelled from any French possession overseas or from the invaded parts of France itself. To all male refugees or deportees over sixty would be paid 3 livres a day; to all females of the same age, 2 livres; to all male refugees or deportees under sixty (the lower age limit is not set), 65 livres a month; to the women and children above twelve, two thirds of this last amount; and to children under twelve, one third. Any refugee or deportee having exercised a trade or profession elsewhere and refusing to employ it in France, though offered an opportunity, would not be eligible for this aid. Those who embraced opportunities to work would be paid one third of the amount of government aid otherwise due them. The instant any returned home, his aid was to cease. The commission of public aid was given control of the disbursement of funds to districts and municipalities, the money coming from a fund of 20,000,000 livres placed at the commission's disposition by the law of 24 messidor. Finally, the decree provided that, conformably to the law of August 4, 1793,

[168] Jean de Servières, "Les refugiés corses à Marseille pendant la Révolution (1793-1797)," *Bulletin de la Société des Sciences historiques & naturelles de la Corse* (Bastia, 1922), pp. 5-10, 58 n. In the appendix (pp. 58-105), the author describes those who came to Marseilles. He says, moreover, that many refugees from Martinique and Santo Domingo were residing in Marseilles at this time (p. 10).

[169] The measure of July 1 provided also for military aid and provisioning of the loyal citizens yet in Corsica. It provided for the continuation of payment of salaries to officials in the islands who were loyal, and for the cessation of the salaries of the others. Finally it assured all loyal Corsicans that France would indemnify them for their losses. As further reports came in telling of the seizures and burnings of property by Paoli's followers, the Convention felt that 50,000 livres was too small a sum, and a motion was adopted to give the Corsicans 600,000 livres as temporary relief (*ibid.*, LXVIII, 36, 536-537).

UNIVERSITY
COLLEGE
LIBRARY
NOTTINGHAM

each refugee or deportee of French citizenship was entitled to the sum of 150 livres, independently of the above terms. Victims of enemy invasion were also eligible for this last sum.[170] Even this did not include all the aid rendered; the refugees were also given bread from the military stores.[171] Complaint was later made by some of the Corsican refugees that they were not paid promptly; moreover, the money was paid in assignats, which had depreciated badly.[172]

Napoleon's mother and three sisters were among the refugees who received aid in Marseilles,[173] and beside their names in the list was written the word *coutourière* (seamstress). Pamphleteers, however, charged that the Bonaparte women worked as laundresses, and had been seen at this work in public.[174] Regardless of whether or not they were actually obliged to work for a living, they did draw refugee aid for a time. By 1794, however, they were receiving some support from Napoleon and Joseph, the former having been made a brigadier general at the close of 1793, with a salary of 12,000 livres, and Joseph in September, 1794, having been given a position as commissioner of war, with a salary of 6,000 livres.[175] Even so, the mother and daughters were occupying the hôtel (residence) of De Cipières, an *émigré*, at Marseilles, and still drawing government assistance.[176]

In 1793 groups of refugees from Belgium and Mainz entered France and were assisted by the French government. For the Belgians, who came in particular from Liège, Franchimont, Stavelot, Logne, and Jemmapes, the sum of 150,000 livres was granted by a decree of 9 frimaire an II (November 29, 1793).[177] These refu-

[170] De Sevières (*op. cit.*, pp. 7-8) quotes the terms verbatim.

[171] *Ibid.*, p. 11.

[172] *Ibid.*, p. 9 n. 1. De Servières (*ibid.*, p. 11) thinks that the aid rendered was inadequate.

[173] For their necessity to leave Corsica, Napoleon himself, it is said, was largely responsible, by getting into "an open feud" with Paoli while on a furlough there (*Cam. Mod. Hist.*, VIII, 560). Their itinerary in Corsica and southern France, for they stopped for intervals at several places (Calvi, La Valette, Brignoles, Antibes, and Marseilles), is given by De Servières, *op. cit.*, pp. 18-19, 22, 36.

[174] *Ibid.*, pp. 15-18. De Servières cites his authorities for these claims.

[175] Lucien had obtained a position as keeper of a warehouse at Saint-Maximin, with a salary of 1,200 livres, besides food (Geer, *op. cit.*, I, 33-35). Napoleon's salary was increased to 15,000 livres in the summer of 1794, and he was given an allowance for quarters and rations.

[176] De Servières, *op. cit.*, p. 36.

[177] *Arch. parl.*, LXXX, 359. Article 2 specifies that the administrators of the

gees were "patriot citizens," who had been obliged to flee from their homes when the Prussian and Austrian forces retook Belgium in 1793.[178] The refugees from Mainz, who were in very much the same predicament, were given 50,000 livres by a decree of September 15, 1793.[179]

On 11 prairial an VII (May 30, 1799) the French government voted aid to a body of Italian refugees, and placed the funds at the disposition of the minister of foreign affairs.[180] The occasion was the expulsion of the French from Italy by Imperial troops while Napoleon was in Egypt. These refugees, of whom there were a "great number," were Italians who had collaborated with the French and feared reprisals at home. For some months they were allowed to remain in southeast France, chiefly at Grenoble. Some, however, were resident at Chambéry, Voiron, Saint-Marcellin, La Côte Saint-André, Tullins, Rives, Romans, and Valence.[181] Their number and the succession of French reverses in Italy increased the uneasiness of Fouché, minister of general police, who became convinced that certain of the refugees were collaborating with the enemy. As a first expedient he asked the minister of war to organize from the refugees an Italian legion; afterwards, in floréal an VIII (May, 1800), he ordered the removal of the men under sixty among the

---

department of Jemmapes were to be paid from this sum the same salaries that they had received when exercising their functions. The funds were placed in the custody of the minister of the interior.

[178] In November and December, 1792, the French army under Dumouriez had expelled the Austrians from Belgium, which by the French decree of December 15 of that year was to be organized under French institutions. On January 26, 1793, the Belgian army was incorporated into the French army. Most of the Belgians were bitter in resentment toward France, but it is clear that these refugees had thrown in their lot with the French. When, later in March, 1793, the French were compelled to withdraw from Belgium, their Belgian collaborators were compelled to seek refuge in France (*Cam. Mod. Hist.*, VIII, 417-421).

[179] *Arch. parl.*, LXXIV, 230. Reference is made to the fact that they had previously been given 2,000 livres (*ibid.*, LXXIV, 33). In 1792 the French forces had occupied Mainz, which in February, 1793, was forcibly annexed to France. In April, however, it was besieged by the Prussians and captured in July (*Cam. Mod. Hist.*, VIII, 422-423). The Mainz refugees, collaborationists with the French, are described in the report of the Barère as some "unfortunate *Mayençais* [who] have preferred to leave their homes and come to enjoy in France some blessings of liberty, rather than to submit a second time to the yoke of slavery" (*Arch. parl.*, LXXIV, 230).

[180] Neither the sum voted nor the number of refugees is given (*Inv.-som* . . . *Isère*, L 236).

[181] The names and professions of about a dozen staying at Grenoble are given. There were professors, artists, physicians, and surgeons.

others to Bourg, near Bordeaux, where they would be less likely to give trouble.

The Russian invasion of Greece in frimaire an VII (late 1798) and Napoleon's conquest of Venice shortly afterwards produced isolated cases of refugees demanding French aid. The merchant Antoine Rogier, native of Tarascon, was one of a number of French citizens resident on the island of Zante when the Russian troops invaded it and made them all prisoners of war. At length, through the aid of some friends on the Turco-Russian commission, he obtained permission to return to France; before he could leave came the news that Napoleon had taken Venice, and the inhabitants of Zante, in anger at this incident, burned the French consulate, where most of the French citizens had sought refuge with their more valuable belongings. After other difficulties he had arrived home in destitution.[182] Talleyrand, minister of foreign affairs, to whom appeal was made for assistance, forwarded the request to the minister of the interior, suggesting that Rogier might be aided in the same way as the French merchants expelled from Spain in 1792.[183]

On 11 brumaire an VIII (November 1, 1799) a so-called Greek refugee in France, Riso Stamati,[184] requested aid of the French government. He was sixty-nine years old, father of a large family, and destitute. His home was Prevesa, which formerly had belonged to Venice, and from Venice he had from time to time drawn slight aid for his family; but lately the Turks had obtained possession of Prevesa, and Stamati did not care to return. Fourteen years earlier he and his brother had sold the French government excellent timber from the Albanian mountains for the construction of ships, but had never been paid for it. One of those who wrote in his behalf thought it well to add that Stamati was greatly attached to the cause of liberty.[185]

So much for refugees coming to France from other lands. Within her own borders were numerous groups of refugees during the 1790's,

[182] The letter says that Bonaparte had heard of the predicament of the French at Zante and had ordered aid rendered, but that thus far none had been given (letter from Rogier to the minister of foreign affairs, Arch. Nat., F15, 103).

[183] Talleyrand to the minister of the interior, 15 germinal an VIII (ibid.).

[184] The name has an Albanian or Italian rather than a Greek ending.

[185] Letters by Sitos Zamates to the minister of the interior, 11 brumaire an VIII, and by Permon to Felix Desportes, secretary-general of the ministry of the interior, 27 germinal [an VIII] (ibid.).

victims of royalist sympathizers or of enemy invaders. Furthermore, many French regions were laid waste by rebels or enemies where the inhabitants did not necessarily turn refugee. To both of these general classes of sufferers, refugees and losers of property, the French government extended aid.

On September 19, 1791, the administrators of the department of Bouches-du-Rhône voted to extend 400 livres to the families from Arles (of whom there were four hundred) who had taken refuge at Aix.[186] On November 27, 1792, the National Convention voted to indemnify the commune of Voncq, in the department of Ardennes, to the extent of 200,000 livres, because of enemy invasion and fire on September 24, 1792.[187] In his report of January 9, 1793, to the National Convention, Roland, minister of the interior, stated that his office was distributing 5,000,000 livres placed at its disposal for the relief of communes devastated by the enemy.[188] On August 27, 1793, on the motion of Barère, the Convention voted to place the sum of 15,000,000 livres at the disposal of the minister of the interior for aid to citizens whose harvests had been destroyed by the enemy.[189] On September 18, 1793, the Convention placed the sum of 100,000 livres at the disposal of the minister of the interior for the relief of the most pressing needs of the women and children of

[186] *Inv.-som* . . . *Bouches-du-Rhône*, LI 3. On November 29, 1791, the Legislative Assembly, on the recommendation of its diplomatic committee, passed a measure to indemnify all foreign (German) princes for "outrages" to their estates in Alsace and for their losses in feudal dues resulting from legislation. This action was taken in order to prevent war and the possible loss of Alsace, for already hostile troops were being assembled along the frontier, and France hoped to placate the offended princes if possible (*Arch. parl.*, XXXV, 439-443). It had been with reluctance that the ancestors of these princes in the 1690's saw French gains in Alsace and the loss of that province to the Empire. The German princes in 1789-91 insisted that events of the Revolution had nullified the terms of the treaty of Ryswick, and that Alsace should revert to the Empire. (For the names of the princes involved, and an interesting historical discussion, see *ibid.*, XIII, 159-162.) An indemnity for the princes had been suggested since December 28, 1789. It is not clear how many millions were expended for this purpose, but in the "Etat comparatif des besoins de l'année 1792, qui doivent être payés en assignats par la caisse de l'extraordinaire" is an item calling for 40,000,000 livres to be used as "indemnities promised to the princes owning property in Alsace, to the pope, or aid for our colonies" (*ibid.*, XLII, 178).

[187] Damages were estimated at 772,623 livres (*ibid.*, LIII, 609-610). By a decree of December 31, 1792, the Convention decided that a portion of the *dons patriotiques* would be placed at the disposal of cities which had suffered the ravages of war (*ibid.*, LVI, 79).

[188] *Ibid.*, LVI, 642.   [189] *Ibid.*, LXXIII, 96.

citizens of the departments of Morbihan, Loire-Inférieure, Maine-et-Loire, and others, who had been killed or made prisoner "by the rebels of la Vendée."[190] Article 2 of the same decree provided an additional 30,000 livres, for the same reason, to the neighboring department of Deux-Sèvres.[191]

To the republicans of the *faubourg* La Guillotière, Lyons, the Convention on August 23, 1793, voted the gift of the confiscated property of the counterrevolutionaries there, by way of partial indemnity for their losses in the recent hostilities in that city. Another decree six days later appropriated 500,000 livres for indemnities to the commune of La Guillotière.[192] On October 13 the Convention placed at the disposal of the minister of the interior the sum of 100,000 livres for aid to the citizens of Arche, department of the Basses-Alpes, who had been forced to abandon their homes because of an invasion by the Piedmontese.[193] On November 21 the Convention appropriated 50,000 livres for aid to "fugitive patriots of Toulon, Marseilles, and the Commune-Affranchie, victims of their civism, persecuted by the enemies of the country, and who have been obliged to abandon their *foyers* and their properties."[194] The sum of 100,000 livres was voted by the Convention on 29 frimaire an II (December 19, 1793) as aid to those communes of the district of Bergues, department of the Nord, which had suffered from Austrian invasion.[195] Finally, on 27 vendémiaire an III (October 18, 1794) the Convention voted aid to French citizens that were still refugees, the funds to come from the appropriation of 24,000,000 livres which had been placed at the disposal of the minister of the interior by the decree of 24 messidor an II (July 12, 1794).[196]

---

[190] *Ibid.*, LXXIV, 352-353. The term "Mayenne-et-Loire" is used evidently in error for Maine-et-Loire.

[191] This supplemented temporary aid rendered by the decree of August 4-6. This measure of August 4-6, 1793, provided 100,000 livres for "the most pressing needs of women and children of citizens of the department of Deux-Sèvres." Wives and children of citizens of the Vendée who had been killed or imprisoned "by the rebels" were to have a share of it (*ibid.*, LXX, 218, 372).

[192] *Inv.-som . . . Isère*, L 229. There was bitter fighting at Lyons in 1793, and harsh reprisals were taken.

[193] *Arch. parl.*, LXXVI, 483. For an account of this invasion and of the cooperation of the Lyonese with the invaders, see *ibid.*, pp. 177-178.

[194] *Ibid.*, LXXIX, 587. A general law determining conditions for the granting of aid to refugees, but carrying no new appropriation, was passed on 6 frimaire an II (November 26, 1793). It supplemented other laws of this type passed on February 22 and August 14, 1793.

[195] *Ibid.*, LXX, 390, 704.   [196] Adher, *Recueil de documents*, p. 490.

From this time forward there was little need to appropriate funds for devastated districts or refugee French citizens, since the tide of battle favored the French. Indeed, French successes in the autumn of 1793 expelled the invaders from all of French soil save Valenciennes and Condé, on the Belgian frontier, and Roussillon, on the Spanish.[197] From these remaining footholds the enemies were driven by the end of July, 1794.[198]

Early in 1794 the minister of the interior sent out forty-six commissioners, with a salary of 600 livres a month and 6 livres per league for traveling expenses, to determine the extent of damages done to French territory by enemy and rebels.[199] If these commissioners traveled only 100 leagues a month, the average monthly traveling expenses of each commissioner amounted to 600 livres, and the monthly cost of all forty-six commissioners, in salaries and traveling expenses, to 55,200 livres. What was ironical was that so much money went for "overhead expenses" when aid was so niggardly—a paradox that perhaps always, and necessarily, has marked relief work. To avoid waste and corruption, it has long been found well for church or state or private relief agency to engage administrators of character and ability. This necessitates good salaries and sometimes considerable expense, but it justifies itself in freedom from abuses and in eventual saving.[200]

That these victims of enemy invasion had arrived at their predicament through no fault of their own gave them a just claim to greater assistance than claimants of certain other types, such as fathers of large families or transients. But too large a pension risked the ruin of the refugee by making him averse to work, and claimants of property losses had a tendency to exaggerate. French officials always had to reckon with this tendency. Thus when the National Convention in November, 1792, made its grant of 200,000 livres to the inhabitants of Voncq, on the estimate by the committee

---

[197] *Cam. Mod. Hist.*, VIII, 432. Alsace, the French Alps, and nearly all of the French territory facing Belgium had been retrieved.

[198] *Ibid.*, VIII, 432-440.

[199] Letter by Goujoin to the committee of public aid, 18 germinal an II (Arch. Nat., F15, 102).

[200] Whether or not it was necessary to send out as many as forty-six commissioners on such a task in 1794 is, of course, another matter. Many sections of France had been devastated by rebels or enemies in 1793. Since the commissioners perhaps went in groups of two or three to inspect different districts, the number need not have been excessive.

of public aid that the damages suffered had been 772,623 livres, a speaker rose and insisted that the damages had been twice that amount. The Convention naturally ignored him.[201]

After 1792 the tendency of the French was to take insults from none, and any seizures of French vessels by Barbary pirates or demands for ransom money from the Barbary States for the release of French captives would probably have led to war. When a Moroccan vessel, with captain, a Spanish pilot, and eight Moroccan sailors, was shipwrecked near Marseilles early in the year VIII,[202] the administrators of the central bureau at Marseilles asked for and no doubt obtained aid from the minister of the interior.[203]

An unusual form of state aid was proposed on 27 frimaire an II (December 17, 1793) when the committee of public works recommended to the Convention the grant of 1,000,000 livres to be placed at the disposal of the minister of the interior for the maintenance of needy families of prisoners, some of whom were foreigners residing in France. Many foreigners and others had been thrust into French jails as suspects since the outbreak of war. In some instances their families were suffering. In February, 1794, the Convention perhaps provided for them in its grant of 500,000 livres toward the care of indigents.[204]

Even under the Old Regime, according to Necker, the government assumed an interest in prisons. During his first administration (1776-81) many grants were made to French cities for the construction of more sanitary and spacious prisons, to promote better health, and to separate debtors from criminals.[205] But in general

[201] *Arch. parl.*, LIII, 609-610.
[202] There really were two shipwrecks of the same vessel, the first off Agde, where the captain and pilot remained. The French commissioner of marine directed that the vessel be sent to Marseilles. The eight sailors attempted to take it, but experienced a second shipwreck en route. The vessel was lost, but the sailors were saved.
[203] Letter of 5 germinal an VIII (March 26, 1800) (Arch. Nat., F15, 103). The National Convention on October 8, 1792, even granted a reward of 1,960 livres to Mathieu Christien and others of Saint-Nazaire who had rescued from shipwreck forty-one seamen of the vessel *Deux Frères* (letter from the administrators of the department of the Loire-Inférieure to the commission of public aid, 24 prairial an II, Arch. Nat., F15, 103).
[204] Tuetey, *L'assistance publique à Paris pendant la Révolution*, IV, 507-508. These suspect foreigners had been arrested by virtue of the law of August 7, 1793, whose terms are given in *Arch. parl.*, LXX, 452-453.
[205] *Compte rendu au roi*, pp. 101-102.

the government of the Old Regime prior to the publication of the works of Beccaria (1764) and Howard (1777) had been indifferent to the lot of prisoners, though their welfare had been espoused in many cities by private charitable societies, such as the Philanthropic Society of Paris, the Mercy of Grenoble, and the Dames of Charity of Bourg. Even in the last years of the century the government showed little interest in the improvement of prisons.[206]

In 1790 an attempt was made by certain members to prevail on the National Assembly to restore to the proper heirs the goods of Protestants confiscated in execution of the Revocation of the Edict of Nantes (1685).[207] Speaking against the measure, Dupont de Nemours and D'Estourmel declared that a similar law had already been passed in 1787; D'Estourmel stated that he had had a part in returning goods to Protestants. Camus declared, however, that the edict of 1787 merely announced the law and did not in itself provide for action. The Assembly dropped the proposal.

Thus during the century both the problem of refugees and the government's measures to meet it grew apace. The Revolutionists made the largest appropriations for war and refugee relief, but during their period came the most extensive invasion of French soil and the greatest amount of internal turmoil. If the appropriations were larger, they were not more liberal to the individual sufferer, nor were the payments more regular. The new features, if any, were the aid to promote the education of certain refugee children and that given the families of suspect foreigners who had been imprisoned; in other respects, the Revolutionists merely carried on the policies of the Old Regime.

[206] Throughout the century the government from time to time, especially at moments of national rejoicing, at the accession of a new king or the news of a great victory, had released groups of prisoners. This was different, however, from improving the lot of prisoners in general.

[207] The Comte de Mersenne-Fontjulianne, deputy for the nobility from Dauphiné, and Bouché, deputy for Aix, were those proposing the new decree (*Arch. parl.*, XVII, 35).

CHAPTER XVII

EDUCATIONAL AID

Before 1789

At the top of the complex educational system of eighteenth-century France were more than a score of universities,[1] several theological seminaries,[2] certain schools of medicine, numerous schools of surgery (most of them with low standards), certain lecture courses in science such as those at the Jardin des Plantes,[3] and lectures on various subjects given under the auspices of the Société Apollonienne.[4] On a somewhat lower level, because they received students either at earlier ages or with less training, or both, were several hundred colleges maintained by the various religious orders, several score technical schools, military and naval schools, and other institutions of a specialized character. The number of the colleges in France in 1789 was given as 562 by Villemain, and estimated by a later writer, Augustin Sicard, as 900 or more.[5] This number was probably smaller than it was before 1763, when the Jesuit colleges were confiscated and some of them closed.[6]

Theoretically the colleges trained students for the universities, yet rivalry sometimes developed between the two types of institu-

[1] Albert Duruy (L'instruction publique et la Révolution, Paris, 1882, p. 48) reports that there were twenty-one; Marcel Marion (Dictionnaire des institutions de la France, pp. 547-548) lists twenty-two; F. de la Fontainerie (French Liberalism and Education in the Eighteenth Century, New York and London, 1933) gives the number as twenty-nine in 1789.

[2] Founded since the Council of Trent. For brief accounts of them, see W. Henley Jervis, A History of the Church of France, from the Concordat of Bologna, A.D. 1516, to the Revolution (London, 1872), I, 332, II, 1-7; and P. Levot, op. cit., II, 221-227.

[3] The lectures, many of them by men of distinction, were given from about 1630 to 1789 (Marion, op. cit., p. 304).

[4] Also known as the Musée de Paris and the Lycée de Paris. It was organized by the famous Freemason Lodge of the Nine Sisters under the inspiration of Benjamin Franklin in the latter half of the century. Lectures were given on history, literature, politics, philosophy, and the sciences. Among the lecturers were Laharpe, Laplace, and the balloonist, Pilâtre de Rozier (Bernard Fäy, Revolution and Freemasonry, 1680-1800, Boston, 1935, pp. 268-269).

[5] L'Abbé Augustin Sicard, Les études classiques en France avant la Revolution (Paris, 1887), p. 536.

[6] The larger number were turned over to other orders for continuation.

tions, as in the notable instance of the University of Paris and the
Collège de Louis-le-Grand. Many students preferred to complete
their training in the colleges rather than in the universities. There
were fourteen military schools, three naval schools, seven schools
of artillery, one school of military engineering, one school of road
and bridge engineering, two schools of mines, three veterinary
schools, twelve schools of drawing, mathematics, and hydrography,
twelve or more (evidently permanent) schools of midwifery, certain riding (or finishing) academies for young nobles, and even other
institutions.[7] For girls, there were a few boarding schools designed
to give polish and religion, but no serious study was undertaken.

Thirdly came multitudes of primary schools, for both sexes, many
run by various religious orders, such as the Brothers of the Christian
Schools, the Ursulines, and the Sisters of Charity, but the majority
maintained by municipal and rural communities and taught by laymen. Many thousands of these primary schools, often but not
always one for each parish, existed in eighteenth-century France, and
taught reading, writing, and arithmetic, sometimes one and sometimes all of these subjects (depending largely upon the willingness
of the parents to pay the trivial tuition fees for each course).[8]

[7] Albert Duruy (*op. cit.*, pp. 48-49) presents a chart of these institutions, borrowed from Villemain. Villemain is certainly wrong in limiting the number of
veterinary schools to two, and he may be wrong also in giving the number of military schools as fourteen.

An excellent study of these institutions, entitled "L'éducation technique en France
au dix-huitième siècle (1700-1789)," has recently been published by Frederick B.
Artz in the *Revue d'histoire moderne* (Sept.-Dec., 1938); also published separately
in 1939, in fifty-one pages.

[8] Duruy gives statistics for several regions of France concerning the number of
primary schools (*op. cit.*, pp. 5-12). An ecclesiastic visiting in 1718 some 1,159
parishes in the diocese of Rouen found 855 boys' schools and 306 girls' schools. In
the district Rouen in 1790 only 15 out of 102 communes were without schools.
In the diocese of Autun around 1789 a traveler found 295 schools in 383 parishes;
in the diocese of Châlons, were found 235 schools in 319 parishes; in the dioceses
of Sens and Coutances almost every commune or parish had a school. In the department of Aube, with its 446 communes, at least 403 were provided with schools
before the Revolution (Albert Babeau, *Le village sous l'ancien régime*, p. 304 n. 4).
In the department of Haute-Marne there were 550 parishes with 473 schools. In
the department of Landes there were 448 communes, with 235 schools, prior to 1789.
Provence had primary schools in all parishes, and the communities often supported
a schoolmistress as well as a schoolmaster.

Armand Ravelet (*Histoire du vénérable Jean-Baptiste de la Salle, fondateur de
l'Institut des Frères des Ecoles Chrétiennes*, Paris, 1874, pp. 24-29) similarly draws
a favorable picture of Paris and the archbishopric of Rouen at the beginning of the
century. In the latter region in 1710 there were 818 schools. B. Bois (*La vie

By a declaration of December 13, 1698, Louis XIV made primary education in France compulsory, at least on paper, in order to force the education of Protestant children by Catholic teachers; to this end, he ordered that all parents and guardians entrusted with the care of children must send them to school (for study of the catechism) until they attained the age of fourteen. All communities without schools were ordered to create them and to tax themselves for the purpose. By the same ordinance he stipulated that the salary of all male teachers should be 150 livres, and that of female teachers 100 livres. In Normandy and other regions where many Protestants were found, the declaration was given force, and many new schools were created, largely from confiscated property of the Protestants; elsewhere it remained for the most part a dead letter. On March 14, 1724, the terms of this ordinance were renewed in a declaration by Louis XV with no greater effect.[9]

Notwithstanding these schools, however, on the eve of the Revolution only one third of the people in some districts, and two thirds or more in others, were able to read and write. In the department of Aube 72 per cent of the men were literate in the 1780's, and 22 per cent of the women.[10] In France in the period 1786-89, according to estimate, 45 to 47 per cent of the men and 22 to 28 per cent of the women were able to write their names.[11] In rural Brittany of the late eighteenth century 60 to 70 per cent of the men could write. In the cities illiteracy was rare.[12] The marriage records of the parish of Bauge, an important town in Anjou, for the years 1786-90 reveal signatures for 39 per cent of the men and 33 per cent of the

scolaire et les créations intellectuelles en Anjou pendant la Révolution (1789-1799), Paris, 1929, pp. 14-15) comments that half the parishes of the diocese of Anjou had educational foundations. There were at least 293 schools, many of them for girls. According to J. Decap (Decap, De la Martinière, and Bideau, L'instruction primaire en France aux XVIIIe et XIXe siècles . . . , Paris, 1914, pp. 1-2), only forty-one of the 139 parishes in the diocese of Rieux, in Languedoc, had schools. In ten parishes the schools were coeducational, with mistresses for teaching the girls. This is the poorest region in schools found, although some mountain sections of the Alps or Pyrenees doubtless were in worse condition.

[9] Duruy, op. cit., pp. 5-6; Babeau, op. cit., pp. 302-303; Decap, op. cit., pp. 42-48.

[10] Babeau, op. cit., p. 317 n. 3.

[11] Ibid., citing Maggiolo, an authority on eighteenth-century France, who studied the records of 344,220 marriages contracted during this period.

[12] Antoine Dupuy, "L'enseignement superieur en Bretagne avant et après la Révolution," Annales de Bretagne, IV (Rennes, 1888-89), 366. Of the literate in the rural regions, 30 per cent could write well, and the other 30 to 40 per cent but poorly.

women. Anjou was one of the less enlightened provinces of the kingdom.[13]

As for students in the higher categories, 72,747 were enrolled in the 562 colleges; of this number 40,000 received their education wholly or in part gratuitously.[14] Between 5,000 and 10,000 students attended the universities.[15]

Of the universities, at least those of Paris and Nantes received aid from the government in the form of money from the *messageries* (a combination of postal and stagecoach system). The right of participation by the University of Paris harked back to the late Middle Ages, when, for want of government service, the University had maintained its own system of mails for the benefit of its students to enable them to receive letters and money from home. When the government in 1676 took over this service and farmed it out, the University was allotted a portion of the returns. The percentage, though fixed, was small. The professors of the University were obliged to charge fees to students attending their classes. Competition and unpleasantness thus developed among the teaching staff, since some professors secured a larger number of students than others.[16]

The University suffered in competition with the Collège de Louis-le-Grand, where tuition was free. In 1719 the government assisted by increasing considerably the allowance to the University from the post and stagecoach service, on condition that the institution thenceforth charge no instructional fees. The professors were then placed on regular stipends, ranging in the departments of philosophy and rhetoric from 600 livres for professors of the fifth and sixth classes to 1,000 for those of the first class. The action was received with

[13] Bois, *op. cit.*, pp. 33-34.

[14] Villemain, quoted by Duruy, *op. cit.*, p. 25. Cf. Artz, *op. cit.*, p. 13 n. Sicard would evidently swell this number of students, along with the number of colleges. Approximately one youth in thirty in France attended the colleges. This does not include the students attending the military, artistic, and technical schools, of whom there must have been several thousand.

[15] No figures are available. The attendance at eighteenth-century universities throughout Europe was small. Moreover, several of the French universities did not possess all of the four faculties. On this point, see Marion, *op. cit.*, pp. 547-548, and De la Fontainerie, *op. cit.*, pp. 11-12.

[16] To a lesser degree there was competition among the colleges of the University. Thus there was much resentment toward the Collège de Mazarin, which was heavily endowed, paid good salaries, and gave free tuition.

rejoicing by both faculty and students at the University, whose rector ordered a *Te Deum* chanted in all its constituent colleges and declared a holiday for two days for the students. The members of the University went in a body to thank the king, the regent, and the guard of the seals.[17] As time passed and living costs advanced, these salaries fixed in 1719 became inadequate, and in 1783 the government again increased the sum allowed the University from the *messageries*. Professors were thenceforth to be paid from 1,000 to 1,400 livres, depending on their rank.[18]

According to Dupuy, the University of Nantes also received a portion from the receipts of the *messageries*. It is possible that other universities received occasional grants, as had been the case prior to the eighteenth century.[19]

The Jesuits in their hundred and twenty-four colleges in France (until closed in 1762) made no tuition charges to day students. At many, perhaps most, of the colleges operated by the Oratorians and other orders the same was true.[20] These religious orders received considerable government aid. Thus the Jesuit seminary at Brest, prior to 1762, had received from the government, the province, and the city, a total of 643,000 livres since its establishment in the 1680's, in addition to certain tax exemptions and the revenues of 1,001,770 livres from two decadent monasteries placed at its disposal by the

[17] Maxime Targe, *Professeurs et régents de collège dans l'ancienne université de Paris (XVIIᵉ et XVIIIᵉ siècles)* (Paris, 1902), pp. 175-200; Duruy, *op. cit.*, p. 30; Babeau, *op. cit.*, II, 309-311; Lecler du Brillet, *op. cit.*, pp. 620-622. The last gives in full two documents on the matter: (1) the letters-patent of April 14, 1719, and (2) the extract of the registers of the council of state. According to Targe, the professors received from 350 to 450 livres each from the *messageries* in 1699, depending on their "nation" in the University. C. P. Duclos (*Oeuvres complètes*, Paris, 1821, VII, 1) states that the sum set aside for the University after 1719 was one-twenty-eighth of the leasing price of the posts and stagecoaches.

[18] Marion, *op. cit.*, p. 209; Duruy, *op. cit.*, p. 30. According to Babeau (*op. cit.*, II, 310) the sum allowed in 1783 was 300,000 livres.

In 1762 the entire property of the Jesuit Collège de Louis-le-Grand was given by the government to the University of Paris (Gustave Dupont-Ferrier, *Du Collège de Clermont au Lycée Louis-le-Grand* (1563-1920), I, Paris, 1921, 307).

[19] For example, the University of Poitiers in 1687 received a royal grant of 3,000 livres (Charles Godard, *Les pouvoirs des intendants sous Louis XIV, particulièrement dans les pays d'élections de 1661 à 1715*, Paris, 1901, p. 368). In a budgetary report to the Estates General on May 5, 1789, Necker listed an item of expense for "Universités, académies, collèges, sciences et arts" at 930,000 livres, but did not indicate the sum for universities in particular (Marcel Marion, *Histoire financière de la France depuis 1715*, I, Paris, 1927, 470).

[20] Duruy, *op. cit.*, p. 30; Babeau, *op. cit.*, II, 309-311.

government. Nor did this aid include the cost of the building, amounting to 300,000 livres, which had been advanced by the government.[21] From the beginning of the seventeenth century until 1762 the Jesuit College of La Flèche received an annual subsidy of 7,000 livres from the province of Brittany.[22] Le Gendre, intendant at Montauban from 1700 to 1713, imposed a tax of 300 livres on the diocese and election in order to support a second course in philosophy at the Jesuit college in that city.[23] Bâville, the intendant of Languedoc, in 1700 recommended to the controller-general of finance that the state subsidize the Jesuits in order to increase their facilities for educating the "newly converted."[24]

These examples of state aid to the Jesuits for their work in education were probably the rule rather than exceptions. Similar aid was given to other religious orders. A notable way of aiding these institutions was to assign to them the confiscated property of Protestants and the property of decadent colleges and monasteries. The Jesuit seminary at Brest, as has been noted, was the recipient of monastic property to the value of a million livres. The Jesuits received much property of this type from the royal hands; when they were suppressed in France, their property, for the most part, was turned over to other religious orders, the disposition being left to municipalities.[25] The Jesuits of Paris in 1762 were receiving from the government 10,000 livres a year for the support and training of ten Armenian students, whom the government designed to use in

[21] Levot, op. cit., 221-227. Certain smaller favors, too, are named. In his chart (p. 226), government aid is reckoned at 276,000 livres, provincial aid at 317,000 livres, and municipal aid at 50,000 livres. When the seminary was suppressed in 1762, the government paid the order 46,000 livres for the buildings and converted them into barracks.

[22] Inv.-som . . . Ille-et-Vilaine, C 4918. After 1762 this sum was divided, 4,000 livres going to an institution for poor girls from the Breton nobility, and 3,000 livres for scholarships in the various colleges of the province to be given to students from the Third Estate.

[23] Godard, op. cit., p. 369. At various places Louis XIV, in the period following the Revocation of the Edict of Nantes, ordered an increase in taxes in order to provide larger buildings and care for the children of Protestants (designated "newly converted") (ibid., p. 368).

[24] Boislisle, op. cit., II, No. 162.

[25] Some cities merely closed the colleges; others continued them, placing them in the hands of other orders. According to Babeau, forty-six former Jesuit colleges were run by other religious orders in 1789. In other ex-Jesuit colleges lay professors were employed (op. cit., II, 313).

the future as interpreters at its consulates and embassy in the Near East.[26]

Throughout the eighteenth century the cities and provinces contributed toward the support of the colleges, paying in numerous instances part or all of the salaries of the principals and regents (professors). The province of Languedoc gave 500 livres yearly to the college of the Doctrinnaires at Narbonne.[27] The city of Angoulême paid an annual sum of 2,000 livres to its colleges,[28] and the city of Angers paid the salaries of its college professors.[29] The extension of aid by city, province, and state enabled them to exert some control over the institutions.[30] For example, the consuls of Forcalquier requested from the intendant of Provence authorization to increase the salary of the three regents of their college from 400 to 1,200 livres, since they were unable to get satisfactory men at the former figure.[31] Sometimes the government or the province made a grant to a college for a particular purpose. The Estates of Burgundy allocated 3,000 livres to the Seminary of Dijon, and 6,000 livres to the Academy (evidently the Academy of Dijon) in 1783 for public courses in botany, mineralogy, chemistry, medicine, astronomy, and for an observatory.[32] Many towns and cities, unable to afford a college, engaged a single regent to teach their youths. Single regents were employed by more than thirty towns in Brittany.[33] Sometimes these solitary professors were paid from provincial funds.[34]

Several free surgical schools were established in eighteenth-century France: one at Rennes in 1748, a second at Nantes in 1760, and a third in connection with the Charity Hospital at Grenoble in 1771. This last was conducted by a religious order. To the first two the Estates of Brittany made several monetary grants of considerable

[26] Barbier, *Journal*, VIII, 29-30. Barbier implies that the practice had been going on for some time. After the youths were trained in France, they were sent to Constantinople and other cities of the Near East for training in Turkish and Arabic.

[27] *Hist. gén. de Languedoc*, XIII, 74.   [28] *Inv.-som . . . Charente*, C 15.

[29] Bois, *op. cit.*, p. 46 with n. 5.   [30] Babeau, *op. cit.*, I, 302-304.

[31] *Inv.-som . . . Bouches-du-Rhône*, C 2610.

[32] *Inv.-som . . . Côte d'Or*, C 3148, f 688; 3237, f 662.

[33] Dupuy, *op. cit.*, IV, 366.

[34] *Inv.-som . . . Ille-et-Vilaine*, C 2531. The intendant paid one Thébault 500 livres for the maintenance of a free school in mathematics at Rennes in 1769.

size.[35] There were also surgical schools at Brest, Aix in Provence, Montpellier, and Paris. The last three received aid from the government, and all doubtless rendered gratuitous instruction.[36] The surgical school at Paris was by far the best and most flourishing in France. According to Mercier it had more than 800 students in 1783.[37] No doubt there were many other surgical schools in France besides these seven.

The Jardin des Plantes was endowed in the late seventeenth century by Colbert with several public lecture courses, on botanical subjects, chemistry, natural history, and surgery. In 1789 Jussieu, Fourcroy, Thounin, Daubenton, and Lacépède were the lecturers. The Jardin in 1782 consisted of 25 *arpents*. It was a government institution, and the lectures were free.[38]

According to the late A. Lawrence Lowell, Vauban (d. 1707) established in Paris a school of military engineering, which became the parent of all schools of military and civil engineering throughout the world.[39] In 1748 a school of military engineering was established at Mezières, which made a brilliant record and lasted down to 1793. In it taught the famous mathematician Monge, and among its graduates were Lazare Carnot, minister of war during the Convention and organizer of the Revolutionary armies, and Cugnot, inventor of the first steam-propelled truck. Each student admitted to this institution had an allowance of 720 livres by the state; his parents contributed 200 livres.[40] Until 1750 civil engineering was taught there along with military engineering; thenceforth it was taught, rather, at the Ecole des Ponts et Chaussées, founded in 1747 by the intendant of finance Trudaine, with Perronet as director. This institution, like the former, was famous in eighteenth-century Europe and turned out

[35] *Inv.-som . . . Ille-et-Vilaine*, C 4935; *Inv.-som . . . Isère*, H, Introduction, p. xxiii.

[36] Levot, *op. cit.*, II, 141-142; *Inv.-som . . . Bouches-du-Rhône*, C 98, f 193v; Garrison, *op. cit.*, p. 409-410.

[37] *Tableau de Paris*, VIII, 126-132.

[38] Marion, *op. cit.*, p. 304. The *arpent* was a French measure of land varying with locality. The *arpent de Paris* was 0.84 acre; the *arpent commun*, 1.04 acres; and the *arpent des eaux et forêts*, 1.26 acres. Cf. *Webster's New International Dictionary*, 2d ed. unabridged, "arpent."

[39] *What a University President Has Learned* (New York, 1938), p. 39. Chéruel (*op. cit.*, II, 906) states that at the close of the seventeenth century France had about 600 military engineers.

[40] Artz, *op. cit.*, pp. 39-42; Chéruel, *op. cit.*, II, 906.

the engineers for the well-developed Administration of Bridges and Highways, responsible for the excellence of certain of the French roads. The school did not engage a regular corps of teachers; instead, the instruction was given by engineers of the highway system. Twelve hundred students were enrolled in 1788. No record has been found concerning the charge for instruction, but to judge from the practice in other state-controlled schools it seems probable that at least a large number of the students enjoyed pensions (or scholarships).[41] In several of the leading towns in Guyenne the intendant Boutin opened free schools in surveying during the years 1763-65. The teaching was done by topographic engineers, the schools evidently being modeled in this respect after the Ecole des Ponts et Chaussées. Despite the gratuitous instruction, the province had difficulty in getting students to take advantage of it, and in most of the schools the enrollment was very small.[42] Finally, the royal School of Mines was established at Paris in 1781, inspired no doubt by the German mining schools at Brunswick (1745), Freiburg (1765), and Clausthal (1775). At the first it had only one professor, the chemist B. G. Sage, a member of the Academy of Sciences; but shortly a second, Duhamel, was added. To be admitted, students were required to be sixteen years old and to pass certain preliminary examinations in German, geometry, and drawing. There were twenty-four scholarships, twelve for the sons of mine-owners and miners, and twelve for capable youths from the provinces who otherwise would not have been able to attend. In 1790 it was closed because of the Revolution, but was reopened in 1794.[43]

Beginning in the 1740's there came into existence a large number of drawing schools (écoles de dessin) and special courses in drawing, painting, or sculpture. Of nineteen of these schools,[44] the one

[41] Artz, op. cit., pp. 25-27; Marion, op. cit., p. 197; Chéruel, op. cit., II, 906.

[42] The seats of these schools were Bordeaux, Périgueux, Condom, Agen, Lesparre, Villeneuve-d'Agen, Excideuil. The attempt to found a school at Bergerac fell through for lack of students. At Lesparre the school began with five students, but the enrollment shortly rose to eight. The most flourishing school whose figures are known was that of Villeneuve-d'Agen, which began with thirty-seven students and later increased to forty-five. Nevertheless, the intendant was obliged to close it. The purpose of these schools to supply the province with trained civil engineers (Inv.-som . . . Gironde, C 3297, 3298).

[43] Artz, op. cit., pp. 28-29; Chéruel, op. cit., II, 792.

[44] Babeau, La ville sous l'ancien régime, II, 331-332; Sicard, op. cit., pp. 333-334. They list eighteen and give dates for some of them; the one established at Bor-

founded by Tourny at Bordeaux in 1744 became a permanent institution and flourished greatly.[45]   Sometimes these schools, like those at Bordeaux, Grenoble, and Aix-in-Provence, began as private establishments,[46] offering instruction in the fine arts and sciences, in which the former predominated.   Later most of their students went into fields of the fine arts for their lifework.[47]   Though called "royal free schools of design," these institutions were supported not only by the government but also quite commonly by the provinces and municipalities in which they were situated.   The Estates of Brittany and Provence paid the salaries of certain professors in them;[48] those of Brittany and Burgundy set aside sums as prizes for pupils.[49]   The Estates of Brittany in 1775 gave three annual prizes of 400 livres each to laureates of the drawing school at Dijon, to enable them to take advanced training at Rome.   The government permitted the drawing school in Marseilles to receive 3,000 livres annually out of the city taxes.[50]   Free courses in drawing were opened by the Estates of Brittany in 1776 at Nantes and Rennes, and in 1758 at Saint-Malo.   At Limoges free lessons in drawing were given every Sunday from 1778 onwards for stonecutters, masons, and carpenters.[51]   Frequently special courses in mathematics were given by professors whose salaries were paid by either the city or the province.

In 1778 the government offered the widow Pallouis a life annuity of 2,600 livres if she would go to Lyons and teach twenty pupils at the General Hospital to card silk.   Some manufacturers, however, persuaded her to remain in Paris.[52]

---

deaux they omit. Sicard is evidently indebted to Babeau. They name the following cities: Rheims (1748), Rouen (1775), Grenoble (1762), Dijon (1766), Troyes (1773), Besançon (1778), Limoges (1778), Orléans, Caen, Beaumont, Langres, Valenciennes, Aix, Arras, Saint-Omer, Ancenis, Saint-Quentin, and Marseilles.

[45] Bernadau, op. cit., pp. 99-101. Many artists trained in painting, sculpture, and architecture came to teach in it, most of them giving their time free.

[46] [Marc Joseph] Frédéric Taulier, Le vrai livre du peuple, ou le riche et le pauvre: histoire et tableau des institutions de bienfaisance et d'instruction primaire de la ville de Grenoble (Grenoble et Paris, 1860), pp. 541-542; Inv.-som . . . Bouches-du-Rhône, C 98, f 57.

[47] Babeau, op. cit. The Royal Free School of Drawing in Paris, founded in 1767, came to be attended by 1,500 students, who were taught practical geometry, architecture, stonecutting, perspective, etc. (Marion, op. cit., p. 197).

[48] Inv.-som . . . Ille-et-Vilaine, C 4919; Inv.-som . . . Bouches-du-Rhône, C 98, f 57 and f 66.

[49] Inv.-som . . . Ille-et-Vilaine, C 4919; Inv.-som . . . Côte d'Or, C 3228.

[50] Babeau, op. cit., II, 334.   [51] Sicard, op. cit., pp. 333-334.

[52] Tuetey, Répertoire général . . . , VII, 260-261, No. 1536.

In the late seventeenth century schools of hydrography, or naval schools, were established at Saint-Malo, Rochefort, Dieppe, Brest, and Nantes; in the eighteenth century others were established at Le Havre, Vannes, Alais, Belle-Isle, Lorient, Nantes, Bordeaux, Bayonne, Agde, Marseilles, and other places.[53] Twenty-four of these institutions were in existence in 1785, and twenty-three in 1791.[54] Colbert was the original inspirer of these schools, his intention being to train officers for the navy. He preferred that they come from the nobility, but it was never possible to recruit enough students from that class to fill the complement. The courses of study were varied and practical.[55] The expense was borne partly by the government and partly by the municipalities, although prior to 1760 the subsidies were not received with regularity.[56] At certain of the schools the state paid 500 livres annually toward the expense of each student, and the youth's family 600 livres.[57] The instructors were named by the state. As a part of their training, the pupils were sent for a while each year for practical experience aboard vessels at Brest, Rochefort, or Toulon. Besides the schools for the training of naval officers, schools were created in 1764 by the Duc de Choiseul, minister of the marine, at Brest, Rochefort, and Toulon, for the training of officers of the merchant marine.[58]

One of the numerous military schools was founded in 1751 at Paris by Louis XV to train five hundred youths drawn from the nobility,[59] preferably the sons or grandsons of officers who had lost life, limb, or health in the king's service; otherwise, young nobles without fortune. They were to enter between the ages of eight and eleven and be trained for four years at government expense. At the end of that time they were to be commissioned in the army as

[53] Artz, *op. cit.*, pp. 42-49, and *Les débuts de l'éducation technique en France (1500-1700)* (Extrait de la *Revue d'histoire moderne* [Sept.-Dec., 1937]) (Paris, 1938), pp. 49-52; Babeau, *op. cit.*, II, 316; *Inv.-som . . . Gironde*, C 3292; Bernadau, *op. cit.*, pp. 351-352; Levot, *op. cit.*, II, 370-371, 376; *Inv.-som . . . Ille-et-Vilaine*, C 563, 740, and 1250.

[54] Artz, *L'éducation technique*, p. 48 n. 3; *Arch. parl.*, XXXI, 102. The latter source carries a list of these schools, and reveals that, at least in 1791, there was only one professor per school.

[55] They are described at some length by Artz, *Les débuts . . .* , pp. 48-53, and *L'éducation technique . . .* , pp. 46-49.

[56] Artz, *L'éducation technique*, p. 48.

[57] *Ibid.*, p. 45.

[58] *Ibid.*, p. 48.

[59] According to Artz (*ibid.*, p. 32), bourgeois youths also attended.

cornettes or *sous-lieutenants*. The expenses of the school were to be derived from an increase in the tax on playing cards and on the receipts from the lottery. Members of the French Academy and the Academy of Sciences, such as Legendre, Laplace, and Berthollet, gave instruction in the institution, which taught scientific studies, as well as Latin, French, English, and German. The record of this school was not altogether successful. Designed for five hundred cadets, it never had more than half that number. A few years after its foundation military tactics ceased to be taught, since many of the students lacked adequate preparation.

In 1764 the former Jesuit College of La Flèche was changed into a preparatory school for the accommodation of two hundred and fifty young students ranging from eight to fourteen years, who were then to pass to the Ecole Militaire. This arrangement was little more satisfactory. Accordingly, in 1776 the Count de Saint-Germain, minister of war, suppressed the Ecole Militaire at Paris and dispersed the cadets among twelve colleges in the provinces, run by various religious orders.[60] Saint-Germain prescribed the curriculum, which was at once modern and utilitarian, consisting of Latin, French, German, history, geography, mathematics and other sciences, drawing, penmanship, the catechism, music, dancing, and fencing. The course of studies in force at all of these colleges was the same. The cadets wore a uniform, and holders of scholarships received from the government 700 livres each toward their expenses. In 1784 a new Ecole Militaire was founded at Paris to serve as a more advanced institution than the twelve provincial military colleges. Napoleon Bonaparte, who attended the school in 1784-85 after completing the course at Brienne, left a favorable account of it: "At the Military School at Paris we were fed [and] served magnificently, [and] treated in all matters as officers enjoying great ease, greater certainly than that of the most of our families, and very much above that which most of us were destined one day to enjoy."[61] After visiting the school on October 20, 1787, Arthur Young, in his *Travels in France*, made scornful remarks on state-paid education.[62] The costliness of the

[60] Of these schools, those at Sorèze, Tiron, Rebais, Beaumont, Pontlevoy, and Auxerre were maintained by the Benedictines; those at Vendôme, Effiat, and Tournon, by the Oratorians; that at Brienne, by the Minimes; that at Pont-à-Mousson, by the canons of the Holy Saviour; and that at La Flèche, by the Doctrinnaires.

[61] Quoted by Artz, *L'éducation technique*, p. 36 n. 3.

[62] Ed. Betham-Edwards, p. 100.

Ecole Militaire, since it could accommodate at most only 140 students, was so disconcerting to the French government that before the end of 1787 it was closed again, and the cadets, 87 in number, were sent in part to the army and in part to their homes. The twelve military colleges in the provinces continued until 1793, when they were suppressed and were replaced in 1794 by the Ecole de Mars at Paris. Between the years 1776 and 1787 a total of 2,381 students attended the military schools, of whom 603 received their education at state expense.[63] After April, 1786, the government required that all students on entering be inoculated for smallpox, unless they had had the disease and could produce a certificate to that effect.[64]

Besides the military schools proper there were several artillery schools with a history dating back to 1689, when Louis XIV founded one at Douai. All of these schools were attached to garrisons; the most important were those at La Fère, Grenoble, and Perpignan. Three days a week were spent in classroom studies, which had many similarities to the studies in the military schools proper. Most of the students' time, however, was given to mathematics and physics. The making of gunpowder, the construction of bridges and fortifications, and methods of defense and attack were also taught. The other three weekdays were spent at maneuvers, artillery practice, and the construction of fortifications.[65]

Also related to the military schools were certain cavalry schools,[66] founded in the 1760's and 1770's, and certain knights' academies or riding schools. The earlier half of the eighteenth century had seen many of the latter existent in France. Paris alone had eight.[67] Bordeaux had one, formed in 1716. Later it was suspended under Tourny, who made plans, however, for the establishment of another.[68] Caen had a riding school, founded in 1728, and supported it with 300 livres annually from the *octrois*, while the state granted it an annual subsidy of 1,200 livres.[69] Rennes was the seat of yet

[63] Artz, *L'éducation technique*, pp. 29-37; Marion, *op. cit.*, p. 196; Sicard, *op. cit.*, pp. 431-438; *Inv.-som* . . . *Calvados*, C 2471, 2474.

[64] *Inv.-som* . . . *Calvados*, C 2475; Tenon, *op. cit.*, p. 16.

[65] Artz, *L'éducation technique*, pp. 37-39.

[66] Those at Metz, Douai, Angers, and Besançon, founded in 1764, were shortlived. In 1771 another was founded at Saumur (*ibid.*, p. 31).

[67] Artz, *Les débuts*, p. 20.

[68] Bernadau, *op. cit.*, pp. 146-147; *Inv.-som* . . . *Gironde*, C 3292. The government accorded a tax in favor of the second.

[69] Babeau, *La ville sous l'ancien régime*, II, 316.

another, called Kergus, after the abbé who founded it in 1748. It continued to the Revolution and received not only 30,000 livres from the Estates of Brittany toward its construction, but other grants afterwards, especially for scholarships.[70] At the riding schools young nobles were trained for a military career and were taught mathematics, music, riding, vaulting, drawing arms, etc. After the establishment of the Ecole Militaire in 1751, they decreased in number; yet in 1780 there were still three in Paris.[71]

Two schools of private foundation existed for the sons of deceased or invalid military men. One, founded in 1773, was partly maintained by an Irish resident of France, the Comte de Pawlet. Two hundred students were received (in 1787, two hundred and twenty-five) and trained according to their aptitude. The curriculum of studies embraced religion, reading, writing, mathematics, Latin, German, English, drawing, painting, music, and various trades (i.e., technical studies). In general the training led to a military career.[72] In 1785 the government agreed to grant a subsidy of 32,000 livres toward scholarships, but by November, 1791, only two installments of 12,000 livres each had been paid.[73] During the Reign of Terror the school was closed. The second school, established about 1780 by the Duc de la Rochefoucauld-Liancourt, was suggested by that of Pawlet. Founded to receive only the sons of poor, crippled, or aged military men, it began with only a score of students, but grew so rapidly that there were 100 students in 1786, 130 in 1787, and 160 in 1789. Each student was allowed for maintenance 160 livres a year, was equipped with a uniform, and was given military and technical training.[74]

The first of three veterinary schools was founded at Lyons by Bourgelat, with aid from the controller-general, in 1761; the second at Limoges, by Turgot in January, 1766. The third at Alfort, near Paris, was established under government auspices, also in 1766.[75]

---

[70] For 1785 and 1786 alone, 28,800 livres were granted it (*Inv.-som . . . Ille-et-Vilaine*, C 1314, 4918).

[71] Artz, *L'éducation technique*, p. 20.

[72] *Ibid.*, p. 24 n. 1; Tenon, *op. cit.*, p. 19. An account of Pawlet is found in *Biographie universelle*, under "Paulet."

[73] Scholarships of 200 livres each were to be given to 260 students annually (Tuetey, *Répertoire général*, VII, Nos. 2007, 2008).

[74] Ferdinand-Dreyfus, *Un philanthrope d'autrefois*, pp. 35-37.

[75] *Encyclopédie méthodique*, Médicine, IX, 463-465; Juvencel, *op. cit.*, p. 267; Dumas, *op. cit.*, pp. 302-304; Arthur Young, *op. cit.*, pp. 98-99.

Those at Lyons and Alfort so quickly attained European fame that students from several countries of Europe, as well as many parts of France, attended them; and they became the precursors of similar institutions in other countries. They were aided by government grants from time to time. In 1781 and 1783, for example, the government màde them grants of 59,000 livres.[76] Many of the provinces gave *bourses* or scholarships to students from their territories in order that they might attend, binding them with a promise to return and work within the province. Thus each of the three provinces in the generality of Tours—Touraine, Anjou, and Maine—supported two students at the veterinary schools of Lyons and Alfort from 1766 to 1777, while in 1769 Maine supported four. Each pupil received 300 livres a year, of which 168 went for tuition and 132 for maintenance. A four-year course of studies was offered, at the completion of which the student received a *brevet* or license. On their return to the province and assumption of work, the graduates were given a uniform, 600 livres, and the promise of 900 livres (extra) in salary over three years—200 the first year, 300 the second, and 400 the third.[77]

Most of the elementary schools were maintained by the municipality or rural community. Permission from the government was a preliminary formality in establishing a school.[78] Little or no expense was incurred for buildings: an old structure might be engaged, or a room or two in the teacher's home might be used. Occasionally expense was entailed for repairs, but no buildings were constructed. Almost the sole expenditure for primary schools was the salary of the schoolmaster or schoolmistress. Sometimes the salary was provided by generous individuals, but more commonly by the community, which raised the funds by a special tax or assessment. In most instances, however, the teacher was given the right to collect a small monthly fee from each student for each course of study. Thus in the earliest years of the century (until 1712) the teacher in the primary school at Cuers, in Provence, was paid a salary of 75 livres annually, and was allowed to charge his pupils for instruction: 5 sous

[76] Necker, *Compte rendu au roi*, pp. 113-114; *Encyclopédie méthodique*, Finances, II (Paris, 1785), 145; Juvencel, *op. cit.*, p. 267.

[77] Dumas, *op. cit.*, pp. 302-305; *Inv.-som . . . Seine-Inférieure*, C 421; *Inv.-som . . . Ille-et-Vilaine*, C 89. A somewhat large number of the *Inventaires-sommaires* refer to the veterinary scholarships.

[78] This was true even in a *pays d'état*, Brittany for example (*Inv.-som . . . Ille-et-Vilaine*, C 618, 692).

for the alphabet, 8 for religious teaching, 10 for French and Latin, 12 for reading, 15 for writing and arithmetic. When in 1715 the salary of this teacher was raised to 150 livres, the fees of the pupils were also increased.[79] Similar fees were demanded in most community schools in France, not only down to, but even beyond, 1789.[80] Even then the teachers, especially in the villages and rural communities, often felt obliged to obtain other work to supplement their salaries. Louis XIV ordered in 1698 that all schoolmasters should be paid at least 150 livres a year, and all schoolmistresses 100 livres. Until the mid-eighteenth century these sums, had they been paid, would have been ample, but in perhaps the greater number of instances they were not paid. During the eighteenth century the cost of living steadily rose, and with it the salaries of schoolteachers. Teachers were never able to live in luxury, but on the other hand they were probably better off than the greater portion of the French people.

Teachers were elected year by year by vote of the citizens of the community at a meeting called for the purpose. It was common for applicants to be required to undergo an examination to show their attainments, but in some instances letters of testimonial were accepted in lieu thereof. Sometimes when there were several applicants a disputation was held, and the competitors were compelled to exhibit specimens of their handwriting, to aid the citizens in making their choice.[81] The curé and the bishop usually had great influence with the citizenry in making their decision; indeed, they were commonly able to dominate the school at all times. The clergy realized clearly the value of the primary schools as an aid to religion, and the catechism was universally taught. Nevertheless, a large percentage of teachers in the community schools were laymen; many of them had university degrees.[82]

[79] Edmond Poupé, *L'instruction publique à Cuers sous l'ancien régime* (Extrait du *Bulletin de la Société d'études scientifiques et archéologiques de la ville de Draguignan*) (Draguignan, 1907), pp. 12-13.

[80] Duruy, *op. cit.*, pp. 15-16; Decap *et al.*, *op. cit.*, p. 51; Frantz Funck-Brentano, *The Old Regime in France*, tr. Herbert Wilson (London, 1929), p. 279. These writers set forth the varying and complicated modes of payment.

[81] Decap and others, *op. cit.*, pp. 21-24; Ravelet, *op. cit.*, pp. 19-20.

[82] Decap, *op. cit.*, pp. 9-10. Decap found that the majority of teachers in the diocese of Rieux were clerical. This does not appear to have been the case for France as a whole. He also inclined to the opinion that the laymen were the better prepared.

The training given in these schools was the simplest kind, rarely going beyond reading, writing, arithmetic, the alphabet (possibly including spelling), and the catechism. The school year, at least in the diocese of Rieux, in Languedoc, commonly ran from mid-October to early September; and the school day ran from 7:00 or 8:00 A.M. to 4:00 or 5:00 P.M., with an extended recess for lunch. Thursdays and fete days were generally holidays, and in some places classes were dismissed on Saturday afternoons.

While it was the usual practice, encouraged by the church, for the sexes to be taught in different schools, many village and rural communities found it necessary to teach them together. In some instances where they were taught in the same building, a man would teach the boys, and a woman (sometimes the wife of the schoolmaster) would teach the girls; but in other instances a schoolmaster would teach both sexes.

The fees charged for instruction were so small that all save the poorest classes could afford to give their children some degree of schooling. Even for the extreme poor, many communities made provision by gratuitous instruction. Indeed, most of the rural schools in Brittany were provided by gifts from the upper classes, and instruction was free to all.[83]

Supplementing the community schools in the field of elementary education were the charity schools run by the various religious orders. Numerous orders of nuns and several orders of monks were engaged in this work.[84] Each province in the eighteenth century tended to have its own order of nuns for the conduct of schools for girls, but this was not always the case. Rouen, for example, had five orders of nuns entrusted with the education of little girls.[85] Of the orders charged with the education of boys, the most prominent by far was that of the Brothers of the Christian Schools, founded in northern France in the late seventeenth century by Jean Baptiste de la Salle, a young priest who held a master of arts degree from the University

---

[83] Dupuy, op. cit., IV, 365-366. Cf. Inv.-som . . . Ardennes, C 370; Inv.-som . . . l'Aube, C 1716; Inv.-som . . . Gironde, C 2670; Inv.-som . . . Ille-et-Vilaine, C 406.

[84] Marcel Marion gives a list of them in his Dictionnaire des institutions de la France, pp. 99-100. Most of them still existed at the time of the Revolution, although the eighteenth century had witnessed a considerable decline in the number of those who joined such orders. Cf. Ravelet, op. cit., pp. 58-61.

[85] Dupuy, op. cit., p. 8 with n. 2.

of Rheims. In 1677 he took over the work of Nicolas Rolland, a priest with whom for a short time he had been associated. Several priests and monks had engaged independently in the opening of gratuitous schools for poor boys in the sixteenth and seventeenth centuries, but their work had not been long-lived because of their difficulty in getting teachers to carry on their enterprise. La Salle solved the problem by opening an institute, or normal school, for the training of teachers and by enlisting them in a special order founded for this mission.

A dozen or more of his schools were established in various cities, chiefly in northern France, before 1700, and they continued to grow rapidly in numbers during the early years of the eighteenth century.[86] Even down to the Revolution the number of schools increased, until almost every city or large town had one or more. In some places there was opposition to education of the poor,[87] and at least for several decades private teachers in writing and spelling strongly protested, with perhaps some justice, that these schools robbed them of pupils. These teachers also declared that the Brothers of the Christian Schools did not always restrict their work to the needy, but sometimes admitted pupils from families that could afford to pay.[88] Charging that the seminary for teachers menaced their corporation, they took the matter to the courts and sometimes won their case.

Most of the Brothers of the Christian Schools, commonly called Ignorantins by the populace because they knew and taught no Latin, indeed, had very little education, but they made up in zeal for their lack of learning. The subjects that they taught were reading, writing, arithmetic, spelling, the catechism and other particulars in religion, and some forms of manual art.[89]

In many cases the schools run by the Christian Brothers and other

---

[86] See Ravelet, op. cit., passim. The rapidity with which they grew is amazing.

[87] Bois (op. cit., pp. 29-30, 49, 50) cites Angers and Saumur as hostile to the work of the petites écoles of the Christian Brothers, which they considered as training only the children of the dregs of the people. Nevertheless, the Christian Brothers had two charity schools in Angers, and the city had several charity schools for girls (ibid., p. 9).

[88] Ravelet, op. cit., pp. 299-317, 329; Bois, op. cit., p. 49.

[89] Preserved Smith, A History of Modern Culture, II (New York, 1934), 431. "The discipline was severe, and the religious instruction plentiful. After suffering a castigation with the whip, a boy was obliged to kneel and thank his teacher for the kindness thereby done him." Cf. Bois, op. cit., p. 31 n. 12.

orders were provided by generous individuals. In others they were provided by the city. In some instances both individuals and city co-operated, one furnishing the building and the other the salary or salaries.[90] Sometimes the schools were aided by the state, as in the Cévennes (a strongly Protestant region of southeast France), at Calais, and Marseilles.[91] Occasionally they were aided by the province, and intendants frequently took an active part in encouraging the establishment of schools within their bounds.[92] The teachers were well paid, sometimes in the early part of the century receiving as much as 200 livres a year.[93] The teachers of the charity schools, moreover, were better off than those of the community schools since they did not have to worry about re-election to their posts each year. They had, however, it might well be imagined, a less desirable type of pupil.

Schools for girls, whether of the community or the charity type, were fewer in number and slower in appearing than those for boys. Nevertheless, they were founded throughout the century. Some were day schools; others, boarding schools. Even the boarding schools sometimes gave gratuitous education to poor girls.[94] Of course every general hospital had a school of free instruction in its halls for the children in its care. Sometimes children from the community were admitted, as was the case of the Hospital of Saint-Etienne, which in 1723 established a free school of instruction for girls or young women (demoiselles) of artisan or bourgeois families in the town who happened to be limited in means.[95] In these schools the girls were taught to read, write, spell, spin, recite the catechism, and to know the moral obligations inculcated by the church.[96]

The government of France contributed little toward either the community or the charity primary schools, save in districts strongly

[90] Ravelet, op. cit., pp. 125-128, 271, 297, 321-323, 325-327, and passim; Poupé, op. cit., pp. 13-14; Inv.-som . . . Calvados, H Suppl. 472-II G 8, 1131-II E 7; Inv.-som . . . Ille-et-Vilaine, C 595.

[91] Ravelet, op. cit., pp. 330-331, 376; Dom Théophile Bérengier, Vie de Mgr Henry de Belsunce, évêque de Marseille, 1670-1755 (Paris, 1886), II, 130.

[92] Inv. som . . . Calvados, C 240; Inv.-som . . . Gironde, C 3292; Bernadau, op. cit., pp. 352-353; Ravelet, op. cit., p. 330; Bois, op. cit., p. 49.

[93] Inv.-som . .·. Calvados, H Suppl. 1131-II E 7.

[94] For example, the school at Provins (Christophe Opoix, Histoire et description de Provins, 2d ed., Provins and Paris, 1846, pp. 361-362).

[95] Inv.-som . . . Charente-Inférieure, H 93.

[96] See Bois, op. cit., p. 9.

Protestant, where the property of self-exiled Huguenots were confiscated and generally given to the schools. The government apparently gave much less to primary than to secondary or university instruction. Near the close of the eighteenth century, however, two special forms of primary education attracted the French government's attention and support. These were the schools for the deaf-mutes and the blind, the former created by the Abbé Charles Michel de l'Epée, and the latter by Valentin Haüy.

The training of isolated individuals who were blind or deaf-mute was a very old practice, but the establishment of special schools for them did not occur until the second half of the eighteenth century. Among those who had previously interested themselves in the teaching of deaf-mutes were Jean de Béverley and the Venerable Bede, of the seventh and eighth centuries, Rodolphe Agricola, Jerome Cardan, Saint Francis de Sales, the Spanish Benedictines Pedro de Ponce and Juan Poblo Bonnet, Pasck of Brandenburg, Ramirez de Carion, Bulwer, Wallis, Dalgarno, Van Helmont, Conrad Amman, Jacob Rodrigues Pereire, and Samuel Heinicke. Several of them had given instruction to deaf-mutes and succeeded in teaching them to talk.[97] Unfortunately, until Pereire appeared, none had left a record of the methods by which success had been achieved, so that each had been compelled to learn anew for himself.[98] It was Pereire, a Jew of Bordeaux, who gave his life to the study and instruction of deaf-mutes, and communicated orally to the Académie des Sciences on various occasions, as well as in writing, the methods by which he had achieved remarkable success with several pupils.[99] He was twice acclaimed by the Académie des Sciences; he was made an associate of the Royal Society of London; the king of France from 1750 gave him a pension of 800 livres a year;[100] and in 1756 the Jews of Bordeaux in return for his services gave him an annual pension of 400 livres.[101]

[97] Eugène Dubief, L'Abbé de l'Epée et l'éducation de sourds-muets (Paris, n. d.) pp. 30-32; Ernest La Rochelle, Jacob Rodrigues Pereire, premier instituteur des sourds-muets en France: sa vie et ses travaux (Paris, 1882), pp. 8-13.

[98] La Rochelle, op. cit., p. 13. He admits that several had left writings on the instruction of deaf-mutes, but says that none had left his secret of achievement. See, however, Dubief, op. cit., p. 31.

[99] La Rochelle has made an excellent study of Pereire's career and has championed his right to be considered the real pioneer in deaf-mute education in France.

[100] La Rochelle, op. cit., pp. 66, 83-84, 86, 151.

[101] In 1762 this was doubled, and at the same time his two sisters were extended a pension of 400 livres (ibid., p. 273-274).

While Pereire devoted his life to the training of deaf-mutes,[102] he taught as a tutor and did not, strictly speaking, open a school for them. The training of deaf-mutes *en masse*, was the work of the Abbé Charles Michel de l'Epée (1712-89), a native of Versailles, a student of theology and law, and a Jansenist priest who suffered persecution from higher ecclesiastical authorities. In 1754 he became interested in a case of twin girl deaf-mutes and, being at the time without ecclesiastical appointment, decided to devote his life to the assistance of those thus afflicted.[103] Some time was spent in study of his problem, and around 1760 he opened a school for the teaching of deaf-mute pupils, which soon won international fame. De l'Epée put all of his patrimony, amounting to 10,000 to 12,000 livres, into the instruction, and gave his own services free.[104] In 1778 the government of Louis XVI took an interest in the project and allowed De l'Epée a part of the old convent of the Celestins, in Paris, for his school. From 1785 it further aided him with a subsidy of 34,000 livres a year.[105] When De l'Epée died in December, 1789, his work was carried on by a former pupil, the Abbé Sicard, who had had several years of practical experience with a similar institution in Bordeaux.

The work of Pereire and De l'Epée attracted the attention of several European rulers, of whom Joseph II and Gustavus III came to witness their work. Thereafter schools for the deaf-mutes rapidly sprang up in different parts of Europe, and some of them were staffed by pupils of De l'Epée.[106] Schools for deaf-mutes were founded at Angers and Bordeaux among other places. The institution at Angers was founded before 1772 by Charlotte Blouin, a pupil of De l'Epée. In 1772 the government (evidently the provincial) accorded it

[102] Some he taught over a period of years and gave higher training than the current elementary education (*ibid.*, pp. 48, 69-70, 106 n.).

[103] Dubief, *op. cit.*, pp. 20-23. Pereire had begun his work of instructing deaf-mutes in 1746.

[104] A brother aided him financially (*ibid.*, p. 37).

[105] Marion, *op. cit.*, p. 517. Dubief (*op. cit.*, p. 55) writes that the transfer to the Celestins was made in 1786, and that at the same time the government granted the institution an annual allotment of 6,000 livres. It seems better to follow Marion, since he cites the specific *arrêts du conseil*.

[106] The Abbé Storck, who was placed by Joseph II in charge of one in Vienna, and the Abbata Silvestri, who was placed in charge of one in Rome (1784), were both pupils of De l'Epée. Other schools were founded in Dresden and Leipzig by Samuel Heinicke, and in Edinburgh by Thomas Braidwood, who, however, were not his pupils (*The Catholic Encyclopedia*, V, 317; Dubief, *op. cit.*, pp. 55-56).

twelve scholarships *(bourses)* for students from the different parishes of the generality. In 1781 and later the intendant of Tours gave further financial assistance to this institution.[107] The institution at Bordeaux was founded in 1786 by De Cicé, the archbishop, who earlier had sent the Abbé Sicard to study under De l'Epée in Paris and to learn his method. The archbishop interested several rich inhabitants of Bordeaux in the projects, and a subscription was made to support several pupils. A lodge of Freemasons gave 1,000 livres. Two years later (1788) the *jurats* (city-councilmen) gave him a pension or salary.[108] Sicard was assisted by Saint-Sernin, a layman, who formerly had taught an elementary school, and who was destined to succeed Sicard when the latter took over De l'Epée's work in Paris in 1789.[109]

Although the school in Bordeaux opened in February, 1786, with an enrollment far below that of De l'Epée's school, it had twenty-two students in 1787 and nineteen in 1789.[110] The course of studies in 1789 embraced grammar, arithmetic, elementary and spherical geometry, geography, metaphysics, religion, and church history.[111]

Similar to De l'Epée's work with the deaf-mutes was that of Valentin Haüy (1745-1822) with the blind. Son of a poor weaver of Saint-Just-en-Chaussée, Picardy, Haüy received his education in a monastic charity school, where he studied calligraphy and foreign languages. Thenceforth he obtained one position after another as interpreter, with bankers, merchants, a university, and eventually, after he had attracted attention through his work with the blind, with the admiralty.[112] He first became interested in the blind when Mlle Paradis, an accomplished blind pianist who read music by

[107] Bois, *op. cit.*, pp. 38, 52-55; Lallemand, *op. cit.*, IV, Part II, 64-65.

[108] Bernadau, *op. cit.*, p. 352.

[109] Much information on these men and on the school in Bordeaux is given by Adrien Cornié, *Etude sur l'institution nationale des sourdes-muettes de Bordeaux, 1786-1903* (Bordeaux, 1903).

[110] Cornié gives a chart on enrollment figures for the Bordeaux institution, 1786-1903 (*op. cit.*, p. 20). De l'Epée had seventy-two students in 1785 (La Rochelle, *op. cit.*, p. 306 n. 1).

[111] Most of these subjects were taught by Saint-Sernin, to whom Cornié gives credit for most of the actual instruction in the institution (*op. cit.*, pp. 21, 24). This range of subjects would take students into secondary work, but it seems unlikely that many of the students advanced that far.

[112] Albert Mathiez, *La théophilanthropie et le culte décadaire, 1796-1801: Essai sur l'histoire religieuse de la Révolution* (Paris, 1903), p. 86. This position with the admiralty continued during the Revolution and under the Empire.

pinpricks on paper, came to Paris from Vienna in 1783.[113] Later in the year his interest was increased by the pathetic spectacle of eight or ten blind musicians trying to play before tittering spectators on the Champs Elysées. His pity was aroused, and he had a long conversation with the musicians.[114] He determined to try to improve the status of the twenty-five thousand blind persons of France and raise them above helplessness and mendicancy. He soon, in 1784, after much insistence, prevailed upon François Lesueur, a blind youth, to become his first pupil.[115]

Following the precedent of Pereire, Haüy, who ever showed a flair for publicity, presented his pupil before the Académie des Sciences in February, 1785, and won praise. In January of that year the Philanthropic Society had opened a school for twelve blind children, and De Vergennes, one of the members, knowing Haüy, asked him to teach in it. At Christmas, 1786, the pupils of Haüy were invited to appear before the court at Versailles and demonstrate their knowledge. They made a splendid impression, and the king promised Haüy the cordon of St. Michel. Haüy invited the public to visit his school on Wednesdays and Saturdays. Several times he had his pupils perform in the ceremonies at Saint-Eustache. Other churches soon asked for them. By these methods he quickly created much publicity for his work. Consequently, the number of students rapidly rose from the original twelve in 1785 to fifty in 1788.[116]

The studies included reading, writing, grammar, arithmetic, geography, history, music, and certain manual arts, such as printing, spinning, ropemaking, leather-work, ribbon-weaving, twinemaking, and bookbinding.[117] Music was perhaps emphasized more than any other subject.[118] Haüy taught by characters made in relief on

[113] She also used geographical maps made in relief (Le Chanoine Pihan, *Eloge historique de Valentin Haüy* . . . , composé pour *l'Annaire de l'Oise*, 1892, Beauvais, 1891, p. 9).

[114] *Ibid.*, pp. 10-11.

[115] *Ibid.*, pp. 10-12; Pierre Villey, *L'aveugle dans le monde des voyants* (Paris, 1927), p. 267.

[116] Villey, *op. cit.*, pp. 267-268.

[117] Boucher d'Argis, *De la bienfaisance dans l'ordre judiciaire* . . . (Londres, 1788), p. 68. Other authorities, however, do not give as impressive a list of studies. See *The Catholic Encyclopedia*, V, 308, and Pihan, *op. cit.*, p. 13. His first pupil, Lesueur, was taught only reading, simple arithmetic, a little geography, and a little music (Pihan, *op. cit.*, pp. 11-12).

[118] Mercier, *op. cit.*, XII, 294.

paper.[119] Mademoiselle de Salignac, a remarkable blind woman, who was known to Haüy, had anticipated him by making letters on paper by means of a pin; and either from her or from certain other sources he doubtless derived his idea.[120]

His work was aided by both the Philanthropic Society and the government. The former supported twelve pupils by giving them 12 livres a month, and also gave the school publicity. The king, too, gave it publicity, and aided it in a material way by making Haüy interpreter for the admiralty, a position that in no way interfered with his teaching, but rather financed him in it.[121]

The influence and imitation of Haüy's school throughout Europe came to resemble that of De l'Epée's. In Great Britain alone four similar institutions sprang up before the end of the century.[122] Either before the end of the century or shortly afterwards schools were established in Berlin, Vienna, Dresden, Copenhagen, Amsterdam, Zurich, and St. Petersburg. Royalty paid honor, and Haüy was the guest of the Prussian king and the Russian czar.[123]

The extent to which the government aided and encouraged education prior to the Revolution is not generally known, but according to Condorcet's report to the National Convention it had allotted previous to 1789 an annual sum of 4,000,000 livres. The total yearly cost of education in France in the 1780's must have been at least 20,000,000 livres.[124] Although the appropriation of 4,000,000 livres was a small item in a budget of approximately 550,000,000 livres, it revealed that the state had some appreciation of education for its subjects.

After 1789

Amid the vicissitudes of the Revolutionary period the educational institutions and ideas of the Old Regime were naturally badly shaken. Temporarily all forms of educational institutions suffered, as funds for their maintenance shrank enormously. Many instructors were

[119] Pihan, op. cit., pp. 12-13.
[120] Villey (op. cit., pp. 256-259, 261-262, 265, 268) states that various persons from the Renaissance to the eighteenth century had suggested or employed the principle of reading by means of raised letters.
[121] Pihan, op. cit., pp. 13-14.
[122] Liverpool (1791), Edinburgh (1793), Bristol (1793), and London (1799) (The Catholic Encyclopedia, V, 308).
[123] Villey, op. cit., pp. 270-271.
[124] Duruy, op. cit., p. 12 with n. 1.

forced to give up their work because of their latent hostility toward the new regime, and all property and assets of the institutions were taken over (in 1792-93) by the state. For several years following 1789 the picture was increasingly dark; all educational elements of the Old Regime were liquidated and thrown into the crucible. Out of this crucible there gradually emerged institutions and ideas, such as had been suggested by apostles of the Enlightenment, and a new day began to dawn in French education. It was thus an age in part macabre and in part hopeful.

The first attack on the educational system of the Old Regime came inadvertently in the stirring events of the night of August 4, 1789, when many nobles and clergy renounced their feudal dues; this was followed by the suppression of the *messageries* in 1790, and of the *dîmes* and *octrois* in 1791. Universities, colleges, and even primary schools suffered greatly in consequence.[125] A large number of colleges in their distress asked aid of the government, and on May 29, 1792, the Legislative Assembly placed 200,000 livres at the disposal of the minister of the interior to aid college and university professors who were suffering because of the diminution or stoppage of their salaries (resulting from the suppression of the *dîmes* and *octrois*).[126] In some instances professors had not received their salaries for many months.[127] The grant of 200,000 livres, however, was a temporary and partial alleviation. The financial distress of the colleges and universities continued, and in March, 1793, the National Convention declared these institutions the property of the nation, confiscating both buildings and endowments, but at the same time agreeing to pay the salaries of the teachers. This action marked the end of the educational machinery of the Old Regime, and ac-

---

[125] "En Anjou, l'Université est appauvrie par la suppression des droits féodaux au 4 août; les collèges le sont par le suppression, dans les villes, des messageries (1790) et des octrois (1791) et les petites écoles, dans les paroisses, sont touchées indirectment par la suppression les dîmes" (Bois, *op. cit.*, p. 97; cf. pp. 103-104). *Dîmes* and feudal dues had been abolished on the night of August 4, 1789, but article 5 of the decree provided that they would continue for the time being to be collected to the extent of supporting the hospitals, colleges, seminaries, and other charitable establishments dependent upon them. By a later decree of April 20, 1790, they ceased to be collected on January 1, 1791 (Duruy, *op. cit.*, pp. 56-57).

[126] *Arch. parl.*, XLIV, 249-250, 251; Duruy, *op. cit.*, pp. 57 n. 1; 58.

[127] Among them were the professors of the Collège de France and the members of the faculty of law of the University of Paris. Their delinquent salaries were paid in July, 1792 (Tuetey, *Répertoire générale*, VII, Nos. 2010-2013).

cording to Duruy (a supporter of the Old Regime) completed the devastation begun in 1789.[128]

Simultaneously with these financial difficulties came the question of loyalty to the Revolution. A decree of November 27, 1790, required all clergymen and members of religious orders teaching in France to accept the Civil Constitution of the Clergy and declare their allegiance to the state. This the majority refused to do. The Oratorians almost without exception responded at once by taking the oath, but they were among the few.[129] Most of those engaged in teaching of elementary charity schools, such as the Brothers of the Christian Schools and the Ursulines, refused to take the oath, though they were allowed to proceed with their work. In several instances they were replaced by lay teachers who took the oath.[130] A later decree, August 18, 1792, suppressed altogether the charity schools run by religious orders; nevertheless, some continued to exist.[131] In universities and colleges the pressure was more stringently applied, and the nonjuring teachers were expelled forthwith when they did not leave of their own accord. Many who did take the oath of allegiance deserted the colleges for curacies, in which the pay was better.[132]

Numerous institutions were closed for lack of finances; others, because the instructors were refractory. In Anjou the smaller colleges were closed in 1791; the three larger ones, at Angers, Saumur, and Baugé, were able with municipal aid to struggle on until 1793.[133] The faculty of theology in the University of Paris was suppressed in March, 1791, because of the refusal of its members to take the oath of allegiance; and on September 15, 1793, all of the universities throughout France were legally suppressed. The University of Angers had already ceased to exist, while in the University of Paris "the best teachers" and the majority of the students had already left

---

[128] *Op. cit.*, p. 63.

[129] Bois, *op. cit.*, pp. 104-105.

[130] *Ibid.*, pp. 110-116. The Brothers of the Christian Schools teaching at Paris refused to take the oath and were expelled. Some went to Italy; others took other forms of work; their superior, however, was thrown into prison and kept there until 1794 (Fosseyeux, *Les écoles de charité à Paris sous l'ancien régime et dans la première partie du XIXe siècle*, Paris, 1912, p. 79).

[131] *Ibid.*, p. 81.

[132] Bois, *op. cit.*, p. 104.

[133] The eddies of the Vendée carried away the last three institutions (*ibid.*, p. 106).

in consequence of governmental interference.[134] Thenceforth universities and university degrees disappeared from France until 1806. Also in 1793 were abolished the various literary, artistic, and scientific academies, the chief of which had always been supported financially by the state, but they were revived in 1795 in the form of the Institut de France.

The suppression or death of the smaller colleges and universities was perhaps more of a service than a blow to French education, for many of these institutions had been poorly attended and poorly staffed, and had provided a stagnant curriculum. Even the best of them taught a curriculum that was obsolete in a dead language. The colleges and universities had given little attention to the rapid and extraordinary developments in science, to modern history, or to modern languages. The Revolutionists insisted that attention be given to them.[135]

The Revolutionists as a whole, and the Jacobins in particular, were interested in making education more practical. Accordingly, they were anxious to preserve and foster institutions of a technical or applied character. The universities and the colleges were destroyed, but an impressive number of the veterinary schools, the engineering schools, the drawing schools, and the naval schools were left in operation, according to the *Almanach national*. In some instances, indeed, there were changes. Thus the military school of the Comte de Pawlet was taken over completely by the Revolutionary government when the Comte fled from France following the abdication of the king on August 10, 1792.[136] Later, on 29 messidor an III (July 17, 1795), it was moved, united with the remnants of two other schools, and given the title of Institute of Orphans of the Country's Defenders.[137] The School of Public

---

[134] Duruy, *op. cit.*, pp. 63-64; Bois, *op. cit.*, pp. 102-103. The medical faculty at Paris was disbanded by a decree of August 8, 1792, and those of the provinces by another of August 8, 1793 (Henry E. Sigerist, *Great Doctors: A Biographical History of Medicine*, tr. Eden and Cedar Paul, London, 1935, p. 267).

[135] Bois, *op. cit.*, pp. 105-107.

[136] Pawlet had already been regarded as "suspect" prior to that date. Moreover, his school had received financial aid from the Legislative Assembly (Tuetey, *Répertoire général*, VIII, 155, 156, 257).

[137] *Institut des Orphelins des Défenseurs de la Patrie*. The new school was closed temporarily in the year IV (1795-96) (Fosseyeux, *Les écoles de charité à Paris*, pp. 81-82; *Almanach national de France, l'an huitième* . . . , Paris, 1799-1800, p. 481).

Works was transformed in October, 1795, into the famous Poly-
technical School.[138]   The School of Mines was unified with that of
Military Engineers at Metz, and called by the latter name.[139]   Certain new institutions were founded, such as a School of Geography,[140]
two new Schools of Navigation,[141] the National Aerostatic School,[142]
the famous Normal School,[143] a School of Powders and Saltpeters,[144]
a School of Mars,[145] and a School of Current Oriental Languages.[146]

The expenses of students in all or almost all of these specialized
institutions, listed in the *Almanach national* under the category of
"Schools of Public Services," were to be paid by the state.   Until
1795 the expenses of students in the veterinary schools at Lyons and
Alfort were paid by the departments that sent them, just as had been
done under the Old Regime.   Thus eight veterinary students were
regularly sent to school by the department of Maine-et-Loire, at an
annual expense of 8,000 livres, with the understanding that after
two years of training they would return to render service in the de-

[138] Bois, *op. cit.*, p. 264.   A somewhat detailed description of this last institution, especially in regard to the courses of study given, is found in the *Almanach
national de France, l'an quatrième* . . . (Paris, 1795-96), pp. 457-459, and in later
issues of this publication.

[139] *Ibid.*, p. 461.

[140] A school of cartography, it was situated at Paris and admitted twenty students who had made preliminary studies at the Ecole Polytechnique (*ibid.*, p. 463).

[141] These were for commercial navigation: one was at Morlaix and the other at
Arles (*ibid.*, p. 464).

[142] *École Nationale Aérostatique*, at Meudon, established by order of the committee of public safety of 10 brumaire an III(October 31, 1794).   Its purpose
was to provide men for air service, or ballooning, in the French armies.   Two such
aerostatic companies were already operating with the French armies along the
Rhine and Meuse.   In the school were apparently only two teachers, but sixty students (*Almanach national de France, l'an sixième* . . . , Paris, 1797-98, pp. 151-152).

[143] Founded in the year III (1794-95) for the training of teachers for elementary
schools.   The students were supposed to be at least twenty-five years of age.   Each
district was to send a certain number of students in proportion to its population; the
sum of 1,200 livres was to be given each student by the state for expense.   Out of a
possible 1,412 students from the 562 districts, 1,258 reported when the institution
was opened.   These students were immature, however, and after a trial of four
months the school ceased (Bois, *op. cit.*, pp. 267-268, 303 n. 5; Duruy, *op. cit.*,
pp. 111-116).

[144] Created in pluviôse an II (January-February 1794), it lasted but one month
(Bois, *op. cit.*, p. 242).

[145] To care for 3,000 cadets, aged sixteen to seventeen, chosen from the people.
The institution lasted only four months in 1794 (*ibid.*, pp. 242-243).

[146] Created in the year III, on the recommendation of Lakanal.   Arabic, Turkish,
Persian, Tartar (of the Crimea), and Malay were taught.   Most of these languages,
interestingly enough, had formerly been taught at the Collège de France.   The new
school was of use to commerce and politics (Duruy, *op. cit.*, pp. 133-134).

partment. The law of 29 germinal an III (April 18, 1795), however, altered this plan by providing that thenceforth one veterinary
student would be sent from each district, and that the maintenance
of these students, fixed provisionally at 1,200 livres, would be borne
by the national treasury. In addition, twenty veterinary students
were to be maintained for the service of the cavalry.[147] Among the
institutions whose students' expenses were paid, were the School of
Mars and the Normal School. The Normal School students were
to receive 1,200 livres for their year of study and transportation
expenses to and from Paris. Unfortunately, both the Normal School
and the School of Mars lasted only about four months each. The
administration and expenses of the National Aerostatic School at
Meudon were controlled by the minister of war, the personnel were
soldiers, and the expense was borne by the government. Finally,
the Institute of Orphans of the Country's Defenders, later changed,
it appears, into the Military School of Pupils of the Country, situated
at Liancourt, was also maintained by the nation. In 1799-1800 it
had six hundred students, sons of "defenders of the country" exclusively, and all their expenses were paid.

The schools for the deaf-mutes and the blind, save in one instance, were continued, and received government aid. The deaf-
mute school at Angers was closed in August, 1792, because of its
protection of nonjuring clergy. From 1790 it had been supported
by the department.[148] The deaf-mute school at Bordeaux struggled
through the early years of the Revolution by means of municipal
and departmental aid.[149] In early 1793 the institution was calum-
niated before the National Convention, and suppression was contemplated. Thereupon Saint-Sernin, the school's director, went at once
to Paris, taking with him one or two of his most clever pupils, and
with them appeared before the committee of public instruction. He
not only was able to save the institution, but even got it placed on
a national basis, with the government thenceforth responsible for its

[147] The terms of this decree are given in the *Encyclopédie méthodique*, Médicine,
IX, 465. See also Bois, *op. cit.*, p. 241 n. 2. The department of Isère previously
had a policy of sending four students every three years, aged sixteen to twenty-five,
to the school at Lyons (*Inv.-som . . . Isère*, L 55, p. 151; 58, p. 135).

[148] Bois, *op. cit.*, p. 114. The pupils were temporarily placed in one of the city
hospitals.

[149] The department of Gironde, for instance, extended it 6,000 livres and the
use of the building of the suppressed Minimes (Cornié, *op. cit.*, pp. 10-11).

expenses. Twenty-four students, children of indigent parents, were each to be allowed 350 livres annually.[150] By a law of July 29, 1791, the government had already rendered similar support to the school at Paris.[151] The Abbé de l'Epée had died in December, 1789, and had been succeeded in 1790 by his pupil, the Abbé Sicard, formerly director of the school at Bordeaux. Sicard neglected to take the oath of allegiance to the Revolutionary government, and narrowly escaped assassination with other nonjuring clergy in September, 1792; he was imprisoned until December, 1793, and then released.[152]

Eventually on 16 nivôse an III (January 5, 1795) the National Convention passed a decree increasing the salaries of those employed at the two institutions, the number of students pensioned, and the amount of the pensions. Thenceforth each school was to receive sixty pensioned students (instead of twenty-four), and to give them five years' instruction. The students of either sex, aged nine to sixteen and indigent, were each to receive 500 livres annually for the first three years, 250 livres for the fourth, and nothing during the fifth save maintenance (given all students), it being assumed that the student by this time would be earning money through the trade taught him. Pupils who distinguished themselves during their five years of instruction, however, would be given 300 livres when they left the institutions, so that they might establish themselves.[153] The terms of this decree remained in force until the time of the Empire, but the vicissitudes of war sometimes made for hard sledding. Thus the number of pupils in the school in 1796 fell to six.[154]

The school for the blind had treatment somewhat similar to that of the Paris school for deaf-mutes. In fact, the two were placed together in 1790 in the old convent of the Celestins, near the Arsenal, and maintained there until 1794.[155] By decrees of July 29 and

---

[150] Teachers and others connected with the institution were paid by the state, and given lodging (ibid., p. 12).

[151] The salaries of instructors and others employed at the institution were to be paid, and twenty-four pupils "without fortune" were each to be given pensions of 350 livres (Tuetey, Répertoire général, VII, 336-337, Nos. 2003-2004). The appropriation to the Parisian institution in 1791 totaled 12,700 livres (Palluy, "Des institutions des sourds-muets en France et à l'étranger," Revue de Paris, VI, Paris, 1829, 33).

[152] Tuetey, op. cit., V, Nos. 182-183, 213-214, and 2382; X, Nos. 534, 745, 1076, 1085.

[153] Watteville, op. cit., p. 36.   [154] Cornié, op. cit., p. 13.

[155] Pihan, op. cit., p. 15.

September 28, 1791, the National Assembly decided that the schools should be nationalized and run co-ordinately, the one to have twenty-four and the other thirty pensions for indigent students. Appropriations were made for one year only, but in September, 1792, they were ordered continued indefinitely, "until the moment of the new organisation of public instruction."[156] The decree of 10 thermidor an III (July 28, 1795) established eighty-six pensions, one for a pupil from each department, with age requirements and monetary allowances the same as those for deaf-mute students. Like those for the deaf-mutes, these pensions covered a five-year course of instruction, which was to consist in part of music and manual training. The pensions, moreover, were to be open to girls as well as boys.[157] Eventually in 1800 the school was attached to the Hospice des Quinze-Vingts.

The institution was fortunate in having Haüy's continued service as director throughout the 1790's. He was a great showman and knew how to advertise his school effectively before those who had political power. This he did by contriving to have his students appear on a multitude of public programs, some religious and others political. They appeared several times before legislative bodies of the Revolution, had a prominent place in the ceremonies of revolutionary fetes, and assisted in many church masses.[158] Along with this theatrical flair he displayed the resilient ability to climb aboard the political "bandwagons" of all the fast-changing Revolutionary governments, save that of Napoleon; and then it was not that Haüy was lacking in willingness or effort, but that Napoleon scorned him. Neither Sieyès nor Talleyrand was more changeable than this chame-

[156] Watteville, op. cit., pp. 9-10, 12, 16-17. The school for the blind asked 24,400 livres to meet expenses for 1792 (Tuetey, op. cit., VII, Nos. 19, 97-98). Pensions were the same in amount at both institutions.

[157] The pupils were to be between the ages of seven and sixteen. For the first three years they were to receive 500 livres each a year, 250 livres during the fourth year, and nothing during the fifth year; but 300 livres was to be accorded each pupil on leaving who had a distinguished record, in order that he might establish himself. Article 1 of this decree alludes to the creation of eighty-six free places at the school by the law of July 21 (or 29), 1791, but there is no mention of such a term in the law of 1791 as published in Watteville (Tuetey, L'assistance publique, IV, 361-364).

[158] Tuetey, Répertoire général, VI, 189-190, Nos. 1561 and 1564; Tuetey L'assistance publique, IV, 349; Arch. parl., LX, 254-255, 521; Villey, op. cit., pp. 269-270; Mathiez, La Théophilanthropie et la culte décadaire, 87-89, 540 n. 3, 573. On one occasion he had the children to appear before the Convention to present their "patriotic gift" of 168 livres 15 sous.

leon, who began life as a royalist, and at length after various gyra-
tions ended it by becoming reconciled to church, if not also to monarchy. He did not deceive everyone, however. There were those,
among them eleven of his students and one of his instructors, who
denounced him as charlatan and royalist, and he became suspect and
had difficulty in keeping his footing.[159] On 11 pluviôse an IV (February 1, 1796) Haüy and his assistants were forced to sign an oath
of loyalty to the republic and eternal hatred of royalty.[160]

The National Convention found that it could not long dispense
with at least one of the faculties of the universities, and on 14 frimaire an III (December 4, 1795) it created three "schools of health,"
at Paris, Montpellier, and Strasbourg, for the training of young men
in medicine and surgery.[161] At Angers, Besançon, and elsewhere
private schools around certain former professors in medical faculties
acquired in some instances departmental support and appealed to
Paris for state support. But both Convention and Directory were
reluctant to establish many "schools of health," and few of these
places obtained their requests.[162] The College of Pharmacy, established in 1777 by the pharmacists of Paris, carrying gratuitous courses
in pharmacy, chemistry, botany, and natural history, was permitted
by the Revolutionists to continue, and in prairial an V (May, 1797)
was extended government support; its name was then altered to that
of the Free School of Pharmacy.[163]

Shortly after the provincial universities were abolished (1792)
the still-surviving colleges entrusted with secondary education also
collapsed or were suppressed,[164] and for the last years of the Convention secondary education in France almost completely disappeared.
But in conformity with the Convention's desire to reorganize the educational system of France, a law of 3 germinal an IV (March 23,
1796) was passed by the Directory that called into being the Central
Schools. They were precursors of the *lycées*. There was to be one

---

[159] Tuetey, *Répertoire général*, VI, No. 1562, and XI, No. 165; Tuetey, *L'assistance publique*, IV, 366-369; Mathiez, *op. cit.*, pp. 701-702.

[160] The document is in Arch. Nat., F15, 102.

[161] Bois, *op. cit.*, pp. 421-422; Sigerist, *op. cit.*, p. 268.

[162] Bois implies that Rennes was successful. Angers and Besançon were unfortunate (*op. cit.*, pp. 422-427). A list of the professors in the School of Medicine
at Paris in 1799-1800, and a list of the subjects taught, can be found in the *Almanach national de France, l'an huitième*, pp. 440-441.

[163] *Ibid.*, p. 450. [164] Bois, *op. cit.*, p. 110; Chéruel, *op. cit.*, II, 1242.

for every 300,000 inhabitants. Each school was to have ten professors, who taught such subjects as chemistry, physics, mathematics, drawing, natural history, ancient languages, belles-lettres, history, grammar, and legislation. The teaching of modern languages was optional.[165] Each professor was to receive 2,000 francs and to be lodged in the school building or buildings unless he preferred it otherwise. On the whole they were men of talent, many of them having formerly taught in the pre-Revolutionary colleges, especially in those of the Oratorians.[166] Some of the movable property of political refugees was appropriated, and receipts from sales of refugee property contributed toward the establishment of the schools.[167] A small portion of the salaries came from the tuition fee of 25 francs a year demanded of at least three fourths of the students. By law it was possible to exempt one fourth of the students from this fee on the grounds of indigence.[168] During the first year of operation the schools received some aid from the state to supplement larger funds from the departments; but a law of 15 frimaire an VI (December 5, 1797) stipulated that thenceforth all expenses must be borne by the department.[169] The departments offered each year prizes to the leading students, after the manner of the Old Regime, in order to increase excellence.[170] Attendance varied from school to school, depending to some extent upon whether the department was in the throes of Chouan disturbances. The Vendée and Vaucluse, which suffered in this respect, had more than fifty and sixty-eight students respectively, while certain other places freed from these troubles, like Rodez, Poitiers, and Besançon, each had several times this number.[171]

[165] Benaerts, *op. cit.*, pp. 192-193; Bois, *op. cit.*, pp. 351-356, 365. Both Benaerts and Bois have excellent chapters on the Central Schools, with especial consideration to their operation at Rennes and Angers, respectively.
[166] Three of the ten teachers at Angers were former teachers in Oratorian colleges, and five of them belonged to the constitutional clergy. At Rennes, Nancy, Poitiers, and elsewhere the proportion of clergymen on the faculty was very much less.
[167] Bois, *op. cit.*, p. 349.   [168] *Ibid.*, p. 358.
[169] *Ibid.*, p. 349. Thus is seen the justification of a statement by Benaerts that in studying the merits of the Central Schools it is necessary to investigate them by departments. The same writer points out that the Central Schools have been as severely criticized by some writers as they have been lauded by others (Benaerts, *op. cit.*, p. 189).
[170] Bois, *op. cit.*, p. 364.
[171] Poitiers, in the year VII, had 500 students (*ibid.*, p. 366).

In the field of elementary education, too, the period of the Revolution was stormy. Until August, 1792, an attempt was made to carry on with the elementary schools of the Old Regime, despite the fact that in 1791 trouble began to develop with the religious orders over their lack of loyalty to the Revolution. By decrees of March 22 and April 15-17, 1791, the National Assembly imposed the necessity of taking the oath of allegiance to the Revolution upon every teacher, lay or ecclesiastical, in all educational institutions in France,[172] which had the effect of forcing large numbers of teachers from elementary teaching. In Paris, for instance, Bailly, on April 5-6, 1791, ordered the closing of all charity schools run by the orders of the nuns of Saint Anne and the Brothers of the Christian Schools.[173] The requirement of the civic oath dealt the primary schools a severe blow, but the coup de grâce was given by the decree of August 18, 1792, which disbanded the religious orders and forbade them to have any part thenceforward in teaching. By the same decree all school property belonging to these orders was confiscated. Thenceforth for a time each municipality or community had to provide its own schools.[174]

On October 2, 1792, the Convention reconstituted the committee of public instruction, already appointed by the Legislative Assembly, and, though many months were wasted in delay because of quarrels between the Girondist and Mountain factions on the committee, much legislation concerning the schools was passed during the next three years. The first legislation, December 12, 1792, amounted to nothing more than a resolution that the "charity schools" would be replaced by "primary schools" in which would be taught only what was "rigorously necessary to all citizens."[175] Shortly afterwards, a law of 29 frimaire an II (December 19, 1793) specified that reading, writing, elementary arithmetic, and certain political charters, such as "The Rights of Man" and "The Constitution," must be taught; that all teachers must take the oath of allegiance to the state and be under the surveillance of municipalities and local citizens; and that these teachers would be paid by the state at the rate of 20 livres a pupil for the schoolmasters, and 15 livres a pupil for the school-

[172] Deries, *op. cit.*, p. 414.
[173] Tuetey, *Répertoire générale*, II, 234, Nos. 2188-2189.
[174] Some took an interest in the matter; others did not (Deries, *op. cit.*, p. 415).
[175] Bois, *op. cit.*, pp. 189-190.

mistresses. Parents were to be required to send their children (six to eight years of age) to these schools.[176]

This law was spoken of as the work of the Mountain. But the Girondists, too, believed that society was obligated to educate all of its members.[177] By a decree of 8 pluviôse an II (January 27, 1794) the Convention, in its effort to unify the nation in speech and thought, declared that only French might be taught in the primary schools, and that Low Breton, Italian, German, and Basque must be dropped.[178] Another school law, passed 18 prairial an II (June 7, 1794), proscribed all usage of patois, insisting that even the differences in dialect in the French language be wiped out; that no priests or members of religious orders, male or female, be allowed to teach in the schools; that teachers receive from the national treasury salaries of 1,500 livres a year; and that parents and guardians be required to send their children (no age specified) to school.[179] Instruction was free.[180] The 27 brumaire an III (November 17, 1794) saw the passage of another school law stipulating, among other things, that there should be a school to every thousand inhabitants; that this school should be divided into two sections, one for boys and another for girls; that the teachers be chosen by examination before special juries and given the salary of 1,000 or 1,200 livres, dependent upon whether the teacher was woman or man; and that "vicarages not sold" be used for school buildings whenever needed.[181]

Nor was this the last school law passed by the Convention: on 3 brumaire an III (October 25, 1795), one day before its dissolution, the Convention passed yet another, of which one of the most interesting features was the cessation of general gratuitous instruction and of state payment of teachers' salaries. One fourth of the students might still be granted free instruction on the ground of indigence, and teachers were to be accorded lodging and a garden. Other features of the schools as prescribed by the law of November 17, 1794, were to remain, save that some forms of manual training were

---

[176] Ibid., pp. 193-237; Duruy, op. cit., pp. 101, 104.
[177] [Louis] Mortimer-Ternaux, Histoire de la Terreur, 1792-94 . . . , VII (Paris, 1869), 196-197.
[178] Bois, op. cit., p. 194 n. 5.
[179] Duruy, op. cit., pp. 109-110.
[180] Bois, op. cit., p. 261. Instruction was free at this time in all types of French schools, elementary and higher.
[181] Ibid., p. 272.

to be provided for the girls.[182]   Thus the school legislation of the period of the National Convention rapidly changed.   It would be erroneous to assume that it was carefully followed throughout the nation.   Revolutionary France displayed much the same indifference toward statutory laws as had the Old Regime.

Throughout the remainder of the eighteenth century—a period of weakness, confusion, and strife—the law of October 25, 1795, governed the elementary schools.   Partly because teachers' salaries were no longer paid by the state but were to come from the fees of their students (or rather from the fees of three fourths of their students), it became exceedingly difficult to get satisfactory teachers. Furthermore, many of the parents were alienated from the support of these schools and sent their children to private schools run by ecclesiastics, which after the beginning of the Directory sprang up all over France.   In the city of Paris were only a dozen public schools, with an average of scarcely forty pupils per school.   Only twenty-seven of some eighty-one were regarded as having their complement.[183]   Throughout France the same conditions prevailed. Guillier de la Touche, a former professor of the University of Angers, asserted in frimaire an VI (December, 1787): "On every hand some men, women, [and] nuns above all, who are not submissive to the laws [and] are sworn and irreconcilable enemies of the Republic, have opened free schools and have brought up children of both sexes in fanaticism, in scorn of the laws and the government, having assured and well persuaded them that to obey it is a source of evil and one of the greatest of all crimes."[184]   Several municipalities undertook to fight the private schools.[185]   In Isère the rural schools found it necessary to adopt the methods of the "refractory preachers" in order to please the parents, whereas the city schools stood stubbornly against compromise and were deserted.[186]   According to an official report of pluviôse an VIII (January-February, 1800), the primary schools of the country districts of the department of the

[182] *Ibid.*, p. 288 with n.   The amount of retribution that each pupil was to make to his teacher was to be fixed by each department (*Inv.-som . . . Isère*, L 172).

[183] Fosseyeux, *op. cit.*, pp. 83-84.   The number of pupils is given as 1,975.

[184] Quoted by Bois, *op. cit.*, p. 322.   Cf. *ibid.*, pp. 328-329, 331.

[185] Angers, Saumur, and Fontainebleau, for example (*ibid.*, pp. 324-326; *Inv.-som . . . Seine-et-Marne*, L 87, f 34).

[186] In the year VI (*Inv.-som . . . Isère*, L 118, pluviôse).

Seine were closed for lack of funds and pupils.[187] In 1801 the commune of Rennes, having more than a thousand children of school age, had only seven primary school teachers, poorly paid and of little ability; yet the same city had twenty-one private schools for boys and three for girls, most or all of them run by ecclesiastics.[188] Official reports were drawn up under the direction of the ministery of the interior in the years VI and VIII that revealed sad results from the primary schools in France. The schools were everywhere deserted, the quality of the teachers was poor, and the people still had a latent desire for their children to be taught religion.[189]

It might naturally be expected that education would suffer greatly during the Revolution in common with other social needs, since the country was confronted with both revolution and war and most of its available funds were needed for their successful prosecution. It is to the credit of the Revolutionists that so much was projected and attempted to make education practical and general. They probably failed in more respects than they succeeded; nevertheless, they rendered ultimate service in preparing the ground for the utilitarian, democratic education of the nineteenth and twentieth centuries. And yet they did not initiate either specialized or democratized education, for both of these forms had made remarkable development under the Old Regime. The Revolutionists merely hastened their progress by special favor and by uprooting the classical educational system, which had outlived its period of usefulness.

[187] A. Aulard, *Paris sous le consulat*, I (Paris, 1903), 165.
[188] Benaerts, *op. cit.*, pp. 188-189.
[189] Duruy, *op. cit.*, pp. 177-178.

CHAPTER XVIII

GOVERNMENT AID IN RELATION TO CHURCH AND PRIVATE CHARITIES

THE FRENCH government in the eighteenth century engaged in charitable activities and administered a measure of relief to almost every form of human need. Though not well developed, these numerous activities included assistance to unfortunate victims of natural disasters, such as famine, fire, flood, hail, insect scourges, drought, shipwreck, and landslides. This government aid, as in the instance of famine sufferers, consisted of either food and seed, or tax remissions and gratifications. Those afflicted with disease and infirmity (the sick, the blind, the deaf and dumb, the crippled, the orphaned) often received aid from the state, directly or indirectly. Toward the maintenance of hospitals in the cities and medical service in the villages and rural regions the state made important contributions. In times of epidemic and epizootic there was an occasional need for military policing to enforce the quarantine. In certain instances tax remissions, gratifications, and pensions were granted. Victims of society's maladjustments (the indigent, the unemployed, the beggars, the prostitutes, the foundlings) aroused less public sympathy, but nonetheless were increasingly treated as wards of the state. Beggars were commonly regarded as parasites, unwilling to work, and consequently received harsh treatment; but sympathy was never absent for those thrown out of work by circumstances beyond their control. Various measures, the most conspicuous of which were charity workshops, were employed increasingly during the century to bring relief.

Other recipients of state assistance, such as pensioners, recipients of gratifications, war refugees, and sufferers from enemy invasion, were more highly esteemed. Fathers of large families, too, had the respect of the public and in many instances received aid in the form of tax remissions, gratifications, and pensions.

Increasingly the state interested itself in education and learning. In a multitude of cases elementary and secondary schools (the latter called colleges), and on occasion universities, received financial support from the government during the century. Many military, naval, and other schools of a technical nature were established and maintained at government expense. Among them were certain engineering and veterinary institutions. Scholarships, too, were provided, either by the royal government or by the provinces. Educational establishments for the blind and the deaf received generous government support. Many poor lads were aided in obtaining their *maîtrise* in a guild or corporation by government or municipal regulations in their favor. Scientific expeditions, the publication of books and maps, and other enterprises designed to advance human knowledge were assisted liberally by royal and provincial governments. This aid was given partly to bring greater knowledge to the state and partly to assist individuals of latent talent but limited resources to develop themselves more fully.

A confusing but important feature of eighteenth-century French charity and assistance, more particularly until the time of the Revolution, was the interplay of royal government, the provincial and municipal governments, the church, charitable societies, and individuals. The church, the oldest of these agencies relieving human misfortunes, still made an impressive record. It constantly received and distributed alms. In times of emergency, such as famine or flood or enemy invasion, special contributions were asked.[1] During famines, periods of severe unemployment, and epidemics, the church furnished food (usually soup) and sometimes fuel and clothing to the poor.[2] Here and there monasteries still distributed alms at their doors, although this practice was far less general than in earlier centuries.[3] The government commonly asked aid of the curés in the distribution of medicines *(remèdes)* among the poor, and not infrequently also of alms.[4] Bishops and curés took an active interest

[1] In June, 1721, the controller-general called upon the bishops throughout France to raise alms for plague-ridden Provence. The replies of many of the bishops are to be found in Arch. Nat., G7, 1731. Some of the bishops stated that their own parishes were too wretched to offer aid; others complied.

[2] Fosseyeux, *Le budget de la charité à Paris au XVIIIᵉ siècle*, pp. 7-8; Gaffarel and Duranty, *op. cit.*, p. 157.

[3] Fosseyeux, *op. cit.*, pp. 7-8; *Hist. gén. de Languedoc*, XIV, 2618; Léon Lallemand, *De l'organisation de la bienfaisance publique et privée dans les campagnes au XVIIIᵉ siècle* (Extrait des *Mémoires de la Société d'agriculture, commerce, sciences et arts du département de la Marne*, année 1894) (Châlons-sur-Marne, 1895), pp. 32-38.

[4] De Juvencel, *op. cit.*, pp. 305-306.

in the administration of hospitals, asylums, schools, and bureaux of charity within their bounds; sometimes their part was dominant. Indeed, a large portion of the smaller hospitals and asylums, most of the free elementary schools, and all of the colleges (or secondary schools proper) were owned and maintained by religious orders. Until the time of the Revolution nursing was almost entirely in the hands of certain religious orders, of which the Sisters of Charity, formed in 1633 by Saint Vincent de Paul and Louise de Marillac, was the largest. In 1789 this order consisted of more than four hundred houses or establishments.[5] During the Plague of Provence (1720-22) the Oratorians and certain of the Jesuits went about Marseilles nursing the sick.[6] While engaged in this or other duty nearly all of the Oratorians died, as did seventeen Jesuits, forty-three Capuchins (out of fifty-five), and twenty Recollets.[7]

Sometimes assistance of uncommon type was rendered by the clergy. For instance, certain bishops in the years preceding the Revolution established fire insurance companies in their dioceses (they were pioneers in this field).[8] In his report to the National Convention Roland praised a certain pastor of the mountain community of Vescors, who some forty years previously had taught the humble people of that region how to spin and weave wool, and so had made their community prosperous.[9] There was a notable lack of interest in mass education in the *cahiers* of 1789. "The clergy (those famous partisans of obscurantism!) were almost alone" in asking for it.[10]

The clergy have been variously praised and criticized in respect to their liberality. According to Marcel Fosseyeux, there was scarcely a curé of the seventeenth and eighteenth centuries who when dying

[5] Marion, *Dictionnaire des institutions de la France*, pp. 86-87.

[6] Gaffarel and Duranty, *op. cit.*, pp. 155-157. The Jesuits, Capuchins, and Brothers of Mercy devoted their labors at this time chiefly to the administration of the last sacrament, but because of their Jansenist opinions Belsunce, the bishop of Marseilles, forbade the Oratorians the right to exercise this function. Thereupon the Oratorians devoted themselves to nursing the sick.

[7] *Ibid.*, p. 155; Dom Théophile Berengier, *Vie de Mgr Henry de Belsunce, évêque de Marseille, 1670-1755*, I (Paris, 1886), 442-444.

[8] Marion (*op. cit.*, p. 28) names four such bishops of the 1780's: Barral, of Troyes; Bourdeille, of Soissons; Fontanges, of Nancy; and Machault, of Amiens. Lallemand (*op. cit.*, p. 17 n. 1) mentions that Talleyrand, bishop of Rheims, set up another (a *bureau des incendies*), supported by alms.

[9] *Arch. parl.*, LVI, 645 n.

[10] Funck-Brentano, *The Old Regime in France*, p. 279.

did not leave a part of his property to the poor of his parish.[11] In
1782 the General Assembly of the French clergy voted the gift of
1,000,000 livres to aid wounded sailors and the widows and children
of sailors lost in the war of the American Revolution.[12] Alms by the
clergy, based on the ecclesiastical *dîme*, should have reached approximately 5,000,000 livres annually, in the estimate of the committee
of mendicity.[13] Sums arising from alms, endowments, and other
sources, should in the opinion of the committee have raised the total
ecclesiastical revenues for charities to more than 10,000,000 livres.
The committee, however, charged that some of the endowments for
the poor had been diverted to ecclesiastical ends, and named several
religious orders guilty of this.[14] Further criticism was made of the
unwillingness of the clergy to tax themselves in proportion to the
other classes in the kingdom. According to long-standing privilege
the French clergy of the eighteenth century paid none of the direct
taxes to which other citizens were subject, and were exempt from
military duty, but once every five years their General Assembly voted
a "free gift" *(don gratuit)* in taxes to the government. During the
reign of Louis XV this averaged merely 3,207,000 livres a year, and
after 1739 the government allowed a certain deduction to enable the
clergy to pay interest on their borrowings. Thus in years when
there was no *don gratuit*, "not only did the clergy pay nothing, but
still they received." "Very feeble then was the clergy's share toward
state expenses, very feeble their contributory part. . . ."[15] Thus the

[11] *Op. cit.*, p. 4. The present writer has examined the records of many such
testaments. Occasionally they were large in size. Thus the nephew of the notorious
Cardinal Dubois, a humble canon, inheriting the remnants of his uncle's fortune,
spent almost the entirety in charity (*Oeuvres complètes de Duclos*, VII, 159-160).
As a second example, the Curé Cochin founded with his own money the small but
excellent Hospice de Saint-Jacques-du-Haut-Pas in Paris in the early 1780's, to serve
old persons possessing some means. The buildings and furniture cost him 180,000
livres. At his death in 1783 there was an indebtedness of 45,000 livres, but he left a
request that his brother pay this. Evidently this was done, since no indebtedness
existed in 1790 when the committee of mendicity undertook its survey (*Arch. parl.*,
XXII, 386-387).

[12] *Inv.-som . . . Calvados*, C 92.

[13] In theory a portion of the *dîme*—in Dauphiné one-twenty-fourth—was destined for the relief of indigents. Estimating the value of the dîme throughout
France at 120,000,000 livres annually, and the percentage allowed for alms in
Dauphiné as average, the committee reached its figure of 5,000,000 livres (Bloch
and Tuetey, *op. cit.*, pp. 555-556).

[14] *Ibid.*, p. 556.

[15] Marcel Marion, *Histoire financière de la France depuis 1715*, I, 39. The
clergy should have paid 319 millions in taxes, on the *don gratuit*, from 1700 to
1750; instead, they paid only 182,750 livres (*ibid.*, I, 48).

clergy failed to carry their proportionate load of the French tax burden, and approximately half of the charity funds at their disposal came from a state tax in their behalf.

Private charities, too, were far from negligible. Gifts large for that day were frequent. On the eve of the Revolution a legacy of 1,200,000 livres was left to the Hôtel-Dieu of Paris by a certain Goudon, but natural heirs contested the will in court, and the Hôtel-Dieu actually received only 320,000 livres.[16] The Chancellor Maupeou, dying in 1792, bequeathed to the nation 800,000 livres.[17] During the Plague of Provence the regent contributed 600,000 livres; the Count of Toulouse, 200,000 livres; John Law and Le Pelletier de la Houssaye, 100,000 livres each; and the Chevalier Roze, 22,000 livres.[18] During the crisis of 1789 the Duc de Charost and Jacques Necker each contributed 100,000 livres; Lafayette, 150,000.[19] At the same time the king and queen sent their silverware to the mint as a contribution (despite attempt at dissuasion by the National Assembly), and the king gave 200,000 livres annually during the emergency for distribution by the church.[20] He also gave life annuities in 1790 to 240 of the most needy widows and orphans of sailors, allotting 120,000 livres for the purpose.[21] Piarron de Chamousset spent his fortune of 500,000 livres in charitable undertakings, mainly in providing hospital expenses for the needy.[22] The La Rochefoucauld family, generous in charitable contributions, gave 60,000 livres for *ateliers de charité* in 1757 and 40,000 livres in 1789.[23] In 1782 one Mme Déjean de Labastide at her death left a legacy of 50,000 écus (150,000 livres) to the Hôtel-Dieu of Toulouse for the purchase of single beds;[24] in 1788 Mme Necker so

---

[16] Möring and Quentin, *op. cit.*, II, 252.

[17] Fernand Mitton, *La férocité pénale: tortures et supplices en France* (Paris, 1909) p. 31 n. 2.

[18] Leclercq, *op. cit.*, III, 89-90; cf. *Pièces historiques*, I, 119-121.

[19] *Mémoires de Bailly*, III, 27, 51; Forado-Cunéo, *op. cit.*, LXXXVII, 29-30.

[20] *Mémoires de Bailly*, II, 389; *Arch. parl.*, XIII, 296-297.

[21] *Arch. parl.*, XVI, 508. Louis XV, in 1751, celebrated the birth of the Duke of Burgundy by giving 400,000 livres in dowries to six hundred poor girls (at 500 livres per girl and a louis d'or for the marriage supper) (Marion, *Dictionnaire des institutions de la France*, p. 86).

[22] Ferdinand-Dreyfus, *Un philanthrope d'autrefois*, p. 139.

[23] *Ibid.*, pp. 8, 100-101.

[24] Patients had been obliged to sleep four and five to a bed. Down to 1789, however, the single beds had not been installed. (Buchalet, *op. cit.*, p. 81).

equipped the Hôpital Saint-Sulpice.[25]   Jean-Baptiste Trincaud (in 1749) bequeathed the Hôpital de la Charité and Hôtel-Dieu of Lyons 221,000 livres, and in 1778 Guillaume Grout left the hospitals of Nantes 200,000 livres.[26]   This list could be greatly extended, more especially for gifts smaller than 100,000 livres, but these should suffice to show the extent that private philanthropy often reached in eighteenth-century France.[27]

These gifts almost without exception were turned over to an organization engaged in charities, the state, the church, the hospitals, or the bureaux of charity.   Rarely an individual administered his own philanthropy, as Joseph Dariot of Le Mans, a poor dealer in second-hand clothes (fripier), who during the famine of 1738-39 undertook to house sixty orphans in his home and to give soup daily to the needy.   Others came to assist him financially, and he was able shortly to feed two thousand indigents daily.   He cared for forty sick persons in a neighboring house, and the surgeon De Villiers came daily to see them without charge.[28]   Similarly the Citizen Verdun before and during the Revolution organized and financed a surprising number of diverse charities and public services.[29]   In Normandy a girl named Elizabeth Lecoq, following the example of her mother, devoted her time to nursing the sick, without recompense.[30]   Numerous physicians and surgeons rendered their services free to hospitals, as did also members of the hospital bureaux of direction.   On the pension rolls of the French government in 1790 were inscribed the names of two individuals with the following unusual citation:

[25] Ferdinand-Dreyfus, op. cit., p. 139.   Earlier she had made a gift of beds for two persons (with wooden partition in the middle) to the Bicêtre (Mercier, Tableau de Paris, VIII, 7).

[26] Dagier, op. cit., II, 118; Inv.-som . . . Ille-et-Vilaine, C 1281.   For several other large gifts to the hospitals at Lyons, see Dagier, op. cit., II, 34, 55, 102, 106, 114, 119, 122, 151, 162, 265.

[27] Mercier in his Tableau de Paris (III, 119) cites an estimate of the alms in Paris at 3,000,000 livres annually.   He comments satirically, however, that about 50,000,000 livres were spent every year on prostitutes.

[28] Paul Delaunay, Etudes sur l'hygiène, l'assistance et les secours publics dans le Maine sous l'ancien régime, 2d ser. (Le Mans, 1923), p. 115; Encyclopédie méthodique, Agriculture, IV, 95.

[29] Tuetey, Répertoire général, XI, No. 1535.

[30] Meeting opposition from the surgeons, she appealed to the intendant De Crosne. He in turn referred the matter to the minister Bertin, and was told to inquire into her ability at nursing and to protect her if she was found competent and genuinely working without pay (Inv. som . . . Seine-Inférieure, C 132).

"In consideration of his (or her) zeal and self-denial for the alleviation of the poor."[31]

Numerous charitable societies existed for aiding unmarried mothers, prisoners, and other unfortunates. Each member was to make an annual contribution (sometimes fixed in amount), and certain of the members were chosen to visit the hospitals and prisons. The Maison Philanthropique, founded at Paris in 1720, charged 2 louis d'or (48 livres) as admission fee and 4 louis d'or annually for dues. The society used this money for providing the needy with food, clothing, and bedcovering. In 1786 it rendered assistance to 300 octogenarians, 48 blind children, 150 women at childbirth, and 36 widows or widowers; during the cold winter of 1788, it fed and clothed 1,500 needy.[32] The Société Philanthropique was founded in Paris in 1780 by the Duc de La Rochefoucauld-Liancourt and others of rank and distinction, and lasted until 1794. It also aided the same needy classes.[33] Other Parisian charitable societies were the Charité de Notre-Dame de Bon Secours, founded in 1773, which provided such diverse aid as food, fuel, drugs, medical attention, and burial expenses;[34] the Association de Bienfaisance Judiciaire, founded in late 1787 or early 1788, an organization whose members paid annual dues of 48 livres for the purpose of aiding needy persons in the courts;[35] and the Société de Charité Maternelle, founded in 1784.[36] Two societies in eighteenth-century Paris were organized for the liberation of debtors from prison: the Compagnie de Messieurs de

[31] One was that of Oliver Descotes, aged eighty-eight, pensioned in 1776; the other, that of Demoiselle Françoise Descotes, aged 49, pensioned in 1787. Each was pensioned at 400 livres (*Arch. parl.*, XIV, 546).

[32] Fosseyeux, *op. cit.*, pp. 9-10.

[33] Mercier, *op. cit.*, XI, 113-115; Ferdinand-Dreyfus, *op. cit.*, p. 46 with n.; Tuetey, *L'assistance publique*, IV, 517-521.

[34] Itemized expenditures for the chief forms of aid in 1773 are reproduced by Fosseyeux, *op. cit.*, p. 6 n. 4.

[35] Fosseyeux (*op. cit.*, p. 10) gives the date 1767, evidently a misprint; Bloch (*op. cit.*, pp. 358-359), 1787; Boucher d'Argis (*De le bienfaisance dans l'ordre judiciaire* . . . , Londres, 316-318), 1788. Boucher d'Argis, founder of the Association and speaker on the occasion of the opening, January 14, 1788, asserted that the Association was designed to aid the poor by assigning a lawyer to defend them in the courts. The magistrates of the Châtelet agreed to make available one of its rooms for the Association's use.

[36] Lacroix (*op. cit.*, VII, 242-247) sketches the history of this organization; F. Gille has written a book about it: *La Société de charité maternelle de Paris, origine, fonctionnement et marche progressive de l'oeuvre, de 1784 à 1885* (Paris, 1887), 300 pp.

la Charité, formed in 1728 to aid prisoners and obtain the freedom of fathers incarcerated because of debt for the *mois de nourrice* (inability or refusal to pay toward the support of their foundling children), and the Compagnie de Messieurs qui Travaillent à la Deliverance des Prisonniers pour Dettes dans toutes les Prisons, interested chiefly in those imprisoned for commercial debts.[37]

Similar societies existed in the provincial cities. Lyons had a society of legal aid for the poor, founded in 1731 by the archbishop, with judges, lawyers, and other citizens as members, and having a revenue of 20,000 livres a year, more than half of it supplied by the archbishop.[38] Melum in 1790 had a Bureau de Paix et de la Jurisprudence Charitable.[39] Bordeaux from 1781 to 1790 had its Société Philanthropique;[40] Bourg, its Société des Dames de la Croix, founded in 1760;[41] Toulouse, its Société Populaire.[42] Doubtless there was one in every city of appreciable size.

Closely akin to the voluntary charitable societies were the bureaux of charity, of which a multitude existed in eighteenth-century France. There was often if not generally one in each parish.[43] Sometimes they went by different names. In Lille during the 1770's there were seven of these parishional organizations. The smaller places had them too.[44] Their membership apparently was limited to a committee, commonly headed by the curé, the other members being the leading political and judicial figures in the locality and possibly other citizens of prominence.[45] In Paris there were parish-

[37] Boucher d'Argis, *op. cit.*, p. 67 n. 20.

[38] *Ibid.*, pp. 25-26. At Nancy, in Lorraine, Stanislas in 1750 set up a Chambre des Consultations, or free legal clinic, composed of lawyers to whom he paid salaries to the end that they might give free legal advice to the poor. This, however, was a ducal rather than private enterprise (*ibid.*, pp. 20, 61-62).

[39] *Inv.-som . . . Seine-et-Marne*, L 6.

[40] Composed of many leading citizens. Their voluntary subscriptions were used for the relief of a number of aged persons, widows with children, and indigent women at childbirth (Bernadeau, *op. cit.*, p. 375).

[41] With forty-three women as members. Its funds were to be raised by contributions *(quêtes)* throughout the city and in the church. It was under the guidance of the curé. Certain members were to visit the poor, the prisoners, and a school for girls. The Society was still existent in 1845, with an active record to its credit (Ebrard, *op. cit.*, pp. 161-182).

[42] Adher, *Recueil de documents*, p. 373.

[43] Bloch, *op. cit.*, pp. 122-126.

[44] Xavier Renouard, *L'assistance publique à Lille de 1527 à l'an VIII* (Lille, 1912), pp. 74-77.

[45] Babeau, *La village sous l'ancien régime*, p. 325; Bloch, *op. cit.*, pp. 122-123. The leading political and judicial personages were always included.

ional charities of this type,[46] and yet over all there was the Grand Bureau des Pauvres.[47] Revenues for this Parisian institution amounted to 45,000 livres a year in the mid-century, coming from legacies, gifts, alms, and a poor tax that fell upon all individuals save servants and indigents.[48] Other cities, too, commonly had their poor tax, which helped to supply their bureaux of charity (a feature that set apart the bureaux of charity from the purely voluntary philanthropic societies).[49] At all places, however, there were supplementary revenues from alms, gifts, and legacies.[50] The services rendered were similar to those of the philanthropic societies: food, clothing, baby-linen, medicines were distributed; dowries for poor girls, and on occasion other monetary gifts, were given; visits were made to the poor in their homes.[51] As much assistance as possible was rendered in kind; rarely in money. Attention was given to the moral and religious character of the recipients: inebriates, debauchees, swearers, and "those who did not send their children to school and the catechism" were considered undeserving of aid.[52] Thus the bureaux of charity and philanthropic societies strove to serve the deserving poor in their homes; the vagabonds, beggars, and others were to be cared for, and if need be incarcerated, at the general hospitals. These respective institutions, therefore, supplemented each other. Above all, the bureaux of charity were "to combat mendicity in the country" where no general hospitals existed.[53] In the late seventeenth and early eighteenth centuries Père Guévarre and certain other Jesuits traveled widely in Provence, Languedoc, Gascony, and elsewhere in France, encouraging the establishment of general hospitals and bureaux of charity, with much success.[54] After 1776

[46] See Mercier's description of the charities of the parish Saint-Sulpice (op. cit., IV, 140-142). Fosseyeux (op. cit., p. 6) says that this parish received and spent 143,605 livres in 1778-79 and 150,000 livres in 1780-81.

[47] The best description of it is found in Léon Cahen's Le grand bureau des pauvres, already cited. See also Bonde, op. cit., pp. 9-10, and Fosseyeux, op. cit., pp. 2-3.

[48] This tax was scaled at different amounts for the different professions and ranks of society (ibid., pp. 2-3). Cf. Bloch, op. cit., p. 274.

[49] Bloch, op. cit., pp. 196-197, 275-276.

[50] Adher, op. cit., Introduction, p. xx; Bloch, op. cit., pp. 125-127; Lallemand, op. cit., p. 44.

[51] Dowries were sometimes given also to indigent youths on marriage (Bloch, op. cit., p. 126).

[52] Lallemand, op. cit., p. 44.   [53] Paultre, op. cit., p. 229.

[54] Ibid., pp. 218 with n., 233-235, 259-266, and passim.

Necker, too, greatly encouraged the formation and work of these bureaux.[55]

Fraternal orders, guilds, and mutual aid societies were other agencies engaged in private charity. The order of Freemasonry in late eighteenth-century France gave "aid of every type" to its members in need.[56] The masters and *compagnons* (journeymen) of many guilds and corporations had chests for the relief of needy members. The gravediggers' guild or association in Paris (formed in 1725 with thirty-six members) had such a chest, to which members paid 4 sous every workday. The 4,000 to 5,000 livres annually raised in this manner was used to aid *compagnons* when sick with hospitalization and to support them during periods of enforced idleness.[57] The glassmakers of France had similar charities for themselves and their workers, offering in some instances old age pensions, death benefits, medical attention, and monetary aid during sickness.[58] The printers *(corps typographique)* had a charity chest formed by a contribution of 12 livres from each member. Sick members were entitled to 15 livres a week for three months, and pensions were paid to members too old to work.[59] Of thirteen "mutual aid societies" existent in eighteenth-century Paris,[60] some were organized for members of a single trade, others were open to members of all professions or trades. Only four were existent prior to 1789; the others came into being between that date and 1800. Besides these thirteen were a fire insurance company (a form of mutual aid society), established at Paris in 1786,[61] and an association of domestics, with elaborate rules and protective benefits, established there in late 1789.[62]

[55] Bloch, *op. cit.*, pp. 198, 222-223.

[56] C. Bernardin, *Histoire de la Franc-Maçonnerie* (1910), p. 42, quoted by Fosseyeux, *op. cit.*, p. 9 n. 4.

[57] Franklin, *op. cit.*, VII, 222.

[58] Warren C. Scoville, "Labor and Labor Conditions in the French Glass Industry, 1643-1789," *Journal of Modern History*, XV (Dec., 1943), 287.

[59] Jaffé, *op. cit.*, p. 104.

[60] Martin-Doisy, *op. cit.*, I, 1002-1007. For their names, dates of origin, dues, and other details, see *ibid.*, I, 1007.

[61] Permitted in 1787 to deal also in life insurance (Marion, *Histoire financière de la France depuis 1715*, I, 367 with n.).

[62] Treated at length in a pamphlet entitled *Etablissement sous la protection de la municipalité, d'une caisse de secours & d'un bureau d'administration pour tous les domestiques de l'un & de l'autre sexe, employés dans la ville de Paris* (Paris, 1790), pp. 4-28. Archives de l'Assistance Publique (Paris), D¹ 12 A. In short, members paid a small fee to the organization and obtained monetary aid for a

Similar mutual aid societies existed in other parts of France.[63]   In
the Basque country mutual aid was often given, although no society
existed.   Thus when a home was burned, neighbors in the village
came forward to aid in its restoration; when a family lost its support,
the neighbors supplied monetary aid; when a flock of sheep died,
neighboring landowners gave lambs from their flocks to help rebuild it; when a conscript left for the army, a contribution in his
behalf was taken from the young men and women of his village.[64]
Eighteenth-century *compagnons*, although forbidden by law to organize themselves, had secret associations with charity chests and
even *auberges*, where members in need might find lodging and food
until they obtained employment.[65]   Sometimes an organization undertook the dispensation of charities to others than its own needy,
an example being the Jacobin club (Friends of the Constitution) of
Limoges, which in 1791 had a committee of health, composed of
physicians, surgeons, and apothecaries, for giving free medical treatment to the poor at the club's expense.[66]

Related to the mutual aid societies were the tontines, called after
their founder, Tonti, an Italian of the mid-seventeenth century.   The
tontines were in one respect an anticipation of endowment life insurance, in another an imitation of the lottery.   There were ten
classes of members, according to age, and dues varied according to
class.   Membership was open to any person from one to seventy.
Dividends were paid after a period of years to surviving members,
and continued throughout their lives.   As beneficiaries died, their
dividends went to the members or member still existing.   The last
survivor was thus able to draw an appreciable sum.   In 1726 a
woman died in Paris at the age of ninety-six who had collected the
dividends (or annuities) of the class of 1689 to the value of 73,500
livres.   Her investment in the tontine had been merely 300 livres.
Thus the longer the members lived, the more they benefited.   In
1770 the Abbé Terray removed the lottery feature and transformed

period of three months when unemployed and medical attention when sick.   An
employment bureau was set up to aid those out of work.   High moral character
was demanded of the members.

[63] *Ibid.*, I, 1004; Saunois de Chevert, *op. cit.*, p. 15.
[64] *Idem.*
[65] Marion, *op. cit.*, p. 125; Jaffé, *op. cit.*, pp. 68, 72.
[66] *Révolutions de France et de Brabant*, ed. Camille Desmoulins, No. 64 (VII,
552-553).

the tontines into mere life annuities.[67] The tontine Lafarge still existed in Paris in the early years of the Revolution and was the subject of much press discussion and parliamentary debate.[68] On 29 prairial an II (June 17, 1794) the National Convention suppressed the various philanthropic societies throughout France which had been helping the indigent, since the state had assumed responsibility for all such aid,[69] but this did not affect the mutual aid societies or the tontines.

There were also the municipal and provincial charities, supported by funds derived from taxation. Nearly all of the cities and towns had a tax on certain incoming goods, the *octroi*, whose funds in large part they were allowed to use for the support of their hôtels-Dieu and general hospitals. Toward the same end they were allowed to use a portion of certain other taxes, such as the tax on public entertainments and that on certain professions. They were permitted to use one third or one half of the sums derived from fines imposed in the magistrates' courts, and moneys derived from the lottery, trade concessions, and other traditional sources.[70] Communities contributed toward the support of their local charity workshops (both *ateliers de charité* and *ateliers de filature*). Most of those provided in Languedoc during the active period from 1760 to the Revolution were maintained by local funds.[71]

Down to the time of the Revolution it was the policy in France that so far as possible the problems of relief should be handled locally. Only when they were too large for the local community, should they be brought before the provincial government; only when too large for the provincial government, should they be brought before the officials of the royal government. In short, it behooved each community to care for its own indigent, sick, afflicted.

[67] Marion, *Dictionnaire des institutions de la France*, p. 536. Here one will find the age-limits of the various tontine classes.

[68] Bloch, *op. cit.*, p. 419.

[69] Tuetey, *L'assistance publique*, IV, 519. During the period of the Directory an attempt was made (law of 27 frimaire an V [Dec. 17, 1796]) to create *bureaux de bienfaisance*, with functions similar to those of the old *bureaux de charité*. Each bureau was to be composed of five members, who were to distribute aid to the resident poor. The funds came from gifts and a tax on spectacles (public entertainments) (Balch, *op. cit.*, pp. 72-73); Parturier, *op. cit.*, pp. 225, 232-233; Gabriel Cross-Mayrevieille, *Traité de l'assistance hospitalière* (Paris and Nancy, 1912), I, 258-261; Martin-Doisy, *op. cit.*, II, 160.

[70] See the chapters on hospitals and asylums.

[71] Buchalet, *op. cit.*, p. 43 n. 2. Buchalet presents much material on city charities.

Vagabonds were returned (with passports and a small allowance for travel expenses) to their home communities, and the sick and afflicted had difficulty in obtaining admission to a hospital or asylum in a city where they were not resident.

There were two types of provincial government or administration. The *pays d'élection*, representing the older portions of France historically, had no legislatures and were ruled in all respects by the royal government and its representative in their midst, the intendant. The intendant was assisted by a small number of subdelegates, seated in the more important towns of his generality. While this intendant was required by the royal government to keep on hand a small fund of several thousand livres from the *capitation* (poll tax), for meeting trivial and unexpected relief cases, he was always obliged to appeal to the controller-general of finance at Paris for aid in other cases; indeed, he commonly had to obtain this approval to disburse the "free funds" at his disposal.[72] On the other hand in the *pays d'états*, comprised of Brittany, Languedoc, Provence, Burgundy, and certain other generalities, provinces on the fringes of France, added in the late Middle Ages, much local control existed. These were federated states, allowed to continue their time-honored legislatures, called assemblies or estates, which met periodically to consider all matters of provincial concern. One of these was relief to the needy. In theory the *pays d'états* had complete control over the collection and use of their taxes, and each year (or biennially in certain cases) they voted a *don gratuit* in tax money to the royal government, as did the assembly of the clergy.[73] In theory, too, the *pays d'états* had complete jurisdiction over their own disbursements for assistance to the needy, but the provincial intendant always had to be consulted, and through him the controller-general at Paris. Aid rendered by the provincial governments was almost as varied as that granted by the royal government itself. It rested upon such taxes as the *capitation*, the *vingtième*, and the *taille*.

On multitudinous occasions, many of which have been cited in earlier pages of this study, the charitable aid came from not one but

---

[72] In 1789 the "free funds of the *capitation*" throughout France amounted to 1,196,577 livres (*Arch. parl.*, XIII, 293).

[73] The *pays d'états* did escape with much lighter loads in taxation than those of the *pays d'élections* (Marion, *Histoire financière de la France depuis 1715*, I, 37-38). Cf. *Encyclopédie méthodique*, Finances, II, 86, 368.

several sources. In meeting famines, floods, fires, periods of severe unemployment, and epidemics, there was a combination of private and church charities, municipal and provincial aid, and government assistance. Instances of friction were exceedingly rare.[74] Ordinarily there was cordial collaboration. It was common for the government to ask the curés to aid in distributing medicines and food among the needy, and not infrequently in other ways.

Throughout the century there was a steady shift of burden from private and church charities to state charities, from local to provincial and governmental assistance.[75] There was no desire on the part of the government to increase its power; on the contrary, down to the Revolution the government tried to make aid to the needy a matter of local responsibility.[76] The change resulted from the repeated failure of church, private, and municipal charities to meet the situation, the state being forced to intervene with its aid, in response to piteous appeals. This tendency grew so rapidly in the second half

[74] Only a few have come to the writer's attention. (1) During the cold winter and famine of 1709 there was dispute between certain *parlements* and the clergy over jurisdiction in charitable matters. The *parlements* criticized the clergy for standing apart selfishly in their charities on this occasion; the clergy fought back (Boislisle, *op. cit., Revue des questions historiques*, XXIX, 491-493). (2) In a letter to the controller-general, December 8, 1721, De Bernage, intendant of Languedoc, referred to the bitterness of the bishops toward the government (evidently because of government action on the Bull Unigenitus), and implied that they were not giving full co-operation in meeting the situation created by the plague (Arch. Nat., G7, 1735). Many of the bishops did refuse to raise contributions for Provence when so requested by the controller-general in June, 1721. (3) De Tocqueville (*The Old Regime and the Revolution*, tr. John Bonner, New York, 1856, p. 284) describes a squabble that arose in 1748 between the intendant and the archbishop of Tours concerning the jurisdiction over the distribution of 20,000 pounds of rice that the king had granted for distribution among the needy of that region. The archbishop insisted that he had obtained the gift, and that it should be distributed by him alone, in his diocese. The intendant, on the other hand, argued that the gift had been made to the generality, and should be distributed in all its parishes, by him. At length the king, to settle the quarrel, doubled the amount of rice to the province, "so that the archbishop and the intendant might each distribute half." Strangely enough, both agreed that it should be given to the poor by the curés. In the correspondence that was provoked, the intendant accused the archbishop of desiring to show favoritism in handling the matter. (4) Again, in 1751 in a dispute between the archbishop and the *parlement* of Paris over the appointment of a Dame Herbert de Moysan as superior of the General Hospital, Jansenist sentiments were involved (Bloch, *op. cit.*, pp. 324-325).

[75] Buchalet, *op. cit.*, p. 14; Cross-Mayevieille, *L'assistance publique et privée en Languedoc*, pp. 86 ff.; A. Prudhomme, *Inv.-som . . . Isère*, H, Introduction, p. xxix; Cahen, *op. cit.*, p. 65; Ferdinand-Dreyfus, *Un philanthrope d'autrefois*, pp. 44-46.

[76] Bloch, *op. cit.*, p. 55.

of the century that prior to the Revolution the opinion had come to be rather general that care of its needy subjects was a state obligation.[77] During the period 1790-94 the Revolutionary governments moved by rapid strides toward the full realization of this ideal. All endowments and other revenues of eleemosynary institutions were suppressed or confiscated by the government; church property was seized and church moneys for charities disappeared; even the philanthropic societies were abolished in 1793.[78] Despite the destruction of so much of the machinery for charitable expression under the Old Regime, and the centralization of this work in the hands of the government during the Revolution, local and private charities were not exterminated. Except for them, the hospitals and other philanthropic agencies would have suffered even more wretchedly in the last years of the century than they did.[79]

It would be desirable to give summary figures, by chart or otherwise, for the various forms of charities (church, private, municipal, provincial, and state) at different periods of the century. Unfortunately these are not available. No such figures are available for any of these groups at any period of the century, except possibly those of the state in 1781 (in Necker's *Compte rendu*) and in the early period of the Revolution. The committee of mendicity in 1790 set forth the sum of 51,500,000 livres as the amount needed (annually) in maintaining state assistance.[80] Roland in 1793 proposed the same budget of 51,000,000 livres (36,000,000 for hospitals and

[77] *Ibid.*, pp. 384-385, 397, 407. As early as 1748 Montesquieu had set forth this view in his *Esprit des lois.*. See translation by Thomas Nugent (6th ed. rev., London, 1793), p. 324.

[78] Each canton was directed to form a committee for extending work and alms to the needy. Paris formed a *Commission Central de Bienfaisance* composed of forty-eight committees, one for each section (Martin-Doisy, *op. cit.*, II, 159).

[79] Various gifts and loans are mentioned in the documents of the period quoted or cited by Adher (*Recueil des documents sur l'assistance publique dans le district de Toulouse*). See, for example, pp. 128, 142-144, 219, 222, 223, 347-348, 361, 425-426, 458, 472, 510. An appeal for private donations to charities, made by the administrators of the department of Bouches-du-Rhône, April 27, 1793, can be found in *Inv.-som . . . Bouches-du-Rhône*, L III, 10.

[80] Bloch and Tuetey, *op. cit.*, pp. 451-452, 473. Of this sum, 12,000,000 livres were needed for support of the hospitals, 27,500,000 for the asylums, 5,000,000 for public works and charity workshops, 3,000,000 for suppressing mendicancy (by *dépôts de mendicité* and otherwise), and 4,000,000 livres for the expense of administration. Necker (*op. cit.*, pp. 111-114) sets forth a list of figures for government aid in 1781, totaling 19 to 22 millions (reproduced by Bloch, *op. cit.*, p. 315).

asylums) for that year.[81] This sum, however, did not include the expense of pensions and gratifications or of education, the figures for which were large. In its closing years the government of the Old Regime was contributing 4,000,000 livres annually toward the nation's education bill, and in 1793 it would doubtless have been more. In 1789 it was paying 29,000,000 livres toward pensions and gratifications, irrespective of ecclesiastical pensions, which amounted to some 2,500,000 livres more. Camus, chairman of the pensions committee in 1790, indeed charged that the total bill for pensions, gratifications, and largesses direct and indirect, cost the French state more than 80,000,000 livres annually. While all of this sum can by no means be considered as devoted to needs strictly charitable, much of it was. In short, the student of charities discovers himself in a bog almost as soon as he sets out on his attempt to reach a summary figure. There is first the problem of deciding what items of expense should be included, and secondly the more difficult problem of finding summary figures for any single form of expense. No less a scholar than the erudite Marcel Marion asserts that the French figures for pensions and other expenses in the eighteenth century are baffling and lacking in accuracy.[82] Those for hospitals and asylums have been cited in an earlier chapter. Contemporary authorities on the eve of the Revolution differed considerably in their estimates.[83] In accepting any figure one accordingly must realize that there may be an error of 10 to 20 per cent. Nevertheless, one can make some important gauges from figures that are available. By taking the figure for pensions in the year 1701 (3,105,213 livres)[84] and comparing it with the sum of 38,000,000, the revised sum for the same ends in 1790, one may see the tremendous expansion of government assistance in this field. For hospitals and asylums, revenues rose from 7,000,000 livres in 1752 to 14,000,000 in 1764 and 20,000,000 or 30,000,000 in 1789.[85] Expenses for the repression of mendicity increased from 600,000 livres in 1770 to more than a million annually before the end of the Old Regime.[86]

[81] *Arch. parl.*, LVI, 648.
[82] *Histoire financière de la France depuis 1715*, I, 456. To quote his summary statement: "Aussi ne peut-on jamais être assuré de saisir la totalité d'aucune catégorie de dépense: les singuliers procédés de comptabilité de l'ancien régime ne le permettent pas."
[83] Bloch, *op. cit.*, pp. 281-282.
[85] Bloch, *op. cit.*, pp. 281-282.
[84] Boislisle, *op. cit.*, II, 600.
[86] *Ibid.*, p. 266 with nn.

There was, to be sure, an increase of population and government receipts and expenditures during the century. Around 1701 the French numbered approximately 19,000,000; in 1784 they were estimated at 24,800,000; in 1801, according to the first census, they numbered 27,349,003.[87] As for state finances, revenues in 1701 amounted to 121,253,624 livres (of which, however, only 73,404,505 livres went to the royal treasury for expenditures); expenses were 159,381,525 livres.[88] In 1769 net revenues were 169,458,348 livres, and expenditures 222,675,344 livres. In 1789, according to Necker's report to the Estates General, gross revenues were 475,294,000 livres; expenses, 531,444,000 livres.[89] Thus these figures reveal that the population-increase during the century was around 43 per cent, the increase in receipts was threefold, and that in expenditures slightly more than threefold. Since total figures for government expenditures on charities early in the century are unknown, it is impossible to give the rate of their increase. Certainly the tenfold increase in payments for pensions is not representative of that in all other fields of assistance. The threefold or fourfold (the latter more likely) increase in the revenues of hospitals and asylums from 1752 to 1789 does not, alas, reveal the ratio of increase in government grants to this end, as only a portion, and an uncalculated portion, of these revenues came from the government. Nevertheless, the increased allotment for government relief after 1760 was great. While it is hazardous to guess, the rate of increase must have increased greatly in the period from 1701 to 1789.[90]

To what extent did government aid and other charities meet the needs? Perhaps never in history have charities reached all of those in need. This at least was the story in eighteenth-century France. That many persons reportedly died of hunger in the famines of 1709 and 1789 and during the Plague of Provence attests the fact

---

[87] Chéruel, *op. cit.*, II, 999.

[88] Boislisle, *op. cit.*, II, 584, 600.

[89] Marion, *Histoire financière de la France depuis 1715*, I, 245, 454-455. It is observed that in all these years the royal treasury ran a deficit.

[90] In the expense sheets of the royal treasury for the years 1701-07, as reproduced by Boislisle (*op. cit.*, III, 600-604), no items for charitable expenditure are given save pensions, gratifications, indemnities, and gifts. The last varied from 300,000 livres to 441,000 a year; the pensions, from 2,000,000 livres to 3,409,389; gratifications and indemnities, from 1,200,000 livres to 11,434,570. The accounts are not sufficiently detailed to enable one to determine precisely the figures for relief.

that aid did not reach all the needy. Multitudes suffered privation short of death, from famine, flood, fire, and other disasters, being relieved only in part. It was never the intention of the state or other charitable agencies to restore all of the loss or to maintain the recipients of relief at the level maintained by citizens in prosperity. The relief was partial, designed to tide the unfortunates through a desperate situation, and afterwards to help them regain their footing. The committee of mendicity in 1790 considered that hospital expense for the needy in Paris should not be over 17 or 18 sous (less than a livre!) per day, and for those in provincial hospitals not above 12.[91] The committee criticized as extravagant some hospitals which reported daily expenses rising above a livre. It estimated the average provincial hospital as having a daily expense of 15 sous. In terms of twentieth-century costs these figures are amazingly small, but there was a great difference in the comforts, sanitation, and treatment given. The committee estimated that the cost of rearing *enfants trouvés*, of whom there were approximately forty thousand in France, at 40 livres a year; the expense of maintaining old and infirm persons, at 70 to 80 livres a year; and indigents in the country, at 55 to 60 livres a year.[92] The Acadians were given pensions of 6 sous a day, and this same sum was given to certain pensioned noncommissioned officers. The highest sums paid to workers in the charity workshops were 20 and 30 sous (the latter only in exceptional cases), given at Paris in 1789. Previously and elsewhere smaller sums were given, and indeed early in the century, only food. Even in 1789 and later women and girls worked in the Paris spinning workshops of charity for sums that appear to have ranged from 4 to 10 sous a day. How did they live on it? It must be borne in mind that money purchased much more than today. The normal daily market wage of the Paris workman in 1789 was 30 to 40 sous. Rural workers around Toulouse prior to the Revolution received only 6 to 12 sous a day, according to the season; in the commune of Saint-Luys they received merely 6 to 8 sous, and women, 3 to 4.[93] Unskilled men working in the French glass industry were paid 8 sous per day in 1701, and in 1761, approximately 10; women worked for relatively half these figures; children and youths, for one third or one half the sum paid

[91] Bloch and Tuetey, *op. cit.*, p. 470.
[92] *Ibid.*, pp. 471-472.
[93] Buchalet, *op. cit.*, p. 27 with n.

adults of their respective sexes.[94]   Certain of the servants employed at the provincial hospitals received not above 50 livres a year in wages.[95]   In view of these wages and the large percentage of people living below or near the borderline of poverty, this aid was less niggardly than it appears on first observation.   Nevertheless, it fell far short of what was desired even in that day, as shown by the correspondence of the intendants, contemporary books and pamphlets, and *cahiers* of 1789.

The government's intentions were good.   The intendants, more especially in the latter part of the century, were for the most part men of ability and integrity.[96]   Certain of the controllers-general, notably Terray, Turgot, Necker, and Calonne, in the period after 1770 zealously extended to the needy all the aid they could muster. Apparently none was callous or indifferent to the cries of distress. Sympathetic attention was given by the intendants and controllers-general to the requests for aid from the suffering and needy.   Often the cases were trivial.   As the century progressed and the state budget increased, it became necessary for the controller-general to delegate to subordinates much of his labor in administration of charities.   In 1764 De Boulogne, an intendant of finances, was given charge (under the controller-general) of hospitals and asylums; in 1775, Ormesson *fils*, another intendant of finances, was similarly given oversight of charity workshops and public works; the intendant of finances Albert was given jurisdiction over food supplies; the intendant of Paris, Bertier, was given special powers in the oversight of indigents; and at length in 1781, Chaumont de la Millière, intendant-general of bridges and highways, was placed in charge of the hospitals, asylums, prisons, and the distribution of gratuitous drugs.   Later the supervision of the depots of mendicity was added to his care.[97]   These men examined the merits of individual cases and sent their decisions to the controller-general for ratification.

There were also inspectors of hospitals and asylums in the last years of the Old Regime.   Names of some appear on the *Etat nominatif des pensions*.   Chaumont de la Millière himself under-

[94] Scoville, *op. cit., Journal of Modern History*, XV, 282.

[95] See above, p. 184 n. 18.

[96] See the complimentary remarks of Bloch (*op. cit.*, pp. 320-321) and Louis Legrand (*Sénac de Meilhan*, p. 147).

[97] Bloch, *op. cit.*, pp. 317-318.

took the inspection of institutions under his care, traveling extensively at this task. Numerous inspectors of *enfants trouvés* traveled through the countryside for periodical investigation of the conditions under which the children were being tended. Interestingly enough, a royal declaration of June 16, 1716, stated that financial inspectors would be named by the government to verify the receipt and expenditure of tax money in the various provinces. The inspectors were to take oath in the generalities where they were employed and were to be subject to orders of the intendants. Accounts of their findings were to be rendered to the council of finances.[98] The inspectors were appointed. Their creation illustrates a spirit of desire in the eighteenth century toward better administration of finances. The degree of care taken in auditing expenditures for relief is not clear, but little if any scandal has come to light. Hospitals and other philanthropic institutions had private audits. Malversation of funds was rare, but theft of goods less infrequent.[99] The inspection of conditions in the hospitals and asylums, and in the homes where *enfants trouvés* were nursed, left much to be desired. To the credit of the government, however, it gave increasing attention to the betterment of conditions.

No student of government aid in eighteenth-century France can limit his consideration to the allotment of aid for this or that cause of distress. The government of the Old Regime, as later also that of the Revolution, made the most assiduous efforts to better the conditions that led to distress. These efforts have been discussed at length in preceding chapters. There were attempts to improve agricultural conditions through drainage, new crops, and the encouragement of agricultural societies. There were attempts of various kinds to improve the livestock. Encouragement was given to the increase of home manufacture throughout the countryside. Better communication was fostered by the development of an elaborate system of highways and canals, built at state expense under the direction of the administration of bridges and highways. Education in all forms, especially technical schools, was greatly encouraged. Earnest efforts were made to give the countryside improved and gratuitous medical attention, and to better sanitary conditions everywhere.

[98] L. Bouchard, *Système financière de l'ancien monarchie* (Paris, 1891), pp. 419-420.
[99] Bloch, *op. cit.*, pp. 88-89.

Bounties were given to inventors, aid to cartographers, scientists, scholars, and men of letters; books were published and scientific expeditions financed. Attempts were made at removing the causes of fires and floods. In short, the French officials of the eighteenth century realized very clearly the need of bettering conditions in France, and to their credit they labored diligently at the task. Since their day, science, communication, and transportation have advanced enormously and tended to bring success in France at many points where eighteenth-century officials met only partial results.

BIBLIOGRAPHY

I. Manuscript Material

Archives Nationales

F15: 101, 102, 103. Diversified aid, 1790's: fires, floods, hailstorms, shipwrecks, explosions, landslides; mendicity, unmarried mothers, foundlings, free baths, free medicines, public works, refugees, sufferers from enemy invasion.

F15: 230. Epidemics.

F15: 396. Epidemics, pensions, hospitals, mendicity.

F15: 3494, 3495. Aid to Acadians.

F15: 3596, 3602. *Ateliers de Filature.*

G7: 1667. Epizootic of 1714-15.

G7: 1729, 1730, 1731, 1732, 1733, 1734, 1735, 1736, 1737, 1738-45. Plague of 1720-22.

H 565. Bad harvests, public works, epidemics, floods.

H 834. Floods and epizootic of 1745-46.

H 1156-57. Epizootic of 1783.

H 1418, 1419, 1420. Flood of 1784, public works.

H 1644. Plague of 1720-22, epizootic of 1774-76.

Archives de la Gironde

C 33, 61, 79, 2478, 2494, 2510, 2512. Aid to large families.

C 79. Epizootic of 1774-76.

C 1650, 2510, 2512, 2513, 2514, 2515. Pensions and gratifications to the "Newly Converted."

C 2494, 2495, 2496, 2497, 2498. Gratifications to wounded French sailors and the widows and children of sailors killed in the American Revolution.

Archives de la Seine-Inférieure

C 101. Epizootic of 1774-76.

C 1005. Aid given because of losses by hail, floods, fires, epidemics, etc.

C 1006, 1007. Aid to large families in the generality of Rouen, 1764-86.

Bibliothèque Nationale
Fonds français

6793. Epizootic of 1714-15, encouragement of cultivating the potato.

6801. Food relief, mendicity, public works.

6802. Aid to large families.

6950, 8956, 8960. Provisioning of Marseilles, 1719-20.

6950. Government grants to hospitals.

II. PRINTED MATTER

ADHER, J. "Les colons réfugiés d'Amerique pendant la Révolution," *Bulletin de la Société de géographie de Toulouse*, année 34 (1915), 152-168.

ADHER, J., ed. *Recueil de documents sur l'assistance publique dans le district de Toulouse de 1789 à 1800.* Toulouse, 1918. Pp. xxviii, 606.

Almanach national de France, I-VIII. Paris, 1793-1800.

Archives parlementaires de 1787 à 1789. Recueil complet des débâts législatifs & politiques des chambres françaises imprimé par ordre du Sénat et de la Chambre des Deputés sous la direction de M. J. Mavidal . . . et de M. E. Laurent. . . . Première série (1787 à 1799). 2d ed. Paris, 1879-1913. 81 vols.

ARTZ, FREDERICK B. *L'éducation technique en France au dix-huitième siècle (1700-1789)* (reprinted from the *Revue d'histoire moderne* [Sept.-Dec., 1938]). Paris, 1939. Pp. 51.

―――. *Les débuts de l'éducation technique en France (1500-1700)* (reprinted from the *Revue d'histoire moderne* [Sept.-Dec., 1937]) Paris, 1938. Pp. 55.

BABEAU, ALBERT. *Le village sous l'ancien régime.* 3d ed. rev. and enlarged. Paris, 1882. Pp. 415.

―――. *La ville sous l'ancien régime..* 2d ed. rev. and enlarged. Paris, 1884. 2 vols.

BACHAUMONT, L. P. DE. *Mémoires secrets pour servir à l'histoire de la république des lettres en France, depuis MDCCLXII jusqu'à nos jours; ou, journal d'un observateur.* Vol. XXV. Londres, 1786.

BAILLY, J. S. *Mémoires, avec une notice sur sa vie, des notes et des éclaircissements historiques* par MM. Berville et Barrière. Paris, 1821-22. 3 vols.

BALCH, EMILY GREENE. *Public Assistance of the Poor in France.* (Publications of the American Economic Association, VIII.) Baltimore, 1893. Pp. 179.

BANÉAT, P. "L'incendie de Rennes en 1720," *Bulletin historique et philologique du comité des travaux historiques et scientifiques* (Paris, 1909), pp. 258-266.

BARBIER, E. J. F. *Chronique de la règence et du règne de Louis XV (1718-1763), ou Journal de Barbier, avocat au parlement de Paris.* Paris, 1857. 8 vols.

BAVARD, ETIENNE. *Hôtel-Dieu de Beaune, 1445-1800*. Beaune, 1881. Pp. xvi, 365.

BAXTER, JAMES P. "What Caused the Deportation of the Acadians?" *Proceedings of the American Antiquarian Society*, N.S., XIII (Worcester, 1901), 74-100.

BENAERTS, LOUIS. *Le régime consulaire en Bretagne.. La départment d'Ille-et-Vilaine durant le consulat (1709-1801)*. Paris, 1914. Pp. xv, 383. (Thèse pour le doctorat-ès-lettres, Paris.)

BÉNET, A. *Le grand hiver de 1709 à Macon*. Paris, 1884. Pp. 16.

BERNADAU, PIERRE. *Histoire de Bordeaux, depuis l'année 1675 jusqu'à 1836.* . . . Bordeaux, 1837. Pp. 603.

Biographie universelle, ancien et moderne, with *Supplément*. Paris, 1811-62. 85 vols.

BLOCH, CAMILLE. *L'assistance et l'état en France à la veille de la Révolution (généralités de Paris, Rouen, Alençon, Orléans, Chalons, Soissons, Amiens) (1764-1790)*. Paris, 1908. Pp. lxiv, 504. (Doctoral dissertation in law, Paris.)

BLOCH, CAMILLE, AND TUETEY, ALEXANDRE, eds. *Procès-verbaux et rapports du comité de mendicité de la Constituante, 1790-1791*. Paris, 1911. Pp. lx, 847.

BOIS, B. *La vie scolaire et les créations intellectuelles en Anjou pendant la Révolution (1789-1799)*. Paris, 1929. Pp. 611.

BOISLISLE, A. DE. *Correspondance des contrôleurs généraux des finances avec les intendants des provinces*. Vol. II (1699 à 1708). Paris, 1883. Pp. 696.

———. "Le grand hiver et la disette de 1709," *Revue des questions historiques*, N.S., XXIX (Paris, 1903), 442-509; XXX (Paris, 1903), 486-542. Also published separately.

———, AND BROTONNE, P. DE. *Correspondance des contrôleurs généraux des finances avec les intendants des provinces*. Vol. III (1708 à 1715). Paris, 1897. Pp. 805.

BOISROUVRAY, FRANCOIS RENÉ JACQUELOT DE. "Journal inédit d'un deputé de l'ordre de la noblesse aux Etats de Bretagne pendant la Régence (1717-1724)." *Annales de Bretagne*, XXV (Rennes, 1909-10), 279-286.

BOISSONNADE, P. *Essai sur l'organisation du travail en Poitou, depuis le XIᵉ siècle jusqu'a la Révolution*. Paris, 1900. 2 vols.

BONAMY. "Mémoire sur l'inondations aux mois de décembre 1740, comparée aux l'inondations précédentes; avec des remarques sur l'elevation du sol de cette ville," *Mémoires de littérature, tirés des registres de l'Académie Royale des Inscriptions et Belles-Lettres, depuis l'année M.DCCXLI, jusques & compris l'année M.DCCXLIII*, XVII (Paris, 1751), 675-708.

BONDE, AMÉDÉE. *Le domaine des hospices de Paris depuis la Révolution jusqu'à la Troisième République.* Paris and Nancy, 1906. Pp. 338.

BONDOIS, PAUL M. "La protection des jardins et des cultures au XVIIIᵉ siècle: la première loi d'échenillage (1732)," *Revue d'histoire économique et sociale*, XIV (Paris, 1926), 447-457.

————. "La protection du troupeau au XVIIIᵉ siècle: l'épizootie de 1763," *Revue d'histoire économique et sociale*, XX (Paris, 1932), 352-375.

————. "Un essai de culture exotique sous l'ancien régime: la 'Peste de Riz' de Thiers (1741)," *Revue d'histoire économique et sociale*, XVI (Paris, 1928), 586-655.

BONNEFOY, GEORGES. *Histoire de l'administration civile dans la province d'Auvergne et le département du Puy-de-Dôme, depuis les temps les plus reculés jusqu'à nos jours.* . . . Paris, 1895-1902. 4 vols.

BONNEFROY. *Mémoire sur la mendicité.* Paris, 1791.

BORD, GUSTAVE. *Histoire de blé en France: le Pacte de Famine; histoire, légende.* Paris, 1887. Pp. 248 + 60.

————. *Les inondations du bassin de la Seine (1658-1910).* Paris, 1910.

BORDERIE, ARTHUR LE MOYNE DE LA. *Histoire de Bretagne*, continuée par Barthélemy Pocquet. Vol. VI. Rennes, 1914.

BOUCHER D'ARGIS. *De la bienfaisance dans l'ordre judiciaire.* . . . Londres, 1788.

BOUCHER, LOUIS. *La Salpêtrière, son histoire de 1656 à 1790, ses origines et son fonctionnement au XVIIIᵉ siècle.* Paris, 1883. Pp. 137.

BOUGOÜIN, E. "Une disette en Guyenne à la fin de l'ancien régime (1777-1778)," *Revue historique de Bordeaux et du département de la Gironde*, XI, 143-161, 208-229; XII, 98-115, 178-182, Bordeaux, 1918-19.

BOUVIER, L'ABBÉ [HENRI B.]. *Histoire de l'assistance publique dans le département de l'Yonne, jusqu'en 1789* (Extrait du *Bulletin de la Société des sciences historiques et naturelles de l'Yonne* [1899-1900]). n.p., n.d. Pp. [69]-129, 235-318.

BRAMARD, AUGUSTE. *La dernière famine: l'hiver et la famine de 1709 en France, en Bourbonnais.* Moulins, 1932.

BREBNER, J. B. *New England's Outpost: Acadia before the Conquest of Canada.* New York and London, 1927. Pp. 291.

BROSSARD, E., AND FREMINVILLE, JOSEPH DE. *Histoire de départment de la Loire pendant la Révolution française (1789-1799)*. Paris and Saint-Etienne, 1907. 2 vols.

BRU, PAUL. *Histoire de Bicêtre (hospice-prison-asile)*, d'après des documents historiques. . . . Paris, 1890. Pp. xviii, 480.

BUCHALET, M. F. *L'assistance publique a Toulouse au dix-huitième siècle*. Toulouse, 1904. Pp. 171.

BURGADE, J. B. J. EUGÈNE. *Histoire de l'hôpital de Libourne*. Bordeaux, 1867. Pp. vii, 316.

CAHEN, LÉON. *Le grand bureau des pauvres en Paris au milieu du XVIIIᵉ siècle*. Paris, 1904. Pp. 78.

The Cambridge Modern History, ed. by Sir A. W. Ward and others. Vols. VI and VIII. New York, 1925, 1907.

CARAMAN, PAUL. "La disette des grains et les émeutes populaires en 1773 dans la généralité de Bordeaux," *Revue historique de Bordeaux et du département de la Gironde*, III (Bordeaux, 1910), 297-319.

———. "Le journal d'un curé de campagne (1763-1792)," *Revue historique de Bordeaux et du département de la Gironde*, VI (Bordeaux, 1912), 329-343.

CASTIGLIONI, ARTURO. *A History of Medicine*, translated from the Italian and edited by E. B. Krumbhaar. New York, 1940. Pp. xxviii, 1013.

CERISE, G. "La lutte contre l'incendie avant 1789," *La controverse et le contemporain*, N.S., IV (Paris and Lyon, 1885), 275-305, 382-412.

CHAMPION, MAURICE. *Les inondations en France depuis le VIᵉ siècle jusqu'à nos jours*. Paris, 1858-64. 6 vols.

CHAUDRON, EMILE. *L'assistance publique à Troyes à la fin de l'ancien régime et pendant la Révolution, 1770-1800*. Paris, 1923. Pp. xxiii, 548. (Doctoral treatise.)

CHÉRUEL, A. *Dictionnaire historique des institutions, moeurs et coutumes de la France*. 4th ed. Paris, 1874. 2 vols.

CHILDS, FRANCES SERGEANT. *French Refugee Life in the United States, 1700-1800: An American Chapter of the French Revolution*. Baltimore, 1941. Pp. 227.

CLÉMENT, P. *La police sous Louis XIV*. Paris, 1866. Pp. 478.

COIFFIER, JOSEPH. *L'assistance publique dans la généralité de Riom (au XVIIIᵉ siècle)*. Clermont-Ferrand, 1905. Pp. 288.

CORMOULS-HOULÈS, EDOUARD. *L'assistance par le travail*. Paris, 1910. Pp. xxiii, 870. (Doctoral treatise, Toulouse.)

CORNAZ, C. A. E. *Une épizootie aux joux de la ville en 1701 et 1702.* Neuchâtel, 1864.

CORNIÉ, ADRIEN. *Etude sur l'institution nationale des sourdes-muettes de Bordeaux (1786-1903).* 2d ed. enlarged. Bordeaux, 1903. Pp. 145.

CRÉTIN, A. *Organisation de l'assistance hospitalière libre et liberale.* Paris, 1886. Pp. 63.

CREVEAUX, EUGÈNE. *Le ravitaillement de Paris par le département de l'Aisne pendant la Révolution.* [Paris, 1936.] Pp. [105]-234.

CROSS-MAYREVIEILLE, GABRIEL. *L'assistance publique et privée en Languedoc.* Montpellier, 1914. Pp. xii, 175.

———. *Traité de l'assistance hospitalière.* Paris and Nancy, 1912. 3 vols.

CROUSAZ-CRÉTET, P. DE. "La question du pain à Paris en 1709," *La revue hebdomadaire,* XI (Nov., 1917), 451-479.

CUZENT, GILBERT. *L'hospice civil et les hôpitaux de Brest.* Brest, 1889. Pp. 436.

DAGIER, ETIENNE. *Histoire chronologique de l'Hôpital Général et grand Hôtel-Dieu de Lyon.* [Lyon] 1830. 2 vols.

DAKIN, DOUGLAS. *Turgot and the Ancien Régime in France.* London, 1939. Pp. xi, 361.

DANJOU, F. "Histoire de l'Hôtel royal des Invalides," *Archives curieuses de l'histoire de France depuis Louis XI jusqu'à Louis XVIII . . . ,* 2d ser., II (Paris, 1840), 71-118.

DAVIES, C. M. *History of Holland . . . ,* III (London, 1884), 449-454.

DÉCAP [JEAN], LA MARTINIÈRE [JULES MACHET DE], and BIDEAU, eds. *L'instruction primaire en France aux XVIIIᵉ et XIXᵉ siècles: Documents d'histoire locale publiés et analysés.* Paris, 1914. Pp. 212.

DELAMARE, NICOLAS. *Traité de la police.* 2d ed., enlarged. Paris, 1719-38. 4 vols. (Vol. IV, edited by Lecler du Brillet, is entitled *Continuation du traité de la police.*)

DÉPARTEMENT DE LA SEINE. *Supplément à l'inventaire sommaire des archives hospitalières antérieures à 1790,* rédigé par M. Brièle. Paris, 1889. Pp. lii, 366.

DÉPARTEMENT DE SEINE-ET-OISE. *Les subsistances dans le district de Versailles de 1788 à l'an V,* documents recueillis et publiés par A. Defresne et F. Evrard. Rennes, 1921-22. 2 vols.

DERIES, MADELINE. *Le district de Saint-Lo pendant la Révolution, 1787-an IV.* Paris, 1922. Pp. xxix, 515. (Doctoral treatise, Paris.)

DRIAULT, EDOUARD, AND LHÉRITER, MICHEL. *Histoire diplomatique de la Grèce de 1821 à nos jours.* Vol. I. Paris, 1925.

DUBIEF, EUGÈNE. *L'Abbé de l'Epée et l'éducation de sourds-muets.* Paris, n.d. Pp. 74.

DUFRESNE AND EVRARD. *Les subsistances dans le district de Versailles de 1788 à l'an V. Documents recueillis et publiés.* Rennes, 1921-22. 2 vols.

DUMAS, F. *La généralité de Tours au XVIIIe siècle: administration de l'intendant du Cluzel (1766-1783).* (*Mémoires de la Société archéologique de Touraine,* XXXIX.) Tours, 1894. Pp. 437.

DUNBAR, ROBERT G. "The Introduction of the Practice of Vaccination into Napoleonic France," *Bulletin of the History of Medicine,* X (Dec., 1941), 635-650.

DUPIN, BARON. *Histoire de l'administration des secours publics, ou analyse historique de la législation des secours publics.* . . . Paris, 1821. Pp. xiv, 470.

DUPONT-FERRIER, GUSTAVE. *Du Collège de Clermont au Lycée Louis-le-Grand (1563-1920).* Vol. I. Paris, 1921.

DUPUY, A[NTOINE]. "La Bretagne au XVIIIe siècle: l'affaire de la constitution municipale; épisode de l'histoire de la ville de Rennes (1757-1782)," *Annales de Bretagne,* I (Rennes, 1886).

———. "L'administration municipale en Bretagne au XVIIIe siècle," *Annales de Bretagne,* III (Rennes, 1887-88), 299-371, 541-612; IV (Rennes, 1888-89), 29-66, 234-295, 553-585; V (Rennes, 1889-90), 3-81, 153-190, 662-692; VI (Rennes, 1890-91), 179-223, 283-373.

———. "L'enseignement supérieur en Bretagne avant et après la Révolution," *Annales de Bretagne,* IV (Rennes, 1888-89).

———. "Les épidémies en Bretagne au XVIIIe siècle," *Annales de Bretagne,* I (Rennes, 1886-87), 115-141, 290-308; II (Rennes, 1886-87), 20-49, 190-226; III (Rennes, 1887-88), 175-204. Also published separately.

DURUY, ALBERT. *L'instruction publique et la Révolution.* Paris, 1882. Pp. 502.

DUTENS, J. *Histoire de la navigation intérieure de la France.* . . . Vol. I. Paris, 1829. Pp. 651.

EBRARD, E[LIE]. *Misère et charité dans une petite ville de France de 1560 à 1862.* . . . Bourg, 1866. Pp. xlix, 492.

Encyclopédie méthodique. [Ed. by Charles Panckoucke and son.] Paris, 1782-1830. 202 vols.

FORADO-CUNÉO, YVONNE. "Les ateliers de charité pendant la Révolution, 1789-1791," *La Révolution française*, LXXXVI-LXXXVII (Paris, 1933-34).

FABRE, AUGUSTIN. *Histoire des hôpitaux et des institutions de bienfaisance de Marseille*. Marseilles, 1854-56. 2 vols.

————. *Histoire de Marseille*. Marseilles, 1829. 2 vols.

FERDINAND-DREYFUS, F. *L'assistance sous la Législative et la Convention (1791-1795)*. Paris, 1905. Pp. 180.

————. *Un philanthrope d'autrefois: La Rochefoucauld-Liancourt, 1747-1827*. Paris, 1903. Pp. xvi, 547. (Work crowned by the Académie française [Prix Montyon].)

FLEMING, GEORGE. *Animal Plagues: Their History, Nature, and Prevention*. London, 1871. Pp. xxxiv, 548.

FONCIN, P. *Essai sur le ministère de Turgot*. Paris, 1877. Pp. 622.

FOSSEYEUX, MARCEL. *Le budget de la charité à Paris au XVIIIe siècle*. (Extrait de la *Revue des études historiques*, année 85 [juillet-octobre, 1918], 253-264.) Paris, 1919. Pp. 12.

————. *Les écoles de charité à Paris sous l'ancien régime et dans la première partie du XIXe siècle*. Paris [Nogent-le-Rotrou], 1912. Pp. 144.

————. *L'Hôtel-Dieu de Paris au XVIIe et XVIIIe siècle*. Paris and Nancy, 1912. Pp. 437.

————. *La Maison des Cent-Filles ou de la Miséricorde au faubourg Saint-Marceau (1623-1795)*. (Extrait du *Bulletin de la Société de l'histoire de Paris et de l'Ile-de-France*, L [1923].) Paris, 1925. Pp. 15.

FRANCE. ARCHIVES DE LA GUERRE, MINISTÈRE DE LA GUERRE. *Inventaire sommaire des archives historiques (archives anciennes—correspondance)*. Vol. I. Paris, 1898.

————. MINISTÈRE DE L'INTÉRIEUR. *Collection des inventaires-sommaires des archives départementales antérieures à 1790*. 1858 et seq. *Série* B. Isère. *Série* C. Ardennes, Aube, Aude, Bouches-du-Rhône, Calvados, Charente, Charente-Inférieure, Côte d'Or, Gironde, Hautes-Alpes, Ille-et-Vilaine, Loire-Inférieure, Seine-et-Marne, Seine-Inférieure. *Série* D. Charente, Charente-Inférieure, Loire-Inférieure, Seine-Inférieure. *Série* E. Charente, Charente-Inférieure, Hôpital de Grenoble, Isère. *Série* F. Hôpital de Grenoble. *Série* G. Charente-Inférieure, Hôpital de Tulle. *Série* H. Calvados, Charente-Inférieure, Isère.

————. MINISTÈRE DE L'INSTRUCTION PUBLIQUE. *Collection des in-*

ventaires-sommaires des archives départementales postérieures à 1790. Série L. Bouches-du-Rhône, Isère, Seine, Seine-et-Marne.

FRANKLIN, ALFRED. *La vie privée d'autrefois; arts et metiers, modes, moeurs, usages des Parisiens du XIIe au XVIIIe siècle, d'après des documents originaux ou inédits.* Paris, 1887-1902. 27 vols.

FRÉGIER, [HONORÉ ANTOINE]. *Histoire de l'administration de la police depuis Philippe Auguste jusqu'aux états généraux de 1789. . . .* Paris, 1850. 2 vols.

FREMINVILLE, EDME DE LA POIX DE. *Dictionnaire ou traité de la police générale. . . .* New ed., rev. and corrected by himself. Paris, 1771. Pp. 783.

FUNCK-BRENTANO, FRANTZ. *The Old Regime in France,* tr. by Herbert Wilson. London [1929]. Pp. 376.

GAFFAREL, PAUL, AND DURANTY, LE MARQUIS DE. *La peste de 1720 à Marseille & en France, d'après des documents inédits.* Paris, 1911. Pp. viii, 630.

GARRISON, FIELDING H. *An Introduction to the History of Medicine.* 3d ed., rev. and enlarged. Philadelphia and London, 1921. Pp. 942.

GAXOTTE, PIERRE. *Louis the Fifteenth and His Times,* translated by J. Lewis May. London, 1934. Pp. 357.

GEER, WALTER. *Napoleon and His Family: The Story of a Corsican Clan.* Vol. I. New York, 1927.

GÉORGEL, J. F. *Mémoires pour servir à l'histoire des événements de la fin du dix-huitième siècle depuis 1760 jusqu'en 1806-1810.* 2d ed. rev. Paris, 1820. 6 vols.

GIRAUDET, ALEX. *Recherches et statistiques sur l'hygiène de la ville de Tours et sur le mouvement de sa population depuis 1632 jusqu'à l'époque actuelle.* Tours, 1853. Pp. xxxiii, 288.

GODARD, CHARLES. *Les pouvoirs des intendants sous Louis XIV, particulièrement dans les pays d'élection de 1661 à 1715.* Paris, 1901. Pp. xv, 543. (Doctoral thesis, Paris.)

[GOIFFRON, JEAN BAPTISTE.] *Relations et dissertation sur la peste du Gévaudan. . . .* Lyon, 1722. Pp. 8 + 188.

GOMEL, CHARLES. *Les causés financières de la Révolution française. Les derniers contrôleurs généraux.* Paris, 1893. Pp. 645.

GRANIER, CAMILLE. *Essai de bibliographie charitable.* Paris, 1891. Pp. 450.

HAMILTON, EARL J. "Growth of Rigidity in Business during the Eighteenth Century," *American Economic Review Supplement,* XXX (March, 1940), 298-305.

————. "Profit Inflation and the Industrial Revolution, 1751-1800," *Quarterly Journal of Economics*, LVI (Feb., 1942), 256-273.

HARVEY, D. C. *The French Regime in Prince Edward Island*. New Haven, 1926. Pp. xi, 265.

HASSAL, ARTHUR. *Louis XIV and the Zenith of the French Monarchy*. New York, 1899. Pp. xvi, 444.

HERLAUT, COMMANDANT. *La disette de pain à Paris en 1709*. (Extrait de *Mémoires de la Société de l'histoire de Paris et de l'Ile-de-France*, XLV [1918].) Paris, 1918. Pp. 100.

————. "Les enlèvements d'enfants à Paris en 1720 et en 1750," *Revue historique*, CXXXIX (janvier, 1922), 43-61, 202-223.

Histoire générale de Languedoc, avec des notes et pièces justicatives par Dom Cl. Devic & Dom J. Vaissete. [. . . continuée jusques en 1790 par Ernest Roschach.] Toulouse, 1872-92 [93]. 16 vols.

HUTYRA, FRANZ, AND MAREK, JOSEF. *Special Pathology and Therapeutics of the Diseases of Domestic Animals*, edited by John R. Mohler and Adolph Eichhorn. 3d authorized American ed. Vol. I. Chicago, 1926.

ISAMBERT, FRANÇOIS ANDRÉ, ed. *Recueil général des anciennes lois françaises, depuis l'an 420 jusqua'à la Révolution de 1789* . . . par MM. Jourdan . . . Decrusy . . . [et] Isambert. . . . Vols. XX-XXIX. Paris [1821-33].

JAFFÉ, GRACE M. *Le mouvement ouvrier à Paris pendant la Révolution (1789-91)*. [Paris, 1924.] Pp. 215.

JUSTIN, EMILE. *Les sociétés royales d'agriculture au XVIIIᵉ siècle (1757-1793)*. Saint-Lo, 1935. Pp. xv, 371.

JUVENCEL, HENRI DE. *Le contrôleur général des finances sous l'ancien régime*. Paris, 1901. Pp. 430.

LABUCHELLE, M. "Bordeaux il y a 200 ans, la misère à Bordeaux de 1709 à 1713," *Revue historique de Bordeaux et du département de la Gironde*, II (Bordeaux, 1909), 30-52, 119-130, 266-275, 317-333.

LACROIX, PAUL. *XVIIIᵉ siècle: lettres, sciences et arts*. Paris, 1878. Pp. xiii, 560.

LACROIX, SIGISMOND, ed. *Actes de la commune de Paris pendant la Révolution*. Paris, 1894-98. 7 vols.

La grande encyclopédie. Paris, 1886-1902. 31 vols.

LALLEMAND, LÉON. *De l'organisation de la bienfaisance publique & privée dans les campagnes au XVIIIᵉ siècle*. (Extrait des *Mémoires de la Société d'agriculture, commerce, sciences et arts du département de la Marne*, année 1894.) Chalons-sur-Marne, 1895. Pp. 52.

————. *Histoire de la charité.* Vol. IV. Parts 1 and 2. Paris, 1910-12. Pp. 624 + 527.

————. *Histoire des enfants abandonnés et délaissés.* Paris, 1885. Pp. 791.

————. *La Révolution et les pauvres.* Paris, 1898. Pp. 398.

————. *L'assistance medicale au XVIIIe siècle* (Extrait du *Bulletin des sciences économiques et sociales du comité des travaux historiques et scientifiques*). Paris, 1895. Pp. 22.

L[APOULAYE], M[ENDRE] DE. "Le blocus des côtes de France et la disette à Bordeaux en 1793-95," *Revue historique de Bordeaux et du département de la Gironde,* VIII (Bordeaux, 1915), 46-49.

LA ROCHELLE, ERNEST. *Jacob Rodrigues Pereire, premier instituteur des sourds-muets en France: sa vie et ses travaux.* Paris, 1882. Pp. 576.

LAUVRIÈRE, EMILE. *La tragédie d'un peuple: histoire du peuple acadien de ses origines à nos jours.* New ed. rev. and corrected. Paris, 1924. 2 vols.

LECLER DU BRILLET. *Continuation du traité de la police* (constituting Vol. IV of Delamare's *Traité de la police*). Paris, 1738.

LECLERCQ, DOM HENRI. *Histoire de la Régence pendant la minorité de Louis XV.* Paris, 1921. 3 vols.

LECOQ, MARCEL. *L'assistance par le travail en France.* Paris, 1900. Pp. 455. (Thesis for doctorate in law, Paris.)

LEFEBVRE, GEORGES. *La grande peur de 1789.* Paris, 1932. Pp. 272.

LE GRAND, LÉON. *Les Quinze-Vingts depuis leur fondation jusqu'à leur translation du faubourg Saint-Antoine (XIIe-XVIIIe siècles).* Nogent-le-Rotrou, 1886-87. 2 vols.

LEGRAND, LOUIS. *Sénac de Meilhan et l'intendance du Hainaut & du Cambrésis sous Louis XVI.* Valenciennes, 1868. Pp. 486.

LEGRAS, P. THÉOD[ORE]. *Notice historique sur les deux hôpitaux et l'asile des aliénés de Rouen, avec remarques sur les enfants trouvés et assistés.* Rouen, 1827. Pp. 143.

LÉON, PAUL. *Les Invalides: les fastes de l'hôtel, ses musées, ses églises, le tombeau de l'empereur.* Paris [1929]. Pp. 423.

LEROY, STÉPHEN. *Franc-Comtois pensionnés sur le trésor royal en 1789.* (Extrait du *Bulletin de la Société grayloise d'émulation,* année 1899.) Gray, 1899. Pp. 23-92.

LETACONNOUX, JOSEPH. *Les subsistances et le commerce des grains en Bretagne au XVIIIe siècle; essai de monographie économique.* Rennes, 1909. Pp. xxxvii, 396. (Doctoral treatise.)

————. "Les subsistance et le commerce des grains en Bretagne, au XVIIIᵉ siècle," *Annales de Bretagne*, XX (Rennes and Paris, 1905).

LEVASSEUR, E. *La population française. Histoire de la population avant 1789 et démographie de la France comparée à celle des autres nations au XIXᵉ siècle. Précédée d'une introduction sur la statistique.* Vol. III. [Paris, 1892.]

————. *Histoire des classes ouvrières et de l'industrie en France avant 1789.* 2d ed., rev. Paris, 1901. 2 vols.

————. *Histoire du commerce de la France.* Paris, 1911-12. 2 vols.

LEVOT, P. J. *Histoire de la ville et du port de Brest.* Brest, 1864-66. 3 vols.

LHÉRITIER, MICHEL. *Tourny, intendant de Bordeaux.* Paris, 1920. Pp. 813. (Doctoral dissertation in letters, Paris.)

[LYON.] *Exposition universelle de 1900: l'économie sociale et l'histoire du travail à Lyon.* Lyon, 1900. Pp. xxviii, 661.

MARAT, J. P. *L'ami du peuple.* Paris, 1789-93.

MARION, MARCEL. *Dictionnaire des institutions de la France au XVIIᵉ et XVIIIᵉ siècles.* Paris, 1923. Pp. ix, 564.

————. *Histoire financière de la France depuis 1715.* Vols. I and II. Paris, 1927. (Work crowned by the *Académie Française*.)

————. "Les fugatifs alsatiens sous la Révolution," *Revue historique*, CXLII (janvier, 1923), 210-228.

————. "Une famine en Guyenne (1747-1748)," *Revue historique*, XLVI (mai-août, 1891), 241-287.

MARSEILLE. Chambre de Commerce. *Inventaire des archives historiques de la Chambre de Commerce de Marseille. . . .* Marseilles, 1878. Pp. 515.

MARTIN, ERNEST. *Les exiles Acadiens en France au XVIIIᵉ siècle et leur établissement en Poitou.* Paris, 1936. Pp. 333.

MARTIN-DOISY. *Dictionnaire d'économie charitable, ou exposé historique, théorique et pratique de l'assistance religieuse, publique et privée, ancienne et moderne.* (Constituting Vols. V-VIII of the *Troisième et dernière Encyclopédie théologique* . . . , publiée par M. l'Abbé Migne.) Paris, 1855-64. 4 vols.

MATHIEZ, ALBERT. *La théophilanthropie et le culte décadaire, 1796-1801. . . .* Paris, 1903. Pp. 753. (Dissertation for doctorate in letters, Paris.)

————. *La vie chère et le mouvement social sous le Terreur.* Paris, 1927. Pp. 620.

MATHOREZ, J. "Les éléments de population orientale en France," *Revue des études historiques*, 83ᵉ année (Paris, 1917), pp. 176-203. Harvard University Library.

MAURICET, ALPH[ONSE]. *Etudes historiques sur les épidémies dans le Morbihan. Histoire des épidémies de maladies fébriles de 1792 à 1851, avec les pièces pour servir de preuves à l'appui.* Vannes, 1883. Pp. lxxi, 181.

McCLOY, SHELBY T. "Charity Workshops during the French Revolution," *South Atlantic Quarterly*, XXXV (Oct., 1936), 446-454.

————. "Charity Workshops for Women, Paris, 1790-95," *Social Service Review*, XI (June, 1937), 274-284.

————. "Flood Relief and Control in Eighteenth-Century France," *Journal of Modern History*, XIII (March, 1941), 1-18.

————. "French Charities to the Acadians, 1755-1799," *Louisiana Historical Quarterly*, XXI (July, 1938), 3-15.

————. "Government Aid to Large Families in Normandy, 1764-1786," *Social Forces*, XVIII (March, 1940), 418-424.

————. "Government Assistance during the Plague of 1720-22 in Southeastern France," *Social Service Review*, XII (June, 1938), 298-318.

————. "Some Eighteenth Century Housing Projects in France," *Social Forces*, XVI (May, 1938), 528-529.

MERCIER, L. S. *Tableau de Paris.* New ed. Vols. VIII, XII. Paris, 1783, 1788.

MERLET, LUCIEN. *Inventaire sommaire des archives hospitalières antérieures à 1790*, rédigé par Lucien Merlet, archiviste d'Eure-et-Loir. *Hospices des Chartres.* Chartres, 1890. Pp. 224.

MONFALCON, J. B. *Histoire monumentale de la ville de Lyon.* Vol. III. Paris and Lyon, 1886.

MONTARLOT, P. "Un bureau de secours aux incendiés du diocèse d'Autun en 1787," *Mémoires de la Société Eduenne*, N.S., XXV (Autun, 1897), 333-354.

[MONTLINOT, C. A. L. DE.] *Etat actuel de la maison de travail de la généralité de Soissons..* [1781.] Deuxième compte. Année 1782. Troisième compte. Année 1783. IV compte. Années 1784-85. 4 vols. in 1. n.p., n.d. Pp. 40, 46, 75, 39.

MÖRING, MICHEL, AND QUENTIN, CHARLES. *Collection des documents pour servir à l'histoire des hôpitaux de Paris*, commencée sous les auspices de M. Michel Möring, continuée par M. Charles Quentin, publiée par M. Brièle. Paris, 1883-87. 4 vols.

MUTEAU, CHARLES. *Les écoles et collèges en province depuis les temps les plus reculés jusqu'en 1789.* Paris, 1882. Pp. xiv, 601.

NECKER, JACQUES. *Compte rendu au roi.* Paris, 1781. Pp. 186.

————. *De l'administration des finances de la France.* Paris, 1785. 3 vols.

OPOIX, CHRISTOPHE. *Histoire et description de Provins.* 2d ed. Provins and Paris, 1846. Pp. 584.

P. G. "Pensionnaires écclesiastiques de 1790 à 1797," *Annales des Alpes,* année 1903 (Gap, 1903), pp. 261-272.

PAILLOT, J. B. J., ed. *Manuel complémentaire des codes françaises et de toutes collections des lois. . . .* Paris, 1845. 2 vols.

PALLUY. "Des institutions des sourds-muets en France et à l'étranger," *Revue de Paris,* VI (Paris, 1829), 32-42.

PAPON, JEAN PIERRE. *Relation de la peste de Marseille, en 1720, et de celle de Montpellier, en 1629. . . .* (Abridgment of his *De la peste ou époques mémorables de ce fléau et les moyens de s'en préserver,* 1800.) Montpellier, 1820. Pp. 93.

PARTURIER, LOUIS. *L'assistance à Paris sous l'ancien régime & pendant la Révolution.* Paris, 1897. Pp. 256.

PAULET [JEAN JACQUES]. *Recherches historiques et physiques sur les maladies épizootiques, avec les moyens d'y remédier, dans tous les cas.* Paris, 1775. 2 vols.

PAULTRE, CHRISTIAN. *De la répression de la mendicité et du vagabondage sous l'ancien régime.* Paris, 1906. Pp. 639.

PETETOT, L'ABBÉ. "Des hôpitaux," *Annales de la charité* (1846), 2-22.

Pièces historiques sur la peste de 1720. n.p., n.d. 2 vols.

PIHAN, LE CHANOINE. *Eloge historique de Valentin Haüy . . .* (composé pour *l'Annaire de l'Oise,* 1892). Beauvais, 1891. Pp. 32.

POUPÉ, EDMOND. *L'instruction publique à Cuers sous l'ancien régime* (reprinted from the *Bulletin de la Société d'études scientifiques et archéologiques de la ville de Draguignan*). Draguignan, 1907. Pp. 27.

PRIESTLEY, HERBERT INGRAM. *France Overseas through the Old Regime: A Study of European Expansion.* New York and London, 1939. Pp. 393.

POWER, THOMAS F., JR. "Emergency Relief in France in 1788," *Journal of Modern History,* XIII (June, 1941), 218-221.

PRUDHOMME, A. *Histoire de Grénoble.* Grenoble, 1888. Pp. xiv, 683.

QUYNN, DOROTHY MACKEY. "Recruiting in Old Orleans for New Orleans," *American Historical Review,* XLVI (July, 1941), 832-836.

RAMBAUD, PIERRE. *L'assistance publique à Poitiers jusqu'à l'an V.* Paris, 1912-14. 2 vols.

RAVELET, ARMAND. *Histoire du vénérable Jean-Baptiste de la Salle, fondateur de l'Institut des Frères des Ecoles Chrétiennes.* Paris, 1874. Pp. 496.

RENOUARD, XAVIER. *L'assistance publique à Lille de 1527 a l'an VIII.* Lille, 1912. Pp. 177. (Doctoral treatise in political and economic sciences.)

Révolutions de Paris . . . , publiées par le sieur Prudhomme. Paris, 1789-1791. 10 vols.

Revue d'assistance; bulletin de la Société internationale pour l'étude des questions d'assistance. Paris, 1900-1901. 2 vols. (Merged with the *Revue philanthropique* in June, 1901.)

Revue philanthropique, edited by P. Strauss. Paris, 1897-1934. 54 vols.

RIVIÈRE, LOUIS. *Les oeuvres d'hospitalité de nuit en France: leur developpement, leur état actuel, leur avenir* (reprinted from the *Revue philanthropique*). Paris, 1898.

ROSCHACH, ERNEST. "Etudes historiques sur la province de Languedoc," *Histoire générale de Languedoc, . . .* par Dom Cl. Devic et Dom J. Vaissete, XIII-XIV. Toulouse, 1876. (Awarded the Prix Gobert, second place.)

ROUCHEFOUCALD, FRANÇOIS DE LA. *Souvenirs du 10 août 1792 et de l'armée de Bourbon,* publiés par Jean Marchand. Paris, 1929. Pp. lix, 245.

ROZE, ERNEST. *Histoire de la pomme de terre. . . .* Paris, 1898. Pp. 464.

SAINT-SIMON. *Mémoires. . . .* nouv. éd. . . . par A. de Boislisle. Vols. XIV-XVII. Paris, 1899-1903.

SAUNOIS DE CHEVERT, G. *L'indigence et l'assistance dans les campagnes depuis 1789 jusqu'à nos jours.* Paris, 1889. Pp. viii, 552. ("Ouvrage recompensé par l'Académie des sciences morales et politiques.")

SCHÖNE, LUCIEN. *Histoire de la population française.* Paris, 1893. Pp. xv, 428.

SCOVILLE, WARREN C. "Large-scale Production in the French Plate-Glass Industry, 1665-1789," *Journal of Political Economy,* I (Oct., 1942), 669-698.

——. "State Policy and the French Glass Industry, 1640-1789," *Quarterly Journal of Economics,* LVI (May, 1942), 430-455.

——. "Technology and the French Glass Industry, 1640-1740," *Journal of Economic History,* I (Nov., 1941), 153-167.

SÉE, HENRI. "La mise en valeur des terres incultes: défrichements et desséchements à la fin de l'ancien régime," *Revue d'histoire économique et sociale,* XI (Paris, 1923), 62-81.

————. *Les classes rurales en Bretagne du XVIe siècle à la Révolution.* Paris, 1906. Pp. xxi, 544.

————. *L'évolution commerciale et industrielle de la France sous l'ancien régime.* Paris, 1925.

————. *Remarques sur la misère, la mendicité et l'assistance en Bretagne à la fin de l'ancien régime* (reprinted from the *Mémoires de la Société d'histoire et d'archéologie de Bretagne*, VI). Rennes and Paris, 1925. Pp. 26.

SERVIÈRES, JEAN DE. "Les refugiés corses à Marseille pendant la Révolution (1793-1797)," *Bulletin de la Société des sciences historiques et naturelles de la Corse* (Bastia, 1922), 1-105.

SICARD, L'ABBÉ AUGUSTIN. *Les études classiques avant la Révolution.* Paris, 1887. Pp. 590.

SIGERIST, HENRY E. *Great Doctors: A Biographical History of Medicine,* tr. by Eden and Cedar Paul. London, 1935. Pp. 436.

SMITH, PRESERVED. *A History of Modern Culture.* II. New York, 1934. Pp. 703.

SPENGLER, JOSEPH J. *France Faces Depopulation.* Durham, 1938. Pp. xi, 313.

————. *French Predecessors of Malthus.* Durham, 1942. Pp. ix, 398.

————. "Messance: Founder of French Demography," *Human Biology,* XII (Feb., 1940), 77-94.

————. "Moheau: Prophet of Depopulation," *Journal of Political Economy,* XLVII (Oct., 1939), 648-677.

STODDARD, T. LOTHROP. *The French Revolution in San Domingo.* Boston and New York, 1914. Pp. 410.

TARGE, MAXINE. *Professeurs et régents de collège dans l'ancienne Université de Paris (XVIIe et XVIIIe siècles).* Paris, 1902. Pp. viii, 318.

TAULIER, [MARC JOSEPH] FREDERIC. *Le vrai livres du peuple, ou le riche et le pauvre: histoire et tableau des institutions de bienfaisance et d'instruction primaire de la ville de Grenoble.* Grenoble and Paris, 1860.

TENON, JACQUES. *Mémoires sur les hôpitaux de Paris.* Paris, 1788. Pp. 472.

TISSIER, J. *L'hiver de 1709 dans le diocèse de Narbonne* (reprinted from the *Bulletin de la Commission archéologique de Narbonne*). Narbonne, 1895.

TOURNEUX, MAURICE. *Bibliographie de l'histoire de Paris pendant la Révolution française.* Paris, 1890-1913. 5 vols.

TUETEY, ALEXANDRE, ed. *L'administration des ateliers de charité, 1789-1790. Rapport de J. B. Edme Plaisant.* Paris, 1906. Pp. 170.

———. *L'assistance publique à Paris pendant la Révolution: documents inédits.* Paris, 1895-97. 4 vols.

———. *Répertoire général des sources manuscrites de l'histoire de Paris pendant la Révolution.* Paris, 1890-1914. 11 vols.

TURGOT, A. R. J. *Oeuvres.* Nouv. éd. . . . par MM. Eugène Daire et Hippolyte Dussard. . . . Paris, 1844. 2 vols.

USHER, ABBOTT PAYSON. *The History of the Grain Trade in France, 1400-1710.* Cambridge, 1913. Pp. xv, 405. (Doctoral treatise, Harvard.)

VALRAN, GASTON. *Assistance et éducation en Provence aux XVIIIe et XIXe siècles.* Paris, 1900. Pp. viii, 219.

———. *Misère et charité en Provence au XVIIIe siècle; essai d'histoire sociale.* Paris, 1899. Pp. xxiv, 422. (Doctoral treatise, Aix.)

VAUBAN. *Project d'une dixme royale.* 2d ed. [Paris], 1708.

VIAUD, J. T., AND FLEURY, E. T. *Histoire de la ville et du port de Rochefort.* Rochefort, 1845. 2 vols.

VIGNOLS, LÉON. "La caisse des Invalides et les dilapidations gouvernementales du XVIIe au XXe siècle," *Revue d'histoire économique et sociale,* année 1936-37 (Paris, 1937), pp. 143-181.

VILLE DE MENDE. *Inventaire-sommaire des archives communales antérieures à 1790,* rédigé par M. Ferdinand André. Mende, 1885. Pp. 333.

VILLEY, PIERRE. *L'aveugle dans le monde des voyants.* Paris, 1927. Pp. 333.

VOLTAIRE. *Siècle de Louis XIV (Oeuvres de Voltaire,* édition Beuchot, vols. XXIX-XXXI). Paris, 1830.

WATTEVILLE, AD[OLPHE] DE. *Législation charitable; ou recueil des lois, arrêtés, décrets, ordonnances, avis au conseil d'état* . . . , 2d ed. enlarged. Paris, 1847. Pp. xv, 711.

YOUNG, ARTHUR. *Travels in France during the Years 1787, 1788, 1789, with an Introduction, Biographical Sketch, and Notes by M. Betham-Edwards.* 2d ed. London, 1889. Pp. lix, 366.

INDEX

Académie des Sciences, Paris, hears paper on hospital sanitation, 186; advocates abandonment of Hôtel-Dieu, 198; honors Pereire, 429; receives in audience Haüy and pupils, 432.

Academy of Surgery, founded 1731, 168; abolished, 176 n. 93.

Acadians, number, 370; expulsion in 1750's, 369-372; support by French government, 372-383, 464; in colonization projects, 374-380; migration to Louisiana (1785), 380-382; other migration schemes fall through, 382; sums spent on them, 382-383; one arrested and released, 358, 393; during Revolution, 389-393; comment on their success and citizenship, 383.

Accusation, of speculation by government officials, 1709, 18; of graft, 1793-95, 46 n. 120; of excessive spending on charities by estates of Languedoc, 72; of squandering government money in Auch, 1775-76, 129 n. 106; against meat-dealers of Auvergne, 1721, 151; against the board of health at Orange, 1721, 154; against hospital finance and service, 209-210; of abuses in pensions, 312, 314 n. 14; few instances of malversation, 466.

Agai, d', intendant of Brittany, 287.

Aged, the, care of, 217-222; annual cost of maintenance, 464.

Agriculture, Royal Society of, 58, 103, 104, 124.

Agricultural societies promoted, 67-68.

Argenson, d', lieutenant general of police, 12, 116.

Armenians, ten students trained, 415-416.

Arpent, unit of measure for land, 417 n. 38.

Association de Bienfaisance Judiciaire, 453.

Association of domestics, 456.

Audits, 466.

Badou, Père, flood victim, 71.

Bailly, mayor of Paris, role in supplying food for city, 1789, 38; on committee concerning Hôtel-Dieu, 197; action toward the charity workshops, 290-291, 306; orders closing of charity schools, 443.

Barère, author of law to aid invalid farmers and artisans, 279.

Bastille, seizure, 221; removed, 277; its "conquerors" aided, 279, 344-346; its former prisoner Latude pensioned, 1784, 331.

Baths, free medicinal, 167-168, 177-178, 347; cold, for insane, 226.

Bathtubs, request for, at Val-de-Grace, Paris, 185 n.

Bâville, intendant of Languedoc, 415.

Beggars (and vagabonds), in crisis of 1709, 7-8; a continual horde, 50, 53, 278; dig burial trenches during plague, 137; numbers, 260-262, 265 n. 22, 274-275; part in crime, 261, 274-275; causes, 262-264; methods used for eradication, 264-271, 272-274, 275-283, 298; numbers arrested, 265 n. 22, 272 n. 58; majority of them agricultural laborers, 269; often forced to work, 285, 298, 302; attitude toward, 447; aided by *bureaux de charité* and philanthropic societies, 455.

Belsunce, bishop of Marseilles, forbids Oratorians to administer extreme unction, 139; his labors during the plague, 139-140; carries *parfum*, 145; marches barefoot, 146 n. 46.

Bénezech, minister of the interior, 1797, 258.

Bernage, de, intendant of Languedoc, on destruction of insects, 66; remark on government fund, 151; his appeals for aid, 152; comment on the poor grain harvest of 1721, 152 n. 74; suggestion on free trade adopted, 154; recommended for honors, 157.

Bernage de Saint-Maurice, intendant of Montpellier, dispenses flood relief, 71-72.

Bernières, intendant of Flanders, 109.

Berthier, intendant of Paris, distributes food in 1788, 34; plans for charity workshops, 288.

Bertin, minister, gives support to Bourgelat, 132; matter referred to him, 452 n. 30.

Bertrand, physician of Marseilles, comment that charity was stifled, 139; criticizes haughtiness of imported physicians during plague, 144; advocate of theory of germ origin of plague, 146 n. 46.

Bertrand de Molleville, intendant of Rennes, 161-162; comment on midwives, 171.

Ormesson *fils*, intendant of finance, on aid to large families, 356; given custody of charity workshops, 465.

Orphans, war, aided, 195 n. 77, 350; institutions for them in Paris, 214-215, 304-305; some institutions consolidated in Revolution, 216; apprenticeship, 243; designation for foundlings, 1793, 255; military schools for, 423, 436, 438. *See also Enfants-trouvés.*

Orry, controller-general, 74.

Ovens, public, for poor, 10, 46.

Papion *le jeune*, estimate of beggars, 260, 275.

Papon, his *Histoire de Provence* subsidized, 332.

Paris, grain agent, 13.

Patras, Antoine, physician at Grenoble, served hospital gratis 30 years, 187 n. 26.

Paulet, physician, author of work on epizootics, 106 n. 1, 109, 113, 116, 117, 120, 123-124, 127; his book published by government, 332.

Pawlet, Comte de, 423, 436.

Pensions, awarded for heroic service during plague, 157; awarded Doulcet and his family, 164; to farmers, artisans, widows, etc., 1794, 279; sums expended (1700-87) 310, (1789) 313 n. 12, (1790) 333-334, 342-343, 462; attempts at reduction, 1710-1787, 310-311; *Livre rouge*, 311-312; abuses revealed, 312, 314 n. 14; majority given for faithful service, 312, 313; *Etat nominatif des pensions*, 312; groups listed therein, 312-313; military and naval, 313-320, 337, 339, 341-342, 349, 351; for politicians and civil servants, 320-323, 337, 351; ecclesiastical, 324-329, 342-344, 353; for favorites and servants of the royal household, 329; for physicians and surgeons, 329-330, 361; for inventors, 330; for professors and academicians, etc., 330-331, 339-340, 351; for lesser groups, 331-332; provincial and municipal, 332-333; revision, 1790, 333-343; to the "conquerors of the Bastille," 344-346; to the "heroes" of Aug. 10, 1792, 346-348; deprivation of *émigrés* and refractory priests, 352; used for building loyal faction, 352, 354; payments often delinquent in 1790's, 352, 353 n. 217, 354; more generous than other forms of government aid, 354; to

large families, 355-358, 361-362; to Pereire, 429; attitude toward recipients, 354, 447; by glassmakers, 456; estimate of total by Camus, 462; size of pension to Acadians and noncommissioned officers, 464.

Pereire, instructor of deaf-mutes, 429-430.

Perronet, engineer, 82 n. 35; director of Ecole des Ponts-et-Chaussées, 417.

Pérusse, Marquis de, settles Germans on his lands, 65 n. 81; his land bought for Acadian settlement, 376-377, 391.

Petites-Maisons, asylum, Paris, 217, 223, 225.

Pied (12.787 inches), 137 n. 10.

Pinel, Philippe, work with the insane, 227-228; attempts vaccinations, 1800, 179.

Pisé, houses of, 102-104.

Plague of Provence, origin, 135-136; panic resulting, 136, 137; death rate, 137; characteristics, 137; burial of victims, 137; isolation of Marseilles and Provence, 137-138; extent of pest-region, 138; total sick and dead, 138; aid rendered by individuals, church, and state, 139-153; precautions at disinfection, 145-146, 155-156; quarantine, 146-147, 155; accompanied by starvation, 148; total expenditures necessitated, 156; remissions in taxes, 157; awards for heroic service, 157.

Ponantois, Captain, shipload of codfish, 149 n. 62.

Pons, physician, extorter, 142 n. 33.

Pope, the, sends three vessels with grain during plague, 140.

Pontchartrain, serves food to needy, 10; observations on French colonies, 246.

Popular Society, Toulouse, its work, 279, 454.

Population of France, estimate, 275 n. 76.

Potato, Irish, cultivation encouraged, 57-59; its history, 57 n. 29.

Printed matter circulated by government, 1793-94, 47; on agriculture, 63; on extermination of various crop pests, 67; the *Instruction* of June, 1721, 155; Tissot's *Notice to the People on Health*, 165.

Prison reform, 179-180, 408-409.

Prison relief, government interest in, 408-409; societies to aid prisoners, 409, 453-454; societies to visit prisoners, 454 n. 41.

Prisoners, ransomed from Algerians, 384-385; aided by societies, 409; released at